D1570028

Edwin Arlington Robinson

William Gropper's drawing of Robinson in his ubiquitous rocking chair. (*In House Photo.*)

SCOTT DONALDSON

Edwin Arlington Robinson

A POET'S LIFE

COLUMBIA UNIVERSITY PRESS   NEW YORK

Columbia University Press

Publishers Since 1893

New York   Chichester, West Sussex

Copyright © 2007 Scott Donaldson

All rights reserved

Library of Congress Cataloging-in-Publication Data

Donaldson, Scott, 1928–
Edwin Arlington Robinson: a poet's life / Scott
Donaldson
p.   cm.
Includes bibliographical references (p.) and index.
ISBN-10 0–231–13842–3 (cloth : alk. paper)
ISBN-13 978–0–231–13842–0 (cloth : alk. paper)

ISBN-10 0–231–51099–3 (e-book)
ISBN-13 978–0–51099–8 (e-book)
1. Robinson, Edwin Arlington, 1869–1935.   2. Poets,
American—20th century—Biography.   I. Title.

PS3535.O25Z645   2007
811'.52—dc22
[B]
2006015660

∞

Columbia University Press books are printed
on permanent and durable acid-free paper.

Printed in the United States of America
Designed by Lisa Hamm
c 10 9 8 7 6 5 4 3 2 1

Contents

Edwin Arlington Robinson

Introduction

This book derives from the conviction that Edwin Arlington Robinson was a great American poet and an exceptionally fine human being. The story of his life deserves telling and has not been told.

Robinson was born December 22, 1869, at Head Tide, Maine, and died in New York City on April 5, 1935. He grew up during the latter days of the Victorians—Tennyson, Browning, Arnold—in England and the Fireside Poets—Longfellow, Lowell, Bryant—in the United States. But the energy was waning, and by the turn of the century most poetry had degenerated into prettified evocations of the natural world. From the start, Robinson declared his independence from that genteel tradition. A few others joined him, among them in England A. E. Housman, whose *A Shropshire Lad* appeared in the same year—1896—as EAR's first volume, *The Torrent and the Night Before*. Among the British poets Robinson most admired, Housman (1859–1935) was a decade older than he, Thomas Hardy (1840–1928) a generation his senior, and Rudyard Kipling (1865–1936) his near contemporary. Robinson, who was to become our first truly modern poet, goes back a long way in time.

When he died in 1935, Robinson reigned as the nation's leading poet. "With the death of Edwin Arlington Robinson," the *New York Times* editorial declared, "America has lost not only one of the finest poets of our time, but one who ranked with the great poets of the past." Robinson was the only poet of his time and place, the *Washington Evening Star* observed, whose name could "be associated with the very greatest names in the history of letters." From newspapers around the country came similar encomiums reflecting patriotic pride in his accomplishment: he was the nation's "preeminent poet," our "most distinguished poet."

That was 1935. Over the succeeding seventy years, Robinson's reputation has declined. True, there was a flurry of attention during his centenary in 1969. Then three separate volumes of selections of his poems appeared in the 1990s, making his best work—the short- to medium-length poems—more easily available to the reading public than it had been for years. This state of affairs did not last for long; only one of these collections remains in print. Hence it remains compelling to reiterate Donald Hall's plea in *The Essential Robinson* (1994), for restoration of EAR to the American pantheon. Robinson's reputation, it seems clear, declined in the wake of the triumph of such modernist poets as Eliot, Pound, Stevens, and Williams. Unlike them, Robinson remained devoted all his life to traditional forms. His poetry on the page came to look almost old-fashioned in its use of meter and rhyme. Yet, as Hall pointed out, that twentieth century generation of great modern poets actually began with Robinson "in his realism or honesty, and his relentless care for the art of poetic language."

Robinson's strongest partisans still are found among fellow poets like Hall and Robert Mezey, editor of the Modern Library's 1999 volume of Robinson poems. One example: During a June 2003 heat wave in Paris, the poet W. S. Merwin, winner of both the Pulitzer and Bollingen prizes, read from his poems in a crowded upstairs room at the Village Voice bookshop in Saint Germain des Pres. With the windows open, Merwin had to compete with traffic noises, but the ease of his manner and the grace of his poetry commanded the attention of a sweaty audience. Afterwards, books were signed and questions asked.

"Were you influenced by Robinson?" someone asked Merwin. Without a second's hesitation, he began reciting "Reuben Bright," one of Robinson's best early sonnets.

> Because he was a butcher, and thereby
> Did earn an honest living (and did right),
> I would not have you think that Reuben Bright
> Was any more a brute than you or I;
> For when they told him that his wife must die,
> He stared at them, and shook with grief and fright,
> And cried like a great baby half that night,
> And made the women cry to see him cry.
>
> And after she was dead, and he had paid
> The singers and the sexton and the rest,
> He packed . . .

Here Merwin stalled momentarily, looking for the rhyme, and the woman poet next in line to have her book signed spoke up to provide it.

> . . . a lot of things that she had made . . .

That was all Merwin needed. He sailed on to the end, declaiming the final couplet in triumph.

> Most mournfully away in an old chest

Of hers, and put some chopped-up cedar boughs
In with them, and tore down the slaughter-house.

"Does that answer your question?" he said.

Great writers must find their distinctive voice, and you can hear Robinson's in "Reuben Bright"(1897). He uses simple rhetoric, the emotion compressed in spare language. As the poet Winfield Townley Scott observed in his notebooks, there are basically two kinds of poetry. One is represented by Hart Crane's line "The seal's wide spindrift gaze toward paradise," the other by Robinson's "And he was all alone there when he died." One is a magic gesture of language, the other "a commentary on human life so concentrated as to give off considerable pressure." The greatest poets combine the two, Scott believed: Shakespeare often, Robinson himself now and then.

When Robinson wrote, it was in a way manifestly his own. His work is highly susceptible to parody, like that of most major writers. What was new about him, as Archibald MacLeish wrote in 1969, was the speaker, "the Voice" whose tone, touched by irony, suggests truths about his characters (and about ourselves) that we almost but don't quite recognize. "We don't despair—not quite—and neither does Robinson," MacLeish commented. "His is the after voice, the evening voice, and . . . we know the thing it means."

Robinson used that voice to present a new subject matter. He was the first of our poets to write about ordinary people and events. No one before his time would have thought it possible to write sonnets about an honest butcher consumed by grief, about a miser with "eyes like little dollars in the dark," about ancient clerks in a dry goods store measuring out their days like bolts of cloth. When Robinson did so in his earliest book, he opened the door for other poets to follow. His best work looks closely at the people around him, exploring for secrets within. In 1926 Ben Ray Redman called him "a biographer of souls . . . bound to humanity by the dual bond of sympathy and humor." Time and again, his poems insist that we cannot really know others, that we do not even know ourselves. Yet Robinson was uncannily perceptive, and we come away from regarding his portraits with a glimmer of understanding. As he himself put it, "poetry is a language that tells us, through a more or less emotional reaction, something that cannot be said."

In "Calverly's," an elegiac 1907 poem, Robinson laments the passing of former companions at a New York City tavern. They had not amounted to much, as judged by worldly standards, yet he will not let them go unremarked.

No fame delays oblivion
For them, but something yet survives:
A record written fair, could we
But read the book of scattered lives.

Usually he took for his subjects those who had failed in life and love. He wrote about the derelict and downtrodden, the old and bereft. Who wanted to read about successful aldermen, anyway? Those who led "scattered lives" interested him, not least because for a long time he thought of himself as one of them. Recognition came late to Robinson. He spent two decades struggling to get his poems published, surviving on the edge of poverty. Drink and depression dogged his days, yet he was sustained by a persistent belief in his calling—that he had been put on the earth to write poems. It was the only thing he could do, and he meant to do it, no matter how few seemed to notice.

In a 1952 libel on poets of his generation, Edmund Wilson maintained that they had too much time on their hands. As a consequence, they formed into groups to engage in "debates, practical jokes and fierce battles" that kept them in a state of excitement. Wilson had a point, for the physical and mental labor of setting poems down on paper hardly qualifies as a full-time occupation. When Teddy Roosevelt provided Robinson with a sinecure at the New York Custom House from 1905 to 1909, it was almost as if the free hours *prevented* him from getting poems written. "Work with me," he said at the time, "means studying the ceiling and my navel for four hours and then writing down perhaps four lines—sometimes seven and then again none at all." But Robinson did not use the time to join organizations, and he was never drawn into the squabbling of literary factions. All his life he remained very much his own man.

It was not that he didn't care what others thought of his poetry. A bad review could summon despondency and a good one inspire him to make a friend of the reviewer. He felt a kinship for anyone who understood and liked what he had written. They had in common, after all, a mutual respect for the power and importance of language. For him, as for Henry in Tom Stoppard's play *The Real Thing*, it was the words that mattered. Writers were not sacred, but words were. If you got the right ones in the right order, you could "make a poem which children will speak for you when you're dead."

That was what Robinson was after. Though utterly unwilling to indulge in advertisements for himself, he was tremendously ambitious about his poetry. "I don't expect recognition while I live," he said early in his career, "but if I thought I could write something that would go on living after I'm gone, I'd be satisfied with an attic and a crust all my life." When critical and popular success finally did come his way, he was wary of the praise. Only time—perhaps a century—would determine whether his poems would survive. "If you will look in on me sometime in the summer of 2026," he wrote a friend from the Mac-Dowell Colony on August 20, 1926, "I may be able to tell you whether my things are going to last."

Robinson also realized that there was no necessary connection between genius and character. In correspondence with older women such as Lilla Cabot Perry and Laura E. Richards, he found himself defending the behavior of great artists of the past. Lord Byron "was a bounder, no doubt, but his heritage accounts for a good deal." Richard Wagner "could not possibly have found the time to be so wicked as his enemies would have him." Yet even if the enemies were right, what did it matter? Wagner "left the world a different place for his having lived in it—which is a good deal for one neurotic little man to do."

What he could easily forgive in others, Robinson could not countenance in himself. Enough of his Puritan heritage remained to guide him both toward his calling and toward a life of kindness and charity. He cared deeply for his family and friends. As troubles threatened to overtake them, Robinson came to their aid with sympathy and understanding, money and counsel. He had a knack for anticipating and untangling the most intricate of emotional complications. Time and again he served as a *fixer*, one whose insights helped relieve those in distress. When Robinson died, a number of his friends insisted on his greatness as a man as well as a poet. "Most great artists are great only in their art," as one of them observed. Another thought him the best man he had ever known.

A Man Almost Without Biography

Before her memoir about Robinson was published, Laura Richards—the other well-known writer from Gardiner, Maine—sent him the manuscript for comments. EAR had but one revision to propose. Richards had written that he was "shy," and, he objected, "no man likes to be called shy." The word carried connotations of weakness. He did not mind being called "reticent," and many chose that adjective to describe his poetry and personality. In fact, Robinson was one of the most private persons who ever lived. With a secretiveness that went beyond the customary Yankee standard, he concealed himself behind barriers, and rarely spoke of the most important events of his life. "Now to one, and then to another, he vouchsafed an item," as his friend Mowry Saben said, "but there was much that he never vouchsafed to anyone."

Robinson's reticence was strikingly apparent in his dealings with those seeking information for publication. As he admitted—with a touch of humor and a touch of pride—he resembled "some sort of a New England shellfish—probably a Maine clam." He retreated into the shell when asked for personal details. "In looking over my life," he told Amy Lowell, "I find that I have no life to speak of, much less to write about." Newspaper reporters found him extremely difficult to interview, for he was reluctant to discuss himself or his way of life or his methods of work. Nor would he promote himself in public. No readings from the platform. No talks to college audiences or women's groups. The poems would have to speak for themselves.

As the perceptive poet-critic J. V. Cunningham summed him up, "Robinson was a man almost without biography who became a legend to his friends." Despite the silences and withdrawals, Robinson had a gift for friendship. At the same time, he was notorious for keeping his friends in separate compartments.

During his most productive years, he divided his time between New York City (from late fall to early spring), the MacDowell Colony in Peterborough, New Hampshire (where he spent twenty-four successive summers and did almost all of his writing), and Boston (during a month or two in the spring and fall). He traveled light, a nomadic minstrel living out of two suitcases. In each place he put them down, he developed a separate cadre of friends that knew little or nothing about those who lived elsewhere. In New York itself, he segregated the bohemian companions of his struggling years from the well-to-do patrons who later came to his rescue. Rarely did any of the friends of his mature years, wherever they encountered Robinson, hear a whisper about his origins in Gardiner.

By any normal criterion, EAR led an undramatic life. He fell in love more than once, and once most permanently and painfully. But he never married, thus cutting himself off from the privileges and obligations of domesticity. This was hardly surprising, considering the catastrophes that befell his own family.

Behind the impressive facade of the Robinson home at 67 Lincoln Avenue in Gardiner, Maine, was enacted a tragedy of Gothic proportions. His parents, he once wrote, would have been among the happiest people on earth if they had not had children. EAR himself was the last and late-begotten child and was given less attention than his two older brothers. During the decade (1888–1898) between his graduation from high school and his departure from Maine for New York, "the town down the river," the Robinson family disintegrated. Oldest brother Dean, a doctor, became a morphine addict and returned to the homestead to be cared for, a ghostly figure treading down the carpet as he shuffled through the night. Robinson's once vigorous father went downhill precipitously in mind and body, taking up spiritualism and table rappings before his death in July 1892. Middle brother Herman, handsome and extroverted, married the girl EAR loved, lost the family fortune in the panic of 1893, and succumbed to drink.

It fell to impractical young Win Robinson, as he was then known, to function as the male bulwark of the family. As the townspeople in Gardiner were wondering when he would settle down and get a job, he did the chores around the house and grounds—planted the vegetables, picked the apples, painted the fences—and continued his efforts to become a published writer. In November 1896, a few days before he received the slim blue copies of his first book, *The Torrent and the Night Before*, his mother died suddenly of black diphtheria: so infectious a disease that the undertaker left the coffin on the porch, the minister intoned a few words from behind a handkerchief, and the sons had to attend to the burial themselves. Win wished his mother could have seen the book, which—subsidized though it was—offered testimony that he had not been wasting his time. Neither of his parents, he felt sure, could possibly have thought of him as in any way successful.

In the following summer, Robinson made a declaration of love to Rosalind Richards that ended in embarrassment to both parties. Daily, also, he saw his brother Herman's beautiful wife Emma, the one lasting love of his life, and the

little nieces who disturbed his work and captured his affection. Finally there
was a confrontation between the brothers, and Win Robinson was exiled to
New York and a life of poetry.

No wonder, then, that he resisted attempts to draw him out about the circumstances of his life, even if they came from the most sympathetic and admiring of supporters. Edith Brower, a magazine writer from Wilkes-Barre, Pennsylvania, was captivated by the poetry in Robinson's first book and wrote to tell
him so. The fledgling author was pleased, and an extensive and lively correspondence ensued. Early on, Brower asked him to tell her about himself, but he
could do so only in part. "If I were to tell the whole story, it would make sorry
reading indeed—so I won't tell it," Robinson wrote her in April 1897. Especially
he would not speak about "family matters . . . of which the knowledge would
only disturb" her. There were some things not worth looking into.

When he addressed those questions that mattered most to him—the judgment of posterity, for instance—he did so obliquely. In a 1918 letter to Laura
Richards, Robinson imagined a one-paragraph summary of his life and career,
as it might be written half a century later.

E. A. R., born, etc. He expected to die young, and should have done so. Owing,
however, to some slight cosmic error, he was allowed to live beyond the logical
time and to write divers books of verse, mostly about corpses and things, and
lost illusions—never having had any of his own worth mentioning. For about
ten years of his life he drank too much rum (chiefly as a more or less ingenious
occupation for his idle hours, which began at noon and ended any time between
two and five in the morning). He wrote some fairly good metres, at times, and he
died owing money. When he was gone, his friends—of whom, for some altogether
unexplained reason, he had several, in spite of the fact that he never said anything
to them to let them know how much he liked them—all said, in a sort of hesitat-
ing unison: "Well," with a rising inflection. He was unpopular during his life, on
account of his incurable optimism, which was always a source of wonder to those
who did not know better. Many seemed to think he should have fussed and cussed
more than he did for having been born to such an ornery lot as that of an "intellectual poet"—when, as a matter of fact, anything like a proper comprehension of
his product was, and is—so far as it is at all—a matter of feeling, not of cerebration.
It has taken a long time to find this out, and a few of the prodigiously faithful are
still at it.

Here Robinson, forty-eight years old, regarded himself wryly, admitting from
behind the humor to his long battle with the bottle, to his debts that were eventually repaid, and to his hapless incapacity to express emotions out loud, while repudiating the public misperception of him as a pessimistic and philosophical poet.

To date, there has been no thoroughly documented biography of Edwin
Arlington Robinson. Hermann Hagedorn's 1938 book, while lively and not

without charm, was disadvantaged by emerging only three years after Robinson's death. Family members turned against the biographer, who refused to ignore the skeleton of Dean's addiction and cast a patronizing eye on the citizens of Gardiner. Then, too, Hagedorn was deprived of access to important caches of letters as a consequence of feuding cliques among Robinson's friends. He was seen as representing the respectable New York establishment, against whom was aligned a group of antagonists convinced that only they knew and properly valued Robinson. "How strange it is," the poet Ridgely Torrence observed at the time, "that a gentle, reasonable spirit like E.A. should have his afterglow clouded by a mist of hates, envies, selfish ambitions and blindnesses."

A decade later, Emery Neff wrote the Robinson volume in the American Men of Letters series. Neff unearthed only a few sources that had been unavailable to Hagedorn, and his book remains more valuable for its discussion of EAR's poetry than for any extensive exploration of his life. In 1965, Chard Powers Smith brought out *Where the Light Falls*, a memoir that rides its thesis—that EAR was in love with Emma—hard, discovering traces of the relationship in almost everything Robinson wrote. Smith, like Hagedorn, encountered resistance from family members and was able to tell only part of the story. Now, fortunately, enough time has passed so that it is possible to fill in the blanks that marred the work of previous biographers. Or most of the blanks, that is, for as Freud warned us, the entire truth about anyone is "inaccessible."

Louis Untermeyer, the poet, critic, and anthologist, knew Robinson fairly well and was a close friend of Robert Frost, the other great New England poet of Robinson's generation. In a harsh review, Untermeyer criticized Hagedorn's 1938 biography for its "failure to record, let alone reconcile, the contradictions of Robinson's mood and character." Despite hints about the poet's combination of evasiveness and candor, "his personality never really emerges." Too many things were left out, among them Robinson's relationships with other poets and particularly with Frost—a crucial one where the issue of reputation is concerned. "Some day," Untermeyer concluded, "a biographer will explore the depths beneath Robinson's deceptive surfaces, the intensity under the detachment, the anxiety manifest in the over-concern with his own work." Such a biographer "will explain the reasons back of [Robinson's] distrust of most men and his fear of almost all women, the causes of his limitations, and the desperate sublimation of the laconic, lonely man, a man obsessed with failure and in love with death." One does not have to agree entirely with Untermeyer's psychological assessments about EAR's "desperate sublimation" and his being "in love with death" to recognize that they carry partial validity. Untermeyer's charge—to dig deep beneath the surface for the reasons behind such behavior—sets the would-be biographer a well-nigh impossible task. But at least, in the first decade of the twenty-first century, he has substantially more information to build upon than has ever been available before.

New Resources

I was first smitten by the poetry of Edwin Arlington Robinson a fast sixty years ago, when Prescott C. Cleveland introduced his Blake School seniors—all boys, at the time—to the revelations of "Richard Cory" and "Miniver Cheevy." Recently it had been brought home to me that not everything worked out for the best in these our lives, and the tale of Richard Cory undoubtedly appealed to a certain teenage tendency to court the melancholy. But Mr. Cleveland—only when not in his presence would we call him Cleve—also opened my eyes to the delightful fact that poems could be wonderfully funny and perceptive at the same time, as Miniver's plight proved. And then, as always, I was moved by the poet's obvious empathy for his characters. At Yale, Robinson was one of the very few twentieth-century writers taught by Stanley T. Williams and Norman Holmes Pearson in a large lecture course on American literature. A few years later, working toward a doctorate in American studies at Minnesota, I had the good fortune to study under, and read papers for, the brilliant J. C. Levenson. A paper I wrote under his direction, on characters in Robinson's poetry, was converted into my first literary article, for the flagship journal *American Literature.*

So it was not at all unnatural that in 1977 I began assembling materials toward a biography of Edwin Arlington Robinson. I had just published *By Force of Will: The Life and Art of Ernest Hemingway* and was eager to write a book about Robinson. Malcolm Cowley, mentor and editor on the Hemingway book, discouraged me. Much as he admired Robinson, he doubted the commercial prospects for a biography. I was preparing to go ahead anyway—I had been teaching EAR's work regularly to my students at the College of William and Mary—until his minuscule and idiosyncratic handwriting stopped me cold. During a summer research trip to the extensive Robinson collection at Colby College in Waterville, Maine, I read, or tried to read, a number of letters that Robinson had written. The scrawls on the page resembled hieroglyphics. It took an hour to decipher a single letter, and even then I could not be entirely sure of a word here or there. I knew, however, that Wallace L. Anderson, the author of the fine *Edwin Arlington Robinson: A Critical Introduction* (1968), was in the process of locating and transcribing Robinson's letters. In due course, the Robinson letters as edited by Anderson would be available. Meanwhile, I could work on other literary biographies.

So I committed books on F. Scott Fitzgerald and John Cheever and Archibald MacLeish and, most recently, the troubled friendship between Hemingway and Fitzgerald. After *Hemingway vs. Fitzgerald* was launched in the fall of 1999, I circled back to Robinson as a biographical subject. This looked no more financially feasible than it had twenty years earlier. Robinson, I knew, threatened to become a casualty in the shifting values of the literary marketplace. Yet I knew, too, that there was no adequate biography and that if there were it might help give his marvelous poetry the attention it deserved.

Above all, the poems continued to exert their appeal. I could not help admiring them, and I shared (or wanted to share) his admirable attitude of sympathy with the fellow mortals he wrote about and the misfortunes that beset them. I would write the biography, then, as a labor of love. Or at least I would try to, if only the letters could be deciphered. What had happened to the letters Anderson was working on? I made a couple of telephone calls and found out. Clifford A. Wood, chairman of the English Department at Bridgewater State College in Massachusetts, provided the unhappy news that Anderson, who had risen to become dean and vice president of the college, had died in 1984. Wood kindly put me in touch with Anderson's widow, Mary, who confirmed that her husband had finished transcribing the Robinson letters he painstakingly tracked down in libraries and in private hands—wonderful!—and that he had completed annotating perhaps three quarters of them.

Working with the aid of a Guggenheim grant, Anderson found about 4,000 letters, and nearly nine-tenths of them had never been printed. What's more, during the two decades devoted to his quest, Anderson acquired the Rosetta stone that enabled him to decode Robinson's handwriting. Here was an invaluable trove for anyone interested in Robinson's life and art, but the trove was languishing in a warehouse in Raynham, Mass.. Having discovered this fact, I urged Mary Anderson, and her son Hale, to transfer these papers to a research library where they could be safeguarded and processed so that students and scholars could read them. Because of its sizable Robinson holdings and its Maine location, Colby College seemed the ideal repository. Early in 2002, the cache of letters was delivered to Colby, where curator of special collections Patricia Burdick assembled them into an exemplary and well-organized archive.

In three separate visits to Colby's Miller library over the next eighteen months, each lasting a week or longer, I read all of these letters and made copies of a good many of them. The more time I spent consulting the archive at Colby, the more I came to admire Anderson's mastery in deciphering Robinson's letters and his professionalism in annotating them. He was so proficient a transcriber that he was able to correct many errors in three previously published volumes of Robinson's letters: the 1940 *Selected Letters* and those written to Harry deForest Smith (1947) and to Edith Brower (1968). Appearing only a few years after the poet died, the *Selected Letters* sanitized his image through a process of omission. When Robinson told a friend of his youth that he had quit chewing tobacco, *Selected Letters* cut the passage. It might be all right to stop chewing tobacco. Having to stop was not. Some wild misreadings were made by the editors and stenographers who did their best to figure out his handwriting. Where Robinson wrote "tadpole," *Selected Letters* rendered it "temple." And the book contained only 181 letters, none among them to Smith and Brower. Those letters, published somewhat later, provided valuable insights into Robinson's early manhood and career but also contained various misspellings and omissions that Anderson was able to put right.

The detailed notes Anderson wrote to accompany the letters demonstrate a wide-ranging knowledge not only of Robinson's life and work but also of the times and the culture. In them he presented capsule biographies of correspondents, information from historical and bibliographical sources, and references to relevant books and articles. It came as something of a blow to discover that the annotations ceased as of the letters of 1916. Still, what Anderson was able to accomplish in the time allotted to him represents a remarkable achievement. In presenting his work to the Colby College library—twelve boxes containing 200 linear feet of file folders—his family has made a major contribution to American literature in general and Robinson in particular.

The letters themselves are characteristically reticent and at the same time engagingly self-deprecatory. One sees Robinson in his embodiment as a practicing writer, deploring the cheapness and materialism around him, making witty comments, arranging for social engagements, giving advice and comfort and money to colleagues and friends. One does not see him announcing his love or campaigning for causes, except for doing away with Prohibition. The letters reflect the reserve and the dignity of the man who wrote them, and demonstrate the good nature with which he confronted his often difficult days. Sometimes, one can read between the lines for emotions concealed. What goes unsaid can say a lot.

In the forty years since the last biography was essayed by Chard Powers Smith, many other documents by or about Robinson have come to light. Smith, for example, was denied permission to quote from the letters Robinson wrote about his occasional visits to Boston's houses of prostitution during the two years (1891–1893) he studied at Harvard. Propriety ruled in this instance, but propriety run amok, for the letters reveal not a callous college youth but a sensitive observer appalled by the degradation of sexual commerce and intensely sympathetic to the women driven to engage in it. Other important, long-withheld material has become available through the generosity and thoughtfulness of the poet's grandnephews David and William Nivison and grandniece Elizabeth Calloway. Included are important and incisive comments on specific poems made by Emma Robinson and her daughter Ruth Nivison (the oldest of EAR's beloved nieces), extensive corrections of Hagedorn's biography made by Emma and Robinson's friend George Burnham, reminiscences of her youth by Ruth Nivison, and significant revelations about the injustice done to Win's brother Herman when he was accused of thievery and banished from the family.

Through the agency of Mrs. Eliot T. Putnam, Robinson's letters to Rosalind Richards were lifted from restricted status at Harvard, along with Rosalind's revealing correspondence with the college librarian. I was directed to Mrs. Putnam as to much else by Danny D. Smith, who knows more about the history and people of Gardiner, Maine, and about the Richards family than anyone else on the face of the earth, and whose willingness to share what he knows extends well beyond the bounds of professional courtesy. During my several visits to Gardiner and environs over four years, Danny served as the most expert and helpful of guides. He also supplied voluminous information from his own files and from the holdings at the Gardiner Library Association.

Two memoirs about Robinson, both running to 150 pages, surfaced during 2003. The first was written by EAR's friend Carty Ranck, who Boswellized the poet over the course of two decades and was disappointed not to be chosen as official biographer. Through diligent digging, the scholar Arnold T. Schwab recovered this typescript from the office of Ranck's lawyer in Louisville, Kentucky, and kindly allowed me to make a copy. The second was the work of Mowry Saben, who met Robinson as a fellow student at Harvard and remained a lifelong friend. Saben's reminiscences were fetched down by Patricia Burdick from the attic at Colby's Miller library, where they reposed—uncatalogued—among the papers of Richard Cary, a Robinson expert and former professor at the college. In addition to these two long accounts, various libraries around the United States provided copies of briefer recollections that have only recently become available and of letters acquired since Anderson's death in 1984. I have been able to write Robinson's life story in the confidence that very little remains restricted or has been overlooked. The greatest resource of all, of course, is the poetry.

"Don't look for me in my writing," Robinson cautioned. Among poets he *was* unusual in that he avoided the presentation of self on the page as assiduously as he did in person. Still, the caveat cannot be taken literally. In a few poems he does portray himself, in disguise—as "Aunt Imogen" (Uncle Win), who gives so much of her love to the children of her sister, or as "Miniver Cheevy" himself. Usually, though, he remains in the wings, bringing other figures on stage. But the thoughts and emotions in the poems are ones he has experienced or can imagine experiencing. And the voice—even when someone else is speaking—is unmistakably his own. "Poets don't have biographies," Octavio Paz contended. "Their work is their biography." To know Robinson, we must let the poems bring his life into focus.

In an essay on literary biography, John Updike points out that most writers "lead quiet lives, or at least are of interest to us because of the words they set down in quiet moments." Only rarely does a writer make sensational news, like Byron in the nineteenth century or Hemingway and Mailer in the twentieth. Robinson's life was quiet enough; there are no scandals. Yet he was one of those marvelous human beings who made it his business to enrich the lives of others.

His closest friends thought of EAR as both a great poet and a great man, and after five years of reading and writing about him, I have come to share that view. This is my seventh literary biography, all dealing with twentieth-century American writers, beginning with the minor poet Winfield Townley Scott and going on to major figures such as Hemingway, Fitzgerald, Cheever, and

MacLeish. Obviously, I admired all of them as writers; otherwise, why undertake the task of telling the story of their life and work? But none of them rank alongside Edwin Arlington Robinson as a human being. In this book, I set out to convey a sense of that man—and through discussion of a number of his best poems, to stimulate a heightened understanding and appreciation of the work that makes him worth knowing about.

A Hell of a Name for a Poet

Anything but Eddie

Edwin Arlington Robinson detested the name that he was given, "and," like Miniver Cheevy, "he had reasons."

The very sound of the name hurt his ears. It seemed overly long and pretentious, offending his natural modesty. In later years, he repeatedly complained to friends about this name he had been saddled with. "Ed-win Ar-ling-ton Rob-in-son!" he would say, hammering out each syllable with profound disgust. Pronounced that way, it sounded "like a tin bathtub bumping down an uncarpeted flight of stairs." In particular, his poet's ear objected to the "n's" at the end of each word. "Ar-ling-ton" jarred on him worst of all, putting the curse on the rest of the name. It was "a hell of a name for a poet."

One of those who heard Robinson denigrate his name was James Norman Hall, novelist and coauthor of the famous *Bounty* novels. In a reminiscent poem, Hall summed up the poet's objections.

> Once he said that 'Edwin Arlington'
> With 'Robinson' attached, was such a load
> As few beside himself had had to hoist
> And stagger under toward a distant grave.
> Eight syllables, and one of them a 'ton'
> Was too much for any Robin's son.

So in conversation Robinson made sport of his unwieldy three-part appellation. The humor concealed a deeper antipathy. "I have always hated my name," he wrote in 1926, "with a hatred that is positively pathological."

Naturally he looked for shorter versions of his cumbersome cognomen, but most abbreviations sounded wrong to him, too. "Ed" no more fitted his buttoned-up personality, as Richard Cary pointed out, than a sweatshirt would have. "You may call me anything you like," he told Edith Brower, "anything but Eddie." He had an aunt who called him that once, "and now she doesn't call me at all." As he was growing up, family and friends shortened Edwin to "Win." A few boyhood companions altered "Win" to "Pin" or "Pinny." Then he became "long Robinson" for a time as he stretched toward his full six feet two. But it was "Win"—or "Uncle Win," to his nieces—that stuck in his home town of Gardiner, Maine.

Robinson published his first two books—in 1896 and 1897—as Edwin Arlington Robinson, and so established his authorial name. Besides carrying reminiscences of *Robinson Crusoe* and *Swiss Family Robinson*, two classics that dealt with shipwrecked sailors, the three-part appellation resonated to the turn-of-the-century audience as properly poetic. Robinson was writing in the aftermath of a number of distinguished New England writers known by three names: Ralph Waldo Emerson, Henry David Thoreau, Henry Wadsworth Longfellow, James Russell Lowell, Oliver Wendell Holmes, John Greenleaf Whittier, William Cullen Bryant. Only Emily Dickinson in Amherst and Walt Whitman, down in New York, got along with two names. The trouble was that Robinson's three-part name tended to associate him with the old guard, and not with fellow innovators like Whitman and Dickinson. (Latterly, he has been confused with the excellent Robinson Jeffers, who was writing a very different kind of poetry at the other end of the continent).

In his personal relations, Robinson sought out alternatives to his trinomial title. As early as his two years at Harvard (1891–1893), where he made several lifelong friends, he began to adopt the British style of using last names only. So he was "Robinson" to (George) "Latham," say, and vice versa. In correspondence, though, he could not sign himself by one name alone.

For a time, in the early 1900s, he signed letters as "Edwin A. Robinson." Later he settled on "E. A. Robinson" as a signature and on "E. A." as what he preferred to be called. "My only name now," he wrote a friend of his youth in 1922, "is 'E. A.,'—which is easy to say and to write, and serves every purpose." When Laura Richards was writing her memoirs in 1931, Robinson instructed her to refer to him in this way. Mrs. Richards made the change in print, although, like others in Gardiner, she would always think of him as "Win."

It was easier to convert his friends in New York and at the MacDowell Colony. He became "E. A." for them, "Uncle E. A." for their children, and "E. A. R.," when referred to in his capacity as a poet. It was as if by taking a new name Robinson had entered into a new transaction with the world. Besides, as Donald Hall was to point out, the bare initials in their near-anonymity "fitted the shadowy silence of his character." Characteristically, though, there was a small segment among his closest friends—concentrated in Boston—that did not fall into line. Thomas Sergeant and Lilla Cabot Perry called him "Rob." To George Burnham, best friend of all, he was "Robbie."

FIGURE 1.1 Edwin Arlington Robinson in the first photograph to appear with a review of his poetry, March 1903. He was identified as "Mr. Edward A. Robinson."

Source: Colby College Special Collections.

Edward Arlington Robinson, Pulitzer Prize Winner

Whatever others may have called him personally, it was Robinson's professional name that gave him the most trouble. A good many people seem incapable of uttering "Edwin Arlington Robinson" correctly. In any company of the reasonably well read today, most will know about Robinson. At least half of them, however, will remember him as "*Edward* Arlington Robinson." This mistake is not a latter-day phenomenon. "Edward" for "Edwin" dogged him from the beginning of his career to the end. Often the error was committed by those who should have known better, sometimes by those who *did* know better.

In a brief comment on the publication of Robinson's first book, when he was still living in Gardiner, Maine, the *Gardiner Daily Reporter-Journal* referred to him as "Edward A. Robinson." Four other times during the first twenty years of his career, his hometown paper ran stories about books he had published, each time identifying him as "Edward" instead of "Edwin." The problem followed him to New York, where, in March 1903, the *Critic* in New York printed the first published photograph of Robinson, accompanying Clinton Scollard's review of *Captain Craig*. The caption read "Mr. Edward A. Robinson."

President Theodore Roosevelt, Robinson's most illustrious benefactor, took time off from his duties at the White House to write a laudatory review of *The Children of the Night* for the August 12, 1905, *Outlook*. Roosevelt did much for Robinson, but did not get his name right. The review referred to the poet twice by his full name, both times as "Edward Arlington Robinson." Twenty-five years later, Theodore Roosevelt Jr. wrote Robinson for permission to quote from his work. Robinson assented, adding a caveat. "Will you kindly see that my name (not *Edward*) is printed correctly? There appears to be a sort of fatality in getting it wrong."

In a 1916 advertisement, Macmillan offered for sale at $1.25 each the plays *Van Zorn* and *The Porcupine*, by its newly acquired author "Robinson, Edward A." Upon election to the Authors Club in 1922, Robinson sent in his dues along with a request that the secretary "correct error in my name as it appears to have been entered on your records." In May 1925, Robinson was delighted to hear that he had won the second of his three Pulitzer Prizes for *The Man Who Died Twice*, less pleased that the official citation read "Edward Arlington Robinson." In his review of *Tristram* (1927), Theodore Spencer rang a change on this usual mistake. "No one but Mr. *Robertson* could have written [the poem]," Spencer commented. "And that is high praise." High, indeed.

Misrenderings increased during the decades following Robinson's death in 1935. A bibliography published in 1971 referred readers to C. B. Hogan's article on "Edward Arlington Robinson: New Bibliographical Notes." Running heads for the chapter on Robinson in *Sixteen Modern American Poets* (1990) uniformly presented him as "Edward." Indexes for the annual edition of *American Literary Scholarship* over the last twenty years run about fifty/fifty between "Edwin" and "Edward." These errors occurred in publications that pride themselves on their accuracy, for the most part justifiably. So pervasive has "Edward" for "Edwin" become that reference librarians regularly direct researchers to look for Robinson under both names.

During his lifetime, Robinson became increasingly annoyed by the mistake. "You'd think some of them would be getting it right by this time," the sixty-year-old poet complained to Rollo Walter Brown. It seemed to him, as he told Carty Ranck, that there was "something weird" about it—something that went beyond a natural inclination to convert the uncommon "Edwin" to the more everyday "Edward." As far as he was concerned, "no name in the language . . . [had] so many wrong connotations as Edward." Some of this animus may have derived from the fact that he, Edwin Arlington Robinson, was the son of Edward Robinson: a circumstance that helps to explain why his hometown newspaper called him "Edward" not only early in his career but also, sadly, in the headline over his obituary.

Edward and Mary

The American origins of Edward Robinson, father of the poet, traced back to the arrival of Gain Robinson in the early eighteenth century. The son of Scottish Presbyterians who had been driven into exile in northern Ireland, Gain came across the Atlantic in search of a sunnier future. His descendants settled in a watery section of southeastern Maine, halfway between Augusta and the coastline, and went into shipbuilding. EAR's grandfather, also named

Edward, owned a shipyard in Newcastle. The poet's father, born in 1818, worked for a time as a shipwright in Boston and New York, then at thirty came back to Maine to serve as schoolmaster in the town of Alna. There he met Mary Elizabeth Palmer, who was herself teaching school in nearby Whitefield. They were married in October 1855.

Mary Elizabeth Palmer's roots sank even deeper into colonial New England than her husband's. Thomas Dudley (1576–1653), governor of the Massachusetts Bay Colony, founder of Cambridge, and an early overseer of Harvard College, was a direct ancestor. His daughter Mercy married the accomplished Rev. John Woodbridge, a Harvard graduate who was among other things a preacher, a writer of instructive verse, and the author of a treatise on banking. (Another daughter of Dudley's was Anne Bradstreet (1612–1672), the eminent Puritan poet hailed in England as "The Tenth Muse Lately Sprung Up in America.") The Woodbridge line eventually extended to Mary Ayer Woodbridge, who was born in Newcastle, married Edward Palmer of Whitefield, and gave birth to Mary Elizabeth in 1833.

In her youth Mary Palmer took an active interest in literary pursuits. She participated actively in the Alna lyceums, contributing poetry and prose of her own to manuscript "publications." At nineteen, she painstakingly copied her favorite poems into a scrapbook. Like all of the Palmers, she was tall and good looking, with attractive coloring that photographs failed to capture. Mary was twenty-two to Edward Robinson's thirty-seven when they were married, and she was the loved one. Her husband hated to be separated from her for any reason.

FIGURES 1.2 AND 1.3   The poet's parents, Edward and Mary Palmer Robinson.

Source: Colby College Special Collections.

FIGURE 1.4 The house where Robinson was born in the village of Head Tide.

Source: Colby College Special Collections.

To improve the family finances, Edward gave up schoolteaching in favor of a career as a buyer and seller of lumber. He prospered at the trade, for he had an uncanny gift for estimating the value of timber. When Ranck was assembling material toward a Robinson biography in the early 1930s, EAR provided him with information about his father's occupation. "He was a shipbuilder and a buyer of standing timber," Robinson wrote, adding, with a trace of pride, "he could tell how much a tree was worth by looking at it." Or a stand of trees, for that matter.

Edward and Mary's first child, Horace Dean (called Dean), arrived in May 1857, less than two years after their marriage. There followed a gap of eight years before a second son, Herman Edward, was born. Dean was a serious child, for whom the family had high hopes. Herman, outgoing and athletic, charmed everyone, most especially his father. By the time he was born, in January 1865, the family was living in a handsome house Edward Robinson had bought in Head Tide, only a few miles from their previous home in Alna.

Head Tide, or Head-of-the-Tide, as it was then known, took its name from its location at the headwaters of the Sheepscot, nine miles above Wiscasset and a dozen southeast of Gardiner. Twice a day the river turned back on itself as the tide struggled upstream from the Atlantic. A tiny New England village, Head Tide fits the guidebook description of "picturesque." Situated off the main roads, Head Tide is no longer the bustling community where Edward and Mary Robinson brought their young family in 1863. Still remaining are half a dozen handsome houses and the high-walled bridge over the boulder-strewn Sheepscot. Gone are the narrow gauge railway, the mill, the grain warehouse, and, just east of the bridge, the general store Edward Robinson owned and operated from 1863 to 1870.

The store served as Edward's headquarters while he continued to build his fortune speculating in lumber. He established himself as a smart and reliable citizen of the village—a one-price merchant who never discounted or marked up his goods, a man who could sit and whittle much of the day and still make money. He had his share of the region's dry sense of humor. When alone, he would sometimes engage himself in conversation. "Part of the time," he explained, "I like to talk to someone with common sense." Edward Robinson was a large man, and the neighbors took to his bluff and hearty ways. Successively he served Head Tide as banker, postmaster, selectman, and representative to the state legislature in Augusta, where he immediately became lonesome for his wife.

The Robinsons' house in Head Tide stood facing the road and the elm-shrouded Sheepscot beyond: a handsome two-story late Federal home, five windows over four in the colonial style, with twin chimneys at either end to accommodate the fireplaces below and a broad Greek Revival doorway to welcome visitors. It was there that Edward and Mary's third son was delivered on December 22, 1869, on the morning after the longest night of the year.

Edwin, Drawn from a Hat

The circumstances surrounding the arrival of Baby Boy Robinson were anything but auspicious. His parents had not planned to have a third child. Edward was fifty-one years old, worth nearly $80,000, and ready to move to the lively town of Gardiner on the wide Kennebec river. There he could enjoy semiretirement while Dean and Herman received better schooling. Mary was content with her two sons and not eager to add to the number. When she became pregnant, she consoled herself with the thought that this time she might produce a daughter, but that was not to be. The birth itself was extremely difficult. In the aftermath, she suffered from hemorrhaging and depression.

Day after cold winter day, she lay sorrowing in the small room with the fireplace at the west end of the house, out of the way of the foot traffic between the kitchen and front parlor. Herman, his fifth birthday only a week away, announced his reaction to the new brother by climbing up and falling off a pile of logs. No one paid much attention to the baby or bothered to provide him with a name.

Mary Robinson felt a strong kinship with her lively older sister Lydia Anne, who had married distant cousin Seth Palmer and so evaded a change in her maiden name. As a matter of course, Lydia Anne came to assist during delivery of the new baby. When she returned to the Palmer homestead on Blen Hill, half a dozen miles away in Pittston, she sent her daughter Clara, then twenty-two, to help care for Mary and the family. The kind-hearted Clara cheerfully performed

FIGURE 1.5 Baby boy Robinson at three months.

Source: Colby College Special Collections.

the everyday tasks that Mary could hardly manage in her postpartum distress, and she formed a bond with the Robinson boys that would last all their lives.

In April, as the trees and flowers renewed themselves, the Robinsons sold their home in Head Tide and, as negotiations for the purchase of a house in Gardiner had not been completed, were temporarily without a place to live. The Palmer relatives came to the rescue, taking in Edward and Mary, Dean and Herman, and the baby boy with the flashing dark eyes who at four months was still without a name. In June the Robinsons moved again, accompanied by Clara Palmer as a nurse and companion. Clara's younger brother, Oakes, drove the party to Dresden. There they caught a boat that carried them down the Kennebec through Merrymeeting Bay to Bath and on to South Harpswell.

Harpswell Neck, a narrow peninsula extending thirty miles from Burnswick to the sea, was originally settled by farmers and fishermen. With the development of steamboats in the mid-nineteenth century, a tide of visitors ventured across Casco Bay from Portland and points south, and the area was transformed into a flourishing summer resort. The Robinson family settled in at Seaside House, one of several boarding houses catering to visitors after the two hotels at South Harpswell burned down in the 1860s. The Seaside House, no longer extant, stood on a sliver of land jutting out into the bay. There, on a late June weekend, Mary and Edward's six-month-old third son finally acquired his name.

It was a magical summer day on the Maine coast, the sun burning off the fog to reveal a sparkling-blue, waveless sea. Mary Robinson gathered wildflowers on a morning walk, while Clara looked after the boys. After lunch mother and baby boy Robinson joined the ladies on the screen porch to watch the men setting out the wickets for croquet. The child with the large eyes was much admired by the women visitors, and there arose a general consternation that he had not yet been given a name. One visitor had the bright idea that all present should jot down names on slips of paper, and Mary Robinson should draw one of the slips from a bonnet. The slip that came out of the hat read "Edwin." The woman who suggested the plan happened to come from Arlington, Massachusetts, *et voila*!

Mary Robinson, with her ear for poetry, must have had reservations. Edwin was obviously an awkward name for a child with a father named Edward, and his three names linked together sounded rather highfalutin. But it was high time, and she had agreed to the lottery, and so the baby boy who had gotten along with no name at all for the first half of his first year became Edwin Arlington Robinson.

EAR knew how he got his name, but the episode at the Seaside House in South Harpswell has come down to us from other members of the family. There is no record that Robinson himself ever told the story to anyone.

EAR as Bestower of Names

The tardy and offhand manner of his own christening may well have inspired Robinson's penchant for finding curious and sometimes outlandish yet invariably felicitous names for his characters. From boyhood on, he was interested in unusual biblical names, in particular such conveniently iambic four-syllable ones as those of the humorous "Two Men" (1897):

There be two men of all mankind
    That I should like to know about;
But search and question where I will,
    I cannot ever find them out.

Melchizedek, he praised the Lord
    And gave some wine to Abraham;
But who can tell what else he did
    Must be more learned than I am.

Ucalegon, he lost his house
    When Agamemnon came to Troy;
But who can tell me who he was—
    I'll pray the gods to give him joy.

There be two men of all mankind
    That I'm forever thinking on:
They chase me everywhere I go,—
    Melchizedek, Ucalegon.

Many of Robinson's early poems focus on the inhabitants of Tilbury Town, a fictional community bearing considerable resemblance to Gardiner, Maine. Commentators differ about the origins of "tilbury." Robinson chose it to criticize the materialistic bent of his home town, Hagedorn contended, with "Tilbury" evoking "a cash box, a till, this modern age in miniature." Neff maintained, more persuasively, that the name referred to "the tilbury, a smart two-wheeled open carriage" of the late nineteenth century. In support of that view, Anderson added the useful information that in Thackeray's *Pendennis*, one of EAR's favorite novels, such a carriage functions as a status symbol. The name, obviously, was carefully chosen, as were the names of his characters. Consider Aaron Stark, for instance, and Reuben Bright, John Evereldown, Richard Cory, Luke Havergal, Miniver Cheevy, Cliff Klingenhagen, Fleming Helphenstine, Flammonde, Tasker Norcross, Bewick Finzer, Eben Flood, Roman Bartholow, many others.

From the beginning of Robinson's career, reviewers called attention to his "fancy for curious names." Most agreed that odd as these names were, they were also oddly appropriate. Even the sound of the names suggested what his characters were like. No ordinary mortal could be called "Flammonde," Ellsworth Barnard observed, for the name struck the ear with heroic overtones. "Miniver Cheevy," on the other hand, could only belong to a person others would not take seriously. As the *Chap-Book* observed in its review of *The Children of the Night* (1897), the names of Robinson's characters fitted them like a glove, often carrying deeper connotations. They were not assigned haphazardly, not drawn from a hat.

2

A Manor Town in Maine

67 Lincoln and Oaklands

In correspondence, Robinson at sixty reflected on the origins of creativity. Where did the artist get his talent, his drive? Characteristically, he was of two minds on the question. He felt certain that heredity supplied "the original juice" without which artistic achievement was impossible. Yet he was equally sure that environment "might strangle or even destroy" genius. "So in one sense," he summed up, "I see heredity as everything, and in another sense I see environment as almost everything."

At the time of these observations, Robinson was at the height of his reputation, regarded by critics and the public alike as a poet of great accomplishment. In addressing this topic, he must to some degree have been thinking of his own case. He must have believed that his forebears, particularly his parents, gave him enough of "the original juice" to make him a poet. He may also have thought that had he stayed in his home town throughout his life, the environment might eventually have "strangled" his talent.

Robinson lived for all but two of his first twenty eight years in Gardiner, Maine, a town of about 4,500 when his father brought the family there in September 1870. Thus he spent his formative years and those of his young manhood, as one dissertation writer patronizingly put it, "in the provincial fastness of a small Maine community" where a handful of poetasters and literary ladies "passed as members of the intelligentsia." Few poets of major stature "have had to contend with a poverty of circumstance so acute." So it might seem, until one thinks, for example, of Emily Dickinson, another poet who learned to see New Englandly, shut up alone in her second-story bedroom in Amherst, Massachusetts. Besides, Gardiner was no ordinary place (nor was Amherst, for that matter). Together with young Win Robinson's troubled family, the town and its inhabitants shaped him into the artist he became.

Edward Robinson spread himself when he bought the S. W. Bates house at 67 Lincoln Avenue. He liked elbow room, and the new home and its surroundings amply provided it. Situated at the intersection of Lincoln Avenue and Danforth Street, high above the Kennebec river, it comprised four lots on two acres. The two-story, white clapboard house, much larger than the one in Head Tide, stood on the rear center of the property, the front door facing south, with an ell and a stable to the west running along Danforth Street and its Cemetery Street extension. An evergreen hedge and berry bushes fringed the property on the west, providing a border for a kitchen garden where small vegetables were cultivated. Corn and potatoes grew on the hillside to the northeast. An ample orchard—an advertising flyer for the property listed eighty-four apple trees, sixty-three pear trees, forty-three plum trees, and ten grape vines—lay behind the house, where the land fell away to a ravine with a brook running through it. The boys did much of the outdoor work around the place, while Mary Robinson canned the raspberries, made blueberry pies and muffins, coddled the sweet apples and Bartlett pears, and baked the winter apples—the Northern Spies and Bellflowers. Chickens were kept, and the horses needed tending to. It was not a farm, really, but the Robinsons, like many another family of the time, took what advantage they could of the short growing season.

In the main house, there were four bedrooms and a bath upstairs—one bedroom for Edward and Mary, one for Dean, one for Herman, and one reserved for guests. The bathroom was a distinction: the first one in town. Two small servant rooms were situated to the rear. In the ell, kitchen and woodshed occupied the ground floor, with three rooms above, one of them Win's. From his windows, he could observe nature taking its inevitable course. On the east side, perennially, the brook wound through the hollow. On the west, from time to time, funeral processions made their way to nearby Oak Grove cemetery.

The Robinson home was handsomely furnished. A Brussels carpet of oriental design covered the entire lower floor of the main house. Most of the furniture was mahogany, but the Robinsons bought a new suite of walnut for the

FIGURE 2.1 67 Lincoln Avenue, the Robinsons' substantial home in Gardiner, Maine.

Source: Gardiner Library Association

south parlor, transferred "the grape set" from Head Tide to the north parlor, added a piano of carved rosewood, and installed two rocking chairs: a Boston rocker and the wicker rocker that became Win's favorite. The outlines of the original house were also altered—not for the best aesthetically, some felt—by the addition of a wraparound porch and bow windows. Towering maples and elms punctuated the front yard. One elm near the driveway was said to be almost two hundred years old.

Altogether the house proclaimed itself as an impressive establishment, the residence of a man of importance. What's more, both Edward and Mary Palmer Robinson came from solid old New England stock. Yet wherever they might have lived and however they might have prospered, the Robinsons were not going to gain acceptance among the aristocracy in Gardiner, a town that stood as a last remnant of feudal aristocracy. "I know of no place in America so English in atmosphere as Gardiner," the poet Amy Lowell, of the Boston Lowells, wrote in 1917. "Standing on the broad blue Kennebec, the little town nestles proudly beside that strange anomaly in an American city—the manor-house. For Gardiner, so far as custom is concerned, possessed a squire for over two hundred years. And this gentleman's house is as truly 'the great house' as that in any hamlet in England."

The history of the town, as recorded by historian Danny D. Smith, traced back to the Pilgrims who came over on the *Mayflower*. They were granted title to Kennebec Valley lands by the English court and sold it to a group of Boston merchants in 1660. Nearly a century later, in 1754, Dr. Silvester Gardiner (1708–1786), a leading surgeon and businessman in Boston, acquired the best land in the entire 1.5-million-acre grant, located at the confluence of the Cobbossee stream and the Kennebec River. Between them, the two watercourses made the future of Gardiner possible. The narrow Cobbossee ran fast, dropping 130 feet in its last mile. Eight dams were built to harness its power for sawmills, gristmills, and lumber and paper mills. Ocean-going vessels plied the Kennebec, wide and deep, providing access to the Atlantic and to trade with cities along the East Coast. Dr. Gardiner left his land in trust for his grandson Robert Hallowell (1782–1864), who according to the will had to fulfill two provisions before assuming title. First, young Hallowell had to reach legal age. Second, he had to change his surname to Gardiner.

In 1803 Robert Hallowell Gardiner I (the name has been passed down the generations to Robert Hallowell Gardiner VI) took over his grandfather's property and began fashioning it into the thriving river town that carried his name. As an important first step, Squire Gardiner commissioned a survey of his land lying west of the Kennebec, and by 1808 he was selling lots to settlers. He repaired mills and dams, built stores, and established the Gardiner Savings Bank. Edward Robinson later served as a director. He erected the Gothic-revival Christ Church, donated five acres in the middle of town (bordered north and south by Lincoln and Dresden Avenues) for a handsome common, and started

FIGURE 2.2
Oaklands, Gardiner's
manor house designed
by Richard Upjohn.

Source: Photo by James
Arthur Hayes, Maine
Historic Preservation
Commission.

the Lyceum, the first industrial arts school in America. And in 1836, he constructed Oaklands, the family's manor house.

Located a discreet two miles south of town on an estate of 400 acres, Oaklands was designed by the eminent Richard Upjohn. With its crenellated turrets and long access road stretching from the Kennebec, the massive mansion resembled a medieval fortress. European nobles in exile came to visit there, as well as three presidents and the near-president James G. Blaine, the Plumed Knight from Maine defeated by Grover Cleveland in the election of 1884. Paintings by Copley and Stuart hung on the walls, and in the front hallway a portrait of Dr. Gardiner the founder, bewigged and with a hand tucked into his waistcoat like Napoleon.

The Gardiners and Hallowells, and such close relatives as the Richardses, who were to play an important role in the life of EAR, maintained their ties to England. Sons were sent to public school there—Rugby for a time—and on to Cambridge. Even as their fortune dwindled and their influence lessened, the Gardiners and their kin continued to think of themselves as lords and ladies of the shire.

Henry Richards, grandson of Robert Hallowell Gardiner I and husband to the writer Laura E. Richards, got his education in England and upon his return took up the practice of architecture in Boston. He was summoned to Gardiner in 1878 to take over operation of the Richardses' paper mill and settled his family right in the middle of town, in the handsome Yellow House on Dennis Street. Sixty years later, he looked back on the period of Maine's greatest prosperity from a patrician point of view. "A prominent group from Massachusetts developed the district of Maine," he wrote, and among them it was "pretty safe to say . . . that the people of importance came from people with a tradition of importance." One "tiny hallmark" of social position, Richards observed, was the use of " 'Esquire,' the plain gentry's title." Many of the colonial fathers had been so addressed when they came across the ocean. The custom, hardly democratic, lingered long in Maine, so that John W. Hanson's *History of Gardiner* (1852) contained references to "Rufus Gay, Esq.," "Frederick Allen, Esq,," "R. H. Gardiner, Esq.," and so on. Even Edward Robinson is referred to as "Esquire" as late as 1876, although he was not among the gentry, the "people of importance" whose forebears brought English customs and prejudices from Massachusetts to Maine. Such distinctions may seem trivial, but, as Louis Coxe comments, the matter of "not being quite right socially" had its effect on EAR's life and on his poetry. He never really belonged to Gardiner's elite. He knew it as a boy, and he would be painfully reminded of it before he left his home town for good.

The Golden Age

Maine enjoyed its period of greatest economic growth during the middle decades of the nineteenth century. As the writer Robert P. Tristram Coffin put it in 1939, the years from 1820 to 1880 were the only ones "when the State of Maine was able to keep her smartest children home and give them all something to do," instead of shipping them westward. In Gardiner, the peak of prosperity came rather later: in *Gardiner on the Kennebec*, Danny D. Smith and Earle G. Shettleworth Jr. designated 1861 through 1896 as the city's golden years. The wealth of the region derived from the combination of the great pine belt and the availability of navigable rivers, and Gardiner was ideally situated to take advantage of both. As the forests of central Maine were cut, logs were floated down the Kennebec and diverted into the mill pond at the bottom of the Cobbossee. From there, the timber was processed into boards, paper, and sawdust at the mills upstream.

The city grew along with the economy. The Gardiner Public Library went up in 1881–82, with Henry Richards as architect. Two years later, the Gardiner Coliseum, the state's largest convention hall, was built. The auditorium housed a stage and a roller-skating rink and could seat up to 2,500 people. The Robinsons' high school graduation ceremonies were held there.

Win Robinson was no country boy, then. He grew up in a busy river town where private enterprise flourished, encouraged by the improvements of Squire Gardiner. Hotels and shops went up along busy Water Street, by the river. Above them rose the steep hill—Church Hill or Nobility Hill, as it was variously called—where the Robinsons and the rest of the rising capitalists lived. Steamboats brought access to seaboard cities and the world beyond. From 1866 to 1889, Capt. Jason Collins piloted the *Star of the East* twice a week between Boston and Gardiner, excepting winter months when the Kennebec was frozen. Leaving Boston at six p.m., "the Splendid Sea-going Steamer" brought passengers to the Gardiner wharf early the following morning. From there, they could board a smaller steamer to negotiate the eight miles upriver to the state capital, Augusta. During the summertime, the popular *Islander* made daily round-trip journeys from Gardiner to the resorts of Boothbay Harbor. By the 1890s the Maine Central Railroad had largely supplanted the steamboats as carriers of passengers and freight. But the memories of youths like Robinson, whose childhood coincided with the boom, forever carried them back to the Kennebec and the sea beyond.

In 1916, Rosalind Richards, daughter of Henry and Laura Richards, and a woman Robinson fell in love with, published a book called *Northern Countryside* about her origins. Without naming the town, the state, or anyone who lived there, Richards used description to evoke Gardiner's atmosphere and way of life. For the most part, she sang a hymn of praise to her surroundings. It was true, she acknowledged, that the inhabitants tended to hug their own firesides in solitude during the six months of winter. But that was because they enjoyed "too little the elixir of our still winter days": days whose splendor she attempted to recreate in rhapsodic prose.

> Like the inside of a pearl; like the inside of a star-sapphire; like a rainbow at twilight. We are in a white world, and save for the rich warmth of the pines and hemlocks there is no color stronger than the delicate penciling of the woods; but the whiteness is softened all day by a frost-haze which the sunlight turns into silver. . . . It is a very still time of year, there is a wonderful uplifting quiet.

Later, she observed that the "white months" provided valuable time for solid reading, writing papers for literary societies, getting up plays and tableaux, and doing the best work in the schools. "Nobody minds the long evenings, the lamplight beside the open fires is so infinitely cozy; and on moonlight nights, all winter, the long double-runners slip past outside, with joyful laughter and clatter, as the boys and girls . . . take one hill after another."

Such passages challenged credibility, for the people of central Maine, like all those living through extended periods of short days, long nights, and bone-chilling cold, were more than ordinarily subject to bouts of depression. Yet Gardiner did put its harsh winter to good commercial use. Ice harvested from the Kennebec—"the frozen-water trade," as Gavin Weightman called it in his book of 2003—kept the area prosperous considerably longer than other northern regions.

From the beginning, the ice business was closely related to Gardiner. In June 1805 Emma Tudor of Boston married Robert Hallowell Gardiner I. Later that same year, her brother Frederic Tudor sketched out his initial plan to transport ice to tropical climates. The techniques he and his employees developed for cutting, shipping, and storing ice soon became standard. Once the water had frozen to a depth of eighteen to twenty-four inches, horses and men scraped the surface clear of snow and used iron cutters to mark out two-foot squares. Next, horse-drawn plows cut the grooves deep enough to allow workmen to pry the squares free. Then the cakes of ice were hauled by conveyer belts to icehouses along the shore, where they awaited the spring thaw and a journey to distant markets. As the use of ice to keep food fresh and drinks cool increased throughout the United States, it was the cities down the coast that bought most of the "frozen gold": Boston, New York, Philadelphia, Baltimore, and Washington, D.C.

By 1860, the Kennebec had become the Northeast's largest single source of ice. There were two principal reasons. First, the river was regarded as uncommonly pure, since it flowed on a steep gradient from north to south and the freshwater fought back the saltwater of the tides. Second, and still more important, the Kennebec invariably froze hard enough to allow for a winter harvest. Frederic Tudor had begun cutting ice at Fresh Pond, near Boston, and competitors in New York used the Hudson river as a source of supply. But the Massachusetts and New York winters sometimes were too mild for effective harvesting. Not so in Maine, so that in a region where the topsoil was too thin and the growing season too limited for more conventional farming, ice became the leading crop. In 1860, James L. Cheeseman moved his operations from the Hudson to Farmingdale, the town adjoining Gardiner to the north. In 1868, the Knickerbocker Ice Company of Philadelphia also relocated to the Kennebec. David C. Shepherd—the father of Emma Shepherd, who was to mean so much to the Robinson family—was sent along to supervise the company, the largest ice producer in Maine. In subsequent years, both Dean and Win Robinson, along with many other local citizens, found part-time employment on the river

FIGURE 2.3 Horses and men going out to harvest ice on the Kennebec river.

Source: Photo by James Arthur Hayes, Maine Historic Preservation Commission.

during the six weeks or so—from late January to early March—when the ice was cut and collected.

In 1869–70 and again a decade later, business on the Kennebec boomed when warm weather kept waterways to the south open throughout the winter. On both occasions, the harvesters worked two shifts—the night crew under the blaze of torches—to cut as much ice as possible and so benefit from rising prices in New York and elsewhere. In 1870, the two firms operating in Maine managed to cut some three hundred thousand tons of ice. That bonanza attracted more competition, so that by 1880, thirty-six companies and fifty-three icehouses were located on the stretch of the river from Bath to Hallowell. A passenger on the *Islander* one late spring day counted seventy-four schooners anchored on the still shorter reach of the Kennebec from Richmond to Gardiner, waiting to take on cargo at the icehouses. The frozen-water trade, although doomed to fail with the advent of artificially manufactured ice, helped keep Gardiner afloat from the 1870s through the last years of the century.

The Duke of Puddledock

Edward Robinson arrived in Gardiner just as it was embarking on its period of greatest growth. Officially he was retired from business, but he was still hale and hearty in his early fifties and by no means inactive. He devoted himself to his investments, drawing 10 percent interest from farm mortgages in Midwestern states and from the Little Androscoggin mills in nearby Auburn. Exercising his Yankee shrewdness and robust charm, he became a trustee of the Gardiner Savings Bank and a director of the Merchants National Bank. As a leading citizen, he was called upon to serve the community: as a member of the Gardiner school committee in 1872, of the common council in 1873–74, and of the board of aldermen in 1876–77. "His whole life has been one of usefulness," his obituary would declare, "and he was in the truest sense of the term, a self-made man."

Edward Robinson was canny in money matters but also uncommonly principled. Daytimes, Nat Barstow remembered, "he and Mr. Swift and Ephraim Hatch and one or two others of those moneyed men" would sit around the savings bank and talk. One day, a banker warned him that it might be best to unload one of his stocks. The company seemed likely to fail, and the bank was selling its shares. "I see," he said. "Then whoever I sell to would lose his money." The banker allowed that was the probable result. "Well then," Edward said, "I guess I'll keep my stock."

EAR knew this story about his father and, in *The Glory of the Nightingales* (1930), effectively paid him tribute by dramatizing the behavior of a less honest man. Nightingale in that poem ruins the life of Malory, his partner in business and rival in love, by selling out his shares in a firm he has learned is about to go on the rocks and withholding the information from fellow shareholder Malory. At the end, the contrite Nightingale confesses his duplicity to Malory.

> I sold all mine
> For someone else to lose, which is finance,
> And somehow failed—I'll hardly say forgot—
> To show you the same seasonable way
> Out of that golden hole.

The word that Gardiner folk used to describe Edward Robinson—a startling word, considering the contrary inclinations of his famous son—was "jolly." He was "very jolly," one recalled, "quite jolly, always in great spirits," another said. He was an accomplished dancer who could perform a difficult "trimming the pigeon" and add impromptu fancy steps at the beginning and end of conventional square dances and contra-dances. He was also a fine singer with a big baritone voice. In the evenings, Mary Robinson would play the piano and Edward would lead their sons in singing such favorites as "The March of the Cameron Men," a Scottish song that EAR would one day transform into a poem. Edward also liked poetry, especially Shakespeare. Asked to account for the sources of his talent, EAR mentioned in a March 1922 letter that his father, "who was otherwise a hard-headed businessman, had a queer fondness for poetry and was always quoting it."

To an extent, Edward's jolliness may have been encouraged by drink. Perhaps the strongest evidence of this came from Harry Swanton, one of Win's boyhood playmates. Writing his recollections for the E. A. Robinson files at the Maine State Library, Swanton included a page of copy about Edward's drinking. In 1935, Henry E. Dunnack, the state librarian, sent all of his files to Laura E. Richards, who in reply urged Dunnack to delete Swanton's passage "about E. A. R.'s father being intemperate." It was easy to see how young Swanton may have come to that conclusion, she wrote. Mr. Robinson had wine on the table and took a glass with dinner. He also had a ruddy complexion, including a red nose. This was enough to start "a neighborhood rumor which would naturally impress a child." But, Richards added, she had been assured by Mrs. Herman Robinson (Emma) that the rumor was false. Emma knew, of course, of the family history of addiction and undoubtedly wanted to conceal it from public view. Dunnack did what Mrs. Richards asked, whiting out the passages on pages three and four of Swanton's account that dealt with Edward Robinson's drinking. In retrospect, it seems likely that he had a drinking problem, one severe enough not to be spoken of.

Perhaps it was the drink, perhaps the jolliness, perhaps the lack of gentlemanly polish, perhaps the jaunty way he carried himself. For whatever reason, and respected though he was by most people in Gardiner, the town's aristocracy regarded Edward Robinson as a somewhat pretentious figure. "His people were not of the very small group of the *statelier* families," Henry Richards wrote by way of fixing his status. Instead, Robinson "fitted entirely" among the good solid families of the community, "practical-minded rather than scholarly" and with "some slight rusticities of speech." Almost everyone in town knew of his pronouncing "corps" as "corpse" during a school board meeting. But it remained for General John Richards, Henry's older brother and the acknowledged snob of the family, to denigrate EAR's father as the "Duke of Puddledock"—Puddledock being a slighting name for his native Alna, Maine. The young poet in the making, listening and looking around him, must have heard—and winced at—the belittling title.

A Pair of Scissors

"My father was to me a mighty stranger," the title character of Robinson's *Roman Bartholow* (1923) says, and adds, "For the most part he let me go my way." So it was between Edward and Edwin. They were not close, the fifty-year gap in age militating against a strong bond.

The boy formed a far closer attachment to his mother, who by all accounts had a tender and loving nature and a strain of poetic idealism in her makeup. Where Edward was vigorous and hearty, Mary Robinson was sensitive, even delicate. No doubt her inability to care for Win as a baby had its psychological effects on his relations with her, as with all future love objects. As the object-relations theorist Nancy Chodorow put it, an infant deprived of nurturing maternal care is prone to develop "an all-pervasive sense, sustained by enormous anxiety, that something is not right, is lacking in him and her." Subsequently, such a person may shrink from emotional commitments, because of the risk of loss.

The Robinson household was not one where family members openly declared or displayed their affection for one another. But the feeling between Mary Robinson and her last-born boy went singularly unarticulated, in its lack of expression extending beneath the standards of New England reticence.

Photographs do not do justice to Mary Robinson. Her fellow townspeople remembered her as a lovely woman, but she did not smile for the camera, and black-and-white prints could not capture her coloring. "She had the satiny skin and delicate peach-blossom coloring which we used to associate with hidden disease," one neighbor recalled. "Her manner was ultra-refined, contrasting strangely with the rugged individualism of her big, powerful husband." Win looked much like her, inheriting the pink cheeks and the low forehead with soft hair growing close. His brothers, especially Herman, took after their father.

In *Where the Light Falls*, biographer Chard Powers Smith reads much into the crayon portrait of Mary Robinson that for many years hung in the house at Head Tide. From the portrait, Smith wrote, she looked out at the world "with hyperdelicate concern." In a family beset by one demon or another, her demon was "obviously that of high breeding run thin, of delicacy spun down into frailty, quality frittered into worry, of selflessness so utter that one wonders if she had anything more substantial than tremulous abstraction to give her sons." That is a great deal to conclude from a crayon portrait made from photographs, particularly so when most such portraits made around 1880 tended to look very much alike. But Smith was right about Mary Robinson's neurasthenia. She usually had a hired girl to help around the house, and though she did the cooking herself, she left ordering the groceries to her husband. In fact, she stayed dependent upon him in almost everything. It was as if—being fifteen years younger—she were his child. The roles were reversed in his final illness when Edward lay for hours, his head in her lap. After he died in 1892, she felt terribly bereft. "Married people are like a pair of scissors," she said to Emma. "One is no good without the other."

Until he fell ill, Edward Robinson functioned as unquestioned master of the household. He made all the important decisions, including the ones that sent Dean to Bowdoin and medical school, launched Herman into a career in business, and downgraded Win—who seemed hopelessly uninterested in worldly success—into the "scientific" high school curriculum where he might be prepared for one modest career or another. Both parents worried what might become of him. Dean and Herman would make their way in the world, Mary Robinson felt sure, but Win's future looked bleak to her. His parents were not the first or last to misjudge their children so completely.

Interviewed after Robinson's death in 1935, companions of his youth repeatedly mentioned his deep attachment to his mother. Among his siblings, Win was the son who was most loyal and most helpful to his mother for the longest period, the one who stayed at home until nearly thirty: obviously, he wanted to please her. And as a mother Mary Robinson gave the youth and young man the kind of attention she could not, because of her postpartum depression, bestow on him in his infancy, during the crucial pre-Oedipal period of object relations. Eventually—as Rosalind Richards put it in her extensive notes on EAR—they "understood and adored each other [like] two quivering halves of the same entity." The statement invites Freudian interpretation, never mind that the understanding and adoration went unexpressed. "To a Freudian," as Louis Coxe remarked, "all things are Oedipal and indeed there is a case for seeing in Robinson's life the familiar pattern of the unwanted third son," rejected by a stern older father and obsessively devoted to a gentle youthful mother.

Robinson rarely spoke about his parents, so that two instances when he did briefly unburden himself about his father assume considerable importance. In the fall of 1892, a few months after Edward Robinson died, EAR and Mowry Saben attended a performance in Boston of James A. Herne's *Shore Acres*. Afterward, he told Saben that the elderly merchant in the play reminded him of his father. This merchant is in love with a young woman, who is also being courted by a young man nearer her age. In conversation with the woman's father, the merchant attempts to undermine his younger rival by making fun of his interest in impractical matters. This "not over-illuminating" remark, Saben observed, was almost the only key Robinson ever gave him "to unlock the secret" of his relationship with his father, and, he concluded, "it was not much." Enough, however, to suggest that Robinson may have envisioned himself in the role of the young suitor vying with a powerful father.

In the early 1930s, Robinson struck up a friendship with the poet and psychiatrist Merrill Moore in Boston. Moore, who was fascinated by the psychological makeup of creative artists, managed to draw from Robinson an account of a dream he'd had. Three men had fallen into a well, and were about to despair of surviving when someone lowered a thread to them. "Here is our chance," one of them cried, grasping the thread, and was drawn upward with the others clinging to him. But as they were about to reach the surface, one of the three succumbed to doubt and they all dropped, sinking under the water. The "someone" in this dream, as the critic and lay analyst Jay Martin interpreted it, represented "the tormenting father-figure" Edward Robinson, and the three men the sons he "had abandoned . . . to their personal disasters." So construed, the dream served to demonstrate that even in his final years EAR "harbored an oedipal hostility toward his father." In discussions, Moore told Hagedorn, he was able to get the poet to acknowledge and accept his long-suppressed resentment of the mighty stranger who ruled his childhood.

3

Never So Young Again

First Light

Mary Robinson dressed up her lastborn Win, aged four, in Little Lord Fauntleroy costume for a trip downtown and secured him in a high chair while she shopped. Other women, attracted by his long brown curls and enormous brown eyes, invited him to talk. "You're a big boy, aren't you?" they asked. Silence. "What's your name?" Silence. "Cat got your tongue?" Silence. "I know why this little boy doesn't talk. He doesn't *have* a tongue." The fussed-over child, keeping silence, stuck out his tongue for reply.

So began Robinson's lifelong struggle with social helplessness. With one or two others, he could conduct a conversation. In larger groups, he found it difficult to say anything at all. "I realized at the age of five," he wrote Jean Ledoux in December 1915, "that I was never going to be able to elbow my way to the Trough of Life." At that age, he often perched on the front end of the rocking chair in the Robinsons' front parlor, lost in introspection. "When I was a small child," he wrote Amy Lowell two weeks earlier than his letter to Mrs. Ledoux, "I used to rock myself in a chair many sizes too large for me and wonder why the deuce I should ever have been born." This made him indignant for a time, but, he assured Lowell, he'd got over all that. Or possibly not. "I don't believe E. A. was ever happy," concluded Laura E. Richards, who knew him well for nearly forty years. He was *born* with a tendency to somberness, she thought. "The effervescence of childhood" was not for him.

At five or six, however, the lad discovered reading, opening a world that seemed to have been made for him. The sound of language captivated him first, as in the rhythmical beat and sonorous rhymes of Edgar Allan Poe's "Raven" and Thomas Campbell's "Lochiel's Warning." He would sit on the kitchen floor and recite "The Raven," much to the delight of his mother.

"Leave no black plume as a token of that lie thy soul has spoken!
Leave my loneliness unbroken!—quit the bust above my door!

FIGURE 3.1 A worried-looking Edwin
Arlington Robinson at three years old.

Source: Wallace L. Anderson Papers, Colby College
Special Collections.

Take thy beak from out my heart, and take thy form from off my door!"
    Quoth the Raven, "Nevermore."

In the evenings, he astounded his father with his command of Campbell's stirring Scottish ballad. "What was it the wizard said to Lochiel?" Edward Robinson would prompt, and his six-year-old would respond:

"Lochiel, Lochiel! Beware of the day
When the Lowlands shall meet thee in battle array,
For a field of the dead rushes red in my sight,
And the clans of Culloden are scattered in flight."

But the brave Lochiel will not heed the warning. "Go preach to the coward," he
tells the wizard. "I trust not the tale!" Forth into the fray he goes, "leaving in
battle no blot on his name."

"Lochiel's Warning" was but one among several "Poems of Patriotism and
Freedom" in William Cullen Bryant's popular *Library of Poetry and Song*.
(Another was the inspirational "Battle-Hymn of the Republic," written by Julia
Ward Howe, the mother of Laura E. Richards.) First published in 1870, Bryant's
thick anthology went through twenty editions in its first six months and found
its way onto the bookshelves at 67 Lincoln Avenue—in a household of readers.
An engraving of the patriarchal Bryant, with long white hair and long white
beard, ran as the frontispiece. In the introduction, he dispensed the critical
wisdom of the time. "The proper office of poetry," Bryant wrote, is to fill the
mind "with delightful images" and awaken "the gentler emotions," a Victorian

standard that Robinson—and the wider culture of modernism—repudiated as unduly limiting the boundaries of what poems could do and say.

At seven Win was reading Shakespeare, understanding little but taking pleasure in the music of the verse. A few years later he kept a small scrapbook wherein he copied poems, just as his mother had before him. Drawn to poems about people instead of the natural world, and about children of more or less his age, he duly copied into his scrapbook Eleanore Myers Jewett's "Little Louise" from *St. Nicholas* magazine and Margaret E. Sangster's "Elizabeth, Aged Nine" about a sampler that a little girl named Elizabeth had made a hundred years before. At ten, he began collecting words from his reading in the Bible and elsewhere. To acknowledge his heroes, he installed a likeness of Poe and a drawing of Ophelia among the willows on his bedroom wall.

Win Robinson was not an entirely literary child, though. He collected butterflies and stamps as well as words. He played along the brook behind his house, sculpting images out of mud. He went to school and made friends.

In the autumn of 1875, Win started school under the instruction of Mrs. William (Mary) Morrell. Mrs. Morrell, rotund and efficient, ran a private school at her house on 83 Dresden Avenue, only a block away from the Robinson's. She had fifteen to twenty students of varying ages in her charge and, with her size and air of command, had no trouble maintaining discipline. Win sat at a long low table with the youngest pupils. Almost all were boys—there seem to have been no girls of his age in attendance—and they soon became playmates as well as schoolmates.

Among his companions were Harry Morrell, the son of the schoolmistress; red-haired Willis Atwood; two Longfellow boys, and three Swantons—Walter,

FIGURE 3.2 Schoolmistress Mrs. Mary Morrell, Win's first teacher.

Source: Wallace L. Anderson Papers, Colby College Special Collections.

John, and Harry. The group played oftenest at the Swanton place on Kingsbury Street, house and barn and shed on two and a half acres of hilly land extending down to Water Street. The boys bounced balls off the side of the house and generally made noise, Win contributing "considerable under his share" to the racket. The amiable Mrs. Swanton didn't mind a group of lads tramping around her house and grounds: at least she knew where her sons could be found. But also in residence, upstairs, was the blunt-spoken Aunt Dorcas, who wryly observed that Pinny Robinson and Will Atwood spent so much time at the Swantons' that they should have been charged for room and board. Aunt Dorcas inspired awe in young boys. Harry tried to lure Win (Pinny, as the boys called him) into her room one afternoon. "Is she in there?" he whispered to Harry, pointing at the closed door. "Is the old lady in there?" When Harry admitted that she was, he flatly refused to enter.

The lads swung on the barn door or tried to negotiate the length of the picket fence without falling. They were city boys, but nature lay all around them. Summertimes, they swam at Bradstreet's Wharf or White's Ice House on the Kennebec. Win loved the swimming, especially at low tide when the side-paddle *Star of the East* rolled waves toward the shore. In the winter, he skated on the river and coasted down Gardiner's hills on the beautiful black walnut, hand-me-down sled—the Hum-Strum—his father had made for Herman. Spring and fall, Win and Herbert Longfellow explored Deane's Grove to capture butterflies or blueberries. One day, they caught a mouse and laid it to rest on a loose leaf. Next morning, they found the mouse under six inches of loose soil, the beetles who had performed the burial standing guard. Every Decoration Day, Win and Will Atwood and the others would pack a lunch and hike south on Lincoln Avenue and through the woods of Oaklands to the waterfall at Rolling Dam brook. Robinson memorialized the site in the title poem of his first book: "I found a torrent falling in a glen / Where the sun's light shone silvered and leaf-split."

In this boyhood activity, Robinson knew he was different from the rest, and it troubled him. He grew up ungainly and poorly coordinated. He could hike or swim or skate adequately but had no facility whatever for playing ball. By the time he was eight or ten, his companions were increasingly devoting themselves to competitive athletic contests. When the others staged running races or chose up sides for baseball, Win stayed inside, reading. The children decided he was lazy and let it go at that. He could bear their indifference. It was more difficult dealing with the disapproval of a father who from time to time urged his son to put down his book and go outside to play.

For fresh air, his parents saw to it that Win was assigned his share of the "farming" tasks around the place. By the time he was ten, he was working in the garden and picking apples, mucking the horses and feeding the chickens. When Harry Swanton came to visit one afternoon, he found Win weeding the strawberry bed and slandering the robins who attacked it. Mary Robinson was a devout churchgoer, her husband less so. They sent their sons to Sunday School at the Congregational church, where Win liked the music and not much else. One sunny Sunday, he and a friend watched until his parents were safely inside the church, then slipped out to play in the Robinsons' barn.

A favorite outing transported Win by horse and buggy to grandfather Seth Palmer's farm across the river. He probably inherited his incapacity to make casual conversation from the Palmer side of the family. But he also found among them the models for tenderly drawn characters like the two old men of "Isaac and Archibald" and the brothers of "Two Gardens in Linndale." He always felt a deep affection for Clara Palmer, the kind and generous cousin who stayed with the Robinsons so often that she became like an older sister to all three sons. Her siblings, all of them substantially older than Win, awaited him at Pittston. The youngest—tall, gaunt, and taciturn Oakes—was thirteen years his senior. Oakes never married, and his spinster sister Clara kept house for him throughout their days. Next youngest was Fred, a schoolteacher, who became Win's friend despite the fifteen year difference in their ages.

Always hovering on the edge of the boy's consciousness, as for every Gardiner child, was the tremendous fact of the sea. Lest they forget, the Atlantic sent regular reminders upstream. Six feet of tide at Gardiner bridge; the daily flight of gulls thirty miles back and forth to the sea; salt on the lips after a southerly blow; coal and oil brought by water; twenty or more schooners lying at anchor, their riding lights bright at night; bones of old wrecks on the white beaches; the lighthouse tender resetting channel buoys every spring and autumn; every day all summer, the little steamer *Islander* taking passengers down to the spruce-wooded islands at the mouths of the Kennebec and Sheepscot.

At ten or eleven, Win made his first journey to the islands with Leonard Barnard, Seth Ellis Pope, and Arthur Blair. When the *Islander* put in at Boothbay Harbor, the other boys bounded ashore. Win stayed on board, transfixed by the sight of the sea. All the time they were at the harbor, and all the way home, he sat looking and looking, absolutely quiet, his hand on the iron stanchion. Afterwards his companions "joked him," Barnard remembered, "because one side of his face was sunburned and the other wasn't."

The "authentic beat and rhythm" of the sea were woven into much of his poetry—most noticeably in *Tristram* but also in other poems such as "Ballade of a Ship," "The Return of Morgan and Fingal," "Lost Anchors," and "Pasa Thalassa Thalassa." The last-named poem—Robinson supplied "The sea is everywhere the sea" as a translating subtitle—paid tribute to the memory of Captain Israel Jordan.

The Jordans lived diagonally across Lincoln Avenue, the Robinsons' nearest neighbors. In boyhood Win occasionally played with Gus and Alice Jordan. Like all of the neighborhood children, he was fascinated by their romantic father who sailed the seas. When Captain Jordan returned from one of his voyages, he dispensed nuts and oranges to the youngsters, along with a whiff of his adventures. Then, alas, he sailed on a ship that foundered at sea. Since there was no report of what happened, for a long time the family hoped for the best. Finally they accepted the worst and erected a gravestone in Cedar Grove cemetery: "Lost at Sea." Robinson told what happened and asked the questions it raised, in "Pasa Thalassa Thalassa."

> Gone—faded out of the story, the sea-faring friend I remember?
> Gone for a decade, they say; never a word or a sign.
> Gone with his hard red face that only his laughter could wrinkle,
> Down where men go to be still, by the old way of the sea.
>
> Never again will he come, with rings in his ears like a pirate,
> Back to be living and seen, here with his roses and vines... .
>
> Where is he lying tonight, as I turn away down to the valley,
> Down where the lamps of men tell me the streets are alive?
> Where shall I ask, and of whom, in the town or on land or on water,
> News of a time and a place buried alike and with him?

If the drowning of the sea captain reminded Win of mortality, so did the sudden death of Harry Morrell at age twelve. They were in school together one April day in 1881. A few days later, Harry died of diphtheria, the disease that was to carry off Robinson's mother, and just as suddenly. The textbooks his brother Dean brought home from medical school, with their vivid representations of hideous diseases, exacerbated Win's incipient hypochondria. "When I was a kid," he wrote Arthur Gledhill, "I had lockjaw, lupus, leprosy, cancer, elephantiasis, Bright's Disease & falling of the womb, and all at once": imagined maladies contracted from the "infernal pictures" in Dean's medical books.

In the fall of 1881, he suffered a very real injury that would affect him all his life. His parents had withdrawn him from Mrs. Morrell's tutelage to attend the public grammar school in Gardiner. Finding him daydreaming in class, his teacher struck him under his right ear with the edge of her hand. The show of discipline got Win's attention. Eventually it led to an operation for necrosis of the inner ear, almost total loss of hearing in that ear, and recurrent episodes of tormenting pain.

Sibling Connections

On January 5, 1882, twelve-year-old Win Robinson wrote a letter to his cousin Fred Palmer, then twenty-seven and teaching school in North New Portland, Maine—the first letter of the poet that has been recovered.

FIGURE 3.3 The twelve-year-old lad
· who wrote his cousin in January 1882.

Source: Colby College Special Collections.

Dear Cousin,

*I guess I will try to write a few lines to you tonight, but let me give you a description
of the table. It is in the little room and has got a pile of papers & books on one end
and a dish of apple-skins and "chompings" on the other but I guess I will not talk
about that any more, because you have been here enough to have it look natural to
you. I want to ask a favor of you if you will do it that is, not to show this letter to
anybody, and "I mean business and no joking" but don't be in such a rush.I want to
ask you another and that is: Please don't name any more branches of the Kennebec
not at present at any rate. School commenced last Tuesday. We had about five inches
of snow Sunday night and Monday morning it was blustering hard and we (please
excuse that tall e for it was an accidental slip of the pen) had some large drifts to
wade through. I suppose you got it bad up there. James I weighs between nine and ten
pounds and is as black as your boots.*

*Herman got a watch Christmas and a few other things. The upper story of Joshua
Gray's office burned off last Tuesday forenoon & came near burning some other buildings laying near it. It has been 'bully' skating on the river all the week and good sleigh-
ing since Tuesday. Herman has gone skating this evening and Dean has gone to a
party, mother is knitting and father has just got done reading a paper,—and I'm here.*

As a first letter, this one reveals a good deal about its author. He begins as if
in response to a request from Fred—*I guess I will try to write a few lines*—and
goes on to the descriptive passage about the pile of papers and apple chompings. As Wallace L. Anderson speculated, the lad may have confessed his literary ambitions to his older cousin, who offered himself as a sounding board.
If so, that might explain Win's request for secrecy. *It's all right for you to know*

about my dreams, but don't let's tell the others: they might not understand, they might make sport of me.

Then the letter proceeds more conventionally to report the news from Gardiner: the snowstorm and drifts, the progress of James I (a dog, presumably, and, considering his weight, perhaps a Scottie, and in the light of Edward Robinson's pride in his origins, undoubtedly named for James I, king of Scotland from 1406 to 1437, and not for the less valiant James I, king of England from 1603 to 1625); the fire at the office of Joshua Gray, the town's leading entrepreneur; the after-dinner tableau of mother-father-son, and—not least—the mention of Win's brothers.

In the diary that Fred Palmer kept during the 1880s, there are several mentions of Dean and Win Robinson. Dean and Win came down to the Palmer farm on the morning of July 11, 1880, Fred noted. The following month, Dean brought Win to "stop a while"—longer than a week—with the Palmers. During that visit, Win and Fred "went to a show" in Dresden together. On July 8, 1881, Oakes and Fred Palmer concluded a trip to Gardiner by bringing Win back to Pittstson with them. On November 23, 1882, when Fred was visiting Gardiner, Dean—then city physician for Gardiner—diagnosed him with a fever, and the following day Dean accompanied Fred on the journey back home, where Fred was "pretty badly off" for more than a month. And so on, ending with a visit from Win on October 15 through 17, 1887, when Fred was teaching at North Conway, New Hampshire. The two cousins, Win then seventeen to Fred's thirty-two, went to the opera the night of the fifteenth.

Two things are striking about Fred's diary. First, he seems totally unselfconscious about his companionship with Win, his much younger cousin. Second, there is no mention whatever of Herman. It is Dean and Win throughout.

FIGURE 3.4 Win's brother Dean as Bowdoin graduate, 1881.

Source: Colby College Special Collections.

At the Robinson household, the oldest and youngest sons formed a close bond. Dean had a brilliant mind, loved to read, was ingenious with his hands, and shared his mother's gentle nature. As a friend of his high school days remembered, "he had . . . a high-minded fine look, and he had very good features. . . . He planned to give himself to [whatever] was best and highest in life." Dean did not particularly want to practice medicine. He went to Bowdoin—where he graduated cum laude—and to medical school largely to please his father. Even then, Dean would have devoted himself to medical research, had not Edward ordained otherwise. Between him and his much younger brother Win, there was no rivalry whatever. Dean recognized the boy's intelligence and gave him affection and encouragement. As for Win, he looked on Dean, twelve years his senior, with something like adoration. "Dean knew more at twenty than I shall ever know," he said.

Herman was different: the handsomest of the three, though all of them were good-looking; the most outgoing; the best athlete; the most popular. All three Robinson boys shared "a natural, quiet dignity," Bertha (Partridge) Allen recalled, and a certain shyness as well, but with distinctions. "Win was the shyest, but they were all three naturally a little shy, only we young folks wouldn't let Herman be shy." Just so: he was everyone's favorite, and especially his father's. "Herman got a watch Christmas and a few other things," while nothing Win may have gotten is mentioned. Herman also got the prize room in the house at 67 Lincoln, the one behind his parents' bedroom and equal in size. When the *Youth's Companion* arrived, Herman had first crack at it. When his mother baked the first blueberry pie of the season, it was his to devour. Win curried the horse that Herman drove. After a time, it could rankle.

FIGURE 3.5 Favored son Herman as high school senior in Gardiner, 1882.

Source: Colby College Special Collections.

"A brilliant, winsome young man and a devastating extrovert, he was doubt-less the petted darling of his parents, in whose eyes he could do no wrong." So Ruth Nivison, Herman's oldest daughter, described her father. "Even his older and younger brothers were made to bow to his wishes, as were his parents." At Gardiner's high school, Herman also impressed instructor Laura (Lewis) Macomber, who taught there two years as a "substitute" for going to college. He "was as handsome as a young fellow could possibly be . . . and he was oh so *merry*—sweet—everything delightful, and he was friends with everybody. . . . Of all the boys I was teaching, Herman was *my boy*; but I never thought he would amount to much—he was the kind that everybody would love, and that would never grow up." EAR would portray him time and again, in his poetry: as the shining albeit inconsequential son in "The Gift of God," as the man who "glit-tered when he walked," like the unfortunate Richard Cory.

Unlike his brothers, Herman liked turbulence and craved excitement. He was a risk taker, avid for adventure and lithe and lucky in its pursuit. At twelve, he nearly got himself killed when he fell off his horse and was dragged by one foot for some two hundred yards. "They supposed him dead when they res-cued him," according to the story in the local newspaper, "but strange to say no bones were broken, although he was very seriously bruised, nearly all his clothes being stripped from his body."

His athletic ability introduced Herman to the more or less exclusive society of the Richards family. Soon after he moved down from Boston in 1878, Henry Richards organized a four-man crew for rowing on the Kennebec. Richards chose young Herman Robinson as one of his oarsmen. Herman possessed "the muscular ease and grace" of the born athlete, Richards recalled, and "he took to good rowing form like a duck to water." Though much the youngest member of the crew, he also proved a pleasant companion. "He was merry and full of charm in those days," as Richards remembered, "a lightsome creature in our little rowing group."

Another fifteen years would elapse before Henry Richards encountered Win Robinson, and he was struck by how dissimilar the two brothers were. Although strong and muscular, Win totally lacked Herman's ease of movement. He "did everything stiffly and awkwardly, and seemed conscious of his awkwardness," Richards observed. "I should think that probably all through his growing-up days he had been very conscious of this difference between himself and Her-man, and that it had stung." At the same time, he speculated, Win's "marked physical awkwardness" must have constituted one of the difficult things he steadily adjusted himself to, in his silent way, and that this process "strength-ened his fiber, all through his boyhood and youth."

Personally and physically, Herman and Win were so unlike each other that it seemed odd they should have been fetched from the same pond. Win stood in awe of Herman's youthful triumphs but did not look up to him as he did to Dean. Nor did he "tag after" Herman, though there were only five years between them. "Charming and gay, and loved by girls and boys and elders all together," the gregarious Herman kept so busy a social calendar that he did not bother to accompany his brothers when they visited their Palmer cousins. Herman's admirers and companions were his alone. It was left to Win to make his own friends.

Dickens, Deadwood Dick, and Don Cesar

Both Edward and Mary Robinson valued reading, and they saw to it that the family library was well stocked with the classics. Edward proudly entered his name in the more impressive sets: the *Works of Shakespeare*, the fifteen volumes of Dickens, the eleven of Thackeray. There were also "many books of poetry on the shelves," EAR recalled, "and I must have read nearly all of them."

He also read the popular fiction of the time aimed at a youthful audience. "When I was young," he wrote Mrs. Richards in 1929, "I read mostly Dickens, Dime Novels (which cost five cents), Elijah Kellogg, Harry Castlemon, Oliver Optic, Horatio Alger, Bulwer-Lytton, Thackeray and Bryant's Library of Poetry and Song." Dickens and Thackeray were already in the canon when Win first immersed himself in them, and Bryant collected the work of the most established poets. Edward Bulwer-Lytton, a best-seller among Victorian novelists, is now best remembered for launching a novel with the now-hackneyed phrase, "It was a dark and stormy night." The other writers Robinson cited were all producing adventure stories for juvenile readers during the 1870s and 1880s. Win probably read their offerings in series: Alger's Pluck and Luck series (*Bound to Rise*), Castlemon's Frank Nelson series (*Frank on a Gun-Boat*), the Rev. Elijah Kellogg's Elm Island series, and Optic's Lakeshore series.

Then there were the dime novels, or more properly the half-dime novels—shorter and less respectable than the works of Alger and Kellogg but equally insistent on the truism that those who lived good lives could surmount all obstacles and prevail. Among the obstacles were Indians—"The deadly rifle spoke—and then/Another redskin bit the dust!"—and Tories, thieves and mustache-twirling scoundrels, brutes and bullies competing against Yale. The heroic figures who defeated them, not without difficulty, included Deadwood Dick, the Liberty Boys, Nick Carter and his faithful Chick, Young Wild West, Frank and Dick Merriwell, and many others.

Erastus Beadle's "Half-Dime Library" turned out more than 1,000 titles during the late 1800s. These "were not for persons of consequence" to read, Edmund Pearson observed in his 1929 history of the phenomenon, "but for boys, for travelers, for soldiers, for sailors, for brakemen on the railroads, and hunters in camp." The soft-cover books were light enough to be carried in the pocket. And they were small enough that they could be read in school, concealed from the teacher inside a textbook, which is exactly what Win Robinson and his friends did in the early 1880s. "I think of the days," he wrote to former schoolmate Arthur Davis Variell in 1926, "when we used to read Beadle's Half Dime Library behind our geographies in the old school house in Neal Street . . . and learn much to our advantage about Tornado Tom and Shorty and Chips and Chin-Chin."

A similar nostalgia permeated Robinson's other reminiscences of youthful adventures—his apple feasts, for example, and the traveling circus that came to Gardiner every summer. He conceived a passion for apples early, inspired by the fruits of the family orchard and the "sopsy-vine" produce of the Jordans' tree across the street. He had his particular favorites, among them firm, juicy Northern Spies and Baldwins, Seek-no-Farthers, and Gravensteins. "I remember one rainy afternoon, the deuce knows how long ago," he wrote in November 1899, "when I went down to the orchard with a tin pail and an umbrella and got Gravensteins. When I got back I washed off the dried grass and the mud and had a solitary orgy by the fire. After I had eaten about ten I began to blow scales on [brother Dean's] clarinet. I have not a doubt but that I had an enormous supper that night and read *The Raven* with unaccustomed force."

Substantial fare was the norm at the Robinsons' table. Win there acquired a lifelong craving for beefsteak and potatoes, as well as for such New England staples as fish chowder, boiled lobster, and pork-and-beans with brown bread. His sweet tooth, too, was developed under the spell of his mother's pies and preserves. This hearty but not particularly healthy diet may have contributed to the digestive problems that disturbed EAR in his mature years.

Gardiner, though only a small city, maintained cultural connections to the greater world down the coast. In the 1880s and 1890s, theatrical troupes came through on tour. James O'Neill, Eugene O'Neill's father, dazzled the local audience as the Count of Monte Cristo. Still more memorable to Win was the performance of Alessandro Salvini in *Don Cesar de Bazan* that he commemorated in *Captain Craig*. With his flashing sword and overblown rhetoric, Salvini may have seemed "flamboyant and old-fashioned, overdone, romantico-robustious" to the sophisticated theatergoer but not to Robinson and his Captain Craig, who maintained that "If you decry *Don Cesar de Bazan*, / There is an imperfection in your vitals."

The traveling actors might come in any season, while the summer offered seasonal entertainment. A merry-go-round set up business on a wharf throughout the warm weather, tooting its whistle to attract customers. And for a few days each summer, the circus came to town, an event Robinson wistfully recalled in "Plummer Street, Gardiner, Maine," an amusing sonnet he embedded in a May 1900 letter to William Vaughn Moody.

If it was not last year,
When was it, then, the place was all arrayed
With tents and elephants and lemonade,

Lifting-machines, freaks, peanuts, and pop-beer?
Where are they gone now? Tell me, if you can,
Where is the giant? And the tattooed man?
Where are the clowns that once were garrulous?
Where are the people who "performed" on bars?
Where are the targets and "ten-cent cigars"
Gone now? Where is the Hipper Pottermus?

The League of Three

Win Robinson was growing fast—too fast—as he embarked on the "scientific course" at Gardiner's mansard-roofed high school just off the common. In his early teens, he "used to grow about an inch in seven minutes" and lie awake wondering if "the shin-bones of all the rest of the world ached" as much as his did. He was taller than his fellow students, and more awkward both physically and socially. They started calling him "long Robinson" and regarded him as lazy—inattentive was more like it—as he was consigned to the back of the schoolroom, his legs sticking out into the aisle.

A few years before entering high school—as early as eleven or twelve—Win had been stealing away to the hayloft or the barn to make his first attempts at writing verse. He told no one about this, not even his parents. Edward Robinson had a healthy respect for literature but did not fancy one of his sons undertaking an unremunerative career as an artist. He hoped that by taking typing and stenography as well as math and chemistry in high school, Win might acquire the practical skills to earn an honest living. It did not bother the boy's father that by skipping the "classical course," with its emphasis on Greek, he was disqualified from entering most colleges. College did no one any good, Edward

FIGURE 3.6 Lizzie Austin, who guided EAR through the classics.

Source: Danny D. Smith Papers.

Robinson announced, and before long his sons Dean and Herman would seem, in their different ways, to prove him right. Besides, Win had not—so far—distinguished himself as a student.

Whatever the curriculum, the boy enjoyed high school, and particularly his classes in Latin and English under the guidance of veteran teachers Giles Stuart and Lizzie Austin. Still, he was "conditioned" when passing from his second to his third year, a sanction he was inclined to think unfair when he thought of "some that were not conditioned." During that third year, he astounded his classmates and delighted the bespectacled Miss Austin when—assigned to translate Cicero's first oration against Cataline into English—he went to the extensive pains of rendering the entire text into blank verse.

> "O Cataline, how long will you abuse
> Our patience?"

his version of the diatribe began. The result, he observed many years later, "may not have been poetry and probably wasn't, but many portions of it had music and rhythm" and even " 'punch'—for which Cicero may possibly deserve some credit." Next he applied himself to transforming portions of Virgil's *Aeneid* into English verse, another laborious self-invented project demonstrating that where poetry was concerned, long Robinson was anything but lazy. Doing the work taught him much about the rigors and pleasures of the craft.

In the middle of Robinson's third—and supposedly final—year of secondary school, Giles Stuart was installed as principal. Sharp eyed and strict, Stuart felt certain that Gardiner High's standards were too low. As a partial remedy, he persuaded the school board to add a year to the curriculum. Win was pleased to continue his studies under the faithful Lizzie Austin, for he had no other plans. Besides, the extra year gave him an opportunity to solidify his friendships.

His closest friend was Harry Smith, who as Giles Stuart's best scholar was already committed to Bowdoin and did not stay for the additional year. Still, the two youths spent long hours together during the summer holidays, smoking their pipes and discoursing about life and literature. Starting in 1890, they began a practice of writing once-a-week letters—letters in which Robinson felt unusually free to unburden himself.

With Smith departed, Win formed the first of a series of "clubs" that would enliven his youth and young manhood with Edward (Gus) Moore and Arthur Gledhill. The League of Three, they called themselves, and adopted a silver triangle with the figure 3 inside as their emblem. As second-year seniors, they were exempted from study hall during school hours. Instead, they betook themselves to the building's belfry, where in privacy they could gossip about girls, play cribbage, and pursue the illicit enjoyments of tobacco: both pipes and the popular "Check" chewing tobacco, each package including a brass replica of a railroad baggage check. The boys plastered the beams with these mementoes.

FIGURE 3.7   Arthur Gledhill, boon companion in the League of Three.

Source: St. Lawrence University.

In their long talks, Win proved himself as always a good listener. Occasionally, in this group of the like-minded, he abandoned his native reserve and spoke forcefully and eloquently on those subjects that interested him most: books and people, in particular. Unlike many poets, Win was not particularly interested in the natural world. He was, however, immensely curious about other human beings. Gledhill and Moore were struck by his insights into the lives of students, teachers, and parents they saw every day and were inclined to take for granted.

All three youths had some intellectual attainments, but only Gledhill shone in the classroom. He wrote Latin poetry, for example, and with him as with Smith, Robinson was later to establish an avenue of correspondence. Gledhill was also his partner in the crime that almost got them both kicked out of school. They had persuaded principal Stuart to install a Franklin stove in the school laboratory. One bitter cold night Win and Art ventured there to partake of hot toddy and smoke the water-pipe they had improvised. With their capacities somewhat impaired, when the boys ran out of wood they broke up an eight-foot settee and burned it for heat. The janitor discovered the crime, Walter Swanton and Billy Gay "blew on" them (as Robinson put it), and Giles Stuart had to take action. He called the boys on the carpet and told them in no uncertain terms that they had violated his trust. Only reluctantly did he allow them to pay four dollars for a new settee instead of dismissing them.

Robinson did not soon forget the disappointment on the principal's face. Three years later, he confessed his feelings to Smith. "When [Giles Stuart] caught Gledhill and [me] in the settee business his heart was well-nigh broken. So was mine, for that matter." The incident cost them their "good character and four dollars. I think we regretted the latter more than the former, at the time, but now I would willingly give as many dollars as I could conveniently muster if the whole thing could be forgotten."

That single episode aside, Robinson looked back on the adventures of the League of Three with euphoria. The past, he knew, could not be recovered. He could never again revert to a callow schoolboy begging ten cents for a plug of "Check" and talking away the hours with a few close companions. Yet in letters to Gledhill written from 1890 to 1892, as his friend was busy completing college and launching his career, Robinson insisted on the importance of their "clandestine symposia." From a practical standpoint, the world at large might consider the time they spent together wasted, but "in after years, when we are fairly well established in the arena (if we ever are) the memories of those days will come back and we will regard them, not with contempt, but with a finer sense of realization of contentment than we have ever known."

As much as any youth, Win felt compelled to make something of himself. But during high school and especially during the 1887–88 postgraduate year, it was as if he had been granted a kind of special dispensation for idleness, with no apologies required. One summer day, he and Moore were sitting in a woodshed door when a census taker came along with his routine inquiries. What occupation was being pursued there? he asked. "Farming," Win said. How many months employed? "Better ask how many unemployed," Win suggested. All right, then, how many unemployed? "Eleven," Robinson gravely responded. The farm in question consisted of six cabbage plants well eaten with bugs.

We were all boys, and three of us were friends;
And we were more than friends, it seemed to me:—
Yes, we were more than brothers then, we three . . .
Brothers? . . . But we were boys, and there it ends.

Gledhill, Moore, Robinson bonded together, but Win had other friends as well. When Edward Robinson acquired a choice sack of sugar, the Swanton lads came over to make caramels. At the Barstows, Win sat in the little telephone room—telephones were a rarity at the time—and read Shakespeare aloud, slapping his knee in admiration of the best passages. The Barstows and Robinsons had much in common. Both fathers were offspring of Maine shipbuilders, and both had gravitated to Gardiner late in their careers. A susceptibility to drink and a series of tragic endings dogged both families. Of the four Barstow brothers, all of them intelligent, Win was closest to Joe in boyhood, and later to George and James.

Apart from poetry, nothing mattered more to Robinson than friendship. Socially compromised though he was, he had a rare capacity for making—and keeping—friends. Often they went out of their way to support or encourage him. Just as often he did the same for them. As the critic Richard Crowder observed, EAR "made almost a cult of friendship"—not a universal embrace of mankind "but a select process in which he could know intimately a few under-standing people and experience a warm exchange of affection and concern." His friends, he used to say, were "a source of grateful wonder" to him. He gave them the absolute loyalty other men invest in their wives and children.

Around girls, he remained incurably shy. To unlimber his social paralysis, his parents sent him to dancing school in the winter of his repeated senior year. There he met the stunning Emma Shepherd and was immediately smitten. Emma lived in Farmingdale, only a mile and a half from the Robinson's house, but she had been sent upriver for her schooling at Hallowell Classical Academy and St. Catherine's Hall in Augusta and knew almost no one in Gardiner before she appeared at dancing school. As a singularly beautiful girl, Emma was used to male admirers, and at twenty-two going on twenty-three, she was four and a half years older than Win. Still, she saw something in the tall, bright-eyed boy who was growing into his body, and did not discourage him when he walked over to her house and diffidently showed her the poems he had been writing. At graduation time she sent him a bouquet of roses.

The League of Three more or less took over the preparations for graduation, collecting funds from classmates to pay for dances and suppers and a brass band from the nearby Soldiers' Home. The commencement exercises were held in the outsized Coliseum on a stormy June day. As the rain pounded on the roof, leading scholars Will Atwood and Art Gledhill presented orations in Latin and Greek, respectively. Robinson was called on to deliver the Class Ode, a satirical piece he called "Mulieria, A Metrical Discourse." He looked incredibly handsome, Harry Swanton thought, but spoke so softly that only those in the first few rows could hear him. Never again, in the course of a long and distin-guished career, did he consent to read from a public platform.

Robinson's satire dealt with the gulf between the sexes, taking a less than gallant view of females. A solitary man wanders into a town inhabited solely by women, "wherein could be seen / Not one single pair of pantaloons." The intruder is taken into custody by a policewoman in petticoats. How is he to break free? The male tries one device after another, before finding the solution:

And then at last, still trusting to their natur'
I thrust into their hands the last *Delineator,*

a popular fashion magazine of the time. As the women fall to quarreling over who may examine the magazine, the prisoner makes his escape.

The Gardiner Poetry Society

Often to the neglect of his schoolwork, Win wrote many sonnets and short poems during his high school years. When he tried them out on his friends, sitting around a hot stove on a chilly afternoon, the friends decided to be unimpressed, and Robinson threw his efforts into the fire. So, as Mrs. Richards was later to lament, "we have no juvenilia." Even those companions who recognized the boy's skillful way with words were unable to conceive that he might actually pursue a career in poetry. The American poets they knew about wore chin whiskers, and most of them wrote the kind of ornamental language Win was forever poking fun at. Looking back at their adolescent days, Harry Swanton could summon from memory only one of Robinson's youthful ventures into verse.

> With deep affliction
> And malediction
> I often think of those Randolph bells.

Randolph was the town across the river from Gardiner. In his comic complaint about the incessant bell ringing from that direction, Robinson was parodying Francis Mahony's well-known "Shannon Bells," not that he expected Harry to know that. For a more appreciative audience, Win had to look to his elders.

In what passed for Bohemia on the Kennebec, a group of three professionals—a retired schoolteacher who had gone to Radcliffe, a probate court judge, and a homeopathic physician—met one evening a week to discuss the latest developments in poetry and criticize one another's attempts to produce it. Caroline Davenport Swan, a spinster with an excellent command of French, served as the presiding spirit of what was variously called the Gardiner Poetry Society or more simply, the Club. Generally, the group foregathered at her house. Judge Henry Webster brought a scholar's temperament and dedication to the assembly. Then there was Dr. Alanson Tucker Schumann, the homeopathist who lived in the next house south of the Robinsons' on Lincoln Avenue. It was Schumann, a generation his senior, who gave young Robinson the encouragement he craved.

One afternoon when he was seventeen, Win walked down the street to call on the forty-year-old Dr. Schumann. Word had reached Robinson about his neighbor's obsession with poetry—"Dr. Schumann was a fairly successful and contented local doctor until poetry got him," he later said of him—but did not really know Schumann except as an adult to nod at, should their paths cross. Only by abandoning his usual reserve and screwing up his courage was Win able to negotiate the hundred feet or so to knock on Schumann's door, a sheaf of manuscripts in hand. The doctor's mother answered the door to behold the shyest of adolescents, and upon his halting request fetched her son from his study.

Robinson presented his manuscripts. "Would you be kind enough to read these?" Of course he would, Schumann agreed with a deprecatory smile. He suggested that Win return in a couple of hours and carried the boy's poems off to look them over. As a poet, Schumann was only a dedicated amateur, but he knew the craft well enough to recognize talent when it lay in front of him. When Robinson returned for the verdict, Schumann proclaimed his work "Wonderful. Very wonderful," thereby making a lifelong friend. Would Robinson be interested in attending the next session of the Gardner Poetry Society? he asked. Oh, yes, sir, he would.

Miss Swan had her doubts about Schumann's youthful disciple but agreed to let him come to their meetings, more as an observer than a participant. The regulars had work to do, after all. "The idea was to go over each other's verse, and read the current verse in the magazines," as she described the Club's procedure. The object was to keep "in touch with what was current and what was developing, rather than what was already between covers," and then, in their own writing, to try to be themselves. Interviewed in her nineties, Miss Swan recollected the first visits of Win Robinson, a good-looking youth with high color in his cheeks. "He sat very quiet, listening. He did not talk, but his eyes were bright, and I noticed that he listened intently for the whole evening." Sometimes Schumann brought along a poem of Robinson's for discussion or persuaded the lad to bring something himself, and the group went over it. "He was learning every day. Our little Club was of great use to him." Yet she doubted that the Club, or anyone in it, had strongly influenced Robinson. The boy was "very determined," she recalled. "He had his own notions, went his own way. He was one of those persons you could not influence, *ever*."

An accomplished linguist who had once translated a French novel into English, Miss Swan introduced her fellow aspirants into the intricacies of the medieval French verse forms then in vogue: triolets, ballades, rondeaux, and villanelles. Schumann, especially, was fascinated by the French forms, which demanded great subtlety and command of technique, and he acquired considerable proficiency in their use. Robinson, who had studied no French whatever, also tried his hand. Together they struggled against the restrictions of the forms—the repetition of lines and rhymes, the use of the refrain—that presented challenges to versifiers writing in English. Then the fallen-away doctor and the poet-in-training tackled the Shakespearean sonnet: another structure with strict formal limits. Schumann had acquired a remarkable facility and could turn out technically flawless sonnets in short order. Robinson worked more slowly and sometimes would consult the maestro down the block for assistance: "find me a word that will fit." It was valuable training for a poet discovering how to think and feel within the boundaries of meter.

Robinson wrote some interesting early poems in the French forms, most notably the villanelle "The House on the Hill." Before long, however, he found that their formal demands fitted better with archaic language and sentiments than with the plain speech and portraits from everyday life he was committed to. "I am too fussy," he told Harry Smith in November 1893. " I have fiddled too much over sonnets and ballades." In his "Ballade of Broken Flutes," dedicated to Schumann, he depicted a once fertile but now desolate Arcadia where the shepherds can no longer make music.

> No more by summer breezes fanned,
>   The place was desolate and gray;
> But still my dream was to command
>   New life into that shrunken clay.
>   I tried it. And you scan today,
> With uncommiserating glee,
>   The songs of one who strove to play
> The broken flutes of Arcady.

Schumann (the "you" of the poem) might well be amused, Robinson acknowledges, at his futile attempts to resurrect the past. He decides to leave the broken flutes behind, "to crumble as they may."

What did Win Robinson learn from the Gardiner Poetry Society? That there were others, even in his small segment of the world, who cared about poetry. That poetry was a craft as well as an art, and that in order to become a poet one had to master the craft. That, as J. V. Cunningham put it, meter is "a language which, like any language, must be learned young or never. And as a language it must have an audience; this the doctor and a cultivated local poetic circle provided." That it was best, as Caroline Swan advised, to avoid "the polish of over-elegance so fast undermining our social life." And, not least, as he discovered by silent observation, that other human beings had their fascination, even—or especially—if they were afflicted with moral and social shortcomings.

FIGURE 3.8 Alanson Tucker Schumann, Win's mentor in the Gardiner Poetry Society.

Source: Colby College Special Collections.

By that standard, Dr. Schumann qualified as the most interesting figure in the Gardiner Poetry Society. Robinson respected the doctor for his technical skill and "his almost finical precision in the use and pronunciation of words." And he felt deeply indebted to Schumann for taking an interest in his work during his apprenticeship. Yet he knew, soon enough, that he had outstripped his mentor. Despite his status as "one of the most remarkable metrical technicians who ever lived" (Robinson's words in 1930), Schumann lacked the fire to transform himself from an expert versifier into a poet. As early as 1894, Win was deprecating Schumann's efforts to Harry Smith. The doctor had produced "some very warm-blooded sonnets lately," he wrote Smith, too warm-blooded for his taste. "He runs Love a little hard, it seems to me." In the same letter, though, Win said that the doctor had done him "a great deal of good by the negative example" of his life and opinions.

By which he meant that Schumann had his faults. He drank too much, and he pursued women too eagerly—facts that could not go unnoticed (though for Robinson, they would go unmentioned) in a small town. In fact, Schumann was regarded as something of a pariah in Gardiner. He had been trained as a doctor, but even before substantially abandoning the profession for poetry, he had not managed to attract many patients. When Win's ear was whacked in grammar school, his parents took him for treatment not to Schumann next door but to Dr. Gertrude Heath, another local homeopathic physician. Dr. Schumann's limited medical practice undoubtedly owed something to his unsavory reputation in other respects. Miss Swan, who had known Schumann since he was a high school student in her class, never forgave him for his drinking.

Others in Gardiner censured Schumann for his womanizing. He had an eye for the ladies and was as aggressive in approaching them as Robinson was backward. "He was very foolish," Bertha Allen remembered, "always getting engaged and then backing out of it." In a November 1899 letter to Josephine Preston Peabody, Robinson expounded on the same theme. EAR had heard from Schumann that he planned to be married, but then again "he has been going to get married for the past twenty years." So long as the doctor's mother was on the scene, "a dictatorial old lady who rules him with a rod of iron," Robinson thought marriage unlikely. Yet in the following year Schumann did in fact marry Emma Hatch, the daughter of the wealthy Ephraim Hatch of Farmington. The marriage was the culmination of the couple's second engagement—Schumann's mother having scotched the first—and set up the doctor for life.

Robinson was also introduced to the ways of the world through observation of two people—Kate Vannah and William Henry Thorne—who moved on the periphery of the Gardiner Poetry Society. The daughter of a German father and Irish mother, Vannah became a successful songwriter whose waltzes and marches enjoyed considerable popularity. Her rough-hewn manner did not sit well with Gardiner's elite, nor did her serial infatuations with other young women. But she was a wonderful storyteller who rolled out Irish stories in a golden brogue. "I'm told that it takes young Robinson six weeks to write a sonnet," she once said. "It takes *me* ten minutes. *One* of us is a fool!"

Vannah's professional career took her often to Boston and New York, and it was through her auspices that the cosmopolitan William Henry Thorne materialized in Gardiner. Thorne (1839–1907) was born, bred, and educated in England. He arrived in the United States as a Protestant clergyman, then segued into a freethinking "cosmotheist" and devout Roman Catholic. He married, fathered five children, and was divorced. In 1890 Thorne founded the *Globe* in New York, a "New Review of World-Literature, Society, Religion, Art and Politics." Thorne wrote most of the articles for the review himself, but he required financing for his magazine, and it was that which brought him to Gardiner.

Thorne was an impressive figure of a man, and carried with him an aura of the wider world beyond. "The man Flammonde, from God knows where, / With firm address and foreign air," paid suit for a time to Kate Vannah, presenting her with a splendid English setter and a fund of flattery. She soon concluded that Thorne was a sponge and passed him along to Caroline Swan, who did not see through him at all and became his patron. She sank her inherited funds into the *Globe* and followed Thorne to New York, where she undertook much of the work of the magazine herself. She also converted to Catholicism. Even when Thorne married another woman, Swan continued to support him. The relationship constituted a scandal of sorts in Gardiner.

Whatever his imperfections, Thorne had the sense to detect a touch of genius in young Win Robinson. Miss Swan herself saw to it that Win was first published. Three poems of his, none very memorable—"Thalia," "The Galley Race," and "The Clam-Digger"—appeared in 1890 in the poetry section of the *Gardiner Reporter Monthly* that she put together. Thorne introduced Robinson to a wider audience in the July–September 1894 issue of the *Globe*. He had previously inveighed against the "general dilettante dullness" of verse from the region, Thorne acknowledged, but he had discovered that there was "still a good deal of literary genius in New England" and especially "in the little town of Gardiner, Maine." Thorne therefore printed poems by all of the Club's members—"Miss Swan, Dr. Schumann, Judge Webster and Mr. Robinson"—adding that in his judgment the young Robinson "bids fair to outshine all competitors in his native state." Not an overwhelming notice, but one that spurred Robinson toward his career.

The question of vocation loomed early and large in his thoughts. Looking backward in 1930, he wrote that "it must have been about the year 1889 when I realized finally, and not without a justifiable uncertainty as to how the thing was to be done, that I was doomed, or elected, or sentenced to life, to the writing of poetry." He was not ready, fresh out of high school, to confide this realization to most other people. He could talk to Schumann, however, who after all shared his obsession. Schumann told Win that he "should have to write poetry or starve," and that he might do both. But probably he wouldn't starve, not exactly, and that at least, Robinson recalled, "was encouraging." In the long years of obscurity ahead, there would be times when he suffered poverty and had to struggle to ward off despair. But the darkest period of all lay in the decade before him. Not much of it had to do with writing poems.

4

Fall of the House of Robinson

Like most Greek tragedies, the Robinsons' began at home. During the terrible decade from 1888 to 1898—as Win Robinson grew from an inexperienced youth to a mature man of nearly thirty—his family collapsed around him in a series of terrible misfortunes. The story reads like a nightmare, Irving Howe commented, in "an atmosphere painfully similar to that of a late [Eugene] O'Neill play."

Edward Robinson degenerated into a pale shadow of his once vigorous self—his body failing first, then his mind—as his youngest son kept watch.

Win's beloved brother Dean became incurably addicted to drugs, and brought his malady home to 67 Lincoln Avenue.

Win lost to brother Herman the hand of Emma Shepherd, a romantic blow with lifelong effects.

Herman squandered the family fortune in a series of misguided investments, then took to drink.

Robinson became Uncle Win to Emma and his three nieces, a bond ripped asunder in an awful confrontation with Herman.

As Jane Mollman summarized matters: "Three brothers, all addicted: one to drugs, one to drink, and the third to poetry. One pretty young wife with three small daughters. The father dead, the mother failing, the money gone." It was more like an O'Neill drama every month, and then . . .

Mary Robinson died in circumstances of gothic horror.

Hyatt Waggoner, in his comprehensive *American Poetry from the Puritans to the Present*, adjudged Robinson's to be "a family history more tragic and terrible perhaps than that of any other major American poet." Robinson was reluctant to talk about it. He spoke often of "living in hell" but would not provide specifics. The details stayed off-limits, save for oblique use in his poetry. "I am afraid

I cannot go into all the domestic hell of my past life," he wrote George Latham in January 1894; it was bad enough to drive him to the brink of madness. "Say anything you like about me," he told putative biographer Carty Ranck. "But leave my brothers out of it." When he left Gardiner for good in 1898, "he locked the door like a stone, and sealed it."

Summer of '88

The series of family disasters did not conveniently occur separately, allowing time to recover from them. Instead, the blows fell concurrently. In the summer of 1888, for example, as Win was spending long hours in the care of his weakening father, Herman arrived like young Lochinvar out of the west and stole Emma away.

As he neared seventy, the spring went out of Edward Robinson's step. His heart was troubling him, so were his kidneys, and he no longer had energy to devote to bank boards and civic enterprises downtown. He lay on the couch in the parlor, his head in the lap of his beloved wife, or he sat on the front porch, stroking his beard and watching passersby. Once the liveliest of dancers, he now found it difficult to walk, and on occasion the muscularly strong Win was called on to hoist him in and out of bed. He was the only son at home at the time. Dean had been sent to Alna, and Herman was in St. Louis, investing Maine money in Missouri real estate. It fell to the youngest son to take care of chores around the house and garden and to entertain a father who in his decline seemed to lack resources of his own. They whiled away the time over checkers and seven-up, as Win dodged a topic on both of their minds: what he was going to do with his life

Since the early 1880s, the Robinsons like several Gardiner families had been spending their summers at Capitol Island, which measured but three-quarters of a mile north to south below Southport in Boothbay Harbor. Edward Robinson liked it there, close to the sea. In the summer of 1888, Win and his parents occupied the Collins's white cottage on the southeastern seaward cliff. Emma Shepherd arranged to spend several weeks on Capitol visiting her friend Maud Kane, three cottages away. On that rocky island, where the swimming and boating were excellent and the mild summer nights summoned the young out of doors, the triangular relationship involving Win, Herman, and Emma took shape.

Emma Shepherd was well worth competing for. The photographs testify to her extraordinary good looks. She was dark haired, short, and quick of movement—everything Win Robinson was not—yet, like him, her most prominent feature were her eyes: very large, dark blue, and disturbingly intense. The eldest daughter of David C. Shepherd, manager of the Kennebec operations of the Knickerbocker Ice Company, she inherited a fund of native intelligence, and during her education in the best finishing schools of the area, she learned to value literature. Despite the family's privileged status, her mother trained Emma and her two younger sisters in the domestic arts. Emma became extremely adept at sewing, a skill that was to serve her well in the troubled times ahead. Her nimble fingers fairly flew as she talked; sometimes, she would pause and look at them "as to be sure again how many of them she had."

Emma had all the advantages that nature and upbringing could supply, and young men found her well-nigh irresistible. "My mother was an adorable person," Emma's daughter Ruth Nivison recalled, "and a great beauty, and she was also a coquette." She came to Capitol Island in 1888 largely to see Win Robinson, although she was engaged to another suitor at the time. By any reasonable standard, Win did not qualify as a good catch. He was fresh out of high school, with no apparent prospect of being able to support a wife and family. Yet, from the evidence of his graduation photograph, he too was remarkable for his looks. Chard Powers Smith, who was to write an extensive book tracing a great many of Robinson's poems to the Emma-Win-Herman triangle, called him a Young God—albeit a rather soulful god. From the start there was a bond of understanding between Emma and Win. They communicated according to a private code of gestures, glances, and phrases no one else could decipher. Her facile ways softened his dignified reserve. She put him at ease as other women did not.

In the long summer evenings on Capitol, the young people gathered on one front porch or another to sing and laugh and talk together. Win, who was "never much of a light in company," rarely took part in these festivities. His style was to wander the island, staring at the Burnt Island lighthouse and eastward past Squirrel Island to the Atlantic, occasionally clambering down a rocky slope to the sea itself, storing up impressions that would resurface in poems like

FIGURE 4.1 Win Robinson's high school graduation picture, 1888.

Source: Colby College Special Collections.

FIGURE 4.2 Emma Shepherd in her youthful beauty.

Source: Colby College Special Collections.

"Eros Turannos" (1914) and *Tristram* (1927). When Emma arrived for her summer visit, the two of them walked together, sharing a silent communion that for Win spoke louder than words. He idealized her, and that was enough for him. As he was soon to characterize his feelings in verse,

> I loved that woman!—
> Not for her face, but for something fairer—
> Something diviner—I thought—than beauty:
> I loved the spirit—the human something
> That seemed to chime with my own condition,
> And make soul music when we were together.

To try to express this "soul music," in life or on paper, would only degrade it, Win thought. He looked askance at any hint of carnality in literature, more out of idealism than prudery. In a September 1890 letter, he inveighed against Leo Tolstoy's *Kreutzer Sonata*, a novel of sex and marriage that had been banned from circulation in the United States. "We are not all rakes," he objected, "and there is such a thing in the world as a good woman." The following March he condemned "the recent deluge of literary nastiness" in American novels that confused lust with love. What he deplored in books, he would hardly practice in action. He did not make physical approaches to Emma. He did not declare his love for her: *surely they knew how they felt about each other*. He did not propose marriage.

Unspoken though it was, Emma was conscious of Win's love for her and pleased by it. She was also sensitive enough to recognize his youthful talent.

But there lay between them the gap of more than four years in age, a chasm that yawned wider at nineteen and twenty-three than it would a decade or two later. Besides, Win was an extremely young nineteen. He had no experience in the culture of courtship—there had been no high school girlfriends—and very little in the ways of the world. Emma was ready for marriage, and he was not.

Although she detected the faint stirrings of the "soul music" that meant everything to Win, Emma yearned for a more vigorous and forceful melody. When Herman Robinson came to Capitol Island and Win introduced him to her, she was simply swept away.

While Win was in high school, Herman was establishing himself as a young capitalist to reckon with. At his own high school graduation in Gardiner, Herman had been chosen—not for his academic attainments but as the most popular boy in his class—to deliver the Class Oration. After taking a short course at a business school in Portland, he returned to Gardiner in 1884 to become assistant cashier at the savings bank. He concentrated on investments, especially in real estate, and rose swiftly in the councils of the bank. In 1886, when Herman was only twenty-two, the bank appointed him its western representative. In that position, he traveled widely and began purchasing plots of land from Minnesota to Kansas, with a particular interest in property in and around St. Louis, Missouri. At the time, investments in rapidly growing western areas seemed almost certain to appreciate in value. There was some risk, to be sure, but taking risks did not disturb Herman Robinson. He persuaded his father to transfer the conservatively invested family funds into his real estate ventures. He also persuaded a good many other customers of the bank in Maine to follow his lead.

FIGURE 4.3 Herman Robinson, rising young businessman.

Source: Colby College Special Collections.

As a salesman, Herman had few peers. He was almost blindingly handsome, and his ready smile and laughing eyes radiated good will. In his frock coat and longhorn moustache, he looked every inch the promising young businessman his father had determined he should be. And for a time he seemed to have the Midas touch, so that any shortcomings in his makeup were obscured. "As we all know," Louis Coxe summed up the situation, "charm and good looks will get you almost anywhere in an entrepreneurial world—as long as you are tough, hardheaded and financially shrewd. Herman was none of these."

Ah, but his weaknesses, like the family predilection for alcohol, lay below the glittering surface, so that when he swept down to Capitol Island, fresh from making an apparently triumphant deal in St. Louis, he captured Emma's affections overnight. The St. Louis *Weekly Real Estate Bulletin* of August 25, 1888, ran an interview with the "eastern capitalist" who had bought Audobon Place for the considerable sum of $30,000 and hoped to subdivide it. This capitalist was "Mr. H. E. Robinson" himself, only twenty-four years of age and full of blue-sky ideas for the future. He planned to move to St. Louis permanently, Herman said, and meant to develop property there. What was most needed, he declared, was an elevated railway like those going up in Chicago and New York. Then elevated trains could carry those living at Audobon Place to and from their jobs in the city. The following year, he resigned from the Gardiner Savings Bank to join the Dundee Land & Investment Company in St. Louis—and in that post, too, he lobbied for elevated trains, this time to carry passengers the ten miles west of town to Forest Park. The area eventually grew and prospered, but not soon enough to profit Herman Robinson or his investors and only after the advent of the automobile, not on the tracks of a phantom elevated railway.

Herman's dreams of gold would turn to dross, but no one knew that in August of 1888 when he arrived at Capitol Island. He was handsome of form, engaging of manner, and a few months older than Emma. Above all, he was bold and not halting in his approach. He wanted to marry Emma, not worship her from afar. They went walking one night to the promontory at the southeastern end of the island and became engaged on that rocky ground. They decided to keep the engagement secret because, as Emma recalled, "it would be more fun to keep busybodies guessing"—and also, probably, because she had to break another engagement first. By the late fall of 1888, though, Emma had her ring.

Win, who had been so hesitant in pressing his own suit, openly tried to argue Emma out of marrying his brother. She and Herman had nothing in common except their good looks and popularity, he insisted. She was *his* soul mate, not Herman's. Emma's parents had their doubts, too, for they thought Herman unduly extravagant. For Christmas 1888 he gave Emma an elegant, blue plush toilet set with ivory fastenings and placed a dozen French-embroidered handkerchiefs and a dozen pairs of kid gloves inside. Engaged or not, the Shepherds felt their daughter could not accept so much from a man. She could keep the toilet set but would have to return the handkerchiefs and gloves. "Well, I don't want them," Herman said. "Throw them in the river."

During his journeys, Herman acquired expensive habits. If you were to succeed, he felt, you had to look and act like a success. And if you made mistakes, you could buy or talk your way out of the consequences. When he came to Gardiner in the summer of 1889, he made plans to join Emma at Capitol Island for a Fourth of July party. Possibly after over-celebrating the night before, Herman missed the *Islander*'s seven-thirty a.m. departure. Altering course, Herman decided to take the nine-thirty train to Brunswick, hire a ride to Bath, and take the Bath boat down to Boothbay. But he missed the train, too. Finally he hitched up the carriage and drove overland all the way to Wiscasset, where he hired a small boat to take him to Capitol. Herman arrived about eleven p.m. and went "tooting down the island" to join the party. Emma, who had every right to be annoyed, was instead excited. No one had *ever* gone down to Capitol Island that way before. Herman the dazzler blurred her vision, and he radiated the kind of worldly assurance she sought in a husband. Win did not have a chance.

Marking Time

Once he had graduated from high school, Win Robinson knew that he was expected to go to work. He was unprepared for college, and for young men fresh out of high school, a proper job was really the only viable option. The good, solid New England values of Gardiner, values that Win himself subscribed to, mandated that he find useful employment. But he had no stomach for business, and no talent for it. And the family situation complicated matters. He had things to do around the house at 67 Lincoln Avenue and a father in decline to look after.

As a temporizing measure, he wangled still another year of study, a post-postgraduate year, with the faithful Lizzie Austin at Gardiner high. During 1888–1889, he read under her supervision the lyrics and satires of the Roman poet Horace and the work of John Milton. In the pages of *Paradise Lost*, he learned much about the structure and music of blank verse. On his own, he read the *Aeneid* (a note in his copy of Virgil reads: "Finished *Aeneid*, May 12, 1889. E. A. Robinson") and translated some of Virgil's eclogues into blank verse. Once a week, he continued to meet with the Gardiner Poetry Society, presenting for group discussion his own sonnets, ballades, and villanelles. In effect, Robinson was doing everything he could to apprentice himself to the career in poetry he was not yet ready to talk about publicly. He knew what Gardiner's reaction would be: "there's no money in it."

To salve his conscience and the town's expectations, Win took occasional odd jobs of short duration. During the winter of 1889 he worked as a time-keeper for the Oakland Ice Company. He complained about it in a letter to Art Gledhill, who was away at St. Lawrence University in Canton, New York. "I have had the very devil of a cough for the past week and I assure you that it has been no pleasant affair to get up at 5 a.m. and go down on the river to shiver all day." Another job, which paid him fifty dollars for a month's work on the River Survey, was not much better. "We have been sounding the river for the past week," he wrote Harry Smith at Bowdoin. "At times I don't care if the river is one fathom deep or forty, as long as there is water enough to take us home." Dollars were mighty convenient things to have, he admitted, but he preferred to labor "under the delusion that [there] is something to life outside of 'business.' Business be damned." He looked forward to summer afternoons when he could read Virgil under a tree and smoke a companionable pipe with Smith.

Robinson was finding out more about himself and what he could accomplish. He studied stenography and gave it up as a waste of time. He practiced on brother Dean's clarinet, learning to play "Abide with Me" and "The Man on the Flying Trapeze." At first the family tomcat fled from the room whenever he drew the clarinet from the drawer. Later, when the cat seemed to tolerate Win's playing, he took it as a sign of musical progress. It turned out that the poor animal "had built up its own defense and gone deaf."

In letters to Gledhill and Smith he revealed miscellaneous information of this sort, along with considerable detail about books he was reading: he preferred Kipling's poetry to his prose, for example, and thought Bret Harte's "Outcasts of Poker Flats" one of the best stories in the English language.

He said not a single word to his correspondents about his disappointment in love, however. The subject of marriage came up only in the context of its capacity to undermine friendships. "If one of our old set should drop out," he wrote Gledhill, "there would be something gone from our own lives." Away at college, Art had found a girl to admire. At home, Win saw less and less of Gus Moore, who was working for his father and also harboring thoughts of matrimony. In a merry November 1889 letter to Gledhill, he proposed that all three of them might "get married the same day," although he did not have any female partner in mind. "Pick me out a good promising specimen," Win suggested to Gledhill. Otherwise he might be reduced to advertising for a wife in the *Police Gazette*: "A young man of good character and unquestionable ability having wearied of his hitherto celibate life has decided to appeal to the affections of the gentler sex through the columns of this periodical."

Three months later, on February 12, 1890, Emma and Herman were married. The wedding, twice delayed, took place in the home of her parents and was covered in detail by the *Kennebec Reporter*. The bride, "a universal favorite" among the young ladies of the region, "was attired in a handsome gown of white faille francaise, en train, with a petticoat of silver and gold brocaded silk, square corsage and short sleeves filled in with trimming of ostrich feathers and a pendant of diamonds, the gift of the groom." (The wedding dress, now at the Maine Historical Society, had a twenty-two-inch waistline!) The groom was described inaccurately as "one of the rising young railroad men of the West" and more accurately, at the time, as "one of the most prosperous and energetic young men who have gone from our city." To launch their life together, Emma's father presented the couple with a check for $1,000; Herman's father gave them $500. After the ceremony and an "elaborate wedding supper," the newlyweds left for their honeymoon on the eleven o'clock Pullman to Boston. The marriage represented "the social event of the season," according to the *Kennebec Reporter*, and was attended by a "large number of . . . society people" from Gardiner, Farmingdale, Hallowell, and Augusta.

It was not attended, however, by three of the couple's four siblings. Emma's much younger sister Josephine, who was to have strewn the bride's path with rose petals, spent the evening in tears. Dean Robinson, addicted to drugs and—according to family legend—also in love with Emma, ran away and was found after midnight, unconscious, by the river. Win, using his father's illness as an excuse, stayed at home writing the first draft of "The Night Before." In that dramatic monologue, the speaker (EAR) confesses to the imaginary murder of "the cad" (Herman) who seduced his wife (Emma). It was the first of many poems he was to write, projecting the same triangle from varying avenues of approach.

Win skipped Herman and Emma's wedding as a gesture of protest. But he did attend the bachelor party. No sooner had Win returned from Herman's "hymeneal symposium" than a letter from Gledhill arrived, revealing in "rather tempestuous rhetoric" his emotional commitment to a young lady who was having second thoughts about him. Conflating his feelings with those of Gledhill, Win responded that if "she goes back on you, Art," he could either become a practicing misogynist or console himself with the thought that "'Tis better to have loved and lost / Than never to have loved at all." In the same letter, before closing, Robinson cited another Tennyson quotation: "But the jingling of the guinea helps the hurt that honor feels." That somewhat cynical sentiment comes from "Locksley Hall," which relates a story—as Wallace L. Anderson noted—"of love rejected for a marriage of worldly gain." Win let literary references testify to the pain in his heart.

The newlyweds planned to begin married life in St. Louis, where Herman's business enterprises were concentrated. In April they boarded the afternoon train for their new home. It took Win twelve years to come to grips with their departure in a poem called "Cortège."

Four o'clock this afternoon,
Fifteen hundred miles away:
So it goes, the crazy tune,
So it pounds and hums all day.

Four o'clock this afternoon,
Earth will hide them far away:
Best they go to go so soon,
Best for them the grave today.

Had she gone but half so soon,
Half the world had passed away.
Four o'clock this afternoon,
Best for them they go today.

Ostensibly the poem—the first half of which appears above—describes a funeral procession, but it is about the death of Robinson's hopes. For him, half the world *did* pass away when brother and sister-in-law left at four o'clock for St. Louis, fifteen hundred miles away. These details, as Robinson's grandnephew David S. Nivison pointed out in a seminal essay, located the lament in the world of actuality, not of fancy, and conveyed "a despair close to distraction." Only a few people, Nivison observed, could possibly understand the personal circumstances that moved Robinson to write "Cortège." But a great many readers could, and did, respond to the depth of emotion beneath the insistent beat of the verse.

Once he was married, most of Herman's business ventures turned sour. He and Emma stayed in St. Louis through the early May land sales and then journeyed north to look after another initiative in Minneapolis. A few years earlier, the Gardiner Savings Bank had invested in the area, and three Gardiner citizens were dispatched west to supervise. The plan was to develop the land around Minnehaha Falls, ten miles south of the city center, into a park, to lay out the land around the park into house lots, and then to sell the lots at a tidy profit.

His eyes fixed on the ever-receding bonanza, Herman bought a lot just above the falls for Emma and himself; invested in other lots in the names of Dean, Win, and his mother; and sold lots to customers in Gardiner. The venture, as Emma put it, "proved to be a millstone around our necks." In January 1891, Herman turned over his interests to another investor, for whom—despite having "been bled right and left in Minnesota" himself—he painted a rosy future. "I doubt there is any chance for loss," Herman assured him.

In St. Louis, Herman and his partners made unfortunate miscalculations about growth patterns. They bought substantial land on speculation in the Tower Grove area south of downtown, while the city grew to the north. In another blunder, Herman persuaded his father to remove his investments from Bates Shirts in Lewiston, Maine, which were drawing 14 percent interest, and place them in mining operations in Missouri. Most of the funds were sunk in the lead and zinc mines of Jasper County, near Joplin, which—as Emma remembered it—"required more and more cash and never paid." Herman was not defeated, quite, but the reverses were serious enough that he lacked the funds to build a cottage on the pinnacle of Capitol Island where he and Emma had plighted their troth. Her father came to the rescue and saw the project through to completion. The Robinson cottage became the Shepherd cottage. People noticed.

From the first, Emma was uncomfortable in the west. She became pregnant as soon as she and Herman were married and felt terribly homesick on the May trip to Minneapolis, where the wild violets around Minnehaha Falls and the board sidewalks downtown reminded her of Maine. In St. Louis, she found the June heat almost unbearable. Emma was glad to spend the summer of 1890 at Capitol Island and to return home to Farmingdale for the birth of the first of her three daughters. Ruth Robinson, nine pounds, was born on November 13, 1890, in the same house where her parents were married, nine months and a day earlier. Her two sisters arrived at two-and-a-half-year intervals thereafter, Marie on April 24, 1893, and Barbara on December 28, 1895. All of them endeared themselves to Uncle Win.

Two Invalids

Hurt by Emma's marriage to Herman, Win was also suffering daily as a witness to his brother Dean's breakdown. After 1889, Dean joined his father as a second invalid in the Robinson house. The good burghers of Gardiner whispered about him, but brooked no *public* discussion of the tragedy at 67 Lincoln Avenue. Alcoholism was bad enough, and widely regarded as the result of moral rather than chemical weakness. Addiction to drugs was beyond the pale. Win also maintained silence about Dean's dilemma, although sometimes, in letters, he groused about caring for his infirm father.

Dean Robinson's malady was the more poignant because it befell so promising a young man. His father sent him off to Bowdoin and medical training on the advice of Dr. Albert Card, a well-respected doctor and businessman who had grown up in Head Tide as the Robinsons' neighbor and who had his practice in Alna. Card, who had himself taken his medical training at Bowdoin, felt sure that a sensitive, brilliant, and studious lad like Dean would make a fine doctor. Initially, it seemed that he was right. Dean graduated cum laude in 1881 and returned for a two-year stint as city physician in Gardiner. During that time, he met and fell in love with Ardell Toby from Hallowell. They were engaged by 1884, when Dean relocated to Camden, on the Maine coast, again at the suggestion of Dr. Card. Dean spent three years there, from 1884 to 1887, and two awful things happened. His fiancée unexpectedly died, and he became enslaved to drugs.

As the youngest practicing doctor in Camden, Dean was assigned the calls to remote areas and the outer islands. In the fierce Maine winter, he contracted an excruciatingly painful case of facial neuralgia. It seemed the most natural thing in the world to treat it with the laudanum he carried in his doctor's bag. He would have prescribed the same remedy to any of his patients suffering similar agonies. The strongly addictive property of opium, and of its derivatives like morphine and laudanum, was not recognized at the time, and the drugs were freely dispensed as specifics against pain. Captain Collins carried laudanum in the medicine chest aboard the *Star of the East* to soothe any passenger's discomfort. Advertisements in *Harper's Weekly* sang the praises of opium to a national audience. So when Dean's neuralgia recurred, he took laudanum again to ameliorate his pain. The deadly cycle had begun, with larger doses needed over time to secure the blessed relief. Dean came back to Gardiner in 1887 in the grip of an addiction he could not overcome. Seeking a solution, Edward Robinson arranged to dispatch his son to Alna as town physician. Perhaps, he thought, Dean could right himself in the surroundings of that small community, with Dr. Card to look after him. Location was not the answer. In 1889 Dean came home for good, to live his last decade in misery.

During his high school years Win had largely been spared the sight of his brother's ruin. After 1889—living in the same house—he witnessed the daily disintegration of the intelligent and gentle older brother he loved just short of adoration. Win was not for a moment disposed to judge Dean in his distress. Instead, he suffered along with his brother as he watched his slow pitiful descent. Except for occasional hallucinations, Dean's mind remained alert, but his body wasted away and his visage went dull with despair. In the "insufficient eyes, forever sad" of his character Charles Carville, Win set down how it must have been.

Dean struggled through the days, his gaze blank to the world. He could do odd jobs, help prepare the bank's books, perform minor medical tasks. But it was as if he had no *affect*. He rarely talked, and when he did he sometimes talked of suicide. The family hired a man named Edgar C. Wakefield to look after him in the bad spells. Wakefield was not invariably a reliable caretaker, for he drank, and on occasion—as on the night of Herman and Emma's wedding—he let Dean drink too.

With Herman away in St. Louis and Dean in the throes of addiction and depression, the Robinsons' youngest son devoted more and more of his time to taking care of the "farm" and looking after his father. Win was glad to do the work for his mother but increasingly felt that he must accomplish something else to justify his existence. In the meantime, he endured periods of loneliness. "[Father] is no better," he wrote Gledhill in July 1890,

> and taking things all around my life is rather a dull one, though of course I can't complain. But still it makes one uneasy to realize that he is sliding off into the majority [Robinson would reach his "majority," his twenty-first birthday, later that year] and as far as a regular occupation is concerned is nothing but a drone, with no particular opening for the future. I tell you what it is, Art, sometimes a week

or ten days goes by without my seeing one of the boys and girls (I believe I never saw much of *them*, anyway) unless I happen to run across them down street in the afternoon for a minute or two.

With Gledhill and Smith away at college and Gus Moore launched in a "regular occupation," Win was short of companions. On New Year's Eve of 1890, however, he made "a damphool excursion" with George Barstow to the Barstows' camp at Oxbow. The two of them endured a bitter cold ride—the thermometer reached twenty-five below zero in Gardiner that night—and hiked the last half-mile to the camp through two to three feet of snow and a final patch of ice that threatened to give way at every step. But they reached the camp safely, kindled a fire, had a beef-steak supper "which went to the spot," smoked their pipes, and read Shakespeare and Tennyson aloud. At midnight George read "The Death of the Old Year" with "great pathos": he had been drinking and Win had not. The poem was singularly appropriate to the occasion:

Full knee-deep lies the winter snow,
  And the winter winds are wearily sighing.

Win had a wonderful time. In the years to follow, he would spend many such happy evenings with friends, combining food and tobacco and alcohol with the recitation of poetry—but never after so adventurous a journey or in such frigid weather.

As the calendar turned into 1891, Robinson became increasingly restive at home and worried about his future. Toward the end of January, he wrote Smith that he was still "dragging along in the same old rut" and mightily annoyed when "pleasant people" asked him, "Well, now, Robinson, what do you intend to do?" All he could say in response was that he didn't know. It must "look a little queer" for others to see him doing practically nothing at his age, he admitted, but for the moment there was "no getting out of it. Someone must be at home to run the place." While he ran it, he could hardly be expected to get ahead. He consoled himself with Richard Blackmore's sentiment that "The more we have in hand to count / The less we have to hope for." But he was aware that while he was moralizing along those lines, someone else might be *getting* what he hoped for. The parade was passing him by. He had to strike out on his own, and soon.

The solution came to him gradually: he would go to Harvard as a special student and continue his preparations for a literary life. The successful college careers of Gledhill and Smith, whom he had visited at nearby Bowdoin, undoubtedly inspired him to take this step. At Harvard, he could pursue his education on a scale, and among scholars, quite unavailable in Gardiner. Going to Cambridge for that purpose would help justify the three years that had passed since high school. He could not feel that those years were "altogether wasted,"

Win wrote Smith. He never would have been satisfied had he "taken up . . . some work with the sole incentive of 'doing something' and given up the idea of a further literary knowledge." But he withheld his dream of a serious writing life from Smith, maintaining that he would be "perfectly satisfied" to work in a publishing house or for "one of the higher grade of newspapers." Whatever the future held, Win knew he did not know enough to reach his potential. He could only go so far as an autodidact.

Throughout 1891 Win's hopes for Harvard wavered back and forth. In January he spoke of having but one more garden to put in at 67 Lincoln Avenue. During the spring he turned down an interim appointment to serve as high school principal in China, Maine—a post in which, he feared, his ignorance of mathematics might prove embarrassing. By April, when he was deep in "cucumbers, cauliflowers, onions," he said only that he would "trust in Providence" to liberate him. Providence chose to intervene, twice. First came the onset of agonizing pain in Win's damaged right ear. For a time there were three male invalids at the Robinson home. On Dr. Schumann's suggestion, Win went to Boston in July for an expert consultation. Necrosis had destroyed the eardrum and infected the bones, the doctor found. Periodic treatments at Massachusetts General Hospital were advised. Second, Herman unexpectedly pleaded Win's case with his father. Herman had no particular sympathy for his brother's literary hopes, but felt he should at least be given a chance. Edward Robinson found it difficult to refuse Herman anything, and Win's ear needed regular treatment. In the light of the twin persuasions, his enfeebled father's resistance to higher education faded away. Win left for Harvard at the end of September. The two years he spent there would change his life.

5

A "Special" at Harvard

College Days

Would he make a fool of himself at Harvard? Could he handle the intellectual demands? Would the whole experiment—at first he envisioned only one year away—be a waste of time and money? So Robinson queried himself in letters to Harry Smith, before arriving at a justification that had nothing to do with academic success. Books and conventional learning aside, he reasoned, the experience "among new forms and faces would do [him] a world of good."

Robinson saw Harvard as an ideal location for escape from the limitations of his hometown. He could extricate himself, at least briefly, from the daily misery at 67 Lincoln Avenue. In Cambridge, he could not only further his literary education under expert instruction but learn something of the larger and more variegated world beyond. And, not least, he could seek new friends, "new forms and faces," to assuage his loneliness.

"The truth is," he wrote Smith two weeks before getting on the train to Boston, "I have lived in Gardiner for nearly twenty-two years and, metaphorically speaking, hardly been out of the yard." This was all wrong, for solitude drove a man to excessive introspection even while it "sharpened his sympathy for failure" and rendered him "suspicious of the whole natural plan." Living alone was a bad business, and he had had more than his share of it.

So he rode the smoking car to Boston, inhaling more cigars than were good for him, and settled into quarters at 717 Cambridge Street, halfway between the university and Massachusetts General Hospital, where his ear could be regularly treated. His furnished room, "no palace," cost $180 for the academic year, and his landlady oversaw her renters with a dispiriting grimness. Robinson would rather have been among the freshmen in Harvard Yard, whom he heard "practicing their yell and making night most damnably hideous." He envied them the four years of college life they could look forward to, as compared to his nine months.

Robinson arrived at registration with a schedule in mind. He would take elementary courses in French and German, to repair his lack of knowledge in those languages. And he would take upper division courses in English literature intended primarily for juniors, seniors, and graduate students. Those in charge blanched at his audacity. Harvard had a reputation for rigor to uphold, and it looked—on the surface—as if this "special" with no further qualification than "a diploma from a second rate high school" might be trying to advance himself toward an A.B. degree in jig time.

An instructor was summoned from the English department to resolve matters. The deliberations took time, so that by twelve-thirty p.m., with registration to end at one, Robinson was still not enrolled. Then the mandate came down. Robinson would be required to take English A (Composition and Rhetoric), the huge beginning course that accommodated 500 students. Anglo-Saxon was added for discipline. French was all right, but German went by the boards because of scheduling problems. Somewhat grudgingly, the special student from Gardiner was admitted to advanced courses in Shakespeare and Nineteenth-Century Prose Writers.

The alteration in his curriculum turned out much as Robinson feared. English A, especially, he regarded as a colossal waste of time, consisting of "watery lectures" and compositions read and graded by instructors no better qualified than himself. Anglo-Saxon was "hellish," and, by EAR's lights, quite unnecessary for his literary development. After a spell of conjugating Saxon verbs in his dreams, he was permitted to withdraw from the course with the approval of his teacher, the eminent Francis Child. Professor Child was also Robinson's instructor in Shakespeare, a course which proved a disappointment. He cut so many lectures that he was given a "condition" in the course, necessitating extra work and makeup exams.

With his study habits rusty, Robinson was nearly overcome by the sheer pace of Harvard education. "To be candid," he wrote Smith after two weeks at Harvard, "I am working about three times as hard as I expected to." This was especially true in French, where students plunged into translating difficult material after only a few meetings. Robinson was somewhat buoyed, however, by the instructors' assurance that at the end of the year he (like the others in the class) would be able to read "an ordinary French novel" without the aid of an English translation. Nineteenth-Century Prose Writers, which also required a great deal of work, ranked as far and away the favorite course of his first year in Cambridge. Robinson was excited at the prospect of reading Austen and Dickens and Thackeray, and Professor Lewis E. Gates, "a fluttering gray moth" of a man and rather younger than most of his colleagues, delivered brilliant lectures. Gates was "a teacher of rare emotional and artistic temperament," with a talent for exposition and the ability to relate "the great social, literary and spiritual movements" of the time to the lives of his listeners. Robinson did not cut a single class of his.

He was fortunate to be attending Harvard during what became generally known as its Golden Age. President Charles W. Eliot oversaw the institution with enthusiasm and reshaped it by instituting a revolutionary elective system. The campus was enlivened by teachers "so full of vitality that they brought healthy disquietude and doubt to whomever they touched." Philosophy was recognized as the most distinguished department—Robinson would sample its offerings during his second year—with such famous figures as William James, Josiah Royce, George Herbert Palmer, and the young George Santayana on the faculty. But English had its share of stars too, including Child, Gates, George Lyman Kittredge, Dean Le Baron Russell Briggs, A. S. Hill, and Barrett Wendell. In fine arts, Charles Eliot Norton, a confidant of Ruskin and Emerson, opened his students' eyes and ears to beauty, which was rare, and to vulgarity, which was not. Most of these professors were accomplished writers as well. James could write like a dream. Royce had written a novel. Santayana was an accomplished poet. Palmer translated the *Odyssey*. Wendell wrote novels and plays. Even Nathaniel Shaler, in geology, had written a five-volume epic poem on Elizabethan England. With professors like that to study under, there was—so Norman Hapgood asserted—no "intellectually more attractive" place than Harvard University near the end of the nineteenth century.

The faculty may have been writers, but they all agreed that the academic environment was not conducive to a writing career. Students were advised not to teach if they wanted to write anything other than textbooks. As to actual instruction in writing, Harvard was no further advanced at the time than any other American institution of higher learning. The lessons in composition that Robinson encountered in English A seemed designed to stifle the least sign of individuality. Hays Gardiner, who taught English there, felt that the department "conscientiously and successfully" impeded the development of literary talent. Santayana went further, declaring that "a whole string of Harvard poets . . . were visibly killed by the lack of air to breathe." Barrett Wendell was to tell Robinson, a decade later, that he was lucky to have escaped from Harvard after only two years. EAR was inclined to agree.

Yet as a place to learn about literature, to make friends, to become acquainted with music and theatre, to drink beer and smoke cigars and talk into the wee hours—in short, as a place to grow up—Harvard could not have suited him better. President Eliot's radical elective system was a godsend to Robinson as a "special" who knew he could not stay for a full four-year curriculum. Robinson concentrated on subjects that would best serve his education as a poet. In classes, he sat alongside freshmen three or four years his junior, graduate students committed to a life in the academy, and the occasional odd duck who, like himself, had landed there as a special student. (Later in the decade, two other great American poets, Robert Frost and Wallace Stevens, followed him as "specials" at Harvard.)

Ideal though it was for enabling—indeed, requiring—the individual student to fashion his own curriculum, the elective system had the unanticipated effect of intensifying class consciousness. "No longer," Larzer Ziff observed, "were the students members of a democratic community of learning made homogeneous by the fact that they had, in great part, to pursue the same discipline. . . . As a result, discrepancies in social status were exaggerated, preparatory-school background was emphasized," and many withdrew into class-defined groups. Robinson, of course, could not qualify for the elite. He came from the public high school of a small town in Maine and knew no one from the prestigious New England schools that supplied a substantial percentage of each Harvard class. He had no connections, no money, no influence. He was to find his friends, for the most part, from among other "specials" like himself, some of them misfits or outcasts: older, less polished, and rather more eccentric than most undergraduates.

During his first weeks at Harvard, Robinson noted the existence of two different cliques, the "fast set" and the literary insiders. The fast set—the young men of privilege—"keep themselves severely away from the common herd," Robinson wrote six weeks after arriving at Harvard. The group had some distinguishing characteristics in common. They rarely got up in time to attend classes, and they hired tutors to prepare them for examinations in which they aimed for nothing higher than "Gentlemen's C's." They affected a blasé air on all issues and would have died rather than betray enthusiasm for anything. They objected to the way that "the over-aggressive Jews or the over-aggressive Westerners or the over-aggressive sons of New England mill hands" disturbed the genteel atmosphere of Harvard Yard. And by virtue of birth they were granted every social distinction that the undergraduate world, and the arbiters of Boston society, could bestow. "I can generally tell one [of these privileged young men] when I see him," Robinson wrote, "and he is not much to see either."

The second group—the literary coterie assembled around the dominating figure of George Santayana—was the one that Robinson wanted to join. After study abroad, Santayana returned to Harvard as an instructor in philosophy. In this post, he chose to spend more time with undergraduates than with faculty colleagues. With his piercing eyes and withering wit, he tended to dominate any gathering and make disciples of the young. He thus became the central figure of the Laodicean Club, which he formed along with William Vaughn Moody, Norman Hapgood, and half a dozen other students. The club took its name from the biblical attack of Paul on the church in Laodicea for being neither hot nor cold. There was much to be said, the members believed, for a temperate approach to all questions—a posture well suited to their sense of aesthetic superiority. In effect, as Ziff suggested, the club adopted a code of intellectual detachment paralleling the studied casualness of the privileged elite.

Robinson may not have known about the Laodicean Club by name. He did not take a course with Santayana at Harvard, and probably the two did not even meet. He did know about the *Harvard Monthly*, the literary journal that Santayana and his friends had founded in 1885, with its reputation outshining that of the more established *Harvard Advocate*. A healthy rivalry existed between the two magazines. "The Monthlies," Malcolm Cowley recalled, "thought that the board of the *Advocate* . . . was composed of journalists, clubmen, athletes, and disciples of Teddy Roosevelt," who had in fact edited the journal while at Harvard. "The Advocates suspected that the Monthlies were aesthetes [a code word for those with homosexual tendencies] . . . scruffy poets, socialists, pacifists, or worse." Within a month after arriving in Cambridge, EAR sent a few poems to the *Monthly* for consideration, while at the same time trying his luck with the *Advocate*.

As it turned out, Robinson published five poems in the *Advocate* during his time at Harvard, while never gaining acceptance to the more glamorous *Monthly*. He wished it were the other way around. Early in November 1891, he alerted Smith to the impressive news that there was a poem by the *Monthly* regular William Vaughn Moody, only a junior at Harvard, in the last *Scribner's* magazine. He had not met Moody—they were not to become friends until 1900—but as soon as his academic requirements allowed, Robinson said, he planned "to make a strong attempt to get in with the *literati* at Harvard." A month later, Robert Morss Lovett, the editor of the *Monthly* and "perhaps the leading spirit of Harvard outside of athletics," knocked on his door. Lovett brought with him the sonnet on Thomas Hood that Robinson had submitted to the *Monthly*. The editors rejected the sonnet, but Lovett thought enough of it to meet Robinson, engage him in pleasant conversation, and ask for another contribution. "I actually felt honored to receive a call from him," Robinson wrote Smith, "being a Special and a first year man at that. . . . If I am a little foxy," he added, "I may get in with the whole gang." Foxiness was not his forte.

Robinson's worshipful attitude toward Lovett was matched by a proper Laodicean indifference from the editor. Lovett, who subsequently achieved a distinguished career at the University of Chicago, admitted in the nineteen-forties that he had no memory of calling on Robinson in 1891. He did remember, oddly enough, that during the following year Robinson had submitted his poems in a blue examination book and that he had included—apparently "as a joke"—a poem by Wordsworth along with his own. "It was rejected with the rest," Lovett wrote, adding that the *Monthly* board at the time was "strongly aesthetic." EAR took some comfort in the realization that the *Monthly*, like many undergraduate literary magazines, "seemed to be a medium for airing the work of its editors."

The *Harvard Advocate's* editors were more hospitable to Robinson's work, publishing three poems during his first semester. All three were couched in the French forms he worked on with Dr. Schumann in Gardiner. Probably the first two—a ballade and a villanelle—had been written in his hometown. But the third, a rondeau called "In Harvard 5," manifestly stemmed from his experience as a Harvard student.

> In Harvard 5 the deathless lore
> That haunts old Avon's classic shore
>   Wakens the long triumphant strain
>   Of Pride and Passion, Mirth and Pain,
> That fed the Poet's mind of yore.
>
> Time's magic glass is turned once more
> And back the sands of ages pour
>   While shades of mouldered monarchs reign
> In Harvard 5.
>
> Thin spirits flutter through the door,
> Quaint phantoms flit across the floor:
>   Now Fancy marks the crimson stain
>   Of Murder . . . and there falls again
> The fateful gloom of Elsinore
> In Harvard 5.

The poem is remarkable as a formal tour de force, Robinson nimbly handling the rhythm of the four-beat lines and the restrictive limit of but two rhymes in fifteen lines, not counting the title refrain. The title alerted his college audience at once to the subject: well into the twentieth century, the lectures in English 9, Shakespeare, were presented in the Harvard 5 classroom. But his readers may have missed the implications conveyed by the repeated images of decay and death. In Harvard 5, "mouldered monarchs" have the floor, "thin spirits" infiltrate the room, the lecture hall takes on a deadly gloom.

The ghostly atmosphere of Robinson's rondeau may have owed something to his father's interest in spiritualism. As Edward Robinson, confined to the house at 67 Lincoln Avenue, approached his own death, he attempted to summon the spirits of the departed, apparently with some success. Win, home for Christmas, was called on to observe and participate in these sessions of spiritualism. Table rappings were heard. Books flew off the shelves. The table itself came off the floor, "cutting [his] universe clean in half." Walking through the cemetery at night, Win's horse shied as from an invisible ghost. With an attitude halfway between terror and skepticism, he concluded it was "best not to monkey with such things."

"The Friends of My Life"

It was at Harvard, Robinson wrote, that he was to meet "with one or two exceptions, the friends of my life." Throughout his life, he depended on friends as a stay against despair and as a means to get through one day after another. "Friends came to mean family, in a sense," Louis Coxe sagely commented, "but less simply they meant release from himself." In Gardiner, he had begun to doubt whether he could achieve his literary goals and even whether they were worth achieving. At Harvard, he found reassurance in the companionship of those who set similarly unmaterialistic goals for themselves. Most of his college friends pursued careers as teachers or professors, ministers, or journalists. They understood, and encouraged, his desire to make a poet of himself.

As many as 2,500 students at Harvard ate every day in the two huge dining halls—Randall and Memorial—that served as a democratizing influence for the university. Robinson took his meals at Memorial, alongside callow freshmen and third-year law students. George W. Latham, a junior, joined his table one evening, and the two men discovered a community of interests. Latham, who was to go on to a career as a professor of English at McGill University, thought Robinson "extraordinarily shy," even repressed, with deficient hearing in one ear and no capacity to push himself forward. Yet occasionally the dam burst, and "it was amazing to see the reticent Robinson transformed" into a lively conversationalist retailing risqué stories and gossip about his origins. Still, Latham concluded, "few then realized what a genial man he was, and what a gift for friendship he had."

Another acquaintance of Robinson's first months was James L. Tryon, a serious-minded young man from the state of Maine. Tryon, a fellow student in Lewis Gates's classes, was fascinated by the Oxford Movement and bound for a career in the Episcopal church. Looking back at his Harvard years, Tryon described Robinson as "a gentleman, dignified but democratic, and naturally hospitable." Tryon was struck by his willingness to share his allowance with college friends who needed help.

Latham and Tryon became members, along with Robinson, of the Corn Cob Club, a loosely organized group of students who met from time to time for lively discussion. The leading light of the Corn Cob Club—and one of the lasting friends of Robinson's life—was the iconoclastic Mowry Saben. Saben grew up a childhood prodigy in Uxbridge, Massachusetts, supposedly having read the Bible before he was seven. His father, a noted mathematician, took pride in his precocious son until it turned out that, unaccountably, Mowry had inherited no talent whatever for mathematics. There followed rejection, a nervous breakdown, and a regimen of cold baths and graham flour. By the time Saben arrived at Harvard as a special student, he was in rebellion against all authority, as represented by his father, his doctors, his instructors, and anyone who dared to criticize his pursuit of pleasure.

Robinson encountered the free-spending Saben not in cavernous Memorial hall but at a restaurant in Harvard Square. Saben was engaged in a vigorous argument with another student, Robinson interceded mildly, and when the meal was over, the two repaired to Saben's room to continue the discussion.

Fifty years later, Saben told the story of that evening in considerable detail, and not to his disadvantage. No sooner had they left the restaurant than Robinson asked Saben if he smoked. He said he did, although to that date his entire previous experience with tobacco had consisted of two cigarettes and one cigar. Thereupon Robinson went into a shop and emerged with twelve cigars, half of which he gave to Saben. Their subsequent bull session lasted well into the night, and when they parted, all of the cigars had been consumed.

It was for Saben a liberating experience, inasmuch as his family physician had decreed that he was in such poor health that to indulge in smoking, drinking, or sex would put his life at risk. At Harvard, Saben proceeded to violate all of the rules the physician laid down for him to follow. "By the time I had violated the last rule," he declared with obvious satisfaction, "I was cured."

In his teenage years, Saben read widely and remembered almost everything, so that he could hold forth on a variety of subjects—literature, history, philosophy, religion, and politics—with the aid of a vast store of quotations. Expansive, overweight, ever convivial, Saben led frequent excursions into Boston for visits to the theatre and the beer halls. Money seemed of no concern to him, and he gave of his purse as freely as he borrowed from others. Robinson had never met anyone like him. Fascinated, he stopped by Saben's room almost every day of his first year at Harvard. Their friendship was cemented when Saben began telling anyone who would listen that Robinson had a genius for poetry.

It was not in Saben's nature to praise anyone without qualification. Thus in his reminiscences about Robinson, Saben celebrates him for his generosity and loyalty to his friends, and for his accomplishment as a poet, while finding fault with a lack of consistency and rigor in his thinking and—most seriously—with his sexual repression and social reticence. At meetings of the Corn Cob Club, Saben thought Robinson "afflicted with a kind of intellectual timidity" and victimized by "a strange abhorrence of all controversial discussion." Argumentative disagreement on any subject was as painful to him, Saben said, as the loud ringing of bells might be to a dog with sensitive ears.

When unavoidably confronted by argument, Robinson tried his best to smooth things over. In May 1892, he wrote Harry Smith about an afternoon when two of his Harvard friends, "at swords' points" with each other, happened to stop by his room. After a few conciliatory words, the two were reunited as friends. The incident moved Robinson to reflect that life was too short to nourish foolish enmities. "I am not setting myself up for a professional peace-maker, but I honestly think that in this case I was the indirect mean of bringing two people together who might have otherwise hated each other to the end of their lives." It meant a great deal to him that he had helped heal their hatred.

When Hermann Hagedorn was writing his 1938 biography of Robinson, he asked Saben for information about the Harvard years. Saben responded with ten typewritten pages, and a decade later he wrote another 150 pages (unpublished) about his memories. "Nobody knew as much of Robinson at Harvard as I did," he declared. Robinson unburdened himself to Saben as he rarely did to anyone, while keeping the excruciating details to himself. "Life is a terrible thing," he told Saben, time and again. And once, "I have forgotten how to laugh." Opposite in personality as they were, the two men became fast friends.

Saben later pursued a career as a journalist, a lecturer, and a writer of speeches for the secretary of the interior. In his one published book, *The Spirit of Life* (1914), he expatiated on a wide variety of topics, in particular advocating the benefits of sexual license. Although he did not share such opinions, Robinson always remained Saben's supporter. As his star ascended and Saben's failed to rise, Robinson devoted a good deal of his time, and a share of his resources, to ameliorating his friend's disappointment

The other lasting friendship Robinson formed during his first year at Harvard was with George Burnham. Burnham, in fact, was to become the single closest friend of EAR's life. Although Robinson did not spend nearly as much time with Burnham as with Saben at Harvard, he was attracted to both men for much the same reason. Each of them had fallen out of favor with his father, and each had rebelled against parental authority. Robinson did not break with his father—it is likely that both of them wanted to avoid confrontation—but manifestly sympathized with his friends' family disputes.

Burnham ran away from his prosperous Hartford home at seventeen to knock about the west, earning room and board through temporary jobs as farmhand, bartender, and hotel worker. He was heading on foot to Butte, Montana, when he was caught in a blizzard and spent a freezing January night kicking the trunk of a tree to ward off deadly sleep. The next morning, Burnham dragged himself to a nearby town where both feet were amputated. He did not arrive at Harvard until he was twenty-four, as a special student in the law school.

FIGURE 5.1 George Burnham, friend to the end.

Source: Colby College Special Collections.

Slight and fair-haired, Burnham became perhaps the most volcanic member of the Corn Cob Club. "He agreed with nobody, and disagreed with everybody," Saben recollected. No one enjoyed argument more than Burnham, making him "the complete antithesis" of Robinson. Arguing with more vehemence than grace, he was inclined to regard anyone who disagreed with him as morally flawed. Yet there was a rugged honesty about Burnham that people were drawn to. Anyone could see that he hated sham and pretense.

Burnham practiced law for only a short time after leaving Harvard, abandoning the field after deciding that he could not in good conscience represent the interests of his corporate clients. By 1901 he had become a disciple of Hindu Vedanta philosophy that extolled the benefits of spiritual growth through personal impoverishment. Burnham thereupon took a lowly clerk's job for the New York, New Haven, and Hartford railroad, and lived much of his celibate life "in what was little more than a cubby-hole, eating lightly, and spending little that was not absolutely necessary." Following this spartan regimen, Burnham lost much of his choler. Robinson, who had his own quarrel with materialism, admired him increasingly as the years wore on. He dedicated *Merlin* (1917) to Burnham and left him $3,000 in his will. No one outside the family meant more to him.

A Social Education

Even before he went to Cambridge, Robinson was warning himself about the "unlicensed deviltry" of college life. Nonetheless, he was surprised by his fellow student's indulgence in drink and debauchery. "Rum was rampant last night," he reported to Smith on 18 October 1891. "The very buildings and trees were drunk." Already in thrall to tobacco—one of his first Harvard purchases was a Sherlock Holmes bulldog pipe—Robinson had little previous experience with alcohol. His first companions in conviviality were fellow exiles from Gardiner: Leonard Barnard at MIT, Dexter Whitney at Boston University, and on occasion Dr. Schumann himself, come to Boston on holiday. Schumann arrived for a visit in mid-November, and together they enjoyed "the most thoroughly Bohemian evening" of Robinson's young existence, replete with "beer, oysters, pipes, cigars, and literary conversation."

Before long, EAR began to make a regular practice of joining his fellow Harvard students on Saturday night forays into Boston. These could prove expensive—he complained about spending up to four or five dollars per trip—but, as he rationalized to Smith, those Saturday nights constituted his sole release from the rigors of study. Besides, he was not "a very wild youth." By the time of midyear examinations, he was going into town several times a week for a bottle or two of "Guinness' Dublin." The night before his exam in English Rhetoric and Composition, George Barstow came to Boston, and Robinson made a night of it with him at the Old Elm. He felt like a bloody fool the next day but managed to sit at his desk "for three mortal hours in a hot room in the upper story of University Hall"—and to emerge, as it turned out, with a B-plus.

That was the best mark he was to receive at Harvard, save for a long paper on *Pendennis* that Professor Gates marked A-minus. Some of the other grades were much lower.

During his first year Robinson was more or less terrified that he might be dismissed. When he discovered that he could get passing grades, he did not particularly aspire to do better. His marks, according to Lucius Beebe, who followed him at Harvard a generation later, ranged from "creditable mediocrity to . . . the narrowest possible escape from failure." But this is not to say that he did not educate himself for the future at Harvard, both in and out of the classroom.

Robinson's assigned advisor was Professor Fréderic César de Sumichrast, who was also one of his instructors in French 1A. Sumichrast (who added the "de" to his name after arriving at Harvard, according to Saben) advised special students as well as a number of young women enrolled at the Annex, though not at Harvard proper. On Thanksgiving night, he and his wife held an evening reception for more than a hundred students and faculty. It was there that Robinson met James Tryon, who remembered seeing EAR "standing by himself against the wall, silent and shy, a tall, handsome young man, with an expression of wonder on his face, as if he were studying the company, had no acquaintance in it, and needed a welcoming hand. He seemed like a person who had character behind his silence." At that reception Robinson also met an earnest Annex girl whom he fed "on chocolate and bilious coconut cakes" and "wheedled" into the library for private conversation. Nothing came of the encounter, he wrote Smith, although the young woman "was apparently growing quite fond" of him when they parted. "Her nose was a trifle one sided," he ungallantly observed, "and she carried a whole arboretum on her bosom."

Despite the apparent success of that evening, Robinson complained to Smith that he had no talent for "society chatter." He could handle one person well enough but felt "like a lost orphan" when compelled to make himself agreeable to a multitude. He went to two subsequent receptions at the Sumichrasts' then promised himself to attend no more. Passing through Cambridge "at-homes" was like passing through hell. At such gatherings, he watched, astounded, as polished young gentlemen "float[ed] from one girl to another, keeping their tongues wagging," but the performance only served to remind him how different one man was from another. He preferred talking with "one or two congenial souls . . . on some congenial subject, and smoking the pipe."

He was not averse, however, to smallish parties, such as the one Saben threw to celebrate the end of midyear exams. "There was quite a jovial time at Saben's room last night," he wrote Smith on February 21, 1892: jovial enough that the Cambridge police arrived some time after midnight to call a halt to the festivities, the Harvard faculty was alerted, and Saben—whose grades were worse than Robinson's—was temporarily kicked out of college. In interviews with authorities, Saben steadfastly refused to name his fellow celebrants. "He would not peach if they put him on the rack," Robinson observed in admiration. Nonetheless, he was worried that news of the incident might leak and a reprimand might be sent home to make an "elegant stink" in Gardiner. People did not understand how strict the rules were at Harvard, EAR told Smith. "The fact is that it does not take but a very little to get a man in trouble, and one is not obliged to murder more than three professors to get his walking ticket." Students had recently been expelled for playing poker.

Fired from Harvard, Saben relocated to Boston, where he spent his time reading, smoking, and buying sets of books charged to his father's account. Voluble as ever, Saben told half the first balcony at the Hollis Street Theatre that "he would be without his books—in hell" and mounted a soapbox on Boston Common to discourse on free trade. "I don't think I could take things so easy under his circumstances," Robinson commented. "I surely hope I could not."

Even before Saben's misadventures, Robinson had begun a practice that, had it come to the attention of Harvard, would have resulted in his expulsion. On February 6, he joined a group of nine young men who concluded their usual Saturday night outing in an unusual way. As Robinson told the story to Smith, by midnight the treasury of the whole party had dwindled to a mere $1.75, "so we decided to make an inspection of Boston's houses of seclusion. We inspected eight between midnight and 4:00 A.M. finding everything satisfactory but the prices. I enclose a souvenir of the trip. Etta will be overjoyed to see you at any time. She is a robust creature and her fold is intensely 'chic.' I have no interest in them myself, but such a journey as we made may be beneficial as a study of humanity—or inhumanity."

That concluding remark undercut Robinson's otherwise jaunty account of boys'-night-out naughtiness. During the month that followed he visited "something like thirty or forty" houses of prostitution. The experience, he reported to Smith on March 6, 1892, "has done me more good than all the ministers in the world could do, if they preached till their lungs rattled." After observing "the real elephant" of female degradation at first hand, it was hard for him

> to understand how a man of any feeling or intellect [could] frequent these holes with no other motive than that of pleasure. . . . You know I have always told you that I had more than ordinary reverence for womankind, and disliked to hear them made light of. The fact that perhaps a little over one half of them are more or less blistered does not seem to me to be any defense for the average man's indifference to their condition, beyond those in whom he has some immediate interest.

The double standard was a vicious thing. A week later, he wrote Smith that his "anatomical investigations grated" on his nerves, and he doubted that he should "ever enter one of the damned holes again." Still, he was gratified to learn that "one of the damsels" had inquired about him: "'Tis sweet to be remembered." Almost certainly, Robinson had treated her as a human being worth his notice and not as a mere purveyor of carnal pleasure.

A disciple of evoking the real rather than the idealized in poetry, Robinson drew on what he had seen in Boston brothels for his own work. In 1902, he published "The Growth of 'Lorraine,'" a double sonnet on the life and death of a prostitute.

I
While I stood listening, discreetly dumb,
Lorraine was having the last word with me:
"I know," she said, "I know it, but you see
Some creatures are born fortunate, and some
Are born to be found out and overcome,—
Born to be slaves, to let the rest go free,
And if I'm one of them (and I must be)
You may as well forget me and go home.

"You tell me not to say these things, I know,
But I should never try to be content:
I've gone too far; the life would be too slow.
Some could have done it—some girls have the stuff;
But I can't do it: I don't know enough.
I'm going to the devil."—And she went.

II
I did not half believe her when she said
That I should never hear from her again;
Nor when I found a letter from Lorraine,
Was I surprised or grieved at what I read:
"Dear friend, when you find this, I shall be dead.
You are too far away to make me stop.
They say that one drop—think of it, one drop!—
Will be enough,—but I'll take five instead.

"You do not frown because I call you friend,
For I would have you glad that I still keep
Your memory, and even at the end—
Impenitent, sick, shattered—cannot curse

The love that flings, for better or for worse,
This worn-out, cast-out flesh of mine to sleep."

Robinson pulls us into the poem by gradually uncovering Lorraine's situation. The two sonnets, brilliant in converting the colloquial into metrical form, come to us primarily in her words. She cannot break free, she tells the narrator, but not until she compares herself to "other girls" and announces that she is going to the devil does it emerge that what has enslaved her is sexual passion. Her rather romantic name, rendered within quotation marks, helps to establish the point: it is her professional *nom de salon*.

The narrator has tried, without success, to convert "Lorraine" to a more conventional life. She appreciates his interest and addresses to him as a friend the suicide letter that might have gone to a devoted parent or partner. Much of the poignancy of the poem derives from an awareness that apparently she has no one else to reach out to. In what sense may it be said that Lorraine has grown? In self-awareness, surely and even, perhaps, in her willingness to end the misery that her passion and sensitivity have led to. She is one of several Robinson characters unaccommodated to life.

Boston whorehouses opened Robinson's eyes for the first time to what it meant to be a woman. His education was furthered along more decorous lines by visits to the theatre (especially during his first year at Harvard) and the concert hall (during his second). The leading actors and actresses of the time routinely performed in Boston, and Robinson watched them with a sharp critical eye. In mid-November he saw Richard Mansfield in *Dr. Jekyll and Mr. Hyde* and reported his displeasure to Smith. There was not much to the play beyond the transformation scenes, he pointed out, and since these took place in total darkness, an usher might as easily have played the part.

The actress Julia Marlowe, however, was a revelation. There was something "unprofessional" about her acting that Robinson found refreshing, and he was in the audience as often as possible when her company came to Boston to put on Shakespeare. "Have seen her four times," he wrote Smith in February 1892, "and [would] like to see her in a dozen more pieces." A year later, Marlowe was back on the boards in Boston, and Robinson went to see her in *Twelfth Night* and *Much Ado About Nothing*. She was best, though, as Rosalind in *As You Like It*. In that play, besides, he thought that Jacques's speech "mimicking the fool moralizing on time" was well worth the price of admission—at his student rate, fifty cents.

In addition to Shakespeare and Stevenson, Robinson attended a number of the new plays performed in Boston. Except for farce, he liked almost everything. On theatre evenings, he was sometimes accompanied by Shirley Everton Johnson, an outspoken Kentuckian and Corn Cob Club member. Johnson had his faults, Robinson acknowledged, but also "enough gall to carry him beyond the need of all friendly sympathy." (After Harvard he became a journalist and wrote a rather precious novel of college life called *The Cult of the Purple Rose*.) Other companions at the theatre included Saben, Barnard, and—when he came to Boston—Schumann. Those evenings fell into a regular pattern. After the production, often on the stage at the Boston Museum, the theatergoers went across the street to the "Museum Exchange." There EAR could stretch his legs under one of the black-topped tables, "surround" a few bottles of Dublin Stout, and watch the actors come and go. Later they might proceed to Vercelli's or Jakey Wirth's or the Old Elm for further sustenance.

It was also in Boston that Robinson cultivated what was to become a lifelong love of music. He wrote Smith in March 1892 that he planned to pay the sizable sum of three dollars to hear the celebrated soprano Adelina Patti in *La Traviata*, adding that it was the only grand opera that much interested him, except for *Il Trovatore*. This was a false show of erudition, for Robinson had at the time enjoyed very little exposure to any serious music whatever. The following fall, he addressed the subject more straightforwardly in a letter to Gledhill. He might delay his trip home for Christmas in order to go to the symphony, Robinson said. "Symphonies and grand operas are a perfect revelation to me and I am cursing myself for letting so many go by last year."

As his first year at Harvard drew to a close, Robinson felt increasingly loyal to the place. The class games in early May, pitting the freshmen against the sophomores, did not much interest him; he belonged to neither side and did not care who won. But he expressed considerable enthusiasm for the Harvard-Yale baseball games, and where they were concerned, he was a devoted supporter of his college. Sometimes, he wrote Smith near the end of May 1892, he got "rather blue" thinking what a different person he would have been had he come to Harvard as a freshman three years earlier. At least it was settled that he would spend one more year there.

The June issue of the *Harvard Advocate* printed Robinson's "Supremacy," a sonnet confronting an issue—the unreliability of conventional judgments—that was much on his mind as he prepared to return to Gardiner for the summer.

> There is a drear and lonely tract of Hell
>   From all the common gloóm removed afar;
>   A flat, sad land where only shadows are,
> Whose lorn estate no word of mine can tell.
> I walked among the shades and knew them well:
>   Men I had scorned upon Life's little star
>   For churls and sluggards: and I knew the scar
> Upon their brows of woe ineffable.

But as I moved triumphant on my way,
  Into the dark they vanished, one by one.
Then came an awful light, a blinding ray—
  As if a new creation were begun;
And with a swift, importunate dismay,
  I heard the dead men singing in the sun.

The overconfident speaker is quite wrong about the shades he encounters. He may regard them as "churls and sluggards," but they are triumphant in the eyes of God. The poem can apply to many cases. Saben, confident that he was unfairly undervalued by almost everyone, construed it as applying to himself and declared it a masterpiece, which it is not. To a certain extent, Robinson undoubtedly had the need to justify himself in mind.

A few days before he returned to Gardiner for the summer, George Latham stopped by his room to pose a philosophical quandary. "I can't see what this life of ours amounts to anyway," he began. "What is the object of it? What are we here for?" Robinson, having no answers, blew a stream of Bull Durham smoke into the air, and in a characteristic gesture shook his head and opened his eyes wide as if in astonishment. The question itself—the meaning of life, and of death—was one he would face as soon as he got back home.

6

Farewell to Carefree Days

Second Time Around

In an April 1892 letter, Win Robinson imagined what the future might hold for him. "Sometimes I have visions of a comfortable home with a wife, pipe, books, cat, and all that sort of thing and again I see myself in a garret without anything to keep the furnace of my stomach from growing cold." He felt compelled to accomplish something, if only to please his mother. "Father never lived (I may as well say that) to see me anything but a parasite, and I have enough manhood in me to feel rather mean over it." At the time of the writing, Edward Robinson had three months left to live. But his mind was gone already, his body was succumbing to cardio-renal failure, and it was as if he were already dead.

Win provided what help he could at Edward's bedside when he returned from Cambridge in mid-June. His father died on July 22, saluted in the obituaries as "a man of sterling integrity" with a proverbial "kindness of heart." EAR would never be entirely quit of his father's ghost. In 1921, he wrote a sonnet about it called "Why He Was There."

Much as he left it when he went away from us
Here was the room again where he had been
So long that something of him should be seen,
Or felt—and so it was. Incredulous,
I turned about, loath to be greeted thus,
And there he was in his old chair, serene
As ever, and as laconic and as lean
As when he lived, and as cadaverous.

Calm as he was of old when we were young,
He sat there gazing at the pallid flame
Before him. "And how far will this go on?"

I thought. He felt the failure of my tongue,
And smiled: "I was not here until you came;
And I shall not be here when you are gone."

Although Mary Robinson felt bereft and Dean's condition made the atmosphere at home "pretty stark," she insisted that Win go back to Cambridge in
the fall. Three months to the day after his father's death, he underwent an operation for necrosis of the inner ear. The doctors recommended the procedure on
the grounds that if left unremedied, the disease might affect his brain. Besides,
the operation might relieve his persistent pain. Robinson anticipated the event
with terror. "I have made arrangements to submit myself to the carver's hands
on Saturday next at 3:00 p.m.," he wrote Smith on October 19. "I have not much
faith [in] the business, though; I have had an idea all along that the necrosis
has got in beyond the small bones. If it has, I may hear a trumpet blow a little
sooner than I would ordinarily—that's all."

Despite his fears, the operation went well, and Robinson felt encouraged
afterwards. "Two bones were removed—hammer and anvil, I suppose—and
about half of the anvil was gone or eaten up. The fact that [the surgeon] left the
third one is enough to make me feel as if I were not in quite so bad a condition
as I supposed." His ear troubles were far from over, however. During 1894 and
1895 he suffered spells when his ear "ran like a brook" for days at a time. His left
ear began acting up in sympathy with the right. "What with threatened caries of
the temporal bone of the right side of my cranium and 'sub-acute inflammation
of the middle-ear' on the left," he sarcastically commented in August 1895, "I am
having a fine summer."

What Robinson knew for certain, after the operation, was that he would face
all of the seasons unable to hear out of his right ear. It troubled him in social
gatherings, where his inability to make out what was said exacerbated his shyness. But he did not complain about it and did not invite the commiseration
of others. When asked which ear had gone deaf, EAR wouldn't say. "It doesn't
matter," he proclaimed. "I hear well enough."

The operation on his ear interrupted an otherwise auspicious beginning to
Robinson's second year at Harvard. He moved ten blocks, into pleasant quarters at 1716 Cambridge Street, started a regimen that forbade tobacco until the
evening hours, buckled down to his studies, and rooted for Harvard in their
annual football game with Yale. Now a dedicated loyalist, he was outraged by
the tactics of the visitors from New Haven. "Yale's deliberate plan to physically
disable Harvard's strongest end was so obvious that it was disgusting," he wrote
Smith.

In the classroom, Robinson took a second year of French, added the beginning German that he'd been scheduled out of the year before, continued his
English prose studies (eighteenth century, this time) with Lewis Gates, and

signed up for two of Harvard's most celebrated courses: philosophy under the instruction of professors George Herbert Palmer, William James, and Josiah Royce, and fine arts, taught by Charles Eliot Norton. In French, Robinson did moderately well, and he might have done better if he had not read so widely among books not assigned. German was very nearly a disaster: after a year of spending ten to fifteen hours a week on the language, he finished with a D-minus, his worst grade at Harvard. Robinson did not like Gates's eighteenth-century course nearly so well as the previous year's nineteenth-century one. He managed to complete the 8,000-word paper on the English periodical essayists by the January deadline but was forced to cut the midyear exam he had not prepared for adequately. He also cut the midyear in Philosophy I, which covered logic ("worse than hell itself to me") and psychology (not much better). Robinson made up the exams in the spring, although not before his adviser was alerted to his derelictions.

His favorite course was Norton's famous Fine Arts 3 and 4, wherein the stoop-shouldered, white-haired, bright-eyed aesthete lectured to legions of undergraduates. The course was regarded as a "snap," and 500 students signed up for it each year. Many of them clambered down the fire escape after the roll was called, and on football Saturdays, only a handful might be in attendance. Robinson, who stayed, thought Norton's lectures magnificent. "I suppose there is no doubt that he is by all odds the greatest man in America," he wrote Smith at Thanksgiving time.

What most pleased him about Norton was his ability to relate observations about ancient art to the present day. He preached against materialism, a gospel Robinson eagerly embraced. In one lecture, Norton made sport of the World's Fair and the Chicago man who said they might not "have much culture out there yet, but when they got it, they were going to make it hum." He also discoursed about the great figures he had known: Ruskin, who called him his "first tutor," and Carlyle and Emerson. It was a considerable privilege, Robinson declared, to sit within six feet of Norton three times a week and hear him talk.

Josiah Royce, though, he did not cotton to. With his homely appearance and raucous voice, Royce was hardly prepossessing on the platform. More importantly, Robinson lacked a philosophical mind. His talent lay in intuitions about others, sometimes uncanny in their insight, not in systematic thought. He was particularly critical of Royce's lectures on psychology, which was not, after all, the professor's field of expertise: apparently, he was filling in for his colleague James. "I get absolutely nothing from what he says," Robinson observed. He read the poems of Elizabeth Barrrett Browning all through one lecture and skipped the next one, on neural activity, to attend a Friday-afternoon symphony concert. Robinson became more interested in what Royce had to say toward the end of the year, when the famous professor's lectures supplemented the course reading in his *Spirit of Modern Philosophy*.

Willie Butler and Others

As with most collegians, Robinson absorbed much of what he learned at Harvard from fellow students and not from professors. In the Corn Cob discussions, for example, his friends clashed vehemently over issues of religion. Saben and Burnham, for once of a single mind, assaulted conventional Christianity, while Tryon and Chauncey Hubbell, a Swedenborgian, rose to its defense. Robinson adopted a middle ground. On the one hand, he could see the merit of the atheist Robert Ingersoll's attacks on popular religion. On the other, he felt sure of the existence of a mystery beyond ordinary understanding.

On occasion, Saben—who had managed to get himself readmitted to Harvard as a law student—simply took over the proceedings of the club. "Saben got drunk, as I expected, and made a learned ass of himself," Robinson wrote to Smith in February 1893. "He read Bob Ingersoll, Coppée, Omar Khayyam, and [Gray's] 'Elegy in a Country Church Yard' as only a drunken man can." The audience was amused, but Robinson thought the performance degrading. Weeks later, Saben and another friend, Philip Crapo, stopped by Robinson's and started a quarrel that lasted from seven p.m. to midnight. "I do not know that I passed through the mental suffering in my life that I did during those five hours," Robinson said.

Robinson saw considerably less of Saben during his second year at Harvard, solidifying other relationships and making several new friends. He was particularly fascinated by the complicated George Latham. In the spring, the two made a literary-historical bargain: Latham agreed to read Hardy's *Tess of the D'Urbervilles*, if Robinson would read Henry Cabot Lodge's biography of Alexander Hamilton. (The bargain worked out well for EAR. Years later, he wrote a long poem about Hamilton and consulted Lodge to ensure the accuracy of his details).

Also in the spring of 1893, Robinson remembered, he invited Latham to come around and visit him after dinner. He waited, but Latham did not arrive. When Robinson asked him the following day what had happened, Latham said he had forgotten all about it. This shook EAR, for it made him doubt Latham's friendship, and as he put it, a "friend is a good deal to me." Latham's reserve inspired Robinson to make "a kind of recreative study" of him during their two years at Cambridge. "You will not think any less of me for confessing this as it is a part of my nature to do such things," he wrote Latham, embedding in that comment the habit of mind that led to many of his most powerful poems.

In a letter of October 1894, Robinson went so far as to present a thoroughgoing analysis of Latham's psychological makeup: "you are far more alive to the aesthetic side of things than you are willing to confess. . . . you also have a practical power of absorbing living questions, and considering them from a purely intellectual point of view. . . . you do not always stop to ask yourself how near or how far from the truth are the opinions you express. . . . you have a slight leaning for the eccentric, and should be glad of it," and so on.

The sheer audacity of the letter must have staggered Latham, who delayed before replying. But Robinson's diagnosis of his friend was not the product of a dispassionate observer. Far from it: it was proof of his involvement with mankind. By way of justification, Robinson pointed out that he had only his thoughts to help people with and he had expressed them in the hope that they might make Latham better acquainted with himself. "If I seem to take an undue interest in your affairs," he added by way of apology, "you must remember that my friends are all part of myself." So too were the characters in his poems, the good and the bad alike, part of himself: human beings for whom he felt an abiding kinship.

In describing Latham to Smith, Robinson characterized him as "one of those complex men whom we can never understand." Latham had suffered a great deal, and his troubles, combined with his unnatural pride, made it almost impossible for him to "render confidences." Robinson might have been describing himself. Indeed, in Latham, he beheld someone concealed within a protective carapace of reticence yet—and this was encouraging—well on the road to accommodation with life. "You must remember that you had an influence over me which you may never have suspected and that influence was for the good," Robinson wrote Latham. "In spite of the cold glazing you seemed to put over your feelings, there was a depth—a complexity—in your nature that made me—very slowly, I must confess—a better man than I could otherwise have been." In his later career, Latham shucked off much of his armor. Biographer Leon Edel, his student at McGill, remembered him as "a lovable—and much loved—man, and an extraordinary teacher."

Latham was one among those he had hoped to befriend at Harvard: "men to talk with whose goddess is not engraved on a silver dollar—men whose literature is not newspapers." Another was the gentle, scholarly Joseph S. Ford, who graduated with the class of 1894 and spent his subsequent career at Phillips Exeter teaching French and serving as director of admissions. Ford was a sensitive soul, who expressed a fervent admiration for Robinson's early poetry. The two men became regular correspondents in the years after Harvard, with Ford ever eager to advance his friend's career.

The most important friendship of Robinson's second year at Harvard, however, was formed with William Edward Butler (1874–1912). Butler, an incoming freshman four years younger than EAR, occupied the two rooms immediately adjacent to Robinson's. The son of a prominent Boston merchant, Butler prepared for college at Exeter and brought with him to college an extraordinary enthusiasm for literature. Early in January 1893, he borrowed Robinson's copy of *Tom Jones* and raced through its 1,000 pages in a marathon sixteen-hour reading binge. Butler was a handsome lad with "charming manners, a face radiant with appreciation, and the soul of a philanthropist." He was also subject to occasional bouts of depression. He completed only one year at Harvard before he was enlisted in the family business: Butler's department store in Boston. During that year, he and Robinson forged a powerful bond.

FIGURE 6.1   Willie Butler in his Harvard digs.

Source: Arnold T. Schwab Papers.

Willie Butler believed in Robinson's genius absolutely. No one did more than he to support EAR during the long period of poverty and lack of recognition that lay ahead. Butler sent him money and sent him books, including both a complete set of Shakespeare and a selection of newly published works from England. He offered him the use of his quarters in Cambridge and Boston whenever Robinson wanted to use them. He came to visit Robinson in Gardiner in the summer of 1893, the only Harvard friend other than Ford to do so. In 1897, he underwrote the publication of EAR's second book, *The Children of the Night*. Twice he offered Robinson jobs that would bring him to Boston, first as a night watchman at the department store in 1898 (an offer Robinson turned down in order to take a clerkship at Harvard) and early in 1905 as a part-time writer of advertising copy for the store (an offer Robinson accepted).

The story of the friendship between the two men can be reconstructed only in hazy outline. None of the correspondence between them has survived. That letters went back and forth is certain, for in writing to others, particularly during the years immediately after Harvard, Robinson repeatedly mentions the latest news from Butler. These secondary accounts make it clear that the relationship was an extremely important one in EAR's life.

In his memoir, Saben asserted that during the 1892–93 year Robinson "had quite fallen in love" with "the handsome youth" (Saben does not use Butler's name) who occupied the rooms next to his. "I have often wondered," Saben writes, "whether the warmest affection that Robinson ever felt for any human being was not for the youth . . . and I have also wondered whether it is quite possible to get very deep into [Robinson's] psychology without knowing something of the attachment." Saben's interpretation of events must be regarded with an awareness that, as "an Epicurean," he zealously advocated sexual activity in all its forms and that, as a Freudian, he was persuaded of the ill effects of repression.

Saben cites three separate incidents as evidence that Butler and Robinson felt something more than friendship for each other. The first is that they once spent a night together in the room of a student at MIT, information that—Saben said—came to him independently from both Butler and Robinson. "What induced them to join thus in contiguous slumber," Saben commented, "has always been one of the minor mysteries that I have never solved, for both were not far removed from their college rooms, and the home of the youth could not have been many blocks distant." There is of course no way of corroborating this story, or the others that Saben related in the late 1940s, long after the deaths of both Robinson and Butler

The second piece of evidence involves a nightmare. As Saben related it, one night after both men had gone to bed in their "adjacent apartments" in Cambridge, Butler "had a dream that he was being assaulted, not by a creature of flesh and blood, but by a bright shining object, a kind of prism." Awaking from his dream, he knocked on Robinson's door in terror. Robinson let him in, and the two sat together "in long conversation" for two hours. "Just what passed between them, just what was discussed," Saben did not know, but when Robinson told him about it, he said, "'I could have taken [Butler] in my arms.'" A decade or more later, Saben asked Robinson whether he had not felt the stirrings of homosexual desire on that occasion. Robinson thought not. Anyone would have wanted to comfort a friend in such distress as Butler's, he said. Ah, Saben countered, but would that have been true if the troubled youngster had not been physically attractive? By all means, Robinson said. However it may have been, Saben felt certain that Butler's dream called for Freudian interpretation, its significance "apparent to a psychoanalyst at a glance."

According to Saben's third tale, on a winter evening in 1893 Robinson went to "a lupanar [brothel] for the purpose of gratifying the desire that lupanars are designed to gratify." This was the only time, Saben maintained, that Robinson actually enjoyed the favors of a prostitute during his time at Harvard, despite his repeated visits to houses of prostitution during the previous year. Robinson told Saben about what he had done the night after it occurred, and Saben relayed the news to Butler. "With the insouciance of a young collegian," Saben writes in characteristically ornate prose, "without the faintest suspicion that my tittle-tattle would be provocative of anything but a broad grin or faint smile of amusement, I blundered into blurting out to the youth [Robinson's] amorous adventure . . . only to find that something expressive of horror, not of amusement, mantled his countenance." A few days later, Robinson asked Saben "in an aggrieved tone of voice, tinged with a wholly unfeigned melancholy," why he had seen fit to tell Butler about it. "I would not have minded your telling it to anyone else," he said, "but I would not have had [Butler] know it for anything."

Saben did not contend that Robinson's feelings for Butler, or vice versa, found physical expression. Saben thought this regrettable: he believed it would have been far better for EAR had such a consummation taken place. Writing half a century after the event, Saben concluded that Robinson was bisexual in nature, having both heterosexual and homosexual inclinations, and because of his repression he was reluctant to indulge himself in either direction.

Robinson's relationship with Butler continued to develop after EAR left Harvard in the spring of 1893. On a trip back to Cambridge in December of that year, he saw Butler in an entirely different environment—in his office at the Butler store. In response to a business emergency, Willie had left Harvard to become treasurer of the family's mercantile enterprise. Detesting the world of business, it was difficult for Robinson to think that the change would benefit Butler. But he came to the conclusion that it was "the best thing" after all. As he wrote Latham with unaccustomed candor in January 1894, "Butler is young and last year acquired an almost abnormal liking for me. I was sorry to see it for I knew well enough that it could not last." When Butler left for a long visit to Europe that winter, Robinson obviously missed him. He complained to Latham that Butler sent him only one "illuminated photograph" from Rome. "He seems to be my friend, though he has a queer way of neglecting little courtesies and saying rather sharp things."

On May 1, 1894, as he was contemplating his forthcoming trip to celebrate Class Day at Harvard, Robinson wrote Smith that he was "getting to think more and more of Butler every day—not because he sends me books, though of course that is pleasant—but because I am beginning to realize that he is an exceptionally fine fellow." Smith had met Butler on a trip to Boston, and Robinson rather envied him the pleasure. "He is a pretty good man to meet in a strange land," he wrote from his confines in Gardiner, "and you doubtless welcomed his broad smile. I think a great deal of that smile, and wish that I had even the ghost of it to lighten my semicadaverous countenance."

In subsequent letters, Robinson fretted over Butler's depression and his father's failure in business—a failure apparently imminent when he was called back from Harvard. Should you go to Boston, Robinson wrote Latham in June 1895, "do not forget to call upon Butler. He is not enjoying himself over much just at present and I know that a call from you would put new life into him." In these ways Robinson took it upon himself to look after the youth who had lived next door to him during his second year at Harvard. Erotically driven or not, it was one of the closest relationships of his life. He dedicated *The Man Against the Sky* (1916) to the memory of William Edward Butler.

Harvard and Its Effects

The days rushed by during Robinson's last weeks at Harvard. Even the changeable springtime weather reminded him how little time remained. On a glorious Sunday morning in mid-March, he took a walk out to Longfellow's house in Elmwood. By the time he returned, it had started snowing under a dark, gray sky. As he was writing Smith his weekly letter an hour later, the snow was still coming down, but under a mostly sunny sky. Things changed fast, and there was much to do. Robinson had a thesis to write for Professor Gates but was doing most of his reading off the syllabus, in Moliere, Kipling, and the popular English novels of the day. For entertainment he went to see Lillian Russell in a comic opera, the Hasty Pudding burlesque, and the Italian opera. Knowing he would not return to college, Robinson could not muster much enthusiasm for final examinations. "I suppose I had better finish up the year's work," he wrote Gledhill resignedly. Still, what was the point of grinding for tests he could see no "possible use in taking"?

Final exams did furnish him with a convenient excuse for skipping Gus Moore's marriage in the middle of June. The fact was, as Robinson put it, that he did "not care for that kind of entertainment." Were he to get married himself, he wouldn't want anyone around besides the principals. But his own marriage was hardly imminent, he told Gledhill. "You and Gus will probably be rearing brats while I am hunting for a job." He could not ignore the "'job' question" much longer: all of Gardiner would want to know what he had in mind. For the moment, though, he was encouraging hometown companions Gledhill and Smith to come to Cambridge for the end-of-year observations. Specifically, he urged Smith to spend a few days there around the summer solstice. They could take in the Yale-Harvard baseball game, see a pop concert "with music and beer galore," and go back to Gardiner together.

In his correspondence with Smith, Robinson reflected on his time at Harvard. He had no particular desire to spend another year there, he wrote early in June, but he "would hate to part with the experience of the past two." He had seen things that he "could not possibly see at any other place, and [had] a different conception of what is good and bad in life." His marks were not good, but that was "the last thing in the world" he cared about. On Class Day, Robinson went to Harvard Yard, which was abloom in wisteria and lilacs. Families of the graduates moved about beneath the elms, listened to the music of the bands, and dodged the Chinese lanterns swaying from tree to tree. "I feel I have gotten comparatively little from my two years," Robinson observed in his final letter to Smith from Harvard, "but still, more than I could get in Gardiner if I lived a century."

It was friends, most of all, that Robinson sought and found at Harvard. "It makes me shudder sometimes to think . . . of what I might be by this time had I never gone to Harvard and met the fellows I did," he wrote Latham. He only regretted that during those two years he had been so often "out of sorts"— afflicted by his diseased ear and mindful of the troubles at home. To maintain those friendships, he returned to Harvard for Class Week both in 1894 and 1895, spending time with Ford, Tryon, and Butler. He contemplated the departure of the last of his college friends from Harvard with sadness: "we meet and get acquainted, and then we are scattered over the country." Saben was scattered furthest of all, sailing for graduate study in Europe in the spring of 1894.

What Robinson carried away with him from college, to buoy him for the rough passage ahead, was a conviction that it was perfectly all right to follow your dreams, however impractical they might seem to most observers. Within a year after leaving campus, he became effusive in his praise of the institution and its effects upon him. Although he was "only half a Harvard man," he wrote Gledhill, he had absorbed enough of the spirit of the place to invest in it "almost the only" patriotic feelings he possessed. "I am a better man with better ideals than I was before I went, but I am afraid they are not the ideals to help me in the active walk of life." And more vigorously to Smith, "my life is infinitely larger" for going to Harvard after twenty years of living "like a snail." There was "a human largeness" about the place that developed a man's mental intensity and awakened "his latent comprehension of the 'greater glory'": a glory beyond the rewards of the marketplace.

As Louis Coxe summed up his time at Harvard, Robinson came there from provincial Maine, deeply discouraged, and emerged two years later with the strength of purpose to survive "the still lower circles of hell that awaited him."

7

Shaping a Life

Becoming a Writer

Win Robinson came home to Gardiner in the summer of 1893 and stayed there another five years. During that half decade, he made the most important decisions of his life about the interrelated issues of career and of love and marriage. There was no one in Gardiner to confide in, much, so that the story emerges in Robinson's correspondence. In letters to Smith and Gledhill, close companions of his youth now living elsewhere, and to Latham and Ford, friends from the Harvard years, he wrote openly of his hopes and ambitions as a writer. The topic of love he addressed only obliquely.

Herman Robinson also returned in late June, disgraced and defeated. The panic of 1893 effectively wiped out the resources he'd invested in western lands. In St. Louis auctions, Herman sold off these holdings at ruinous prices, as well as those of other Maine men he'd talked into making similar investments. Emma was already living with her parents in Farmingdale, having come there for the birth of their second daughter, Marie, on April 24. She and the children lived in Maine from that time on, although for at least two more years Herman spent part of the year in Missouri, attempting to breathe life into dying endeavors.

The panic stretched nationwide, leaving four million unemployed. Coxey's army marched on Washington; tramps knocked on doors everywhere. The Robinsons were not quite impoverished, although most of the money Edward Robinson left behind evaporated with startling rapidity. There was not much Herman could have done to prevent this patrimony from slipping away, but in the aftermath he felt that he had been betrayed by his associates and turned to drink for solace. A defeated man, he spent much of his time with local fishermen and sometimes peddled fresh-caught lobsters in downtown Gardiner. Almost every night, he drank, leading to family quarrels with Emma.

"My money has all gone to the devil in a bad investment and I am as poor as need be," Win told Gledhill. He had his own problems to confront, besides. Early in July he feared that he was going blind. The oculist fitted him for glasses, but for the next six months he could not read more than a few minutes at a time "without paying [a] penalty." His ears occasionally acted up. He was troubled by constipation, as he had been at Harvard and would be all of his days. Physical ailments were as nothing, however, compared to persistent worrying about the future.

"I am getting to be an old man," he wrote Gledhill, "and must do something to bring in the ducats instead of throwing them out all the time." He didn't want "to teach school, or work with tools or much of anything else that brings money to a man." He deplored "the feverish drudgery of business," having no sympathy "with the cold, matter-of-fact contriving nature" of the capitalist. What he wanted was to write, even though there might be little money in it, but he was visited by humiliation about his situation at home. "You, who are making a living," he wrote Smith, then teaching at Rockland, "cannot imagine how cutting it is for a man of twenty-four to depend upon his mother for every cent he has and every mouthful he swallows."

As he debated the issue of occupation, Robinson made what small contributions he could to his own and the family's welfare. Over the summer of 1893, he tutored James Barstow in French to prepare him for college entrance examinations. The lessons were conducted in the Barstows' warm and comfortable cellar while Robinson happily munched on apples. By way of comparison, he told Barstow, pears were "nothing but sand and sweetened water." Tending to the apple orchard was only one of the several chores he undertook at home, where he assumed the job of caretaker. Dean was in residence but hardly healthy enough to undertake the outdoor work. By helping around the place, Win could assuage some of his guilt and embarrassment as a fully grown dependent son.

In letters to Smith and Ford, Robinson regularly reported on his accomplishments in "farming," a term which encompassed gardening, tending to the chickens, cutting firewood, and general upkeep. In May 1894, for instance, he itemized the vegetables he'd just completed planting: eggplants and okra, five kinds of tomatoes, big red Victoria onions that promised wondrous smells come fall, and above all beans. "A man who does not like beans is only partly constructed," he told Ford. He would not consider leaving for an October holiday in Cambridge until he'd finished picking all of the beans. He acquired "a farmer tan," his face and neck burned to the color of leather, and felt proud of it.

Win also got to be handy with an axe, splitting "slab wood of every shape and length imaginable—full of splinters and conducive to all sorts of swear words." There was a certain poetry in reducing a sprawling apple limb to stove wood, he thought. He could find no poetry whatever in *gathering* apples, though. "It is the worst work I know except washing dishes and listening to a debate." The workload at 67 Lincoln accelerated in the autumn and again in the spring, when the northern land awoke from a long winter's sleep. Every May, Robinson was busy scrubbing around the house, cleaning out the barn, planting the garden, and generally brightening up the place. One spring he painted the dining room floor.

If he had not discovered a form of compensation in his various chores, Robinson would not have made so much of them in his letters. "Well, I must put on my old duds and clear the ashes out of the cellar," he wrote Smith. He used to think that kind of work was beneath him, but had changed his mind. "Such things do a man a world of good, if he can only bring himself to think so." Even as he complained of having to rise before dawn "to work in that cursed raspberry bed of ours," uttering the complaint made him feel of some use in the world.

Useful as Win may have been around the house and grounds, most people in his hometown were still asking what he meant to do, with the strong implication that he ought to get a job and the sooner the better. In a letter to Gledhill of October 28, 1893, he declared his intention to try writing as a career, chancy and impractical as that might seem. "This itch for authorship is worse than the devil and about spoils a man for anything else. . . . I will make a clean confession and say that writing has been my dream ever since I was old enough to lay a plan for my air castle. Now for the first time I seem to have something of an opportunity and this winter I shall make a beginning. If I make a failure of it, and the chances are about ten to one that I shall, my life will be a disappointment and a failure."

Mary Robinson approved, or at least did not object. She assigned him the small square room adjoining his bedroom for a study, in hopes that his smoking might not contaminate the air in the rest of the house from that remove. Win set about fixing up the room as a workplace. His grandfather Robinson's desk and the wicker rocking chair came upstairs from the sitting room. A radiator was installed to ward off Maine weather "too cold for free thought." He put in a bookcase along the west wall, and got a typewriter for formal correspondence and for making legible copies of the serious writing he'd done by hand.

Having declared himself "a literary man," Robinson was determined to work every bit as hard as a lawyer or banker or businessman. After breakfast each morning, he went to the post office to pick up the mail and spent the rest of the day in his den. What he wrote there, during the next year and a half, were stories, mostly, not poems. Robinson's capacity to read French was one of the lasting benefits of his years at Harvard, and the contes of François Coppée and Alphonse Daudet came to him as a revelation. He valued Coppée for relating the struggles of "the humble, the forgotten, the unknown" without resorting to maudlin sentimentality, and he admired Daudet for his extraordinary condensation and for making every sentence count. In attempting his own sketches, Robinson adopted Coppée's straightforward and unornamented depiction of ordinary people as his model, and like Daudet he sought to eliminate all nonessential language.

There was plenty of material to be found, even in Gardiner, for those who stopped gazing inward long enough to really look at the people they encountered every day. Robinson had been doing a "considerable amount of observing," he wrote Smith in March 1894. "In fact, I observe so much that my feet often slip and I am forever stumbling over little things that other men never notice." He hoped for a "clear view of the wrinkles on the cerebrum of the men and women" he met, and if he could not achieve that, at least for "some idea of their characters." All of Robinson's concentrated observation did not mean that he was enamored of his fellow man, in general. To Smith, he confessed "the dismal truth that the majority of mankind interest me only as studies." But these were hardly objective studies, for he undertook them with fascination and, as any reader of his poetry knows, he felt a profound compassion for the disadvantaged and bereft among them, and had an uncanny knack for understanding their inner makeup.

Like the best of his poetry, the prose sketches concentrated on characters and relationships. Some of them derived from his own experience. One dealt "with the selfishness of self-denial—a peculiar but by no means rare flaw of human nature," another with "the philosophical enmity of two brothers who were not born for the same purpose." A third sketch about marital conflict bordered on the ridiculous: "It is not an easy task," Robinson said, "to kill a woman in childbirth brought on by excessive clarinet playing on the part of an over-enthusiastic young husband." There was "a marionette story touching lightly on divorce," a somewhat queer sketch reflecting "the wasted part of a brilliant but 'unruddered' man in the company of a poor devil he has taken as a companion for the simple reason that he can master him," a portrait of a philosophical tramp, and a "reincarnation story" that gave him trouble because he had to keep "the idea of destiny ever present without saying much about it."

As a "penniless prospective literatus," Robinson hoped that his sketches could be sold to the magazines and collected in a book. That would scratch his itch for authorship and earn him the self-respect that he was seeking. "Two or three years at the most ought to tell me something," he wrote. If the verdict went against him, it would be "another case of a disappointed life, blasted hopes, and the usual accompaniments." But it would not be too late "to start out for an occupation and a living."

At first the fiction came fast. Robinson discovered he could write a 4,000-word piece in a week's time, working four hours a day or until his head began to spin. By March 1894 he had finished seven sketches. In May he sent three of them to the *Atlantic Monthly*. Editor Horace Scudder sent them back with a conciliatory comment: "These sketches seem to me not without some claim to notice. They show restraint and an effort at telling something worth while." Swallowing his pride, Robinson pronounced this reaction "far from discouraging" and kept at his desk. In September he set up a timetable for a volume of twelve to fifteen stories, to be completed by May 1895. Then he sped ahead of the timetable, so that by late January he had enough on paper to make a book of 350 to 400 pages. Poetry kept getting in the way, however. His "worst and most persistent enemy," he declared in March, was the "constant inclination to write poetry." Sometimes he feared that "the damned stuff would kill what little ability" he had for fiction.

Retrospectively such sentiments sound ironical, given that Robinson was to become a major American poet, but he meant them seriously at the time. His goal was to publish a volume of stories, and he resented anything that got in the way. "I have made up my mind that I am going to do this thing, and that is all there is to it," he told Smith in April 1895. "Some day you will see a printed edition of *Scattered Lives* even though it be printed on toilet paper with a one-hand printing press." In addition to the sketches, he wrote Ford, he "had three novels well under way—in his mind." He proposed to send Ford the manuscript of *The Book of Scattered Lives* to pass on to an editor friend. Much of the summer was spent revising and reshaping the sketches. Smith thought them extraordinarily good. Butler read them on his visit to Gardiner and praised them extravagantly in a letter to Saben. But when they were finally shipped out—"The expectation of a returned manuscript is better than no excitement at all"—no publisher could be found.

In a letter to Latham, Robinson imagined how he might react to such a rejection. "Not that I shall be discouraged, or anything of the kind, but I shall be most damnably disappointed—which is the same thing, after all." He took that disappointment hard. In the fall of 1895, he destroyed the manuscript that had been his major project for the two previous years.

One can hardly judge Robinson's early fiction without access to the sketches, but it seems probable that in his case, too much space was the enemy. Prose fiction allowed a wider latitude for elaboration of detail, for parenthetical qualification, for peripheral comment, for complicated questioning. All of these were tendencies in his thinking that the exigencies of form required him to suppress in sonnets and three- or four-stanza portrait poems. So it was just as well that he reversed direction and concentrated his ambitions on the poetry, which kept reemerging, hard as he tried to "tread [it] under." The poems yielded sketches in verse of Edgar Allen Poe, which *Lippincott's* actually bought, and of Thomas Hardy, taken by the *Critic*, as well as of such local citizens as the skirt-crazed reprobate John Evereldown—a subject Robinson treated humorously with tongue in cheek—and the miserable Aaron Stark.

Withal a meagre man was Aaron Stark.
Cursed and unkempt, shrewd, shrivelled, and morose.
A miser was he, with a miser's nose,
And eyes like little dollars in the dark.

His thin, pinched mouth was nothing but a mark;
And when he spoke there came like sullen blows
Through scattered fangs a few snarled words and close,
As if a cur were chary of its bark.

Glad for the murmur of his hard renown,
Year after year he shambled through the town,
A loveless exile moving with a staff;
And oftentimes there crept into his ears
A sound of alien pity, touched with tears,—
And then (and only then) did Aaron laugh.

There is very little action in the poem. Robinson tells us what Aaron was like, with sound reinforcing the point. The alliterative hiss in "shrewd, shrivelled, and morose" is picked up in Aaron's own speech, "a few snarled words and close" that fall like sullen blows. The entire sonnet is stitched together by aural imagery. Aaron's bark ending the octet gives way to the town's murmuring about his "hard renown." Aaron covets the murmur as evidence of his notoriety, and even more the "sound of alien pity" and crocodile tears of the townspeople. That they should presume to feel sorry for him moves him to contemptuous laughter. His name itself contributes to the effect, through the harshness of Stark and the biblical appropriateness of Aaron. The staff that he carries is a latter-day version of Aaron's rod, symbolizing the authority he and his brother Moses exerted in Israel. Aaron's great sin makes him a singularly fitting ancestor for the miser. In Moses's absence, he melted down the ornaments of the people into a golden calf for them to worship.

This was strong stuff, not at all in line with magazine editors' ideas about what constituted poetry. They would print laudatory literary poems about Poe and Hardy. "Aaron Stark" they would not.

"Dear Friends"

In his 1852 history of Gardiner, J. W. Hanson characterized the town as "masculine in the extreme," by which he meant, among other things, that the inhabitants were far more concerned with making a living than with making art. Denham Sutcliffe, writing in the Bates College magazine in 1935, cast a baleful eye on Gardiner and other Maine towns of the late nineteenth century. In that environment, he wrote, any man "who would command the respect of his fellows must vote a straight Republican ticket, work willingly, spend less than he earns, discreetly conceal his sins, and pray loudly in meeting." The "long-haired cigarette-flickin' fellers" who scribbled poems or dabbled on canvas could expect no respect at all.

Yet was it so surprising, after all, that the citizens of Robinson's hometown wondered why he didn't follow the ordinary path and get himself a job? He didn't seem to be publishing much of anything or otherwise supporting himself. As Gardiner native Jane Mollman observed in 1976, her "grandparents, a few blocks away from Lincoln Avenue, could never have comprehended Robinson. And not because they were insensitive. Because 78 hours a week in a paper mill, and raising three children in a house with no central heat, no electricity, no bathroom, no hot water, and almost no money, left them little time or strength for anything else."

Robinson knew people like that and respected them, even as he found himself unable to "swallow [the] teaching of our poor old grandfathers who worked sixteen hours and sang psalms and praised heaven that a life is what we make it." For the most part, he shared Gardiner's "masculine" values at the same time that he was repudiating them. Hence his humiliation at living off his family's diminishing income and his willingness—even eagerness—to do the odd jobs around the house even as he was crafting his stories and poems. Win understood that he was different. He could not bring himself to admire "Merchant A and Barrister B," the "so called successful men" pointed out to him as examples to follow. Unlike the lawyer in one of Dr. Schumann's poems, he refused to sell his soul "for a paltry fee."

In his letters, Robinson returned time and again to the problem confronting him. He wanted to go his own way and at the same time was reluctant to separate himself from the community. "I am half afraid that my 'dear friends' here in Gardiner will be disappointed in me if I do not do something before long," he wrote Smith on October 1, 1893. "I suspect that I am pretty much what I am, and that I am pretty much a damned fool in many ways; but I further suspect that I am not altogether an ass, whatever my neighbors may say." He heard what they were saying and intuited what went unsaid. So he addressed the "dear friends" in a sonnet that amounted to a literary declaration of independence.

> Dear friends, reproach me not for what I do,
> Nor counsel me, nor pity me; nor say
> That I am wearing half my life away
> For bubble-work that only fools pursue.
> And if my bubbles be too small for you,
> Blow bigger then your own: the games we play
> To fill the frittered minutes of a day,
> Good glasses are to read the spirit through.
>
> And whoso reads may get him some shrewd skill;
> And some unprofitable scorn resign,
> To praise the very thing that he deplores;
> So, friends (dear friends), remember, if you will,

The shame I win for singing is all mine,
The gold I miss for dreaming is all yours.

In the first eight lines, the aspiring poet addresses the "dear friends" directly and with little apparent sarcasm. He does, however, assume a position of authority, telling them to forgo pitying him and giving him advice, to leave him alone to blow his bubbles in peace. Then in the sestet, he slyly converts the message to a materialistic context designed to appeal to his audience. Their scorn for him may be "unprofitable." They might acquire "some shrewd skill" should they look more closely. They might even decide to praise him (which would please him). The repetition in "friends (dear friends)" brings irony overtly into play, leading to the prudent reminder of the last two lines that the singer makes no claim on their pocketbooks.

Written sometime in 1894 or 1895, "Dear Friends" artfully states the case for Robinson's career. In a sense, the eminently respectable people of this poem were brothers under the skin to the town miser Aaron Stark. It was their shared obsession with gold that Robinson objected to. There were three basic tenets in Gardiner's creed: a devout materialism, a strict Victorian morality, and a Puritan work ethic. Robinson accepted the last two without dispute, just as he adopted the town's Republican politics. But he rose up in defiance against the strain of materialism. It "makes me positively sick to see the results of modern materialism as they are revealed in a town like this," he said. Tilbury Town (Gardiner in creative disguise) became for him the "antagonist of . . . the gifted or far-seeing individual who, a failure by conventional standards, dedicate[d] himself to the interior life." The place gave Robinson a standard to measure himself against, a barrier to try to surmount.

There were times when he yearned to escape the town: when he got tired of listening to the brook eternally running below his window or when he read of a performance of Brahms's second symphony in Boston. He lived in hopes of having the music of Brahms near at hand and the brook only a memory, but that day had not yet dawned. There was "no prospect of [his] getting out of Maine for a long time to come," he wrote in the spring of 1894. He would not go away for another four years.

Occasionally, his sentence was lightened by amusing items in the local news-paper. A news item reported the adventures of two Gardiner men jailed for drunkenness, one of whom—"an old acquaintance" of Win's—escaped through the transom. Another read as follows: "I, Sam'l H. Potter, forbid all persons trusting or harboring my wife, Abbie Potter, as I will pay no bills of her con-tracting from this date as she has left my bed and board between three and half past five in the morning while I was gone down to Wiscasset after clams. But the cars will run just the same." The daily paper, Robinson dryly commented, "was a gold mine." In the pages of the *Gardiner Reporter Journal*, he also discov-ered a poem that began

Down Water Street Bill Jewel walks
In the cold and frosty morning,
And after him, Ed Nevins came
Just as the day was dawning.

"If [the poet] could have kept it going," he declared to Ford, "he would have written one of the best ballads in the English language."

Engagements

Everywhere Robinson looked, he beheld friends well launched on their careers, often with a wife at their side. "Did you know Gledhill was married?" he inquired of Smith in October 1893. Not only married but working as a professor of mathematics? With both companions in the League of Three committed to matrimony and respectable occupation, he could hardly avoid feeling that life was passing him by. So in January 1894 he reported "a new employment" with some enthusiasm. "Next week I shall begin to tutor a young lady in French preparatory to her entering Wellesley College," he wrote Smith. The tutoring might make him feel "of a little use in the world."

The young lady in question was Mabel Moore, a slender, good-looking girl in the class behind Robinson and her brother Gus. Win admired Mabel for having the courage to embark on a college education five years after graduating from high school. It gave them something in common. He admired her in other ways, too. Originally the plan was that he would tutor her until September, but it did not work out that way. The tale emerges from between the lines of four letters he wrote Harry Smith in May and June.

The gray sticky weather on May Day reflected his spirits, Robinson acknowledged in the first of these. "Perhaps you will understand my feelings . . . better, and perhaps not, when I tell you that my French lessons are over. You may interpret this as you like, but I fancy you will not get far out of the way in your conclusions. Anticipation and realization are two different things." It was remarkable, he thought, that Butler should have so recently sent him Hardy's *Life's Little Ironies* and Beatrice Harraden's *Ships That Pass in the Night*, with its epigraph "So, on the ocean of life, we pass and speak one another, / Only a look and a voice, then darkness again and a silence."

As in many Robinson poems, in his personal life we are left often to wonder precisely what happened. It seems likely that there had been an understanding between Mabel Moore and him, even an engagement, that was broken. Robinson hinted at such an interpretation in his letter of May 20, responding to Smith's announcement that he was engaged. "You are engaged to be married, you are happy, and the world and the future look bright in your eyes," he wrote: "I am not (now) engaged to be married, I am not happy, and the world and the future look so dark and gloomy that I look mostly into the past."

Asked about the relationship many years later, Mabel Moore denied that there had been anything beyond friendship between them. But Alice Jordan, Win's neighbor, remembered his saying he was thinking of her as a wife. What is clear is that he had anticipated much and been disappointed, leaving him with a "horrible dose of the blues." On June 3, he spoke of "separation from the one who is and always will be a part of my daily life." Thereafter, silence descended as to "the one," "the young lady," the "girl": the terms by which Robinson protected Mabel's privacy in correspondence.

Robinson took the news of Smith's impending marriage as hard as the end of his French lessons. Smith was, at the time, his closest friend in the world. During summers, when Smith was on vacation from his teaching duties, they spent long afternoons together in the grove of evergreens back of the Smith homestead on Iron Mine Hill. There the two young men smoked and talked about books and what the future might hold. Both of them were captivated by literature. Smith was "born for learning," Rosalind Richards said. "He foamed to it, as a stream rushes down hill." In due course, he was to become professor of Greek at Amherst. He was a man Robinson could "take to [his] soul."

During the long winters, they kept in touch with weekly letters. Robinson unburdened himself to Smith as to no one else. He trusted Smith, admired him, respected his judgment, rejoiced in his company. So when Smith sent him the tidings, "Her name is Adela—and we are engaged. That's all," Robinson was nearly devastated. His long letter of May 20, 1894, stands as testimony. It began, unpleasantly enough, with the comment that Win disliked Smith's "big sprawl-

FIGURE 7.1 Harry Smith at Bowdoin, 1891.

Source: Colby College Special Collections.

ing lines," symptomatic as they were of his elation. Next he asserted that word of the engagement came as no surprise. For six months, Robinson said, he had felt that Smith was slowly putting him off to make way for the woman he was going to marry. He did not think Smith ceased to value his friendship. It was "merely a case of 'not that I loved long Robinson less, but—oh, yes, Adela—more.'" They would surely sit and read and smoke together under the pines during the summer to come, the last of Smith's bachelor days, but it would not be the same. "In short, I have lost you, and, for your sake, I am heartily glad of it."

In the letter Robinson insisted five times how "*glad*" he was about his friend's engagement. He "was *glad*, upon the whole" to discover that his suspicions about Smith's being in love with somebody were accurate. He was "*glad* for what seem[ed] to be in store" for Smith. He was *glad* Smith was "going to be married. I have always looked upon a bachelor as only half a man. . . . I have always believed in love and always shall believe in it." And, finally: "Do you fully understand that I am *glad* that this change has come to you—that your life is beginning, in the true sense of the expression, to mean something to you?" But all that gladness was compromised by a prescient sorrow for his own solitary fate. "I see myself—sometimes in the light of a partial success—living alone in some city—Boston, most likely—with a friend or two to drop in upon me once in a while, and a few faithful correspondents." And further undercut by the mandate he issued at the end of his letter. "When you are married," he wrote Smith, "you must not ask me to come to your wedding."

Over the course of several summers, Smith and Robinson devised various plans together. One was to build a cabin of field stone at their evergreen hideaway. They collected a few boulders toward that end, then let the project lapse. Early in February 1894, Robinson proposed an idea better suited to their mutual interests. "My scheme," he wrote, "is to make a metrical translation of the *Antigone*." Smith, the Greek scholar, was to translate Sophocles's play into English prose. Robinson would then convert the prose into blank verse. When they were done, they could have the result printed in a limited edition: "*The Antigone of Sophocles: A translation by Harry de Forest Smith and Edwin Arlington Robinson.*" As preparation for the task, Robinson familiarized himself with the Greek alphabet, but did not undertake to learn the language. His very ignorance, he thought, might save him from slavish literalness. Instead, he immersed himself in reading about Greek culture, in the process deciding that he possessed "something of the Hellenic spirit" himself.

Initially, Robinson thought they could finish over the summer, a timetable that proved unduly optimistic. The translation went forward intermittently over a period of more than three years. In the end, though, Robinson set it aside in favor of his own writing. He left the manuscript behind when he left Gardiner for good in 1898. Two decades later, when Smith inquired about its whereabouts, EAR replied that he'd boxed it up with some books, but that "the children" (Emma and Herman's three young daughters) had opened the box and "more or less scattered" the contents. Robinson's niece Ruth recalled using the clean side of the sheets of paper for drawing and coloring.

Although it did not lead to publication, the *Antigone* enterprise bound the friends together throughout the summer of 1894. When the summer was over, so too—Robinson clearly felt—was the friendship itself. "Smith and I," he wrote Ford in mid-September, "have had our last fire in the woods, roasted our last corn, and he has gone away, and I am alone. There is a kind of poetry about the whole thing, but it isn't the kind that pays." That Christmas was the "sorriest" of his life. He felt "hollow and vaguely conscious of wasted time." His friends were marching ahead of him into professional careers, settling down into marriage, getting on with their lives. Probably he was "a damned fool to be disturbed by the progress of others," but he couldn't help it.

Melancholy overtook him again in the spring, when "Reece's band" played all week in Gardiner. The performers stood up and played "Auld Lang Syne" at the last concert, sending "seven distinct kind of crinkles" up Robinson's spine and through his hair. When they put up their instruments, he felt as if an epoch in his life were over. True to his word, Robinson could not bring himself to attend Smith's wedding in June. "I only know that it is better for me to stay where I am, and also better for you," he wrote Smith.

Some of the emotional attachment Robinson felt for Mabel Moore and Harry Smith was redirected toward Emma and her nieces. From 1893 on, they spent their summers on Capitol Island, and during the rest of the year resided with Emma's parents in Farmingdale. But there were long periods during the fall and winter months, with Herman out of town trying in vain to recover the family finances, when the little girls stayed at the Robinson house. Mary Robinson—"Daomina" to her grandchildren—doted on Ruth, particularly. At the beginning, Uncle Win seems to have regarded his nieces as a considerable annoyance. "Since the middle of last week," he wrote in mid-November 1894, "I have been hopelessly 'out of sorts' on account of the kids, who keep running by my door and shake the house generally." At times the racket got so loud that he had to go for a walk to cool off. On a rainy day in late January 1895, he prayed for a howling wind to "drown [out] a baby's yelling. That is the only sound I hear nowadays." In October 1895 he concluded that babies were "a mistake."

Yet all the while, the curmudgeon was giving way to the adoring uncle. Ruth was busy around the kitchen, "helping" grandmother Robinson as she canned raspberries and baked apples. One day, Daomina allowed Ruth to help her pare turnips. When the knife slipped, the little girl saw the spurt of blood and cried terribly. The uncles came to her rescue. Uncle Dean drew Ruth's wound together with a piece of court plaster, and Uncle Win took her for a ride on his shoulders and told her the story of "Brave Horatius at the Bridge." In the joy, Ruth forgot her woe—and captured a corner of her uncle's heart.

Then there was Emma herself to disturb his feelings, even in her young motherhood. In the spring of 1894, Robinson was constructing his "Parable of the Pines," the sketch about the enmity of two brothers "not born for the same purpose." At the very same time, he went back to "The Night Before," the long poem about a lover's betrayal and his subsequent murder of the "cad" who stole his true love away. Robinson obviously had the Win-Emma-Herman triangle of 1888 in mind as he rebuilt this dramatic monologue, in which, in effect, he confesses to the imaginary murder of his brother Herman. He also allowed the narrator (himself, in this case) to learn from his terrible experience that suffering could lead to compassion, and compassion to art. "The woes [he] suffered / After that hard betrayal made [him] / Pity, at first, all breathing creatures / On this bewildered earth." Then he began to study their faces and to create for himself "the story / Of their scattered lives."

Tilbury Townspeople

In a letter to Smith of December 14, 1895, Robinson mentioned "Tilbury Town" for the first time. It was the place, he pointed out, where John Evereldown "had all the women under his wing, or thought he had." Tilbury Town had a tavern, and Robinson was writing a series of tavern songs that were "villainously hard to make." He included the opening stanza of one of the best for Smith to enjoy.

> Look at Edward Alphabet
> Going home to pray!
> Drunk as he can ever get,
> And on the Sabbath day!

He had also completed "a piece of deliberate degeneration called 'Luke Havergal,'" which unlike "Edward Alphabet" was not at all funny. These characters and more he intended to bring to light in a book of poems called *The Tavern and the Night Before*, a volume to take the place of the aborted fictional sketches.

He devoted the winter of 1895–96 to assembling the contents of this book. By March 7 he had finished the work and sent his poems off to the publishers. "I am sure of one thing," he told Smith jauntily, "and that is that they are to be printed by somebody." When a month passed with no word, though, he began to prepare himself for rejection "with a kind of optimistic desperation." On May 13, when the bad news arrived, he added a couple of new poems and tried another publisher. Once again the manuscript came back. The same Horace Scudder who had administered the coup de grace to Robinson's prose sketches at the *Atlantic* performed the same service for his book of poetry at Houghton Mifflin. Scudder "recognized the individuality of the poems" but advised against publication. The firm's recent experience with volumes of verse had been "so very discouraging that we cannot think it advisable to attempt a wider circulation to Mr. Robinson's poetry than he is likely to secure through friendly means"—that is, by a privately subsidized printing. Robinson took the hint, and decided that the someone who would publish his first book of poems would have to be himself. In the long run it would not matter. "If [the poems] are really good for anything," he wrote Ford, "they will make their own way, though the process may be rather slow."

Working as his own editor, Robinson scrapped the tavern songs and revised and rearranged the other poems. There remained forty-six short poems that would appear on forty closely printed pages in a slim collection retitled *The Torrent and the Night Before*. Edward Proby Fox, an uncle in Boston who worked for the Riverside Press, agreed to oversee the production. While he waited for the blue-backed booklets to appear, Robinson tinkered with his stamp collection and practiced on the fiddle. "If there are half a dozen poems in the whole lot," he wrote Ford, "I shall be satisfied." By "poems," Robinson added, he meant something different from "what goes nowadays for poetry." He feared that his style was "too much from the shoulder" to suit the general public.

As with his prose, Robinson was shaping his poetry after the approach of a master. His model was George Crabbe (1754–1832), the English poet who had "demolished [Oliver] Goldsmith's idealized pastoral" by describing with accuracy and sympathy the squalid, blighted, and eccentric lives of the poor folk of his native town. Robinson acknowledged the debt in a sonnet celebrating Crabbe's "plain excellence and stubborn skill." Like his predecessor, Robinson was interested in telling the "fearless truth" about the people he had been observing. "You won't find much in the way of natural description," he warned Gledhill about his book-in-progress. "There is very little tinkling water, and . . . not a red-bellied robin in the whole collection." Taking their place were "The Clerks."

I did not think that I should find them there
When I came back again; but there they stood,
As in the days they dreamed of when young blood
Was in their cheeks and women called them fair.
Be sure, they met me with an ancient air,—
And yes, there was a shop-worn brotherhood
About them; but the men were just as good,
And just as human as they ever were.

And you that ache so much to be sublime,
And you that feed yourselves with your descent,

What comes of all your visions and your fears?
Poets and kings are but the clerks of Time,
Tiering the same dull webs of discontent,
Clipping the same sad alnage of the years.

Beginning in the summer of 1893 after his return from Harvard, Robinson had been sending his poetry to every reputable monthly and weekly periodical in the country. Three years later he had accumulated "one of the largest and most comprehensive" collection of rejection slips in literary history. "The Clerks" was one of many poems that went the rounds, and finally came back from the editor of the *New York Sun* with a cryptic, one-word comment written in blue pencil on a sheet of white paper: "Unavailable. Paul Dana." In the early days of his career, Robinson invested a great deal of time on his poems. He'd struggled with "The Clerks" for a month and did not submit it for consideration until he felt confident that it represented his best effort. Indeed, as the poet Henry Taylor observed in 1997, the sonnet has proved to be "as durable as anything he ever wrote." But a century earlier, its repeated refusal troubled him.

There were two related reasons why Robinson's clerks were thought "unavailable" at the time. First, the poem was written in a conversational voice devoid of the flowery touches most editors expected from verse.

I did not think that I should find them there
When I came back again; but there they stood

What could be simpler, and more elegant? Nineteen words, eighteen monosyllables, and a story on its way to being told. But, as Robinson put it, the words "might as well have been written, so far as possible attention or interest on the part of editors and publishers was concerned, in the language of the Senegambians." The second difficulty was posed by the aggressively mundane subject matter. Exhibiting his career-long empathy for the old, Robinson focused his gaze on the "ancient" clerks that he and everyone else in Gardiner might encounter any day at J. T. Stone's Dry Goods shop on Water Street.

Robinson wrote within the conventional boundaries of form—meter and rhyme—and for that reason has been too much thought of as a merely traditional poet, a latter-day survivor of the New England Fireside poets. But if the form was familiar, the language and subject matter marked a revolution in American poetry. "Robinson was the first American poet of stature," Irving Howe wrote, "to bring commonplace people and commonplace experience into our poetry." He was convinced that there was poetry in all types of humanity, and he set out to prove it in his Tilbury sonnets and lyrics.

The poem itself does not contain much explicit description of the clerks. In their youth they dreamed of doing great things. In their old age they settle for a fellowship among others of their occupation. They are clerks, that is all: "just as good, / And just as human as they ever were," but how good and how human goes unspecified. The homily comes in the sestet, where those beset by ambition and unduly proud of their forebears are reminded of their unimportance in the larger scheme of things. What rules is Time, hence capitalized. As against its supremacy, even poets and kings can be classified with the clerks whose lives are measured out not in coffee spoons but in the tiers of cloth on the shelves or, when they were brought down to be scissored and sold, in "the same sad alnage of the years."

Robinson loved the English language—he often read in the dictionary as a warm-up for writing—and sometimes became so taken with a word that he would write a poem to put it to work. Here, the word is "alnage," which according to the Oxford English Dictionary dates back to 1477 and denotes "measurement by the ell, specifically official inspection of woolen cloth and attestation of its value by affixing of a leaden seal." "Ell" itself has become an archaism, although the American Heritage Dictionary continues to define it as "an English linear measure equal to 45 inches" and deriving from the Old English "eln," representing "the length from the elbow to the tip of the middle finger." Hence the picture Robinson surely had in mind: the clerks he had thought gone and forgotten, still measuring off cloth for customers by extending it down their arm, one ell at a time, much as their own remaining days were being measured off. Robinson presents a world of diminished possibility, where all of us are "tiering the same dull webs of discontent." Yet he grants dignity to those who do their work, cast off delusion, and reckon with mortality.

A corruption of "ell" survives in the popular adage: "Give them an inch and they'll take a mile," where "mile" is a whoppingly exaggerated version of the original "ell," at forty-five times the inch more than adequate to make the point. Robinson was fond enough of the word to reuse it in "Rembrandt to Rembrandt" (1921), where he writes of the painter smearing "[a] few more perishable ells of cloth" with ochres and oil.

In February 1896, Robinson read Henry James's "Lesson of the Master" and proclaimed it a work of genius. In James's story, he found a cautionary tale that applied to his situation. Aspiring young writer Paul Overt comes to seek advice from Henry St. George, the literary "master" of the title. There has been a falling off in quality in the novels of St. George, Overt knows, but he is hardly prepared for the bitter life lesson the older writer provides. To all outward appearances, St. George has enjoyed a successful career. People read his books. He has a comfortable home, an attractive and adoring wife, admirable children. Yet he knows he has not accomplished what he might have and regards himself as a failure. "As an artist, you know, I've married for money," he tells young Overt. Not his wife's money, but that of "the mercenary muse."

St. George proceeds to instruct Overt how to avoid the pitfalls that await him. Let us suppose, he posits, that "a certain perfection is possible and even desirable" in one's art. "Well, all I say is that one's children interfere with perfection. One's wife interferes. Marriage interferes." An artist who marries "does so at his peril." The young writer concludes, at the end of the story, "that Nature had dedicated him to intellectual, not to personal passion." He will pursue his career without the encumbrance of a wife and family. St. George's warning and Overt's decision stayed in Robinson's mind as he regarded the marriages of his friends and considered the possibility of his own.

Gardiner in Decline, 1896

In the fall, as he waited for delivery of his copies of *The Torrent and the Night Before*, Win was paid two dollars to serve as ward clerk for the elections. Villanelles and sonnets ran through his head as he sat at a desk chewing tobacco and checking names against a list of eligible voters. It marked the pinnacle of his political activity. Like almost everyone else in Republican Gardiner, Robinson voted for McKinley, but he did so without enthusiasm. Politics stimulated his sense of humor, not his passion.

In a celebratory piece for the *Kennebec Reporter* of 1888, editor Will Landers itemized "What Gardiner Has." It made for an impressive list.

> Four banks, two grist mills, an axe factory, five saw mills, two fine hotels, three laundries, five paper mills, seven churches, a public library, two large bakeries, an edge-tool factory, a large shoe factory, 7,000 inhabitants, five pleasant boarding houses, 17 passenger trains a day, two large bed-slat manufactories, a free bridge across the Kennebec, three large carriage manufactories, two foundries and four machine shops, two granite and marble manufactories, a brass band that is a credit to our city . . .

and so on for another ten lines. Eight years later, however, the city had passed its peak.

After half a century of growth, the boom was over. As if to mark the end, the Kennebec spilled its banks in the great flood of March 2, 1896. A sudden thaw and persistent rain broke up the ice much earlier than usual. Great cakes crashed against the ramparts of the bridge, followed by a huge mass of logs drifting downstream. Laura E. Richards watched the bridge shake, rise for a moment, and then fall, its timbers "dropped like a child's jackstraws." By late afternoon Water Street looked like a Venetian canal.

Robinson witnessed the flood as he witnessed the beginning of the end of Gardiner's prosperity, following the example of the family fortune. The panic of '93 took its toll. Fewer ships pulled alongside the piers. Paper and lumber mills closed down or were sold off to conglomerates who moved operations to the southeast. The ice business vanished entirely as refrigeration captured the market. With exquisite irony, the Gardiner board of trade chose the moment to celebrate the city's economic future in a publication called *Picturesque Gardiner* (1896). Few documents could more effectively have conveyed the boosterism and dominant commercial spirit of the time.

In its closing appeal, *Picturesque Gardiner* called for an influx of newcomers. "Come to us, manufacturers," and come to us also, capitalists, men of push and enterprise, men of thought and study. When you do, you will find "no idlers among us. Everybody is trying to make the wheels go faster, and to hasten the time when the census-taker shall find our present population multiplied by five." This was pie in the sky. Six thousand people lived in Gardiner in 1896. During the succeeding century, the number remained substantially the same.

A generation and more later, the poet Robert P. Tristram Coffin traced "the color of futility and air of decayed greatness" in Robinson's poetry to the rotting piers and abandoned houses along the Kennebec. Van Wyck Brooks went further in assessing the effect of the region's decay on the poet's writing.

> Gardiner abounded in men who had once been important and who had no life any longer to shape to their code. . . . There never was a more wintry world, as Robinson saw it. The sun rose dull there. Brown weeds grew through the floors of houses. Torn curtains flapped in broken windows. The trees were leafless, a ghostly band in cold array, and the thin leaves skipped on the stones with a freezing whisper. . . . Spring never came there.

In fact, Robinson left Gardiner for good before the city suffered its worst reverses. Yet in poems like "The Dead Village" and "The House on the Hill," both in *The Torrent and the Night Before* (1896), he predicted what was to come.

"The Dead Village" begins ominously, "Here there is death," and ends with "The music failed, and then / God frowned, and shut the village from his sight." In between, Robinson portrays a place inhabited only by "the ghosts of things . . . No life, no love, no children, and no men." So much for pastoral. "The House on the Hill" captures the sense of desolation more subtly and powerfully.

> They are all gone away,
>   The House is shut and still,
> There is nothing more to say.
>
> Through broken walls and gray
>   The winds blow bleak and shrill:
> They are all gone away.
>
> Nor is there one to-day

To speak them good or ill:
There is nothing more to say.

Why is it then we stray
　　Around the sunken sill?
They are all gone away.

And our poor fancy-play
　　For them is wasted skill:
There is nothing more to say.

There is ruin and decay
　　In the House on the Hill:
They are all gone away.
There is nothing more to say.

Despite (or because of) its technical limitations, this villanelle came to Robinson rapidly, in the course of but twenty minutes. Unsurprisingly, some important revisions followed. As written out for Smith on February 25, 1894, the day after its composition, Robinson's poem carried a subtitle "(Villanelle of Departure)" that was later dropped. So were the second and third tercets, as illustrated below.

Malign them as we may,　　　　　　Through broken walls and gray
　　We cannot do them ill:　　　　　　　The winds blow bleak and shrill:
They are all gone away.　　　　　　　They are all gone away.
(1894)　　　　　　　　　　　　　　　(1896)
Are we more fit than they　　　　　　Nor is there one to-day
　　To meet the Master's will?—　　　　To speak them good or ill:
There is nothing more to say　　　　　There is nothing more to say.

Robinson told Smith that "The House on the Hill" was "a little mystical perhaps" but at the same time "poetry of the commonplace." In revision he eliminated the "mystical" concept of a meeting with the Master in the next world, along with the moralistic message that we do well not to judge others. In addition, the changes move from the particular to the universal. The original second tercet, especially, seems to refer to specific people slandered by their neighbors. As revised, they are subsumed within the generalized company of those "gone away."

Both "The Dead Village" and "The House on the Hill" evoke an atmosphere rather than a particular location. In them, Robinson circled around the topic of the inimical social forces—among them the materialistic spirit behind the Board of Trade's promotional piece—that he felt were undermining his hometown. His apprehensions about heedless progress emerged in a number of early poems, as Alan Trachtenberg has noted: in "Amaryllis," where he deplored "The calling of loud progress, and the bold / Incessant scream of commerce"; in the reference in "The Torrent," recalling his father's career as a speculator in lumber, to "the coming of hard men / To cut those patriarchal trees away, / And turn to gold the silver of that spray"; in "the isolation and murderous envy wrought by class division" of "Richard Cory." Everywhere in Tilbury Town, he beheld exploitation and decay, although the outlines of the place itself remained shadowy. As the incisive Irving Howe expressed it, Robinson eyed Tilbury Town "obliquely, half in and half out of its boundaries, a secret sharer taking snapshots of decline."

The snapshots are what matter. Robinson brings Tilbury townspeople to life in their foolishness and sorrow, their redundancy and superannuation. Coffin compares them to seashells fetched from the shore and left in unaccustomed sunlight. The landlocked shells have a loveliness still, but "they are not the shells they were in the ocean. A touch will powder them to dust." So with the people Robinson writes about: "lovely human designs, but stranded in a cruelly hostile place, lost and wasted on the world."

The Death of Mary Robinson

Win was looking forward to showing his mother the printed copies of *The Torrent and the Night Before* due to arrive before the Christmas season of 1896. She did not live to see them.

After the death of her husband, thin, quiet, unassertive Mary Robinson was left to preside over a family in distress. Dean could not shake off his addiction. Herman lost the family money. Win had no regular job. Occasionally she had to escape, and early in November 1896 she went to Boston on a two-week holiday. Emma and her three girls—Barbara, the youngest, was now eleven months—came up from summer residence in the Shepherd cottage on Capitol Island to take care of matters at 67 Lincoln Avenue.

Ruth was eating her supper of blueberries, oven toast, and milk when her Daomina returned, on Saturday, November 14, and rushed out to give her a big kiss. The following day, Mary Robinson complained of a sore throat. As a precautionary measure, Dean decided that Emma and the children should go to the Shepherds' house in Farmingdale. Before they left, Daomina helped Ruth into her leggings and gave her another kiss smack on the mouth. Dean had written his thesis on diphtheria, which was then reaching epidemic proportions as a common cause of death in children, and he may have suspected the worst. Either in Boston or on her journey home, Mary Robinson had been infected with diphtheria.

On Wednesday the 18th, Emma was called back to Gardiner when Mary Robinson did not improve, and she brought along Barbara, whom she was still nursing. Upon opening the door, she was met by the maid, who said she felt an attack of asthma coming on and had to leave. Mary Robinson was much worse on Friday morning when Dr. Wooster P. Giddings made his morning call. He exiled Emma and her baby to the back of the house, and did not return. Dean took over as best he could. That night, Emma, too, was troubled by a sore throat, and the three Robinson boys put her to bed and plied her with whiskey until she was unconscious. When she awoke, her sore throat was gone, but she always remembered the worried faces of the Robinson sons looking down at her. For forty-eight hours, Mary Robinson "suffered the tortures of hell," fighting for breath as the poison spread through her body. On Sunday, November 22, she became unconscious and died during the night.

The funeral was held the next afternoon. Terrified by the deadly contagious disease, no one would come near Mary Robinson's body or set foot inside the house where she had died. The undertaker left the coffin on the porch, and the boys tenderly laid their mother inside. They hired a delivery wagon for the casket, conveyed it the block and a half down Cemetery Street to the Palmer-Robinson plot, and lowered it into the grave. The Reverend J. Langdon Quimby, the Congregational minister, read the service with a handkerchief across his face and did not come near the coffin. It was snowing. There were no other mourners in attendance. During the funeral, one kind neighbor took the risk of hanging a bag of doughnuts on the front doorknob of the Robinson house.

None of the Robinson boys were infected. But both Emma in Gardiner and Ruth in Farmingdale were diagnosed with diphtheria and given serum to ward off the disease. For six weeks, Ruth and Marie were quarantined at their grandparent Shepherds' house, while Emma and Barbara remained at 67 Lincoln Avenue. Not until after Christmas were they reunited. From that time on, Emma, Herman, and their three children lived in the Robinson house, where Emma tried to take Mary Robinson's place. As Ruth observed, "it was quite a household" for her mother to supervise: "three men and three little girls, Dean up and down, and my father becoming an alcoholic." The family closed in upon itself as fear of diphtheria kept visitors away. It was three months before the maid returned, and five months before a neighbor paid a call.

On the night of Mary Robinson's death, Win began writing a long poem he called "The Book of Annandale." Annandale, in his work, stood for Robinson, and he portrayed all three brothers in various poems that use the name. In "The Book of Annandale," the narrator (based on Win himself) is troubled by his inability to feel grief after the death of the "pretty wife" (a camouflage for his mother) they had "buried . . . that afternoon, / Under the leaves and the snow."

How could he be so frigid and inert,
So like a man with water in his veins
Where blood had been a little while before?

Had he become hardened "into a loveless, feelingless dead thing?" All he knew for certain was that he was exhausted. "Something supreme had been wrenched out of him." A year later, when they were walking together, Rosalind Richards spoke to Win of his mother and had the "impression as of a person turned to stone" beside her.

His mother's death reinforced Robinson's growing dedication to "idealism as the one logical and satisfactory interpretation of life." He consoled himself with the thought that in dying she had been released from a suffering not to be borne. "I thoroughly believe that my mother has gone ahead," he wrote Ford a week after her death, "and I thoroughly hope that no memory of this life will follow her." In the ensuing months he began to read Emerson—and particularly his essay "The Over-Soul"—with real enthusiasm. But it was a struggle, he wrote Smith on March 15, 1897, to keep his thoughts in rational order. "The one great pleasure of my life is the knowledge that my poor mother is out of it. I can't quite understand—yet—the laws of compensation that make a woman suffer what she did and from so many causes. We say she died of diphtheria. What does that mean? It means just this: she had endured all [she] could and was ready to die."

8

Loves Lost

The Torrent Descends

Ten days after his mother died, Robinson received 312 copies of the "inconspicuous blue-covered little pamphlet" he had named, "rather arbitrarily" in recognition of its first and last poems, *The Torrent and the Night Before*. On first glance, Win didn't think much of them. The books "looked so small and so devilish blue," he felt like kicking them all the way to Augusta. At the same time, though, he clung to the "same old ridiculous notion that they [might] amount to something some day." The entire edition cost him $52. Nowadays, a single copy in mint condition would fetch upward of $1,000.

Robinson sat down at his desk and began inscribing copies of *The Torrent* to be dispatched into the world. He sent thirty to forty copies of them to friends and acquaintances. Most of the others were posted "unsolicited and unannounced" to periodicals in hopes of a review or to prominent figures—strangers to Robinson—in the literary establishment. Among these leading poets and critics and editors were Thomas Bailey Aldrich, Robert Bridges, Witter Bynner, Bliss Carman, Richard Watson Gilder, Louise Chandler Moulton, Clinton Scollard, and Edmund Clarence Stedman: names to be reckoned with at the time. Three pamphlets crossed the Atlantic to Edmund Gosse, Thomas Hardy, and Algernon Charles Swinburne. A few Harvard professors received copies, as did William Vaughn Moody, Robinson's much-admired contemporary at Cambridge. All of this was rather brash, but as EAR said three decades later, he "wanted a hearing . . . and that seemed to be about the only way to get it."

Remarkably, it worked. This "book of untried stuff, more or less poetical," written by an unknown and without the imprimatur of an established publisher, attracted an unusual amount of attention, most of it extremely encouraging. In the front matter of the book, Robinson aimed to shock. The title page included an italicized witticism from Coppée: "*Qui pourrais-je imiter pour être original?* [Whom should I imitate to be an original?]" and proclaimed its self-published status in bold capital letters, PRINTED FOR THE AUTHOR. The book was dedicated "to any man, woman, or critic who will cut the edges of it—I have done the top." He would just as soon forget that "rather cocky" dedication, Robinson told an interviewer in 1928. He "must have been conceited and still a bit mad" at editors and critics.

The most heartening response came in the form of letters. "Very rarely, I think, does one find such work as yours—where every line that meets the eye proves itself at a glance real literature"—Barrett Wendell. "I have read enough . . . to recognize the debt of gratitude which you owe to the Muse for the gift with which she has enriched your life"—Charles Eliot Norton. "I should like to know you. When you come to Boston, please let me shake hands with you and thank you by word of mouth for your book which I have read with unconditional delight"—Nathan Haskell Dole. "A man who can do the things you have done in *The Torrent* does not need the small praise of a small man like me. . . . The world may not have it, but go on doing it just the same"—Joseph E. Chamberlain of the *Boston Transcript*. "I call it unmistakable poetry—most of it, indeed, of the 'inevitable sort': and in many of the lines there is a deep and moving music. . . . Your gift seems to me quite a certain thing"—Dr. Titus Munson Coan of the New York Bureau of Revision. "I don't thank you for sending me a book, for I get books of poetry until I haven't shelf-room for them. But you have given me a rare sensation: you have sent me a book that I can read, and for that I thank you. I am a very busy man but you have sent me a book I cannot help reading, and for that I praise you"—Edward Eggleston, author of *The Hoosier Schoolmaster*. Robinson copied out these and other laudatory comments and mailed them to Smith. "I would not send them to anyone else," he said by way of apology, "and I look to you to burn them up when you have read them."

These letters would help give Robinson courage "through the years of obscurity and material uncertainty" that lay ahead. Yet to advance his literary reputation, he needed public reviews, not private correspondence. In this respect, too, *The Torrent and the Night Before* fared unusually well. Robinson scholar Richard Cary of Colby College unearthed "twenty reviews in newspapers and magazines of substantial circulation and prestige—not a bad record for a first, minuscule volume of verses in paper wrappers by an utterly unknown poet who . . . issued them under his own auspices and . . . distributed them personally." Not all of the reviews were "especially complimentary or true," Robinson commented. He thought himself especially misunderstood by Harry Thurston Peck of *The Bookman*.

Peck acknowledged the "true fire in [Robinson's] verse" but detected an unfortunate limitation as well. The author's "humor is of a grim sort, and the world is not beautiful to him, but a prison-house. In the night-time there is weeping and sorrow, and joy does not come in the morning." In thanking Peck for the review, Robinson tried to set matters straight. "I am sorry to learn that I have painted myself in such lugubrious colors. The world is not a 'prison-house,' but a kind of spiritual kindergarten, where millions of bewildered infants are trying to spell God with the wrong blocks."

This exchange raised an issue—whether Robinson was unduly pessimistic—that was to bulk large in criticism of his work. As he saw it, to take him "for a yelling pessimist" as *The Bookman* had was to miss the point entirely. Robinson wrote Smith that his verses were "written with a conscious hope that they might make some despairing devil a little stronger and a little better satisfied with things—not as they are, but as they are to be. . . . Because I don't dance on [an] illuminated hilltop and sing about the bobolinks and bumble-bees, they tell me that my world is a 'prison house, etc.'"

The goal of his life was to combine the two impulses that drove him. "I want to give my whole life to the uplifting of others," he wrote Ford, "but at the same time I want to be successful in literature." He was, he said, "the very incarnation of theoretical altruism and intellectual selfishness": a sentiment that might have been uttered by a Massachusetts Puritan of the seventeenth century, sure that a gift for literature was of no worth unless employed in the service of a higher cause.

Among the incoming letters of praise for *The Torrent*, there was nothing from a publisher offering to bring out his next book of poems. It looked as if he might have to "begin a search for that most perilous of all worldly things—a job," Robinson wrote in mid-December 1896, but he gave himself the coming winter and spring in which to accomplish something. New poems kept arriving, and as he set them down he went back over *The Torrent* to excise some of his earlier work. On a trip to Boston in late March 1897, he looked for a "respectable imprint" for a second book of poems that would reflect these changes.

In Boston, Robinson was surprised to find himself recognized as a promising young author. He was put off by the obsequiousness of Harvard "men who never knew me" and "by the sight of that blue-backed experiment of mine on Barrett Wendell's desk." Chamberlain of the *Transcript* hosted a literary luncheon for him at the St. Botolph Club, and there was another luncheon in his honor at the Colonial Club. He had interviews with a number of publishing firms. One showed considerable interest in bringing out his work before backing off. It was discouraging. "To spend four or five years in getting a small book together and have it just fall short 'is a damned tough bullet to chew,'" he said.

Looking backward near the end of his life, Robinson articulated the stubborn faith in himself that made his career possible. "I was unable to foresee oblivion for the [early] poems, though I could foresee too surely a long and obscure journey for them before they should have more than a small number of friends." He was right about the arduous path, and right about the eventual recognition.

Seventy-five years after its publication, the critic Harold Bloom proclaimed *The Torrent and the Night Before* "one of the best first volumes in our poetry" and singled out "George Crabbe," "Luke Havergal," and "The Clerks" as poems

Robinson was never to surpass. The poet Donald Justice, writing on the hundredth anniversary of the book, saw its publication as a historically important event. Once Robinson opened the package of small, blue-backed books and began to address them, "he was—he had become—the first modern American poet."

Light Through the Clouds

The winter of 1896–97 amounted to a season in hell for Robinson. If the preceding three months had come two years earlier, he wrote Smith on 15 March 1897, they would have finished him off. The trouble started in the household at 67 Lincoln Avenue, where his mother had died, Dean had become a hopeless burden, and Herman was sinking into the grip of alcoholism: "things here at home that [were] pulling [him] back." He could not see his way clear to leaving, not for a year at least.

On a broader plane, Robinson deplored "the whole trend of popular thought," not only aimed in the wrong direction but seemingly proud of it. "The age is all right, material progress is all right, Herbert Spencer is all right, hell is all right," he bitterly spat out the received wisdom of the time. Bad as things were, he assured Smith that he would not succumb to despair as long as he could catch "a glimpse of the real light through the clouds of time." That glimpse was enough to make him "wish to live and see it out." Without it, he would be tempted to stick his nose into a rag soaked with chloroform. Here, for the first time, Robinson invoked the transforming power of "the light"—his symbol for salvation in a world gone wrong—that that was to mean so much to him and his poetry.

During the early and middle 1890s, Dean Robinson had been able to control his addiction well enough to hold down occasional temporary jobs. He worked as a time keeper on the ice, for example, and as a teller at the savings bank. Then in February 1897, even though Dean was going downhill rapidly, Herman and Win drew funds from their mother's estate to provide their older brother with a legitimate occupation. For $2,700 they purchased the stock of the drug store at 207 Water Street and installed Dean as proprietor of "H. D. Robinson and Co." This arrangement had the advantage of supplying Dean as druggist with the daily morphine he required, even as he continued to battle his addiction. Both in May and in October of 1897, he traveled to Illinois to take the Keeley cure. The Keeley cure did not work for Dean, and neither did the drugstore.

As his illness worsened, Dean became a pathetic and somewhat frightening figure. Laura Macomber, who had known and liked him in high school, remembered seeing Dean stumbling along, only partly conscious, and crossing the street to avoid meeting him. He was gentle for the most part at home, where an atmosphere of sympathetic friendliness prevailed. But there were nights when, in the throes of withdrawal, he shuffled back and forth for hours at a time. As Win expressed it in "The Dark House,"

> in one room
> Burns a lamp as in a tomb;
> And I see the shadow glide,
> Back and forth, of one denied
> Power to find himself outside.

One night, Ruth awoke to see Uncle Dean coming out of his room, weaving unsteadily and dangerously tipping the oil lamp he was carrying. Her mother came to the rescue, steering him back to his room as docile as could be. On another occasion, Ruth recalled, Dean was acting strange and moaning, and Emma was so frightened that she collected all three children and curled up with them outside in the hammock. Uncle Win, who had been downtown, came back around eleven o'clock, "quieted Uncle Dean and got us all into bed and all cheered up very quickly."

Two women came along to brighten Robinson's dark days. Both were about twenty years his senior, and both were accomplished writers. The first was Edith Brower, a woman of letters from Wilkes-Barre, Pennsylvania. Exceptionally sensitive to art, music, and literature, Brower had published more than a score of articles and stories in leading periodicals like the *Atlantic Monthly* and *Harper's Weekly*. She also served as a reader of manuscripts for the "New York Bureau of Criticism and Revision," run by Dr. Titus Munson Coan. It was through Coan that she heard of Robinson.

FIGURE 8.1 Edith Brower, who admired and befriended the young poet.

Source: Colby College Special Collections.

On a trip to New York early in January 1897, Brower stopped by Coan's office. Nearly always he had something amusing to show her: a hilariously unfixable manuscript, for example, to be returned with a letter conveying "a minimum of justice and a maximum of mercy." The motto of the bureau, in dealing with impossible submissions, was "the truth, and nothing but the truth, but not all the truth." This time, however, Coan handed her a small thin pamphlet with blue paper cover that had recently been sent him from Maine. Brower began to read the opening sonnet, "The Torrrent," and exclaimed "But this is poetry!" "Read on," said Dr. Coan, and on another page she found "Dear Friends." "But this is Poetry!" she repeated, her tone supplying the capital. "Read on," Coan repeated.

After a few more investigations, Brower asked for a corner of Coan's desk and for paper, pen, and ink. "Please send me at once a copy of your book, if you have to beg, borrow, or steal one," she wrote Robinson. "Should it be necessary, kill somebody to get it." Thus commenced a correspondence and friendship that lasted for more than thirty years.

Robinson was more than a little intrigued about this "unknown female who seem[ed] to be in a very bad way about [his] verses." Through letters he concluded that she was an "infernally bright" professional writer and twenty-one years older than he, so that there need be no romantic nonsense between them. From photographs and from Brower herself, he found that she stood five feet six in her stocking feet and was "not at all ugly," with "dark sharp eyes" and "dark hair (gray on the forehead)." And, further, that she rode a bicycle and didn't "eat any meat to speak of, but subsist[ed] for the most part on bananas and graham and the elixir of her own thoughts." Best of all, she was instantly and permanently captivated by his poetry. Almost immediately, Brower encouraged Robinson to visit her in Wilkes-Barre, promising that she would put him at his ease.

Brower was no ordinary woman. A near agnostic, she held radically flexible religious beliefs. A progressive in politics, she campaigned for abolition of child labor and equal rights for African Americans. An active feminist, she enthusiastically supported women's suffrage and pestered the local government to clean up and beautify her hometown. Brower had a strong philanthropic streak in her nature and did whatever she could to promote the young poet from Maine: writing a favorable review, praising his work to other writers and critics, and offering him a well-informed and sympathetic ear. She considered herself to have more or less "discovered" Robinson and took a proprietary interest in his career. Repeatedly, she asked him to tell her more about himself and his circumstances, but only rarely did Robinson respond with personal revelations. The correspondence centered instead on literary matters—he thought she knew "a great deal more . . . about books and things" than himself—and on the beginning of his career. He wrote her 110 letters between January 1897 and October 1902.

Brower did more than praise Robinson's poems. She also convinced him that his work could do some actual good in the world, just as he hoped. "My female correspondent," he wrote Smith in April 1897, "has done wonders for me, and has proved to me that I possess the power of helping others, which, after all, is about the greatest thing a man, or a book, can do." Reading his poetry, she told him, swept "no end of cobwebs from her brain."

Robinson's other benefactress during this time of distress was his Gardiner neighbor, the well-established writer Laura E. Richards. Mrs. Richards came from patrician roots in Boston. Her father was the philanthropist Samuel Gridley Howe; her mother, Julia Ward Howe, had written "The Battle Hymn of the Republic." She married Henry Richards, a cousin of the Gardiners who gave the town its name, and moved there in 1876 when Henry, an architect by training, was called upon to manage the family paper mill. They bought a house on Dennis Street, painted it a shocking intense yellow, and settled there for the rest of their days. At the Yellow House, as it was called, they brought up seven children and devoted themselves to the betterment of the community.

Mrs. Richards was blessed with an abundance of energy and a relentless brightness of outlook. She was also a prolific writer, producing eighty books during her ninety-three years. Daily, she sat down at her roll-top desk in the North Parlor, warmed up by reading one act of a Shakespeare play and twenty minutes of H. W. Fowler's guide to usage, and settled down to write. She wrote several volumes of light verse—she claimed the hurdy-gurdy, not the lyre, as her instrument—and of fiction aimed at young readers. *Captain January* (1890) sold 750,000 copies, and was made into a movie starring Shirley Temple. She also wrote more serious work for adult audiences, including a two-volume biography of her mother that won the Pulitzer Prize.

FIGURE 8.2 Laura Richards: prolific author, lifetime supporter of EAR.

Source: Maine Historic Preservation Commission

FIGURE 8.3 The Richardses' Yellow House in Gardiner.

Source: Maine Historic Preservation Commission.

Laura Richards was, far and away, the leading author in Gardiner, and as a courtesy Win Robinson sent her a copy of *The Torrent and the Night Before* in December 1896. They were not acquainted at the time. As a practicing professional, Mrs. Richards eschewed involvement with the amateurs of the Gardiner Poetry Society. And as transplanted Bostonians with friends in that city, in New York, and in England, she and her husband did not as a rule look to the local citizenry for companionship. They knew of the Robinsons but did not see them socially. This changed when EAR's slim pamphlet arrived. Mrs. Richards could recognize talent when she saw it and was eager to get to know the young poet, nineteen years her junior, who lived only a few blocks away. Her son, Henry Howe Richards, ran across Win at the Barstows, and she proposed that he bring Win to the Yellow House. It could not be done, her son assured her. Robinson was shy of social gatherings and would not come.

Undeterred—in her positive thinking she was rarely deterred—in the early spring Mrs. Richards sent Robinson a brief note inviting him to call. "Prithee, good Hermit Thrush, come out of thy thicket!" Win did not know quite how to respond, but Dr. Schumann insisted that an invitation from Laura E. Richards was an honor and that he must accept. "Dear Mrs. Richards," Win wrote back with gravity, "I shall be glad to come to see you on Monday. I am not a Hermit Thrush."

He came that first Monday, and came again on subsequent Monday evenings when there was talk of the latest books from Kipling and Stevenson and Meredith and Housman (he could hold his own in that discourse) followed by music from Alice Richards on the grand piano. Alice, the oldest daughter, had an extraordinary musical talent. It was said that she could sight read a symphony score and reduce it to a piano part. Robinson sat, silent and absorbed, while she played Beethoven, Bach, Schumann, some Chopin, sometimes Wagner. He admired the family busts and portraits and took time to examine the materials on the Treasure Table, among them a pencil made by Henry David Thoreau and given by Ralph Waldo Emerson to Julia Ward Howe. Hays Gardiner, who taught at Harvard when his health permitted, came over from Oaklands to say "all the pleasant things that were necessary between selections."

In late April, Robinson revealed to Smith that, to his surprise, he had had "a good time" at the Richards' home. It had been "a devil of a while" since he last had one. He and Hays Gardiner became friends, and before long Win was visiting Oaklands for conversation beneath the Copleys and Stuarts. Win was also attracted to Alice's beautiful younger sister Rosalind, who hoped to write books herself. They began to take walks together.

But it was Mrs. Richards who took the strongest interest in Robinson. He presented himself at her home: "a slender figure, erect, distinguished, breeding and race in every line of it; dark, glowing eyes; brilliant color," and at once she set about advancing his career. The snobbishness implicit in her description of Robinson was characteristic of her, but so was her determination to do good.

All of the enlightened local reforms of the time, Gardiner historian Danny D. Smith pointed out—the water district, the public-health nurse, the library, the hospital, the Red Cross chapter, the new high school—stemmed from initiatives undertaken by the Richards family. For their social improvement, Mrs. Richards also invited the more promising boys of the town to her home for meetings of the Howe Club. She gave them tea, lessons in good manners, and conversation on topics not broached at their own dinner tables. It was Mrs. Richards's conviction that, although things might not be for the best in the best of all possible worlds, they could be considerably improved through a little judicious counsel and illustration by example.

Her joyful outlook clashed with Robinson's skepticism. He was the consummate introvert, she the epitome of outgoing cheerfulness. As he wrote Smith on May 17, 1897, "the only trouble with that family is they are too abnormally happy and unconscious of the damnation that makes up nine tenths of life." The opposite viewpoints only served to bind them together. Upon leaving Gardiner, Robinson began a correspondence with Mrs. Richards that lasted all his life.

In his April 4, 1897, letter to Harry Smith, Robinson discoursed widely on his recent activities. He told Smith about the unsuccessful attempt to locate a publisher in Boston, about his female admirer in Wilkes-Barre, about his reading in Stevenson and Kipling and Zola ("the greatest worker in the objective that the world had ever seen"), and about having rented "a down-town den to crawl into" with three other young men in Gardiner.

This loosely knit and short-lived group, the Quadruped, offered Robinson a welcome refuge. After dinner he could walk downtown, join his friends, and temporarily forget the troubles at home. The principals were Arthur Blair, the banker; Seth Ellis Pope, the pedagogue; Linville Robbins, the scientist; and

FIGURE 8.4 Robinson, Pope, and Robbins: Three Legs of the Quadruped.

Source: Colby College Special Collections.

EAR, the poet. For two dollars a month they engaged a third-floor room above Brown's dry-goods store on Water Street, overlooking the Cobbossee and the mill pond. It was sparsely furnished with a table, a few wooden chairs, and a wood stove, and when the wind was wrong the stench from the paper and saw mills upstream pervaded the place. Nonetheless, the group met almost every evening. Blair, who shared Robinson's interests in music and literature, played the fiddle. Robbins argued with Robinson about religion and philosophy. Pope was unpolished, overweight, somewhat oafish, and worshipful toward Robinson. "Pope is in love, and is one of the most harmless creatures in existence," Win characterized him in a letter to Brower. "He worries about the grossness of his features and makes epigrams. . . . The worst thing I have against him is that he sings in a church choir." Pope taught school in Gardiner for a time, not particularly well, and then trained to become a librarian. He and Robinson became the closest of friends.

Thwarted Love

It was "rather queer," Robinson thought, that Butler should have sent him a copy of George Moore's *Celibates*, accompanied by an announcement of his engagement to be married. In each of the three novelettes in *Celibates*. which arrived on the day after Mary Robinson's death, the leading character struggles against social and economic pressures mandating "marriage, marriage, always marriage . . . as if there were nothing else in the world." After reading the book, Robinson wrote Ford, "I rather think I am booked to be a celibate myself, for I don't think there is a woman in the world who could live with me." As a breadwinner, he had precious little to offer any potential wife.

Yet he was hardly ready to write off marriage entirely. His friends gave him promising examples to follow. On his visit to Boston in March 1897, Robinson had dinner with Butler and his wife. She was "very fair to see" and thought Hardy's *Jude the Obscure* a great book: "rather a remarkable combination." The couple seemed very happy indeed. He could not help wondering if he might find such a companion himself. He looked around him, and beheld the fine features and red-gold hair of Rosalind Richards.

Socially it was all wrong, and both of them knew it. The wellborn Richardses stood at the pinnacle of Gardiner society. The respectable Robinsons did not. But Win was taken with Rosalind's looks and her intelligent eagerness to learn about writers and writing. During much of 1897, they took weekly walks together, usually through the Oaklands pastures and woods. Rosalind, at twenty-two to Win's twenty-seven, knew well enough what such walks might lead to. In adolescence she had been sent to Boston to live with her grandmother, Julia Ward Howe, and at dancing school encountered her share of "sighers" among the boys who sought her attention. She had spent a schoolgirl year in Paris, and on the way home visited Oxford for "a fairyland fortnight and Eight's Week." Then, back in Boston, her grandmother organized Rosalind's "very shy Coming Out."

Despite her experience, Rosalind was quite unprepared for "the declaration of passionate affection" that was to come from EAR. She thought of him primarily as a friend and contemporary of her cousin Hays Gardiner, who was eleven years older than herself. During the summers, Hays oversaw the swimming and the tennis, the reading and the manners, of his dovecote of young Richards cousins. On their walks together, Robinson adopted a similar schoolmasterly role for Rosalind, offering comments and suggestions on her reading. With his gravity of manner, he struck her as well along into his thirties and, though "very handsome," not a candidate for romance at all, the issue of social distance aside. Beset by recurring illnesses throughout her life, just being out of doors was enough to stimulate "a sort of ecstasy" for Rosalind. She was "not too much aware of which kind strong one, Hays or E. A. R.," strode alongside her on those walks.

Robinson's declaration came at the end of a visit to Camp Cobbossee, on Cobbosseecontee Pond (only ten miles long, and hence, in Maine parlance, not deserving the designation of "Lake"). At the camp, the children plunged into fishing, swimming, and canoeing. Mrs. Richards offered amiable supervision, and her husband Henry arrived for the weekends, taking time off from his duties at the family paper mill. His brother, "Uncle Bob," was always there: Professor R. H. Richards of MIT, known as King of the Camp. The merry and delightful George Hodges, dean of the Episcopal Theological School in Cambridge, came in 1897, along with Hays Gardiner and the young scientist Lawrence (Chug) Henderson. So, too, for a week late in August, did E. A. Robinson.

FIGURE 8.5 At Camp Cobbossee, summer 1897, Win Robinson joined the Richards family and friends at their lakeside camp in August. Seated in the middle row are Reverend George Hodges, Rosalind Richards, Laura E. Richards, and EAR. Mrs. Richards is apparently conversing with James Barstow (with the bike). Wearing knickers in the middle of the first row is John Hays Gardiner, who worked to advance Robinson's career, on both sides of the grave.

Source: Yellow House Papers, Gardiner Library Association.

Robinson did not easily fit into the outdoor life. A photograph shows him seated in a boat with others, uncomfortably overdressed in a dark suit and wearing the white, Italian fisherman's hat Mrs. Richards presented him with as "becoming to [his] somber beauty." He shone, however, in the word game Dean Hodges introduced, called "The 'Tionaries Ball." The imaginary ball was a festive party given by Mr. and Mrs. 'Tionary for their son Mr. Dick 'Tionary and his Gramma(r). The object was to suggest additions to the guest list for the ball. EAR came up with Mr. and Mrs. Aritan and Good Sam Aritan, and Mr. and Mrs. Buck and Tim Buck Too.

Mrs. Richards recalled another day at the camp: a group gathered under the trees, laughter and song; Robinson, as so often, listening, cheerfully silent. Before him sat Julia Richards, then ten years old, her hair braided in one massive pigtail reaching to her waist. Win looked at it intently. After considerable observation he leaned forward and gently but firmly tweaked the pigtail. The child turned; there was no word, only an exchange of smiles.

It was Julia's much older sister Rosalind who commanded most of his attention, though. All week long his feelings smoldered. The night before he was to leave the camp, he let them emerge. After supper, he took Rosalind for a fare-well walk among the birch trees. He could conceal his love no longer, and he felt obligated to say how he felt, after having spent a week under the Richardses' roof. But Robinson knew nothing of the art of courtship, and the words burst forth in a passionate tirade. Rosalind was startled, even slightly frightened, as she took it in and kept her silence. It was going to turn out just as he had feared, Win thought. Had she responded in kind, he did not know what he would have done next. When she did not, he reassured her that he had not really expected her to reciprocate his feelings.

"All through it," Rosalind remembered, "he kept repeating, as if to shield me from self-reproach, 'I have always known, from the first, that you would never have anything to say to me.'" The incident shook them both, Robinson because his worst expectations were realized, Rosalind because she could do nothing to assuage his anguish. They were to remain friends throughout their lives, but neither of them forgot that shattering evening at Camp Cobbossee.

Rosalind Richards never married and may over time have inflated the seri-ousness of her relationship with a young man who became the country's pre-eminent poet. Certainly that was the view of Emma Robinson and her daughter Ruth, who recalled asking EAR if he had been in love with Rosalind and his replying, "well, the Richardses can be fanciful."

Robinson's letters to Rosalind, restricted until 2002, proved somewhat dis-appointing. EAR's invariable reluctance to commit himself on paper militated

FIGURE 8.6 Rosalind Richards as Undine for a fancy dress frolic, 1898.

Source: Yellow House Papers, Gardiner Library Association

against any startling disclosures. He called Rosalind "Person" as a private name between them, and in one note mentioned a possible "reagitation of that autumn night." Otherwise, the correspondence might have been addressed to any reasonably good friend, with one notable exception. Robinson was often asked to evaluate others' writing, and he usually consented to do so. But where art was concerned, he made little room for false politeness, and his comments on the writing of his friends were almost always brutally frank. Not so with Rosalind Richards, "R.R.," "Dear Person." When she sent him her work, he responded with unusual thoroughness and an obvious desire not to disappoint.

The strongest evidence of Robinson's continuing feeling for Rosalind Richards is contained in the photograph album he carried with him and had among his possessions at the end of his life. As an itinerant minstrel without a home of his own, Robinson invariably traveled light, with two suitcases at most. But this photo album, marked in his hand

E. A. Robinson
His Book

went back and forth between New York and Boston and New Hampshire. Inside were several pictures of the Richards family, most prominent among them three separate photos of Rosalind alone. One, showing her at full length, wearing a long tie and smiling, was taken at Camp Cobbossee in the fateful summer of 1897: Robinson labeled it "Before the War." A second, more romantic photograph depicts her as Undine for the fancy dress frolic of 1898. A third, undated, shows her standing on a rock with a writing tablet in hand.

Both Rosalind in reminiscence and EAR in correspondence used a similar metaphor to describe what happened at the camp. Their friendship had been "painfully broken across, once and once only," she wrote upon donating her letters from EAR to Harvard in 1946. He had "made breaks," he wrote Edith Brower on September 15, 1897, in an account of his week at Camp Cobbossee. The letter to Brower gave him a chance to unburden himself, if only by indirection. He began with a promise to visit Brower before long, in New York or Wilkes-Barre or wherever. He warned her that he was a much better listener than a talker. Then he told his cryptic story.

> When I do talk, I am likely to say too much and so hurt people's feelings. Feelings are a mistake; we ought not to be bothered by them. Mrs. Richards (*Capt. January*, etc.) had me out to her camp on Cobboseecontee Pond . . . and there I was compelled to make [myself] agreeable and interesting to five females, one Episcopal Dean, one scientific Professor, one Harvard instructor and one small dog that snored so that he had to be sent back. I washed dishes, lugged wood, stirred porridge and made breaks—some of them pretty bad, I'm afraid. I don't know why it is, but I've done this sort of thing all my life. It is only . . . the innate godliness of

humankind that permits people to stand me at all, and I am not altogether sure that I am not a beast. I'm not a gentleman—never can be one – don't want to be one. I've lived alone so much that I have lost all desire to conform to the ways of decent people. All I am good for is to live by myself and write.

Read in the light of his repudiated overture to Rosalind Richards, this passage takes on a poignancy. "Feelings" were a mistake, he began, and so was talking about them: people got hurt. Then, after an engaging sentence or two about camp chores and the unfortunate dog, Robinson comes haltingly to the point. He'd made pretty bad "breaks," and not for the first time. Unlike his male companions at the camp, he was not a "gentleman." Had Rosalind or someone else said as much to him after his declaration? He was not cut out for "the ways of decent people," including marriage. It was better to live alone and write.

Puzzled, Brower challenged Robinson about not being a gentleman. He could not have written his poems without the kindness and compassion for others that were part of the gentlemanly code. That was true, EAR acknowledged, but he was thinking of the "external side" of the question. (On the inside, he might be a gentleman; on the outside, he was not.) Too often he meant one thing and suggested another. His good instincts bumped up against what he sometimes did and said, thoughtlessly. When that happened, he was liable to hurt people's feelings, though never intentionally. At the same time he almost always hurt his own feelings and wondered why he kept doing so. All of this made a certain sense when applied to the last evening at Camp Cobbossee. But Brower could hardly have broken the code.

The "gentleman" issue was much on Robinson's mind at the time, having recently committed to paper his most famous poem:

Whenever Richard Cory went down town,
We people on the pavement looked at him:
He was a gentleman from sole to crown,
Clean favored, and imperially slim.

And he was always quietly arrayed,
And he was always human when he talked;
But still he fluttered pulses when he said,
"Good-morning," and he glittered when he walked.

And he was rich—yes, richer than a king—
And admirably schooled in every grace:

In fine, we thought that he was everything
To make us wish that we were in his place.

So on we worked, and waited for the light,
And went without the meat, and cursed the bread;
And Richard Cory, one calm summer night,
Went home and put a bullet through his head.

Almost surely, "Richard Cory" had its immediate origin in the suicide of a local citizen of Gardiner. He wrote to Smith on April 24, 1897, "Frank Anne blew his bowels out with a shot-gun. That was hell." And to Brower, on July 31, 1897, "I've written a nice little thing called 'Richard Cory.' . . . There isn't any idealism in it, but there's lots of something else—humanity, maybe. I opine that it will go."

Go it did, and then some. "Richard Cory" has been repeatedly anthologized, so much so that it is the single Robinson poem many casual readers recall from their schooldays. Its popularity became a source of annoyance to Robinson while he lived and has probably done his reputation considerable harm. In 1948, Yvor Winters, otherwise one of Robinson's most enthusiastic admirers, savaged the poem as "a superficially neat portrait of the elegant man of mystery" that "builds up to a very cheap surprise ending." As a critic, Winters did not mince words, and although few subsequent commentators would condemn the poem as ruthlessly as he did in 1948, many have patronized it as too facile, too dependent on the shock of its ending, and above all, too well known.

On this last point, Robinson agreed. When a fellow poet asked him in 1924 to write out "Richard Cory" to frame and hang in his bathroom, EAR wryly complied. "It may be a good thing to shave by—assuming that you use a safety-razor," he observed. A few years later, though, he told Hermann Hagedorn that he was getting tired of anthology makers who kept asking for that one poem. "I suppose it is because it is so concise and clear and has a sharp conclusion that people like it and remember it," he told an interviewer, with a sigh, in 1933. He did not mean to deprecate "Richard Cory," but after all he had written "quite a variety" of poetry to select from.

The poem has prompted a considerable amount of speculation about who Richard Cory "was." Frank Anne, the West Gardiner river man who killed himself, hardly qualified as the slim elegant aristocrat of the poem. In his biography, Hage-dorn proposes that Robinson modeled his character after Sedgewick Plummer, a wealthy Gardiner attorney who lost his fortune in drink and gambling. Robinson would have known about Plummer, who slept in alleyways and cadged scraps of food downtown before dying in the city poor house in 1884. Robinson family members, on the other hand, felt sure that Herman Robinson's days of glory and rapid downfall inspired the portrait of Cory. It hardly matters, for on the page Richard Cory emerges as a generic figure. Robinson probably drew him from multiple sources: from Plummer and brother Herman, from the wellborn idlers he scorned at Harvard, even from the Gardiner aristocrats who adopted him as their erstwhile companion at the Yellow House and their camp at the lake.

The character of Richard Cory is sketched impressionistically in the poem. Robinson furnishes no concrete information about his occupation or family. When Paul Simon rewrote the poem for his 1960s song, he decided to give Robinson's shadowy character greater definition.

> They say that Richard Cory owns one half of this whole town,
> With political connections to spread his wealth around.
> Born into society, a banker's only child,
> He had everything a man could want: power, grace, and style.

In two following verses, Simon further delineates Cory as a contradictory figure: a celebrity whose picture appears everywhere and who is rumored to have "orgies on his yacht", a philanthropist who gives to charity and has "the common touch."

Wisely, though, Simon followed Robinson in not supplying Cory with reasons for his despondency. Speculative readers, missing the point of the poem, have rushed to explain *why* Cory shot himself. As in most cases of suicide, there were probably multiple causes. But this is not what "Richard Cory" is about. "Not surprise but paradox and irony provide the structure of the poem," as Edwin Fussell observed. The central irony has to do with the wrongheaded attitude of the Tilbury townspeople, the "we" of the poem, who commodify Cory into the embodiment of their own avaricious dreams. Things are not what they seem, especially when those observing shared the values of the marketplace.

The final quatrain underscores how morally obtuse the townspeople are.

> So on we worked and waited for the light,
> And went without the meat, and cursed the bread;
> And Richard Cory, one calm summer night,
> Went home and put a bullet through his head.

As J. C. Levenson construed these lines, "Those who count over what they lack and fail to bless the good before their eyes [consider the sacrilegious implications of cursing the bread] are truly desperate. The blind see only what they can covet or envy. With their mean complaining, they are right enough about their being in darkness, and their dead-gray triviality illuminates by contrast Cory's absolute commitment to despair."

Only superficially does "Richard Cory" deal with the truism that wealth does not guarantee happiness. What troubled Robinson, looking carefully around him in Gardiner, was the confident way in which his fellow citizens collectively misjudged others and refused to confront their own failings. It is no surprise that it was written by a man who would soon bid farewell to his home town and its inhabitants. He had another compelling reason to leave, too.

A Crisis at Home

In the Robinson household under Emma's supervision, beginning at the end of 1896, Herman drifted into his own "dark house" of alcoholism and was often unavailable for fatherly duties. When he was around, there was a perceptible chill between him and his wife. The children did not know what was wrong as they heard their parents' wrangling over "Madame Clicquot," their code word for Herman's drinking. Under those circumstances, Uncle Win began to assume the duties of a surrogate father. It fell to him, for instance, to help determine the course of Ruth's schooling.

Ruth was not quite six when her grandmother died, and she was held out of school that year because of her quarantine and because of Win's strong opinion that children should not start school too soon. The next year, he escorted her on her first day at the kindergarten Rosalind Richards had begun in the Episcopal parish house. Rosalind never forgot the sight of the two of them as they approached. "It wasn't just that her hand was in his, all the way down the street, she looking up at him, laughing and talking and frolicking along; it was the way in which he held her hand, protecting, owning; and the utter confidence with which she seemed to own him." Win, who had persuaded Rosalind in advance to admit his niece, brought along a little stick to be used at her discretion, should Ruth require disciplining. Rosalind treasured that small private joke between them. She kept the stick as a memento all her days, and presented it to Ruth herself sixty years later.

During the year after his mother died, Robinson's workdays fell into a pattern. He rose at seven and performed a few chores around the place before settling down in his den to write. He fed the five family hens, for example. Why bother? Emma asked. The chickens didn't lay any eggs. "We have always had hens," Win replied. She found a more useful task for him instead. He asked her why she was carrying wood and coal into the house when there were three men in the house and she only had to ask them. "Well, I guess it's because I have to ask them." Thereafter he fetched fuel for the fire himself.

Chores done, Robinson worked at his desk from nine in the morning until nearly five in the evening. Then came the children's hour. He would emerge from his room at the top of the stairs and romp with the youngsters, carrying them piggyback and tossing them in the air. Then he would bring out his fiddle and play—not expertly—English and Scottish ballads and Stephen Foster songs for them all to sing. It made for a joyous time. At dinner there was talk with Emma, who encouraged his poetry and stuck up for him against any aspersions from Herman. Then Win walked down town to the Quadruped hideaway and returned in time for a good night's sleep. So the time passed in the spring of 1897, and so it passed after Emma and the girls returned from Capitol Island in the fall. He might almost have been married.

Of course it could not last. Herman could not help feeling jealous about his younger brother's obvious compatibility with his wife and about the growing attachment between Win and his children. On a pleasant night in the fall of 1897, the tension between the brothers erupted.

Win had gone to join his friends at the Quadruped when Herman staggered home, the worse for wear after a fishing trip and considerable drinking. There were words between husband and wife, but Emma helped Herman into bed and, with the children asleep, went out on the porch to collect herself. When Win returned, he sat down beside her and put his arm around her as she cried herself to sleep. Nothing more. They were still sitting there, in a scene of apparent domestic tranquility, when Herman awoke, came downstairs in the darkened house, lit the gas lamp in the parlor, and spied them through the window. With the indignation of one who fancied himself wronged, Herman raged at his younger brother. They carried the argument upstairs to Win's study. No blows were struck, but Emma heard loud and angry talk from behind the closed door.

That night, the brothers reached an agreement of sorts. Win must leave the house. He would draw an allowance—possibly about $750 a year—to support him for the four years or so until his portion of the estate was gone. But he was not to show any further affection for Emma, and he might as well give up any hope of making her his wife one day. Herman would see to it that it never happened.

The next morning Herman said to Emma, "A man's a scoundrel who will come into another man's house and steal his wife's love—and she is just as bad." She spoke not a word in reply. Win spent the forenoon packing his belongings and preparing to leave what had been his home since his infancy. It was his house as much as Herman's: more so, considering the effort he'd put into it. But it was an impossible situation, and he was prepared to leave. He did not chastise himself. It was true that he cared for Emma. He always had and always would. And it was true that as Emma's confidant and comforter and, most of the time, the man around the house, he had tried to make her care for him. But they had done nothing to violate the sanctity of the marriage. "I thought I could help you by staying here," he told Emma as he walked out the door, "but I find I can't and I have to go."

The estrangement between brothers was painful, and Win's hopeless love for Emma hurt even more. Yet what it took from his life was more than redeemed in his art. The love triangle was to appear continually in his work, in scores of short poems and most of the long poems. The unhappy marriage of his brother and wife formed the basis for many others, including "Eros Turannos," one of his most admired and enduring poems. In these works, EAR did not try to recreate the crisis at 67 Lincoln Avenue in photographic detail. To do so would have violated all sense of decorum. Besides, he was more interested in the wider psychological resonances than in the particularities of a single instance. Love gone wrong remained a dominant theme in his work; he examined his disastrous triangles and failed marriages from any number of different perspectives.

9

Breaking Away

The Children of the Night

In the months following his mother's death, Robinson was groping for a way of looking at life. He found it in the gospel of idealism, not as it might have been preached from the pulpit but as embedded in the thinking of Thomas Carlyle and Ralph Waldo Emerson and even, for a time, though he could not in the end accept "a system . . . too dependent on unsubstantial inferences," in the Christian Science of Mary Baker Eddy. He had long talks with an older fellow in Gardiner named Jones, probably Samuel W. Jones, a painter who lived a few houses away at 76 Lincoln Avenue. A dedicated idealist, Jones led Robinson into the study of comparative religion. He was struck by the similarities between Christianity and Buddhism. "Nirvana and Heaven are from the idealist's point of view—which is to me the only point of view—pretty much the same thing." The only thing that kept him going, he wrote Latham, was the belief that he had "an inkling as to the spiritual scheme of things."

By the spring of 1897, EAR had substantially arrived at a creed that would serve him and his poetry all his days. He set out to articulate it in a series of "Octaves," eight-line unrhymed poems addressing religion and philosophy. In September, he told Edith Brower that he had written sixty-four of them, but only "about 25" survived his own pruning and "the merciless scavenging" of his friend Seth Pope when he tried them out, of an evening, on the Quadruped. (Later, he cut the number to twenty-three for his *Collected Poems*). The "Octaves" were very different from the portrait poems and stories he had been writing. Dealing in abstractions and proclaiming their conclusions in an oracular voice, they do not make for easy reading. But they had to be written. Robinson needed a faith to live by to replace his "optimistic desperation," and in these eight-line poems he spelled it out.

Throughout the "Octaves" runs Robinson's conception of life as "a spiritual exercise." The world is a terrible place, but we must accept it in the hope that "something better will come sometime." Death itself is a release, not a source of sorrow.

> And when the dead man goes it seems to me
> 'T were better for us all to do away
> With weeping, and be glad that he is gone.

Hard though life might he for the living, there was compensation in our common plight.

> There is no loneliness:—no matter where
> We go, nor whence we come, or what good friends
> Forsake us in the seeming, we are all
> At one with a complete companionship;
> And though forlornly joyless be the ways
> We travel, the compensate spirit-gleams
> Of Wisdom shaft the darkness here and there,
> Like scattered lamps in unfrequented streets.

In that vivid final image lay the glimmer of the light that was to illuminate so much of Robinson's later work. In questing for it, he warned, we must look ahead and not to the past.

> We lack the courage to be where we are:—
> We love too much to travel on old roads.
> To triumph on old fields; we love too much
> To consecrate the magic of dead things.

It is no good romanticizing our existence, yet despite all doubts, we should not succumb to faithlessness.

> Forebodings are the fiends of Recreance;
> The master of the moment, the clean seer
> Of ages, too securely scans what is,
> Ever to be appalled at what is not;
> He sees beyond the groaning borough lines
> Of Hell, God's highways gleaming, and he knows
> That Love's complete communion is the end
> Of anguish to the liberated man.

To avoid a disastrous loss of faith (recreance), one must learn like "the master of the moment" to catch a sight of heaven beyond hell and to find "complete communion" in an altruistic love for one's fellow man that parallels the love of God.

Salvation depends upon developing the capacity to look and listen. To ward off despair, we must see beyond "the onslaught that awaits this idiot world" and read the "record of All-Soul whereon God writes" the truth. And we have to open our ears to "the timeless hymns of Love," to the "cadence of that infinite plain-song / Which is itself all music." This was, to be sure, an antinomian process. The individual had to find his way without the guidance of any churchly establishment.

As such, Robinson's "Octaves" elicited the condemnation of the passionately Catholic William Henry Thorne, who read them in *The Children of the Night* and thundered his disapproval in the *Globe*. Thorne admired Robinson's talent and was sure that his purposes were "high and pure," his former companion in the Gardiner Poetry Society wrote. But he could not tolerate the young poet's "infernal philosophy." With an arrogance characteristic of Yankees, Thorne maintained, EAR made "his own definition of God" and admitted "no higher mind or power than his own untaught and youthful intellect." Where was it written that this world was hell? What was this of the All-Soul? From whom had Robinson learned that "if God be God, He is Love"? From Jesus Christ or the atheistic Thomas Paine?

Thorne's charges, though expressed in inflammatory language, were valid enough. Confronted with the "Octaves" as a proclamation of beliefs arrived at without the validation of authority, the Puritans among Robinson's ancestors would have exiled him from Massachusetts Bay as surely as they did Roger Williams and Anne Hutchinson. Or they would have exacted an even more severe penalty, for Robinson's tampering with church doctrine was every bit as heretical as that of his freethinking New England predecessor Emily Dickinson. As Allen Tate sagely remarked, the stern and saintly "Cotton Mather would have burnt her for a witch."

The Children of the Night, published on December 6, 1897, combined all but two of the poems from the privately printed *The Torrent and the Night Before* of the previous year with forty-three new poems, among them "Richard Cory," "Cliff Klingenhagen," "Reuben Bright," and the "Octaves." By midsummer, Robinson had settled on a publisher. "I'm going to get out my book again in the fall—this time as a 'legitimate' publication," Robinson wrote Joseph Ford in August. The quotation marks around "legitimate" were well-advised. Unable to interest the larger and better-known houses in bringing out *The Children of the Night*, Robinson entrusted it to Richard G. Badger & Company of Boston, a notorious vanity publisher of the time, with a specialty in poetry. For a fee, Badger would publish the work of anyone desiring to see his name on the jacket of a book.

Reviewers were liable to turn up their noses at any volume with a Badger imprint. New York–based critics, especially, made sport of what they called Badger's "Boston bards." Still, on occasion Badger printed the early work of very good writers indeed, including Willa Cather, Edgar Lee Masters, and Eugene

O'Neill along with Robinson. In any case, EAR must have felt that a Badger imprint was better than none at all. Eager as always to help his friend, Willie Butler agreed to pay all costs.

As EAR anxiously awaited the book's publication, he shuttled between self-deprecation and self-justification. He wrote Edith Brower that he knew his book was "full of flaws," but he hoped it might make him "a little more certain in regard to what I am here for." He expanded on the topic to Harry Smith. "From the *Children* I do not expect much, if anything, in the way of direct remuneration but I shall always feel, even if I starve to death someday, that the book has done a good deal for me. . . . When I think of the hours I have spent over some of the lines in it I wonder if it is all worth while; but in the end I cease wondering. If anything is worthy of a man's best and hardest effort, that thing is the utterance of what he believes to be the truth."

Despite its disreputable imprint, his book attracted a fair share of attention from reviewers. Richard Cary located two dozen reviews, most of which greeted the book with commendation. Three separate notices announced the discovery of "A New Poet" in their headlines. The *Boston Evening Transcript* even reviewed *The Children* twice. The *Transcript's* first, anonymous reviewer praised the poet's "simple and direct" style and his "deep sympathy for all who suffer and struggle." The second, much longer review, from Harvard's Hays Gardiner, noted that the slender volume was "essentially a modest effort," not long, and of limited range. But its modesty, Gardiner went on, should be interpreted not as a sign of weakness but "of reserved strength." Robinson's sonnets and lyrics, with their sketches of "imaginary characters," reminded Gardiner of Wordsworth, aligned with a "shrewd and Yankee directness which is like nothing we remember."

In an omnibus review of "Recent American Poetry" for the *Nation*, the eminent Thomas Wentworth Higginson, once mentor to Dickinson, singled out Robinson as far superior to the other twenty poets under consideration. EAR wrote "of men and women, not external nature" with admirable vigor and creative imagination, Higginson commented, and seemed to have the power to encompass a whole life in fourteen lines.

Robinson was delighted with the review, but it might have galled him had he known that Mrs. Richards had intervened on his behalf with Colonel Higginson. On *The Torrent's* publication day, she wrote Higginson asking that he read and consider Robinson's book "and, it may be, give it your good word . . . when next you are reviewing recent poetry for the 'Nation.'" Robinson was a friend of hers whom she valued highly, Mrs. Richards said. More than that, she thought his poems of real merit: "strong, genuine, and individual." It was the first of many boosts she was to give EAR as he tried to catch a foothold on the ladder of recognition.

As with *The Torrent*, there were those who read *The Children* and thought it unduly pessimistic. Dean L. B. R. Briggs at Harvard proposed that Robinson should follow *The Children of the Night* with a sequel called *The Children of the Light*. But the book struck others with great force. The young poet Ridgely Torrence, working late at the New York Public Library, came across a copy of the tan-covered volume on a shelf of new publications, read a few poems, caught his breath, and read on through to the end as if spellbound. The critic William Stanley Braithwaite, who knew all about Badger books, picked up Robinson's *Children* and came away convinced "that here was a major poet." Over the course of time, the book has taken its place as one of the revolutionary publications in the history of American poetry. It marked "the beginning of a new era in American poetry," Tate commented. Louise Bogan called it "one of the hinges upon which American poetry was able to turn from the sentimentality of the nineties toward modern veracity and psychological truth."

It appeared for a time that *The Children* might do better as a commercial enterprise than Robinson anticipated. Two months after publication Badger announced that he had sold three hundred copies. EAR could account for about 150 of them purchased by friends and well-wishers, but the rest had gone off "into the unknown and the unknowable," which was where he liked to have them go. Some of the sales were attributable to the advertisement Badger placed in the *Bibelot*, consisting of quotations lifted from various reviews of the book. In composing the ad, Badger used a technique that has become a staple in motion picture advertising: he included the good parts of a review and omitted the bad. When one reviewer commented that "on one page is poetic sentiment, graceful play of fancy, powerful imagery and strength of diction, while the next page may hold the rudest twaddle," Badger judiciously left out the clause beginning with "while."

There were no further advertisements, sales of *The Children* slowed precipitously, and Robinson received nothing in the way of royalties. When he was in Boston in the winter of 1899, Robinson presented himself at Badger's office and demanded payment on the spot. He left with $17 and a sense of satisfaction. "I had no scruples at all," he remembered thirty-five years later. "I was more hard up than Badger." Later that year Badger was glad to sell Willie Butler all the remaining copies of *The Children of the Night*. They were placed on sale in Butler's department store, not customarily a venue for books of poetry by virtually unknown authors.

Winter in Bohemia

Warned out of the family homestead, Robinson grew increasingly uncomfortable in Gardiner. "I have lived this sort of life about as long as I can," he announced to Smith on November 1, 1897, "and my system—physical, intellectual and spiritual—demands a change." His nerves were as taut as the E string on the fiddle. He couldn't sleep and couldn't work. It was time to strike out on his own, escaping the quarrel with Herman, the emotional pull of Emma and the girls, and the steady and inevitable deterioration of Dean. Win set his sights on New York City, the town down the river. In cosmopolitan New York, he fancied, he would encounter the bohemian life he'd read about in Thackeray's *Pendennis* and George du Maurier's *Trilby*.

He went to see Kate Vannah before leaving. As a successful songwriter, Vannah knew her way around the cafes and coffee houses of the metropolis. "Win Robinson marched bravely in the other evening about 7:45," she wrote a friend, "and by 10:40 his shyness had thawed *consibble* . . . He longs to be away from Gardiner and I can understand how he is at war with his surroundings. . . . It was pathetic to hear him say he would be willing to live on $4.00 a week (if he *could*) in N.Y. He knows nothing of N.Y. and hasn't a friend there. Poor boy." Vannah exaggerated Robinson's plight. George Burnham, his friend from Harvard's Corn Cob Club, was living in a rooming house on West Sixty-fourth Street and was glad to take him in. Nor would poor Win have to subsist on $4 a week. Probably through the agreement with Herman, a check for $600 descended from the Robinson estate, a windfall that could finance him for a year at $12 a week.

Professionally, too, Robinson could count on making some contacts among the literary-artistic community. Publication of a book of poems, even under a suspect imprint, would give him a measure of recognition. And he had a standing invitation from Dr. Titus Munson Coan, the manuscript doctor who admired the poems in *The Torrent*, to look him up whenever Robinson came to the city. At the end of November, Win packed his things and took the train to New York. He planned to stay until June, and perhaps longer. He did not know it was to become his home base for all of the winters to come.

FIGURE 9.1 Titus Munson Coan, Leader of the Clan.

Source: Collection of the New-York Historical Society.

As soon as he'd unpacked, Robinson made his way to 70 Fifth Avenue, where Coan directed his bureau of manuscript revision. Small in stature and a generation older than EAR, Coan had been born to missionary parents in Hawaii, fought with Farragut in the Civil War, and graduated from Williams College and from the New York College of Physicians and Surgeons. In addition to fixing the work of aspiring authors, Coan published both prose and verse in the leading periodicals of the day. He belonged to the eminent Century Association and to the Authors' Club. He was also something of a showman. Along one wall at his apartment, he displayed an extensive collection of pornographic photographs.

Coan was the leading light of a group of writer-drinkers called the Clan. He took it upon himself to introduce Robinson to the members of this bohemian group, which gathered frequently for convivial evenings out. In addition, he arranged for Robinson to be invited to the Authors' Club and gave him a card to the Century. "I like this man, the Doctor," Robinson wrote Edith Brower on December 17, not for his favors but for "something in his personality." The previous evening, he and Coan had attended a dinner at the Authors' Club, where EAR shook the hand of the novelist Hamlin Garland, who seemed to be a very good fellow. Otherwise, he was put off by the "general suggestion of swelled head" among the participants and was more impressed by the stomachs than the minds of the assembled luminaries. He got along much better with members of the Clan.

Robinson's closest friend in the Clan was a baldheaded Canadian from Nova Scotia named Craven Langstroth Betts. Betts sold law books for a living but spent much of his time cranking out hundreds of ornate overwritten poems. He met Robinson at Coan's apartment and was attracted to his "unusual and detached" manner. Robinson maintained a sphinxlike calm, never raised his voice, and rarely showed emotion. Betts, who had detected the depth of feeling in Robinson's early poems, felt sure that this placid exterior concealed "a personality throbbing and burning with suppressed fire." At the same time he could see that EAR was "in the main unskilled in the material things of the world, and had no notion of how he was to keep himself in New York."

Also a member of the Clan was Thorne, the egocentric fire-breathing Catholic who had come to Gardiner, acquired the sponsorship of Caroline Swan, and returned to New York to disgorge his thoughts in the *Globe*. Thorne was well along in years and susceptible to ranting on the page and in person. He was often at loggerheads with Alfred H. Louis, the most interesting and eccentric figure in the group.

Robinson met Louis for the first time in a basement café at the southwest corner of Broadway and Thirteenth Street. Diminutive and ill-smelling, Louis looked like a prophet out of the Old Testament. He had grown up in England, excelled at public school and Cambridge, converted from Judaism to Catholicism, taken a law degree, gone into politics only to have his career thwarted by

FIGURE 9.2 The amazing, unkempt Alfred H. Louis, model for "Captain Craig."

Source: Arnold T. Schwab Papers.

Gladstone, come to the States, lived for a while in Chicago, done time in an mental hospital, and landed in New York without any apparent means of support.

Robinson was immediately fascinated by this ancient English Jew. A polymath familiar with all the religions and philosophies of the world and well versed in art, music, literature, and international affairs, Louis was the most learned man EAR had ever known. He spoke casually of great figures who had once, he claimed, been his intimate friends. He had gone to school with E. W. Benson, the Archbishop of Canterbury. He knew Ruskin, Meredith, and Trollope. George Eliot, he said, had fashioned the character of Mordecai in *Daniel Deronda* after him. There was even a rumor that he was the illegitimate son of Prime Minister Benjamin Disraeli. In the United States, he had befriended Longfellow and Howells.

Coan and Betts were inclined to dispute the veracity of Louis's claims, but their doubts melted away when the old man sat down at the piano and played Chopin beautifully or when he raised his mellifluous voice to recite poetry. "Recitation" hardly did justice to his delivery: one evening he read Robert Browning's "The Bishop Orders His Tomb" for Betts and Robinson, evoking all of its "hatred, vanity, lust of the flesh, grief, pathos, and suspicion." He could have been a great actor, Betts thought.

Yet for all his brilliance and ability, and in spite of the shafts of wisdom he could launch, Louis was a troubled human being. When you made an engagement with him, you could never be sure who would keep it: the charmer who could flatter with the most insidious grace or the madman who would fly into a passion and seize you by the collar. Louis lived in a hovel on Eighth Street, wore a filthy great coat, and stunk like a goat. He was poor beyond the ordinary sense of the word and constantly sponged off his friends. "Some way or other he managed to live," Robinson wrote of him thirty years later. "Somebody gave him enough to keep him alive. Doctor Coan helped him out, and there were others. One way or another the ravens looked after old Mr. Louis."

Robinson, holding his nose, listened and learned. He began to think of writing a long poem that would do Louis justice. At first, the working title was "The Pauper." Later, he decided to call him "Captain Craig." For his part, Louis detected the gleam of genius in Robinson's writing and sought to know him better. Before EAR returned to Maine in the summer of 1898, Louis sent him a postcard proposing a private meeting. He had some ideas about EAR that he wanted to go over with him. Besides, Louis wrote, "I so much wish some communion of our selves undiluted by other personalities."

As Louis's note suggested, the Clan usually assembled in groups of more than two. At various restaurants and bars in lower Manhattan—Raganachi's, The Cave, Zum Praelaten, Cavanaugh's—Coan and his cohort met for food, drink, and extended discussion of life and letters. As at Harvard, Robinson's tongue needed loosening, a process now abetted by the consumption of whiskey instead of beer or ale. As the night wore on, he could hold his own in lively conversation with everyone on hand—except the amazing Louis. This, then, was his Bohemia.

Robinson welcomed the new year of 1899 at another Authors' Club party. He met E. C. Stedman that evening, a stockbroker, critic, and poet in his mid-sixties who had a reputation as the "dean of American poets, the friend and helper of young aspirants." Stedman was to be of assistance in launching Robinson's career, and once again, Mrs. Richards was working behind the scenes. She and EAR had begun their regular correspondence—she wrote weekly, on Fridays, and he biweekly—and in his first letter of the new year he told her he'd had the pleasure of meeting Mr. Stedman. She at once took pen in hand to tell Stedman about Robinson and the difficulties he had had to overcome. "He has lived too much in the shadow," she pointed out. "His life, in the very spring of manhood, has been saddened by much physical suffering, by cruel bereavement, and by other domestic trials of a painful nature, for none of which he has been responsible, and in which he has shown an unselfishness almost heroic." Robinson was noble, high-minded, and had a very real gift for poetry. She urged Stedman to take an interest in him but without letting him know about her letter. "A proud, shy, super-sensitive lad does not like to be talked about, even in the most friendly way."

Early in January Robinson took the train to Wilkes-Barre to meet Edith Brower, who like Laura Richards was his fervid supporter. For fully a year he had been promising to pay Brower a visit, but this only became feasible after he set up headquarters in New York City. He made the journey out of curiosity and to express his gratitude for Brower's continued encouragement, most recently evidenced in her long and laudatory review of *The Children* for the Wilkes-

Barre daily newspaper. The book had been put together, at least in part, on the strength of her belief in him.

Before undertaking his visit, Robinson warned Brower that he was long and awkward, a very poor talker, and "no special chrysanthemum" in any way. She shouldn't expect too much. "I tell you very frankly that I shall disappoint you. I disappoint everybody and almost everybody disappoints me. I make free to say this, knowing that you will do nothing of the kind." She should be prepared to play the piano much of the time, though, and would have to promise not to ask him how he planned to earn a living.

In reply, Brower struck a cautionary note of her own. She had a fifteen-year-old cat, Rory O'Moore, who all his life had fled when "anything wearing boots and trousers" entered the house. EAR was not to be offended when the cat took refuge. "The cat and I are going to get along first-rate," he assured her, and so it proved to be. The moment Rory laid eyes on Robinson, Brower recounted, "he went straight to him, jumped upon his knees and made believe he had found a lap—which he hadn't, for R. [was] very long and was at that time very thin."

Brower's response to Robinson coincided with the cat's. Domestically and socially, she decided, Robinson had what the English called "homely" ways, combining "a curious mixture of New England reserve and blunt outspokenness." She thought EAR "the most utterly unaffected person" she'd ever known. He stayed two days and made a good impression not only on Brower and her aunt but on Brower's close friend Jean Gordon Hansen and especially on her attractive daughter Marjorie, who was produced as a possible romantic attachment. According to Mrs. Hansen, Marjorie had met "one poet—Robinson—whom she thinks very beautiful." EAR corresponded with Marjorie for a time but let the connection go no further.

A week after his two-day visit to Wilkes-Barre, Robinson wrote Brower that it had been "one of the greatest pleasures" of his life. He had not said much, he might have seemed "rather wooden for the most part," but he felt comfortable there. A reluctant traveler, he did not return; in fact, he never ventured that far west again. But the journey had been worth making, he told Harry Smith, for he'd "had a good time and found a good friend, which is not a combination to be laughed at." The letters to Brower continued. She valued his work and understood what he was aiming for.

Last Days at Home

New York was doing him good, Robinson felt sure, but he had no idea yet of making it a permanent part of his life. He was in "a transition stage," as he wrote Smith in February. Throughout the spring of 1898, he vacillated about where to spend the summer. Edith Brower proposed that he might come to

Dallas, a pleasant country town near Wilkes-Barre with boarding houses for summer visitors. His Quadruped friend, Arthur Blair, was managing a branch of the Augusta Safe Deposit & Trust Co. in Winthrop, Maine, about fifteen miles northwest of Gardiner, and urged EAR to join him there. Gardiner itself offered a less inviting prospect. Dean's condition was worsening, and Win was still at odds with Herman. "There are things to make me go to Maine," he wrote Brower, "and there are things to keep me away." He was not at all sure he could get his work done there.

Nonetheless, it was back to the house on Lincoln Avenue that he came at the end of May. He was needed to help take care of Dean while Herman, Emma, and the three girls summered on Capitol Island. Ruth and the other nieces were glad to see him. He laughed hard, an extremely rare occurrence, when five-year-old Marie chastised him. "I looked all the way through *The Children of the Night*," she said, "and there wasn't a thing about babies in it." He roughhoused with the youngsters as of old, although otherwise maintaining his usual gravity. Those images went with him downtown to the Quadruped's room. There, he could work on his poetry in relative peace and look in on Dean's drug store from time to time.

His friendship with Pope solidified. "A great tall stoutish ungainly young man" (as Rosalind Richards described him), Pope had been brought up on a farm, graduated from Bowdoin, and was struggling as a schoolteacher at Gardiner's Highland Avenue grammar school. A lovable if somewhat lazy fellow, he regarded Robinson as a kind of young prince, "a victim of suppressed immortality." It didn't matter if EAR ever made a cent, Pope told him, so long as his poetry "g[ot] itself uttered." He played the role of Robinson's "laudator," then and later. EAR coveted the friendship and needed the praise.

Life in Gardiner was far from ideal, however. "I'm here in the wilderness for God knows how long," Robinson wrote Dr. Coan in June. He was feeling homesick for New York. "I would give a good deal, if I had it, to walk down Broadway to-night and find you all together as I used to." The weather in Maine could not have been lovelier, but he was unwilling to see the beauties of a place that was hell to him. The "asinine" city authorities, he complained indignantly in a letter to Brower, kept the Common "clipped like a prisoner's head and not a blessed young one was allowed to play on it." The children played in the streets to keep the Common looking pretty. Having lashed out at the powers-that-be, Robinson kept silence about matters closer to home.

At his aerie over Brown's dry goods store, EAR smoked "Before the War" cigars, gazed at the mill pond below, and began to rough out 120 lines "making a regular analysis of an Old Maid." The mill pond must have had something to do with it, he said after finishing the poem two years later. "Maybe I thought she ought to have drowned herself."

The poem was his blank verse narrative "Aunt Imogen." In it, Robinson movingly portrayed a figure more common in 1900 than in 2000: the solitary spinster living in reduced circumstances upon whom the relatives must pay duty calls on birthdays and holidays. Robinson observed his share of these women, growing up in his New England town; he was to depict yet another, again with great poignancy, in "The Poor Relation" (1915). Aunt Imogen was more fortunate than many of these lonely women, for once a year she was invited to stay with her sister Jane and her family for a month at a time. Jane's three children—two boys and a girl—looked forward to her annual visit. All of September became "a Queen's Festival" during which Aunt Imogen entertained them tirelessly.

With genders reversed, the situation of the maiden aunt paralleled Uncle Win's own relationship with his sister-in-law and her nieces. And, in fact, EAR confessed both to Emma and to Ruth that he was revealing—or concealing— himself in the character of Aunt Imogen, a woman who over the course of the poem comes to realize that her dreams of what might have been will not come true. Characteristically, Robinson evades any full-scale revelation of himself in the poem. There is a hint of rivalry between the two sisters when Imogen reflects that she

> Was there for only one month of the year,
> While she, the mother,—she was always there;
> And that was what made all the difference.

But no husband appears on the scene to complete the triangle.

Yet in the text of "Aunt Imogen" as it was printed in 1902's *Captain Craig: A Book of Poems*, and again in the 1915 reprinting of that book, Robinson did include a male figure—a brother to the two sisters—who was deleted for the *Collected Poems* of 1921 and thereafter. Here is part of the passage that was cut, midway through the poem:

> Even her big bewhiskered brother Giles
> Had called her [Imogen, that is] in his letter, not long since,
> A superannuated pretty girl;
> And she, to do the thing most adequate,
> Had posted back sarcastic sheets enough
> To keep the beast in humor for a month.

The brother, in his insensitivity to Imogen's spinsterhood and his beard, bears a more than passing resemblance to Herman Robinson. One wonders what Herman might have said to Win about his bachelorhood.

Jane's children, "little savages / Who knew no better than to be themselves," more or less attack Aunt Imogen each times she appears. Frowzle-headed little Jane strangles her, Sylvester thumps his drum, Young George howls. Metaphorically, the youngsters launch a military campaign that ends by overwhelming their aunt and relieving her of her long-nurtured illusions. The poem reaches its climax as Imogen is rocking Young George and he is moved to tell her what a fine place the world is and what a good game life is, especially when she is around.

> And something in his way of telling it—
> The language, or the tone, or something else—
> Gripped like insidious fingers on her throat,
> And then went foraging as if to make
> A plaything of her heart.

As George celebrates an existence of boundless profusion, Imogen sees how little awaits her.

> The blow that she had vaguely thrust aside
> Like fright so many times had found her now:
> Clean-thrust and final it had come to her
> From a child's lips at last.

She knows that there will be "no love / Save borrowed love" for her, nothing to savor but "the blank taste of time." She was "born to be Aunt Imogen," nothing more. Having at last abandoned all dreams of fulfillment, she can submit to her fate gracefully.

> Now she could see the truth and look at it;
> Now she could make stars out where once had palled
> A future's emptiness; now she could share
> With others—ah, the others!—to the end
> The largess of a woman who could smile;
> Now it was hers to dance the folly down,
> And all the murmuring; now it was hers
> To be Aunt Imogen.

By virtue of its subject matter alone, "Aunt Imogen" runs the risk of descending into sentimentality. Robinson uses imagery to ward it off. Truth is depicted as a commedia dell'arte Harlequin who leaps out from ambush, complementing the martial activity of the "tumultuous" children. At the very end, a resigned Aunt Imogen turns the tables on her attacker by holding Young George close and "crush"ing him until he laughs. Aunt Imogen, as Robinson earlier told us, "made everybody laugh."

Some critical commentators on EAR have purported to find him "cold" or "distant." It is hard to understand how anyone who has read about Aunt Imogen, or the poor relation shut up in her New York apartment or old Eben Flood climbing alone to his upland hermitage or a dozen other bereft human beings, could possibly arrive at such a judgment.

In midsummer, a marvelous funeral procession wound past the Robinson house: the Gardiner brass band blaring away and the Knights of Pythias in full regalia ushering E. R. Protheroe to his resting place. Protheroe, a much-admired little Welshman, had come to Gardiner to put on an oratorio and stayed twenty years to teach music to the city's children. It occurred to Robinson to weave Protheroe's funeral into "The Pauper," the long poem he was constructing about Alfred H. Louis, another immigrant from the British Isles.

Near the end of September, Robinson wrote Brower that he wanted to go back to New York "as a cat wants to go home" but was committed to stay in Maine for the time being. Not at 67 Lincoln Avenue, however. Herman, strapped for funds after his return from Capitol Island, rented the house to another family. He and Emma and the children moved into a second-floor apartment two doors west on Danforth Street. Dean, ill, put up temporarily with a neighbor. Win went to stay with Arthur Blair in Winthrop.

There would be occasional visits in the future—and one longer stay in 1909—but in effect, when Robinson packed his bag in the fall of 1898, he left Gardiner for good. Before his departure, he took leave of those who most mattered to him. He couldn't do anything but write poetry, he told Emma. Maybe he couldn't even do that, but he was determined to try and willing to wait for recognition. "If I thought I could write something that would go on living after I'm gone," he told her, "I'd be satisfied with an attic and a crust all my life." The next fifteen years were to test that resolve.

At the Yellow House, Mrs. Richards presented him as a farewell gift with a parody of *Don't!*, a then-popular manual of manners she had given, earlier, to the "very rustic" Seth Pope. Such a gesture was not at all unusual for Laura Richards. She had already tried, without much success, to coach EAR in the proper method of shaking hands: firmly, with full eye-contact. Robinson rather resented her patronizing, but he could not help laughing at her clever parody. "Don't write to your hostess after a visit," she advised. "Don't, above all, express pleasure in everything that is done for you."

Robinson did not stay long at Winthrop. He made some progress on "The Pauper," but the winter scenery got him down. "The sight of those eternal white fields and gray stone walls" gave him indigestion, he wrote Coan in New York. "I know them too well. I have had too much of them. They can

FIGURE 9.3 Charles W. Eliot, president of Harvard and EAR's employer, briefly.

Source: Picture Collection, New York Public Library.

feed me at a distance and agree with me but no longer when I am with them."

Two friends in Boston and Cambridge offered to liberate him from such bleak surroundings. Willie Butler promised him a job as a night watchman/janitor at his department store. For a time, EAR planned to take it. Five or six hours of sweeping out the store every night might not sound promising, he reasoned, but looked at as a miserable means to a worthy end, he was prepared to go through almost anything.

Hays Gardiner suggested the more attractive alternative of a position at Harvard and consulted Robinson about what he might be able to do. Teaching was out of the question, EAR insisted. He could rake the college yard, but he refused to read themes and he didn't know enough about rhetoric to teach English composition. A post as a clerk would be better and not overly demanding. The idea was to find some way for EAR to perform his duties and still have the time and energy for his writing. Thereupon Gardiner wrote Harvard president Charles W. Eliot advancing Robinson's "exceptional" case. He called attention to *The Children of the Night*, alluded to the troubles EAR had gone through, stressed his good sense and manliness, and appealed to Eliot's sense of thrift. "Altogether it seems to me that this may be a chance to get a superior man" at a clerk's pay, he pointed out. Over the Christmas holiday Robinson took a trip to Cambridge for an interview with Eliot, who offered him a job in the college office. Early in the new year, EAR moved to Cambridge to try it out.

IO

Poetry as a Calling

Six Months in University 5

Working at Harvard, Robinson figured he could make a living and keep his trousers creased at the same time. It was not a post he was "hungering for," but it was better than sweeping out Butler's store. Besides, the respectable academic "atmosphere must inevitably count for something." He rented a room at 1716 Cambridge Avenue, the same place he had lived during 1892–93, and went each day to University 5, a spacious well-lit room tucked between President Eliot's office and the chamber where the faculty held its meetings. "The office of a big college is a new thing to me," he wrote Harry Smith during his first week on the job, "and I ought to find something in it—something human and interesting." The expectation was not fulfilled. Robinson was put to work reading and filing graduate school applications. The sole benefit of this unrewarding process was that his eye happened to light upon the Divinity School candidacy of one Louis Craig Cornish, whose middle name he filched for his "Pauper" poem. His subsequent duties as "a sort of assistant secretary and metaphorical bottle washer" were similarly dull and unchallenging. He might have perished from boredom were it not for President Eliot himself.

An Olympian figure in the history of Harvard, Charles W. Eliot (1834–1926) was a man of seemingly limitless accomplishments. He took over as president of the university in the year of Robinson's birth, and was still vigorously running it thirty years later. During the interim he converted Harvard into one of the world's great universities. Nor did Eliot confine his abounding energy to that institution alone. He also helped to develop the entire system of elementary and higher education in the United States, was prominent in shaping the course of modern medicine and modern science, and participated in every struggle on behalf of greater respect for human beings from the days of Negro slavery to the fight for a World Court in 1925. Nothing much good could be done without a fight, he believed. Robinson remembered to his dying day Eliot's comment that when a tiger kills a lamb we all say "poor lamb" and never think of saying "happy tiger."

A whirlwind of activity, Eliot did not know what to make of EAR's deliberate ways. From time to time, Robinson was conscious of the president secretly watching him, as if he were a strange animal. Finally, Eliot drew Robinson aside one day, "Are you married?" he asked. Robinson answered that he was not. "A great mistake," Eliot declared. "A young man should marry." Judgment delivered. End of conversation. EAR was put off and never quite forgave Eliot.

Less than six weeks after undertaking his duties at Harvard, Robinson had an opportunity to escape to a job in the Midwest. Through the offices of James Barstow's sister Mary Louise, who was supervising a private school for girls in Kansas City, Robinson was offered the position of literary editor of the *Kansas City Star*. The two-thousand-a-year salary was much higher than he was earning in Cambridge, and the work promised to be more suitable to his talents. A few years earlier, he would have leaped at the proposal. Now he turned it down, and in a letter to Edith Brower, he tried to explain why.

He was "in the power of an ideal," EAR explained: an ideal of creating poetry that would do some good in the world. He feared that the kind of writing the newspaper would demand might be "positively repulsive" to him. Then too, he was reluctant to launch himself into unknown territory. He stayed on at Harvard, where at least there was "something familiar and congenial in the atmosphere."

James Barstow took the *Kansas City Star* post himself and stayed for three years. Robinson wrote him a Polonius-like letter about how to conduct himself as a reviewer. "Be a little sparing in your use of clever ridicule," he advised. Don't write down for your audience. Show them you have something to say and your own way of saying it. Barstow was annoyed by the tone of this directive. EAR was some years his senior but not his father, or uncle. Still, he admired Robinson's poetry. During his first six months in Kansas City, Barstow reprinted half a dozen poems from *The Children of the Night* in the *Star*.

At Harvard, Robinson labored through the spring months joylessly. He concluded that for good or ill, he made a lousy employee. He didn't want to be anyone else's boss, but when orders were issued to him, he at once became "either an independent ass or a groveling and idiotic slave." The problem, he wrote Gardiner, was that he had "only half a brain." Those who had whole ones could hardly understand how "a creature of passable intelligence" such as himself could cut such a pathetic figure.

Worst of all, he wasn't getting poems down on paper. People at the Harvard office were generally sympathetic with his ambitions as a poet. At the same time, most of them regarded literature as a sideline, "an extra" that a reasonable fellow might outgrow while he was "starved into a little common sense." For a while, EAR tried to write at night, from eleven p.m. to one a.m. But he didn't have the stamina to live two lives, he wrote Brower. The position ended with the close of the academic year, and not too soon. "Three months more of the life I have lived for the past half year would make an imbecile of me if not a corpse," he told Smith. As for future employment in the college office, in resigning Robinson told his superiors that he was in the wrong place. They agreed with him, heartily.

EAR stayed on in Cambridge through the summer. "I am in ridiculously good spirits," he declared in the middle of July, "sending the Pauper along at a rate that makes him red in the face, eating anything that comes along, drinking nothing unpermitted by the laws of Cambridge, and feeling every morning the joy of a liberated idiot for the thought that I am no longer a 'necessity' in University 5." Halfheartedly, he angled for a civil service job. More seriously, he made plans to go to New York in the fall.

Dan Mason and Josephine Peabody

Robinson's servitude at the Harvard office was lightened by two important friendships made during his six-month sentence. Daniel Gregory Mason, four years younger than Robinson, established his aesthetic credentials while an undergraduate at Harvard. With Winthrop Ames, he composed an operetta produced by the Hasty Pudding Club. Santayana accepted him under his wing as a member of the Laodiceans. Mason befriended the much-acclaimed Harvard poets William Vaughn Moody and Philip Henry Savage. After graduation in 1895, he and Will Moody took a walking trip to Europe together.

Music was Mason's vocation. He was to become a well-known composer, a distinguished professor at Columbia, and "the most widely read author in America of books about music." But when he and Robinson met in March 1899, Mason "was drawing small checks for assisting in the [Harvard] English courses of Barrett Wendell." He had taken the job as a temporary measure while recovering from a severe "pianist's cramp" that made it impossible for him to play the piano. The cramp was getting better, but Mason was troubled by two other circumstances that eerily coincided with Robinson's. His family finances, like EAR's, had substantially diminished following the death of his father and the panic of 1893. And, like Robinson, he had fallen in love with his older brother's wife. These mutual misfortunes drew the two men together.

Mason recorded his initial impressions of Robinson in his 1938 book, *Music in Our Time*. He described EAR as "tall and in a sensitive way handsome, with dark, fine hair, flowing moustache, and fresh healthy color. Beautiful were his large and peculiarly limpid dark eyes. They gleamed and glowed behind his spectacles, alternately quiet with poetic penetration and dancing with humorous irony." It was the dry irony that particularly struck Mason, especially in contrast "with the romantic warmth of Will Moody and the delicate idealism of Phil Savage."

Mason also noted in Robinson that same streak of helplessness that had brought Betts to his aid in New York City. Robinson "has so little prehensile power," Mason commented in his journal, "so little knack at making people give him what he wants. . . . Yet transcendentally he is richly endowed." From a pianist's perspective, he focused on Robinson's hands, whose long fingers seemed "made not to grasp objects" like saws or hammers or even pens but rather—a characteristic gesture of EAR's—to rub his forehead in thought.

The friendship between the two men developed rapidly, even though, as Mason wrote in his journal, "you have to wait hours for him to say anything." Music and literature forged the bond. Mason loaned Robinson his copy of Henry David Thoreau's poems, which EAR had not previously read and immediately embraced. One day when Betts came to visit, Mason played Brahms all afternoon, much to EAR's delight. Robinson inscribed Mason's copy of *The Children of the Night* and in August sent him a photograph of himself to paste inside. The letter enclosing the picture (taken by Willie Butler) apologized for his lugubrious appearance. "I have a look that might lead one to think that I had just been eating the lining out of my own coffin, but that is the fault of an uncomfortable feel somewhere in my spinal column. I was not properly adjusted for the interminable two minutes."

When the aspiring poet Philip Savage died of appendicitis in June 1899, Robinson was moved to inveigh against the ill effects of Savage's employment as a secretary in the Boston Public Library. Most of those who knew Savage felt that securing such a post had been a stroke of luck for him. For Robinson, however, nothing was lucky which deflected a poet from his career.

Mason commemorated his friend Savage in an "Elegy for Piano," first performed in Boston in September 1899. On that occasion, Robinson met Mrs. Edward (Mary) Mason, the object of Dan's affection, for the first time, and was most favorably impressed. "To my great surprise," the poet Josephine Preston Peabody wrote her afterward, "[EAR] even admitted that he liked you,—that you seemed neither ill-favored nor lacking in intelligence. I gather that you exercised many and varied wiles upon an unusually discriminating man." Peabody was a friend and confidante of Mrs. Mason and also became Robinson's close friend during his stay in Cambridge. They had poetry in common, and something of a spark besides.

Robinson knew of Peabody's poetry before they met. He wrote an extended review of her first book of poems, *The Wayfarers* (1898), while still living with Arthur Blair in Winthrop. It was the only review he ever wrote—he did not think it appropriate to sit in judgment on the work of other writers—and was undertaken at the behest of Badger for his *Literary Review*. By and large he found Peabody's poetry first-rate. Here is "the real thing," he announced, and backed up the statement with quotations from the title poem and others. With his strong preference for the language of the street, EAR took exception to Peabody's use of such archaic words as "glamourie" and "enringing." Still, there

FIGURE 10.1 The poet Josephine Preston Peabody, admirer of and admired by Robinson.

Source: Picture Collection, New York Public Library.

was in her work "a union of art and substance, of wisdom and imagination, that amounts almost, if not quite, to genius."

Peabody was pleased with the review and still more pleased when Robinson proposed a meeting in Boston. They met on March 29, when Robinson called— an hour late, having underestimated the distance—at the modest Dorchester home where Peabody and her mother lived. "In those days," Mason said of her, "she was a very beautiful girl in her twenties, dark, with a peach-bloom complexion, wonderfully clear eyes, and a voice of thrilling low sonority." She was incandescent, vibrant, talkative: everything EAR was not. Yet as young poets at the beginning of their careers, they shared an ambition to make their mark. Forgotten now, Peabody (1874–1922) carved out a substantial niche in her time, publishing six books of poems and six plays. Mason, Robinson, and Moody called her "Bard" with a capital B, and sometimes "the Little Singer," meant affectionately and not dismissively.

In her journal for March 30, 1899, Peabody described the awkwardness—and the success—of the first visit from Robinson.

Last night, Mr. Robinson came to see me. . . . He was not at all what I expected. His biting strength of insight and expression were hidden somewhere behind a gentleness and a quiet [reticence].

He spoke of moody tendencies and a dislike of meeting people now & then, but looked at me very directly when he did so, and with an odd something of sweetness and humor and especially modesty in his look.

He doesn't talk readily; but I was prepared for that . . . once in a while we were silent, taking thought, and staring at each other a bit, with a funny keenness. It seemed to me that he regarded me with a good deal of almost compassionate friendliness. And after the others [more aggressive gentlemen callers?], it seemed a very new thing.

We spoke of the two books [her *Wayfarers*, his *Children of the Night*] a little and of theories of work. . . . I hope he will come again. He's to be heard from, certainly.

He *has* been heard from, very much. His book is the strongest thing I've seen in several years.

By the summer, Peabody had moved to Cambridge, where Robinson came to see her on several occasions. On July 8, she wrote Mary Mason that he had called twice and they talked at length on both occasions. She found it easy enough to get on with him, even though his conversation was sometimes cryptic and he put up barriers against intimacy. "It is queer, isn't it, that anyone so distinctly gifted should seem to suffer a kind of helpless imprisonment within his own personality." By the end of August, EAR had seen her six or seven times, even though "the eternal bumpkin in me is a little more than she can stand and a little more than I can overcome." In mid-October, Peabody confided to her journal that "E. A. Robinson has gone to New York for the winter; and I'm very sorry to know that he won't be here."

Over the course of the next two years, they continued their relationship by way of correspondence. Much of this was devoted to criticizing each other's work in progress. Robinson proved to be a daunting editor who delivered judgments with alarming candor. Many comments dealt with diction.

May I suggest that you be careful in your use of 'o''. It is always bad; and in 'the greatest o' his day' it is needlessly awkward.

'You look *palely*' would stagger a modern purist. Certainly you will take it out.

'Sweetened corse' is awful. Take it out.

'Belike' will make the judicious grieve.

'Perfect' is an overworked word. Don't use it if you can find anything else.

Isn't 'clear, benignant eye' a bit suggestive of the Poet's Corner—say in the Podunk Gazette?

Somehow their friendship survived the barrage. Peabody could hardly doubt Robinson's sincere interest in her poetry and respected his judgment enough to make most of the alterations he recommended. Still, it was with some trepidation that she sent him the manuscript of *Fortune and Men's Eyes* in April 1900. "I wager my last hat that he sees 1000 horrors in it and as in duty bound tells me so, and that I pine of remorse and vacillating attempts at revision," she wrote in her journal. When word came back that Robinson actually liked the blank verse play that gave her book its title, she was delighted. He said it was "far better than he expected." It was a remarkable piece of writing. He felt sure it would act. Praise from Robinson was worth celebrating. "Three cheers for him:—three more for me!" Peabody wrote. Much as he admired the play, Peabody admitted in her next entry, EAR "had many curses, though, for some of the shorter poems."

Early in the fall of 1899, as he was dining alone at the Old Elm, Robinson was accosted by Joseph Louis French, a man who was to haunt him until his dying days. French (1858–1936) was nothing if not colorful. Richard Cary described him as "a Dickensian figure—flamboyant, garrulous, crapulous, unpredictable, short-fused this side of madness." To Hermann Hagedorn, who had his own encounters with French, he looked "somewhat like a punctured John Bull, on the verge of tears." Pudgy and heavy-jowled, French was given to dramatic effusions. At the end of these performances, he would seek compensation by borrowing small sums that were invariably not repaid. But he had a story to tell and spent half a dozen hours telling it to Robinson on their first meeting. French "had ears like other men but he put them to no social use," Hagedorn said.

The son of a wealthy New York importer who lost his fortune, French ran away from home and traveled west. He rode the Santa Fe trail with a rifle on his hip, explored Arizona and Mexico, worked as a reporter on newspapers all over the United States, helped to found a monthly in Kansas City and a weekly in San Francisco, and landed in Boston as a salesman for Badger's disreputable publishing house. Badger told French that Robinson was "a real poet," not one of his amateur Boston bards. That was enough to inspire French to read *The Children of the Night* and—having decided that Badger was right—to intrude himself with journalistic brashness into Robinson's rather restricted universe.

Difficult and dangerous as French was to become, he had the virtue of genuinely admiring Robinson's poetry, which was enough to earn EAR's gratitude. Robinson recognized French's weaknesses and saw through his pretensions (French managed to get himself included in *Who's Who*, where he claimed to have written two dozen books), but felt compassion for him as a man touched by tragedy and doomed to failure. Taking advantage of this feeling, French persistently dogged Robinson's footsteps. Over a period of thirty years, he repeatedly borrowed money from EAR, stole clothes from him, praised him, abused him, campaigned to get him the Nobel prize, threatened his life, and when EAR lay dying, wormed his way into his New York Hospital room to demand a last "loan."

Dr. H. D. (Dean) Robinson, forty-two, died on the morning of Friday, September 29, 1899. The death was caused by "apoplexy," according to the Gardiner newspaper, and "was not expected." Win was summoned from Cambridge to pay final respects to his much-loved oldest brother and left the next day in a drizzling rain. Ruth Robinson, then nine years old, vividly remembered the funeral. Dean had been a Mason, and the Knights Templar marched in uniform to the "Dead March" from *Saul*. Ruth gazed at her uncle's "sad pinched face lying in the casket" and listened afterwards to the adults "arguing why and how he died." The consensus was that Dean, depressed and unable to shake off his addiction, "saved a little of each potion sent up from the [drug] store until he had accumulated a lethal dose." A decade later, Win wrote a poem about it, "How Annandale Went Out."

> "They called it Annandale—and I was there
> To flourish, to find words, and to attend:
> Liar, physician, hypocrite, and friend,
> I watched him; and the sight was not so fair
> As one or two that I have seen elsewhere:
> An apparatus not for me to mend—
> A wreck, with hell between him and the end,
> Remained of Annandale; and I was there.
>
> "I knew the ruin as I knew the man;
> So put the two together if you can,
> Remembering the worst you know of me.
> Now view yourself as I was, on the spot—
> With a slight kind of engine. Do you see?
> Like this . . . You wouldn't hang me? I thought not."

Here Robinson artfully presents the case for his brother's taking his own life, concealed behind a plea on behalf of euthanasia. The sonnet consists entirely of what a physician says, presumably to a jury, about the death of his friend Annandale. The first line establishes Annandale's plight; he has descended from person to object, from "him" to "it." There is nothing the doctor can do to remedy this broken "apparatus." He knows that the tortures of the damned await this "ruin" of what was once a man. He asks those sitting in judgment to put themselves in his place: there, on the spot, alone with this poor wreck, yet armed with "a slight kind of engine" in his doctor's bag. "Engine" here takes on its tertiary dictionary meaning of "a mechanical appliance, instrument, or tool," a hypodermic needle (!) to be used "like this" (the physician demonstrates) to summon blessed oblivion. Knowing the situation, who would convict him of wrongdoing?

David Nivison, Ruth's son, has written insightfully about "How Annandale Went Out." The poem works well enough, he points out, as "presenting the imaginary defense of a doctor who has performed a mercy killing of a patient who has over time become a wreck, delivering him from excruciating awareness of what he is and what he was." Yet our reading of the poem, and our understanding of the man who wrote it, can only be enriched by "another, hidden meaning . . . : the patient and the doctor are the same person, who is Robinson's elder brother Dean, and the 'crime' is both euthanasia and suicide." *Dean* is the physician asking forgiveness of himself and family and friends for what he has done to end his own suffering.

Ruth Nivison articulated the biographical interpretation in her exhaustive annotations of Uncle Win's poetry: "HOW ANNANDALE WENT OUT. H. D. R. to himself—The doctor who thrice took the Keeley Cure to no avail and at length took an overdose of morphia with his hypodermic." Robinson's relatives were inclined to think that this reading was "a dark family secret." So David Nivison was startled one evening in the spring of 1953 when, in the course of a lively discussion with the Boston psychiatrist-poet Dr. Merrill Moore at the Harvard Club, the talk came around to "How Annandale Went Out." "That poem," Moore said, "is about your Uncle Dean." Dumbfounded, Nivison tried to draw Moore out further on the subject. But all he could ascertain was that EAR must have talked to Moore about it during their meetings in Boston in the early 1930s. The subject would have fascinated Moore, who took a professional interest both in the psychology of poets and the psychology of addiction.

Although EAR apparently revealed Dean's suicide to Moore, there is no evidence that he told anyone else. Even his closest friends knew little about Dean, Herman, or Emma. The outlet of poetry aside, Robinson ordinarily kept his feelings to himself. Once in a while, he would drop hints in passing. Edith Isaacs, who with her husband Lewis M. Isaacs became Robinson's friends and benefactors after 1912, remembered EAR telling her about the time his brother was struck by lightning, when they were out walking. He lay unmoving for a long time and EAR thought he was dead, but after a while, the fingers began to move.

"Poor fellow," EAR said, "he had on rubber boots."

"Was that what caused it?" Isaacs asked.

"Good gracious, no, that was what saved him for so many years of unhappy life."

The lightning strike has not been corroborated in the reminiscences of others, suggesting that it may have been invented. Robinson did not specify which brother he had in mind. Considering their misfortunes, it could have been either one.

New York, New York

In the middle of October 1899, Robinson returned to New York "maybe for six months, maybe for the rest of [his] natural life." The second "maybe" ended up closer to the mark. During his remaining thirty-six years, Robinson spent an average of more than eight months a year in New York City, usually from October through May. "There is no other place," he wrote Brower, "where I can feel easy or half comfortable. I shall eat some queer things and very likely live in a queer place, but I must have the town." The city's size and impersonality appealed to him. He wanted nothing less than "the biggest conglomeration of humanity and inhumanity that America affords."

Robinson came to New York without a job, in reduced if not yet straitened circumstances, to try to make his way in a profession notorious for not rewarding its practitioners. He arrived full of high spirits, nonetheless. If necessary, he wrote Betts cheerfully, he could "work most of [his] meals out of the ash cans that spot the landscape between Fourth and Eighth Street." The Eighth Street fare was more nourishing, he'd heard.

Robinson found a room in Washington Square but was driven out twenty-four hours later by the "familiar and irrepressible Bed Bug." Next, he secured a small box of a room at 71 Irving Place, just south of Gramercy Park, where Burnham was also in residence. The bed was too short for him, even the sheets, but everything was new, the board "particularly good for the price" and the company reasonably amiable.

"My wall decorations," he wrote Mason, "consist of a red match box and a fifty cent photograph of Beethoven for the sake of having the presence of a fellow who did things without ears." His own difficulty in hearing militated against conversation around the communal dining table, which so far as he could tell seemed to concentrate on art, the drama, and vegetarianism. On the other hand, the same poor hearing left him largely undisturbed by the "thirty-five thousand drays loaded with sheet iron" that passed every hour, as Moody humorously put it when he moved into 71 Irving Place the following year. Robinson curled his toes around the rods at the end of the bed, and slept happily in the confidence that the bedbugs had not followed him north from Washington Square. "On the whole, I am well fixed," he wrote Hays Gardiner.

In New York as nowhere else, Robinson could cultivate his tastes, and do so on the cheap. He located "a permanent dago around the corner" who would sell him three big Northern Spies for only a nickel. Often he consumed the apples in lieu of lunch. They were like the ones he had grown up on, and he didn't mind "the occasional nostalgic disturbances" they brought on. EAR was always to be afflicted, to some degree, by digestive difficulties, but he had a healthy appetite nonetheless. New York below Thirtieth Street—his New York—was full of unpretentious French, Italian, and German restaurants serving good food at reasonable prices. At Signor Bossi's in MacDougal Street, the host strode among the tables ladling minestrone out of a giant tureen and pouring wine from the cantina on his shoulder. Mouquin's, on Sixth Avenue at Twenty-sixth Street, featured admirable French cooking. Dinner with wine never cost more than fifty cents. At Riggs's, Robinson discovered he "could do very well for a quarter—provided he ha[d] faith. To him that hath shall be given, but it depends a good deal on how much he hath."

Robinson spent many evenings with the Clan. Betts was as engaging and full of the joy of life, Dr. Coan as lively and sardonic, Louis as down-at-heel and triumphant as ever. EAR kept silence until a few beers or a whiskey allowed him to join the conversation, haltingly. After half a dozen drinks, he would announce, "Now I'm up to where you people are," and talk fluently and well. He could consume vast amounts of liquor without showing ill effects. Drink had not yet become a problem.

Robinson sent Mason regular bulletins on musical performances in New York. "Last week we had the *Fourth Symphony* of Brahms," he wrote, "and it took hold of me like the jaws of something—something that never lets go." Robinson's musical tastes were catholic. In addition to Brahms, he reveled in Stephen Foster's melodies and frequented one particular saloon because the bartender could be counted on to sing a sentimental song from "The Trumpeter of Säckingen." Light opera had its appeal as well. Then there was Wagner's *Tristan und Isolde*, which he saw twice in the spring of 1900 and declared to be "the only opera, as such, ever written."

Best of all, he could work in New York. Even in Boston, once liberated from his duties at Harvard, he had been advancing his long "Pauper" poem at a healthy rate. In New York, he kept it moving and attended as well to the other poems that kept invading his consciousness. He thought optimistically in terms of publishing two books before long: *Captain Craig* and a separate volume of shorter work. "I am mighty glad to be here," he wrote Joseph Ford. "Everything goes well and I am undoubtedly working."

What lay immediately ahead, though, was an extended period of poverty and disappointment. Robinson at twenty-nine, aiming to become a professional poet, found that the culture was not ready to repay its artists. The magazines would not buy his poems. The two books he had in mind were put off for a couple of years. The last of the family money ran out. Skating close to despair, Robinson found solace in drink. "For seven years," as he said late in life, "I had ab-so-lute-ly nothing but the bottle." The bottle—and a powerful determination to do what he had been put on earth for.

New England Ways

Invariably traveling light, Robinson carried with him the standards of behavior and the habits of thought of the native New Englander—and not only a New Englander but someone born to the rockbound coasts of northern New England. "The simple needs of existence required so much labor" in that environment, Louise Bogan argued in a 1931 review, that the life of the imagination was forced underground. The Yankee's wit went dry. If he felt or thought deeply, he was wise not to let on. So Robinson—very much a son of Maine—carried himself with dignity, maintained his reserve, and balked at emotional displays.

Only rarely did he follow the path of the lyric poet and write unguardedly of himself.

Robinson's literary sensibilities manifestly derived from New England. Like Hawthorne, he borrowed from the Puritans the concept of life as a dramatic struggle between good and evil, and the habit of intensive scrutiny into human motives. Like Emerson, he felt a yearning toward transcendence that was religious without being conventional. His weaker poems, as Irving Howe observed, followed the Emersonian track. The stronger ones shared with Hawthorne "a cast of mind that is intensely serious, convinced of the irreducibility of moral problems, and devoted to nuance of motive with the scrupulosity his Puritan grandfathers had applied to nuance of theology."

One could not begin to understand the nuances of others' motives without understanding—and challenging—one's own. "The belief that we have done well does not amount to much if we cannot bring ourselves to feel that we deserve the credit," he wrote Harry Smith in March 1894. The previous day he had given some old postage stamps to a neighbor lad. "That youngster went away with a glad heart, and I felt a quiet satisfaction myself—until some devil or other made me ask myself why I did it. . . . I did it because I enjoyed it— because I was prompted to do it by some inner selfishness over which it seems that I had no control." From such a standpoint, all seeming virtuous acts must be regarded as suspect. It was not easy for Robinson to congratulate himself. He was more charitable with the people who found their way into his poems.

Robinson descended from New Englanders on both sides of the family, and on his mother's, from the Puritan leaders of the Massachusetts Bay Colony. Much Puritan rigor had vanished by the time he came of age, but the concept of the "Christian Calling" took him by the throat and never let go. The idea, as expressed by John Cotton in a famous essay, was that God assigned each of his saints—those elected for salvation—a particular calling they were to follow all their days. They were to do so not for material advantage but for the good of the community, their own spiritual well-being, and the honor and glory of God. Only in that way could they attain justification, the heartening sense that they had justified their existence here on earth, and with it the assurance that they were among the elect.

Without adopting the theological underpinnings of this doctrine, Robinson keenly felt the need for a proper calling. He felt called to a life of poetry but worried whether it constituted an acceptable vocation. According to the conflicting principle of the Protestant ethic, a man was supposed to *earn* money. To do so was itself a sign of grace, although any ostentation in *spending* it would only besmirch his accomplishment. But writing poetry was hardly likely to produce wealth.

Fortunately, the heaping up of riches was not the sole road to justification. One could also validate his existence by being of service to others. Several of Robinson's friends in high school and college chose such occupations: Gledhill and Tryon in the ministry, Smith and Ford and Latham as educators. Was poetry really a vocation of the same kind? Tryon, who read Carlyle with Robinson at Harvard, drew no basic distinction between their apparently divergent career paths. Writing after EAR had died, Tryon said that "Robinson stood for the Everlasting Yea [of Carlyle's *Sartor Resartus*] as he went forth from college into active life, Puritan like, duty bound, after pondering over the mysteries of being, to make the most of his talents." What Tryon could see, retrospectively, was not a view widely shared at the turn of the twentieth century. Robinson had been called to a vocation that possessed little value in the eyes of the world.

He did not for a moment want to escape his obligations through inhabiting a universe of the imagination, building ideal dream castles where art ruled reality. Art for art's sake seemed to him a contradiction in terms. Nor did he seek to retreat into nature. After reading Thoreau's *Walking* in 1899, Robinson denounced its "glorified world-cowardice" in a letter to Mason. "For God's sake says the sage, let me get away into the wilderness where I shall not have a single human responsibility or the first symptom of social discipline. Let me be a pickerel or a skunk cabbage or anything that will not have to meet the realities of civilization. There is a wholesomeness about some people that is positively unhealthy, and I find it in this essay."

Robinson required a commanding and fortifying purpose to guide him in the real world. For him, there could be no worthy calling that did not help others. As a poet, he might not serve as overtly as a pastor comforting parishioners or a college professor mentoring students. Nonetheless he wanted desperately to believe that by writing poetry he would do some good in the world. It did not matter if following his vocation brought him material rewards. In a sense, it was almost better that he go unrewarded, so that poetry might represent both a calling and a renunciation. Time and again, as he was shaping his career, Robinson explicitly made the link between a life of poetry and a life of service.

To Harry de Forest Smith, May 13, 1896: "If printed lines are good for anything, they are bound to be picked up some time; and then, if some poor devil feels any better or any stronger for something I have written, I shall have no fault to find with the scheme or anything in it."

To Edith Brower, April 2, 1897: "I am doing what I can for myself and a little for others; and I am very glad to know that I have been of some slight service to them. There are two or three fellows whom I have really helped. I know it; they have told me so; and their actions prove the truth of what they say. And now you—a total stranger—tell me that I have helped you. What more can I ask?"

To Josephine Preston Peabody, September 14, 1900: "I cannot, in the nature of things, help you to any great extent; but as I look back on thirty years of somewhat ridiculous existence, I find that I have helped others, and sometimes (which is the real thing) without their knowing it. And this discovery is, it seems to me, about the only thing that really counts. If I could turn about and help myself a little, I might be much better off, but my attempts in that direction just now are not altogether golden in their results."

To Craven Langstroth Betts, March 1, 1905: "It's high time that you have a few of the many things that you deserve. You deserve them so much that I wonder sometimes if you will ever get them. . . . Whatever comes you will have the satisfaction of having done things and of having been of some use in the world."

To William Stanley Braithwaite, May 1913, upon being asked whether his poetry had a message to impart: "I suppose a part of it might be described as a faint hope of making a few of us understand our fellow creatures a little better, and to realize what a small difference there is, after all, between ourselves, as we are, and ourselves, not only as we might have been but would have been if our physical and temperamental make-up and our environment had been a little different."

To Louis V. Ledoux, December 14, 1921, after the first publication of his *Collected Poems*: "Meanwhile I shall have brightened the way for a few groping wanderers without lanterns, and shall have comforted them with the assurance that, generally speaking, they haven't a damned thing to say about it. Somehow or other I suspect that my rather rickety existence has justified itself, but I don't recommend its equivalent to anyone else."

All of these remarks testify to Robinson's belief that poetry should both please and instruct. His goal was not only to delight his readers, but to give them insights into themselves and others that might lighten their way. During the long hours and days when he wasn't writing poetry, he sought to bring his own often uncanny insight to bear on the problems confronting his friends. He also gave them encouragement when needed and financial support when possible. Robinson wanted success like any other man. If he could help to mend or repair a few scattered lives in the bargain, he wanted that too.

The Climate for Poetry, 1900

New York was the right place for Robinson, the fast-growing, discordant city having supplanted staid and respectable Boston as the literary capital of the nation. But he could hardly have chosen a worse time to launch his career. It was a time, as Amy Lowell put it, "when America was given over to pretty-prettinesses of all kinds." While still languishing in Gardiner in 1894, Robinson lashed out at the popular taste of the day. *Munsey's* magazine, he observed, was ubiquitously displayed on the parlor tables of the city's prominent citizens. *Munsey's* seemed to him a magazine full of sentimental slop, lacking any redeeming virtues beyond its pictures of dogs and horses. "If the end of our century encourages such rot what will the twentieth be like?" he wondered. Then, two years later, he concentrated his fire on one of the most successful contributors. "When Mrs. Burton [Constance Cary] Harrison is the highest paid writer in the country it is time to stop and think. It is also time to stop buying magazines."

Those magazines had little use for the kind of poetry he was writing: realistic, true to life, without affectation. Their editors provided an audience for a few score "gifted singers," whose verse decorated their pages. Month after month, Robinson's poems were rejected by editors choosing instead from their choir of singers. Month after month, Robinson gagged on the archaic language and artificial sentiment of their printed offerings. Finally, in one of his earliest published poems, he let his frustration boil over.

Oh for a poet—for a beacon bright
To rift this changeless glimmer of dead gray;
To spirit back the Muses, long astray,
And flush Parnassus with a newer light;
To put these little sonnet-men to flight
Who fashion, in a shrewd mechanic way,
Songs without souls, to flicker for a day,
And vanish in irrevocable night.

What does it mean, this barren age of ours?
Here are the men, the women, and the flowers,
The seasons, and the sunset, as before.
What does it mean? Shall there not one arise
To wrench one banner from the western skies,
And mark it with his name forevermore?

Light was the answer: light to shatter the flickering grayness of the "little sonnet-men." In the last three lines, calling for a light-bringer, Robinson announced his ambition. "Shall there not one arise . . . ?"

It seemed not. The little sonnet-men, the gifted singers, "the tea-pot poets" in Whitman's phrase, carried the day. "In this period," Cary pointed out, "the keynote was a distant temple bell, the vista an incandescent twilight, the goal a castle in the air. The poetic product was hollow, torpid, exuding an air of perfumed decay." Poetry had become a parlor game for the wealthy, a suppressed instinct whose chief function was ornament, an avocation unattached to and uninterested in American life. At the forefront stood a few local colorists who touched up their portraits to remove the least imperfection: James Whitcomb Riley, Eugene Field, Edwin Markham. In the next ranks, as Richard Cary listed them, were Thomas Bailey Aldrich, Richard Henry Stoddard, Edmund Clarence Stedman, Clinton Scollard, Henry Cuyler Bunner, Madison Cawein, Henry Van Dyke, Richard Watson Gilder, Louise Imogen Guiney, Henry Underwood Johnson, Celia Thaxter, Louise Chandler Moulton, et alia. Whitman and Dickinson—and Robinson—would have to wait for recognition.

To do them justice, some of these figures detected Robinson's genius and helped him along—Stedman and Gilder, in particular. Both these men were major figures in the New York literary world in 1900. Yet they did not, themselves, write poetry worth reading. It says much about Gilder, editor of the influential *Century*, that he styled himself "the Squire of Poesy."

Both Robert Mezey and Robert Faggen, in their selections from Robinson's poetry, take a crack at Gilder. Mezey let Gilder indict himself in a few lines.

> What is a sonnet? 'T is the tear that fell
>   From a great poet's hidden ecstasy;
>   A two-edged sword, a star, a song—ah me!
> Sometimes a heavy-tolling funeral bell.

"Ah me indeed," Mezey comments, followed by the observation that "inept sonneteers [of the period] were addicted to writing sonnets about the sonnet." Faggen cites as an egregious example the conclusion of Gilder's "The Master Poets," another poem about poetry.

> O, these are they
> Who on men's hearts with mightiest power can play—
> The master poets of humanity,
> From heaven sent down to lift men to the sky.

"Whoever these poets were, are, or will be," Faggen observes, "Gilder was certainly not one of them."

To editors who fancied this sort of high-minded drool, Robinson must have seemed a creature from another planet. He wrote in meter and rhyme, to be sure, but in no other respect did he resemble the upholders of the Genteel Tradition. He was revolutionary in his diction, in his subject matter, and in his attitude toward the pieties.

Even as a child, Robinson could never see "why the language of verse should be distorted almost out of recognition in order to be poetical." He especially disliked stilted and archaic diction. Why say *thee* and *thou*, why *forsooth*, why *whilom*? Why not use the words of people talking? He was powerfully attracted to Rudyard Kipling's daring use of common speech in *Barrack-Room Ballads* (1892). Kipling was much better as a poet than as a fiction writer, he thought. In 1895, he went so far as to declare him "the greatest poet now writing English." But what English! In New York, when drinking, Robinson recited favorite passages as much for his own delight as for his companions.

> "As I was spittin' into the Ditch aboard o' the Crocodile,
> I see a man on a man-o'-war got up in the Regulars' style.

'E was scraping the paint from off of her plates an' I sez to 'im, 'Oo are you?'
Sez 'e, 'I'm a Jolly, 'Er Majesty's Jolly,—soldier an' sailor too!' "

Robinson was rarely so colloquial himself, though occasionally—as in "Isaac
and Archibald"—he captured the tone and timbre of Down East dialect. What
he learned from Kipling was that the prosaic could become the stuff of poetry
and that this principle applied to subject matter as well as to language.

There was poetry to be discovered, Robinson famously said, in all kinds of
humanity, even lawyers and horse jockeys. This dictum ran up against the prevailing aesthetic norms. According to Calvin T. Kindilien's study of American
poetry during the 1890s, the standard volume published during that decade
contained "a stereotyped title, a laudatory or self-effacing preface, a moral or
didactic poem, one discussing religion more concretely, a nature description,
a sentimental verse, one idolizing women, a humanitarian reflection, a patriotic poem, and one or more tributes to famous men." That was what readers
expected. They were unprepared for Robinson's butchers and misers, dry-goods
clerks and maiden aunts, and readers were doubtful that they belonged on
the page at all. Instead of "the tributes to famous men," Robinson paid hom-
age to Crabbe, to the dissolute Paul Verlaine ("Song sloughs away the sin to
find redress / In art's complete remembrance"), and to the naturalistic novelist
Emile Zola, who wrote about coal miners and prostitutes and was the target in
the United States of a "squeamish and emasculate crusade / Against the grim
dominion of his art."

Robinson went his own way, writing brilliantly about people on the street
and interestingly if less well about his quest for a way of thinking to live by. He
set himself a near-impossible goal: to make a living out of writing poems, and
he complicated the task by refusing to accept conventional views. As the poet
Donald Justice said, in Robinson's poems "the pieties [were] not quite in place."
Against the bedrock of moral certitude, he offered doubt. He would not reduce
the natural world to tinkling water, nor shove his characters into pigeonholes.
He was trying, as the critic Ellsworth Barnard said, "to bring poetry back into
touch with life; to take it out of the drawing room, out of the realm of hearts and
flowers, and onto drab small town streets and dusty country roads; to tell the
stories of humdrum and even sordid lives and show that these were after all the
lives of human beings; and to tell these stories in 'the real language of men.'"

The reading public was not ready for him. "Poetry was one thing and reality another. Poetry was for ladies and lady-like professors." He would have to
wait a long time for an audience. "My poetry is rat-poison to editors," he said.
There was a gap of eleven years, from 1894 to 1905, between the first and second
poems Robinson actually *sold* to magazines.

Like any beginning poet, Louis Coxe wrote, Robinson was "left to his own
resources of influence, money, self-advertisement, friends and genius. Of all

but the last two he was destitute," and his genius would barely survive the long period of neglect. He could not have persisted through those years without the inner assurance that his life had a purpose, that he had been called to poetry.

"If I could have done anything else on God's green earth, I would never have written poetry," he told a friend. "There was nothing else I could do, and I had to justify my existence."

II

City of Artists

Three Benefactors

In New York, Robinson found what Gardiner and even Boston had failed to provide: a substantial coterie of fellow artists trying to make their way in a materialistic universe. Here were people who understood what EAR wanted to do, people willing to offer him companionship and support without begrudging him a talent superior to their own. Chief among these was the beneficent Craven Langstroth Betts—to Robinson, simply "Betts."

Betts was forever joyful, forever optimistic, and like Robinson in thrall to poetry. Betts published four books of poems, much of it about remote or imaginary worlds and written in an overblown rhetoric. His taste and Robinson's could hardly have been more divergent. Nonetheless, Betts gave EAR unquestioning admiration and, at sixteen years his senior, looked after him like a benevolent older brother.

Betts functioned as Robinson's banker, for instance, cashing the checks that floated down from a rapidly vanishing estate in Maine. He also loaned Robinson small sums of money and became his most frequent dining and drinking companion. In a letter of March 15, 1900, EAR made an appointment for a night on the town with Betts that suggests their good-natured intimacy. "Say Saturday evening, if you have nothing better to do. We will have deep brained sonnets for a couple of hours, and then go out to some hellish resort for a hot scotch or a dish of beer. Why not dish of beer as well as dish of tea?"

Recognizing Robinson's yearning for friendship, Betts introduced him around among an extensive circle of acquaintances, women as well as men. One of these was Mrs. Henry Guy Carleton, the divorced wife of a playwright with a predilection for young artists. In writing about her, Betts protected Mrs. Carleton's identity while emphasizing the importance of the relationship. "A lady belonging to the fashionable set, but in poor circumstances, the wife of an irresponsible literary man who had left her with a small stipend, became much interested in Robinson, and . . . welcomed Robinson and myself frequently to

FIGURE 11.1 Craven Langstroth Betts, an "older brother" in New York.

Source: Arnold T. Schwab Papers.

her apartment. In fact, the devotion of this lady kept Robinson during this try-ing period from a despair which might have had fatal consequences."

Sometimes Betts and Robinson went together to visit "Mrs. C." Sometimes each of them went alone. It was best, they found, not to drop in without notice. Betts called on her one time, heard voices inside, and was not admitted. This bothered him a good deal, but Robinson advised forgiveness. The same thing had happened to him, he told Betts. Besides, he said, "I can't help suggesting that as long as women do not hold themselves to any particular code of honor in regard to door-bells and the like, it may be just as well not to mind their lapses." Betts simply rang her bell at the wrong time.

In the summer of 1900 and again the following year, Robinson and Betts lived together at 450 Manhattan Avenue, a few blocks from the Sixth Avenue Elevated stop at 116th Street in Harlem. The house was vacated during the hot weather by Betts's mother and aunt, and Betts invited EAR to "help him cook" while they were away. This arrangement enabled Robinson to avoid paying rent for a couple of months. It also showed him what a wonderful fellow Betts was.

As Robinson lay asleep one morning on the hospital cot provided him—he was a notoriously late riser—Betts regarded him with benign amusement. He looked like the dog in Dürer's "Melancholy," Betts told him. "Now of all [the] damned dogs that have ever been littered or sketched," EAR objected, "Dürer's is undeniably the least desirable as a prototype." After two months as Betts's housemate, Robinson concluded that "no orthodox heaven could give him more than he deserves. Almost the whole of his life has been given up to oth-ers and he is now well along on the road to fifty years old." He contrasted Betts to "the active and supposedly successful fellow who makes a lot of money and cuts his figure in Wall Street." As opposed to him, Betts "knows in his heart that he is looked upon by his friends as one condemned to mediocrity and yet goes on . . . trying to make life a little pleasanter for all the hungry-looking victims who come his way." He was nothing less than "a bald-headed angel." He ought to be "calendered" as "Saint Craven of Harlem."

The two men remained friends throughout Robinson's life. As his fortunes improved in later years, EAR was able to repay his debt to Betts several times over by presenting him with original manuscripts to sell. He dedicated *Dionysius in Doubt* (1925) to Betts and bequeathed him $1,000 in his will.

In the fall of 1899, the ebullient E. C. Stedman, promoter of all things poetic, decided, with a shove from Laura Richards, to print some of Robinson's work in his forthcoming *An American Anthology*. On July 16, 1899, writing to thank the broker-poet for including *her* poems in the anthology, Mrs. Richards pleaded Robinson's case. "His little volume, 'The Children of the Night,' seems to me of real and permanent value," she wrote. Whether influenced by this appeal or not, Stedman chose five Robinson poems to be "soused in anthological pickle": "Luke Havergal," "Ballade of Dead Friends," "The Clerks," "The Pity of the Leaves," and "The House on the Hill."

When word reached Stedman that Robinson was living to New York, he went to call on him, and "the young celibates" (as Stedman, twice EAR's age, called them) soon became friends. They made an unlikely pair, Stedman a small slender man of tremendous vitality and a playful disposition, Robinson tall and awkward and quiet.

Beginning in May 1900, Robinson began spending his Sundays visiting Stedman at his house in Bronxville. The first time he came, Stedman greeted him at the door, made a sweeping gesture toward another visitor, and announced "Torrence—and the Night After." In his role as mentor, Stedman had befriended Ridgely Torrence, whose first book of poems, *The House of a Hundred Lights*, was published in 1899. Five years EAR's junior, Torrence was tall, thin, elegant, and a splendid mimic. Hagedorn described Torrence as a "sprightly, mischievous being, [an] incarnation of youth, so individual, yet so free of pose, so fluid, so witty, so imaginative, yet so honest, and so loyal . . . a social being to his fingertips, picking adventure from every bush; a fountain of gracefully rising and falling entertainment, giving himself with careless generosity, yet, like Robinson, wholly self-sustaining; unpossessed and unpossessable." If Hagedorn was captivated by Torrence, so was Robinson. The two young poets took the train together back into the city, and stayed up until all hours talking in EAR's box of a room.

At midsummer, Laura Richards intervened once more on Robinson's behalf with Stedman. The manuscript of EAR's *Captain Craig* had come back from Scribner's, and Richards wanted Stedman to encourage Robinson to submit it elsewhere. And also, if he were feeling well and could spare the time, to write her "a line about the book itself" that she could pass on to other houses. Mrs. Richards had, obviously, become Robinson's most dedicated advocate. As she wrote Stedman, "he is a kind of adopted son of mine, and a very dear one."

FIGURE 11.2 Edmund Clarence Stedman, poet, anthologist, adviser.

Source: Picture Collection, New York Public Library.

Stedman did not advance the cause of *Captain Craig*, a poem not to his taste. But he continued to entertain Robinson on Sunday afternoons and to suggest ways that he might support himself. Even to Stedman, the concept of a poet actually making a living out of poetry seemed outrageous. Poetry might be a man's calling, but he could not expect it to pay. For a livelihood, he would have to find a peripheral field that actually paid. Do library work, like Torrence at the New York Public, or teach in universities, like William Vaughn Moody, or edit magazines and put together anthologies, as Stedman did once he'd abandoned Wall Street. Then there was freelance journalism, and this was what he had in mind for Robinson.

"My chief recreation," Robinson wrote Dan Mason late in August, "is riding to Bronxville on Sundays and consuming Mr. Stedman's tobacco." Stedman was not well, and his doctor would not allow him to smoke. Yet despite his illness, EAR wrote, Stedman "keeps up a show of cheerfulness and really likes to have all sorts of damned things come to see him." They took walks together and talked of farming and art and how EAR might support himself. Stedman was well connected with the leading daily newspapers and gave Robinson letters to present to the editors of the *Times* and the *Post* and the *Tribune*. The idea was that EAR should write short pieces for the editorial pages: not necessarily about politics or the news of the day, but "fourth leaders"—witty and entertaining observations on almost any subject.

From August to October 1900, Robinson attempted to establish himself as a contributor to these dailies. He fashioned a number of articles that he thought might do. Only a few titles survive: "Puns," "Sophisticated Reader," "Friendship and Reason," "Peaches and Ether." The articles tended to run rather long for newspapers, up to 1,200 words, but he assured Stedman that at least they seemed to amuse Betts. Armed with these submissions and an introductory letter from Stedman, Robinson went to call on the city's leading editors. They returned his work as "almost but not quite good enough."

Stedman told Robinson that he was the victim of bad luck. If editor A at the *Post* had seen "Peaches and Ether" instead of editor B, he would have taken it at once. Conversely, B would undoubtedly have bought "Puns," which did not appeal to A. The thing to do was to keep trying. "In fact, if I were in your place," Stedman advised, "I would write etc. to leading dailies, *and weeklies*, until I made a breach somewhere, then the woods will open amazingly."

Robinson followed this advice, but his efforts yielded only one actual publication: an unsigned editorial titled "The Balm of Custom" in the *New York Daily Tribune* for Sunday, October 7, 1900. The piece satirized the supporters of William Jennings Bryan, the Democratic candidate for president. With the election looming, the topic was a timely one, and its message fit nicely into the Republican leanings of the *Tribune*. Robinson's basic theme was that Democrats could be expected to vote for Bryan not because they believed in him and his fiscal policies but simply because they had gotten used to him (he had run in 1896 as well) and were no longer afraid of him as a novelty. "Custom has so staled [Bryan's] infinite monotony that he does not seem to them to be half so dangerous as he used to be." Whether the *Tribune*'s readers caught the Shakespearean allusion to Cleopatra's "infinite variety" may be in doubt. Robinson's style, as Betts put it, "was not in keeping with the downright quality of a newspaper editorial."

The woods did not open amazingly, or at all. "The Balm of Custom" represented the beginning and the end of EAR's newspaper career. "I confess I looked forward to some financial recognition," Robinson told an interviewer in 1931. "They paid me"—a slight pause—"$4.25."

In Gardiner, the Richards paper mill was sold to a larger firm and then closed down, leaving Henry Richards unemployed. As a means of support, he decided to start a summer camp for boys—Camp Merryweather—in the Belgrade Lakes, with the considerable aid of his wife and children. Mrs. Richards made no mention of these setbacks in her letters to Robinson: she was too busy trying to cheer him up. The letters he wrote her from this period are gone, destroyed at his request. In them, as she recalled, "*gloom* was the prevailing note: self-dissection, self-analysis, self-depreciation." To Mason and Peabody and Brower, EAR wrote witty and engaging letters. To Laura Richards, he denigrated himself as a "half-man" and wondered how she or anyone could think well of him. In reply, she chided him to think more *of* himself and less *about* himself. But "the first motive" of her letters was "trying to convince him that the sun continued to shine." She cited his own words against him:

It is the crimson, not the gray,
   That charms the twilight of all time.

It is the promise of the day
  That makes the stormy night sublime.

The quatrain came from "The Children of the Night," the poem that gave Robinson's 1897 book its title. Twenty years later, when time came to choose what would go into his *Collected Poems*, he cut the poem. It is easy to see why. Much as Mrs. Richards might have approved the quoted lines, their easy affirmation rubbed against the grain of Robinson's experience. More important, their preachy didacticism sounded like the worst of the prettified verse he was rebelling against. They might have been written by Richard Watson Gilder himself.

Despite their different sensibilities, Robinson and Mrs. Richards conducted an amiable correspondence for more than thirty years. On a personal level, Robinson disparaged himself, and she bucked him up. But he did not reveal his innermost troubles, or complain of poverty. More than anything else they wrote about books and their authors. She sent him a subscription to the *Spectator* each year. Only once, early on, did he erupt into anger.

The dispute involved Seth Ellis Pope, Robinson's Quadruped companion and worshipful admirer. With Mrs. Richards's endorsement, Pope had landed a job teaching at the Highland Avenue Grammar School in Gardiner. But he proved unequal to the task, for he could not control the unruly boys under his charge. When she wrote Robinson that Pope had been let go, EAR erupted. The letter nearly burnt the paper, Rosalind Richards remembered. In it, Robinson damned Pope's dismissal as a case of social injustice. He must have been fired

FIGURE 11.3 Robinson in hat given him by Mrs. Richards, ca. 1900.

Source: Colby College Special Collections.

"because he was poor, because his clothes were shabby, etc." Mrs. Richards calmly responded that Pope's failure had nothing to do with his clothes. After a while EAR's wrath subsided.

To the Richards family, Pope seemed a nearly hopeless case. Robinson had brought Pope along to the Yellow House on one of his first visits. He struck Mrs. Richards at once as "an underdog, gently timid, adoring 'The Man' as he called E. A., clinging to him, looking to him for strength, for initiative, for everything that he himself had not." Yet Pope was clearly intelligent—he'd graduated from Bowdoin—and he was one of Gardiner's own, so after the school-teaching fiasco, Mrs. Richards set about finding a career for him. She and her husband and Hays Gardiner concluded that Pope was probably best fitted for library work. After consulting with EAR and Pope himself about this plan, they formed a small consortium to send him to library school in Albany.

Armed with a library qualification, Pope married a divorcée named Florence Peltier. She was a writer herself, who published on Japanese manners and culture. They moved to New York in due course, after Pope landed a job at the Brooklyn Public Library. Robinson spent many weekends with the Popes in Brooklyn, generally without disclosing his whereabouts to his literary companions in Manhattan. This practice led to rumors about possible love affairs. When the marriage broke up, Robinson moved to Pope's apartment in Brooklyn and stayed there until his friend died years later. Robinson modeled the character of Killigrew, in *Captain Craig*, on Pope, and never forgot the compliment Pope paid him by reading the entire two thousand lines of the poem, in manuscript, at one sitting. He was to be, always, EAR's "homespun, uncouth, loving friend and disciple."

The Mason Triangle

In a very real sense, Robinson's friends took the place of wife and family. "I shall always have friends enough—there's a fate that seems to take care of that," he wrote in August 1899, "but I shall never see the day when mosquitos will settle on the neck of one of them if I am anywhere in reach." He gave his friends unswerving loyalty and did everything in his power to be of service to them. His efforts to smooth their path were closely related to his sense of the calling conferred on him. To justify himself, he had to help others. It was only natural for him to rise in wrath when he imagined poor Pope under attack. In a similar spirit, he made himself of use to Dan Mason.

That the two men came from entirely different backgrounds did not trouble EAR in the least. He could and did befriend the rusticated and downtrodden Pope every bit as easily as the well-bred and cultivated Mason. At the same time, though, he understood that the two of them would not mix well and began the lifelong process of compartmentalizing his friends: bohemians of Coan's Clan in one segregated group of acquaintances, Harvard-trained artists in another, companions from Gardiner in a third, elegant and well-to-do New Yorkers in a fourth. He did not introduce Betts to Moody, or Pope to Louis Ledoux. Some of those from different compartments were startled to learn of one another's existence after EAR died.

Dan Mason underwent a personal crisis during 1900 and 1901, even as Robinson was struggling against poverty and obscurity. Their "common misfortune" brought them together, Mason said, along with the uncanny parallel between the emotionally charged triangular relationships both men faced. In living vicariously through Mason's crisis, Robinson revisited his own.

Daniel Gregory Mason fell in love with Mary Mason, his older brother Edward's wife. She reciprocated his feeling, but divorce was not lightly undertaken at the time. As the apparent injured party, Edward seemed unlikely to cooperate. For Mary to leave him and marry his brother would cause a social scandal. At the very least, she and Dan would have to leave Boston. Then, as with Emma and Herman, there were children and custody to consider, and the terribly important question whether Dan could make a living to support them and still continue his work as a composer. Similar issues had run through Robinson's mind as he contemplated the possibility of marrying Emma.

In the spring of 1900 Mason issued a two-part invitation to Robinson. EAR could come to see him in Boston, or he could join a July gathering with Edward and Mary, and with Josephine Peabody and Will Moody, at Falmouth on Cape Cod. The second was the more daring alternative. Like all lovers, Dan and Mary needed to see each other, and the presence of their poet friends during a family vacation made doing so seem more acceptable. Robinson, who had just moved to Harlem with Betts, decided to stay in New York. The sea waves had a mighty attraction to someone who could see nothing from his window "more sparkling than Grant's Tomb," he acknowledged, but he had "an exceptionally good opportunity to go on with some work": the re-creation of "Aunt Imogen," begun two years earlier in Gardiner. He was also in the midst of his extended campaign to place *Captain Craig* with a publisher.

In August, Mason and Moody went off on a working vacation at the house of Truman H. Bartlett in Chocorua, New Hampshire. Bartlett, father of a famous sculptor, was a genuine eccentric who liked to give young artists a leg up when they were still unappreciated by the public. In a letter to Robert Morss Lovett, Moody called him "a magnificent old goat." In person, Moody and Mason referred to him as "Pere Bartlett," the title quite inadequate to convey (in Mason's description) "his skittish independence and unconventionality, his gusto in denunciation of servile respectability, his boyish zest in profanity and in the wildest exaggerations. . . . There was about him always something of the free air, the untrammelled good nature, of his intimate friend Walt Whitman." Robinson was fascinated by what he heard of Bartlett. Ten years later, he too would be Bartlett's guest during the summer season.

Dan and Mary Mason's affair intensified after his return to Boston. Soon, he felt, he would have to do something about it, and Robinson was one of those he gravitated toward for counsel. Mason was impressed by EAR's "half serene, half humorous detachment from his surroundings, the long stride and quizzical smile with which he walked through all incongruities." He also respected his patience in the face of repeated disappointment. "The great art of life," Robinson had told him, "is to suffer without worrying." Finally, Mason wrote EAR a painfully frank letter about his dilemma, then admitted that he could not bring himself to put it in the mail.

In response, Robinson expressed his eagerness to help however he could:

> In regard to the long letter which you wrote but did not send there is nothing for me to say except that if any suggestion of mine, or any safety valve of sympathy, can be of any worth to you, it is always ready. I have supposed that things were somewhat snarled with you, but of course I have not carried my supposition any farther than that. I appreciate your confidence in me, and I want you to know it; and at the same time I ask you to believe that I have always had a good deal of sympathy—more or less vague, but still of what I may call the solid sort, with your ambitions to do what you were born to do and with your difficulties of which you say so little.

In his patent appeal for Mason to unburden himself, written at the end of December 1900, Robinson emphasized the interconnection between the artist's ambitions, and the "difficulties"—emotional or economic or whatever—of leading his life.

Six weeks later, Mason came to New York to spend five days with EAR. They drank highballs together and talked of their careers. Mason was working on a trio, and Robinson praised the first movement as a work of genius. If Mason could keep up the pace, he wrote Josephine Peabody, "he will be not only heard from but heard—which is quite another thing." On this visit, Mason spoke openly about the family triangle and discovered in Robinson someone who could understand and relate to the problem he faced. EAR sent him back to Boston feeling much more sprightly than when he arrived. In his journal, Mason noted: "February 9–14. Visit to New York. The beginning of my deeper friendship with Robinson."

With the passage of another six weeks, Mason's personal crisis reached a climax. At Harvard, he consulted the "incomparably sympathetic and wise" Josiah Royce about what to do. Royce advised him to go away for a time, and see if distance might serve as a remedy. In Paris, he suggested, Mason could compose music in an ideal artistic ambience. When he returned, if he and Mary still felt the same, they could seek a confrontation with Edward. Before making his decision, Mason consulted Robinson as well, and received from him a letter of "clairvoyant sympathy" exhibiting "his insight into poetic truth." In addressing Mason's situation, Robinson had much to say about his own. The entire letter—and it is a long one—appears below.

29 East 22nd Street,
March 26, 1901

Dear Mason,

I don't want you to go anywhere with the idea of giving up anything, but I can't help telling you that Royce's advice seems to me to be the wisest you could receive just now. If you go to Paris you will have at least the satisfaction of knowing that you have made a definite move in the matter and the probabilities are that you will not find the separation so hard to bear as you think now that it must be. And then again, the very question of test and probation, or whatever you choose to call it, comes to me now in the light of something like a duty. You will say to yourself that I am thinking only of you, perhaps, and I assure you that I do not forget that there is the other and that it is more on her account than on yours (you will not misunderstand me) that I hesitate at all in advising you to go away at once. The man can always get along somehow, and the woman knows it; and in this case, I doubt if there is any real question in her mind as to her own belief that she can do the same. It is easy, of course, for me to say all this; but I cannot be quite honest and say anything else. When two people are sure of each other, as you are, perhaps it is not so much a question of what one of you can bear as it is of how the other is going to suffer while he is bearing it; and when it comes to a solution of this difficulty I suppose there is nothing better or less emotional to be said than that she must look on it as the price she has to pay for the right to believe in the possibility of a great happiness. As things are going, I find it utterly impossible to disagree with Royce; and as I am sure that both of you agree with him I can only hope that you will be able [to] make the change without losing any of your courage or your faith. There is no reason why you should lose either; on the contrary, there is every reason why you should have new surroundings for a time and a better opportunity for new ideas. You know by this time that there is a good deal of the brute in the artist, and you know it is chiefly to him that I am appealing when I venture to remind you of the other side of the question at a time when you are not expecting this sort of treatment from a friend. What I am most afraid of in your case is that you are in danger of forgetting that even the most hellish of human complexities are not to be considered too bitterly in the beginning. We cannot measure anything until we have seen it through; and I am sure that she will be willing to make this trial if you are, and to do all she can for you and for herself. God knows it is a bad business at the best—bad, I mean, as we see things—but I believe that some definite measure like this that you are contemplating will end in making the whole thing clearer. If you will put away all thoughts of hopelessness and start out with thoughts of strength and faith, she will do the same. And this, as I see it, is all that either of you can do just now. As there is no immediate solution possible, you must have courage to do what you believe to be the wisest thing, no matter how hard it may seem at first. If you make up your mind to do it, you will soon find a kind of joy in the sheer intensity of the immediate sacrifice and another in the consciousness that you have not only a moral but an artistic ideal to live for. You must remember, even when it seems almost like selfishness to do so, that your art is to be the concrete expression of your life. If you are loyal to that, you cannot be disloyal to yourself; for all of your largest ideas have come from this new life, which you think just now to contain nothing but unhappiness. Refuse for once and all to measure anything by the moment and you will realize before long that the picture will take on new colors—and brighter ones. This, again, is easy enough to say.

Personally, I shall be sorry to have you go—but of course there is no need of my telling you this. Thank you very much for the photograph, which is remarkably good. I am glad to have it.—I am sorry that I cannot be of more service to you—but you understand all that.

Always sincerely yours
E. A. R.

All this is horribly "preachy," but I won't try to improve matters by saying the same thing in a different way. This pen is particularly damnable, also.

R.

In this letter of "profound spiritual understanding," Robinson addresses three issues that he knew must have been weighing on Mason's mind, as they were on his own. He had, after all, left Emma Robinson behind to face her problems alone while he pursued his life's work. (It is hard to imagine that Robinson, after hearing out Mason, did not reveal the similar triangle in his own family. But nothing in his letter, and nothing in what Mason subsequently wrote about the affair, hints at any such revelation.)

Would not going away mean that Mason was giving up the love of his life? Not at all, EAR argues. The separation might put that love to the test, but since they were sure of each other it would surely pass the test.

Would not his departure impose an intolerable burden on Mary Mason? Possibly, but this was both unjust and unavoidable. She must look on it as "the price" not of their future happiness together but "for the right to believe in the possibility" of that happiness.

Four days later, after word arrived that Mason was going to take Royce's (and Robinson's) advice and go abroad, EAR expanded on the point in a letter to Josephine Peabody. The affair was a pretty bad one, he wrote, but he could not justify advising Mason to break it off entirely. "It is almost brutal of me to say so, but I believe a year or two of exile will prove in the end to be a benefit to him, but what the exile will be to her I don't know. Sometimes it looks to me like one of those cases where the woman is fated to pay for the man's salvation, but then I remember that I am not wholly indifferent to melodrama. . . . If there were anything under heaven that I could do, I should have the most selfish sort of pleasure in doing [it]; but as it is, I can only look on and hope."

What effect would the separation have on Mason's career as an artist? Here Robinson seems to be addressing himself as well as Mason. Leaving would not only be the right "moral" decision but might well represent a good thing for his art as well. He should not forget that his art was to be "the concrete expression" of his life. And, hellish though his emotional trouble might be, it had already–in Mason's music as in Robinson's poetry—produced some of his "largest ideas." As artists, they must refuse "to measure anything by the moment." In the long run, the darkness might well lead to light. Though he did not quite say so, Robinson implied that the demands of art should outweigh those of love.

Mason's exile lasted only a few months, not a few years. By early July, Mason was back in Boston, once again inviting Robinson to come north for "part of the sweltering season." Once again EAR declined, having already committed to occupy the flat in Harlem with Betts. But he continued to worry about the Masons' difficulties, not the least of them financial.

Writing Josephine Peabody early in September, he admitted that he knew very little about "the question of dollars," but felt certain it was an important consideration.

> If D. and M. . . . can get along and keep their share of the bewildered offspring, and if the impressionable Edward can be persuaded not to do a new "turn" oftener than once in six months or so, I see no reason why the affair may not be settled. The children might well be sent away to school for the greater part of the time—if there is money to send them—and by this means our unfortunate friends might have a chance to breathe and be happy. I have never felt entirely sure about the happiness, no matter how free they might be—but of course this is horribly confidential and none of my business. All I think I know is, if things keep on as they are their lives will [be] ruined; and this is why I am unable to see anything attractive in any half way measures.

Here Robinson ventured a solution for Dan and Mary Mason that he had been unable to find for himself and Emma: that in order to avoid ruining their lives, they should "breathe and be happy" together. Confidentially, though, he harbored doubts about that happiness. The doubts were caused, at least in part, by the conflict Robinson envisioned between the artist and the husband. To reach his goals, he felt, the artist must totally commit himself to his work and, inevitably, neglect his obligations to wife and family. Was it right to marry and force a wife to share the costs of poverty and discouragement? What if the artist achieved nothing remarkable, so that the sacrifices were made to no purpose? And what if success did finally come, but too late? He addressed the issue in a poem first called "The Wife of Palissy," then "Partnership."

A sixteenth century French potter, Palissy spent sixteen impoverished years looking for the secret of white enamel. He sacrificed everything during his long quest, even feeding his kiln with the household furniture, before finally achieving success. Longfellow wrote a poem, "Keramos," celebrating the artist's victory. As Robinson embarked on his own writing career in 1893, he quoted Longfellow's lines in his support.

> Tomorrow the hot furnace-flame
> Will search the heart and try the frame,
> And stamp with honor or with shame
>   These vessels made of clay.

His work too would "go into the oven before long," he wrote Harry Smith. He hoped that his vessels would be stamped with honor.

When he transformed Palissy's tale into poetry eight years later, Robinson told the story from the standpoint of the potter's wife. In "Partnership," a dramatic monologue, she speaks from her deathbed as her husband presents—at last—the gleaming evidence of his ceramic triumph. Ah, yes, it is beautiful, she agrees.

> Lift it where the beams are bright;
> Hold it where the western light,
> Shining in above my bed,
> Throws a glory on your head.
> Now it is all said.

But she has had a hard time of it through the years, toiling and weeping, "clashing and unreconciled." Having shared the sacrifices, she has no energy left to share the victory.

> But the clashing is all past,
> And the gift is yours at last.
> Lift it—hold it high again! . . .
> Did I doubt you now and then?
> Well, we are not men.
>
> Never mind; we know the way,—
> And I do not need to stay.
> Let us have it well confessed:
> You to triumph, I to rest.
> That will be the best.

By the spring of 1902, the Masons had settled on a course of action. Mary Mason and her children separated from Edward and moved to New York. Dan took a job at Princeton and came to the city often. Robinson saw a lot of both of them during the two succeeding years. During the summer of 1903, Mary Mason kindly loaned him the use of her room at 500 W. 121st Street while she went to Connecticut and Long Island. The room was vastly more spacious and comfortable than anything he was used to. Sending her a copy of *Hedda Gabler* in gratitude, he headed his note "Pisgah," as in Mount Pisgah, where Moses was taken to view the Promised Land.

The Masons' story had a happy ending. By the spring of 1904 Mary's break with Edward must have become final, for Robinson, mindful of the proprieties, began addressing letters to her as "Mrs. Mary L. Mason" instead of "Mrs. Edward P. Mason." She and Dan were married on October 8, 1904, and set up housekeeping with her two younger children, while two older boys attended boarding school. Mason wrote Robinson a letter announcing the news and thanking him for his part in making it possible.

EAR would have none of it. He was naturally delighted to know that Dan had "wrestled with [his] worst difficulties, and beaten them. . . . If ever two people deserved to be happy in this life, I know who they are." He was also pleased that Mason thought of him "as a good friend through it all," but would take no credit for the outcome. "I am . . . at a loss to know what in the name of Jehosophat and the Delectable Mountains I have ever done, or what I have even been able to suggest," he wrote. "Beyond the honor of your confidence, I have [had] no part in the clearing up of one of the worst tangles that the gods and devils ever delighted themselves with."

Circling Moody

No one attending Class Day at Harvard in June of 1893 could have been in doubt about the identity of the university's fair-haired young poet. There he was on the platform, reciting the Class Day poem: William Vaughn Moody, son of an Indiana riverboat captain come east to dazzle everyone in Cambridge. E. A. Robinson watched with a trace of envy as the glamorous Moody, entirely at ease, captivated his audience. Only six months older than he, Moody had leaped years ahead in the race for recognition.

Moody was one of those rare creatures who did everything well. As an undergraduate, he edited the esteemed *Harvard Monthly* and began publishing his poetry in leading national magazines. He finished his course work in three years, graduating second in his class. During his senior year, he tramped around Europe in charge of a young pupil, returning in time for graduation. Moody planned to stay at Harvard for a few years, studying medieval philology and assisting Lewis E. Gates, Robinson's favorite English professor. He could look forward to the brightest of futures.

After Mason's graduation in 1895, he and Moody embarked on a summer walking trip in Europe. Mason regarded Moody worshipfully, celebrating "the fascination of [his] imagination-releasing figures of speech, his fertile silences, his irresponsible humor, comical slang, and shouting gusto of laughter, his deep, contagious sense of the infinite mystery and richness of life." "Lover of Life," Mason called him.

Maurice F. Brown, Moody's biographer, noted the striking differences between Moody and Robinson. In personality, Moody "was spontaneous and emotional, 'florid and careless' in dress, with a 'barbaric taste for extravagance in waistcoats' . . . while Robinson tended to be quiet and self-conscious. Robinson's sensitivity to the potential misery and the quiet ironies of human experience were balanced by Moody's buoyant enthusiasm and his love of the grand and dramatic." In poetry, the contrast only intensified. "Where Robinson understated, Moody overstated. Where Robinson found pathos and irony, Moody found vibrant passion or heroic drama. Where the surface of Robinson's poetry was matter-of-fact, that of Moody's was richly sensuous or emotional. Where Robinson's diction was plain, Moody's was luxuriant."

Despite these differences the two men respected each other and became friends. Moody initiated their meeting after *The Children of the Night* was published. By that time, Moody was teaching at the University of Chicago. "Note what you say of Robinson with interest," Moody wrote Mason in May 1898. "Do not know his work. Wish you could get me a line of introduction from some friends."

The following year, Mason arranged a meeting of the two poets. Their friendship developed during the period from 1899 through 1901 when Moody was enjoying a great vogue and Robinson could sell nothing at all, either to magazine editors or book publishers.

In his correspondence, EAR consistently disparaged himself in contrast to the widely talented Moody. In August 1899, for example, Robinson wrote Moody how poorly equipped he was for even the most menial tasks. He couldn't be "a motor-man," for he was too absent-minded and might bowl over prominent citizens. He might possibly be capable of operating a newsstand and he'd thought of finding "some sort of useful occupation in the Morgue," where he wouldn't have to talk to everyone who came in. Moody possessed a "chronic ability to make [a] living," and he did not. Moody could do the world's work, he told Mason, because he had a brain. As for himself, he was "simply incomplete, and made up . . . of what must have been left over after the manufacture of some sixteen or seventeen fellows."

When it came to poetry itself, however, Robinson was less inclined to adopt a stance of self-deprecation. In letters to Dan Mason, Josephine Peabody, Edith Brower, Hays Gardiner, and Moody himself, Robinson frequently commented on Moody's work as it emerged on the pages of national magazines and books. His usual practice was to praise Moody's work, then to qualify the praise with reservations.

Moody's "Ode in Time of Hesitation," which appeared in the *Atlantic Monthly* in the spring of 1900, provided an interesting example of this process in operation. Moody's poem caused a considerable stir by rebuking the policy of "Manifest Destiny" that led the United States to occupy the Philippines. Dan Mason alerted Robinson to Moody's "magnificent" work in advance of publication, and Robinson responded before actually reading it. "I am glad to know that Moody has written another poem but I am sorry that he calls it an ode. . . . I could no more get together a poem on the Philippines than I could write a description of the human brain."

Two weeks later, having read the poem, Robinson wrote Moody about it directly. "You have done a stunning piece of work and you have done it in the spirit of the new age . . . and you have proved a modern ode to be a possibility," EAR observed. "By some diabolical method of your own you have written a political tract in the form of a romantic sermon, and you have kept the 'tune' going from beginning to end." He had, though, a few objections. It seemed to him that Moody had tangled up the geography somewhat and that in his "apparent determination to be commonplace" he had communicated "a passing suggestion of self-consciousness." But no matter. Moody had captured exactly how EAR felt when he looked at the Shaw memorial in Boston, and this inclined Robinson to believe he was "a genius—more or less."

Moody prefaced his ode with the note: "(After seeing at Boston the statue of Robert Gould Shaw, killed while storming Fort Wagner, July 18, 1863, at the head of the first enlisted negro regiment, the 54th Massachusetts)." The statue, by Augustus Saint-Gaudens, along with the valor of Gould and his men, was evoked again in one of the twentieth century's most famous poems, Robert Lowell's "For the Union Dead."

EAR followed this letter with another a week later, retracting his "idiotic remarks" on the way Moody dealt with American geography. He had read the poem carefully now, and declared it to be *"big," "even bigger"* than he'd thought at first glance. The adjective (italicized for emphasis) was one Robinson frequently used in describing Moody and his accomplishments. *Big* though he might be, Robinson could not resist adding that Moody sometimes seemed "given to what [Hays] Gardner call[ed] an 'occasional affectation of the vocabulary' ": to showing off, in other words.

In September 1900, when Moody's "Gloucester Moors" came out, Robinson told Mason he liked it "better than [Moody's] more splendiferous ode." The same message went to Moody, sort of. "You have done it this time with a bang," EAR wrote him, "but . . ." and there followed a spate of criticism every bit as harsh as that he was leveling at Josephine Peabody during this same period. The last three verses of the first stanza were "just a little too 'creative,' " he wrote Moody. He disliked Moody's "use of archaic monstrosities like 'lifteth' [and] 'doth,' " pointing out correctly that "ten years from now this sort of thing will not be tolerated." The phrase "like a gallant gallant ship" struck him "as a trifle sophomoric."

Robinson's criticisms, he understood, might seem offensive, but where artistic questions were concerned, he felt an obligation to speak out. Moody received his judgments in the same spirit. An honest and expert critique was worth a dozen unthinking eulogies. There was a climate of mutual respect between them, just as there was between Robinson and Josephine Preston Peabody. The difference was that both Moody and Peabody were being welcomed into the literary world while Robinson was not.

In the first decade of the new century, Moody was to publish seven volumes—books of poetry, plays, and even, in 1902, *A History of English Literature* coauthored with his Harvard friend Robert Morss Lovett: an enormous undertaking by two men barely thirty years old. In 1906, Moody's play *The Great Divide* became a hit on Broadway. In 1908, Yale gave him an honorary degree, and he was elected to the American Academy of Arts and Letters. All auspices pointed to Moody as a major figure, perhaps the major figure, of his generation. Then he was unexpectedly taken ill and died in October 1910, at the age of forty-one.

In the fall of 1900 Moody came to New York for a few months, and the two young poets saw a great deal of each other. EAR called on Moody in his quarters on West Twelfth Street, and Moody visited EAR in Yonkers, where he was boarding with two kind-hearted old ladies. They took several-mile walks together along the Hudson between Yonkers and Riverdale, where fellow Harvard man Fullerton Waldo played his viola for them. They talked enthusiastically of their work in progress and got along extremely well, yet there inevitably remained a vestige of rivalry between them. Robinson was torn between admiration of Moody's victories and the frustration of his own hopes. He did not wish Moody ill. He simply wanted a few crumbs of recognition for himself.

"My friend Moody has just published *The Masque of Judgment*, which I want you to read," Robinson wrote Edith Brower on 10 November 1900. He promised to let Brower look at his unbound copy as soon as Betts was through reading it. "I have been reading the *Masque*, and I call it a *pretty big thing*," he wrote Peabody late in November. "But I don't know how many will make anything more of it than a general attack on traditional theology," Early in December, EAR wrote Gardiner that he was seeing Moody once or twice a week and thought him "likely to do *something big*. In one way he has done it in the Masque," which had "*the big quality*" about it. In a Christmas day letter to Peabody, he went further, declaring the *Masque* to be "really great." He took comfort from the fact that it was "so ridiculously different" from his *Captain Craig* as to rule out odious comparisons.

Early in the new year Robinson wrote Mary Mason that he thought Moody had written the greatest American verse since Emerson. He also let Moody— now returned to Chicago—know that he'd read the *Masque* again and thought it "*one of the big things* in literature." Moody, who had felt Robinson's lash, replied with gratitude. "What you said gave me the deepest—joy, I was going to say; but

FIGURE 11.4 The star-crossed William Vaughn Moody, October 1906.

Source: Photo by Daniel Gregory Mason.

remembering your distrust of exuberant language, I will say satisfaction. Still, it was joy, all the same—the feeling was exuberant enough to warrant, this once, my florid vocabulary."

In the same letter, Moody fondly recalled their recent encounters in New York. "I like to hark back and mouse dreamily over . . . those walks we had from Riverdale to Yonkers, especially the last one." It may have been during that walk that the two of them had a moment of quiet confrontation. "I'll never forget it," EAR told Torrence later. They had walked a long time in silence, when he turned to look at Moody and found Moody looking back at him. "We were watching each other. He wanted to know what I was up to, and I wanted to know what he was up to."

When Robinson repeatedly referred to Moody's "bigness," he had in mind a number of things, chief among them the application of his rhetorical gifts to ambitious subject matter. Moody was writing about American imperialism abroad ("Ode in a Time of Hesitation") and the justification of man to God (*The Masque of Judgment*), while Robinson in everyday language was finishing poems about a maiden aunt invited once a year to entertain the children ("Aunt Imogen") and a penniless derelict savant (*Captain Craig*), topics that were large only in the compassion and conviction he brought to them.

Then too, Moody qualified as "big" because of his ability to succeed in a variety of fields: as a student and then a professor, as a poet and playwright, as a scholar-author mastering all of English literature. Robinson had no such versatility, and he knew it. As he told Harry Smith: "If I were a *big* man, I should do this and that—manufacture ten-penny nails and get into the common council, and in my old age with a competence and plenty of time, I should write and study Spanish. The *big* men can do this, perhaps, but I can't."

Poetry was, at best, an unaccredited profession, but Robinson stuck to it when it would have been easy to quit, investing all his energy in one direction, and he became a master. As a craftsman, Robinson was more than big enough to warrant Moody's glance. The two of them circled each other warily, in a spirit of shared admiration and unspoken rivalry.

Still, Robinson was unable—even after their bonding in the fall of 1900—to praise his friend without qualification. "Moody is beyond doubt the coming man," he wrote Brower in January 1901. With the *Masque* published and a book of poems on its way from Houghton Mifflin, "he can hardly fail to take something like the place he deserves; and beyond all this he is a rattling good fellow." Then, though, EAR launched into a series of reservations. Moody was "a jaynius, and he will be a good deal more of a jaynius when he really finds himself—sometime in the course of five to ten years." Moody had not entirely grown up, EAR went on, but "he will indubitably be making *a big noise* in very short order." Robinson wanted to be the first to let Brower know about Moody: "I like to pose once in a while as a prophet." Unpacking these brief quotations, it is interesting to note that EAR could not bring himself to designate Moody as a "genius" plain and simple, that he once more invoked the "big" metaphor, and that he tempered his critique with an irrelevant observation about what a "good fellow" Moody was. Robinson went through similar steps in writing Hays Gardiner: began with praise, segued into adverse commentary, and softened the effect by describing Moody as "one of the most human and attractive of mortals."

There was nothing underhanded or ill-spirited in Robinson's remarks—or in his nature, for that matter. What he would say about Moody to others, he said to Moody directly. In May 1901, when Houghton Mifflin, with considerable fanfare, brought out Moody's *Poems*, EAR congratulated him at once. "I believe that you, with your extraordinary powers of expression, have it in you to give American literature a new meaning for the new century." Then he proceeded to observe that there was "too much color and not enough light" in Moody's work. He was "*too big*," EAR cautioned, to indulge in purple passages. One poem had about it the aura of "p.r.": public relations. The phrase, "by God's ring-finger stirred," he thought "really damnable."

Having delivered himself of these judgments, Robinson said—and meant it—that his acquaintance with Moody was "one of the things that make life worth while." Because he knew EAR was motivated by fidelity to the highest standards of craftsmanship, Moody was not offended by his criticisms. Because he knew Robinson would not fawn or flatter, words of praise from him meant all the more. Besides, he was one of the first to recognize Robinson's genius. "Well," Moody told Mason, "[EAR] can afford to be generous."

Before long, Moody was to do Robinson a number of favors to advance his career, and whatever "faint periodic jealousy" Robinson may have felt for the brilliant Moody vanished. Given ten years of tolerably decent existence, EAR told Mason, he thought Moody capable of producing "almost anything." "When we're all dead and buried," Moody told Torrence, "E. A. will go thundering down the ages."

12

The Saga of Captain Craig

The Work in Progress

Captain Craig began germinating as early as 1894, when Robinson jotted down, "in a lighter vein," a prose sketch "of a philosophic tramp . . . looking for rest." In the same year, he discovered an approach for his long poem in Anatole France's *Crime de Sylvester Bonnard*, a book written as the "*journal intime*" of an old savant given to eccentric digressions. The role was already taking shape in EAR's mind when he came to New York in 1897 and beheld in the flesh the one man in the world best suited for the part: the tattered and oracular Alfred H. Louis, a down-and-out expatriate who dispensed wisdom bountifully and accepted loans in return. Watching and listening, EAR soaked up from Louis much of what would go into his blank verse narrative.

Robinson started writing "The Pauper" in March 1898. The next year, he did what little he could to advance the poem during his purgatorial service in the Harvard college office. Released from his academic job in June 1899, he sprinted ahead on what had by then become *Captain Craig*. He finished the narrative, nearly 2,000 lines in blank verse, in the spring of 1900.

A number of people came into Robinson's life during the two-year period of composition, and they found their way into the poem. He acknowledged to Edith Brower in September 1899 that he had "made some literary capital" out of these friends. More specifically, he told Laura Richards the following year that he fashioned the character of Killigrew, a doubting Thomas in the poem, after Seth Ellis Pope, then studying in the library school at Albany. Killigrew is one among several young men who to a greater or lesser degree adopt the impecunious Captain Craig as their combination mentor and beneficiary. Others in the group include Morgan, with his fiddle, and the "learned Plunkett," who may have been based on Arthur Blair and Linville Robbins, the other members of the Quadruped with Pope and Robinson. The splendid comic character of Count Pretzel von Würzburger derived from the ubiquitous Joseph Lewis French, who, as if in pursuit, had followed Robinson from Boston to New York.

Captain Craig is a philosophical poem, its ideas shaped both by Alfred H. Louis and by Robinson's brother Dean, who died in the fall of 1899. EAR relocated Handel's Dead March in *Saul* from Dean's funeral to that of his title character and transplanted some of Dean's thinking as well. Chard Powers Smith sensibly proposed dividing the poem's "enormous array of wisdom" into two parts: "an aggressive, self-assertive, essentially pagan part which might be attributed to Louis, and a humble, essentially Christian part which might be attributed to Dean." The pagan wisdom, associated with the sun, recommends enjoyment of living and interprets the whole "Scheme" to be God's joke, so that both life and death should be confronted with a sense of humor. The humbler, more idealistic wisdom attributable to Dean "was congenital with Robinson, and . . . eventually led Captain Craig's hot 'sun' to fade into the selfless 'Light.'" Both strains share an antimaterialistic bias, recommending artistic self-expression as far preferable to financial advancement.

Although the learned old pauper Louis and his troubled brother Dean each made his contribution, for the most part the opinions expressed in *Captain Craig* are EAR's own. He transferred much of what he had to say in the "Octaves" to the longer poem. There was "undoubtedly a certain amount of self-caricature" in the title character, he said.

From the beginning, Robinson understood that *Captain Craig* would outrage the sensibilities of many readers and critics. The long blank verse narrative, celebrating an unmitigated failure, was sure to offend those who believed devoutly in the gospel of success. In addition, the poem was written in language as close to common speech as he could make it, hence sure to arouse the genteel literary establishment against him. As biographer Emery Neff summed it up in 1948, in *Captain Craig* Robinson made "a twofold assault upon conventional conceptions of beauty and conventional ideals of success." Nor did EAR concern himself overmuch with proprieties of form. Here as never again, Robinson let himself go, giving full rein to the exuberance of his imagination.

In correspondence, EAR consistently made apologies for this "rather particular kind of twentieth century comedy," his most audacious departure from what readers and critics of the time expected. He shared the manuscript sparingly among his most dedicated supporters, especially after it turned out that "Mr. Stedman, who [was] given to look kindly on all sorts of so-called innovations, fought rather shy" of the Captain. Even the faithful Edith Brower would have to wait until it emerged between covers. If he showed it to her too early, EAR felt, she would find five hundred places she didn't like, and some of them were places he couldn't fix. Even the irreverent Titus Munson Coan, he feared, would find the poem "a wicked dose." It did not seem likely to him that any one reader would like the poem in its entirety. "Parts of it," he warned Mason, would jar his nervous system. "I am not altogether certain that [*Captain Craig*] has unity," he told Moody. "I call the book funny, but you may call it prosaic. I call it funny because it begins with a line that will not scan (so I am told) and ends with a brass band." The opening line, "I doubt if ten men in all Tilbury Town," did in fact pose a problem in scansion, and if Moody did not find the poem "prosaic," a number of reviewers certainly did.

Despite these reservations, Robinson remained confident that he had "done something" fresh and original in writing *Captain Craig*. It did not fit into the rather narrow territory poetry was supposed to occupy, but, as he boldly declared to Josephine Peabody, "my definition of poetry includes almost everything." He hoped that the poem's message might get through. "I can see how it will repel a good many delicate readers," he told Harry Smith, "but I don't see [how] it can fail to make them a little more sensible in their attitude toward the sentimental of life and death." Sentimentality was a vice worth exposing, and Robinson meant to do so.

"On the evening of the Eighteenth day of April, in the year of our Lord One Thousand Nine Hundred," EAR finally reached the home stretch with "The Pauper" and prepared to dispatch it to the marketplace. Crossing the finish line gave him a burst of optimism. "[But] by the time the thing has come back from six or seven publishers," he wrote Mason, "I may be more rational."

Robinson's jocular remark proved uncannily prescient. *Captain Craig* was about to begin a tortuous two-year journey among the publishers of New York and Boston, with half a dozen stops along the way. It was enough to discourage any ambitious young poet. The magazines wouldn't print his shorter poems, and if EAR couldn't find a book publisher, his very reason for existence would be called into question. How could he follow his calling and do some good if no one read his work?

The first stop *Captain Craig* made was at the house of Scribner, where Hays Gardiner prevailed on Pitts Duffield, late of Harvard, to give Robinson's book proper consideration. In the middle of May 1900, EAR shipped his "Big Thing" there, telling Brower (1) that he expected it to come back in due time, as it did and (2) that if it were rejected he would not be unduly disappointed, for he "had no end of other stuff in my head." This was both true and not true. During his first few years in New York, Robinson did indeed produce an extraordinary amount of short- to medium-length work, including the masterly "Isaac and Archibald." But his highest hopes rode with the Pauper, the Captain, the Big Thing—or as he wryly came to call the poem during its protracted travels, the Old Man of the Sea, the Monstrosity, the Serpent, the Incubus.

Captain Craig, Described

Robinson delivers a fierce moral judgment at the beginning of his long poem. Although every inch a cosmopolite, his conversation enlivened by an extraordinary command of classical references, the impoverished Captain has somehow descended in his final years to Tilbury Town. We are introduced to him in extremity, "weak, dizzy, chilled, and half-starved." He ventures "patch-clad through the streets" and lightly touches "a prudent sleeve" for succor, say-ing simply, "My name is Captain Craig, and I must eat." For all answer, "the sleeve moved on."

Those who fail to respond to a fellow human in need are not so much to blame individually as collectively, the poem suggests.

> There was just a false note in the Tilbury tune—
> A note that able-bodied men might sound
> Hosannas on while Captain Craig lay quiet.
> They might have made him sing by feeding him
> Till he should march again, but probably
> Such yielding would have jeopardized the rhythm;
> They found it more melodious to shout
> Right on, with unmolested adoration,
> To keep the tune as it had always been,
> To trust in God, and let the Captain starve.

In their prudential withholding of support for the derelict stranger, the towns-people lose the benefits of sacrifice. Every gift, the Captain observes, can result in

> Two kinds of gratitude: the sudden kind
> We feel for what we take, the larger kind
> We feel for what we give.

Fortunately, five or six young men in town rescue the Captain and allow him to dispense his Socratic wisdom. Some of them regard the old man dubi-ously, and during their evenings at the Chrysalis tavern, they berate the narra-tor—the only one who truly becomes a disciple—for his gullibility. The story, such as it is, goes forward by way of talk between the Captain and the narrator, and through the Captain's correspondence. Very little actually happens in the course of the poem, beyond the eventual decline and death of the title figure. But the Captain speaks and writes with eloquence and an engaging sense of humor. In his youth, he had done well enough in the ways of the world but, like many another, let that early promise wither away. Having wasted his talents, he might have come to despise himself for accomplishments left unachieved. But he is anything but bitter, and he happily holds forth for his young admirer, acknowledging neither shame nor regret.

As much as any character Robinson invented, Captain Craig speaks for his creator. EAR always resisted critical exploration of his philosophy. He was a poet not a philosopher, he insisted, and indeed he did not reason systematically or with consistency. But he was deeply interested in what his eminent predeces-sor Ralph Waldo Emerson—another man obsessed with shaping a vocation for himself—called The Conduct of Life: how to think and act in an often hostile universe. Addressing this question, Captain Craig speaks with a joie de vivre that belies the usual view of Robinson as forbiddingly pessimistic. He advises his young listeners to discover and celebrate the light behind the dark. The affirmation of the Captain's counsel gains a certain authority, coming as it does from a man who lay alone in a grimy hall bedroom, broken, bereft, and barely able to glimpse the sun through an unwashed window.

Despite his destitution, the Captain sings a rhapsody of "irremediable cheerfulness." God's humor, he declares, constitutes the music of the spheres. Old as he is, he can still laugh along with the child within. In the throes of poverty and of war, where he has seen men, women, and children reduced to "things without shape or name," Captain Craig sometimes had "half a mind to blow [his] brains out."

> But what has this to do
> With Spring?—Because one half of humankind
> Lives here in hell, shall not the other half
> Do any more than just for conscience' sake
> Be miserable? Is this the way for us
> To lead these creatures up to find the light,—
> Or to be drawn down surely to the dark
> Again? Which is it? What does the child say?

The critic Jay Martin describes Captain Craig as "a Platonic hero of the Ideal, defined by light and music." But his idealism is always accompanied by an awareness of mankind's very real inhumanity. He rejects equally the heedless optimism of the escapist and the determined pessimism of the cynic. In a letter to the narrator, he draws vivid pictures of two such single-minded people he had known during his salad days, when he "had hounds and credit and grave friends / To borrow my books and set wet glasses upon them."

The first is "a woman cursed with happiness" and wealth. Robinson, through the Captain, depicts her with a coating of sarcasm. She possesses everything except "an inward eye" for the miseries of "this infernal world of ours."

> The cleverness
> God gave her—or the devil—cautions her
> That she must keep the china cup of life
> Filled somehow, and she fills it—runs it over—
> Claps her white hands while some one does the sopping
> With fingers made, she thinks, for just that purpose,
> Giggles and eats and reads and goes to church,
> Makes pretty little penitential prayers,
> And has an eighteen-carat crucifix

Wrapped up in chamois-skin. She gives enough,
You say; but what is giving like hers worth?

The second is her opposite number, a man "who feeds his very soul on poison."

No matter what he does, or where he looks,
He finds unhappiness; or, if he fails
To find it, he creates it, and then hugs it.

Some critics have accused Robinson himself of adopting just such a jaundiced attitude. Manifestly, Robinson felt an affinity for the defeated people he summoned to life in his poems, Captain Craig among them. But here he rejects the killjoy along with the Pollyanna, and with rather more enthusiasm. What can you do with a man like that? the Captain asks about the hidebound pessimist. Give him a rose, and he'll lament that its beauty must perish.

As his health deteriorates, Captain Craig presents his young acolytes with the "jocund instrument" of his last will and testament. He leaves to them a vast estate empty of negotiable content.

I, Captain Craig, abhorred iconoclast,
Sage-errant, favored of the Mysteries,
And self-reputed humorist at large,
Do now, confessed of my world-worshipping,
Time-questioning, sun-fearing, and heart-yielding,
Approve and unreservedly devise
To you and your assigns for evermore,
God's universe and yours.

As a final piece of advice, he counsels them to join the "climbers and up-fliers" who risk crashing to earth instead of those whose sadness makes their footsteps stumble.

Whatever be the altitude you reach,
You do not rise alone; nor do you fall
But you drag others down to more or less
Than your preferred abasement.

On one afternoon, Captain Craig reads his will. On the next, he delivers his valedictory speech. Dark though the world may be, he warns his disciples against succumbing to despair.

There is no servitude so fraudulent
As of a sun-shut mind; for 't is the mind

That makes you craven or invincible,
Diseased or puissant.

The doctrine sounds a great deal like Emersonian idealism, especially as joined
with the poem's antimaterialism. Fifteen years later, in "The Man Against the
Sky," Robinson wrote another poem about climbing toward enlightenment,
without achieving the jubilant enthusiasm of his "pauper."

All along, the old man has told his followers to celebrate his funeral with a
brass band. With his last word, he smiles, looks around him, and says "Trom-
bones." That night at the Chrysalis, the faithful fiddle and sing as never before.
Soon they will go their divergent ways, carrying with them enough of his legacy so that "neither parted roads nor cent per cent" can "starve out the child"
within. First, though, they have a promise to fulfill, one that goes against all
the proprieties. On the windy, dreary day of the Captain's funeral, they march
along the road with his casket. As they proceed, the bewildered townspeople
stopped

> And eyed us on that road from time to time,
> And on that road the children followed us,
> And all along that road the Tilbury Band
> Blared indiscreetly the Dead March in Saul.

Ellsworth Barnard, one of Robinson's best interpreters, admirably summed
up the virtues of *Captain Craig*. In it, he wrote, the poet achieved a nearly equal
balance "between the general and the specific, the philosophic and the dramatic." Without the philosophy, the Captain's story would be depressing. Without the Captain, the philosophy would be cold. "Taken together, they make a
poem that is not always easy reading, but that quickens our awareness, deepens our understanding, widens our sympathies, and leaves us with a feeling of
renewed well-being." Barnard's favorable judgment of *Captain Craig* came in
1952. In the literary climate that prevailed half a century earlier, EAR's poem—a
radical departure from the practice of the time—had the devil's own time getting any hearing at all.

The *Captain*'s Long Journey

Scribner's kept the manuscript of *Captain Craig* a month before
returning it. When it came back, Robinson decided that he had better let "old
Mr. Louis" have a look at it. He had, after all, put "rather more" of the disreputable but eloquent pauper into the poem than he originally intended. He gave
Louis the manuscript, knowing that he would recognize much of himself in it
and somewhat apprehensive about his reaction. The old man returned it "with

hands trembling and eyes full of tears." Now he knew why he was still alive, Louis said. *Captain Craig* had justified his existence.

On the grounds that his poem might be too experimental for established firms like Scribner's, Robinson next dispatched it to Small, Maynard & Company, a small publisher in Boston. It seemed like a sensible decision. Small, Maynard was bringing out Josephine Preston Peabody's *Fortune and Men's Eyes*, and Dan Mason recommended the firm. As he posted the manuscript to Boston early in July 1900, Robinson adopted a warily defensive attitude about its fate. "It is barely possible that they may care to take hold of it, though I am inclined to believe that I shall print it eventually at my own expense." Still, he hoped for the best.

After two months of silence, Robinson wrote T. T. Bouvé at Small, Maynard that he was willing to let the manuscript stay until the return of editor Laurens Maynard. But, he added with a trace of exasperation, "as the thing involves to some extent the question of What is Art, and as I have but one lifetime, perhaps you will be good enough to tell him that I should like to hear from him at his earliest convenience." More amelioratively, he wrote Mason that the "one thing the Pauper will not stand is a hasty examination." He need not have worried on that score. "My only hope is that people will not read him rapidly; and for once in my life I think my hopes will be fulfilled." They were.

Another month passed before Josephine Peabody came into the picture as Robinson's advocate. EAR had written her that she'd find *Captain Craig* "amusing and sometimes hilarious" and as a whole "elevating." So she was fully prepared to like it—she already liked Robinson a great deal—when the opportunity to say so unexpectedly presented itself. Maynard and his wife came to her house for a social evening on October 18, and in the course of conversation it emerged that the editor was dubious about publishing Robinson's poem.

"I've only glanced through it," he confessed. "It's a long thing, narrative of some sort."

Peabody advised him to reconsider. "Robinson is distinctly a coming man. I know him somewhat, and he's the most *original* mind of all the young men writing now. Without any doubt."

Maynard then asked, "Do you want to read it for us?"

The next day Peabody "hopped and skipped downtown" to pick up the manuscript. She found the poem every bit as amusing and elevating as EAR had predicted. "Now if I can only make them take it, as they ought and must," she confided to her journal. "I had no doubts before I read it, and I certainly haven't any now."

Peabody let Robinson know of her clandestine maneuverings, and he duly thanked her for "stirring Maynard up." Despite the "crudities" of his "monstrosity," he was willing to affix his "long-tailed name" on the title page, in the unlikely event that the firm decided to publish it. Robinson's pessimism seemed well justified by another long silence from Small, Maynard. He couldn't help wondering what the devil they were doing with *Captain Craig*, he wrote Harry Smith at Thanksgiving time. He let another few weeks go by before sending the publishers a polite ultimatum on December 10. "If you do not care to publish 'Captain Craig,' which I took the liberty to submit to you last June [actually, early in July], may I ask if you will be kind enough to return the MS. to me by express as soon as possible."

His letter, seconded by Peabody's glowing recommendation, apparently had its effect. Six days later EAR wrote Edith Brower that "the book business is looking a little better with me and *Captain C.* will be brought out by Small, Maynard & Company sometime in 1901." He kept Peabody's involvement confidential but told Brower of the rumor (false) that the well-known poet Bliss Carman had recommended the book to the firm. On the whole, he was inclined to think that the Captain would "go," even if "the cherrystone critics" couldn't make much of him. The important thing was that the book would emerge at last from Small, Maynard. Or so it seemed.

News of the acceptance of *Captain Craig* stimulated Robinson to work on the book of shorter- and medium-length poems he'd been "pegging at for the past three years." He could have finished it sooner, he wrote Brower, but it had been interrupted by the Captain and "several other people." As he planned it, the new book would include extended poems like "The Book of Annandale" and "Isaac and Archibald," shorter narratives like "Aunt Imogen," "The Return of Morgan and Fingal," and "The Wife of Palissy" (or "Partnership"), and a number of briefer offerings, such as the double sonnet "The Growth of 'Lorraine.'" It would be as unlike *Captain Craig* as any two things of his could possibly be.

On New Year's Day, 1901, EAR wrote Peabody about a strange message he'd recently had from Maynard, to the effect that the firm's long delay in accepting the book was "due to its great merit"—a lie, he maintained, to challenge those of Ananias.

While he waited, and waited, for proof from Small, Maynard, Robinson was feeling uneasy about the extent of his debt to Peabody. "I don't know when [*Captain Craig*] is to be published, if ever," he wrote her in mid-February, "but this does not keep me from being grateful to you for having him taken out of his grave clothes and examined for whatever symptoms of life he might reveal." If it was through her influence that "the thing was taken" he would try to be appropriately appreciative.

Neither Robinson nor Peabody understood how the fates—and human frailty—were conspiring to prevent publication of *Captain Craig*. Normally, EAR would have received proofs early in 1901. He did not and could not, for on a cold winter's night a member of the staff at Small, Maynard paid a visit to a Boston brothel, left the manuscript behind, and quite forgot about it. Robinson wanted the script back for revisions, and the publishers were forced to stall him while they turned the office upside down in a futile search for it. Months went by before springtime, with the sap rising, lured the erring staffer back to the whorehouse. There the madam presented him with the manuscript she had carefully preserved.

Unfortunately, Small, Maynard had by then gone into receivership and decided not to publish *Captain Craig* after all. When Maynard reconstructed the story years later, he failed to mention the incident of the brothel or the unconscionable length of time they held Robinson's manuscript. At first he had been dubious about the financial success of *Captain Craig*, Maynard said, but felt he "could not decline a work of such absolute merit as literature." Nor had it been his decision to break the contract. That was the fault of "new management" that took over the failing firm and sought release from publishing anything that did not promise direct profits.

The disheartening news reached Robinson on May 10, 1901, and had the effect of temporarily spoiling what was otherwise a most pleasant visit from Josephine Peabody. During her fortnight in New York, she and Robinson spent a considerable amount of time together. One day he took her down to the Battery to see the Aquarium, and from there they walked to the Brooklyn Bridge to watch "the marvelous sight of towers and spires and banners of smoke . . . all color of pearl." On another occasion they called on the ailing poet and critic Richard Henry Stoddard, who had been a prominent figure in the New York literary establishment for half a century. "E. A. R.'s light comes out and shines when he is with the aged or afflicted," Peabody wrote in her journal. "So it shone doubly, that night."

Robinson could not quite bring himself to see Peabody, or anyone else, on the day he heard that Small, Maynard would not publish *Captain Craig*, but by the next evening he had recovered from his disappointment enough to welcome her company. The two of them walked along the avenues in a misty light. Now and then it showered, she wrote in her journal, but they put up an umbrella "and continued to saunter and talk of all people and things: oh, good, good talk!"

With the vivacious Peabody, Robinson shook off his carapace of reserve. If the two young poets were not in love, they certainly shared a warmth of feeling for each other. Peabody took the rejection of *Captain Craig* nearly as hard as Robinson. The "detestable" Small, Maynard, she observed in her journal, "lightly fool with the MS for *ten months*—and then send it back." She was even inclined to blame herself for her "little efforts" of helpfulness that contributed to the firm's keeping the manuscript out of circulation for so long. EAR "is such a genius and so delayed," she lamented.

Robinson was embittered by the experience, especially after the whole story—abandoned manuscript and all—finally came out. He found the matter "just a little sickening," for he had "a most unsophisticated liking for common decency" and was not disposed to change. He prayed that he might never have occasion to tell Maynard what he thought of him. That would be too much for his "Puritanical self-restraint."

Toward Peabody, however, he felt only gratitude. He was very glad, he wrote her after she returned to Boston, to have "added anything in my ridiculous way to your enjoyment of this village. As you can never know how much you have done for me, perhaps I may be pardoned . . . for taking more than ordinary satisfaction in the thought that I may be of any service to you at all." Robinson also cut back on his usual critical comments to praise her work without reservation. Her blank verse play on Christopher Marlowe was "a sure thing, strong and clear and true," he told her. He also singled out as a stroke of "pure genius" her line in another poem: "And there were trees, and then there weren't." In a letter to his friend Joseph Ford at Exeter, he struck a more personal note. "Miss Peabody is a good fellow and she is rather stunning. You had better call on her."

There were other options for *Captain Craig*, of course. Hays Gardiner recommended Silver, Burdett in New York, and Robinson tried them next. "All I know," he wrote Mason, "is they will not keep it for a year and then sling it back at me." The book's extended delay in a derelict Boston publishing house left the thirty-one-year-old Robinson in an ugly mood. He let his friendship with Ridgely Torrence lapse, apologizing afterward on the grounds that he was feeling "rather like the devil" and "not much in the mood for seeing anybody." And he broke with old man Louis himself.

In his memoir *Episodes Before Thirty*, the English mystic Algernon Blackwood celebrated Louis's remarkable gift for conversation. Like Robinson, he encountered the old man in New York near the turn of the century, living in the "vagrant and grandiloquent poverty" that proclaimed itself in his filthy garments. But when Louis began to talk, Blackwood wrote, his astonishing voice made it all vanish: "his long frock-coat, green with age and dirt; his broken boots and frayed trousers; his shapeless top hat, brushed the wrong way till it looked like a beehive coated with rough plush; his grimy collar without a tie; the spots upon his grease-stained waistcoat." Robinson was similarly impressed. "I have met some mighty talkers in my time," he said in reminiscence, "but none could compare with Louis. Words poured from him in a never-ending stream." Yet with the onset of old age, even the greatest talkers sometimes succumb to garrulousness. So, with Alfred H. Louis, what was initially enchanting became tiresome.

Then too, having none himself, Louis was forever importuning his friends for funds. Despite his poverty, he continued to see himself as Alfred H. Louis, "barrister-at-law, Esq.," and familiar of the great. He did not beg for money, he demanded it as his due. "Betts!" he said as he and Craven Betts were walking along the street one day, "I'm going to do you a favor. I'm going to let you lend me five dollars." For a time this kind of brazenness had its charm, and then it didn't. One by one his companions sloughed off old Mr. Louis as a persistent pest. Robinson was fond of the old man and grateful to him for supplying so much of the character of Captain Craig. But he was running short of money—and patience—himself. Finally he ordered Louis away from his door and immediately felt contrite about it.

"I have just turned Mr. Louis down in the most brutal manner and with all possible deliberation," EAR wrote Betts on June 21, 1901. "He has been on my nerves for the past day or two, and I have had the devil's own time with my better feelings on his account; but this morning—after another night without sleep—I have kicked my real self out of the way and done a thing that I shall always regret but shall never be able to consider quite unjustifiable under the circumstances." The break was not an easy one for Robinson to make. He believed in "the splendor of the unfulfilled," after all, and was inclined to value failure at least as much as what generally passed for success.

Two years later Louis went back to his native England, where he died in 1915. Apparently he harbored no resentment against EAR for the way their friendship ended. In correspondence with Betts, he praised Robinson's work. "All that he has done grows, grows, grows upon me. It is very great." He also acknowledged his own "persistent and rather unbecoming obstreperousness" and counseled Betts to continue his "watchful and affectionately careful friendship" with EAR. The cycle of forgiveness was completed in 1930 when Robinson dedicated *The Glory of the Nightingales* to the memory of Alfred H. Louis. It was a gesture that might have warmed the old man's bones.

Safe Harbor at Last

Within days after dispatching *Captain Craig* to Silver, Burdett for consideration, Robinson received a letter from Ford offering to present the manuscript to a friend at Little, Brown, the prominent Boston publisher. Robinson continued to think that "the thing will not go with any of the older houses," however, and there is no evidence that his poem was ever submitted to Little, Brown. Instead, it went the rounds of smaller firms in New York City over the summer, including McClure, Phillips after Silver, Burdett. Near the end of September, he wrote Mason that the manuscript had been turned down five times but that the Captain, his trousers pretty badly frayed, was "still on the march." More and more Robinson became convinced that *Captain Craig* would never see the light unless he published it himself—and the prospects of his being able to afford such an undertaking were steadily deteriorating.

Meanwhile, he had higher hopes for the "other book" of poems he was polishing for publication. There was nothing in it to cause discomfort "even to the most conventional and thin-skinned," he assured Ford. First he planned to call it *Isaac and Archibald*, then *The Book of Annandale* after the two longest poems. In the latter guise, Robinson carried the new book to Pitts Duffield at Scribner's, this time with an added incentive from Hays Gardiner. "You will remember," Gardiner reminded Duffield on October 13, "that Mrs. Richards and I—and now [Barrett] Wendell wants to join us—are desirous to give you a guaranty, if the commercial prospects stand in the way of the publication."

Even the promise of a subvention did not sway Duffield. He could see how Gardiner and Wendell might have liked the "quaint contemplative philosophy" of the poems, he wrote on November 21, but he thought they were "at once too simple and too sophisticated" for New York readers. He imagined that they might appeal more to "persons for the most part of the poet's own Brahmin class."

In reply, Gardiner thanked Duffield for his consideration, mentioning only his conviction that in due course Robinson's philosophy and "sophisticated simplicity" would be highly valued. He also discoursed on Robinson's personality in response to a remark of Duffield's. "What you say of Robinson's being hard to know is entirely true: he is the queerest combination of the most retiring shyness with an occasional natural readiness to come forward that I know." Even "when you know him," Gardiner added, "he is not very easy to understand, I suspect."

As this correspondence made clear, Gardiner had taken over the task of marketing *The Book of Annandale* for Robinson. He may have been amused by Duffield's mistaking EAR for a Boston Brahmin but did not bother to correct him. Instead, he took the hint and, early in January 1902, got in touch with Houghton Mifflin, the most certifiably Brahmin of all Boston book publishers and one where both he and Laura Richards had strong connections. To prepare the way, Mrs. Richards wrote a charming letter to writer-editor Annie Fields, whose husband was a principal figure at the publishing house, requesting a "friendly and receptive as well as an intelligent" reading for her protégé Robinson, "a man who has something unusual to say." In closing, she echoed Gardiner's query to Duffield at Scribner's. "Would there be any chance of Mr. Robinson's getting some book (manuscript) reading to do for H.M.?" These appeals for part-time employment for Robinson demonstrate that both Gardiner and Richards were aware of his increasingly straitened circumstances. Neither request led to anything remunerative.

The powers-that-be at Houghton Mifflin directed Robinson's *Book of Annandale* to the attention of the firm's chief literary adviser, *Atlantic Monthly* editor Bliss Perry. Meanwhile, Gardiner enlisted William Vaughn Moody to join those endorsing Robinson's work to the publishers. At Moody's insistence EAR also forwarded *Captain Craig* to Houghton Mifflin, on the grounds that it might function "as a possible reinforcement to the other book." Bliss Perry and his readers thereafter considered the two manuscripts, combined, as the material for a single "rather thick volume" of verse.

In his autobiography, Perry conceded that he had been too timid to accept "Aunt Imogen" for the *Atlantic* but wrote that he "atoned for that blunder by persuading the skeptical House [of Houghton Mifflin] to publish Robinson's *Captain Craig.*" The record shows, however, that he was hardly an advocate for the book. Perry's in-house memorandum characterized it as "a volume of obscure verse, often eccentric and prosaic in character but with flashes of genius occasionally." The only "ground of acceptance," he added, "is the faith of Robinson's friends and the possibility of a more popular book later."

Writing directly to Hays Gardiner on March 14, Perry stressed yet again "the obscurity that characterizes a good deal" of the poetry, striking a note that was to be sounded repeatedly in subsequent Robinson criticism. More favorably, Perry noted the "power of phrase, and the insight into character, as well as the humor and pathos which his poems constantly display." But these admirable qualities were balanced against a "whimsicality, not to say perversity, both of word and technique." In short, Robinson on the page did not sound like the conventional poetry of the time, and Perry found it difficult to envisage "publishing the work successfully." He did, however, extend the possibility of bringing out the book "on commission," the expense to be provided "either by the author himself or by his friends who are particularly interested in this project."

That grudging assent was all Gardiner needed to hear. Two weeks later, he committed $400 toward publication, possibly to be supplied in part by Mrs. Richards. The two of them collaborated to give Robinson's *Captain Craig: A Book of Poems* the best possible sendoff. The price was to be kept low—no more than a dollar—to give the book its widest possible readership. Copies were to be sent to influential literary people like William Dean Howells, R. H. Stoddard, E. C. Stedman, Colonel T. W. Higginson, and William Lyon Phelps; to Harvard luminaries Barrett Wendell and Charles Eliot Norton and William James; to Josephine Preston Peabody and William Allan Neilson, either of whom might do the important *Atlantic Monthly* review; in England to Hall Caine, to Alice Meynell, once the friend of Alfred H. Louis, and to Mrs. Richards's sister Maud Howe Elliott, who knew Henry James well enough to recommend the book to him. Robinson himself was much concerned with securing a British copyright for the volume, which—he wrongly conjectured—might eventually find four readers in England for each one in the United States.

Houghton Mifflin published the book in an edition of 500 copies on October 4, 1902. That evening, Robinson and Torrence dined together in celebration at Zum Praelaten, the book propped on the table between them. Ten days later, EAR sent a copy to Rosalind Richards with a limerick:

To R.R.

Though I got the book first for another—
To wit, your adorable mother—
　　Will you please have the grace
　　Without making a face,
To take it? (Or not, if you'd rather)

Robinson thought about dedicating the volume to Gardiner, but decided that such a salutation might embarrass his friend. Not until the substantially revised edition of 1915 did he add a dedicatory page to Gardiner's memory.

Robinson sat back to await the reviewer's reaction to his oddly configured *Captain Craig: A Book of Poems*: the first half taken up by the 2,000 lines of the title poem, the second half by fifteen shorter works. He had been working on it, off and on, for five years, and invested much of his future in its success. As if to forestall disappointment, he predicted to Peabody that the Captain "will be hooted at, if he is noticed at all." For the most part, he was right. The luminaries to whom Gardiner and Mrs. Richards sent copies did not choose, Higginson excepted, to discourse about the book in public. Instead, it fell into the hands of such influential book reviewers as Frank Dempster Sherman, Clinton Scollard, and Bliss Carman: men aligned with "the hermaphroditic piper[s]" who articulated the fashionable taste of the time. Uniformly, they hooted at Robinson's book, and for precisely those reasons he had anticipated: its plain unprettified style, its concentration on less than heroic figures, its leaving so much to the reader as to be deemed "obscure."

In his review, Scollard (one of the eminences to whom EAR had sent a complimentary copy of *The Torrent and the Night Before* in 1896) deplored Robinson's "frequent disregard for the niceties of form." After acknowledging that the poet had enough to say, Scollard laid down a barrage of metaphors attacking him. Robinson owed it to his readers "to dress his thought in attractive attire, and not let it go slovenly clad," he wrote. "Blank-verse that is little more than inverted prose chopped up into lines is continually elbowing passages that are shot through with real poetic fire in this disturbing volume." Sherman, assessing the volume along with thirty-eight others in an omnibus review, arrived at a similar conclusion. Robinson displayed "a positive talent for narrative verse," but "one cannot forgive him the rough, crude, and altogether prosaic character of the blank verse in which they are written."

Carman, whom Robinson had misidentified as a promoter of *Captain Craig*, concentrated his fire on that long poem alone. Like Scollard, Carman let his critical metaphors run wild. *Captain Craig* was "worse than Browning," he declared. "To read it at a sitting is like a long swim under water—quite as much a feat as a pleasure." Robinson possessed power and ambition, but in this case "his arrow has gone very wide of the mark, not at all because he is a poor shot, but because his vision for the time being is not clear." He agreed with Scollard and Sherman that the basic trouble lay in the way the poem was written. "It was the verse that bored and impeded me, while the story itself and the psychology lured me on."

H. W. Boynton went the logical step further in the *Atlantic Monthly* review that fell to him rather than to Neilson or Peabody. In a "yes, but" assessment, he suggested that Robinson should give up poetry for prose. Yes, there was "much power, even genius" in his book, but "it is reasonably clear that verse is not the medium of expression through which this power, or genius, can hope to become fully articulate."

A number of reviewers exemplified what they found wanting in *Captain Craig* by quoting or citing a poem they liked: the conventional "Twilight Song"

Robinson used in closing. Here they found reassuring evidence that the poet could write traditional verse when he wished. Why didn't he write more of it? Ironically, this was a poem Robinson himself had little confidence in. He tinkered with it considerably, cutting two of its six twelve-line stanzas at Moody's behest and offering to Peabody to cut two more if she so advised or possibly to "throw out" the poem entirely. "I tried to do something 'rather swagger' and I did not quite succeed," he wrote her. The basic problem, he thought, was the poem's fuzziness of meaning.

What the reviewers liked about "Twilight Song" had little to do with its content, however. Given its drumbeat anapests and predictable rhymes, it *sounded* like the kind of verse they were used to, and not at all like "the rough, bathetic prose passages" in Robinson's longer blank verse poems. "Twilight Song" begins:

Through the shine, through the rain
We have shared the day's load;
To the old march again
We have tramped the long road;
We have laughed, we have cried,
And we've tossed the King's crown;
We have fought, we have died,
And we've trod the day down.
So it's lift the old song
Ere the night flies again,
Where the road leads along
Through the shine, through the rain.

Whatever that might mean, it was rhythmic enough to satisfy most of the critics.

There were but two strongly favorable notices of *Captain Craig*, one in a journal so obscure it escaped Richard Cary in his exhaustive collection of early Robinson reviews. Therein, Nathan Haskell Dole, who had been much taken by *The Torrent and the Night Before*, hailed Robinson's work as a promising sign for the future of American poetry. Dole singled out "Isaac and Archibald" for its truth in characterization and "Aunt Imogen" for its dramatic intensity. He went on to say that "Mr. Robinson is a very modest, shy, and retiring man, but if this day may be called the Twilight of Poetry, his verse is a very bright and promising evening star. Great things may be expected of one whose work is already so original and individual."

The second and more significant laudatory review was written by Trumbull Stickney for the *Harvard Monthly*, which had rejected all of EAR's submissions during his college years. It did not appear until December 1903, more than a year after the publication of *Captain Craig*. Stickney had attended Harvard at the same time as Robinson, taken a doctorate at the Sorbonne, and returned to teach Greek at Harvard. He was regarded as a highly promising young poet himself before his death from a brain tumor in 1904. There is no evidence that the two men knew each other, but EAR found in Stickney someone who understood him just as he wanted to be understood.

Stickney concentrated his gaze on the characters Robinson brought to life: "These people are all queer," he observed. "Captain Craig, Carmichael, Aunt Imogen, Lorraine, George Annandale, Vanderberg [in the poem "Sainte-Nitouche"]: they are among those who after experience will curl up in a corner and under persuasion will talk to you. . . . "

"You have met such people and felt that way: if you have not, you care nothing for the various members of your race, you let the faces on the street go by without seeing them, you are putting on your gloves instead of shaking hands. How much you miss!" Robinson showed us such men and women "directly, in their action on each other, moving and lost in the stress of life." His poems read like introductions to his friends, and this was something entirely new and worth extolling.

Stickney also advanced a spirited defense of what other critics derided as Robinson's "prosaic" style. His words might seem simple and straightforward, but they were nonetheless entirely "adequate to the thought. . . . The fact that so much poetry past and present is written in what professors of rhetoric call an elevated style does not necessarily condemn authors who use plain Saxon." Nor did the loose and relaxed metrics of the long, blank-verse poems disqualify Robinson from the company of Milton and Browning. In Robinson, Stickney said, "we have one poet more, one more of those men like us but more than we; who make life richer and clearer, by bringing the smile and the tear nearer together, and in their mixture showing us the human face of men and women, as it looks, on the whole rather anxiously, before and upward."

Best of all, Stickney announced that reading Robinson had succeeded in transforming his life: precisely what EAR aimed to do in pursuit of his calling. In an extravagant sentence, Stickney revealed the extent of what he owed to this new author. "The honesty and simplicity of his mind, the pathos and kindness of his heart, and above all the humor with which his imagination is lighted up continually have made me *begin life over again* and feel once more that poetry is part of it, perhaps the truth of it." It is unfortunate that these two kindred spirits should never have met. As Robinson wrote Peabody upon learning of Stickney's sudden death the following year, "we could not afford to lose him."

Stickney's wonderful review came too late to assuage Robinson's anguish over the reception of *Captain Craig*. "I put everything I had into that poem," he said, and "no more attention was paid to 'the captain' than if he had never been born." As Malcolm Cowley commented, Robinson "painfully rolled a boulder to the edge of the Grand Canyon, pushed it over and waited breathlessly. After a while there was the echo of a pebble-sized splash far below," followed by silence.

By 1922, after his *Collected Poems* had been published and awarded the Pulitzer Prize, Robinson could look back on the neglect of *Captain Craig* with equanimity. It was odd, he wrote Mrs. Richards, that some people didn't care for it at all while others liked it better than anything he had done. If she were to read it again, he directed her to try the version in his collected poems, which he had "pruned and prism'd, and I think improved." In 1934, he looked back on the captain more judgmentally. The poem was full of "metrical and colloquial extravagances" and "the didactic parts" were "overdone." Yet with all its imperfections, "the thing contrives somehow to stay alive. Perhaps it is old Mr. Louis that refuses to die in it. He was pretty tough."

Only a few commentators on *Captain Craig: A Book of Poems* bothered to mention "Isaac and Archibald," which belongs among the great American poems. Robinson placed it immediately following his title poem, and both works touch on what old men may have to teach. But "Isaac and Archibald," at 344 lines, one-sixth as long as *Captain Craig*, avoids the didacticism that occasionally creeps into the Captain's discourse, and the circumstances are quite different.

In the affecting poem, which Louis Coxe called "a small miracle of tone, control, speaking voice, and self-effacing description," Robinson creates a speaker who manages through technical legerdemain to address the audience *both* as the twelve-year-old boy who walked with Isaac to Archibald's farm one sweltering summer afternoon *and* as the mature storyteller that boy became, looking back on a memorable day. The whole texture depends on this interplay between present and past, lending an effect of timelessness. The double point of view is established at the very beginning (and echoed at the end):

> Isaac and Archibald were two old men.
> I knew them, and I may have laughed at them
> A little; but I must have honored them
> For they were old, and they were good to me.

We look back with the boy now grown up, and follow him as he recreates the legendary past in a sun-struck daydream at Archibald's place. Gazing absently down through the orchard across the road, across the river and the hills into the blue forest,

> Now and then my fancy caught
> A flying glimpse of a good life beyond—
> Something of ships and sunlight, streets and singing,
> Troy falling, and the ages coming back,

And ages coming forward. Archibald
And Isaac were good fellows in old clothes,
And Agamemnon was a friend of mine;
Ulysses coming home again to shoot
With bows and feathered arrows made another,
And all was as it should be.

The poem takes the form of journey and return, and here, as in another masterwork, the late poem "Mr. Flood's Party," Robinson invokes an epic connection with gentle irony. The five-mile hike to Archibald's hardly qualifies as a Homeric test. As Isaac and the boy set out, the lad is conscious of "gladness everywhere" in "the warmth and wonder of the land" and "the wayside flash of leaves." Before long, however, he has trouble keeping pace with Isaac's vigorous strides and is "ready to sweat blood" from the heat of the day. Isaac, fit for his age and proud of it, will admit no discomfort from the sun beating down or from the thirst it produces. Tramping down the River Road to Archibald's is no trouble for him, or none he will admit to, anyway. Besides, he has a mission to perform. It is high time for Archibald's oats to be cut, and, as Isaac tells the boy, he "could never feel / Quite sure about Archibald" these days. Soon, however, we discover that the oats have been cut, and that Archibald has similar doubts about Isaac.

"Isaac and Archibald" derived from conversations EAR had in New York with William Henry Thorne (the model, probably, for Robinson's later "Flammonde") and with Alfred H. Louis (who indisputably sat for Captain Craig). Each of them saw the other as slipping into his dotage. Age was changing Louis, Thorne told EAR, and not for the better. Then Louis drew Robinson aside, declaring that Thorne was not the man he once had been. The comic situation inspired the poet to create a glimpse into "the lives of two old men, linked by true friendship, yet not so heroically devoted as not to point out a flaw in the other fellow."

Yet no anecdote, however charming—no snapshot, however engaging—will justify a 344-line poem, much less convert it into a work of art. In his sinewy verse, Robinson took the material and shaped its transformation. The cosmopolitan Thorne and Louis were converted into New England countrymen, taking physical form along the lines of EAR's Palmer uncles from across the Kennebec that he had enjoyed listening to during his boyhood. And the two old men are sharply differentiated as people, so that to follow the hint of the anecdote and conclude with most critics that Isaac and Archibald were cut from the same cloth is to libel Robinson's skill at characterization.

During the course of the poem, both Isaac and Archibald tell the boy of their doubts about the other. In delivering this message, both summon a blessing on his youthful innocence—"God bless you, boy!"—and both ask him to remember and reflect upon what they have had to say. Otherwise, they could hardly be more different. Isaac, for example, consistently emphasizes what he himself stands to lose should Archibald die. For seven years, he says, he has seen

"That Archibald is changing. It is not
So much that he should come to his last hand,
And leave the game, and go the old way down;
But I have known him in and out so long

. . . .
                            that now it brings
To this old heart of mine an ache that you
Have not yet lived enough to know about."

The metaphor is nicely chosen, for there will be a card game to come and another to imagine before the end of the poem. Moreover, Isaac bemoans "the slackening" that has come to Archibald in vivid language. He notices the change

"Now in a common word that would have passed
Uncaught from any other lips than his,
Now in some trivial act of every day
Done as he might have done it all along
But for a twinging little difference
That nips you like a squirrel's teeth."

The twinge works powerfully, even though the image comes from a man primarily concerned with himself. In concluding, Isaac asks the boy to remember him to the end, and beyond. "Look at me, my boy," he directs. "Think of me, to bring me back again."

Self-centered though he may be, in his manner of speaking Isaac pays rhetorical obeisance to the Almighty. At the pump located halfway to Archibald's farm, he drinks deeply and thanks "God for all things / That he had put on earth to drink." Once they reach their destination, Isaac and the boy go down cellar where Archibald has laid away eight barrels of cider, and as they imbibe their fill, Isaac once more acknowledges the bounty of the Lord.

"I never twist a spigot nowadays,"
He said, and raised the glass up to the light,
"But I thank God for orchards."

By way of contrast, a mystical but not godly *light* figures prominently in Archibald's talk, where the word assumes transcendental overtones. Unlike Isaac, Archibald has been declining physically. He limps out to meet his visitors, "one hand on his back, / And the other clutching his huge-headed cane." In due course, Isaac sets out to inspect his friend's farm and leaves the boy and Archibald together.

Archibald, unlike Isaac, has a rare command of the vernacular. He describes the steamy August afternoon as "a master day for sunstroke" and observes that Isaac and the boy must have had "a right smart walk" from Tilbury Town to his farm. Archibald also has wit and humor and few illusions about himself. As he tells the lad how age has diminished his friend, he admits its effects upon himself as well. "I get it here / A little in my knees, and Isaac—here," he says, tapping his knuckles three times to his forehead.

But it is his charge to the boy that most differentiates Archibald from Isaac. "Remember me," Isaac says. "Remember . . . the light behind the stars," Archibald says.

"Let there be no confusion or distrust
In you, no snarling of a life half lived,
Nor any cursing over broken things
That your complaint has been the ruin of.
Live to see clearly, and the light will come
To you, and as you need it."

Back from his inspection trip, Isaac finds fault after all with Archibald's cutting of the oats: not that he neglected to cut them in time, but that he did so a day or two too soon. Archibald signifies his annoyance with a widening and narrowing of the nostrils, as elsewhere he does with mirthless chuckles. Each of the three characters, in fact, has his own distinct way of laughing. The poem is invigorated by such telling observations, by what the critic William Pritchard calls "the energy of noticings."

Because his twelve-year-old imagination is captured by Homer, the boy conceives of Isaac as a latter-day Ulysses but can conjure up no such role for Archibald, who lacks "heroics." Heroic or not, Archibald is the better card player, and wins the game of seven-up with Isaac. After supper and the long walk home, the boy dreams of his companions as angels still bent over their cards, and overhears as a dry voice "Cried thinly, with unpatronizing triumph, / 'I've got you, Isaac: high, low, jack, and the game.'"

Robinson might have ended there, but added a reflective passage bringing his poem full circle. The boy grown to manhood thinks back on Isaac and Archibald, now long dead.

I knew them, and I may have laughed at them;
But there's a laughing that has honor in it,
And I have no regret for light words now.

He remembers them, just as they had wished, and the vitality of those memories "testif[ies] to the warmth of affection" he feels for the old men.

"Isaac and Archibald" is a quiet poem, offering little in the way of emotional fireworks. William James thought it "*fully* as good as anything of the kind in

Wordsworth." Edwin Fussell, who wrote a book about influences on Robinson's work, saw it as "a blend of Wordsworth and Yankee," encompassing the moral idealism and simple rhetoric of the English romantic but adding "a firmer realism, a more complex sense of irony and paradox, and a sense of humor." It tells us something about a few other human beings and ourselves, it stays in the mind, and it repays rereading.

Down and Out

Descent Into Poverty

Upon first settling in New York, Robinson discovered one of the benefits of living unencumbered by possessions. "There was a man and he had nought, and robbers came to rob him," he wrote Josephine Peabody from his room on Irving Place. "They came one day last week about noon and went pretty much through the house, but they found nothing in the man's room but two or three books and some papers which were of no particular value except to the owner; and they were kind enough to leave those things as they found them." The most valuable asset he had, Robinson calculated, was the manuscript of "Aunt Imogen," which he valued at $1.75.

Traveling light had its advantages, and that was the way Robinson chose to live. Before long, he would have no choice in the matter. In the fall of 1900, at about the same time as the robbery, he mentioned to Mason that "the last smash in my western real estate"—Herman's ventures in Missouri and Minnesota—had inspired him to try to "transform a draggle-tailed poet into something practical." At the time EAR's tone was cheerful enough. The discouragement of the whole *Captain Craig* fiasco, from its misadventures among publishers to lukewarm reception, lay just ahead, as did the final dispensations from the once substantial family estate. Within two years, he would descend into the depths of poverty.

The trouble began in Gardiner, where Herman and his family were struggling along on the remnants of his inheritance and whatever assistance might be forthcoming from Emma's parents. As Herman drank away his days, the Shepherds became less and less sympathetic. They urged Emma to leave her husband and move to their house in Farmingdale with her three daughters. When she refused to give up on the marriage, her parents helped support the children and brought groceries when they visited, but they would not give their daughter money. To make ends meet, she was reduced to dressmaking.

Herman was appointed administrator of his mother's estate, which was finally appraised by the probate court in January 1901. The liquid assets had been reduced to approximately $6,000, and there is no record that any of this money reached EAR in New York. The very next month, Dean's estate was settled under the stewardship of Henry S. Webster, Win's onetime companion in the Gardiner Poetry Society. Webster succeeded in disposing of this estate's only appreciable asset, the stock of the drugstore. The proceeds after expenses amounted to $1571.30, half of which was distributed to each of the two surviving brothers. Win received $500 of his share in August 1901, leading him to splurge on opera tickets, in "the peanut gallery of course," and to commit the "moral crime" of buying a writing table for his rented room. The remainder of Dean's estate came to him in decreasingly small installments during the following year. The last four checks were for $40, $14.86, $25, and $12.54. Then there was nothing more. After the autumn of 1902, the poet in New York received no further funds from the capital Edward Robinson had worked a lifetime to accumulate.

During most of the dark days from 1901 to 1905, Robinson lived in a cubicle on the fourth and top floor of a brownstone building at 450 W. Twenty-third Street. His landlord was Jimmie Moore, grandson of the very proper Rev. Clement Clarke Moore, who wrote "The Night Before Christmas." With the passing of two generations, Jimmie Moore emerged as the sort of unapologetic libertine his grandfather preached against: a convivial, riotous, licentious fellow with the red face and black moustache of the villain in the melodrama.

In the spring of 1901, Robinson did Moore a favor. He was then living in a boarding house at 29 E. Twenty-second Street, five long cross-town blocks east of Moore's building. Moore took a carnal interest in a young lady at the boarding house and asked EAR to give up his place next to her in the dining room. Robinson complied, Moore dined with her, and the conquest was made. When Jimmie heard that EAR was short of cash, he offered him a room in the brownstone in gratitude, rent payable at his convenience.

West Twenty-third Street bore little resemblance to Robinson's previous addresses east of Fifth Avenue. "Before there was a Great White Way on Broadway," according to a 1979 New York Times article, "Chelsea's West 23rd Street was a gaslit theater district with an opera house, luxury restaurants, gambling houses, and more hot and cold running scandals than plumbing." Jimmie Moore, as landlord, saw to it that the inhabitants at 450 West Twenty-third enjoyed their full share in the deviltry. Many of his renters were artists or would-be artists given to all-night parties and unsanctioned sexual interludes. No one cared who spent the night, or with whom. In the basement, Moore installed a shooting gallery and bowling alley. Outside, the street was busy with traffic headed for the rumbling Ninth Avenue Elevated, half a block away, and for the ferry beyond Tenth Avenue which plied the Hudson.

Robinson had no quarrel with the Dionysian surroundings. He could write there as well as in more decorous quarters and did not lack for companionship. The faithful Burnham gave up his career as a corporate lawyer—"he could not bring himself to lie," Robinson explained—and moved in next door. The two friends talked and smoked together whenever EAR was not writing, and in the evenings they sought out the best of the saloons and cheap restaurants. Betts also lived at 450 W. Twenty-third for a brief time, as did the inescapable Joseph Lewis French.

There too, Robinson met a number of visual artists the landlord had cultivated. Moore introduced EAR to William Sherman Potts, the first to paint Robinson's portrait. The painter Ernest Lawson, who became a friend, was a neighbor on the top floor. In the basement shooting gallery Robinson met the young sculptor James Earle Fraser. "Are you the poet?" Fraser asked, immediately winning Robinson over. Twenty years later, the Frasers—Jimmy and his wife Laura, also a sculptor—would take Robinson in as part of their family.

The fastidious Fullerton Waldo, a well-bred Harvard man whose music EAR enjoyed listening to, came to visit Robinson in his "dismal cell" and was appalled. The bare furnishings consisted of a bed, a "precarious" rocking chair, a bureau without a mirror, and a wash-stand with a cracked water pitcher. At the time of Waldo's visit, "five bohemians" were crammed into the room, sitting on the bed, the chair, the windowsill, and talking nonsense "about the manufacture of poetry." Awful as the room was, Waldo preferred it to the company.

Years later, Robinson and Burnham joked about Waldo's account. Both of them spent much of their lives in one hall bedroom or another, and in their eyes EAR's room at 450 West Twenty-third Street was more than adequate to the purpose. Though small, it was clean, comfortable, and even quiet, since it faced south away from the bustle of Twenty-third Street. Robinson accomplished a great deal of work there during 1901 and most of 1902.

When his financial emergency struck in 1903, Robinson had few sumptuary habits to give up. He lived frugally, with no expensive tastes. Ostentation and luxury were "as foreign to him as unnecessary speech," Betts said. He liked good food, with a special fondness for the New England dishes of his youth, but could easily be satisfied by the plainest of fare. He dressed simply, more like a clerk than a bohemian. When his best suit grew threadbare, he begged off an invitation from Betts to the Salmagundi Club on the grounds that he looked "too seedy." Still, there were plenty of places they could go for dinner where his clothes wouldn't matter.

Robinson was not out to campaign against middle-class proprieties. He observed them when he could and felt somewhat embarrassed when he could not. Yet he understood that giving up good food and good lodging and good clothes was part of the bargain he had made in order to live a life in poetry.

Robinson hated subsisting off the largesse of others, but he had to for two lengthy periods. From 1902 to 1905, and again from 1910 to 1914, he was almost entirely dependent on the charity of friends. The experience left him both grateful and humiliated, and undoubtedly contributed to the generosity he lavished on others once he had enough money to do so. When success finally did come to him, his financial adviser pleaded with him to stop dispensing his income so lavishly to old friends and new. "You don't understand," EAR said. "You've never walked the streets of New York without a nickel in your pockets." Robinson did that, starting in the summer of 1902.

For a while, he maintained his equanimity under the burden. He took up Greek, reading Homer and the dramatists and—best of all—Mackail's entertaining versions of the *Greek Anthology*. He spoke of finding "more commodious" living quarters. Perhaps, he thought, *Captain Craig* might enrich him or make his verse more palatable to editors. It did not turn out that way. Not a single poem of his appeared in a magazine or newspaper from 1901 through 1904.

"Sometimes I think the funniest thing in my whole life, and pretty much all of it is funny, is my staying alive since 1903—I mean since 1902," Robinson wrote Betts a few years later. At the time, it did not seem funny at all. By the winter of 1903, he was deep in depression. Lawson could hear the creak of his rocking chair, EAR's substitute for pacing the floor, well into the morning hours. When Torrence stopped by to take Robinson to dinner, he invariably found him facing the door, as if anticipating that someone might come along to rescue him and ready to be disappointed when it didn't happen. It seemed to him that he had always been unhappy. "I was born," he told Torrence, "with my skin inside out."

Friends did what they could to help him through his despondency. Once he met his landlord on the front stoop and stammered a promise about paying the long-past-due rent. "Robbie," Jimmie Moore roared at him, "you pay me that rent when you get goddam good and ready." Stedman, past seventy, climbed the stairs to offer his assistance. He had a hundred dollars he didn't seem to need. Could EAR make use of it?

Such kindnesses, invaluable as they were, only worsened Robinson's fear of failure. Lack of money made it difficult to get through one day after another. Lack of recognition made him wonder about his very reason for existence. Really, he valued only two things: poetry and companionship. When the poetry failed to command an audience, EAR in his dejection began to cut ties to those who cared about him. He very nearly stopped writing letters, even to the three women who most believed in him. "I am not writing much to anybody nowadays," he apologized to Josephine Peabody in February 1903. The correspondence with Edith Brower slowed during 1902, with EAR managing a *jeu d'esprit* when he sent her a copy of *Captain Craig* in October:

There was a pale artist named Ransom
Whose hands were exceedingly handsome.
     To be sure they were seen
     He painted them green
And held them all day through the transom.

During all of 1903 and 1904, he sent Brower only one letter, a tardy note of condolence for the death of her aunt.

EAR also tried to break off communication with Laura Richards. They had nothing in common, after all, he said. Probably they would never see each other again. What was the point of continuing? Recognizing the sound of despair, Mrs. Richards categorically refused EAR's suggestion. It was important, she chided him in reply, to keep in touch with one's hometown and old friends. The correspondence continued, with twice as many letters going from Gardiner to New York as in the other direction.

As his funds decreased, Robinson sometimes went hungry. Beneficially, New York City passed a law requiring that liquor could only be served with food. This led to the institution of free lunch counters in saloons, where coarse cheese and pickled pig's feet would be uncovered to anyone who produced a nickel for a glass of beer. Robinson became a connoisseur of such establishments, which enabled him to satisfy two needs at once. He could draw a map, he claimed, showing the location of every free lunch counter in the city. Still, there were times when he didn't have the required nickel. Sometimes he had to make a meal of a roll from the bakery, which could be had for a few cents. Once, eating alone at the Old Homestead on Eighth Avenue, he looked so down-and-out that a waiter offered to lend him two dollars.

There were those who were disposed to see Robinson's poverty as a benefit rather than a hindrance. To some extent, EAR was complicit in fostering this attitude. The English writer John Cowper Powys once made his way to the room on West Twenty-third Street.

"Why do you live with nothing but a bed?" Powys asked Robinson.

"Because," he answered, "I am a faithful servant of Apollo."

The critic and literary historian Van Wyck Brooks met Robinson at about this time and straightway glamorized his "cult of failure—poverty, shabbiness and failure." Brooks, who had family funds enough not to face the worst, liked "mean streets and faded houses" and rejoiced in holes in the seat of his pants and holes in the soles of his shoes. What worried Brooks, in the marrow of his bones, was the danger of being rich. EAR understood that feeling and shared it to a degree. But it was not a danger that he was confronted with at the time; he was down-and-out, as Brooks was not. Cultivating one's muse was "all very well, but a drink and a meal did better on a cold night."

Rightly or wrongly, Robinson felt that only liquor could keep him going. Late at night, after touring West Side bars with Torrence or Betts, the veil of despondency would lift, EAR's eyes brighten, and his tongue loosen. But these were costly excursions. Given his capacity, it took a lot of whiskey to produce the desired transformation, and the next day his depression would return, deepened by remorse.

As he became increasingly dependent on drink, the Dutch uncle in Robinson drove him to warn young James Barstow about its perils. Barstow, who was then tutoring a wealthy youth in Tuxedo, would come into the city flush with money to finance a night on the town. Though grateful for his generosity, EAR could not resist warning Barstow to be more careful "about the too convivial side of life." He advised him to give "up the whole thing, beer and all," and to quit smoking cigarettes in favor of a pipe. "I may not be a shining success myself," EAR admitted, "but that does not prevent my having eyes." What he observed was a young man who needed straightening out. Once again, as when Barstow went to Kansas City to work on the newspaper, EAR took it upon himself to do the job. A few months later, when Barstow left New York to begin his career as a prep school teacher, Robinson sent him off with a piece of advice he himself was quite unable to follow. "You might remember what Stevenson says about leaving off the booze. Something to the effect that a man should quit and then dismiss the incident from his mind. Easy as the very devil to say," EAR concluded, "but still there is something in it."

His involvement in the plight of others was one of the two things that enabled Robinson to outlive his dejection. Even in his despair, he maintained his sense of fellowship with other human beings, especially those whom fortune had not favored. In September 1903, for example, he broke the silence in his correspondence with Peabody to commiserate with her about a financial crisis in her household. "Surely you deserve something better than you are getting," he wrote her. "Maybe that is why you don't get it," he added. Committed to doing what he could for others, Robinson could not abide the callousness or self-centeredness everywhere around him. "This utter lack of consideration for others goes far toward making this life of ours the rat-trap that it is," he told Peabody in March 1904, "With the world so beautiful and life itself so hideous, I don't wonder that [the] closing choruses of the Greek tragedies were all alike."

The other saving grace—what kept Robinson from letting depression become oblivion—was his stubborn faith in the worth of his poetry. A less committed artist would have given up the battle in the face of the reversals he suffered, from the indifference of a reading public that did not buy his books to the lack of acceptance or even outright hostility of magazine editors. One editor summarily forbade him to submit any more poems for consideration.

Herman's Banishment

As Robinson bottomed out in New York, so did his brother Herman in Gardiner. In September 1903 he sold the family's sole remaining asset, the house at 67 Lincoln Avenue. For a few years past, he had been renting the house during all of the summer and part of the winter, but the income was barely enough to pay taxes and upkeep and did nothing to support Emma and the three girls. Finally, Herman put the place up for auction. This insured a quick sale, but not a particularly remunerative one. Ruth Robinson, then twelve, remembered the auctioneer standing on the dining room table and knocking down the house for $2,200, $300 less than it was appraised at two years before and $1,800 less than Edward Robinson had paid for it in 1870. The auctioneer also disposed of most of the furniture and other family possessions.

When the auction was over, Herman asked daughter Ruth to write Win about the outcome. She was to tell Win that he was too tired to write now but would do so later, Herman said. However that may be, no correspondence on the sale of the house survives, and there is no evidence that the poet in New York received any proceeds from the property that belonged jointly to the two brothers. In "Bokardo," an embittered 1915 poem, Robinson expressed his indignation. Bokardo—a name drawn from a figure in logic that no one understood—comes to visit the narrator of the poem, a friend whom he has wronged. The narrator hears him out:

Talk a little; or, if not,
　Show me with a sign
Why it was that you forgot
　What was yours and mine.
Friends, I gather, are small things
In an age when coins are kings;
Even at that, one hardly flings
　Friends before swine.

In apparent remorse, Bokardo speaks his piece. He has been driven to the brink of suicide, he says, and seeks absolution for his dereliction of duty. The narrator, detecting self-pity rather than genuine repentance, is disinclined to grant it. "Your last flight went rather low," he points out.

Written a dozen years after the sale of the house, "Bokardo" reveals EAR's lasting resentment against the favored brother who married the woman he loved and compounded the offense through at best imprudent mismanagement of the family fortune. Still, he would certainly not have condoned the vengeance wrought against Herman by his in-laws. This incident, which occurred only a month after the sale of the 67 Lincoln Avenue property, has remained a skeleton in the Robinson and Shepherd family closet for a century.

The precipitating factor was the sudden death of David C. Shepherd, Emma's father, on October 9, 1903, less than a month after Herman disposed of the house. Shepherd had gone to pick apples after his midday dinner, with the understanding that he would return in time to harness the horse and ride into the country looking for men to work on the ice. Mrs. Shepherd was to accompany her husband, and when he did not call for her by four o'clock, she went looking for him. She found him lying unconscious but still breathing on the kitchen floor. Emma's sister May—"Aunt May" to the family—rushed for the doctor (they had no telephone), but her father died before she came back.

David Shepherd left behind a household full of women: his widow (Nana); her daughters, Emma, May, and Jo; and Emma's daughters, Ruth, Marie, and Barbara, with Herman the sole male relative. Within hours of the funeral, the domineering Aunt May decided to eliminate Herman from the mix. He was sent to the store for groceries. In his absence, May took the japanned tin strongbox her father kept under the head of his bed and sequestered it. Then she announced that the box, containing negotiable securities, was missing. No one outside the family had an opportunity to steal it: ergo, Herman must have stolen it. He was not to be permitted to enter the house ever again, she decreed.

Aunt May was only the most assertive of the Shepherd in-laws aligned against Herman. They knew of his neglect of Emma and her children and were disinclined to excuse it on the grounds of alcoholism. May must have felt that to accuse Herman of an inexcusable act was the only way she could liberate her sister from a disastrous marriage. And her stratagem worked. When Herman returned from his errands, Emma met him at the door and told him of the accusation against him. He denied the charge vociferously, of course, and Emma, though she had grown used to his prevarications, wanted to believe him. But since no one else in the house had any apparent motive for taking the securities, and she had three little children to clothe and feed, and he had failed as a provider, with no money coming in then or in the foreseeable future, she sent Herman protesting into the night.

Thirty years later, Emma told Laura Richards about that moment of separation without revealing the conniving of her sister May. When she barred the door to her husband, Emma said, it was with the understanding that he "could have us any time he provided a home." Herman was thirty-eight at the time, with nearly six more years to live. During much of that time, he scratched out an existence on the water, as a fisherman and clam gatherer. He had dreams of making a fresh start elsewhere and then summoning Emma and the girls, but ill health and liquor prevented him from fulfilling them.

On the night he was turned out of the Farmingdale house, Herman walked the streets much of the night, and then—to find refuge—hiked the fourteen miles across the river to his mother's old home in Whitefield, where his cousin Henry and uncle Kingsbury Palmer took him in. The fatigue and exposure of the journey took its toll, and he came down with a severe case of pneumonia. He spent the winter with the Palmers and in the hospital, losing weight and much of his strength. He and Emma did not communicate for nearly two years.

A Hole in the Ground

"I think I may have a nice job on the subway," Robinson wrote Coan in the fall of 1903. "Nice" was hardly the word, but the job did indeed materialize. The New York subway project was just getting underway, after considerable political maneuvering. Burnham's brother-in-law, one of the engineers in charge of construction, found Robinson a position as a time checker. The job itself required no particular expertise. He was to check the workmen in and out and also to keep count of the loads of material—stone and otherwise—that were delivered. He had the title of inspector, and was paid twenty cents an hour: two dollars a day for ten hours of work.

From November 1903 through August 1904, Robinson staved off starvation by working on the subway. Every morning he descended into the earth, walking south in the damp and gaseous air from 137th Street to 72nd Street, and then north to 159th Street, making entries in his time book of the brass numbers the laborers wore and checking the construction material dumped into the gaping mouths of the tunnel. The very first day, he bruised himself in the dark, stumbling into a pit filled with water, and limped home ready to quit. But he was back on the job in the morning. He could not borrow from his friends forever. The rent had to be paid eventually.

Going down into "a hole in the ground" was hardly tragic, Robinson told Josephine Peabody. "Just what manner of cave I may select for a time is of no real importance." But the job had "a paralyzing effect" on his mind. Long hours on his feet left him too exhausted to write letters, much less poems. Robinson wasn't "much use for purposes of comradeship these days," Moody wrote Harriet Brainard (later his wife) in December 1903. "He is working at a very dreary job, poor chap, and is too tired after he gets through to do much but roll into bed."

Dreary as the job was, Robinson's conscience would not let him leave when, in January, Hays Gardiner offered him a loan. Some time in the future, when he had a new book ready, he might let Gardiner help him out, but not at present. "If my mind is not large enough to include a few months of monotony and dirt, it is not large enough for you to think about," he said. "If I were to come out of my hole now, I should feel that I was making the mortal blunder of my life."

Robinson got along well with the workmen digging underground: Italian immigrants, mostly, and a few Irish. He felt he had more in common with them than with their employers. As a time keeper, he was liberal with his calculations, allowing the men a few extra minutes here and there. The big Irish foreman protected him in turn when he showed up late. One morning when EAR arrived on the job, this Irishman looked downcast. He was going through a family crisis: his brother had died suddenly, leaving a wife and several children without any means of support.

"It's a terrible world," Robinson said.

"Mr. Robinson," said the foreman earnestly, "the world is a son-of-a-bitch."

Determined as he was to stick it out, the long hours walking up and down in a deep gash in the earth took their toll on Robinson's physical and psychological well-being. He hated going down each day into the depths, where the air was fetid and the noise persistently painful to his ears. And he hated the idea of the spying on his fellow workers that the job required. He began, like his brothers before him, to drink for oblivion.

One evening he came back to West Twenty-third Street carrying a bottle of whiskey, something he had never done before. He couldn't help himself, he told Burnham, as he poured a glass three-quarters full and drank it off. So the cycle began: a night of dosing himself with liquor, followed by a dismal day he could only confront as an excuse to drink himself to death. Betts and Torrence and others could see that EAR was destroying himself and pleaded with Burnham, the closest friend of all, to try to make him stop. Burnham, with his newfound Hindu faith in the order of the universe, refused to act. "When the time comes," he said, "Robbie will see the necessity and do the right thing."

In the spring of 1904, the unavoidable French saw a way to turn Robinson's predicament to his benefit. He peddled the idea of a feature on "The Poet in the Subway" to the Sunday *New York World*. To give the story credibility, French brought in Stedman to testify that Robinson was worthy of the title of poet. When EAR heard what was afoot, he was appalled. Such a piece, in French's sensational prose, was sure to humiliate him. He ordered French to cease and desist. French said he would, but went ahead anyway. Nor would Stedman back down. The publicity, he reasoned, might do EAR some good.

The feature ran as a six-column spread on page 10 of the Sunday *World* for May 15, 1904. A head-and-shoulders photograph of Robinson functioned as the centerpiece, with a facsimile of the *Captain Craig* title page to one side and on the other a drawing of the poet in sombrero and mackintosh, toting a lantern as he watched workmen dig the subway tunnel. In a box at upper right, Stedman called Robinson "a man of fine talent" and drew attention to his New England bloodlines. "Some of Mr. Robinson's earlier lyrics and sonnets were beautiful and original," Stedman said, but he waxed less enthusiastic about that "striking bit of realism," *Captain Craig*. Robinson was the kind of poet, he concluded, who "gains at first a select audience if any": implying, quite accurately, that he would have to wait for recognition.

"The Poet in the Subway" story carried an attention-grabbing subhead reading

HAILED AS A GENIUS BY MEN OF LETTERS, EDWIN ARLINGTON
ROBINSON HAS TO EARN HIS LIVING AS A TIME-KEEPER

In the body of the piece, French followed the sensationalist thread in discoursing on Robinson's career and personality. "Even a poet must have the means to live. If his genius, though winning applause, fails to provide the necessities, what then?" Robinson was "a mystery even to his friends," French wrote. Efforts to introduce him to the literary circles of New York and Boston had "only served to withdraw him more and more into his hermit life." French also supplied a summary of the poet's background, riddled with errors of fact. EAR was every bit as dismayed by the article as he had feared.

In *Captain Craig*, he depicted French as Count Pretzel von Würzburger, a drunken artistic pretender and sponger who was nonetheless amusing enough that the Captain advised the narrator "to damn him sparingly." At that stage of their acquaintance, Robinson still thought it possible to restore French to a functional existence. In April 1902 he wrote Mason on his behalf. French was trying to pull himself together, EAR said, but he badly needed "a few acquaintances who will take him with some degree of seriousness and treat him as if he were a human being." He had "an intelligent passion for music and a sort of instinctive adoration" for Mason as a composer. Would Mason be kind enough to let him visit from time to time? It would do a lot for French and might even do something for Mason if he could see through the fellow's "noisy bluff of indifference and egotism (if he tries it on you) and through his real admixture of mild craziness—which can be cured only by a little human interest and sympathy."

On the envelope of Robinson's letter, Mason wrote "French—alas!" Before long, Robinson came to feel the same way. When French appeared, he would praise Robinson extravagantly and demand money. Upon leaving with his dole, he would excoriate EAR just as enthusiastically. The Sunday *World* episode in 1904 was cause enough to break off the relationship, but, EAR discovered, "French isn't a man you can get rid of." Once he attached himself to Robinson, he would not let go. He then expanded his operations to other writers EAR knew. When he attempted to establish a connection with Torrence in August 1904, Robinson warned him off. "French? Crazy as a bedbug. I help him when no one else will and receive the reward that is usual in such cases." The following winter, French "elope[d]" with Moody's only overcoat. "For three days," Moody wrote EAR, "I planned bloody plans for getting it back; at the end of that time I reflected that he needed it more than I did." On the strength of such pardons, French survived to do further mischief.

Robinson was laid off in the middle of August when the digging for the subway tunnel he'd been working on was completed. He plunged at once into more congenial labor, reading about the depths in Maxim Gorky and John Milton. In tribute to his fellow workers, he took up Italian as a recreation, going underground to Dante's *Inferno* and managing to read the tragic tale of Paolo and Francesca in the original before contenting himself with translations.

Within a month, he was ready to return to writing. "I shall soon be at work again in my old unreasonable way," he wrote Gardiner. He was inclined to envy those who had more practical occupations in mind, such as peanut vendors and sword swallowers. "If I were to go into the peanut business I should burn more than I sold. If I were to swallow a sword the results might be more satisfying to some of my friends, though I might not enjoy the process any more than I did the subway." As long as friends like Gardiner believed in him, he could "keep on waiting for some time longer in the dark."

Late in October, the initial segment of the subway opened for business. Robinson took a ride and reported the results to Peabody. "Dark and stuffy, but smooth and otherwise satisfactory. On the whole, I'm rather glad I built it." This was meant to amuse, and Robinson refused to romanticize the experience. He told Torrence, for example, that when he went down into the subway, he was "simply in Hell" and unavoidably so. "I was there because I couldn't get out." Two decades later, after he had begun to receive recognition, a well-meaning young woman tried to draw him out on the subject of the Italians he worked alongside. "How interesting, Mr. Robinson," she said. "You must have enjoyed studying them." No, he replied. He despised himself because he couldn't get a better job.

With his underground employment at an end, Robinson faced his predicament once more. He could get a job, and eat, or write, and give up eating. At the end of the year, Willie Butler proposed a compromise of sorts. He would employ EAR to compose advertisements for his Boston department store at ten dollars a week, with an understanding that he was to devote only one-third of his time to the job.

Robinson assented to these generous terms and was back in Boston at the beginning of 1905. He went to see Josephine Peabody on January 2, "looking well & different somehow" and sensibly prepared to make money. "We talked five hours with much profit," she noted in her journal. For the next six months, EAR was in Butler's employ. Writing copy for dry goods ads a few hours each day did not tax EAR's resources, but he found the work dull and without redeeming social value. During off hours, he resumed attempts to summon the muse, with some success. He could write in Boston all right, but as he wrote Betts, "New York was the best town to live in." Before long, courtesy of the president of the United States, Robinson was back in New York, free of his cumbersome poverty.

Deliverance Through Groton

Robinson's liberation began at an unlikely site: on the waters of the Nashua river, thirty miles west of Boston, where the boys of the Groton School were learning to row in competition.

Groton was founded in 1884 as a preparatory school for boys on the English model. The students—among the most famous of whom were Theodore Roosevelt's sons and their cousin, Franklin Delano Roosevelt—were subjected to a rigorous way of life. They slept in cubicles, thirty to a room, with only a cloth curtain for privacy. Each morning they took a cold shower and washed up at the basin in the soapstone sink assigned to them. After classes and compulsory afternoon exercise, they showered again and changed into stiff collars, patent leather shoes, and coat and tie for dinner. An oblong head table, higher than the others, commanded the dining room, with all the tables covered with linen tablecloths. On Sundays, the boys wore suits to the mandatory services in the chapel.

Groton was very much the creation and embodiment of Endicott Peabody, one of its three founders. At six feet two and more than two hundred pounds, Peabody ruled as rector for over half a century. He had been educated at Cheltenham and Trinity College, Cambridge, and imported English nomenclature for his new school. He was the rector, not the principal or headmaster. Students were divided into forms, not classes. In the winter they learned the English game of "fives" instead of squash racquets or the more plebian handball. Within the compass of a highly disciplined atmosphere, Peabody aimed to break down barriers between students and teachers. In the fall, everyone played football, boys and masters alike, with Peabody himself an imposing figure at tackle. He also was one of the first proponents of the honor system. If a boy broke the rules, by going out of bounds at night or lying or cheating or smoking or drinking during the holidays, he was expected to undertake his own self-discipline. If he did not, he was a likely candidate for dismissal.

Peabody's Groton was designed to mold the character of its students and to instill in them a commitment to serve those less fortunate than themselves. The rector was not an intellectual, and he took little interest in the educational reforms proposed during his tenure, notably by John Dewey. He ran the school his way and brooked no dissent.

"Cottie" Peabody's iron hand, high moral seriousness, and English partialities had their appeal to the American gentry. From the Yellow House in Gardiner, Laura and Henry Richards sent their son Henry Howe Richards to Groton. He graduated in the class of 1894, went on to Harvard, and returned in 1898—the first "old boy" to do so—to teach Latin and English for more than forty years. From the White House in Washington, Theodore and Edith Roosevelt sent their sons to Groton. Himself an advocate of the strenuous life, the president felt a natural kinship with the rector. So in the early years of the twentieth century, Richards became dormitory master to young Kermit Roosevelt, the second of President Roosevelt's four sons. It was, for E. A. Robinson, a fortunate coincidence.

Known to schoolboy generations as "Mister Dick," Richards struck one of his early students as representing "the best of New England" and looking "as if he just stepped off the *Mayflower*." He brought with him to Groton the proficiency as an oarsman he had learned from his father. In the spring of 1903 Richards coached the Squannacook crew in the intramural race against the Hemenways. Kermit Roosevelt, a diminutive thirteen-year-old first former, was his coxswain. The race ended in a dispute. When one of the Hemenway rowers caught a crab on a bend of the river near the finish line, their shell veered into that of the Squannacooks, knocking it off course. The Hemenways crossed the finish line first, and were declared the winners. Richards protested, knowing his boys had been fouled, while Mather Abbott, coach of the Hemenways, maintained innocence. Eventually, it was decided that the race should be called a tie, and the father of one of the Hemenway oarsmen donated individual cups to the members of both crews. Impressed by the vigor with which the coach defended his crew, Kermit joined a small group of boys to whom Richards occasionally read poetry aloud.

According to his mother, in his teenage years Kermit was a rather "solitary, independent character." Unlike his father and brothers, he did not take to horseback riding and shooting. Instead, he was devoted to reading, collecting books, and developing "a finer literary taste" than his siblings. When "Mister Dick" read some of Robinson's poems to his students and told them something about EAR and his difficulties, Kermit was entranced. He particularly liked "The Wilderness," a Poe-like poem in long rhythmical lines that depends more on sound than sense for its effect. On his own initiative, the boy purchased and gave copies of the limited vellum edition of *The Children of the Night* to his father in January 1904 and to his mother in August of that year.

President Roosevelt was an omnivorous reader. The legend holds that he read a book a day, and while that may be an exaggeration, it seems unlikely that any president in the century since he held the office read as much as he, or in such a wide variety of fields, including poetry. But the slim volume of poems Kermit gave him in January 1904 must have eluded his eye. Not until November 3, 1904, days before he was reelected to the presidency, did Roosevelt tell Kermit that he had "taken immense comfort out of the little volume of poems by Robinson, that you gave mother." A week later, when the returns were in, he reverted to the same theme. "I have been reading Robinson's poems again and like them as much as ever," he said. And again, at the end of January 1905, Roosevelt wrote his son that he was "delighted with Robinson's Children of the Night" and had "as usual been reading and re-reading it."

As to Robinson, the newly reelected president paid his son the compliment of adopting the poet's cause as his own. It is clear from President Roosevelt's letters that the youngster at Groton was not only advocating the merits of Robinson's verse but urging his father to do something about rescuing him from indigence. In writing to Kermit, the president referred to Robinson as "your poet." Early in his new term of office, he set aside affairs of state to find a way of alleviating Robinson's poverty while enabling him to continue writing.

Rough Rider to the Rescue

Robinson and Moody stayed up until dawn watching the 1904 election returns. As a Republican from Maine, EAR welcomed Roosevelt's victory over Democrat Alton B. Parker. He had no idea at the time that the president—and his son Kermit at Groton—had already become supporters of *his*.

In the first weeks of his new term, President Roosevelt asked Richard Watson Gilder, poetaster and influential editor of *The Century* magazine, what he knew about Robinson. Not much, Gilder replied, but he offered to find out more. In late January 1905, Robinson received an unexpected letter from Gilder, inquiring about his welfare and offering an invitation to lunch. EAR, by then occupying dingy quarters at 1 Yarmouth Street in Boston, could not very well break bread with the editor in New York, who had previously shown no interest in his work. But he did bring Gilder up to date on his recent activities: publishing *Captain Craig* with Houghton Mifflin, tramping the New York subway for nine months, and in Boston "writing advertisements for a department store and inviting famine by writing more verse."

Six weeks later, on the strength of Gilder's overture, Robinson sent him a batch of poems for consideration. Gilder forwarded them to his associate editor at *The Century*, with a note saying that they were the work of "the Robinson in whom Pres. Roosevelt is interested." What interested the president interested Gilder as well. He proposed that one of the submitted poems, "Uncle Ananias," might do for the magazine's "In Lighter Vein" department. Hence Robinson's portrait of a genial old liar who charmed the children with the "superb magnificence and ease" of his prevarications ran alongside the lightest verse in the August 1905 *Century*. It was the first poem of his a magazine had actually paid for since *Lippincott's* took his sonnet on Poe eleven years earlier.

Gilder was also involved in the discussions that led Roosevelt, in the fortnight spanning the end of March and beginning of April, to offer Robinson a government position. The editor came to see the president in connection with an article he was writing, "The President as a Reader." Roosevelt, who had been prodded on the subject by Kermit, asked Gilder about Robinson yet again and fired off a letter to the poet dated March 27, 1905.

Dear Mr. Robinson:

I have enjoyed your poems especially The Children of the Night so much that I must write to tell you so. Will you permit me to ask what you are doing and how you are getting along? I wish I could see you.

Sincerely yours,
Theodore Roosevelt

The letter was typewritten, except for "especially The Children of the Night," which Roosevelt added in longhand.

When the letter reached him in Boston, Robinson was thunderstruck. His clothes were so shabby that he could not accept the president's implied command to visit him. He responded at once, though, noting that "getting along" barely did justice to his precarious existence. Meanwhile, Gilder and Moody took up the matter at dinner. Things proceeded rapidly, as separate letters of March 31 testify: one from Moody to Robinson, the other from Roosevelt to Gilder.

"It may interest you to know that you have been discovered by the national administration," Moody wrote EAR. "Roosevelt is said to stop cabinet discus-

sions to ask [John] Hay, 'Do you know Robinson?' and upon receiving a negative reply, to spend the rest of the session reading 'Captain Craig' aloud." Upon
hearing this report from Gilder, Moody said, he had made the editor promise
to suggest to Roosevelt that Robinson should be given "a nice lazy berth in
the consular service in England." The next day, Gilder made this suggestion to
Roosevelt, omitting the word "lazy," but the president balked. Writing Gilder,
he expressed his conviction that it would be "inadvisable for [Robinson] to go
to England." Roosevelt felt that "our literary men [were] always hurt by going
abroad. If Bret Harte had stayed in the West, if he had not even come East, he
might have gone on doing productive work. To go to England was the worst
thing possible for him." As an alternative, Roosevelt said, he might be able to
locate "some position in the Government service, just as Walt Whitman and
John Burroughs were given Government positions."

Once that occurred to him, Roosevelt immediately swung into action. He
wired Robinson the next day. "Would you accept the position of immigrant
inspector at Montreal or Mexico at a salary of six dollars a day? I think you
would find the work interesting and later I shall be able to transfer you to some
other position with more congenial duties, though some little time might elapse
before I could do this. Wire decision at once."

EAR's reply, both by telegram and letter, has not survived. But it is clear that
he refused the offer. On April 3, the president tried again, with perhaps a trace
of exasperation, while on a train bound for a bear hunt in the west. "Will you
let me know what kind of place it is that you could accept. I do not want you
to leave the country if it can be avoided. I may not be able to give you the place
you desire, but I shall try."

Again, EARs response has disappeared, but he let his friends know about the
astounding overtures from the White House. In her journal entry for April 10,
Peabody offered "three cheers" for Roosevelt, who seemed "ready and eager to
find for R. such work as he might be ready and eager to do. I don't know when
anything so timely had befallen anyone who so needed a cheering fantasy." To
Betts the following day, EAR revealed that "President Teddy has been trying to
entice me away to Montreal and Mexico with eighteen hundred dollar jobs, but
somehow they don't attract me. I have told him what I want."

He was more explicit about what he wanted in a letter to Gilder of the same
date. Robinson knew that Gilder had been acting as a go-between, and he
undoubtedly sought to explain himself to someone who had the president's
ear. He told Gilder about the initial "pleasant note" from Roosevelt and the
subsequent "offers of employment in strange lands," which he could not see
his way to accept. "Now he understands my situation, and I may or may not
hear from him again. In many respects I am placed fortunately as I am, in that
I have about two-thirds of my time to myself. I have told him this, making it
clear at the same time that if I could have more congenial work, with more
pay and the same amount of leisure, I should be happy to get it. Were I not

cursed with the poetical microbe, of course everything would be different. In fact, I should never have heard from him at all." As always circumspect about acknowledging the help of others, Robinson thanked Gilder for everything he had done and added that he could not find out from Moody "just how far he [was] implicated" in assisting him. "Will you kindly see that he gets his share of my gratitude?"

The schoolboy at Groton continued to jog his father on Robinson's behalf. "Yes, I wrote Robinson, but he could not take what I offered him," the president replied to Kermit on May 7. "I have written him again asking him if there is not some position that he would take. I want to help him if I am able to." Less than a week later, on May 12, President Roosevelt offered Robinson "a $2000 position as special agent of the Treasury, say in New York, although possibly in Boston. It will give you plenty of time to do your outside work. That you will perform your duties in the position I am sure. I shall hope that you will be able to accept."

"Teddy is after me again with a scalping knife and a machine gun," EAR wrote Peabody. This time, he came with an offer Robinson could not refuse. As Robinson told Gardiner, he didn't "know a special agent of the Treasury from the mother of Samson." All he knew was that the job promised $2,000 a year—four times what as he was making in Boston—with ample opportunity to do his own writing. Under those circumstances, he might even "be able to own two pairs of shoes at the same time." Robinson agreed to take the position beginning July 1, and it turned out to be in New York, as he had hoped.

Roosevelt, however, did not want to leave their correspondence on a merely commercial footing. "Some time when you are in New York," he wrote Robinson on May 23, "I shall want to see you, to discuss literature—not the Treasury." Then the president enlightened "Blessed Kermit" about what he'd done and promised to invite Robinson to Sagamore Hill, their summer home at Oyster Bay, Long Island, where "you and I can both see him."

As an enthusiastic advocate of equity in government appointments and promotions, President Roosevelt had fleeting reservations about what he had done for Robinson. For once, he admitted, he had gone back on all his civil service principles to play Maecenas. "Tell it not in civil-service-reform Gath, nor whisper it in the streets of Askelon," he wrote a friend. "I am free to say that [Robinson] was put in less with a view to the good of the government service than with a view of helping American letters." It was the only sinecure he bestowed on anyone during his presidency.

Roosevelt conveyed the same message to Robinson when he visited Sagamore Hill in July. "I want you to understand," he said, "that I expect you to think poetry first and Treasury second." Having done much for Robinson, the president undertook to do more. Not without calculation, he invited Robert Bridges, literary adviser of Scribner's, to the luncheon at Oyster Bay. Kermit was there also, prepared for the poet's notorious reticence by Richards and

FIGURE 13.1 President Theodore Roosevelt, EAR's patron, in 1906.

Source: Picture Collection, New York Public Library.

delighted to see his idol in the flesh. In the course of the conversation, Robinson discovered that the president knew more about contemporary American poetry than anyone he had ever met who was not a professional critic.

The next month, Roosevelt took time off from brokering a peace between the warring nations of Russia and Japan to assume the role of critic himself, publishing a laudatory essay about *The Children of the Night* in *The Outlook*. The piece was dictated by Roosevelt with son Kermit at his side making suggestions. The magazine paid $50 for the contribution, which father and son split down the middle. Kermit's half went entirely for books.

Roosevelt's praise for a book that had been published eight years earlier might have seemed odd, had it not been agreed upon by Scribner's to print a new edition of *The Children of the Night* in October. The publishing firm, which had rejected *Captain Craig* in 1900 and then rejected the book of shorter Robinson poems submitted eighteen months later, even though it came with a guaranteed subsidy, adopted a different stance once Bridges was apprised of the president's interest in EAR.

Roosevelt's article on Robinson in *The Outlook* represents the only instance of literary criticism from the hand of a sitting president. Like so many others Roosevelt spelled the poet's first name as "Edward," but otherwise the president found only good things to say about him and his work. The essay began with a lament that no American poet of recent years ranked as high in the world of letters as American sculptors and painters did in the world of art. Robinson, it was suggested, might help to remedy the situation. It was "curious" that his work had been so little noticed, the president said, for there was "an undoubted touch of genius" in *The Children of the Night*. He touched on the charge of obscurity only to discount it. A poem could not be translated into terms of mathematical accuracy, Roosevelt observed. "I am not sure that I understand 'Luke Havergal,' " he said, "but I am entirely sure that I like it."

His two-page review essay quoted "The House on the Hill" and "The Wilderness" in full, and mentioned briefly "Richard Cory," "Ballade of Broken Flutes," "Amaryllis," "The Pity of the Leaves," and "The Tavern." "Richard Cory" and the ballade were cited as evidence that to Robinson "the most real of lives is the life of the American small town." "The Wilderness," in contrast, offered testimony that he was "a man into whose heart there had entered deep the very spirit of the vast and melancholy northern forests"—a remark which, as a critic later commented, told the reader more about Roosevelt than about Robinson. The piece ended with a minor caveat: "Mr. Robinson has written in this little volume not verse but poetry. Whether he has the power of sustained flight remains to be seen."

Any poet in midcareer, thirty-five years old and little recognized, might have been expected to click his heels upon reading such a glowing notice from a president of the United States. Robinson walked the floor of his room exclaiming, "I shall never live it down! I shall never live it down!" His Yankee reserve was at work here, as it had been with the "Poet in the Subway" article of the previous year. In addition, EAR rightly anticipated that the president would come under fire for presuming to invade a field not his own. "It was very good of Theodore to write me up as he did," he wrote Mary Mason, "though he put himself, and incidentally E. A. R., in a way to accumulate a good deal of cussing."

The cussing began when, less than forty-eight hours after *The Outlook* appeared, the *New York Evening Post*, Roosevelt's political enemy, took the president to task. "This union of political and literary authority in a single man is a dangerous business," the *Post* objected. And the more dangerous, the anonymous editorial writer added, because Roosevelt's judgment was quite wrong. "There are few lovers of fair play who do not honestly regret to see a person in high authority turn from his course to puff a book mediocre in character and little distinguished from scores of similar volumes put out by a busy press." In his "literary ukase," the piece explained, "Mr. Roosevelt has lauded one of Badger's Boston bards; he has thereby given grievance to the thousands unnamed."

The Bookman also took a swipe at EAR while enlightening Roosevelt on his shortcomings. "There are, of course, many poets of the Robinson degree, but the President is not to blame if he has encountered only one of them. It is well known that he has had a number of other matters on his hands of fully equal importance." *The New York Times*, with a defter sarcastic touch, congratulated Robinson on his good luck. He "will doubtless be encouraged to write many more books of verse for the edification of a people enlightened as to their worth by a Chief Magistrate who is also a popular hero." Even at the present, it was something "to be a Roosevelt poet, and it will surely be a glory of the future to have been an acknowledged and officially accredited poet of the Theodorian era."

Though as a consequence of President Roosevelt's venture into literary criticism Robinson was subjected to "the calamities of injudicious praise," the episode made his poetry more commercially viable to the house of Scribner. The publishers initially featured an excerpt from Roosevelt's *Century* article on the dust jacket of the new edition of *The Children of the Night*, scheduled for a publication date of October 14, 1905. The day before, an advance copy was sent to the White House, eliciting a protest from Roosevelt's private secretary, William Loeb Jr. The president was constantly asked for endorsements and invariably refused to lend his name for purposes of advertising, Loeb explained. Would Scribner's "therefore discontinue the use of the President's name in any way in connection with the book?"

Of course they would, but Roosevelt's praise for the book was so well known to the literary community that almost every review reacted to it, either pro or con. *The Dial* took the affirmative: "This time the presidential lightning has struck in the right place, for Robinson's work has never got half the attention it deserved." *The Critic* argued for the negative: if Roosevelt had "kept up with the flood of American minor verse . . . he would think twice before applying the word 'genius' to Robinson." The longest and best review came from itinerant journalist Mowry Saben, EAR's close friend at Harvard. Saben alluded indirectly to Roosevelt's quotation from Wordsworth about the poems radiating "the light that never was on sea or land." But the mysticism in Robinson, Saben remarked, was more apparent than real. He "has seen much in everyday life and everyday things which escapes the eyes of most of us, that is all." His poetry became more understandable with rereading and the acquisition of experience. Some of the poems that bewildered him seven years before, Saben said, were "clear as crystal" now.

Despite the uproar it caused, the president did not disavow his article in praise of EAR. He simply felt that Robinson deserved more attention and that his position as president gave him the opportunity to see that he got it. And he believed that "a poet can do much more for his country than the proprietor of a nail factory."

The public image of the Rough Riding Roosevelt, carrying a big stick and eager for confrontation with political opponents, the nation's enemies, and wild animals in remote places, did not much appeal to Robinson. He knew better than anyone that there was far more to the president than "biceps and sunshine." He had, after all, engaged in a "disinterested and business-like pursuit" of EAR himself and exerted considerable energy toward advancing his career as a poet.

In later years, Robinson established a cordial relationship with Kermit Roosevelt. He sent the young man copies of poems as they emerged and copies of his books as well. After Kermit married, he and his wife often entertained EAR for dinner in New York. Always, though, it was Teddy Roosevelt who had Robinson's gratitude. "I don't like to think where I should be now if it had not been for your astonishing father," he wrote Kermit in 1913. "He fished me out of hell by the hair of the head."

14

Theater Days

Customhouse Duty

Back in New York to take up his government job, Robinson bought himself a derby hat as a token of his rise to bourgeois respectability. "When I paid for the damned thing, I said to myself, Is this the end?" he wrote Betts in mock alarm. He put the derby on his head anyway and reported for duty in June, a month earlier than Roosevelt originally proposed, at the Custom House in lower Manhattan, headquarters of the United States Customs Service, Port of New York.

On his first day at work, he was ushered into an office containing only a desk and chair. Finding nothing inside the desk other than a spool of tape, he went to the head of his department and asked, "What am I supposed to do?" With some embarrassment, the man dodged the question. He knew that Robinson was a political appointee, not expected to do any real work. With some indignation, EAR demanded that he be given something to do; he'd had enough of "empty hours in the office" in Boston. The department chief gave him a set of regulations on imports and suggested he might familiarize himself with them.

For the next month or two, Robinson cheerfully made light of his new occupation. "My days are spent in reading the Customs Regulations and waiting for crime," he wrote. "My well-being depends entirely upon the iniquity of others"—and not only his but the well-being of everyone in the Customs House. They were supposed to stop smuggling and other irregularities and were out of luck when none occurred. "The whole place is languishing for lack of crime." To remedy the situation, he proposed to Mrs. Richards that she initiate some illegal activity. "If you are really a friend of mine you will go abroad at once and smuggle something."

At first his superiors made a few half-hearted efforts to accommodate their new special agent's desire to be of use. They sent him to the wharves of the Fall River line, supposedly to keep his eye open for smugglers on ships that plied their way entirely in American waters. He found nothing, of course. Then his superior officer gave him a small stone that the customs people were supposed to assess. "When you come across some college man among your friends, ask him what it is. No one here seems to have any idea." EAR slipped the stone into his pocket, but neither encountered a friend with the requisite scientific training to identify what it was nor troubled himself to seek expert information on his own. He did tell Betts one day that he exposed a million-dollar conspiracy to defraud the government. The case, Betts thought, "was highly hypothetical."

Before long, Robinson's undemanding days fell into a pattern. He would sleep late, come into the office around noon, eat an apple, turn over a few documents, read the papers—especially the *New York Journal* with the Mutt and Jeff cartoons—and depart. That left the evenings free for "shopping," EAR's term for sampling the wares of various saloons.

Word of Robinson's preferment by the president aroused a certain degree of envy among those less favored. *The Touchstone* for January 1906, a short-lived Chicago periodical, cast a satirical eye on EAR's career, enlivened by humorous drawings of the poet gamboling in the daisy fields of Maine, at his desk in a New York attic, toting a pickax in the subway, and finally languishing recumbent in the customhouse, quill in hand, while his fellow employees snooze away. "Go down to the custom house and sit on one of those comfortable reed-bottomed chairs," the article has President Roosevelt telling Robinson, "or lie on the floor if you like all day long."

Even Ridgely Torrence, a frequent companions of EAR's, could not ward off a certain resentment. In a May 1906 letter to his parents, Torrence waxed indignant over his friend's soft berth. "Robinson will soon get a raise in position and salary in the Customs service," he wrote. "He is certainly very lucky as he does no work whatever. He is frightfully lazy, sleeps until noon and sometimes until four o'clock in the afternoon and complains when he has to go down to the office to draw up his pay twice a month." Hard-working employees were getting fired while Roosevelt kept Robinson on the dole, Torrence maintained. Besides, even with all his free time, EAR wasn't doing much writing.

This was true. With the depredations of poverty behind him and his holding a well-paying post that demanded little of him, the auspices were promising for poetic production from Robinson. Moreover, Roosevelt's intervention opened up certain avenues that had heretofore been barricaded against him. The impressive Richard Watson Gilder followed the president's lead so far as to call on EAR while he was still in Boston and to invite him to dinner once he reached New York. On June 29, 1905, Gilder wrote the president that he had entertained Robinson at his house "for several evenings together. He is a fine fellow—shy, frank, high-toned, and . . . well worthy of your interest." The house of Scribner followed its reissue of *The Children of the Night* by printing six Robinson poems in *Scribner's* magazine between January 1906 and October 1908. In May 1907, the staid *Atlantic Monthly* in Boston ran "Calverly's," Robinson's evocation of likable if unsuccessful comrades in bohemian New York. But this was hardly an explosion of poetry over more than three years' time. EAR's muse did not respond well to good fortune.

There was another reason why Robinson did not write more poetry while in the employ of the Customs Service: he had been bitten by the theater bug. At the time, Broadway offered a literally electrifying prospect to ambitious writers. As early as 1891, the first electric marquee was lit at the intersection of Broadway and Fifth Avenue at West Twenty-third Street, only a few blocks from Jimmie Moore's brownstone. By the middle of the following decade, electric signs announced each show in white lights along Broadway all the way from Union Square to Times Square. The Great White Way was ablaze, and theaters sprang up to take advantage of the boom. Like Hollywood a generation later, Broadway promised substantial financial rewards for those who could or would meet its standards.

The lure was more than Robinson could resist. No sooner had he emerged from his incarceration in the subway than he began roughing out "a comedy in prose" that had been "pursuing" him for two years. This project was put aside but not forgotten while EAR wrote ads for women's millinery in Boston. By the time he relocated to New York, it seemed that almost every poet he knew had turned to drama.

Torrence published a romantic play in verse, *El Dorado: A Tragedy*, in 1903, and was completing another, *Abelard and Heloise*, which Scribner's published in 1907. Peabody's blank-verse *Marlowe* was produced at Radcliffe College in the summer of 1905, with George Pierce Baker—later to earn fame as a mentor to actors and playwrights at Harvard—in the title role. Moody, elected to the National Institute of Arts and Letters in February 1905 under the sponsorship of Stedman and Gilder, put aside the poetry that earned him that distinction and threw himself into writing prose plays for Broadway.

Moody turned up in New York in November 1905, with a mysterious bullet hole in his hat, and invited Robinson to hear Percy MacKaye read his new play, *Jeanne d'Arc*. A tall lean fellow with flashing dark eyes and superabundant energy, poet and playwright MacKaye had grown up in the theatre, with time off for a Harvard education. A few months earlier, EAR had read another of MacKaye's plays, *Fenris, the Wolf*, with little enthusiasm. But MacKaye in person, reading *Jeanne d'Arc* with theatrical flair to a "very select crowd" in Moody's room, was captivating. He "hypnotized us with the first two acts," EAR wrote Peabody. He cited MacKaye as one of the "two geniuses" he met during that autumn.

The other "genius" was the "Lady of the Divine Fire," the English writer May Sinclair. Her 1904 novel about a starry-eyed poet, *The Divine Fire*, had become a best-seller, despite the fact that she had written it without knowing a single poet. On her trip to the United States, she made up for her previous lack of experience by meeting not one but three: Moody, Torrence, and Robinson. Sinclair, in Moody's description, was "a drab and angular little lady, somewhere between thirty and forty by the almanac but in reality quite undated—without a single feather to flaunt, meek-spoken, naïve, wholly unworldly and without guile." She took to Robinson "tremendously," Moody reported. "There is a story of their having been seen at 2 a.m., leaning over the railing in the middle of the Brooklyn Bridge, entirely incommunicative and at one."

In her "Three American Poets of To-Day," which appeared both in the *Fortnightly Review* and the *Atlantic Monthly* for September 1906, Sinclair singled out Robinson, Moody, and Torrence as the leading American poets, with a perceptible tilt in favor of EAR. She noted Robinson's "unerring skill in disentangling the slender threads of thought and motive and emotion" and proclaimed that he had it within him "to write a great human drama, a drama of the soul from which all action proceeds and to which its results return." Such praise was part of her pattern of championing the work of challenging new writers. During a subsequent career that involved writing twenty-four novels, Sinclair spoke out on behalf of Ezra Pound, T. S. Eliot, and D. H. Lawrence.

During the summer of 1906, Josephine Peabody married Lionel S. Marks, a professor of engineering at Harvard. Robinson did not attend the ceremony, but Moody, Torrence, and MacKaye were on hand. They presented the bride with a silver loving cup inscribed with their names (and EAR's), along with a verse from Theocritus: "May there always be concord in the house of the Muses." They were beginning to think of themselves as a group primed for an assault on the American theatre.

Later that summer, Robinson and Moody visited MacKaye at his Cornish, New Hampshire, home. Harriet Monroe, who was soon to launch the influential *Poetry* magazine, stopped by one afternoon. This was her first meeting with Robinson, though she had advance word about him from Moody: "mighty good poet—very simple bare style." Monroe found EAR "shy, quiet, reticent, holding off from easy intimacies." She would have preferred him to be more candid and forthcoming. Afterward, she read *Captain Craig* and discovered that "this poet of the lean phrase and the nutty flavor was no Victorian."

Torrence at the Judson

In the fall of 1906, Jimmie Moore was obliged to sell his building at 450 W. Twenty-third Street (some of the canvases that artists gave him in lieu of rent formed the nucleus of the new Whitney Museum), and Robinson was forced to leave. EAR joined Torrence in moving to the Judson hotel at the south end of Washington Square. The two poets were sometimes at odds, but never for long. Early in their friendship, Robinson was hurt by what seemed to be Torrence's "indifference." During 1903, as EAR's funds were running out, they agreed to meet every Tuesday evening for dinner, an arrangement that turned sour when, as letters between them attest, one or the other of them would fail to show up. Later, Torrence was annoyed not only by EAR's cushy job but also by his excessive drinking. "I found E. A. R. in that hell hole of Guffanti's last night deep in his soup," he wrote Moody. Robinson, for his part, was put off by (in Betts's phrase) "Torrence's fleering ways": his derisive laughter. Yet their relationship lasted to the end, bolstered by a shared love of poetry and a mutual respect for each other's work. They were never closer than during the period of 1906 through 1909 when both were in residence at the Judson.

The Judson hotel provided Robinson with more respectable surroundings than those on raucous West Twenty-third Street. The 1890 building, designed by the brilliant Stanford White, looked to the north through the greenery of Washington Square Park. In addition to its pleasant and variegated rooms, the Judson offered excellent food for its boarders. The place quickly acquired a reputation as a haven for writers and artists. Henry James stayed there for a time. So did Robert Louis Stevenson's widow, and his son. Frank Norris was said to have outlined his novel *The Pit* in one of the tower rooms. The painter John Sloan converted his quarters into a studio apartment.

In residence when Robinson and Torrence moved in during the fall of 1906 were Lyman Beecher Stowe, grandson of the author of *Uncle Tom's Cabin*, Olivia Howard Dunbar, an attractive freelance writer, and a number of other intelligent young women. Dunbar watched with amusement as first one woman and then another tried to break through EAR's reserve and came away defeated. He was sympathetic, polite, considerate, but would reveal nothing of his innermost self.

The Judson served as a gathering place for the circle of poets and playwrights that included Ridgely Torrence and Robinson. Torrence introduced EAR to Louis Ledoux there, a well-to-do young poet—and crack tennis player—who was to became Robinson's lifelong friend and supporter. Moody stopped by when he was in town, as did MacKaye and Mason. The chief entertainer at evening gatherings was Torrence himself. With a long lean face and high forehead, he looked like an ascetic, but his talk uncovered considerable knowledge of the ways of the world. "He was an incomparable mimic," Mason recalled. "He could look drunk entirely by facial expression," with no staggering required. Or he could assume the pose of a Fourth of July orator, one hand between his vest buttons, solemnly addressing his "Fellow Citizens." Torrence's best impersonation of all, Mason thought, was his Missionary, a person of considerable self-importance and equivalent stupidity.

In correspondence as in person, Torrence had a gift for "pure, divine nonsense." From his home town of Xenia, Ohio, he wrote Mason a "wish you were here" letter lamenting that distance prevented their meeting, for,

As the poick nobly sings,

The feathered tribes on pinions cleave the air.
Not so the mackerel, and still less the bear.

I wish that you and I were sitting round some heavenly board, on these hot days, with about half a stigtossel of dogglegammon . . . between us. Wouldn't we be a pair of cool ones as ever went up?

FIGURE 14.1 Ridgely Torrence, poet, humorist, and great friend at the Judson.

Source: Torrence Collection, Princeton University Library.

"Sometimes," Ledoux was to say of Torrence, "I have thought that he was the most charming male human being I have ever encountered."

Of an evening, Robinson and Torrence, one dark and withdrawn, the other blond and engaging, would leave the Judson and make the rounds of the nearby saloons. Upon returning, they would read poetry aloud to each other. Robinson's taste ran to the sorrowful, as in Rossetti's "Lost Days" and Coleridge's "Youth and Age." He seemed happiest when in the vicinity of misery, a habit of mind that Torrence attributed to "Old Puritan stock" and a melancholy like that of Hawthorne. Between the two of them, though, they devised a more gladsome practice, playing an ongoing private game as scandal detectives.

Each week, Robinson received the Gardiner newspaper. When it arrived, he would alert Torrence so that they could examine the social notes together. In these columns, they pretended to discover highly dubious activities involving local residents. There was, in particular, Torrence recalled, "a man whom we will call James Perkins, and a lady whom we will protect by giving her the name of Mrs. Henry Hasbrouck." Both of them were respectably married, with sizable families, yet it was uncanny how often they would be reported as having visited the same place at the same time. When Mr. Perkins took a business trip to Boston, Mrs. Hasbrouck was staying with her cousin in that city. When Mrs. Hasbrouck went to a Job's Daughters meeting in Portland, Mr. Perkins was attending a bankers' conference there. Could this be only coincidence? The poets rarely missed an opportunity to read and interpret the latest dispatches. "We sat above the puppets and watched their innocently suspicious movements with tireless attention," as Torrence said. Some years later, discovering that the Perkins and Hasbrouck names were no longer mentioned in the paper, Robinson wrote finis to the amiable game with a dolorous line from Charles Lamb: "All, all are gone, the old familiar faces."

Torrence's biographer placed considerable emphasis upon his role in brightening Robinson's days. He did not seem to know, however, about EAR's behind-the-scenes efforts to arrange a European vacation for Torrence from the spring of 1907: efforts documented in confidential letters between Robinson and Ledoux. Torrence was in poor health at the time, his lungs ill-equipped for New York weather. He was also strapped for funds, in part because of supporting his younger brother at Harvard. Ledoux, whose father Albert was president of a successful metallurgical firm, asked Robinson privately what might be done for Torrence, knowing that he would not accept an outright gift. On February 19, 1907, EAR replied to Ledoux, "I think it right that I should tell you that R.T. appears to be in a bad way. If anything can be done it ought to be done now." Of course, Robinson added at the end of the letter, he was writing without Torrence's knowledge. "Tear this up, please," he advised.

Ledoux and his father managed to persuade Torrence to sign a loan to finance a journey abroad. "T. is beginning to realize the necessity of his getting away and I feel pretty confident of his yielding to your father's persuasion," Robinson wrote Ledoux on February 26. "He appears to suspect nothing in regard to my letter." Two days later, Moody wrote Harriet Brainard in Chicago that Torrence had secured money for a Mediterranean trip and was wild to have him come along. In mid-March, Torrence and Moody sailed on the *Romanic* for Gibraltar. Apparently, Torrence never knew of Robinson's acting as intermediary on his behalf. Eager to help his friend, EAR did not want to injure his pride or to draw attention to himself.

The Siege of Broadway

At the start of the twentieth century, the principal theaters were controlled by a syndicate more interested in attracting cash customers than in furthering the art of the drama. Dodging the requirements of the International Copyright act of 1891, producers imported material from the London stage; plays by popular English dramatists were almost certain to follow their runs in New York or Philadelphia with lucrative road tours. Otherwise, sentimental melodramas and vapid comedies ruled the stage. Ibsen was regarded as morbid, Shaw shocked the public sensibilities, and there seemed little demand for serious realistic plays by unknown American playwrights.

Then the tide began to turn. In 1904, the actresses Minnie Maddern Fiske and Nance O'Neil each played the title role in Ibsen's *Hedda Gabler*. In the following year, the police closed Shaw's *Mrs. Warren's Profession* after a single performance, but sizable audiences were allowed to see his *Man and Superman* without intervention. The time had come, the energetic MacKaye decided, for "a poets' onset on the theatre" that would advance the cause of American drama. All that was required was talent and imagination, and he found those qualities abounding in the "little group" including himself, Moody, Torrence, Robinson, and Peabody, all in their early thirties.

Robinson was a reluctant member of any group, even one with MacKaye as cheerleader and impresario. But he plunged into playwriting after the extraordinary reception of Moody's *Great Divide*, a play built around the conflict between the New England and Western temperaments.

In March 1906, Moody read this work in progress at Dan and Mary Mason's, with Robinson a rapt listener. Soon thereafter, Moody "gathered in Robinson and Torrence" to celebrate signing a contract for production of the play on Broadway. With this prospect in mind, EAR wrote Peabody on July 4 that he was finishing a poem about a great new period for the American theater. "The White Lights" drew an analogy between the current theatrical renaissance and the past glories of Greek, Roman, and Elizabethan drama. It ended:

Here, where the white lights have begun
To seethe a way for something fair,
No prophet knew, from what was done,
That there was triumph in the air.

Robinson himself was prophesying the triumph, one which—he told Peabody—"you and Von Moody [his favored nickname for Moody] and Torrence and MacKaye will have to make good": leaving himself out of the mix.

The Great Divide opened at the Princess Theatre on October 3, 1906. The reviews were excellent—one critic hailed the author as a "great American playwright"—and the play was a smash hit at the box office. Moody had succeeded in doing what all of the group hoped to accomplish: making a considerable amount of money from an honest and realistic play. "It's like taking candy from a child," Moody wrote MacKaye, who had his own first stage success two weeks later with the opening of *Jeanne d'Arc* in Philadelphia.

By January 1907, both Torrence and Robinson had caught "the dramatic fever" and were turning out prose plays. Torrence wrote a three-act called *The Madstone*, based on an Ohio folk legend about a small porous stone supposed to be able to extract poison when applied to a human wound. In his play, Torrence transformed the madstone into a symbol of a woman's love. "Robinson thinks the play is a great thing," Moody said, adding that EAR himself was working on the first draft of *Ferguson's Ivory Tower* (later called *Van Zorn*), "It would be wonderfully good luck if they both pulled it off. One could begin to think the American drama, long awaited and devoutly prayed-for babe, really about to be born."

Robinson had high hopes that *Van Zorn* might prove "good enough or bad enough to find its way into the favor of a Broadway manager." He gave a full synopsis to Moody, who liked what he heard. In mid-March he took himself and *Van Zorn* to MacKaye's home in Cornish, New Hampshire, where he read the play to his friend and heard his verdict that "it will go." MacKaye used his theatrical connections to try to open doors for Robinson, without notable success. He sent EAR to the distinguished character actor Kyrle Bellew, to Harrison Fiske, dramatist and manager of his wife Minnie Maddern Fiske's theatrical company, and finally to Charles Frohman, producer of E. H. Sothern and Julia Marlowe's Shakespeare plays in 1905 and 1906. Only Frohman promptly read and reacted to *Van Zorn*, and he dismissed the comedy in a few brief words: "good qualities, but not suitable for stage purposes."

Instead of abandoning the field, Robinson decided to make another assault. "I have done a new play—all but the writing," he told MacKaye on April 20. The play occupied a space between comedy and tragedy, he explained, ending "'in two keys,' like R.[ichard] Strauss's *Zarathustra*." By midsummer, *The Porcupine* was completed, and he took it along on another visit to Cornish. He was eager to read it to MacKaye and to spend some time with him and his family away from the August heat of New York.

For the three years from 1906 to 1909, Robinson devoted most of his writing energy to the composition of prose plays. These included several one-act plays that vanished, and at least three full-length plays, of which only *Van Zorn* and *The Porcupine* survived. Throughout this period, he was perpetually aware that he was not writing the poetry that President Roosevelt expected of him. Or at least not much of it. In April 1907 he sent Kermit Roosevelt the manuscript of "Calverly's," which was about to appear in the *Atlantic Monthly*, along with a note accounting for his general lack of poetic production. "About seven months ago I was seized by the hair, dragged out of bed, and pounded into relative insensibility by a tall and uncompromising being called Modern American Drama. . . . I have been in his power ever since."

A similar message went to Dr. Schuman. Schumann, now married, stayed at the Judson on a trip to New York City. One night Robinson and Burnham showed him the white lights of Broadway, where Schumann was relieved of his gold watch by a pickpocket. A few nights later, Schumann and Robinson went roistering again, the doctor having purchased a tin watch in the interim. But that too was stolen, so the story goes, and Schumann returned to Gardiner without a timepiece.

Robinson wrote Schumann in May that "for the past four or five months" the poems had refused to come. He feared that "this drama business [might] be the annihilation of me." His former mentor from the Gardiner Poetry Society attempted to be reassuring. It was a good thing to stick to the drama for a while, Schumann said, "for even if you find you can't do it successfully, the practice will help you in the kind of work which you can and will do again."

Robinson's dream of a career as a playwright brightened briefly in July 1907 when he received an unexpected letter from the manager of His Majesty's Theatre in London.. He had heard about Robinson from Josephine Peabody Marks, who was living in London, and asked to see his work. Robinson dispatched *Van Zorn* across the water and waited in vain for a favorable word in return.

Robinson read *The Porcupine* to Moody in October. He could not have found a more enthusiastic audience. "A stunning play handled with a wonderful deftness and lightness of touch," Moody declared. He took the manuscript with him to beard Charles Frohman in his den. "Before I knew it," Moody wrote about their meeting, "I was pouring out my heart to him on what our little group dreamed of trying to do by way of crusade." In particular, he "swore the daylight black and blue cracking up *The Porcupine*." Moody could speak with some authority, *The Great Divide* having just completed one thousand performances on Broadway and on its way to a production in London's West End.

Frohman heard him out and promised to read Robinson's play at once. Three days later, the producer sent it back to Moody with a terse scribbled comment: "Not available for stage," the language paralleling his judgment against *Van Zorn* five months earlier.

At about this time, in the autumn of 1907, Robinson and Burnham were about to go out one evening when they were accosted by a cadaverous looking man. EAR excused himself to talk with the intruder and only afterwards told Burnham, "That was my brother." Herman Robinson was in a bad way, exiled from his wife and family, scratching out a bare existence in cabins and camps near Capitol Island, trying to shake off alcoholism, and intermittently in and out of a Boston hospital with pneumonia and tuberculosis. EAR, now that he could afford to, agreed to help support his impoverished brother. They had little in common, and Win had reason to be resentful about Herman's past behavior, but the blood tie outweighed those considerations. Besides, the poet in EAR could not help feeling sympathy for a defeated figure who had begun with so much promise.

Soon after appearing on his brother's doorstep, Herman was back in Boston for treatment and tests. "It was a great relief to me to know that there was nothing wrong with your liver and kidneys," EAR wrote him there. "I was pretty well convinced that there was something and had about given you up." He asked Herman to let him know how he was getting along, but it was not really a friendly letter. "I have nothing new to say about myself," he concluded.

Clara Davidge, one of New York's more adventurous hostesses, collected Robinson, Torrence, and Moody for a festive Halloween dinner at her handsome house on Washington Square (MacKaye, in Cornish, was unavailable). A small, lively woman in her middle forties, the widowed Mrs. Davidge had been born into society and good works as the daughter of Henry C. Potter, the Episcopal bishop of New York, and was devoting her time and money to aid artists in their careers. At the Halloween celebration, the three poet-playwrights, along with Dan Mason and Rodman Gilder, "twined [their] brows with grape wreaths and looked like tipsy pagans." It was fortunate that Robinson, a reluctant guest, decided to attend the party. Before long, Mrs. Davidge would single him out for continued support.

In the winter of 1908, E. A. Robinson, Ridgely Torrence, and Percy Mac-Kaye were all elected to the National Institute of Arts and Letters, with William Vaughn Moody sponsoring each of them. Heartening as the recognition from the National Institute was, EAR could not easily escape the despondency caused by the second negative pronouncement from Charles Frohman.

In May, the disheartened Robinson declined Josephine Marks's request for a look at *Van Zorn* and *The Porcupine*. "The two plays you ask for are so bad that I don't want them seen again by anybody in their present shape," he declared. He felt absolutely sure of their lack of merit, "for there is a degree of badness that cannot be mistaken even in one's own work."

Robinson also felt guilty that he had so little to show after three years in his government post. His chief fear, he wrote Mason on July 22, 1908, was that he might prove a disappointment to his "friends and to T.R.—who must be wondering, if he finds time, how long it takes a man to write a hundred pages of verse."

In the same letter to Mason, Robinson revealed that under a new system and with a new boss at the Custom House, he was now expected to be in attendance during all office hours. He felt like "a prisoner in Room 408," he said. "This is particularly rotten just now, as I am in the mood for work (work with me means studying the ceiling and my navel for four hours and then writing down perhaps four lines—sometimes as many as seven and again none at all) while there is just enough going on here, not to mention all hell outside, to keep my poor relic of a brain in a state . . . of semi-agitated punk."

He was reduced to working nights, when his obsession with the theater once more took hold of him. In midsummer, Torrence wrote Moody that he'd discovered EAR "drilling away in the tower of the Judson" on his third three-act play, with a scheme for a fourth in prospect. "He is miserable, of course, because he is happy, but fortunately he is happy because he is miserable," Torrence added, in a reprise of their ongoing joke about Robinson's temperament.

Robinson was drawn back to playwriting both by the heady prospect of financial rewards far beyond the reach of poetry and by his lifelong love of the theater. The stage fascinated him as a boy, and the two years at Harvard confirmed his addiction. He enjoyed "almost anything that a curtain goes up and down on," from Shakespeare and Ibsen to the most facile comedies and mysteries. The experience let him enter into the imagined lives of other people, much as he did when he envisioned them in his poems. In his later years, there were times when he considered moving his winter headquarters to Boston instead of New York. Such plans were invariably abandoned once he got "a sniff of Forty-second Street and a sight of Broadway."

In October 1908, Moody encouraged Robinson to stick to the "playwriting business, despite Frohman and all his works. You have got the technique better than any of us, and it is only a question of time when you will strike it, and strike it hard." Meantime, Moody advised, EAR should "by all means publish *Van Zorn* and *The Porcupine*." He'd already tried to do so, Robinson answered, only to learn "that a play is about thirty-seven times more difficult to place than an epic poem founded on the life of [social butterfly] Ward McAllister."

The group's prospects brightened with a fresh success from the prolific MacKaye, who managed to get a play mounted on Broadway nearly every year. In 1907, his *Sappho and Phaon* bombed, yet back he came the next year with *Mater*, which despite chancy reviews caught on with theatergoers. "Hurray for the continuation of *Mater*," Torrence wrote MacKaye. "E. A. and I rejoice with you. It is our success as well as yours, for it doesn't matter who writes what we all want written." In the following year, MacKaye published his *Poems*, with its dedication—"To W. V. M., E. A. R., and R. T., In Fellowship"—acknowledging the bond between the four literary musketeers. Robinson himself, though hardly a joiner, did the same in subsequent years, dedicating *Roman Bartholow* (1923) to Percy MacKaye, *Cavender's House* (1929) to the memory of William Vaughn Moody, and *Matthias at the Door* (1931) to Ridgely Torrence.

Poems came slowly during the period of intoxication with the theatre, but among them were a few of Robinson's best, including "Miniver Cheevy," a light-hearted satirical portrait unlike anything else he wrote.

> Miniver Cheevy, child of scorn,
>   Grew lean while he assailed the seasons;
> He wept that he was ever born,
>   And he had reasons.
>
> Miniver loved the days of old
>   When swords were bright and steeds were prancing;
> The vision of a warrior bold
>   Would set him dancing.
>
> Miniver sighed for what was not,
>   And dreamed, and rested from his labors;
> He dreamed of Thebes and Camelot,
>   And Priam's neighbors.
>
> Miniver mourned the ripe renown
>   That made so many a name so fragrant;
> He mourned Romance, now on the town,
>   And Art, a vagrant.

Miniver loved the Medici
   Albeit he had never seen one;
He would have sinned incessantly
   Could he have been one.

Miniver cursed the commonplace
   And eyed a khaki suit with loathing;
He missed the mediaeval grace
   Of iron clothing.

Miniver scorned the gold he sought,
   But sore annoyed was he without it;
Miniver thought, and thought, and thought,
   And thought about it.

Miniver Cheevy, born too late,
   Scratched his head and kept on thinking;
Miniver coughed, and called it fate,
   And kept on drinking.

Robinson rightly maintained that most of his poetry carried an undercurrent of humor, but in "Miniver Cheevy" the comic spirit is at flood level. The poem is all uncomplicated delight, the enjoyment coming at the expense of the hapless Miniver. This very lack of complication, and the absence of strong empathy for the figure under examination, distinguish it from the customary Robinson character study. We are not invited to identify with the title figure. It is enough to laugh at him.

Technically, also, "Miniver Cheevy" represents a departure from EAR's customary approaches. There is no choral voice, no "we" to present a point of view from which the narrator or reader may want to distance himself. Instead, an omniscient voice bodies Miniver forth as a very foolish fellow. The stanzaic and metrical forms are radically different from others Robinson used, and perfect for light verse. The finest touch comes with the feminine endings, dangling unaccented syllables at the end of the second and fourth lines. The double rhymes they create produce amusing aural effects, as in "loathing" and the priceless iron "clothing" and in the long *es* of "seen one" and "been one."

In the first line of the poem, we are introduced to Miniver Cheevy as a "child of scorn." The scorn cuts two ways, for just as Miniver deplores the drabness of modern life, he is scorned by others for his ludicrous yearnings and persistent inaction. The word recurs in the penultimate stanza.

Miniver scorned the gold he sought,
   But sore annoyed was he without it;

Miniver thought, and thought, and thought,
    And thought about it.

Here the poem makes fun of Miniver's constant cogitation, along with his hypocritical antimaterialism. His high-minded repudiation of riches is undermined
by the revelation that "Miniver loved the Medici" and that if he had been as rich
and powerful as they, he too "would have sinned incessantly."

The case against poor Miniver is closed in the final line, when we find that
in bemoaning his fate he has turned to drink. That concluding revelation seems
almost an afterthought. The poor fellow has faults enough without an addiction to liquor. The only real justification for this detail derives from the facts of
the case: Robinson drank, and therefore so did Miniver, for "Miniver Cheevy"
exists both as a highly entertaining sketch and a wry self-portrait.

As EAR's grand nephew David S. Nivison observed, "Robinson laughs at
[Miniver] without reserve in every line, and leaves us with no compulsion
to take him seriously or to go deeper into his make-up. . . . [Robinson] talks
about Miniver as he could bring himself to talk about no other man, real or
imaginary—except himself." The excessive introspection, the habit of looking
backward, the derisive attitude toward material success: all were facets of his
own personality. "If we make due allowance for exaggeration," Nivison wrote,
"what is said of Miniver is applicable to Robinson himself—even (for a season)
the drinking part of it." A pleasure to read (preferably, aloud) on any level, the
poem illustrates two admirable qualities of the author: self-awareness and a
willingness to laugh at himself.

In November 1908, after a decade of performing and studying in Europe, the
captivating Isadora Duncan brought her "Dance of the Future" to the United
States. Duncan thought that traditional ballet "deform[ed] the beautiful woman's body," and she argued for less disciplined, more natural movement. Only in
that way could dance regain its status as one of the high arts, "as it was with the
Greeks." She also believed that artists had the right—even the duty—to ignore
conventional moral boundaries. She caused a sensation when she walked down
Broadway in sandals and a diaphanous gown. In more private surroundings,
she indulged her appetites as she pleased, and without apology.

On the night of her first appearance at the Metropolitan Opera House, Percy
MacKaye, Will Moody, and the sculptor George Grey Barnard sat transfixed as
Duncan danced to a full symphony orchestra playing Beethoven's Seventh. The
following evening, MacKaye brought a full complement of poet-playwrights,
including Robinson and Torrence, to call on the "wondrous dancing creature"
in her blue-curtained studio at Fifth Avenue and East Forty-fifth Street. Isadora

FIGURE 14.2 Isadora Duncan, dancer and free spirit.

Source: Library of Congress.

was somewhat hungover from the night before, a reporter for the *New York Sun* observed, but as the champagne flowed, her spirits rose. "It is to revive the lost art of dancing that I have devoted my life," she announced. Then, to piano music, she glided around the room in defiance of gravity, dancing impromptu tributes to each of her poetical visitors in turn. Flirtatiously, she flicked her cigarette under Robinson's nose. With his reserved manner, Robinson interested her more than the others; seducing him presented her with a challenge. "You know," she said coyly as her guests departed, "dancers were made for poets."

On Christmas Eve, dancer and poet met again. Isadora arrived unannounced at the Judson with a motorcar full of revelers and demanded that Robinson and Torrence join the party. The poets were reluctant, for the hour was late, but succumbed when Duncan threatened to make a scene. The celebration moved to her studio, where at about two a.m. she began to send her guests home. Soon there were only half a dozen, and she shunted five of them into an adjoining room, keeping Robinson to herself alone. They were both tipsy, and Duncan let EAR know what she needed from him. Only through the love of a poet, she said, could she achieve fulfillment in her art. Alas, EAR told her, it could not be: the muse was his one true love. He was back in his room at the Judson, virtue intact, when Christmas morning dawned.

EAR's encounter with Isadora Duncan was not to be forgotten. When she died in 1927, he wrote a friend about another well-known overture of hers, to George Bernard Shaw. "As I have the most wonderful body and you the most wonderful brain in the world, don't you think we owe humanity a child?" she wrote the playwright. To which Shaw famously replied, "Has it occurred to you that the child might possibly have my body and your brain?" Two years later, a young poet visiting him at the MacDowell Colony asked Robinson about Isadora Duncan.

"Did you know her well?"

"No, not well"—with the suggestion of a smile. "She wasn't beautiful."

"She was supposed to have preferred a diet of champagne and oysters."

"Well," Robinson said, after a pause, "she didn't refuse whiskey."

15

The End of Something

Herman in Exile

During the entire four-year period when Robinson was supported by the Customs Service and consumed by theatrical ambitions, his brother Herman remained estranged from his wife and family. Throughout this time, Herman was living either on Capitol Island or at nearby Southport on the mainland. Always handy around boats, he survived by fishing and doing odd jobs. But this was only temporary, he told Emma in a series of twenty-one letters written between June 1906 and September 1908.

The dominating theme of these letters was that Herman remained in love with Emma and hoped to win her back. Herman understood that this could not happen until he was able to provide for his family. Although poor health worked against him, he repeatedly asserted that he was feeling better and that a promising future lay ahead. He made plans to return to St. Louis, where once he had been hailed as the very model of the up-and-coming capitalist. He angled for a high-paying position in Toledo. He accumulated letters of reference from men in Gardiner.

He insisted in his often poignant letters to Emma that her family had wronged them both. Just you wait, he kept telling her. They can't keep us apart forever.

Throughout the summer and fall of 1907, Herman pleaded with Emma to visit him, either on Capitol Island or at the Fishers' in Southport. His letters must have softened her resistance, for by mid-August she let him know that she was willing to see him. The question was where and when, for their rendezvous would have to be kept secret from her mother and sisters, especially the domineering May. In mid-September, Herman himself came up to Gardiner to peddle lobsters and made a point of intercepting Ruth and Marie on their way home from school. Ruth was horrified; she'd heard the stories about her father's theft and his lack of support for the family. But Marie, still in grade school, skipped across the street to see her father, who gave her a small unclothed doll she treasured. Herman then took his trip to New York to see Win and proceeded to Boston, where the doctors removed a polyp from his larynx.

When Herman and Emma finally did meet, late in November, she could see that her husband was in no condition to start a new career. With his damaged larynx, he could barely whisper, and he had lost much of his youthful energy. Nonetheless, he collected letters of recommendation from Will C. Atkins, mayor of Gardiner; from probate judge Henry S. Webster in his capacity as treasurer of the Gardiner Savings Institution, and from Henry Farrington, cashier at the Oakland National Bank. All of these men knew of Herman's business failure and of his reputation as a drinker, and their recommendations showed it. Farringston's was perhaps the least supportive. "I hereby certify that I have known Mr. H. E. Robinson for about twenty-five years. During a part of that time he occupied a position of trust, and discharged his duties faithfully. I regard him as a man of good business ability and I believe him to be honest."

Herman obtained these credentials on a trip to Gardiner in June 1908 and apparently got drunk afterwards. So at least Emma heard, and she promptly excoriated him. Herman protested his innocence. Why did she keep waving that whiskey bottle under his nose? Emma did not believe him and broke off the correspondence for nearly three months. On September 1, Herman argued his case yet again. He insisted that he had done nothing to merit her treatment of him. Either she had been lied to and deceived, or she no longer cared about him at all. If it was the first, he could straighten things out in short order. If the second, it would be merciful of her to say so. He left her in no doubt about *his* feelings, closing with

For better or for worse and
Until death us do part.

This cri de coeur brought about a final meeting between Herman and Emma Robinson. She came down to see him at Southport in the last week of September, this time quite openly and accompanied by her mother. Both women had something to say to relieve Herman's distress. Mrs. Shepherd told him that the tin box he was supposed to have stolen had reappeared, its contents intact. Despite all their differences, she wanted to apologize to him and to say that she knew he was not a thief.

Then Herman and Emma had a talk: difficult for him, for his throat was sore from continual coughing. He rasped that he loved her more than she did him. If she were to die he would never remarry, while if he died, she would marry Win. Out of sympathy or love, Emma volunteered a promise that whatever happened she would not marry his brother.

Still cultivating pipe dreams of a prosperous future, Herman had only four months to live. Early in October he went to Boston for a series of medical tests, staying in a hotel. He was admitted to Boston City Hospital on January 25, 1909, complaining of severe trouble with his throat, difficulty swallowing, and a persistent cough. According to the attending doctor, Herman subsequently developed difficulty in breathing "due to a swelling caused by a tubercular ulcer on the vocal cords." A tracheotomy was performed to provide relief, but without satisfactory results. On February 4, Herman E. Robinson, forty-four, once the most popular boy in Gardiner, died of tuberculosis in a public ward of Boston City Hospital, without a friend or relative near.

Emma could not get away from Farmingdale, where she was nursing her mother through what was to be her fatal bout with emphysema. When the end came, she wired Win to go to Boston and bring Herman's body home. He did not reach Farmingdale until Saturday, February 7. "I can [still] see the light of expectancy on [Uncle Win's] face as he came up the front walk," Ruth recalled many years later. The modest obituary in the Gardiner newspaper said nothing about Herman's occupation or about his family, merely remarking that at the funeral "there was a good attendance of old acquaintances and friends, who remembered him for his many good qualities." The funeral was held at the Shepherd home on Sunday. Afterward, Emma and Win took a long walk together. On Monday morning he went back to New York, with things left unsaid between them. He would be back to say them in the fall.

Courting Emma

When William Howard Taft replaced Theodore Roosevelt in the presidency, Robinson's career as a customs officer effectively ended. At the New York Custom House, William Loeb, formerly Roosevelt's secretary and, under the new administration, collector of the port, protected EAR as long as he could before letting him go in midsummer. EAR announced his termination in apocalyptic language. Loeb had issued his "death-warrant," he told Ledoux. His head had "come off with some hundreds of others under the new executioner in the Custom House," he told MacKaye.

Actually, it was just as well. He had unfinished business to tend to, and that could only be completed back in Maine. For twenty years and more he had been in love with Emma Shepherd Robinson. Twelve years earlier, he had comforted her one night and as a consequence been driven away from his boyhood home. During the previous decade, he had returned only twice, and for only two days on each occasion, for the funerals of his brothers. After waiting a patient seven months following the death of Herman, and with no pressing obligations to hold him in New York, EAR seized his opportunity. In September he went to Maine, "to stay the devil knows how long": for more than two months, as it turned out.

It was easy to run to seed in Maine, he told MacKaye, but while there he planned to whip the long-delayed book of poems he owed President Roosevelt into shape. He said nothing, characteristically, of the romantic feelings that drew him back or of his intention to declare his love to Emma and ask her to marry him. They were no longer young. He was in his fortieth year and she several years older. If they were to marry, now was the time.

Robinson tended to idealize women, Emma most of all, so that the courtship proceeded slowly. Win stayed at the Shepherd home in Farmingdale. Emma installed him in a comfortable bedroom on the second floor equipped with a Franklin stove to ward off the chill. There was plenty of room in the house. Emma's mother, Nana, had died in August. May had an office job, and Jo, recently married, lived in a home of her own. During the day, both Emma and Win were busy, she with dressmaking and he with poetry. He worked well there, letting the poems come and the plays recede from consciousness. He did not drink at all. In the evenings, he and Emma made time for themselves. And once again, he forged a bond with his nieces.

Ruth, who reminded him of his own mother, was on a morning schedule at high school and came home for lunch with Win and her little sister Barbara. The lively Marie, at Miss Burleigh's school, would be back by midafternoon. Win took the girls on excursions, collecting mushrooms in the pastures at Oaklands and wandering the hills behind Farmingdale. "The kids coming home from school make me feel like an old [man]," he wrote Ledoux.

Chard Powers Smith, whose biography of EAR, *Where the Light Falls*, is largely based on the Emma-Win relationship, came to believe—though he did not say so in his book—that they consummated their love during his time in Farmingdale. In unpublished notes, Smith speculated that "at her own instance, [Emma] would for his benefit have made the most of those long days when the girls were at school, and of those 'crisp autumn evenings,' to the end that his great love of her should be a complete thing for him, that it should have reality in her female terms as well as in those idealistic terms of his, which she could see as beautiful and good but not quite true."

Well, as Smith says, "perhaps." Neither Win nor Emma ever confessed as much to anyone, but then—as a neighbor observed—"you couldn't get anything out of [either one of them] with a screwdriver." What does seem clear is that Win came to Maine to propose to Emma, and she—at length—refused him. *Why* she did so was to remain a matter of family dispute. According to her youngest daughter, Barbara, who maintained a strong sense of loyalty to her father, Emma always loved Herman and regarded Win only with the affection she might feel for a younger brother. According to her eldest daughter, Ruth, who felt a close affinity to her uncle, Emma loved Win deeply and rejected him out of a conviction that he had outgrown her and she might prove an impediment to his career.

Ruth's opinion stemmed from a conversation in which her mother, then past sixty, for once dropped the veil of secrecy. The two of them were talking about EAR when, surprisingly, Emma asked an atypically revealing question: "Has it ever occurred to you that he cared for me?" The comment opened up much of her uncle's poetry to Ruth, and subsequently mother and daughter embarked on a joint venture to annotate all of Robinson's poems. They worked on the project intermittently over the years. Before she died in 1940, Emma told Ruth to "be sure to finish our work," and she did so. As might be expected, these annotations sometimes discovered in the poems more references to Herman, Emma, and the triangular love affair than are actually warranted.

Still, Robinson's poetry provides the best evidence we have for what happened between him and his sister-in-law during the two months he spent in Farmingdale, from the middle of September to the middle of November 1909. "My poems will have to tell you all I cannot say," as he later wrote her. Two in particular—"Late Summer" (1919), a fine poem, and "The March of the Cameron Men" (1932), an inferior one—seem directly related to Emma and Win's situation. In each of them, a man proposes to a woman whose husband has recently died, and in each case the woman refuses. Otherwise, though, the poems tell substantially different stories.

"Late Summer" depicts a man making his case to a widow whose husband treated her badly and left behind a legacy of lies. The conversation takes place in a setting appropriate to watery Maine, with waves washing up on shore. The suitor implores her to face the truth, for " 'We cannot have the dead between us. / Tell me to go, and I go.' " That is what she does, preferring her illusions to the "needful truth" he has insisted upon. At the end, the man has gone and she gazes, alone, at the shadows covering "the whole cold ocean's healing indifference." Can we assume that Win tried to disillusion Emma about Herman, whom she had come to pity if not to love during their separation? It does not sound like the kind of thing he would have wanted to do, or been capable of doing.

"The March of the Cameron Men," longer and more complicated, presents a more plausible picture of what might have occurred in the fall of 1909. In this case the suitor is a "doctor" come to attend the woman's dying husband. They have had some past history, and the doctor fully expects to marry her after the death of her husband.

" 'You drove me away once,' " the suitor says, " 'but I came back / . . . because you said you needed me/ Because you called me.' " Emma may very well have called for Win to come to Maine; he had no other reason to return there. The doctor, like Win himself, is starkly unsentimental about the dead man. He and the woman row out on the lake for privacy, where he speaks dismissively of the recently departed husband.

"There was no happiness in him alive,
And none for you in your enduring him
With lies and kindness. It was a wrong knot
You made, you two."

To mark the place in her copy of Robinson's *Collected Poems*, Emma left a coil of embroidery silk—true blue, and not knotted—between pages 1220 and 1221, where this passage appears.

The doctor goes on to plead for their life together, but she will not be moved. Her husband was "a devil," she says, and God was afraid to let him live. She is well rid of him, and spent by their unhappy marriage: "as dead emotionally," Emma was to tell Ruth, "as if she were six feet underground." Then she reaches the crux of her case for refusing him.

"As for you and me,
You would have nothing, if you drowned me now,
But sorrow for your work."

He may think he needs and wants her, but she recognizes that he must live for his work. "Is it not better to be wise tonight, / And free tomorrow?'" she asks. The time will come when he will bless her "that all has ended well."

Robinson's trip to Maine in 1909 marked a decisive milestone in his life. Never again would he and Emma be bound together so closely and over so long a period of time as the two months between the middle of September and the middle of November 1909. EAR arrived full of hope and returned in disappointment, without the promise from Emma he had anticipated for twenty years. He risked a great deal in pursuit of her, yet as time wore on he must have realized that she was right to refuse him.

With that rejection, he continued to idealize her as uncapturable and to imagine in dozens of poems how the love triangle might have worked out. And, above all, Emma made it possible for him to follow his calling without the encumbrances of marriage and a family. EAR had been acutely aware of the problem since reading Henry James's "Lesson of the Master" in 1896, and grew dubious about even the most celebrated of romantic unions. "Do you know I have a theory that Browning's life-long happiness with [Elizabeth Barrett] is all humbug?" he wrote Harry Smith. "The man's life was in his art, and he was big enough to make the world think otherwise." And to Edith Brower, he confessed his judgment that Mendelssohn "was a good deal of a man. He had the disadvantage of staying married but even then he wrote some good things." It was wonderful to love, not nearly so wonderful to marry.

The practical Emma, who had learned what it was to be poor during her marriage with Herman, must have seen all or much of this. No matter how they felt about each other, was it not better to be wise today and free tomorrow? Especially since, with President Roosevelt's largesse at an end, Win was without any regular source of income. During the four years immediately before him, he would struggle through a painful period of indigence much like the one of 1902 through 1905. A wife and family would have made the burden insupportable.

Perhaps in partial acceptance of her judgment, as soon as he got back to New York, Robinson wrote "Exit," a poem commemorating the brother who had stolen Emma and squandered his patrimony.

> For what we owe to other days,
> Before we poisoned him with praise,
> May we who shrank to find him weak
> Remember that he cannot speak.
>
> For envy that we may recall,
> And for our faith before the fall,
> May we who are alive be slow
> To tell what we shall never know.
>
> For penance he would not confess,
> And for the fateful emptiness
> Of early triumph undermined,
> May we now venture to be kind.

Some have called "Exit" a tribute, but apologia seems more apt. Herman, he concluded, had been the victim of too much adulation and expectation, and those who envied him—EAR included—had nothing to be proud of. Whatever his brother may have done to injure him, EAR paid him the same courtesy he bestowed on the many other failures who inhabit his poetry: that of trying to understand him.

Despite his disappointment in the fall of 1909, Robinson remained devoted to Emma and her girls throughout his life. They were all the family he had, and family mattered to him. Remembrances went back and forth at Christmas, when the nieces sent Uncle Win embroidered handkerchiefs and he sent them books. Barbara treasured the two witty books on the Goops, rude creatures who behaved so badly as to provide, in reverse, useful lessons in manners. Barbara passed on her enthusiasm for the Goops to her daughter Elizabeth Calloway, who rattled off the verse below one hundred years after her grand uncle Win first acquainted her mother with the Goops' erring ways.

> The Goops they lick their fingers.
> The Goops they lick their knives.
> They wipe their hands on the tablecloth.
> Oh, they lead disgusting lives.

When he stayed in the Farmingdale house during the fall of 1909, Ruth was a blooming eighteen-year-old trying to decide whether and where to go to college. She had almost settled on Smith, but finances were a problem. In the end, Ruth opted for the two-year course at Bradford Academy (later Junior College)

FIGURE 15.1 Uncle Win's beloved
nieces, Barbara, Marie, and Ruth.

Source: Gardiner Library Association

in Haverhill, Massachusetts, then proceeded directly into nurses' training at
Massachusetts General Hospital in Boston. Marie and Barbara followed Ruth's
lead in becoming nurses. All three of them witnessed at firsthand how important it could be for a woman to support herself. And they shared as well a desire
to relieve the pain and suffering of others.

Ruth went through Bradford as "a working student," doing chores to pay
for her room and board, and she was chosen president of the class of 1912. The
next spring, after her first year in nurses' training, Uncle Win came to see her
in Boston. With avuncular concern, he'd warned her to beware the advances
of male interns. Those fellows would "stop at nothing," he declared. With the
protection of innocence, Ruth warded off all assaults on her virtue at Mass
General. But when she and her uncle met, he found something else to trouble
himself about.

Ruth was about to go back to Bradford to deliver a talk to the 1913 graduates. As niece and uncle chatted, he could not help noticing that she was wearing a pair of old shoes with patches. Did she plan to wear them to Bradford?
Well, they were all she had. A week later, a letter arrived from him enclosing
a five dollar bill: not a princely sum, but a substantial one considering his own
impoverished condition at the time. "I worried a good deal over your going to
Bradford with those shoes," he wrote her, "but as it was too late then for me to
do anything, I had to let you go and trust to your personality and general excellence to overcome your temporary pedal defects." She would know what to do
with the five dollars.

16

Down and Out, Yet Again

Friends in Need

In New York one day, the ordinarily uncommunicative Robinson unburdened himself to Ridgely Torrence:

"Do you know," he said out of the blue, "that one of the most terrible things is to walk alone and feel that you are receiving deadly wounds?"

Startled, Torrence asked him what he meant.

The wounds came, EAR said, as he went along the street and caught a glimpse of recognition in the eyes of passersby, only to realize that he would never see them again.

Like Whitman's patient noiseless spider, and nearly as quietly, Robinson was forever casting out filaments, hoping to catch a friend. A number of his poems deal with this quest, bemoaning the frustration of missed connections.

"Fleming Helphenstine" (1896) describes a meeting with Helphenstine, who presents himself amiably, talking "of this and that and So-and-So," laughing and chatting "like any friend of mine."

> But then, with a queer, quick frown, he looked at me,
> And I looked hard at him, and there we gazed
> In a strained way that made us cringe and wince:
> Then, with a wordless clogged apology
> That sounded half confused and half amazed,
> He dodged—and I have never seen him since.

The poem suggests an encounter between two people who mistake each other for former companions and who, in their embarrassment, are rendered unable to communicate.

In "The Corridor" (1902), the speaker laments the loss of one who reached out to him, or tried to.

I keep a scant half-dozen words he said,
And every now and then I lose his name;
He may be living or he may be dead,
But I must have him with me all the same.

The relationship failed to develop

Because silence held us alien to the end;
And I have now no magic to retrieve
That year, to stop that hunger for a friend.

"Alma Mater" (1910) represents Robinson's darkest treatment of the theme of frustrated brotherhood. A nameless, dying creature appears at the door, and the speaker wonders "What battered ancientry is this . . . / And when, if ever, did we meet before?" The wretch dies at his feet, prompting still further questions.

When had I known him? And what brought him here?
Love, warning, malediction, hunger, fear?
Surely I never thwarted such as he?—
Again, what soiled obscurity was this:
Out of what scum, and up from what abyss,
Had they arrived, these rags of memory?

The mystery goes unresolved, even as the theme of an evanescent contact persists.

In "A Song at Shannon's" (1919), a sonnet like "Fleming Helphenstine" and "Alma Mater," Robinson evokes the sorrow of unrealized friendship. Two men emerge from Shannon's tavern after listening to an old song from "some unhappy night bird," and they go their separate ways. The sestet spells out what has been lost.

Slowly away they went, leaving behind
More light than was before them. Neither met
The other's eyes again or said a word.
Each to his loneliness or to his kind,
Went his own way, and with his own regret,
Not knowing what the other might have heard.

These short poems, written over a period of more than twenty years, demonstrate a yearning for human companionship far beyond the ordinary. Without a wife and children, Robinson depended "upon [friends] strangely," as he told Percy MacKaye. Sometimes EAR seemed brusque in his mannered reserve. He had a forbiddingly formal telephone manner. His long silences put people off.

He let correspondence lapse. "And all the time," Robinson insisted, "no man ever lived who cared more for his friends."

Robinson bound those friends to him in two important ways. First of all, he gave them all the distinct sense that they—and they alone—shared a confidential intimacy, Second, he would do anything to assist his friends in time of crisis, offering whatever advice, influence, and money he could muster.

In contemporary American society, as David Halperin has observed, "friendship is the *anomalous* relation. It exists outside the more thoroughly codified social networks forged by kinship and family ties." We are apt to look at a life as dependent upon male friendship as Robinson's and to wonder if he did not live out his days as a closeted gay man (closeted against himself most of all). But EAR's love for Emma—and for Rosalind Richards as well—argues against such a hypothesis. Just as important, there is not a shred of evidence that Robinson ever sought sexual relations with any man. Moreover, his friends were by no means exclusively male, as illustrated by such examples as Laura Richards, Edith Brower, Josephine Preston Peabody, Jean Ledoux, and Lilla Cabot Perry. Only Mowry Saben, among those who knew Robinson well, was moved to speculate that he had repressed homoerotic tendencies. And Saben, as we shall see, was an enthusiastic supporter of love and license in all their forms.

All Robinson asked of his friends was that they believe in him and his calling. Fortunately, he had one such benefactress waiting for him in New York when he returned from Maine, his mission to capture Emma having failed. This was the lion-hunting Clara Davidge, who undertook to improve Robin-

FIGURE 16.1 Clara Davidge, who housed Robinson and tried to reform him.

Source: Princeton University Library.

son while she smoothed his path. Because of her generosity, EAR wrote Betts late in October 1909, he could be sure of a roof over his head without much expense.

Mrs. Davidge had a small, charming studio built to his specifications in the Italian garden in back of her new house at 121 Washington Place. EAR moved there in November and remained in residence for two years. Breakfast was brought to him, and he took his other meals where he wanted. He was on call to appear at occasional social gatherings, but otherwise he was left undisturbed to write. Mrs. Davidge thought that his quiet studio might supply her protégé with an ideal setting for composition. She also endeavored—she was, after all, the daughter of a bishop—to moderate EAR's drinking or to stop it entirely.

Robinson finished a number of poems in his new quarters and shaped them along with others he had written since 1905 into a book called *The Town Down the River*. On March 9, 1910, Scribner's accepted the book for fall publication, at a royalty rate of 10 percent. This businesslike process was unprecedented in Robinson's experience. For the first time, he did not have to shop his wares to various publishers or to lean on others to advance his cause by way of subvention. "The acceptance . . . gives me great pleasure," he wrote his publisher, and he buckled down to polishing and revising and organizing the poems. By early June, the manuscript was ready for the printer.

When the midsummer heat in New York became stifling, Robinson "found a door open" for him at Truman H. Bartlett's farmhouse in Chocorua, New Hampshire. He fled north on the Fall River boat, and before he knew it was buttoning his coat in the cool of the woods and the mountains. With the book of poems awaiting publication, he embarked on a novel, in hopes of producing something that might be "both palatable and profitable." The novel was based on his play *Van Zorn*—"a rehashing of an impossible play, with some added frills"—and before long he had the project "sufficiently in hand" to know that he could finish it. The mountain air seemed to stimulate him.

The eccentric Bartlett, who had played host to Dan Mason and Will Moody a decade earlier, grew up a country boy, without manners. He ate with his knife, wore his hat in the house, and spat on the floor. As a youth he became interested in stone cutting at the village graveyard, and through the generosity of some well-to-do visitors, was sent to Italy and France to become a sculptor. His career did not prosper, but he was supported in his New Hampshire retreat by two Boston physicians. Some people kept yachts or race horses, one of them said. He found it more amusing to keep Bartlett. In turn, Bartlett extended his hospitality to young artists. He enjoyed the company and could unload on them his store of irreverent opinions and personal peculiarities.

Bartlett had been a friend of Whitman and, with his scraggly beard, open collar, and flowing tie, rather looked the part of a latter-day Whitman himself.

FIGURE 16.2 EAR and Truman H. Bartlett at billiards, 1910.

Source: Photo by Hermann Hagedorn.

In his contrary fashion, he railed against sacrosanct institutions like universal education—"the trotting out of a damn fine thing to a pack of idiots"—and the government—"a necessarily constructed bugaboo for the regulation of fools." He'd never met a New Englander, he declared, "who had his navel-string untied. They're all bound up." He scoffed at the world relentlessly, but the scoffing was mingled with poetic insight and a devotion to art.

The primary lesson Bartlett wanted to impart to such visitors as Mason, Moody, and Robinson was that the greatest creative accomplishments could only be achieved against the heaviest odds. "All the concentrated sentences of the best minds are based on blood, grief, and martyrdom," he preached. "Emerson is rotten with good things, but he nailed them with cold hands and an empty stomach. Think of his going lecturing in the wilderness of Illinois, in 1855, for fifty dollars a night, eating tough pork, sleeping in a cold room, and obliged to be pleasant to idiots. That's the price he paid for being remembered by you and me. Every sentence of his cost Pain." So when Mason complained of a bad review, Bartlett advised him to rejoice, not despair. Similarly, when Robinson betrayed a trace of self-pity at his mistreatment in the literary marketplace, Bartlett chastised him. EAR "ought to wear out the knees of his trousers" in gratitude for his troubles, he said.

Robinson wore a dark suit and stiff straw hat at Chocorua, a costume that differentiated him both from the rural natives and the summer visitors. He awoke early, worked six to seven hours, took an afternoon walk, and had his meals with Bartlett, who was a generation his senior. The old man's chief excitement in life, EAR reported, consisted of swatting flies at mealtime and "swearing in a most piratical manner."

On occasion, the two men were entertained at a nearby farmhouse occupied for the summer by Hermann Hagedorn, his wife, and his one-year-old daughter. The ambitious Hagedorn, ten years younger than Robinson, had been chosen class poet at Harvard three years earlier. Now he was writing lyrics to be set to the music of Edward MacDowell for a pageant at Peterborough, New Hampshire, located southwest across the state from Chocorua. Peterborough was the site of the newly formed MacDowell Colony, and the pageant was to be presented, under the direction of George Pierce Baker, as a benefit for the colony. Hagedorn tried to get EAR to accompany him to Peterborough and, failing in that, returned extolling the virtues of the MacDowell Colony. EAR ought to apply there next summer, he suggested. Robinson shook his head. "Artist's colonies," he said, uttering the words scornfully, were not his dish of tea.

For most of the summer, Robinson and Bartlett got on splendidly. "Paradise could not be better than Chocorua, nor the Good Lord God better than Pere B.," he wrote Ledoux at the beginning of September. But EAR stayed at Chocorua well into October, and during the last weeks he and Bartlett began to get on each other's nerves. In a letter to Bartlett written two years later, EAR apologized that he had descended "into the valley of the shadow" (begun drinking to excess) during that time, found himself unable to write, and behaved like an infernal incubus. "I can only say again that I am very sorry," hc said. Robinson, who could ill tolerate the loss of a friend, was relieved that his host at Chocorua bore him no lasting grudge. Bartlett accepted his apology and even blamed himself for supplying the rum.

Robinson was still at Chocorua when *The Town Down the River* was published on October 8, 1910, and still there when William Vaughn Moody died in Colorado Springs on October 17. Moody's attack of typhoid two years earlier had weakened him, and eventually a brain tumor carried him away. His death was greatly lamented. "I cannot think that . . . I shall never see him again, with his pipe and slouch hat and clear, steady eyes and . . . that explosive laugh," Dan Mason wrote in his journal. He had lost in Moody a dear friend, a fine artist, a big-souled poet: "the greatest man" he had ever known. Percy MacKaye, similarly distressed, telegraphed Robinson the news and on the next day wrote George Pierce Baker proposing a Harvard Theatre to be financed by contributions to a William Vaughn Moody Memorial Committee. Harvard balked at raising funds for that purpose.

With Moody's passing, Robinson lost a friend, a supporter, and—inevitably—a rival. He had last seen Moody in the summer of 1908, when the latter was convalescing from typhoid fever, and EAR felt even then that "the real man was gone." Moody had accomplished enough to earn his place among the immortals, EAR wrote MacKaye. Inasmuch "as there was nothing more for him in this life, I say that we ought to be glad that he lived, glad that we could know him, and glad that he is now done with pain. If this sounds cold, you know me too well to mistake it."

The Town Down the River

When Scribner's contracted to publish *The Town Down the River*, Robinson felt that he had at last discharged an obligation. "The President has been expecting work of me, and here it is," he told Torrence. Robinson wanted to dedicate the book to Roosevelt but sought his approval before doing so. "Indeed it will give me great pleasure to have you dedicate your volume to me," Roosevelt replied on June 25, 1910. Remembering the unauthorized use of his name in connection with advertising for the 1905 *Children of the Night*, Roosevelt added a brief caveat: "Of course you will not put this letter in the book— I suppose that is needless advice on my part!" When the volume appeared, Roosevelt read it through "with the utmost delight" and assured Robinson that he believed in him "more than ever." He could never have written the poems, EAR replied, without Roosevelt's "friendly and substantial interest" in his work.

The town in *The Town Down the River* was New York, down river from Gardiner, Maine, and the title came from one of the "Tavern Songs" Robinson had written in 1894. EAR awaited the critical response with ambivalence. When the sun was shining, he felt that the book was "going to make a big difference in his life." When clouds filled the sky, he warned himself and others that its publication was unlikely to produce any "immediate noise." Most of the reviews were respectful—this was Robinson's fourth volume of verse, after all—but few were enthusiastic. The *New York Times Review of Books* waited four months before noticing *The Town*, and then only briefly in connection with two other books of poetry. The genteel approach of the anonymous reviewer may be gauged by the opening sentence: "Three volumes of verse have lately been added to the singing brooks that flow forever to the brimming river of poetry."

The most laudatory review, headed "Down the River: The Spiritual Qualities of an American Poet," came from William Stanley Braithwaite in the *Boston Evening Transcript*. Braithwaite located *The Town* as part of a body of work encompassing *The Children of the Night* and *Captain Craig* as well. These volumes, he declared, represented "the best in contemporary poetry." He singled out EAR's psychological character sketches as "the most wonderful part" of his work. Within the narrow limits of a sonnet, he observed, the poet could draw the lineaments "of a complete character, and in a short lyric a complete story of human fate and circumstance."

Braithwaite's review, EAR told Bartlett, was "the best thing ever written about his work." He made a point of looking Braithwaite up in Boston on his way back to New York from Chocorua. Robinson was not cynically cultivating future applause. He felt it only polite to acknowledge intelligent favorable notices. The best of him was in his poetry, he knew, and he could not resist reaching out to those who understood and esteemed what he was doing. The two men met in the Boston Public Library and formed a lasting friendship. Braithwaite,

FIGURE 16.3 The poet of *The Town Down the River* in William Sherman Potts's 1910 portrait.

Source: Colby College Special Collections.

the grandson of a British admiral who retired to Barbados and married a black woman, was to become an important figure in the literary establishment, editing the book page for the *Transcript* and bringing out annual anthologies of the best poems appearing in periodicals. He also became Robinson's strongest literary partisan.

The Town Down the River included poems based on historical figures, family and friends back in Maine, and Robinson's bohemian companions in New York. Tributes to Abraham Lincoln and Theodore Roosevelt opened and closed the volume, The poems were of identical length and adopted the same metrical and rhyme scheme. The titles were also parallel, with "The Master (Lincoln)" at the beginning and "The Revealer (Roosevelt)" at the end. Robinson obviously meant to suggest that both men had been great presidents. He hailed each of them as a "Titan" insufficiently appreciated in his time.

Other than "Miniver Cheevy," probably the best-known poem in *The Town Down the River* is "For a Dead Lady." It is also one of Robinson's most misunderstood.

> No more with overflowing light
> Shall fill the eyes that now are faded,
> Nor shall another's fringe with night
> Their woman-hidden world as they did.
> No more shall quiver down the days
> The flowing wonder of her ways,

Whereof no language may requite
The shifting and the many-shaded.

The grace, divine, definitive,
Clings only as a faint forestalling;
The laugh that love could not forgive
Is hushed, and answers to no calling.
The forehead and the little ears
Have gone where Saturn keeps the years;
The breast where roses could not live
Has done with rising and with falling.

The beauty, shattered by the laws
That have creation in their keeping,
No longer trembles at applause,
Or over children who are sleeping;
And we who delve in beauty's lore
Know all that we have known before
Of what inexorable cause
Makes Time so vicious in his reaping.

Much of the confusion about "For a Dead Lady" stemmed from the assumption that Robinson was writing a memorial to his mother, a theory advanced by Hermann Hagedorn and subsequently taken up by Louis Coxe and other commentators on his work. Given such a hypothesis, the elegy has usually been read as a heartfelt lament. Neither the biographical evidence nor a careful reading can support such an interpretation.

Even those most moved by the apparent tenderness of the poem have been confounded by such lines as "The laugh that love could not forgive" and "The breast where roses could not live." Edith Brower asked Robinson about the second of those lines. Did he mean that her breast was so lovely that roses could not compare? Not at all, EAR replied. "I never thought of meaning or indicating anything more than her way of presuming on her attractions and 'guying,' so to speak, those who admired her." Nowhere in any account of Mary Robinson does there crop up so much as a hint that she was given to "presuming on her attractions." Win's mother had beauty, to be sure, but it was commingled with modesty rather than artifice. Furthermore, late in his life EAR told a young poet friend that the lady of the poem was modeled on an actress he had met in New York. The phrase about roses may well have been suggested by the proverb quoted in Joyce's *Ulysses*: "They say if the flower withers she wears she's a flirt."

Collateral testimony is hardly necessary to arrive at a sound reading of "For a Dead Lady." On the surface, Robinson presents a moving lament for grace and beauty lost to the seasons. "No more, no more, no longer." Time has its way with lovely women as with mundane dry-goods clerks. But this is an odd elegy, its celebration of the lady's beauty compromised by inklings of anger or bitterness about her actions. Beneath the conventional framework of lamentation, the poet constructs a penetrating portrait of a woman who was not entirely what she seemed.

Each of the three stanzas touches on a particular attribute of the "lady": her wisdom, her grace, her beauty. The pattern used throughout, up to the concluding peroration, is that two lines of regret for what has been lost with the death of the lady are followed by two more calling her character into question. In the first stanza, for instance, the "overflowing light" of her eyes is sadly gone, but so too is what she withheld by drawing into herself. The "flowing wonder" (note the echo) of her ways cannot be restored, but neither can her apparent inconstancy and impenetrability: her "shifting and many-shaded" behavior.

The most forceful accusation comes in the first four lines of the second stanza.

> The grace, divine, definitive,
> Clings only as a faint forestalling:
> The laugh that love could not forgive
> Is hushed, and answers to no calling.

The religious quality of the grace bestowed on her will not last, while the hurtful "laugh that love could not forgive," though quieted by death, threatens to persist in memory. In the concluding stanza, the assertion that the lady "No longer trembles at applause / Or over children that are sleeping" suggests that she may be *performing* rather than *living* her life, in the home as on the stage.

So the poem goes—first granting, then taking back—until in the final four lines Robinson ends in mourning and bewilderment.

> And we who delve in beauty's lore
> Know all that we have known before
> Of what inexorable cause
> Makes Time so vicious in his reaping.

The lady had her vanity along with her loveliness. Still, she was one of us, and deserves our empathy, especially since her beauty was so brutally "shattered." We are alike in our inability to know how to accept or understand such cruelty. The point is made in lines that rush along without end stops, in sharp contrast to the earlier sections of the poem. As Ellsworth Barnard observed, few of the many poems written in protest "against the inevitability of beauty's death have clothed the mystery in words more moving."

If "For a Dead Lady" is not about Robinson's mother, the two brothers in the fine and neglected "Two Gardens of Linndale" surely were drawn from memories of her Palmer relatives. Such other poems as "Pasa Thalassa Thalassa" and

"Uncle Ananias" also traced back to his boyhood in Gardiner. But what most distinguished *The Town Down the River* from his earlier books of poetry was its focus on New York and its bohemians. In a series of four poems, "Calverly's," "Leffingwell" (consisting of three sonnets), "Clavering," and "Lingard and the Stars," Robinson summoned up a group of these men. "Calverly's" set the stage.

> We go no more to Calverly's.
> For there the lights are few and low;
> And who are there to see by them,
> Or what they see, we do not know.
> Poor strangers of another tongue
> May now creep in from anywhere,
> And we, forgotten, be no more
> Than twilight on a ruin there.
>
> We two, the remnant. All the rest
> Are cold and quiet. You nor I,
> Nor fiddle now, nor flagon-lid,
> May ring them back from where they lie.
> No fame delays oblivion
> For them, but something yet survives:
> A record written fair, could we
> But read the book of scattered lives.
>
> There'll be a page for Leffingwell,
> And one for Lingard, the Moon-calf;
> And who knows what for Clavering,
> Who died because he couldn't laugh?
> Who knows or cares? No sign is here,
> No face, no voice, no memory;
> No Lingard with his eerie joy,
> No Clavering, no Calverly.
>
> We cannot have them here with us
> To say where their light lives are gone,
> Or if they be of other stuff
> Than are the moons of Ilion.
> So, be their place of one estate
> With ashes, echoes, and old wars—
> Or ever we be of the night,
> Or we be lost among the stars.

Here Robinson mourns the passing of the "group of incomplete geniuses" he met during his first years in Manhattan. Once they reveled together in song and drink. Now they are "cold and quiet" and "go no more to Calverly's." It becomes the poet's task to bring them flickering to life.

Robinson only hints at what these men were like. In the book of scattered lives, there will be only a page for Leffingwell, and Lingard, and Clavering. When remembered at all, it will not be for their accomplishments. They reached for the heavens and fell short, with no fame to delay their oblivion.

The lunatic Lingard is perhaps the least interesting. He indulges in séances and table rappings and moon gazing and spends his time in full retreat from the everyday world. An engaging ghost raps out what he wants to hear:

> When earth is cold and there is no more sea,
> There will be what was Lingard.

Grateful for the promise of immortality, Lingard still seeks confirmation. "I wish the ghost would give his name," he says, but the séance is over, and he walks the midnight streets with Clavering.

Leffingwell's story emerges sketchily in a group of three sonnets, "The Lure," "The Quickstep," and "Requiescat." In the first sonnet the narrator separates his judgment of Leffingwell, who has recently died, from that of other mourners at his funeral. Forget "your Cricket and your Ant," he advises them, for the chirp of gossip and the condemnation of the industrious who brand Leffingwell as "parasite and sycophant" hardly fathom his case:

> I tell you, Leffingwell was more than these;
> And if he prove a rather sorry knight,
> What quiverings in the distance of what light
> May not have lured him with high promises,
> And then gone down?

Again the light, again the lure, and again the race to ruin, for Leffingwell, like the others who frequented Calverly's, has "played and lost" at the game of renown. When the dirge is played and the burial performed (in the second sonnet), "we smile at his arrears," but cannot reckon what "his failure-laden years" cost him. In the final sonnet the narrator warns against disturbing Leffingwell's ghost with speculation about his whereabouts. "He may be now an amiable shade," enjoying himself in hell, but "we do not ask," for if not allowed to rest in peace, Leffingwell will

>   rise and haunt us horribly,
> And be with us o' nights of a certainty.
> Did we not hear him when he told us so?

One can detect elements of the parasitical Louis and French in Leffingwell, and something of Betts in Lingard. The portrait of Clavering brings Robinson himself to mind. Like Miniver Cheevy, Clavering is not accommodated to the demands of this world. Obsessed by the past and a hinted-at lost love, he composes "metres" (not poems) and steadfastly avoids commerce with the present. He drifts through life without rudder or sails. But Clavering is kind and loyal:

I think of him as one who gave
To Lingard leave to be amused,
And listened with a patient grace
That we, the wise ones, had refused.
. . . .
I think of last words that he said
One midnight over Calverly:
"Good by—good man." He was not good;
So Clavering was wrong, you see.

Wrong, yes, but kind enough not to make sport of Lingard and loyal enough to think the best of his friends.

Robinson provides only fleeting clues about these men. Their depths cannot be sounded, and in writing about them the poet leaves out more than he tells. Yet through all of these poems is woven a pattern of affection for companions he must have thought of in the years between 1900 and 1910 as his fellow failures. The white lights of fame beckoned the regulars at Calverly's, but they found only the dark. They shared a dream and shared disappointment when it did not come true. EAR writes about them with tenderness.

Five years after the publication of *The Town Down the River*, the publisher and diplomat Lincoln MacVeagh wrote his sole essay in literary criticism, a piece that revealed him as Robinson's ideal reader. MacVeagh carried away from his reading of the Calverly's poems precisely that sense of fellow feeling EAR invested in them. "There they all are," MacVeath wrote, "Calverly himself, Lingard, Leffingwell, Clavering, deep in the midst of one of their long silences filled with the blue smoke of pipes. Lingard nurses his knee and laughs softly to himself. Clavering dreams in the legendary past. The big, somber, restless man is Leffingwell. And Calverly, leaning forward a little on the table, embraces them all with his quick glance, for his heart . . . is endlessly hospitable to these men."

The pictures Robinson provided were so sketchy that he more or less invited his readers to flesh them out. MacVeagh took him up on it, adding such touches as Lingard nursing his knee and Calverly leaning in the table. He did not know, MacVeagh admitted, whether the pictures he has formed in his mind "would be recognizable" to Robinson. But that was of little consequence, for "every one who knows the 'Calverly' poems knows each of the four friends better than if he had lived with them." In a few short poems, Robinson had "wrought the miracle" of creating four human beings to care about. "He makes us know

Leffingwell, [Clavering], Lingard, in the most intimate way possible; that is, he makes us know what it would be like to be one of these men, even feel as if we had been each of them." *Even feel as if we had been each of them*: what more could a poet hope for?

Borrowings

The elegiac approach of the Calverly poems was premature, for all of the companions from the early years in New York were still alive: Dr. Coan, Betts, Louis, French. But they had drifted apart for geographical and other reasons, and in those poems Robinson was bidding farewell both to his drinking friends and his own youthful self of the late 1890s, when his hopes were as yet unsullied by poverty and neglect. Robinson was forty years old when he wrote the Calverly poems, and more or less bereft of illusions.

Ahead of him lay another four-year period of destitution like the one that brought him to the brink of despair a decade earlier. To survive, he had to rely on the generosity of Clara Davidge and to borrow from such old supporters as Hays Gardiner and Willie Butler in Boston and such new ones as Hermann Hagedorn and Louis Ledoux in New York.

"The gifts he received," the eminent Malcolm Cowley speculated, "didn't wound [Robinson's] Yankee pride because he felt they were being given, not to him, but through him to poetry. Having taken vows of poverty, chastity, and obedience to his art, he could accept charity as if he were a whole monastic order." Cowley may have oversimplified the matter, for EAR always felt uneasy about asking for help, concealed his financial distress as much as possible (family and friends in Gardiner heard little or nothing about it), and felt bound to repay his debts. But Cowley was certainly correct about Robinson's faithfulness to his calling and what it cost him. "He sacrificed to poetry not only the comforts and luxuries of an ordinary existence, but also some things that are necessary to poets—books, music, travel, the stimulation of meeting other minds as keen as his own. He had to turn in upon himself." These early privations, Cowley thought, robbed some of EAR's later work of body and warmth.

Robinson implied as much himself in a 1916 interview. "Should a poet be able to make a living out of poetry?" he was asked. Whether he *should* or not, Robinson answered, as a practical matter it was "not possible for a poet to make a decent living by his work." What he needed even more than money was an audience. A thousand dollars a year should be sufficient to support a poet "with no obligations and responsibilities except to stay alive," he said. Just how to acquire the thousand dollars was another question.

On the other hand, in 1916 Robinson harbored no romantic notions about poverty as a stimulus to the starving artist. "I don't believe in poverty. I never did. I think it is good for a poet to be bumped and knocked around when he is

FIGURE 16.4 Hermann Hagedorn at Harvard, ca. 1907.

Source: Harvard University Archives.

young, but all the difficulties that are put in his way after he gets to be twenty-five or thirty are certain to take something out of his work. I don't see how they can do anything else."

Following their meeting in the mountains of New Hampshire, Hagedorn and Robinson established an ongoing relationship. The two men were both determined to lead literary lives, but there were significant differences between them. Hagedorn had enough money not to be troubled by the specter of want: his father, a German immigrant, made a fortune on the New York Cotton Exchange. He also had energy, ambition, and talent enough to carve out a long career as poet, novelist, and biographer. When he first became Robinson's financial supporter, Hagedorn was fresh out of Harvard and only beginning that career. A tall, handsome fellow, somewhat authoritarian in his Teutonic fashion, he was, like EAR, totally devoted to his craft and perceptive enough to detect, admire, and eventually envy Robinson's genius.

The letters Robinson wrote Hagedorn during the worst of his poverty-stricken period from 1911 through 1913 invariably addressed literary issues. Robinson would report on the status of his work in progress and offer commentary on manuscripts Hagedorn sent him for criticism. He gave Hagedorn's work the same ruthless honesty he had given Josephine Preston Peabody's a decade earlier, even though it might have been prudent to soft-pedal his comments.

In those same letters, Robinson applied for loans as subtly and engagingly as possible. Sometimes, not always, he asked for specific sums. Sometimes, he tied the request to a particular need, as for the cost of paying a typist to prepare manuscripts for submission. Often, he struggled for the right words to convey his gratitude. It was understood that EAR would repay the debt, should he ever manage to make some money with his writing. A few examples illustrate the process, and suggest Robinson's discomfort as supplicant.

January 24, 1912, after a check had gone astray in the mail: "If you send another check on receipt of this, of course I shall return the other immediately if I get it. . . . I have been warned unprofessionally, by a physician, that I must beware of corpulence in the event of sudden material success. So you will see that I have all sorts of things to worry about."

February 8, 1912: "Your check came like a barrel of manna and set me up strangely."

March 12, 1912: "The novel will be done in three days but I don't see how it will be typed in three years unless you are sufficiently interested to advance the money—about thirty dollars. . . . I shall not be at all surprised if you find yourself unable to do this, and if you are not of course you will say so."

September 8, 1912: "[If] this finds you in a position to gamble a little more on my future, I can only offer in return the one security at my command—and that is that I shall do everything in my power to make good. . . . I am high and dry—or shall be in a few days, and—oh, well, you understand what that means without my going any further into details."

Robinson's friendship with Louis Ledoux and his family was stronger and more lasting than that with Hagedorn. Ledoux joined his father's firm of mining engineers, chemists, and assayers in 1903 and succeeded him as president in 1923. He escaped the business long enough, however, to become an accomplished poet and a connoisseur of Japanese art. He was the author of five books, one of which—*The Soul's Progress and Other Poems* (1906)—he dedicated jointly to Robinson and Torrence. Ledoux married in 1907, and his wife Jean was to become one of EAR's closest female friends. When Robinson's play, *The Porcupine*, was published in 1915, he dedicated it to Ledoux.

During the dark days after 1910, Robinson applied to Ledoux for assistance less frequently than to Hagedorn, and with less sense of a need to justify himself. Ledoux sent him a sum to pay for his expenses at Chocorua. "The X came all right," EAR wrote in thanks, "and if I were even half-civilized I should have acknowledged it at once. It is going to save my life." In addition to providing money, Ledoux was ever on the lookout to advance Robinson's cause. He wrote to thank Braithwaite for his review of *The Town Down the River*, for example. And, knowing that the wolf of poverty was "licking his chops," Ledoux and his wife arranged for EAR to house-sit their apartment when they journeyed to Italy in the spring of 1912.

In December of that year, Dr. Albert Ledoux, Louis's father, sent Robinson a "very substantial indication" of his generosity. When things grew worse in the year ahead, EAR wrote Louis that he'd feel "like a bear on an iceberg unless [he could] raise the wind somehow." He asked for fifty dollars in May 1913, providing the sum didn't "stand in the way of [Ledoux's] doing or getting anything else," and for ten dollars a month later, as part of a blanket solicitation to "a few of [his] long suffering friends."

Hays Gardiner belonged in that company, having interested himself in Robinson's career from the beginning. With the best will in the world, Gardiner argued EAR away from poetry and toward fiction. The reasoning could not have been more logical. Robinson needed to support himself. He couldn't do so writing poetry. Novels sometimes made money. Therefore he should convert himself into a novelist.

Robinson's novelized version of *Van Zorn* was completed by the spring of 1911, and he shipped it off to Scribner's. The firm gave it a polite reception before shipping it back. Robinson's novel "was most carefully read by several people and given every care and consideration," Robert Bridges wrote EAR on July 25, but they were compelled to reject it as "too difficult and too far off the popular key." Disappointed but not defeated, Robinson began converting *The Porcupine* into a novel. He aimed to produce something "less difficult and queer and God knows what else than Van Zorn seems to be to the minds of the Scribner people." The work sped along: "to me the stuff seems as easy as lying," he told Ledoux.

After revisions, the book was "ready for rejection" in the spring of 1912, and rejected it was. At this stage, Robinson abandoned all hope of "getting anything out of [his] novels." They were "extinct," he told Kermit Roosevelt. Hagedorn, who had been holding the typescripts for him, was instructed to destroy the evidence. "It is good to know that my misbegotten novels are now among the things that were," EAR wrote him in January 1914.

In a tribute to Robinson, the poet Vachel Lindsay described him as "a novelist distilled into a poet," capable of communicating the germ of an entire novel in a poem of fifty lines or less. It did not work the other way around. Robinson's technique of distillation and concealment, admirably suited to poetry, did not translate into fiction. "In the novel," as E. M. Forster argued, "we can know people perfectly, and . . . can find here a compensation for their dimness in life." Novels thus solace us. By suggesting "a more comprehensible and thus a more manageable human race, they give us the illusion of perspicacity and of power." EAR's poetry offers no such comfort. He steadfastly refuses to tell us more than he knows, or than anyone can know. He can and does provide suggestions and hints, so that the pleasure of reading him comes in good part from detecting the clues and subjecting them to our own forensic skills.

But Robinson never pretends to omniscience, and—in the absence of the unpublished novels themselves—one is inclined to speculate that it was his unwillingness to assume this position that made his novels "difficult" and "far off the popular key." Robinson's poems, at their best, occupy the shadowlands between imagination and reality. "Your work has none of the shoddy qualities that attract the many," novelist May Sinclair wrote him in response to *The Town*

Down the River, "but it will go straight to everybody who values fineness and restraint."

That was pleasant to hear but buttered no bread. So Robinson turned to plays once again. "With the novels out of my system and poetry out of the question, I see nothing else for me to do," he wrote Hagedorn in August 1912. Besides, the playwriting devil was after him "with a red-hot iron." Amazingly, he decided to reconvert both *Van Zorn* and *The Porcupine* back into dramatic form. In a burst of productivity, he wrote another play, his "Jack and Jill" comedy, and announced his intention to write a half dozen more. "I am really bitten this time," he said. Bitten by his love for the theater and by the heady prospect of a pot of gold at the end of the runway.

In seeking to support himself as a writer, Robinson wasted three full years on unpublishable novels and unactable plays. He stopped writing poems almost entirely. He published none at all in 1911 and 1912 and only one in 1913. The one good thing was that during that time, he discovered a refuge that would last him all his life.

17

Life in the Woods, Death in Boston

A Home at the Colony

Borrowing a few dollars to pay for his travel expenses, Robinson arrived in Peterborough, New Hampshire, site of the fledgling MacDowell Colony, in the middle of July 1911. He came propelled by the continued urging of Hagedorn but arrived with substantial misgivings and in his pocket a fake telegram declaring a family emergency. If he decided to leave, the telegram would give him an excuse.

As it turned out, Robinson liked the MacDowell from the start. Two weeks after arrival he thanked Hagedorn for steering him there. From his corner room in the men's dormitory called the "Mannex," he looked out on stone walls and a rickety gate, a dozen cows, and the finest maple trees he'd ever seen. "I am looking forward to a particularly good summer," he declared.

The colony was situated a mile west of Peterborough, a town Thornton Wilder memorialized as Grover's Corners in *Our Town*. The distinguished American composer Edward MacDowell bought a two-hundred acre farm there in 1885: more forest than farm, really, with Mount Monadnock dominating the view. Upon MacDowell's death in 1908, an association was formed to convert the property into a retreat for creative artists: writers and visual artists as well as musicians. In its first years the place could only accommodate a small number of colonists. In 1911 Robinson was one among seven.

Of the colonists, only Parker Fillmore had read any of Robinson's work, a few poems he had encountered in the magazines. Once they became acquainted, Fillmore paid EAR the compliment of sending to Scribner's for his books of poems, an act that launched a lasting friendship. Fillmore came to the Mac-Dowell from Cincinnati, where he had been toiling in the family bond business by day and writing short stories and book reviews at night. When his fiction began to appear regularly in popular magazines, he packed his bags and escaped to Peterborough, New York, and a career as a writer of fiction.

Conditions were spartan in the early years at Peterborough. The male colonists shaved with cold water and took their baths in the nearby Nubanusic River. Perforce, the small contingent got to know one another well. On first impression, Robinson struck Fillmore as "a quiet, shabbily dressed, discouraged looking man, neither young nor old [he was forty-one] . . . polite enough if you spoke to him but much preferring not to be bothered. . . . He smoked Sweet Caporals and he was hungry": so ravenous, in fact, that Fillmore thought he must have been close to starvation.

As the summer wore on and Robinson realized Fillmore's interest in his poems, he began to unbend and talk more freely. Neither then nor later, though, did Fillmore dare ask Robinson to expand on anything he said. "If by a question you reminded him that he was telling you something, he took fright and shut up." Only momentarily would he reveal something of himself before lapsing into the safety of silence. Fillmore heard a snippet here, a fragment there, about the woes of Robinson's family. Not until EAR died, however, did Fillmore discover that he had more than one brother.

Robinson's state-of-Maine reticence made him particularly uncomfortable at the Sunday evening teas where Mrs. Marian MacDowell, the composer's widow, held weekly court. This practice served to give the housekeepers and cooks a day off and enabled Mrs. MacDowell to introduce her cadre of creative artists to wealthy townspeople and tourists who might be coaxed into making a contribution to the colony. EAR hated these Sunday evening gatherings, which required a good deal of mindless conversation. "Why must people talk?" he protested. "I have never been able to understand why people must talk."

Robinson also disliked the picnic atmosphere of the Sunday teas: balancing a plate on his knees or jostling shoulders at an overcrowded table. Even worse, a summer visitor might corner him to demand, "And what interesting thing do you do?" Once or twice, he snuck into town for a meal and skipped the occasion entirely, but he had to stop when Mrs. MacDowell, noting his absence, made solicitous inquiries about what she assumed must have been his ill health. Thereafter, EAR arrived at the Sunday gatherings at the latest possible hour and made an early departure.

During that first summer at Peterborough, Robinson rarely left his ill-smelling quarters. From his window, he could witness "a beauchus country," and he roused himself for occasional outdoor concerts. Otherwise, he avoided walks in the woods and stayed in his room, smoking and sighing. Fillmore thought he looked hypnotized. Nonetheless, the place worked its restorative powers.

Robinson was a sick man when he came to the MacDowell Colony—sicker than he realized. Not only had liquor become indispensable to him, but he had descended to writing dangerously "easy" prose, trying "to make the Porcupine eat out of [his] hand, keep his quills down, and be a novel." As Louis Coxe speculated, "he must have felt that as long as he worked, no matter how worthless the result . . . he could claim the title of author and a right to drink long and hard." Peterborough cured him. Anesthetized though he seemed to Fillmore, he was imperceptibly recovering throughout the summer of 1911. He found friends, an atmosphere where creative work was valued, and a regular work routine. Colonists ate breakfast and dinner together, but a box lunch was brought to them in the room or studio where they worked and left silently at the door. Otherwise, there were no interruptions. Under this regimen, Robinson had all day to devote to his work.

After his initial exposure to the MacDowell Colony, EAR returned every summer until the year he died: twenty-three years, for stays of about four months each time. He recognized his debt to the colony at once and did what he could to repay it. "If I were a millionaire, or a piece of one," he commented after only a few weeks in residence, "I should like nothing better than to do my part in keeping the [Colony] going." He was one of the founders of the Allied Members of the MacDowell Colony, an organization established that summer for the purpose of making the place "a permanent institution and a vital factor in the development of American music, literature, and art." He wrote testimonials to the colony on request and advised Mrs. MacDowell about which writers to invite.

Robinson stayed at Peterborough longer than expected in 1911. To ward off the autumn chill, he asked Betts to send him the overcoat he'd left, wrapped in newspapers, on the floor of his combination bookcase/clothes closet at Mrs. Davidge's cottage. When the leaves began to turn, he paid a farewell call on Mrs. MacDowell. Both of them had confessions to make. She'd admitted him largely on the recommendation of Edith Brower, a long-time friend of hers, Mrs. MacDowell told him. But she'd been afraid that he wouldn't like the colony at all. In response, Robinson produced the telegram he'd prepared to facilitate his escape, months earlier. They shared a smile about that. She became one of the people he would always care about.

A promising pianist in her youth, Marian Nevins traveled to Germany in hopes of studying with Clara Schumann and ended up instead as the pupil of the brilliant young Edward MacDowell. Once they were married, Marian gave up her career to look after her husband's. He prospered both as pianist and composer, in due course assuming a professorship in music at Columbia. When the duties of that post threatened to sap his creative energy, they bought their farm in New Hampshire as a summer retreat. They moved into the farm house, called Hillcrest, and built a log cabin deep in the woods where MacDowell could see Monadnock through the trees and write his music undisturbed. It was a wonderful arrangement.

MacDowell was not destined for a long life. As his health worsened, he awoke in the wee hours one morning to tell his wife about a dream he'd had about their New Hampshire land. Why couldn't they provide a place for other artists who needed freedom and solitude, just as he had? Marian promised she would do everything in her power to make that dream come true. She assumed the task of creating the MacDowell Colony as a sacred trust and devoted the rest of her

FIGURE 17.1 The composer
Edward MacDowell and his
wife, Marian, who made
his dream of an artists
colony come true.

Source: Library of Congress.

life to it. A small woman with a fluttery manner, she walked on crutches and
was constantly in pain, but she traveled the nation to raise funds for the colony.
"She begged, she charmed, she gave concerts for it till she was practically faint-
ing on the platform."

From 1908 to 1945, the MacDowell Colony grew from 135 acres, one studio,
and one dormitory, to more than 700 acres, twenty-four studios, three dormi-
tories, a dining room-recreation center, and a library. Throughout that time,
Mrs. MacDowell ruled the colony. No specific rules of conduct were spelled
out for those in residence, but if someone's behavior threatened the good name
of the colony or interfered with the work of others, she saw to it that they were
warned and in some cases summarily dismissed. She was, in the words of one
colonist, "a remarkable woman, Elizabethan, enormous, magnificent." Robinson was grateful to her, admired her, and worried about her.

Robinson's first few years at MacDowell introduced him to a number of
people who became lifetime friends and supporters. In 1911, for example, the
writer Anne Shannon Monroe, upon discovering that Robinson liked music,
took him to call on Lewis and Edith Isaacs, who were staying in a cottage across
the Nubanusit river. The Isaacses, like so many of Robinson's friends, were some
ten years younger than he. Somewhat reserved socially, Lewis had graduated
from Columbia law school and gone into the family law firm in New York. His
real passion was for music, however. He completed a master's degree in music
while finishing his legal studies and continued to compose while practicing law.
Edith, cordial and outgoing, was also a person of accomplishment as a playwright and an editor of the *Drama Quarterly*.

The Isaacses took to Robinson at once, and he to them. He could count
on good music and easy companionship wherever they met, whether in New

Hampshire; at their country home in Pelham, New York; or at their apartment in the city. Five years after he met Robinson, Isaacs assumed the role of his chief patron. Twenty-five years later, he served with Louis Ledoux as executor of Robinson's estate.

Edwin Carty Ranck barged into the Mannex in the middle of June 1912. A rough-hewn Kentuckian in his early thirties, Ranck had wandered the country as an itinerant newspaperman before he decided he wanted to be a playwright. He came to the colony fresh from George Pierce Baker's drama workshop at Harvard. Upon meeting EAR, Ranck at once announced that he thought "How Annandale Went Out" the most dramatic short poem he had ever read. "That seemed to thaw the atmosphere a bit," Ranck remembered.

Chard Powers Smith described Carty Ranck as "a short, stocky, ejaculatory, slobbering, popeyed, pugnacious misfit." He was uncouth around the edges and given to bawdy humor and physical confrontations: about as different from Robinson as one man could be from another. Ranck had some talent for playwriting, but when he attempted poetry, he reverted to the slipshod habits of a reporter facing a deadline. "I like your poem as a whole," Robinson said of one of Ranck's efforts, "but there are several lines in it that make me wish you had never seen the inside of a newspaper office."

That judgment did not bother Ranck at all. He respected—even worshipped—Robinson so much that nothing he said or did could ever offend him. It amused Ranck that EAR did not look the part of a poet:

His eyes were never in a "fine frenzy rolling." He wore his hair short, kept his voice down, and listened while others talked. He was the stillest man I have ever known. Except for his strikingly beautiful brown eyes, which his spectacles never successfully hid, he might have been mistaken for a quiet, well-poised business man. But his eyes gave him away. They were extraordinarily large, and, try as he might, he could not keep his poet's soul from peering forth. Most of the time they were kind and sympathetic eyes, but they could be quizzical, whimsical or sophisticated when the mood was on him—and they could burn with a fiery indignation at some story of injustice.

Ranck soon became Robinson's devoted disciple. For years, he dutifully made typewritten copies of EAR's poems for submission to magazines. This was not a simple task, for it required deciphering Robinson's notoriously difficult handwriting. "If you find a word that seems to make nonsense," EAR cautioned Ranck, "leave the space blank rather than guess at it. Perhaps it's all nonsense." Ranck occasionally suggested markets for particular poems. He knew the field; he earned his living freelancing for newspapers and magazines.

Ranck was living in Boston at the time he and Robinson met. There he formed a close companionship with George Burnham, another man who deeply admired EAR as a person and a poet. In later years, Ranck contributed

FIGURE 17.2 Six male colonists at MacDowell, ca. 1912: reading third from left, Parker Fillmore (in profile), Robinson looking stiff and emaciated, and the diminutive Carty Ranck.

Source: Houghton Library, Harvard University

a series of highly laudatory reviews of Robinson's books to the *Boston Evening Transcript*. He also let it be known that he was "Boswellizing" Robinson: setting down entries toward what he projected as a definitive biography of the poet. Because of a number of factors, including Ranck's mental instability, that book was never written. Ranck left behind instead a disorganized memoir of Robinson, only rarely illuminated by a telling anecdote or observation.

It troubled Parker Fillmore, who kept his friendship with Robinson on a basis of equality, that EAR seemed to encourage Ranck in his posture as adoring slave. To a degree, it is undoubtedly true that Robinson accepted Ranck because he could not help liking anyone who thought of him as a great man. There are less understandable vanities. But he also rather enjoyed Ranck and his crudities. "In some strange way," he wrote Hagedorn, "[Ranck] has a stimulating effect on my sluggish creative faculties." Besides, Ranck was at least as poorly equipped to prosper in the world as EAR himself. That gave Robinson the opportunity to do things for his benefit, just as he let Ranck be of service to him. Few things pleased him more than doing a favor for someone else.

During Robinson's third summer at the MacDowell Colony, he met Thomas Sergeant Perry and Lilla Cabot Perry. They were patrician Bostonians, she a Cabot and he the grandson of the naval hero, Commodore Oliver Hazard Perry. The Perrys spent the warm summer months at Flagstones, their country home in Hancock, New Hampshire, one of the most beautiful of New England villages. A man of letters, a scholar, and a gentleman, Perry represented, in Robinson's words, "the perfection of a culture that has passed." In his boyhood, he played on the beach at Newport with Henry James, and in his maturity he maintained a lively correspondence with James, William Dean Howells, and other literary luminaries in the United States and England. Perry taught at Harvard for a number of years, French and German as well as English. An accomplished linguist, he spent three years in Paris and another three years as a professor in Japan. He lived for books. Oliver Wendell Holmes called him "the best read man [he had] ever known."

Perry and Robinson were acquainted with each other through books before they met. In March 1893, his final semester at Harvard, Robinson bought Perry's best-known book, *English Literature of the Eighteenth Century*. In 1896, Perry read Robinson's *Torrent and the Night Before*, and in the following year he gave his wife a copy of *The Children of the Night* as a present. So when Robinson turned up at the Perrys' compound in Hancock on a sunny Saturday in August 1913, one of several passengers in a large touring car, Perry at once "carried him off to his [library] and hermetically sealed the door," leaving Lilla to entertain the rest of the company.

A shy man, Tom Perry more than met his match in Robinson, who often conversed by way of silences. One afternoon, "to avoid painful gaps," Perry talked on until Robinson, a notoriously bad sleeper, felt driven to lie down for a nap. "I was horrified to be interrupted in the middle of a most brilliant exposition," Perry wrote in one of his engaging letters, "but I was glad he got some sleep." Invited to dinner on another occasion, EAR brought with him a single overture to conversation. Looking up from his plate, on which his gaze had been fixed, he asked Perry if he had read Arnold Bennett's novel *Riceyman Steps*. Alas, Perry had not, so Robinson bowed his head again and said no more.

Robinson also established a warm relationship with Lilla Cabot Perry, whose sociable nature broke down his reserve. A talented painter, Lilla Perry shaped her work after the example of the French impressionists; in 1889, she and her husband rented a house in Giverny to be close to the great Monet. She also aspired to poetry, eventually publishing three volumes of verse.

Robinson encouraged her with his usual unrelenting frankness. "I think I'd better try to tell you just how I feel about your poetry," he wrote her in May 1914. "There is no lack of interesting subject matter (the rarest thing in the world), no lack of . . . force, music, or fancy . . . but there is at times . . . an almost exasperating lack of patience with refractory and inadequate lines, and a rather lazy (Lord help me if you ever see me again) tendency to let ancient and once honorable archaisms do the service of original exploration and discovery."

Lilla Cabot Perry took such criticism as a compliment and made sure that she and Robinson met again. He spent many summer weekends at Hancock,

FIGURE 17.3 Lilla Cabot Perry in self-portrait of 1892.

Source: In House Photo.

occupying a room across the road from the Perrys. Of an evening, he and Lilla searched for impossible rhymes, tested new meters, and tinkered with their poems before trying them out on the judicious ear of Tom Perry. Sometimes there was music, Robinson listening enraptured as MacDowell colonists joined Margaret Perry, eldest of the three Perry daughters, for string quartets from Beethoven, Mozart, Schubert, Brahms, and César Franck. The Perrys were old enough to have been Robinson's parents. Robbie, as they called him, became almost a member of the family.

Not wanting to presume too far, he declined most offers to stay with the Perrys in Boston, en route to or from Peterborough. "I could not possibly accept so much hospitality," he wrote Mrs. Perry in December 1915. "Whenever I come to Boston you will see enough of me." On almost all of his visits to Boston, he put up in a modest hall bedroom near that of George Burnham, who was working as a clerk for the New York, New Haven, and Hartford railroad. Staying there, he was able to accept another kind proposal from Mrs. Perry: that he use her studio as a daytime workplace and retreat. In September 1916, he sat for her wonderful portrait in that studio.

Butler and Suicide

At two P.M., Friday, November 1, 1912, William E. Butler, head of Butler's department store in Boston, finished dictating a letter to his secretary and sent her down the hall to see Ralph Albertson, manager of his various enterprises. Butler then left a short note on the secretary's desk, went into his office,

FIGURE 17.4   William E. Butler as successful businessman, ca. 1910.

Source: Arnold T. Schwab Papers.

closed the door, and shot himself in the head with a thirty-two-caliber revolver. Death was instantaneous.

Willie Butler had been "suffering from mental depression for some time," similar headlines in the Saturday *Boston Evening Transcript* and *Boston Globe* proclaimed. The *Transcript* called Butler, only thirty-nine, "one of the youngest of Boston's big business men." He was a director of the Boston Chamber of Commerce and a member of the Boston City Club, the Puritan Club, the Chestnut Hill Club, the Chestnut Hill Golf Club, and the Country Club. He and his wife Harriet owned a summer home in Falmouth. They had twin thirteen-year-olds, a boy and a girl.

In its account, the *Globe*—which ran a sizable advertisement for Butler's Apparel Shops on the day of the suicide—added information designed to suggest that Butler's desperate act did not derive from any business- or family-related problems. Albertson was quoted to the effect that the death would not interfere with the activities of the W. S. Butler Company. "There is no real financial difficulty," he said. The *Globe* also stressed that "the home life of the Butlers was ideal and it was his greatest joy and recreation."

His friend Butler's suicide had a devastating effect on Robinson. EAR invariably visited Butler when in Boston, and as late as 1910 was using W. S. Butler and Co., 90 Tremont Street, as a forwarding address. It is possible that Robinson may have felt in some measure responsible for what happened. He wrote Burnham in August 1912, three months before Butler killed himself, that he had received a letter containing "a check for two hundred dollars—which I thought was rubbing it in just a little. I returned it to the sender." If the unnamed benefactor was Butler, who did much for Robinson when he was in need, he may well have been surprised or hurt when the check came back.

It took Robinson seven weeks to write Butler's widow a letter of condolence. When he did, the letter revealed a depth of feeling he was rarely able to express. "I have intended for some time to write to you," he began,

> and I have often been on the point of doing so, but I have always realized that there is little or nothing that I can say that will do more than assure you again of what you know already. Of course I could not help from seeing for a long time that Will was working under a great mental strain, and I had always known his tendency to periods of depression; but I little dreamed they would have such tragic consequences. I hope that he understood, and that you understand, my great affection and gratitude while he lived. I am sure that I need not tell you of my affection for his memory.

A month later, Robinson wrote Harriet Butler again. "Of course I can say nothing that will do you any good, but you may like to have a word of assurance, or reassurance, that I shall always think of Will as *one of the best men that ever lived, and one of the best friends that any man ever had*" (emphasis added). From the emotionally withdrawn Robinson, that was an unusual outburst.

Robinson did not easily shake off the memory of Butler's suicide. During a visit to the Isaacses six years later, he came down late to breakfast as usual. Edith Isaacs sat with him through three cups of coffee, EAR lost in one of his "talkative silences." His brow furrowed with worry, he suddenly said, "But I never thought he would put a bullet through his head." Then, realizing that he had not been talking to her in his thoughts, he began telling Edith about his "friend Butler in Boston."

The problem of suicide obviously interested Robinson. Ellsworth Barnard counted fourteen suicides in EAR's poems, not including a couple of probables. There was also a genetic strain of depression in his family: his cousin Alice Robinson and his niece Marie manifestly took their own lives, and his brother Dean probably did. Considering the disappointments and defeats he suffered through, at one time or another EAR must have considered doing the same. The literary critic Austin Warren once observed EAR sitting in complete silence with an old Boston journalist friend (probably Carty Ranck) in a "desolate white-tiled lunchroom near Copley Square." Knowing something of EAR's poetry and apparently bleak existence, Warren wondered why he did not choose oblivion and speculated that a certain "bony toughness" inherited from his New England roots—a determination to endure the worst—saved him from suicide.

Perhaps that kind of stoicism helped Robinson ward off "the savage god." As for other deterrents, we have his testimony that "a glimpse of the real light through the clouds" made him "wish to live and see it out." That light—a spiritual beacon most vividly invoked in *Lancelot*—saw him through the despondency caused by the sudden terrible death of his mother. "For all my long lean face," Robinson wrote Harry Smith at the time, "I never gave up; and I never shall give up." Then too, besides the light he was blessed with a saving sense of humor, understated but coursing below the surface.

Robinson refused to be judgmental about those who succumbed to the temptation of suicide. His position was that none of us can know what demons drive people to take their own lives, and he recognized no religious proscriptions against the act. When the poet and music critic Donald Evans died in 1921, EAR assumed that he had "remov[ed] himself from a world that somehow never had a place for him." He wished Evans peace, "wherever and whatever he is now. There was much that was good in him," he concluded in a letter to the poet Arthur Davison Ficke, "and the rest is not . . . our affair." Ficke apparently objected in response that Evans may not have killed himself. This prompted Robinson to observe that he suspected Evans had "helped things along," but whether he did or not was of no matter. "A suicide signifies derangement or despair—either of which is, or should be, too far beyond the scope of our poor little piddling human censure to require of our ignorance anything less kind than silence."

Ten years later, he expressed himself even more vehemently in commenting on another suicide:

When a man finds himself at the end of things and puts himself out, I don't think so much of the act itself as of what he must have been going through before committing it. Nothing offends me quite as much as the cheap and easy criticism that many of us have ready for delivery on such occasions, and nothing is more depressing than the inability of most human minds to imagine anything outside their own experience. You will hear [t]his death explained as one reprehensible thing or another, and mostly by people who have never had anything worse than a stomach-ache.

As a poet, Robinson's job, and obligation, was to make excursions into the hearts and minds of other people: trips he made with empathy and a persistent unwillingness to condemn his fellow man.

"Luke Havergal," written in 1895, is one of Robinson's best poems, as hauntingly beautiful as it is frustratingly puzzling. Allen Tate called it "one of the great lyrics of modern times." Robert Mezey placed it first in his 1999 Modern Library edition of *The Poetry of E. A. Robinson*.

Go to the western gate, Luke Havergal,
There where the vines cling crimson on the wall,

And in the twilight wait for what will come.
The leaves will whisper there of her, and some,
Like flying words, will strike you as they fall;
But go, and if you listen she will call.
Go to the western gate, Luke Havergal—
Luke Havergal.

No, there is not a dawn in eastern skies
To rift the fiery night that's in your eyes;
But there, where western glooms are gathering,
The dark will end the dark, if anything:
God slays Himself with every leaf that flies,
And hell is more than half of paradise.
No, there is not a dawn in eastern skies—
In eastern skies.

Out of a grave I come to tell you this,
Out of a grave I come to quench the kiss
That flames upon your forehead with a glow
That blinds you to the way that you must go.
Yes, there is but one way to where she is,
Bitter, but one that faith may never miss.
Out of a grave I come to tell you this—
To tell you this.

There is the western gate, Luke Havergal,
There are the crimson leaves upon the wall.
Go, for the winds are tearing them away,—
Nor think to riddle the dead words they say,
Nor any more to feel them as they fall;
But go, and if you trust her she will call.
There is the western gate, Luke Havergal—
Luke Havergal.

If Theodore Roosevelt had trouble understanding "Luke Havergal," so have many others. As Robinson wrote Edith Brower, "the meaning is all suggested, and is not capable of a definite working-out by anyone who doesn't happen to sympathize with the writer's fancy." Let people figure it out for themselves, he told Craven Langstroth Betts. If he attempted a prose interpretation, he would only injure the poem. The critic must tread softly too, lest he damage the pure magic and incantatory music of "Luke Havergal." But the best poems not only survive explication but grow in the process.

Most agree that "Luke Havergal" confronts the issue of suicide. A speaker— who may be a projection of the voice of despair within the title character—

comes from "out of a grave" to counsel Havergal to join his departed lover in death. The entire poem thus represents an argument in persuasion, but how far is the speaker to be trusted?

That trust is crucial emerges in the distinction between the sixth line of the first stanza and the sixth line of the last. In the opening stanza, the shade (or shadow self) advises Luke Havergal to proceed to the western gate, the threshold of oblivion. "But go, and if you *listen* she will call," he says. In the final stanza, the speaker has lured Havergal within sight of this destination. "There is the western gate," he says, and "there are the crimson leaves" he spoke of earlier, displaying a burst of color before the wind tears them away. Now the time has come for Havergal, despairing over the death of his lover, to be reunited with her by committing suicide. Now the speaker says: "But go, and if you *trust her*, she will call."

Mere listening is not enough. Trust is of the essence. Yet it is not trusting the lover that matters, but trusting the persuader. He constructs his argument artfully, in the process trying to dismiss any objections Havergal might have. In the second stanza, for instance, he cites the benefits of escaping from an existence so dark that even the dawn brings no relief. Only through the darkness of release from consciousness can Luke end the darkness of his despair. Then the speaker seeks to absolve Havergal of the Christian penalty awaiting suicides.

> God slays Himself with every leaf that flies.
> And hell is more than half of paradise.

Through the cycle of death and rebirth, exemplified by the dead leaves, God has provided ample evidence that self-murder is a natural course of action. And even if a suicide will be dispatched to hell, that may constitute a better fate than an existence distraught with grief.

In the third stanza the speaker switches to the first person to establish his authority as a counselor. He knows the afterworld well: "Out of a grave I come to tell you this." He advises Havergal to abandon those emotions that "blind" him to the course he must follow. There remains but one way he must go: through the western gate.

A key to understanding "Luke Havergal" exists in a letter to Harry Smith of December 14, 1895. Robinson was in the midst of a creative spurt at the time, rewriting "The Night Before," fashioning songs, and producing two of his most memorable poems. One was about "old John Evereldown." The other was "a piece of deliberate degeneration called 'Luke Havergal,' which is not at all funny." Elsewhere he called the poem "my uncomfortable abstraction."

What Robinson meant by "deliberate degeneration" becomes clear in the context of the times. The phrase referred to the German author Max Nordau's *Degeneration*, an enormously influential book that was translated and published in English in 1895 and went through seven editions by the end of the year. *Degeneration* attacked the literature, art, and music of the fin de siècle. Robinson read the book in May, delighting in Nordau's extravagant language. "He thinks no more of calling a man a driveling idiot than he does of calling him dull," he told Joseph Ford.

For the most part, Robinson agreed with Nordau, who was a disciple of the Italian Cesare Lombroso. He much preferred the plain-spoken verse of Kipling, Hardy, and Housman, for example, to the more elaborate and artificial work of Swinburne and Aubrey Beardsley. But even when he disagreed with him—as about the highly emotional music of Richard Wagner, which EAR adored—he could still enjoy Nordau's intemperate assault on the composer. He quoted it for Ford: "The lovers in [Wagner's] pieces behave like tom-cats gone mad, rolling in contortions and convulsions over a root of valerian."

Robinson read not only *Degeneration* but reviews of the book by Israel Zangwill and Lombroso. Moreover, Nordau's ideas gave rise to two poems in *The Torrent and the Night Before*, which Robinson was hard at work on throughout 1895. The first, "A Poem for Max Nordau," presented a parody of the symbolist style considered by Nordau to be degenerate. In it Robinson mocked the inflated rhetoric and embrace of despondency that were hallmarks of fin de siècle poetry:

> Dun shades quiver down the long lone fallow,
> And the scared night shudders at the brown owl's cry;
> The bleak reeds rattle as the winds whirl by,
> And frayed leaves flutter through the clumped shrubs callow.

And so on for two additional stanzas of melodic and insincere overstatement.

The other poem influenced by Nordau was "Luke Havergal," with the significant difference that Robinson offered no explanation in the title or elsewhere as to what he was about. EAR revealed the connection between the poem and *Degeneration* in a October 6, 1895, letter to Harry Smith. He was planning a trip from Gardiner to Cambridge and looking forward to smoking a pipe with Smith, having some talks, and glorying in the autumn weather. "October is the month for me," he wrote. "I like the red leaves. Red leaves makes me think of *Degeneration* and that makes me think of Lombroso's article in the last *Century*." During the next two months he composed "Luke Havergal," importing those crimson leaves to function as the dominant imagery.

Robinson might well have felt "uncomfortable" about "Luke Havergal." In it, he did almost nothing to undercut his persuader's advice: the single possibly ironic note is struck by the qualifying phrase "if anything" in "The dark will end the dark, if anything." The poem reads very much like a straightforward argument for suicide. But we know from other work of his, and from his correspondence, that this does not square with Robinson's own views. In "Credo," another poem in his first book, EAR speaks frankly and in his own voice of the troubled universe he inhabits. The sonnet begins in dejection: "I cannot find my way: there is no star / In all the shrouded heavens anywhere." It ends in a powerful affirmation. Despite "the black and awful chaos of the night," the poet expresses what he called his "cosmic optimism." "I know the far-sent message of the years, / I feel the coming glory of the Light!"

In writing "a piece of deliberate degeneration" called "Luke Havergal," Robinson turned "A Poem for Max Nordau" upside down. Instead of satirizing the excesses Nordau railed against, "Luke Havergal" represented Robinson's experiment in imitating them. The inescapably melancholy tone of the poem defeats attempts—there have been many of them—to make it conform to EAR's general philosophical outlook. "Luke Havergal" expresses a viewpoint entirely opposed to that outlook. Robinson *deliberately* undertook to write a *degenerate* poem, and did it so skillfully as to confound understanding.

18

Reversal of Fortune

Leaving the Dark House

When he got back to New York in the late fall of 1911, Robinson met Hagedorn at the Players Club and surprised him by refusing a drink. He owed it to Mrs. MacDowell, he said, to do the best work that was in him. "And I can't work and drink at the same time." This resolve did not last. Liquor cast a glow and put him at ease with himself and the world. Drinking made it possible to lift for a few hours the burden of failure. Going without drink, he told Torrence, made him feel like "scratching down the stars." So there were times when the Wolf tracked him down, the Demon or the Devil caught him, and he revisited the Dark House yet again.

It was easier to practice sobriety at MacDowell, where his work regimen steadied him, than during less structured days in New York City. Braithwaite, invited to visit him at 121 Washington Place in the winter of 1912, caught Robinson at a moment when his demon was in dominance. The two of them were ushered into the main house where eight or ten others had assembled, among them the artist Henry Taylor, a recovering alcoholic who would soon marry Clara Davidge, and Olivia Dunbar, EAR's former tablemate at the Judson. The gathering stretched on into the evening, unlubricated by liquor, until finally Braithwaite excused himself.

"I'll go with you," Robinson said, rising at once. "I'll go with you."

Outside he thanked Braithwaite for rescuing him. "Let's get something to eat," he said. They walked up Fifth Avenue to Fourteenth Street and then west on Fourteenth, Robinson giving every saloon they passed a sidelong glance. Eventually they went into one, where for every scotch and soda Braithwaite had, EAR downed two or three. It was nine o'clock at night when they walked through the doors of the saloon, and two in the morning before they left.

During the summer of 1912 at the MacDowell Colony, however, Robinson renewed his determination to shake free of liquor. "My devil is so far away at present that I can't see him and the wagon goes without jolting," he wrote

Burnham early in August. "The town may have surprises for me, but I'm no longer scared." He was still sober in October, when he admitted to Ledoux that "the woes of the wagon are many and great, but its rewards are said to be considerable, and I have an eye out for them along the roadside." The woes receded when Robinson buckled down to work.

Others helped steel Robinson's commitment to sobriety. When he told Jean Ledoux that he was tempted to fall off the wagon, she replied that "the bottom would drop out of things for Louis and me" if he did. Jean was musical, cultivated, gracious, and clever. Her marriage to Louis could not have been happier. Robinson wanted to please her, and he promised to report to her if and when he took a drink.

Clara Davidge was also devoted to keeping Robinson away from the bottle. In the fall of 1912 she sold her house on Washington Place, and the adjacent cottage she'd constructed for Robinson went with it. Mrs. Davidge and Henry Taylor moved to an old brick mansion on Staten Island called La Tourette, and they brought EAR along. "Uncle Harry" Taylor, who liked to poke fun at Robinson's social disabilities, showed him around the house, which was said to house a ghost.

"Here is your room," he told EAR. "Here is a bed to sleep on. Here is a desk for writing. You can put your spare possessions here." He had no spare possessions, EAR said. "Then where do you keep your other pocket handkerchief?" Taylor wanted to know. "In my other pocket," Robinson said.

Mrs. Davidge had coaxed Uncle Harry into abstinence, and together the two of them aimed to do the same for Robinson. After dinner each evening, they concentrated their psychic energies on removing all thoughts of alcohol from EAR's mind. Oddly enough, it seemed to work. "She's a witch, you know," he said of Mrs. Davidge. There seemed no other way to explain why he'd lost all taste for liquor.

Living on Staten Island, Robinson felt as out of touch with New York as if he'd moved to New Zealand. He did, however, attend the opening of the famous Armory Show in mid-February 1913 that both Taylor and Davidge had been instrumental in organizing. The exhibition introduced the work of Matisse, Picasso, Cezanne, Van Gogh, and others to the American public. The most controversial painting was Marcel Duchamp's abstract "Nude Descending a Staircase," which reminded Theodore Roosevelt of a Navajo blanket. Robinson had a somewhat similar reaction. Although he professed to approve of experimentation in art as well as in science, his own tastes did not incline to the avant garde. "I went to . . . the big Art Show the other evening," he wrote Hagedorn, "and since then I've been trying to decide who's crazy."

Mabel (Ganson) Evans Dodge Sterne Luhan (then Dodge), a living embodiment of the revolutionary in art and mores, came to lunch at La Tourette and felt an immediate affinity for EAR. In her extensive memoirs, the adventurous Dodge rather uncharitably characterized Mrs. Davidge as a collector of "old furniture and promising artists," including a painter (Henry Taylor) and a poet (Edwin Arlington Robinson), whose shyness only made him a more valuable acquisition.

At the luncheon EAR and Mabel Dodge sat opposite each other. He was "without doubt the most inarticulate man" she had ever met, so that they communicated only through occasional eye contact. But, she recalled, she "had never seen anyone else, except [the acclaimed actress Eleanora] Duse, with quite the depth of somber imprisoned heat in the eyes that this man had." Robinson flashed her "one tiny, shy, burning, and directed glance that conveyed his complete realization of everything any one of us there could know, with something more than any of us knew." In that reciprocal flicker, they "realized each other" as cronies, pals, friends, yet "too much *en rapport* to be lovers." In later years she often invited EAR to gatherings with various artists not too much *en rapport* to be disqualified as lovers. Usually, Robinson made his excuses. He was attracted to Mabel Dodge, but not to her style of life.

In the spring of 1913, Mabel Dodge came back to La Tourette, expecting to stay through the weekend. But she was routed awake at midnight by the mansion's ghost, said to have been poisoned in the room she was assigned. She hurriedly packed and caught the last train and ferry for the safety of Greenwich Village, warning Robinson that the ghost was "getting in his deadly work" on everyone at La Tourette, himself included.

The ghost never troubled him, but his relations with Clara Davidge soured. From Boston in June, he wrote Ledoux that she'd seemed "rather queer and rather high strung" before he left Staten Island for his annual northward journey. He'd been rather grouchy himself, he admitted. It may be that Robinson betrayed a trace of resentment about his treatment at La Tourette: a feeling

FIGURE 18.1 Mabel Dodge, who was transfixed by a glance from EAR.

Source: In House Photo.

that he was being patronized, that though Mrs. Davidge might like to have him around for decoration, neither she nor Uncle Harry took him seriously as a man. "I'm sorry if I made her mad," EAR wrote Ledoux, "but I don't know just what I can do about it."

Turning of the Tide

Interest in poetry, long dormant, was beginning to rise. In the fall of 1912, Harriet Monroe founded *Poetry* in Chicago, the first American periodical devoted solely to verse and criticism. In England, Ezra Pound launched a movement called imagism, a revolt that aimed to replace overblown rhetoric with precision of phrase and a concentration on the image. Amy Lowell preached the same gospel in Cambridge and advocated the looser, more supple benefits of free verse. The new poetry, above all, was more realistic than in the previous generation. No longer a sort of elegant accomplishment, it took itself seriously. It looked at life directly, instead of evading it through the world of fancy.

The revival was all to the good, even if free verse was not to Robinson's taste. "I write badly enough as it is," he said. Before Pound and Lowell and others, he had already achieved a revolution of his own against the genteel tradition. Staying within the boundaries of rhyme and meter, he depicted the lives of men and women in a spare and nearly colloquial diction. His poems were often moving but never sentimental. Suddenly, and without the impetus of a new Robinson book to inspire them, two well-known poets entirely unknown to EAR decided to notice, and they praised his work in the pages of the nation's most prominent newspapers.

In an extensive article for the September 8, 1912, issue of the *New York Times Book Review*, Joyce Kilmer hailed Robinson as "a classic poet." Kilmer, not yet thirty, was to die a few years hence at the second battle of the Marne and to be forever remembered as the author of "Trees." He lauded Robinson for his command of craft, his skill in versification, and his lucidity. Most of all, though, he celebrated EAR for his humanity. In a concluding paragraph, Kilmer summed up his admiration. "Not as a prophet, not as a teacher, but as a student of mankind does Robinson hold his place among poets. Always he looks at humanity patiently, earnestly, searchingly. His poems . . . are compounded of sympathy and humor."

Kilmer's unexpected encomium elicited three letters from Peterborough, where Robinson was still in residence. Mrs. MacDowell seized the opportunity to tell Kilmer about the colony and Robinson's involvement with it. Parker Fillmore sent Kilmer a note: "My feeling for Robinson and his work is so strong that I take another's appreciation of him almost personally," he said. A week after publication, Robinson himself thanked Kilmer for his "friendly notice" in the *Times*. "You say things in it that I have been waiting for someone to say."

Ledoux and Hagedorn joined the chorus with letters to the editor. The principal characteristics of Robinson's poetry, Ledoux commented, were "kindliness, humor, sympathy, and a sort of incurable optimism that sometimes seems to be amused at its own pig-headedness." His characters constituted a sorry lot, "derelicts of all conditions," but he treated them with a willingness to discover the good in apparent failure. Ledoux's letter, which ran in the September 29 issue, represented "the best thing" he had read about *The Town Down the River*, EAR told Ledoux. No other critic had understood so well his "invincible optimism" in the face of a brutal world or his subtle humor that never descended to ridicule.

Hagedorn went even further in celebrating Robinson's accomplishment. On December 1, 1912, he wrote the *Times* that Kilmer's article and Ledoux's "justly enthusiastic letter" pointed to "the cheerful possibility" that Robinson might be recognized as "by all odds the most noteworthy living American poet." EAR hardly knew what to say in response, other than that he thought Hagedorn "one of the best things now engaged in displacing terrestrial atmosphere."

In Boston as in New York, Robinson received an unlooked-for tribute. The young English poet Alfred Noyes came to the United States from February to July 1913 to lecture on poetry and antimilitarism. Interviewed by the *Boston Post* soon after his arrival, Noyes declared his admiration for the younger American poets in general, and two of them in particular: Brian Hooker, who the previous year had written the libretto for the opera *Mona*, and "Arlington Robinson." He called attention to Robinson's "sardonic, powerful" style and described his technique as "perfect." *The Town Down the River*, he said, was a masterpiece.

Three separate features in the Boston newspapers followed up on Noyes's remarks. The first, from Carty Ranck, emphasized Robinson's manliness and vigor while saying almost nothing about his work. "Edwin Arlington Robinson is not a dilettante," Ranck concluded. "He does not write occasional verse. He only writes when he feels deeply and has something to say. He has written three volumes of poetry and there is nothing cheap or unworthy in any one of them. He is real. He is sincere. He is vital."

When Robinson himself came through Boston on his way to Peterborough, Braithwaite sought him out for a *Boston Evening Transcript* article that appeared on May 28, 1913, under the title of "America's Foremost Poet." Not to be outdone by its rival newspaper, the *Boston Post* dispatched a reporter to corner Robinson for a feature article that ran two days after Braithwaite's, accompanied by an artist's sketch of the poet. The *Post* aimed for the sensational, as the headline showed:

GREAT AMONG POETS HIDES IN MODESTY

Edwin Arlington Robinson, Acclaimed Nation's Greatest
    Living Poet, Quietly Living in Boston, Unrecognized

Robinson was not "living in Boston," nor had he been acclaimed as the nation's "greatest living poet" by Noyes (an inaccuracy first perpetrated by Braithwaite).

The *Post*'s anonymous reporter was clearly beyond his depth in interviewing a poet, especially one as unforthcoming as Robinson. Was he going to publish any new poems soon? No, but he'd been reading Constance Garnett's ["Constant Garnet" in the article] fine translation of Dostoyevsky's *Brothers Karamazov*. Would he say why he found that novel so absorbing? Not really: "it explains itself, why it is so great." Queried about socialism, women's suffrage, internationalism, politics, and religion, Robinson offered only the most perfunctory replies. "All these questions," he said, pulling on his cigarette, "are too large for such a short talk." The hapless reporter was nonplussed. "All through the interview [Robinson] showed a great unwillingness to commit himself on any questions, and it was only with difficulty that a few scattered remarks were drawn from him."

The recognition generated by Noyes in Boston and Kilmer in New York undoubtedly gave Robinson a renewed dedication to his craft. Just how he was supposed to support himself remained a mystery. He was as broke in 1913 as he had ever been. Before leaving Boston for the mountains of New Hampshire, EAR decided to ask Robert Bridges for an advance against future poems he would submit to *Scribner's* magazine. Bridges came up with one hundred dollars, despite having seen no poems at all from EAR for the previous three years. More than half of the money went to finance a small operation Carty Ranck had to undergo.

A Devil Done Away With

It was finally time, Robinson decided, to end his disastrous career as a playwright. With the encouragement of Hays Gardiner, Percy MacKaye, and Hermann Hagedorn, and the "playwriting devil" after him "with a red-hot iron," Robinson devoted all of his creative energies during 1911 and 1912 to the composition of plays. He refashioned *Van Zorn* and *The Porcupine* into dramatic form, wrote the "Jack and Jill" comedy in which he professed to detect "the real odor of the stage," and threatened to compose as many as half a dozen other plays.

By late July 1912, Robinson began to have doubts. Prose was not his "natural form of expression," he realized. There were too many words in prose, and they took up too much room. Still, having invested so much time in "the playwriting game," EAR felt compelled to peddle his wares in the marketplace. The marketplace remained stubbornly indifferent. He could not interest theatrical producers in the "Jack and Jill" play, or in either *Van Zorn* or *The Porcupine*, now rewritten for the second time.

Robinson was so busy writing plays that when Harriet Monroe sent him a prospectus for *Poetry* in August 1912, asking him to send "as soon as possible, some poems too fine and rare for the popular magazines to appreciate," he had nothing to submit. His "poetry machine" had run down two years earlier, he

told Monroe, and since then he'd been occupied with "the first and last infirmity of noble minds—the writing of plays." When he'd satisfied himself and
his friends that he couldn't write one, he hoped to be able to write some more
poetry.

Early in 1913, the deciding blow came from Winthrop Ames, the highly
respected director of the New Theatre. Upon reading Robinson's carefully
reworked third version of *The Porcupine*, Ames declared that while he himself
liked it immensely, he thought "it would pass over the heads of an audience and
leave them wondering what it was all about." That finally delivered Robinson
from his "literary gallivanting." Poetry was the only thing he could do and at the
same time have "any clear notion" of what he was about.

Robinson wrote Gardiner this decision on March 9, 1913, enclosing the letter from Ames as a supporting document. He could never make any money
writing plays, he said. "It isn't that I can't write a play, so far as the technique
goes . . . but I can't hit the popular chord, and for the simple reason that there
is no immediate popular impulse in *me*. In poetry this is an advantage, but for
commercial playwriting it is deadly. When I come down out of myself and try
to write for the crowd, I perpetrate the damnedest rubbish." Now that he'd seen
the light, he was going to write another book of poems.

Robinson further explained himself in a sentence designed to mollify Gardiner, who had faithfully supported him during three years of "floundering in
prose." "I feel that I have given the thing a fair trial," he said, "and that it would
be unfair to you as well as to myself to waste any more of my life in doing something for which I have come to see I am not fitted."

A few months later, EAR had occasion to render judgment on the work of
Marian MacKaye, Percy's wife, who had written a play and sent it to Robinson
for criticism. She'd made the same mistake he had, EAR told her. "You tried to
write popular trash and you didn't succeed for the reason that you haven't that
sort of thing to dispense." He felt sure she would be happier "during the rest of
[her] extremely valuable life" if she followed his example and left the writing of
plays to others.

Robinson's return to poetry left him in the worst of financial straits. Matters
only worsened in May 1913, with the death of the generous Hays Gardiner. The
MacDowell Colony provided room and board during the ensuing summer, but
after that he became desperate for funds. He could raise little money from his
writing, and he had borrowed from friends until he could borrow no more. "I
was on my uppers, absolutely," he said years later. "It was the one time in my life
where there seemed to be nothing ahead."

Early in March 1914 Robinson went out with one of his friends in New York
and with the help of alcohol "tried to forget things a little." Lacking fifty cents
for breakfast the next morning, he got up late and went into the hallway for the
mail. There was one letter, typewritten, from a law office in Boston. EAR tore
it open, and a slip of paper fluttered to the floor. It was a check for thirty-six

hundred dollars, the bulk of the four-thousand-dollar bequest that John Hays Gardiner had settled on Edwin Arlington Robinson.

At the rate he was spending money at the time, Robinson said, he "could have lived for a million years on four thousand dollars." After that windfall, he was always able to keep going. It made him feel as if there was "somebody somewhere who made a business of looking out for people." Exercising his Yankee sense of obligation, Robinson at once set about repaying debts, or trying to. He sent Louis Ledoux's father a check for a hundred dollars. Dr. Ledoux sent it right back.

Disappointed as he was that his plays were not produced, Robinson remained determined to see them in book form. Scribner's, which had passed on both *Van Zorn* and *The Porcupine* earlier, was unwilling to publish them, despite the exhortations of Ledoux. Hagedorn then took *Van Zorn* to George Brett at Macmillan, who in March 1914 agreed to publish it as part of a package deal that would include *The Porcupine*, a revised edition of *Captain Craig*, and the new book of poems EAR was working on. In effect, Macmillan was willing to publish the plays in exchange for tying up Robinson's poems.

The offer placed Robinson in a delicate position. He was not used to having publishers competing for his work. Besides, he felt indebted to Scribner's. They had brought out his poetry when other firms were unwilling to, come through with the hundred-dollar advance, and offered a periodical market through *Scribner's* magazine, where Robinson had formed an ongoing relationship with Robert Bridges. So EAR wrote Bridges rather sheepishly to say that Brett, at Macmillan, had made him an offer that he would "in all probability, find [himself] unable to refuse." But he wanted Bridges to know that this was strictly a professional decision, that it had all come about "without any solicitation" on his part, that he felt "great regard" for him, and that he hoped it would not affect his standing as a contributor of poems to the magazine.

Bridges consulted behind the scenes with Isaacs about what might be done to keep Robinson in Scribner's fold. On May 18, 1914, he proposed publishing EAR's collected poetry and invited him to lunch to talk it over. Robinson was not swayed by the idea of a collected edition, at least not yet. It would be four or five years before he was ready for such an edition, he wrote Bridges. They had their lunch, but EAR's mind was made up. Bridges's notes told the story: "Lunch May 20, 1914. Play & Capt. Craig bound to Macmillan. Probably will feel bound to let them have his new book of verse."

Robinson's two published plays—*Van Zorn* (1914) and *The Porcupine* (1915), the first billed as a comedy and the second a drama—are remarkably similar. Each takes place in a contemporary setting. Each has seven characters, four men and three women, whose psychological and emotional difficulties unravel over the course of three acts. Suicide threatens a character in each play. And in each, a "fixer" in the mold of Robinson himself uses an expenditure of funds as well as a gift for understanding in trying to make things right for others.

"A fringe of mystery" hovers about the magisterial figure of Van Zorn, who turns up in Greenwich Village from his foreign travels. By virtue of his genius for intuiting other people's troubles, Van Zorn persuades the once promising but presently dejected George Lucas, who has threatened to "go west" by way of poisoning himself, to give up strong drink so that he can be "born again." Then Van Zorn induces the bright and attractive Villa Vannevar to break her engagement to the successful painter Weldon Farnham in order to marry Lucas.

In his best poems, Robinson leaves something unsaid. He provides hints and clues, but does not reach firm conclusions or stand in judgment on his characters. Instead of revealing what motivates them, he insists that such knowledge is beyond our ken and paradoxically invites his readers to participate in puzzling out what cannot be known. In a play, though, one expects more revelation. Although it is undoubtedly true, as Van Zorn says, that "we mortals know very little of ourselves, and far less of each other," a theatre audience may rebel at a play where too much is left out.

In the case of *Van Zorn*, the crucial missing piece of information is that Van Zorn himself is in love with Villa Vannevar, so that by delivering her to George Lucas he is making a substantial sacrifice to ensure the happiness of others. Robinson was unwilling to make this too obvious. Besides, it seemed to him that he had made the point, albeit indirectly. "The play is for the most part the working of character on character, the plot being left, more or less, to reveal itself by inference," he said. But the inferences remain submerged in dialogue marked by a studied cleverness and a reluctance to come to the point. "The play is tantalizing," the *New York Times Book Review* observed. "It has all the puckered brow and portentous manner of hidden meaning—but the meaning remains hidden even after a most attentive and respectful perusal. . . . *Van Zorn* lacks substance not because it is trivial but because—literally—it is not all there."

Upon reading several reviews like that and discovering that not even Edith Brower had grasped the central emotional dilemma at the heart of his play, Robinson sent her a letter headed by the figure of a tombstone. "Here Lies X. Melchizedek Van Zorn, 1906–1914," the stone was engraved. "And Only Five People Knew What Ailed Him."

The Porcupine is marred by a similar vagueness. Four of the characters are talking:

"I have felt for some time that something is going to happen," one of them says.

"Well, if it's going to happen, we'll have to let it happen," says a second.

"Do you understand these people?" a third character asks.

"I'm not sure that I do," remarks a fourth.

"Well, I'm sure that I *don't*," the third says, "and if they aren't going to tell me what they mean, I'm going to bed."

FIGURE 18.2 *Tombstone Sketch.* Robinson's sketch, committing *Van Zorn* to rest.

Source: In House Photo.

A sentiment that an audience might share, even if they detected that the playwright was making fun of himself.

In *The Porcupine*, the wrong people are already married to each other. One unhappy marriage has united Stuart and Louise Hoover: he a young attorney in a small New England village called Tadmor, she a stage-struck singer longing for the lights of Broadway. Larry Scammon, a Tadmor native come home after making his fortune in Chicago, provides the funds that will enable Mrs. Hoover to pursue her career in New York. Before her departure, he dictates a letter for her to sign and send to her husband, promising to stay out of his life in the future.

Larry understands that "some men and some women have about as much business being married as alligators would have—being vaccinated." Like Van Zorn—and Robinson himself—he aspires to improve other people's lives. He also thinks that all of their problems can be solved, and that he can do the job. "I believe in ways out of places," he declares.

He cannot fix the marriage of his half brother Rollo and his wife Rachel, however. As a dissatisfied wife, Rachel has made Rollo's life miserable. You cannot imagine, Rollo tells Larry, what it is like to be married to a porcupine instead of a woman.

Perhaps Larry cannot. Certainly he is blind to his own complicity in causing the marital discontent. He and Rachel had been lovers in their youth; she did not marry Rollo until after Larry left town. Wise as he may be about other people, Larry somehow does not perceive that Rachel has always been in love with him and that her son, who shows a disturbing fondness for "Uncle Larry," is in fact his child. At the end of the play, when Rachel enlightens him, he offers to run away with her and the boy. She knows that Larry does not really love her, though, and knows as well what damage she has done to her well-meaning husband. "Life is not so simple as you would have it, or so easily changed," she tells Larry. At the end, she takes the vial of poison that will end her life.

Scammon and Van Zorn both seek to redirect the lives of others, but Robinson effectively differentiates them as characters. Van Zorn speaks as he acts, with dignity and deliberation. Scammon talks with the cockiness and buoyancy of a man who has yet to learn that he lacks the power to alter circumstances. The message seems to be that while one can help others with their problems, he cannot do much to secure his own happiness.

Technically, *The Porcupine* represents an advance on *Van Zorn*. In both plays, Robinson handles the staging and the action well and guides the proceedings with copious stage directions. But in *The Porcupine*, he distinguishes characters more effectively through gestures and facial expressions and keeps the play moving through shorter scenes and shorter speeches. Yet neither is a really satisfactory play. Robinson leaves too much unexplained, and the people are not nearly as convincing, or as interesting, as those that inhabit his poetry.

Robinson's career survived two extended periods of playwriting, one beginning in 1905 and the other in 1911. Allowing for interruptions to produce *The Town Down the River* and the failed attempt to convert two of his plays into novels, he devoted nearly six years of his life to the drama. At the beginning, in the 1906 "White Lights," he celebrated a renaissance in the American theatre. After his failed attempts to become part of such a movement, he excoriated the stage in a 1918 poem called "Broadway."

> By night a gay leviathan
> That fades before the sun—
> A monster with a million eyes
> Without the sight of one—
> A coruscating thing with claws
> To tear the soul apart—
> Breaker of men and avenues,
> It throbs, and has no heart.

"When I die," he told Esther Bates, "they ought to put D.D.—Defeated Dramatist—on my tombstone." It took him a long time to admit that defeat and to understand its cause. "I'm not a playwright," he acknowledged in a 1932 interview. "A play must be *direct*—there is no chance for a movement of light and shade."

19

A Poet Once Again

A New Pattern

Robinson lived a migratory life, without a permanent home, but his movements hewed to a regular schedule as he shuttled between the two poles of New York in the winter and the MacDowell Colony in the summer. He usually spent at least six months in the city. In April or May he started north, stopping to visit the Isaacses in Pelham, New York, and the Hagedorns in Fairfield, Connecticut, before staying in Boston for a few weeks. By mid-June he would be in Peterborough for the four summer months, during which he wrote almost all of his poetry. The fall journey down the coast mirrored that of the spring: some time in Boston, most of it spent with Burnham, followed by houseguest appearances on the way to New York, the longest at the Cornwall-on-Hudson home of Louis and Jean Ledoux.

The schedule served Robinson well. He got his work done at the colony, enjoyed the music and the theatre in New York, and had amiable companions to visit as he went from one place to the other. At the Isaacs's home, EAR would propose a musical program for the evening, often involving Gilbert and Sullivan, and Lewis would play from memory. Afterward, Edith would wander off and return an hour of so later to find the two men sitting contentedly in silence, Robinson puffing on his invariable Sweet Caporals. There was music at the Hagedorns, too, where occasionally, in a subdued voice, EAR himself ventured to sing a favorite Tin Pan Alley number.

Robinson usually spent late October and early November at Sengen, the Ledoux's spacious house west of Storm King mountain. Louis and he had poetry in common, and he bonded with the cultivated and intelligent Jean: ten years EAR's junior but otherwise much like his mother. She had a wonderful singing voice and knew how to josh Robinson out of his modesty.

When she and Louis went abroad in the spring of 1914, Robinson felt "rather lonesome" without them. "I go to other places," he wrote her, "but somehow I have never succeeded in acquiring with other people the same sense of freedom, security, rapport, expansion, and general well-being that I begin to feel as soon as I inflict myself upon you and yours." His letters to her were longer than usual, reporting on his life and work and manifestly trying to amuse. He passed on to her, for example, an anecdote about the popular playwright Louis Anspacher, who was observed on a Fifth Avenue bus reading Keats. As the observer watched, Anspacher jotted a note in the margin: "Neat, but not as I should have done it."

During his stays with the Ledoux, Robinson played the part of a lovable if rather crotchety uncle. Urban creature as he was, EAR insisted on being moved from one room to another to avoid the nightly eruptions of a whippoorwill who "thought he was Caruso." He made an uneasy peace with the Ledoux's Airedale, whom he referred to as the Mutt. As a puppy, the Mutt persisted in untying Robinson's shoelaces and trying to persuade him to abandon the rocking chair and take him for a walk. "The Mutt is a bitter disappointment to me," EAR wrote Jean Ledoux. "I shouldn't even call him a gentleman; and yet he seems to be well born, and I know that he has had a good bringing-up."

The autumn visits of "Uncle E. A.," like those of Aunt Imogen, were welcomed by the Ledoux's children. His chief obligation was to carve a Halloween lantern. "It appears," he wrote Isaacs, "that I am supposed to carve the annual pumpkin for the youngsters and that no one else can do it. It is good to be supreme at something." He wrote charming letters to young Renee Ledoux: "Did you ever have an English Sparrow fly up to your window and cling to the screen and look at you as if he liked you? One did that for me this morning. But I forgot. He couldn't do it for you, because you have no screens. That is why you have so many bugs—I mean insects—and reptiles and ornithorhynchuses in your house during the warm weather. . . . The other evening I went to a Pop Concert [in Boston] and heard the fiddlers play 'The March of the [Tin] Soldiers,' and somehow it made me think of *you*. I hope you will hear it sometime yourself, and it will make you think of *me*."

In the country, Robinson sat in a rocking chair all day long, writing or thinking or reading, with his back to the view. As it started getting dark, he went for a walk of three-quarters of a mile—the Mutt trying valiantly to lengthen the distance—after which he considered that he had "done his duty," and spent the evening by the fire being read to. The reading was often from Kipling or Dickens, except when EAR brought along his summer production of poems (typewritten, thankfully) for the Ledoux to read aloud. Robinson wanted to find out how much of what he had written could be instantly comprehended, and comprehension, as Ledoux remarked, "was not helped by [EAR's] eye on the reader or by occasional interruptions such as: 'Did the stenographer leave out the comma? I didn't hear it.'"

Ledoux valued the visits of Robinson, "the gentleman of quiet humor, of subtle intuitions; the man who could be trusted to be loyal and who in all the give and take of life never failed in that kindliness of judgment which though it was in essence an expression of his own marked personality, yet was based on an intuitive and sympathetic understanding of all that is most pathetically human." He could recall no instance when EAR's "attitude toward a fellow mortal . . . was anything but kindly." Moreover, he never lost his ability "to enter into the lives of others"—a quality, Ledoux thought, that signified his greatness as a man as well as a poet.

In the spring of 1914, Robinson had an opportunity to prove himself a friend to the MacKayes. Their son Robin—the oldest of their three "adorable children"—was going through a period of teenage disturbance. After discussion with Jamie Barstow, then teaching at Groton, Robinson concluded that the best course for the family would be to send the lad away to school. He was fully cognizant of "the unusual advantages of Robin's altogether exceptional home life," EAR wrote Percy MacKaye, but was convinced that the boy needed the systematic discipline of a good preparatory school.

Specifically, Robinson recommended Exeter, where Joseph S. Ford, his friend at Harvard, had been in residence for twenty years. This suggestion was offered "with the most damnably good intentions," he assured MacKaye: "the kind, in fact, that often make us wish to murder our best friends." MacKaye was not offended. He immediately got in touch with Ford to make arrangements for Robin as an Exeter student.

The following year MacKaye came to Robinson again for advice regarding the children. Not the sort to hide his light—or that of his offspring—under a bushel, MacKaye conceived the idea that "a little book" containing the poems and drawings of Robin, fifteen, and Arvia, thirteen, should be published. He sent Robinson copies of the "verses of both kiddies," which he thought were "touched with a glow of poetry worthy of preserving." Did Robinson agree? If so, would he write an introduction for such a volume?

Robinson chose to disagree. He praised a few poems written by the "altogether remarkable youngsters," but as "a cold-blooded, mossbacked, sour-bellied bachelor friend," he advised against publication. "If your own childhood stuff were printed in a book," he told MacKaye, "you would probably pay a considerable sum of money for each copy that you could buy and destroy." Why be in such a devil of a hurry?

Ridgely Torrrence and Olivia Dunbar were married in February 1914. In his book on Robinson, Chard Powers Smith printed the rumor that EAR had an affair with Dunbar and was upset to discover that Torrence had, in effect, supplanted him. Smith supplied two items of information in support of this contention. The first, hearsay that would be thrown out in any court of law, involved what Torrence told young poet Boris Todrin that Todrin then passed on to Smith. According to this story, upon returning from Mac-Dowell in the fall of 1913, Robinson went to see Dunbar, who was still living in the "tower room" at the Judson. Discovering Torrence with her and the couple engaged, he bolted from the room. Torrence gave pursuit, found EAR

FIGURE 19.1 The writer Olivia Howard Dunbar, who married Ridgely Torrence.

Source: Princeton University Library.

several blocks away, and persuaded him to come back for a talk that lasted for hours.

The second piece of evidence was Robinson's note to the couple following their marriage in February 1914. "I have no means of knowing how much or how little my best wishes are worth to either of you, but you may be sure that you have them, and that they are entirely genuine," Robinson wrote. "I was not very much surprised by the news, for the occurrence seemed to be in the order of things likely to happen." Even for Robinson, this was less than effusive. If Robinson bore a grudge for whatever reason, it did not last long. He recommended that the Torrences be invited to spend the summer of 1915 at the MacDowell Colony. The three saw a lot of one another during that time, and in conversation with other colonists EAR predicted great things for Torrence in the future.

O Tempora, O Mores

In the fall of 1914, Mowry Saben published a book of his essays under the title *The Spirit of Life*. If anything, the aversion to conventional thinking Saben demonstrated during his college years with Robinson had grown more deeply imbedded over time. Having moved from the study of philosophy to psychology and physiology, under the guidance of Sigmund Freud and Havelock Ellis, Saben set out to shock the sensibilities of the bourgeoisie.

In the book's chapters on "Morals" and "Sex" Saben advocated repudiating all absolute moral standards. "A virtue is only some old sin that has become common. A sin is a virtue that has become obsolete in good society." Besides, sin was of little importance when measured against art. "What does it matter if the author of the Twenty-Third Psalm committed adultery, if Lord Bacon took bribes, if Shakespeare got drunk? Their sins have all passed away . . . but the *Psalm*, the *Essays* and *King Lear* are our delight forever."

Saben aimed his heaviest artillery at sexual intolerance. He had no respect for "fig-leaf morality," which feared "the naked truth as it feared the naked body." There was no organ of the living body, male or female, which offended him, "nothing in the flesh of which one should feel ashamed." From this postulate, he progressed to a defense, even a celebration, of homosexuality. In Whitman's poems, Saben wrote—poems that he and Robinson read with admiration at Harvard—he recognized "the fine thought and feeling of one who was not afraid of sex—not even of his own."

Sexual orientations stemmed from each individual's chemistry, he believed. The "normal" male yearned for the female, and vice versa. "But abnormal individuals of both sexes may have no desire for the opposite sex, and yet possess an intense desire for an individual, or for many individuals, of their own sex." Others were bisexual, and more of them than was generally supposed. To take the curse off the adjective "abnormal," Saben speculated that the "germs of all sexual abnormalities exist in us all," but were held in check by inhibitions. To let such inhibitions govern one's life was foolhardy, he thought.

Even more radically, Saben argued against fidelity and in favor of multiple sexual experiences: "The man or woman who believes that in another has been found all the richness of life has no true acquaintance with life. Let us admit that each has found in the other a piece of pure gold. But are there no other pieces of pure gold?"

These were not views Robinson could share. While he was glad that his friend's book, long in the making, was finally published, EAR more or less agreed with the judgment of the *New York Evening Post*. Saben was to be admired for rejecting the standards of the "inefficient past" and defying those of the "smug present," the *Post*'s reviewer noted. Yet in the name of freedom, Saben led his readers "upon decidedly boggy ground," particularly the ground that defended homosexuality and promiscuity. When Saben was preparing another volume of essays a decade later, Robinson recommended that he omit all reference "to the procreative organs. You can sail all around them and give a sufficiently adequate report without going ashore." Saben ignored the counsel.

Robinson may have been reluctant to "go ashore" on the islands of sexual license, but he addressed himself often—far oftener than has generally been supposed—to the most important issues of his times. As the poet and critic Morton Dauwen Zabel pointed out in an excellent summary of Robinson's career, he lived through a half century "of dramatic and stupefying circumstances in American life" and wrote about most of them. "The age is in his work," Zabel observed. He "observed steadily the crises around him and judged what he saw," even when his views ran counter to those of the culture he inhabited. David Nivison, too, noted that social criticism made up a surprisingly large part of EAR's work.

Robinson did not by any means conceive of poets as the "unacknowledged legislators of mankind." When Josephine (Peabody) Marks joined the Fabian Society, and began writing poems of socialist propaganda, EAR protested that she would only consume herself in trying to reform the world. "I don't mean to be discouraging, but you can't do it." But he did not believe, either, that poets should keep silent about the major events of their time. Even if they could not alter the course of history, they owed it to themselves and their readers to speak out. With the outbreak of World War I, EAR did so.

He was at the MacDowell Colony during the early days of the war, and with Parker Fillmore walked into Peterborough every afternoon to get the news from the Boston papers. The news, during the summer of 1914, was terrible. Seventy-five thousand French soldiers and nineteen thousand British were killed or wounded at the Battle of the Somme. German troops were crashing toward Paris. Robinson was convinced of two things about the war even at that early date, Fillmore recalled. First, that it "marked the end of our time and our era." Second, that "we are all going to be caught in this."

This second point he emphasized in "Cassandra," published—after being rejected by *Scribner's*—in the *Boston Evening Transcript* of December 21, 1914. Although "Cassandra" was "not in any sense a war poem," Robinson wrote, "it may not be entirely out of tune with existing conditions." World War I is not specifically mentioned in the poem, which is primarily concerned with the blindness, arrogance, and materialism of the public. In effect, "Cassandra" attacks the doctrine of American exceptionalism: the mistaken notion that the United States could opt out of history. Robinson was not advocating that we should fight. He was arguing that, like it or not, we would be drawn into the war.

The prophetess Cassandra was granted the gift of foreknowledge by Apollo yet also condemned never to be believed. In Robinson's poem, she speaks sagely of American shortcomings and warns of disasters ahead, but her words fall on deaf ears. The nation's single greatest fault lies in its worship of Mammon rather than God, she observes.

"Your Dollar is your only Word.
    The wrath of it your only fear."

Armed with money, the "children" Cassandra addresses are pridefully blind to external dangers and foolishly confident that nothing can threaten them. She asks a series of questions in an attempt to shake them out of their complacency.

"Because a few complacent years
    Have made your peril of your pride,

Think you that you are to go on
   Forever pampered and untried?

. . . .

"Think you to tread forever down
   The merciless old verities?
And are you never to have eyes
   To see the world for what it is?

"Are you to pay for what you have
With all you are?"

At which point the "laughing crowd / Moved on. None heeded, and few heard."

Robinson, in his late forties, was not a candidate for service in the war, though there were times when he felt he "should be driving a mule in France." He paid tribute of a sort to Alan Seeger, an American poet nearly two decades his junior, who joined the French Foreign Legion and was killed in action in 1916, a year before the United States entered the war. Seeger—"the Hedonist," EAR, called him in a letter to Ledoux—came to see him at MacDowell in 1911, "looking as mediaeval as possible in a fishing jacket, a pair of brown duck trousers, Indian moccasins, and with his hair a little more so than usual." Robinson did not know what to make of Seeger's ostentatiously untraditional garb and manner. Dying in battle, he wrote Jean Ledoux, may have been "the best thing for him, for I don't believe that he would ever have come anywhere near to fitting himself into this interesting but sometimes unfittable world."

Meeting and Passing

It was Braithwaite who brought Robinson together with another poet with a genius for capturing human emotions in what looked like everyday language, another New Englander—six years younger than EAR—who had labored long at his craft without gaining widespread acceptance. Robert Frost, in fact, had to go to England to locate a publisher, and he returned home on the wings of *A Boy's Will* (1913) and *North of Boston* (1914), his first two volumes of poetry.

Frost knew about Robinson before EAR knew about him. He read May Sinclair's 1906 article about Robinson, Moody, and Torrence in the *Atlantic Monthly* and thought she should have "put Robinson ahead" of the other two. As early as July 1913, he asked a friend if he could put him in touch with Robinson. The two poets had no contact, however, until after Frost came back to the United States. When his boat landed in New York City in February 1915, the *Literary Digest* was carrying an article noting that Robinson "had received higher praise from discriminating critics than any other living American poet": an observation certain to arouse Frost's rivalrous nature. When Braithwaite brought the two men together, he made matters worse.

Upon hearing that Frost was anxious to meet Robinson, Braithwaite took him to see EAR in his spartan quarters on Boston's St. Botolph Street. EAR rose from his desk in the corner of the room when his guests arrived. Braithwaite, sensing the importance of the occasion, paused and put his hand out to arrest Frost's entrance. Then he said, "Frost, when anybody thinks of poetry in America, he always thinks of Robinson as our greatest poet." It was exactly the wrong thing to say. Braithwaite had the impression that Frost never forgave him for it.

Soon thereafter, Robinson and Frost met again. At the end of a session of the newly formed New England Poetry Club, EAR drew Frost aside and proposed that they repair to a nearby bar. He'd noticed, Robinson said slyly, that Frost sounded hoarse, and suggested that a dose of bitters might be of help. Not much of a man for barrooms, Frost went along, and at "The Place of Bitters," as they later called it, the two poets had their single extended conversation.

Frost was a world-class talker, Robinson notoriously retiring, but they had shared a similar experience as aspiring poets, suffering through a long period of neglect before beginning to achieve recognition. They both kept writing when nobody seemed interested, sending their poems to editors and wondering what was wrong when the poems were rejected. When the same magazines started accepting their work, it didn't make much sense, for their poetry had not changed, much. Both of them were glad they had stuck to their lasts. They agreed on that and further agreed that it didn't matter at all whether a poem was written in an experimental vein or had a message to convey. All that mattered was whether the poem was any good.

When they parted, Frost and Robinson promised to send each other copies of their latest books. In EAR's case, this was *The Porcupine*, likely the worst book he ever published. Frost responded with generosity—and a telling if subdued point of criticism. He'd read it twice over, Frost said, and declared it to be "good writing, or better than that, good speaking caught alive—every sentence of it. The speaking tones are all there on the printed page, nothing is left for the actor but to recognize and give them. And the action is in the speech where it should be, and not along beside it in antics for the body to perform." Then Frost delivered his critique in the form of a query. "I wonder if you agree with me that the best sentences are those that convey their own tone—that haven't to be described in italics," such as "*with feline demureness.*" Robinson, although undoubtedly pleased with Frost's praise, could hardly have failed to notice that many speeches in his play were accompanied by such stage directions.

After issuing this caveat, Frost resumed his compliments. He'd often been asked to tell others what he thought of their writing, and he shied away from doing so. It was different with Robinson. He was one of the "very few" Frost actually wanted to tell what he thought: "I have had some sort of real satisfaction in everything of yours I have read. I hope I make that sweeping enough." In closing, Frost said he "owed Braithwaite a great deal for our meeting that day."

Robinson in reply commented on both *A Boy's Will* and *North of Boston*. Robinson read the second book first and, in a letter written after the middle of June 1915, said he was glad he had, for he liked it so thoroughly and in so many ways. *A Boy's Will* had "much good stuff in it," he wrote, "and the quality is nearly always authentic, but it hasn't quite the force or the distinction that I looked for after *North of Boston*." Still, there was nothing in that first book "for which [Frost] need ever be sorry," and EAR could not say the same about the "juvenile things" he'd printed in *The Children of the Night*. He also felt indebted to Braithwaite for bringing them together, Robinson said in conclusion.

Somewhere in Robinson's letter (only a fragment of which has survived), he asked Frost two quite uncharacteristic, deeply personal questions. Did Frost care what Robinson thought of him? Was he satisfied with himself? These were questions, clearly, that EAR might have put to himself instead of to Frost. "Both your speculations interest me, particularly the first one as to whether or not I care what you think of me," Frost wrote in mid-September. As long ago as May Sinclair's *Atlantic* article, he had "marked [Robinson] down" as someone he intended one day to know. He'd only held off making an overture for fear that Robinson might not "find anything to like" in his work. He knew he liked Robinson's, Frost said. "But I should never actually seek a fellow author's friendship unless everything was right, unless he saw something in me as I saw something in him and there was little or nothing to cover up or lie about in our opinions of each other."

As to the second question, Frost acknowledged that yes, "in a way" he did feel "satisfied with" himself. "I'm rather pleased to have attained to a position where I don't have to admire my work as much as I had to when no one else admired it." Frost's answers went directly to the issues behind EAR's questions.

FIGURE 19.2 Robert Frost, 1930, in James Chapin's painting.

Source: The Picture Collection, New York Public Library.

Was the career worth the agony? How well should one think of oneself? Did it matter what others thought?

At the end of his letter, Frost proposed a meeting in New York. The two did see each other there, but only at a distance. Robinson was in the audience and Frost on the platform at the Poetry Society of America meeting of January 25, 1916. Supple as he was in private conversation, Frost was only beginning to feel comfortable in front of a sizable group. His talk that evening—a serious defense of his theory of poetry, presented to a gathering of the old guard—did not go well. Moreover, he was followed by Louis Untermeyer, who delighted the audience by reading in deadpan fashion his hilarious parodies of such members of the new guard as Amy Lowell, Vachel Lindsay, Edgar Lee Masters, and—of course—both Robinson and Frost. After the dinner, EAR "oozed out slowly" with the crowd and lost the opportunity to talk to Frost and meet his wife. To make amends, he sent Frost a note of regret about the missed connection and a copy of *The Man Against the Sky*, which was published in mid-February.

Frost did not acknowledge the note or the book. A few months later, in Boston, EAR asked Braithwaite if he'd heard from Frost lately. He wondered, Robinson said, because he'd sent Frost his new book and hadn't received any word back. Was it possible that Frost was offended about Braithwaite's remark when the two men met? Later that year, Robinson did receive a copy of *Mountain Interval*, Frost's new book of poems, which was sent to him in care of Macmillan. The publishers let the volume languish for some time before delivering it to EAR so it was early February 1917 before Robinson wrote Frost a note of thanks. He congratulated Frost on a number of poems, including "Birches" and "The Road Not Taken," that undoubtedly added "something permanent to the world." He liked everything else in the book, EAR added, but "those poems seemed to stand out." Again there was no response from Frost.

In future years Frost and Robinson met only twice, apparently, and the correspondence between them dwindled away. In his biography of Robinson, Hermann Hagedorn speculated that "jealous and defensive" partisans of each poet kept their acquaintance from developing into a friendship. But the two were acutely aware of each other as rivals, without any intervention from others to remind them of it. What mattered was whether the rivalry went deep into jealousy and rancor. With Frost, it did, as he was to prove on a number of occasions. With Robinson, it did not.

20

A Breakthrough Book

Once Robinson abandoned playwriting, it was as if a dam had given way. After "chasing false gods" for so long, the poems poured out of him. In August 1913 he wrote Ledoux that he had enough material "in hand—or rather in head" to keep him busy for the next three years. During that period, he produced some of his greatest work: poems rather longer than his earlier character studies but deeper in their psychological resonances. In addition, his stock had risen in the literary marketplace, and new outlets for his verse miraculously opened up. "Eros Turannos" appeared in *Poetry* for March 1914, "Flammonde" and "The Poor Relation" in *The Outlook* for January and June 1915, "Ben Jonson Entertains a Man from Stratford" in *The Drama* for November 1915. All of these and others went to make up his 1916 volume, *The Man Against the Sky*.

Six months in advance of the book's publication, William Stanley Braithwaite advised his *Boston Evening Transcript* readers to expect "a general and popular acclamation" when it came out. The nation was in the midst of "a wonderfully poetic period," Braithwaite wrote, and he reserved the topmost peak for "the silent and lordly figure" of Edwin Arlington Robinson.

The reviews of *The Man Against the Sky* were not as rhapsodic as Braithwaite anticipated, but they were very good indeed. Robinson had waited twenty years for the kind of recognition that the book elicited. After cordially neglecting EAR's previous books, the *New York Times Book Review* gave *The Man Against the Sky* an unusual amount of space. In attitude, Robinson was like Dostoyevsky, the anonymous reviewer commented, but the darkness was lightened by the growing "penetrative power" of the author's vision, aligned with "a greater mastery of compression and of interpretative conciseness" than in his earlier books.

Additional penetrating praise came from Amy Lowell in the *New Republic*. Robinson's poems were "modern because they [were] universal," she said. They exhibited "great power" and were "dynamic with experience and knowledge of life." So much was conveyed in so little space that to open his volume was like opening "a jar of compressed air." The poems revealed the "great pitying tenderness" of their "magnificently noble" creator. It was generally agreed that *The Man Against the Sky* was his best book, so far. As Ben Ray Redman, Mark Van Doren, and Allen Tate variously observed, EAR's "slender" volume of 1916 "awakened" the critics to his virtues, earned him the "wide attention" he had been seeking, and advanced him into "the front rank" of American poetry.

The collection assembled the results of what had been Robinson's greatest period of production: the work he did in the summers of 1913 through 1915 at the MacDowell Colony. "At least eight of the poems in this volume" [out of twenty-six], Louis Coxe said, "rank with the poet's very best, which is to say, with the best then being written." It is no easy matter selecting which eight. Almost everything in *The Man Against the Sky* exhibits Robinson's mastery of his craft.

Three that surely do belong among the best depict women victimized by life in one way or another. The exquisitely wrought "Gift of God" examines a mother's illusory belief that she has been blessed with a son so wonderful as to make it seem "a sacrilege to call him hers." The implied comparison to the Virgin Mary and Jesus emerges in the first two of six eight-line stanzas, together with the motif of the mother's blurred vision. This vision is so faulty that she forever sees her quite ordinary son as "shining"—a verb five times repeated.

When the mother, overcome with pride, parades her son's virtues to the townspeople, they respond with "many smiles and many doubts." When she further demands that they share her opinion, the kindest "writhe and hesitate." Ignoring their discomfort, she "transmutes him with her faith and praise / And has him shining where she will." The Latinate verb in a poem of Anglo-Saxon diction invites attention to the miracle of the mother's alchemy: her transmutation of base material into precious, of dross into gold.

In the final stanza, the mother is carried away by her imaginings.

> She crowns him with her gratefulness,
> And says again that life is good;
> And should the gift of God be less
> In him than in her motherhood,
> His fame, though vague, will not be small,
> As upward through her dream he fares
> Half clouded with a crimson fall
> Of roses thrown on marble stairs.

She sees her son crowned a king among men, even as Christ ascending to heaven. And the gift of God inheres in her blessed inability to recognize her error. Wrong she certainly is. Foolish she may well be. But despite her delusion, Robinson does not mock the misguided mother. What we feel for her is compassion.

"The Poor Relation" (initially titled "Pauvrette") presents the plight of a woman with no illusions whatever. Despite its title, the poem does not so much as mention her financial situation. The poor relation is poor in the sense that life and love have passed her by. In her youth, she was beautiful and much envied. Now she is growing old, alone, in a city apartment. She is also in poor health, her beauty "blanched with pain." She may even be crippled, the poem suggests by comparing her to a "plover with a wounded wing" and echoing the analogy in the concluding stanza.

> Bereft enough to shame a sage
> And given little to long sighing,
> With no illusion to assuage
> The lonely changelessness of dying,—
> Unsought, unthought-of, and unheard,
> She sings and watches like a bird,
> Safe in a comfortable cage
> From which there will be no more flying.

Robinson structured his poem around the theme of visitors paying duty calls on the poor relation. She is gracious with these callers—the few left who know where to find her—telling them with a smile that it is quite wrong of her to stay alive so long. Their visits are short, but she would not have them longer, knowing that "Pity, having played, soon tires."

Eventually the callers stop coming. Her several visitors are reduced to a single one who "always reappears." This is "the good ghost" of the woman herself as she was in the bloom of youth. With this imaginary companion, she can laugh her slender laugh and sing her childhood songs. (Robinson's "Mr. Flood's Party" was to introduce another solitary character moved to break into song with himself.) Musical imagery further underlines the woman's distress. She is troubled by the city's eternal humming, "like a giant harp," and by the thousand sounds that remind her of "the small intolerable drums/ Of Time."

As a bachelor without home or family, Robinson felt a natural kinship with the bereft. To some extent, he was imagining in "The Poor Relation" how it might work out for himself. But that hardly invalidates the emotional power of the poems.

When the typescript of EAR's "Eros Turannos" reached Harriet Monroe at *Poetry*, she wrote "Jewel" at the top of the page. A jewel it was, and continues to be. Yvor Winters called it "one of the greatest short poems in the language" and maintained that its forty-eight lines (the same length and meter as "The Gift of God") contained "the substance of a short novel or of a tragic drama."

She fears him, and will always ask
   What fated her to choose him;
She meets in his engaging mask
   All reasons to refuse him;
But what she meets and what she fears
Are less than are the downward years,
Drawn slowly to the foamless weirs
   Of age, were she to lose him.

Between a blurred sagacity
   That once had power to sound him,
And Love, that will not let him be
   The Judas that she found him,
Her pride assuages her almost,
As if it were alone the cost.—
He sees that he will not be lost,
   And waits and looks around him.

A sense of ocean and old trees
   Envelops and allures him;
Tradition, touching all he sees,
   Beguiles and reassures him;
And all her doubts of what he says
Are dimmed with what she knows of days—
Till even prejudice delays
   And fades, and she secures him.

The falling leaf inaugurates
   The reign of her confusion;
The pounding wave reverberates
   The dirge of her illusion;
And home, where passion lived and died,
Becomes a place where she can hide,
While all the town and harbor side
   Vibrate with her seclusion.

We tell you, tapping on our brows,
   The story as it should be,—
As if the story of a house
   Were told, or ever could be;
We'll have no kindly veil between
Her visions and those we have seen,—
As if we guessed what hers have been
   Or what they are or would be.

Meanwhile we do no harm; for they
  That with a god have striven,
Not hearing much of what we say,
  Take what the god has given;
Though like waves breaking it may be
Or like a changed familiar tree,
Or like a stairway to the sea
  Where down the blind are driven.

In Donald Justice's summary, "a woman of good standing in a small town marries for love, but marries beneath her; the man betrays her in some fashion, probably sexual; and for reasons the townspeople think they can guess at, the wife, victim of the tyrannical god of love, sticks with the husband." This is not an unusual story. We have heard it before, and read it before too, in Henry James's *Washington Square*. Almost everything depends on how it is told.

Much of the tale emerges in the first stanza. "She fears him" says a great deal, and so does the revelation that she will continue to wonder why predestination and free will in contradictory combination "fated her to choose him." The narrative voice here sounds confidently well informed, using present past and future tenses (in but two lines!) to reveal not only how things are but the way they were and will be. For the most part, though, the story is told in a kind of continuous present, with the chronology left vague. Thus we learn that she found her husband to be a Judas, but do not know whether this happened before or after they were married.

The burden of stanzas 1 through 3 is to present the woman's developing disillusionment with the man love has saddled her with and her reluctant acceptance of her unhappy situation. Along the way, the reader discovers how the man reacts when his treachery is unveiled at no cost to himself. "He sees that he will not be lost, / And waits and looks around him"—safely ensconced in his comfortable situation. Here, as in "Miniver Cheevy," Robinson uses feminine endings, but for dramatic rather than comic purposes. Everything is centered on uncovering the woman's attitude toward the man who wears an "engaging mask" as false as it is calculatedly agreeable. He is there at the end of nine feminine rhymes, just as he will be there at the end. "Choose him," "refuse him," "lose him." "Sound him," "found him," "around him." "Allures him," "reassures him," "secures him."

That last phrase, coming at the midpoint of "Eros Turannos," is both crucial and intentionally ambiguous. As Justice observes, "secures" suggests a spinster's catch of an elusive bachelor—which would place the action in the past. But it also seems to mean that she "secures" her husband *now* by binding him to her despite his betrayal(s). There is the further connotation that by bestowing on him the blessings of a respectable house and background—a sense of tradition and "of ocean and old trees"—she makes him feel secure. To insist on a single interpretation of "secures" would limit the reach of the poem.

In the fourth stanza, Robinson brings imagery to bear on the woman's misfortune.

> The falling leaf inaugurates
>   The reign of her confusion;
> The pounding wave reverberates
>   The dirge of her illusion.

She secludes herself, avoiding contact with those whose incessant chatter makes the town and harbor side "vibrate": a wonderfully chosen word that stands out as the sole trochaic substitution in a poem of iambics. In the succeeding stanza, the emphasis shifts to a closer look at the gossipers.

> We tell you, tapping on our brows,
>   The story as it should be,—
> As if the story of a house
>   Were told, or ever could be;
> We'll have no kindly veil between
> Her visions and those we have seen,—
> As if we guessed what hers have been,
>   Or what they are or would be.

The townspeople may grasp the bare facts of the case: a woman stays married to a man who does not deserve her. But "her visions" and theirs may be entirely different. It is unwise and arrogant to decide about others "as if" we can understand their innermost thoughts and feelings. "There are things about this poem we will never know," to quote Justice yet again, "just as there are things about it we seem to have known even before we started reading it."

The last note is struck through a reinvocation of the images from nature. In the concluding lines, the woman is left to confront the desolation the god of love has wrought,

> Though like waves breaking it may be
> Or like a changed familiar tree,
> Or like a stairway to the sea
>   Where down the blind are driven.

The similes, as the poet Donald Hall has pointed out, are structural and not decorative: "as 'like waves breaking' embodies the relentless dolor of a featureless daily life in a house by the ocean, as 'like a changed familiar tree' alludes to the 'family tree' and combines ancestral pride with debasement, as 'like a stairway to the sea' (ocean, again) foreshadows inevitable descent into death, recalls the 'foamless weirs / Of age,' and suggests possible suicide by drowning—tyrannical Love driving its victim into the sea." It makes for an eloquent, artful, and compassionate ending.

The two longest poems in *The Man Against the Sky* were also the most ambitious. In "Ben Jonson Entertains a Man from Stratford," a dramatic monologue in four hundred lines of blank verse, Robinson attempted to create a portrait in words of William Shakespeare. EAR's youthful admiration of Shakespeare deepened during his own years of involvement with the theater. He got into the habit of scanning scenes from the plays, particularly *King Lear* and *Antony and Cleopatra*, to warm up for a day's writing. He also perused everything available about Shakespeare the man and was especially impressed by Georg Brandes's *William Shakespeare: A Critical Study*. He sent a copy to Lewis Isaacs in December 1912, with the recommendation that Brandes's book, despite its title, read like "one of the best novels ever written."

In the spring of 1915 he converted much of what he had learned about Shakespeare into a single poem. "Ben Jonson" was written not at MacDowell but during a week in the spring of 1915 when he was confined to his room on West Eighty-third Street in New York by a nasty cold. Aware that he was tackling a subject daunting in its magnitude, Robinson struck a note of modesty in writing Arthur Davison Ficke that he didn't "expect anyone to take the thing very seriously as a reconstruction of Shakespeare." He only hoped that it might make "fairly interesting reading." Still, he felt proud enough of the poem to offer it to Winthrop Ames, who had written appointing him class poet, to be read—by someone else—at the twentieth-anniversary dinner of the Harvard class of 1895.

The impressive Ben Jonson (1572–1637), a London literary dictator of sorts during his time, holds forth about Shakespeare (1564–1616) for the benefit of a visiting alderman from Stratford. Jonson speaks incisively and informally—the two men are drinking together—about his fellow and rival playwright.

> You are a friend then, as I make out,
> Of our man Shakespeare, who alone of us
> Will put an ass's head in Fairyland
> As he would add a shilling to more shillings,
> All most harmonious,—and out of his
> Miraculous inviolable increase
> Fills Ilion, Rome, or any town you like
> Of olden time with timeless Englishmen;
> And I must wonder what you think of him—

All you down there where your small Avon flows
By Stratford, and where you're an Alderman.

These opening lines establish the tone and the basic themes of the poem. As a classicist Jonson is appalled at Shakespeare's boldness in conflating historical periods and places yet admiring of his capacity to make his "timeless" characters come to life. His Shakespeare is given to a certain crudity on the stage—the ass in *A Midsummer Night's Dream*—as to the box-office success that may result from it. Jonson makes much throughout of Shakespeare's worldly aspirations, exemplified by the ambition to "have that House— / The best you ever saw" in his native Stratford. He is "manor-bitten to the bone," Jonson says.

Jonson salts his tavern talk with occasional remarks of Shakespeare's. "Ben, you're a scholar, what's the time of day?" he asks on one occasion. "So few of them," he says of women, "are worth the guessing." In a passage remindful of the nihilism of King Lear, Shakespeare is quoted at greater length.

"No, Ben," he mused; "it's Nothing. It's all Nothing.
We come, we go; and when we're done, we're done.
Spiders and flies—we're mostly one or t'other—
. . . .
Your fly will serve as well as anybody,
And what's his hour? He flies, and flies, and flies,
And in his fly's mind has a brave appearance;
And then your spider gets him in her net,
And eats him out, and hangs him up to dry.
That's Nature, the kind mother of us all.
And then your slattern housemaid swings her broom,
And where's your spider? And that's Nature, also.
It's Nature, and it's Nothing. It's all Nothing."

"Bugs and emperors" alike go back to the same dust.

Jonson speculates that the gods, having granted Shakespeare so many things, "left out the first,—faith, innocence, illusion, / Whatever 'tis that keeps us out o' Bedlam." When Shakespeare became disconsolate, the only thing Jonson could do was to lead him to a tavern where he could drink and then be sick.

The great
Should be as large in liquor as in love,—
And our great friend is not so large in either.

This is one of several observations, this time echoing *Othello*, drawn from Shakespeare's plays into Robinson's poem. Jonson's funeral oration for Shakespeare is reflected in still other lines, notably "I love the man this side idolatry."

Jonson's comments on Shakespeare, as Robinson fashions them, also suggest the playwrights' competitive position. In some frustration, Jonson reveals his consternation at the combination of the ordinary and the extraordinary in Shakespeare. On the one hand, he is driven by the most mundane of financial goals. Here, according to the eminent Shakespeare scholar Marjorie Garber, Robinson's portrayal rings true. As the son of an upwardly mobile Stratford family growing up in a market town, it was only to be expected that Shakespeare should have coveted "O Lord, that House in Stratford!" On the other hand, Shakespeare's genius for language and incredible perceptiveness about people seem to have descended upon him so easily and naturally as to confound Jonson, himself a great poet but one who arrived at his accomplishments only after a rigorous process of self-education.

"Ben Jonson Entertains a Man from Stratford" has been criticized for telling us more about Jonson than about Shakespeare and for telling us more about Robinson than about either of the great Elizabethans. It seems fair to say that the poem tells us something about all three. EAR assigns to Shakespeare two of his own disabilities, insomnia and poor digestion. The more telling parallel, though, has to do with Robinson's wanting to prove his worth to the citizens of Gardiner, Maine, in much the same way that Shakespeare sought to impress the good burghers of Stratford.

When Jonson says of Shakespeare that "something happening in his boyhood / Fulfilled him with a boy's determination / To make all Stratford 'ware of him," he might as easily have been speaking of Robinson.

It was probably inevitable that "Ben Jonson" should prompt comparisons of Robinson with Robert Browning (1812–1889). Even earlier, a score of reviewers had cited Browning as an influence on EAR's poetry. In fact, there was only a brief period—during EAR's time at Harvard and immediately afterward—when he enjoyed reading Browning's work, particularly his poem "Waring." Thereafter, he repeatedly denigrated the Victorian poet. Only Browning's lyrics were worth reading, he said. His plays were "deadly dull." He could not get through *The Ring and the Book*. He disliked "Rabbi Ben Ezra" intensely and rejected the "strident optimism and easy metaphysics" of such Browning assertions as "God's in His heaven—/ All's right with the world!"

The two poets had a few similarities, to be sure. Both concentrated their gaze on people other than themselves. Moreover, Robinson borrowed from Browning the structural device of the dramatic monologue as a way to depict these people. But in "their world-view, psychology, tone, diction, and imagery," the two poets were markedly different.

It was with some annoyance, then, that Robinson saw *The Bookman* for July 1917, wherein William Rose Benet presented a full-page drawing characterizing Robinson and Browning as coconspirators. The two, wrapped in long cloaks, huddle close together under a full moon. The caption reads "Edwin Arlington Robinson Meets the Man from Asolo at Midnight."

THE MASQUE OF POETS AS SEEN BY
WILLIAM ROSE BENÉT

EDWIN ARLINGTON 9.8'16
ROBINSON

*MEETS THE MAN FROM
ASOLO AT MIDNIGHT*

FIGURE 20.1 EAR and Browning.

Source: In House Photo.

Robinson thereupon wrote Lewis N. Chase that he had "never at all, so far as I am aware, [been] under [the influence] of Browning" and insisted to Edith Brower that he couldn't "quite see the relation between 'B. J.' ["Ben Jonson . . ."] and R. B. [Robert Browning]." He could never shake free of his supposed connection to Browning, however. "I'm altogether too lazy to kill anyone," he observed in November 1928, "even a critic who calls me the American Browning, meaning apparently to give pleasure."

The title poem for *The Man Against the Sky*, placed at the end of the volume, represented Robinson's "most ambitious attempt to set forth his thought on ultimate problems." The principal problem was that of belief: how could modern man achieve a faith that would survive the disruptions of the early twentieth century, including the Great War? Robinson explored this issue in 314 lines of loosely rhymed verse: ten irregular strophes organized into a three-part structure.

The first two brief strophes introduce the man against the sky, a generalized creature witnessed at a distance and with a kind of wonderment.

Between me and the sunset, like a dome
Against the glory of a world on fire,
Now burned a sudden hill,
Bleak, round, and high, by flame-lit height made higher,

With nothing on it for the flame to kill
Save one who moved and was alone up there
To loom before the chaos and the glare
As if he were the last god going home
Unto his last desire.

As the poet watches, the "dark, marvelous, and inscrutable" figure moves out of sight into the distance.

The second part of the poem consists of speculations about this man "who stood on high / And faced alone the sky." Robinson proposes five possible interpretations about what "drove or lured or guided him":

A vision answering a faith unshaken,
An easy trust assumed of easy trials,
A sick negation born of weak denials,
A crazed abhorrence of an old condition,
A blind attendance on a brief ambition,—

the alternatives confronting the contemporary everyman. No matter what the particular circumstances of the man against the sky may have been, Robinson writes, "his way was even as ours."

In the three long strophes that end the poem, he poses a series of questions in such a way that to answer them in the affirmative would be devastating. As David H. Hirsch points out in his analysis of the poem, these questions fall into two general categories. "If man can no longer believe as he once did, does that mean that he cannot believe at all? And if man has no hope beyond the grave, if he is nothing better than this quintessence of dust, then what is there to keep him from suicide?"

In a concluding passage that led to widespread misunderstanding of his poem, EAR puts one last terrible question and seems to answer it.

If after all that we have lived and thought,
All comes to Nought,—
If there be nothing after Now,
And we be nothing anyhow,
And we know that,—why live?
'Twere sure but weaklings' vain distress
To suffer dungeons where so many doors
Will open on the cold eternal shores
That look sheer down
To the dark tideless floods of Nothingness
Where all who know may drown.

These lines carry a powerful negative charge, but Robinson did not mean them to be taken literally.

"The Man Against the Sky" was "not a dirge," he insisted. In fact, his purpose "was to try to cheer people up and incidentally to indicate the futility of materialism as a thing to live by"—or to die by. Yet intelligent people, including Amy Lowell, read doubt, disbelief, and despair into his poem. By way of enlightening her, EAR pointed out that he intended the ending words ironically. To support his point, he recommended that some time she read the poem again and consider the word "know" in the last line. He had considered putting the word in italics, he said, but felt that would be going too far.

What one can know was always, to Robinson's mind, severely limited. We could not know much even about ourselves or one another, he believed, and correspondingly less about the cosmos and ultimate questions. Robinson and many others in 1916 faced a crisis of belief as the foundations of western civilization seemed to be collapsing around them. But when he seems to be counseling suicide in the closing lines, he twice qualifies the advice as applicable only to those who "know" that "all comes to Nought." If we *know* that, why live? If we *know* that, why not drown in "the dark tideless floods of Nothingness"?

With this characteristic epistemological uncertainty in mind, Robinson's few lines of strongest affirmation—presented two pages in advance of the conclusion—assume tremendous weight. For in them, he asserts what *can* be known.

> Where was he going, this man against the sky?
> You know not, nor do I.
> But this we know, if we know anything:
> That we may laugh and fight and sing
> And of our transience here make offering
> To an orient Word that will not be erased,
> Or, save in incommunicable gleams
> Too permanent for dreams,
> Be found or known.

"But this we know" followed by seven lines (out of 314) setting out the grounds for belief. As strongly as he can, Robinson asserts the reality of some sort of spiritual experience, outside the realm of proof, that makes it possible for us to take pleasure in our brief existence and to struggle against our demons. No matter how dark the sky, he could not accept the view of scientific materialism: that human beings were merely collections of atoms moved about by chance.

FIGURE 20.2 Lewis Isaacs, ca. 1923: lawyer and composer, and coconspirator with Louis Ledoux.

Source: In House Photo.

FIGURE 20.3 Poet and connoisseur Louis Ledoux, ca. 1920, coconspirator to provide Robinson with an annual subsidy.

Source: In House Photo.

Not long after publication of *The Man Against the Sky*, Robinson's friends conspired to brighten his days. With funds from Hays Gardiner's bequest almost exhausted, EAR once again faced the specter of poverty. A "surprising remembrance" in March 1916 from Dr. Albert Ledoux temporarily alleviated his worries. Then, in midsummer, Louis Ledoux and Lewis Isaacs conceived a plan to finance Robinson's poetry for the next five years.

As Ledoux explained it in a letter to Percy MacKaye, the idea was "to get twelve people to put up $100 each yearly for five years." Ledoux wrote MacKaye in hopes that he might be able "to approach" people who would join in this scheme. He and Isaacs were "finding some difficulty" in locating potential donors, Ledoux said, even though he felt there ought to be some patron of the arts who could give the entire amount "without five minutes consideration and without feeling the strain." By the end of the year, Ledoux and Isaacs had found their dozen contributors. On his birthday, December 22, 1916, Robinson received a letter from the New York Trust Company notifying him that for the next five years he would be sent $100 at the first of every month.

The five years stretched to ten, running through 1926, with a one-time contribution raising the annual allowance from $1200 to $1500 in 1921 and 1922. Robinson was fortunate in his friends. To have a subsidy like his was extremely rare in a culture that did not encourage individual patronage or provide government support. Although the sum was modest, less than the salary of beginning college teachers, with royalties and given EAR's frugality it was enough. He never again faced true economic distress.

Robinson always tried to pay back his debts, but the trust company plan, with the identity of the contributors withheld, helped relieve him of his Yankee sense of obligation. He was aware, however, that Isaacs and Ledoux hatched the scheme and in recompense gave them manuscripts of his completed work. In apparently the first such gesture, he offered Isaacs the MS of *Lancelot*, his "Camelot job," in the summer of 1917. "If you don't care for such lumber," he said, "I'll hand it over to Ledoux." As Robinson's reputation rose during the next twenty years, those manuscripts more than made up for any sense of indebtedness that may have been weighing on him.

21

Reaching Fifty

Van Zorn on Stage

Three years after he bade farewell to playwriting, and after both of his published plays had "fallen utterly flat," Robinson continued to "nourish a more or less idiotic faith in their coming to life some day." His faith was rewarded, briefly, when *Van Zorn* was resuscitated for one cold week in February 1917. The play was performed not on Broadway but in the auditorium of the Central YMCA in Brooklyn, as the initial presentation of the Brooklyn Community Theatre Company. Despite its title, this was no ordinary community theatre. The director-producer for *Van Zorn* was Henry Stillman, who was to go on to an extensive career in the theater. Wright Kramer, who had been appearing on Broadway since the beginning of the century, was cast in the title role, with Helen Holmes as Villa Vannevar.

Like many another playwright about to see his work on the stage for the first time, Robinson was elated. He wrote Edith Brower with the news, adding the optimistic note that if *Van Zorn* survived its week's run in Brooklyn, it would be "taken to Philadelphia and New York." At rehearsals, EAR maintained his usual silence, seeming so detached that Kramer found it hard to believe he was the author.

"Do you object to the cuts?" he was asked. "Oh, no. The play was too long." "Do you have any suggestions?" "No, I haven't any at all. I think it's fine."

Whoever was in charge of publicity thought so little of Robinson that advertisements in the *Brooklyn Eagle* did not even mention his name.

To build the audience for opening night—Monday, February 26—Robinson set aside tickets for various friends and benefactors. Teddy Roosevelt and his wife could not attend, but Mr. and Mrs. Kermit Roosevelt made the journey across the river to see the play EAR had spent years writing and rewriting. So did the Hagedorns and Ledoux and Isaacses. The MacDowell Colony was well represented. One of the colony's supporters, who lived in a mansion on St. Mark's Place in Brooklyn, gave a pretheater dinner party with autographed copies of *Van Zorn* as place cards. Parker Fillmore was among the guests, as was Mrs. MacDowell herself.

When the curtain finally went up, Robinson watched his play with his face flushed and tears of excitement in his eyes. The small audience, almost all invitees, called the actors forward five times when it was over. But the applause was directed more toward EAR than his play, which struck Hagedorn as wooden and inert. "The characters," he wrote, "were like exquisite engravings talking."

Van Zorn attracted few viewers during the rest of its run. "Where [Stillman] got the few cents that kept us going for a week I haven't any idea," Kramer remembered. "Certainly none was gathered from the customers." Given the tepid response, there was no question of taking the show elsewhere.

Robinson was disappointed but stubbornly unwilling to dismiss his play entirely. "The thing is given under the worst imaginable conditions," he wrore Josephine Marks, "but those who see it sit through it and appear to be interested, and possibly a bit bewildered. At any rate I have the satisfaction of knowing that I wasn't an ass for believing it would act. It comes out just as I saw it in my mind's eye—only a little more so. It isn't a bad show, but I doubt if there will ever be much of a public for it."

For him, at least, *Van Zorn* played. But he also understood why it was unlikely to attract a wide audience: because those who sat through it would go home "possibly a bit bewildered." Among those who agreed with him on both counts was the newspaperman and humorist Don Marquis. Later to become famous as the inventor of Archy and Mehitabel, Marquis saw *Van Zorn* opening night. He liked the play enough to propose to Kramer—a decade later, after EAR's success with *Tristram*—that he try to reshape it "into a paying proposition." Marquis made the attempt, but decided it could not be done.

"I couldn't touch Van Zorn, and I don't believe anybody could without ruining it," Marquis told Kramer.

What it is, it is, and a well-nigh perfect piece of work of its kind—I realize that more than I did some years ago. . . .

To be a popular success it would have to be "pointed up" as they say in its emotional possibilities; it would have to be broadened and its story slammed and punched home more.

And that would be to destroy its peculiar excellence. Everything is done in it by suggestion, by inference, with restraint. . . .

To treat the story, even here and there, without the suggestiveness, the inferential quality, would be to nullify the feeling of mystery which is its chief effect intended. It is a play which creates its impressions *entirely* in this manner of treatment, and I do not see how part of it could be changed without ruining it all—certainly, nobody could change it except Robinson.

In admitting defeat, Marquis assigned to *Van Zorn* precisely that quality of inferential suggestiveness that gives EAR's poems—on the page—their "peculiar excellence." As Robinson observed in 1932, it might have been better if *Van Zorn* had been written as a long poem rather than a play. By then, he was determined to stick to poetry, "which perishes less conspicuously" than plays. "The drama is a harlot," he wrote Ranck, "and is just about as trustworthy as the rest of them."

Merlin . . .

In the spring of 1916, Robinson read and was much impressed by Hermann Hagedorn's "altogether stunning" poem "The Great Maze," which refashioned the material of Greek tragedy—the story of the house of Atreus—into modern dress. As he contemplated the summer's work ahead of him, EAR began turning over the possibility of borrowing a well-known legend himself and turning it into a book-length narrative poem. By mid-June, Robinson had settled on Malory's King Arthur as the source of his effort.

In nine weeks he wrote and rewrote *Merlin*. During the following summer, he completed yet another Arthurian poem, focusing on the love affair of Lancelot and Guinevere and intended as a companion piece to *Merlin*. They were his longest poems so far, the first of a series of fourteen extended verse narratives he would produce over the next two decades.

In constructing *Merlin*, which was published in March 1917, EAR started the story, as he had his ill-fated plays, just before the "exploding point." Merlin has returned to Camelot to witness the incendiary destruction of Arthur's kingdom, and Dagonet the fool addresses Gawaine from their post atop Merlin's Rock. What is he looking for from that elevation, Dagonet asks Gawaine. For the lady Vivian, for the Holy Grail, or for Merlin himself?

So begins section 1. Then in the concluding section 7, after a flashback to his decade-long dalliance with Vivian, Merlin circles back to refer to Vivian ("the torch of woman") and to the grail ("the light that Galahad found") as "the two fires that are to light the world." This would not happen very soon. Robinson paints a desolate nightscape at the end of his poem.

> Colder blew the wind
> Across the world, and on it heavier lay
> The shadow and the burden of the night;
> And there was darkness over Camelot.

Merlin helped to establish Arthur as king, although aware that Arthur had sinned twice, first by succumbing to an incestuous union with his unrecognized sister and so conceiving the reptilian and vengeful Modred, and then by marrying Guinevere although she did not love him. Arthur committed these acts knowing they were wrong, thinking that he would not have to pay the consequences. And for some years the king "reigned well," though doom awaited. Merlin in his farseeing wisdom understood that there would be a day of accounting, but hoped that the prideful Arthur and his kingdom would serve as "a mirror wherein men / [Might] see themselves, and pause."

Robinson fashioned a Merlin quite different from the stock figure of the medieval wizard with a wand and a conical cap. He is wise but hardly a super-man. He sees far more than most men but cannot see everything and cannot alter the future. Nor does Robinson follow precedent by making Merlin a dod-dering figure approaching his dotage. He is of "indeterminate age" when he joins Vivian at Broceliande. At their first meeting, he tells her that "Whatever I am, / I have not lived in time until to-day."

To some extent, Merlin's vision is dimmed by the enchantments he encoun-ters in the pleasure garden of Broceliande. Songbirds greet him on arrival, and petals flutter down from the cherry trees. The first night with Vivian is described in detail in the long central section of the poem. To prepare for the evening, he submits to the symbolic changes in appearance she requires: his beard is shaved off and his black traveling costume exchanged for robes of purple. He looks so different that the enchanting Vivian, herself transformed "in a fragile sheath of crimson," makes a small joke of it.

> "Go away," she said;
> "I never saw you in my life before."

The night's sumptuary delights then commence. Vivian is like a flower, but no ordinary flower.

> It seemed
> A flower of wonder with a crimson stem
> Came leaning slowly and regretfully
> To meet his will—a flower of change and peril
> That had a clinging blossom of warm olive
> Half stifled with a tyranny of black,
> And held the wayward fragrance of a rose
> Made woman by delirious alchemy.

They kiss, as she calls his lips to meet hers and so surrender "The last of any-thing that might remain / Of what was now their beardless wizardry." At dinner, "dream-weaving" music from distant flutes and viols and hautboys accompanies the food and wine. The black-haired Vivian fills his cup of gold over and again, as her "inextinguishable eyes" flash blindness into his. As he falls asleep later, still flushed with the sensory overload, Merlin envisions Camelot in ruins.

> There came
> Between him and the world a crumbling sky
> Of black and crimson, with a crimson cloud
> That held a far off town of many towers.

The towers sway and shake, then disintegrate in his dreams. He awakes to the sound of birds, and a fainter sound as well, "As if a sleeping child with a black head / Beside him drew the breath of innocence." This passage, members of the Robinson family believe, referred to the fall of 1897, when the dark-haired Emma in her distress rested her head on Win's shoulder and Herman, raging, came home to find them so.

Merlin may dream of Camelot, but Vivian has him in thrall, and he remains ten years by her side. She, like Merlin, belongs to this world, and works her enchantment through artfulness rather than an exercise of supernatural powers. During his decade as her "prisoner," the days pass without arousing in Merlin any desire to escape. Vivian is guileful and gracious and charmingly witty, and she converts Merlin from political genius into lover. Or does so until King Arthur commands his return, with the empire about to be destroyed in a cataclysm Merlin can do nothing to prevent.

In his final leave-taking, Merlin acknowledges that he will never see Vivian again. There is little for either of them to regret. They have had their love, and Merlin departs in confidence that it was her great love as well as his.

> But I shall see
> No more the lady Vivian. Let her love
> What man she may, no other love than mine
> Shall be an index of her memories.
> I fear no man who may come after me,
> And I see none. I see her, still in green,
> Beside the fountain. I shall not go back.
> We pay for going back; and all we get
> Is one more needless ounce of weary wisdom
> To bring away with us.

Carl Van Doren, reading the passages about Vivian, became convinced that in order to create her Robinson must have experienced a deep and lasting love. There are several signs that connect the fictional Vivian to the very real Emma Robinson: their shared coloring and engaging flirtatiousness, for example. If *Merlin* is interpreted as one version among many of that relationship that Robinson explored in his poetry, it would seem to imply that the love between EAR and Emma, powerful as it was, was not strong enough to outweigh his obligation to pursue his calling as a poet. Both in this poem and in *Lancelot*, he was reconciling himself to a life of poetry, minus the comforts of wife and home and family. In his imagination, at least, Robinson like Merlin experienced his great love and understood that going back might tarnish the memory.

It would be wrong, though, to read these poems as autobiographical. Robinson was also writing about the times and the world around him. The terrible sense of waste and folly Merlin feels as he witnesses the darkness descending on Camelot paralleled EAR's distress about World War I. In a January 1920 interview, he said he wrote *Merlin* because he "saw a world symbol in the situation and used the Arthurian method as a peg to hang the picture on." There were two themes he had in mind. "One was that nothing can endure that is built on a false foundation, and the other is that you can't live in two worlds at the same time." At the end of the poem, civil war is about to break out, and the wise fool Dagonet speaks for EAR as he addresses Bedivere:

> When all men are like you and me, my lord,
> When all are rational or rickety,
> There may be no more war. But what's here now?
> Lancelot loves the Queen, and he makes war
> Of love; the King, being bitten to the soul
> By love and hate that work in him together,
> Makes war of madness; Gawaine hates Lancelot,
> And he, to be in tune, makes war of hate;
> Modred hates everything, yet he can see
> With one damned illegitimate small eye
> His father's crown, and with another like it
> He sees the beauty of the Queen herself;
> He needs the two for his ambitious pleasure,
> And therefore he makes war of his ambition;
> And somewhere in the middle of all this
> There's a squeezed world that elbows for attention.

In its catalogue of human hatred, Dagonet's speech illustrates the greatest single difference between Robinson's Arthurian poems and Tennyson's immensely popular *Idylls of the King*. Where Tennyson idealizes his characters, Robinson brings them down to earth. The critic Yvor Winters illustrates the point by comparing the portraits of King Arthur. "Robinson's Arthur is a mirror in which imperfect humanity may view itself; Tennyson endeavors to make of his Arthur a model for imperfect humanity to emulate."

In the years immediately following the publication of *Merlin*, Robinson was inclined to believe that he had done his best work there. Reviewers were of two minds about the poem, however. Those who liked it did so extravagantly; those who disliked it exhibited a similar enthusiasm in their disapproval. Among the admirers was Edward Bliss Reed in the *Yale Review*, a journal that was soon to become a favored repository for EAR's poems.

Merlin, Reed wrote, was "unlike any Arthurian poem [he had] ever read. . . . The characters are not figures in armor; they are men no further removed from us than the characters" in George Meredith's novels. Reed ended with praise for the full range of Robinson's accomplishment. "Each volume of Mr. Robinson's deepens the conviction that he is our foremost American poet. In laying down 'Merlin,' we have but one criticism to offer: it is too soon ended."

The poet Conrad Aiken, in a commentary on Robinson's work through 1920, declared that he had reached his zenith in *Merlin*. "Merlin and Vivien [*sic*] move before us exquisitely known and seen, as none of the people whom Tennyson took from Malory ever did. It is one of the finest love stories in English verse." Like Reed, he drew an analogy between EAR's verse and the prose of a major novelist. Robinson's *Merlin* and *Lancelot*, Aiken observed, "give us a Malory as Henry James might have rewritten and enlarged it, had Henry James been a poet. . . . Everything is hint and gleam. . . . The express is at a minimum, the implications are vast." Here, Aiken was applauding Robinson for the subtle inferences that made his dramas, like James's similar efforts to write for the stage, virtually unplayable. Aiken was among the first to compare Robinson's poetry to James's fiction. Many were to follow.

In late Robinson as in late James, there is a great deal of conversation. Harriet Monroe at *Poetry* had minimal tolerance for "characters unfolding their perplexities, or recording their action upon each other, in long speeches which are not talk, as talk actually was or could be, but which are talk intensified into an extra-luminous self revelation." Robinson's method, she felt, was akin to that of "the psychoanalyst who encourages confessional monologue, or uses dialogue, as a probe to strike through the poison of lies and appearances and reveal the truth."

This was not at all her cup of tea, nor did she have much patience with EAR's abandoning native grounds in favor of medieval settings and circumstances. Monroe admitted that Robinson did not adopt archaic language or forswear "all modern significance" in his Arthurian poems, "but to me at least his modern instinct and habit of mind seem out of place in Camelot." Monroe was never to become a strong supporter of Robinson's work. She preferred Vachel Lindsay to him, and Carl Sandburg and Edgar Lee Masters.

Amy Lowell, who had so much good to say about *The Man Against the Sky*, shared Monroe's disapproval of Robinson for abandoning American subjects and settings. In her *Tendencies in Modern American Poetry*, published in October 1917, Lowell followed a mostly laudatory assessment of EAR's career with an attack on his most recent work. There were some beautiful passages in *Merlin*, she acknowledged. But the retelling of the Arthurian legend was "neither so new nor so different as one might have expected." Reading it, she said, was like turning over "the pages of a picture book, a portfolio of old, rare prints. They have nothing to do with us, nor we with them."

Robinson, who was not insensitive to such matters, was well aware that anything Amy Lowell had to say would have an impact on his reputation. Lowell was notorious for her considerable girth—Ezra Pound called her a "hippopoetess"—and eccentric style of life. As a Boston Lowell whose brother became president of Harvard, she did not hesitate to flout convention. She and the actress Ada Russell openly lived together. She smoked cigars and kept scandalous hours, sleeping much of the day and working on her several volumes of poetry and criticism at night. These established her as a champion of the imagist movement, an advocate of free verse, and a prolific and influential critic.

In correspondence with Amy Lowell, Robinson appeared to be following the advice of the fictional Mr. Nixon in a satirical passage of Pound's "Hugh Selwyn Mauberley." The calculating Nixon, a highly successful writer, counsels the beginning author to "butter reviewers." It had worked for him, he says. Something of a similar careerist motivation undoubtedly drove EAR to tell Lowell (in November 1915) that he'd read halfway through her book on *Six French Poets* before realizing what time it was and to declare (in October 1916) that the poems in her *Men, Women, and Ghosts* struck him with the force of "an avalanche."

When Lowell asked for personal information for *Tendencies in Modern American Poetry*, the compulsively private Robinson deflected the request in engaging fashion. "In looking over my life I find that I have no life to speak of,

Cpt. New York Times

FIGURE 21.1 Amy Lowell: poet and critic to be reckoned with.

Source: Picture Collection, New York Public Library.

FIGURE 21.2 Robinson in fisherman's hat, used as frontispiece for Lowell's *Tendencies in American Poetry*, 1917.

Source: In House Photo.

much less to write about," he told her. Then he went on to provide the basic details in a self-deprecatory way. "I was born at Head Tide, Maine, on December 22, 1869, was educated (?) at the Gardiner (Maine) High School and at Harvard College (1891–93) and after that in the University of Hard Knocks—in which, I fancy, I made out my own curriculum to a large extent. In 1905 President Roosevelt was good enough to give me a position in the New York Custom House, where I stayed for five years and was probably the least efficient public servant who ever drew his pay from the U.S. Treasury Department—which is much for any one man to say of himself. In general I have engaged in what is vaguely called 'literary work', and I have continued somehow to stay alive." Subsequently, he sent her a photograph of himself for use in the book.

Lowell did not want to displease Robinson, either. She used his photo as the frontispiece for *Tendencies*, giving him pride of place among the other poets under discussion, and warned him, twice, that he might be "a little disappointed" by her comments about *Merlin*: "I had to say what I thought about it." Upon reading the book, EAR responded without rancor that her strictures about *Merlin* seemed "entirely sincere" and "probably not far from the truth" and that he was gratified by her copious praise of his other work. "I have never pretended not to be a human being, and I have never been at a loss for the proper word to apply to those people who pretend that they do not care what other people think of them." *Hypocrite*, one presumes, was the word.

Robinson went on to call her book "extraordinarily interesting," particularly her appreciation of Frost, whose work he thought more important that that of the other modern American poets she had written about, among them Edgar Lee Masters, H.D., and John Gould Fletcher. On the same day—October 22,

1917—that he wrote Lowell, Robinson offered a different perspective on her book in a letter to Thomas Sergeant Perry, a Boston Brahmin well acquainted with her. As a private joke, EAR and the Perrys referred to Amy Lowell in capital letters. "Having read what She says about me in Her book, I have to say that she has let me [off] rather better than I expected. Where I looked for the stiletto and the bodkin, I encountered the meat-axe and the shillalah. Some of her remarks are singularly good, and some, to my mind, singularly bad. But I am glad that she wrote the article, and I cannot yet be sure that she means murder."

He had little doubt that Lowell was capable of such a crime. Some years later, he said that she "should have lived in Renaissance Italy. She'd have enjoyed poisoning people." He'd heard her dispose of half a dozen during dinner.

. . . and Lancelot

Once he'd finished *Merlin*, Robinson immediately embarked on "Lancelot and Guinevere" (the working title for *Lancelot*). He did fragmentary sketches for the poem during the winter of 1917 in New York, but found that most of them were unusable. "The thing wasn't ripe then," he wrote Isaacs from the MacDowell Colony early in June, "and I shouldn't have bothered with it but for the annoying feeling that . . . I ought to be doing something to justify my seemingly negative existence." Now that he was working, though, he could contemplate the future with equanimity. "I see nothing for me but a righteous and orderly life, with a book now and then to punctuate its harmless monotony, and then, when I have earned it, a hole in the ground with whatever may or may not come after." This, he thought, was "not a bad or an unpleasant programme."

During the summer, Robinson zoomed along at a giddy pace: 500 lines in the first eight days and a complete draft of 3,400 lines by the end of August. He wrote *Lancelot* "as enthusiastically as if [he] thought someone were going to read it," EAR said, yet he wondered "what kind of face" his publishers would make when he presented them with another long blank verse poem. He had good reason to wonder. Early in December 1917, Macmillan let him know they did not think it "advisable to bring out [*Lancelot*] at present."

Robinson made substantial cuts during the winter and submitted the poem for a prize offered by the bumptious litterateur Samuel Roth. Not having read the fine print, Robinson did not understand that by submitting his entry, he gave Roth the right to publish if *Lancelot* won. It did, and after some delays caused by business difficulties, Robinson's second Arthurian poem came out in February 1920 under the imprint of Thomas Seltzer.

Macmillan apparently thought *Lancelot* too long and convoluted, but that was not the firm's principal objection. The United States had been drawn into World War I by the time Robinson submitted his manuscript—a manuscript with a powerful antiwar bias. To publish it in 1918 would have been widely regarded as unpatriotic.

From boyhood on, Robinson had been fascinated by the legend of King Arthur. Not until the outbreak of the Great War, however, did it occur to him that the collapse of Camelot offered "a perfect symbol" of a world breaking up. Both *Merlin* and *Lancelot* were "suggested by the world war," EAR said, with the analogy much clearer in the second poem. The two poems were intended to "be read together," he said, with the action proceeding chronologically from *Merlin* to *Lancelot* and the message gaining authority when they were considered jointly.

Given his temperamental inclinations, Robinson expected nothing less than the destruction of western civilization from the war. At the same time, he insisted that his was a basically optimistic outlook, for only after such a drastic obliteration could civilization be rebuilt on a sound foundation. "You may still call me an evangelist of ruin when you have read [*Merlin*]," he told Jean Ledoux, "but you mustn't forget the redemption—even if you don't see it." Similarly, he told Edith Brower that there was "nothing especially sad about the end of kings and the redemption of the world." In *Merlin*, the "torch of woman" and the pursuit of the Holy Grail are to bring renewal. In *Lancelot*, a Voice tells the errant knight that "a world has died/ For you, that a world may live."

Robinson did not, however, foresee such a rebirth in his time. The end of World War I made little difference in his outlook. Two weeks after the Armistice, he predicted the onset of a few years of hell in Germany, followed by a constitutional monarchy to keep the Teutons quiet for a while. In another sense, though, "the war has just begun, and I don't even pretend to make a guess as to how far the Bolshevik poison may penetrate."

Without being explicit about the countries and political systems involved, Robinson warned in *Lancelot* against the terrible costs of war in general and World War I in particular. It is love, or the lack of it, that leads to war in the poem: Arthur's arrogant taking of Guinevere as his queen, even knowing that she loved Lancelot; Guinevere's enduring love that leads her to pursue an affair with Lancelot; and Lancelot's passion for Guinevere that deters him from seeking the Light, or the Gleam, or the Grail.

Lancelot is a poem about love and war and the havoc they wreak on human lives. Robinson's Lancelot is not merely a triumphant participant in the tournaments and knightly encounters of Camelot but a man deeply divided and guilt-ridden by his yearnings. And Guinevere, who understands that she has been wronged by her father and husband, becomes a genuine heroine by renouncing the love of her life. Robinson focuses on the inner life of these characters, as it emerges in conversation. The action, and the carnage, take place offstage.

To Guinevere, the war seems little more than a "slow game / Of empty slaughter" that men love to play. Impatiently, she confronts her lover.

"Lancelot,
There must be glimmering yet somewhere within you
The last spark of a little willingness
To tell me why it is this war goes on."

And later,

"How many thousand men
Are going to their death before Gawaine
And Arthur go to theirs—and I to mine?"

Finally, Lancelot too comes to see the matter in the same way. "The world has paid enough / For Camelot," he says, in a phrase EAR cited as the overriding message of his poem.

Arthur's false love born of pride was the real trigger to the war. The king recognizes his error, but cannot undo it.

"Merlin told me:
'The love that never was!' Two years ago
He told me that: 'The love that never was!'
I saw—but I saw nothing. Like the bird
That hides his head, I made myself see nothing."

Lancelot and Guinevere are uncovered as lovers by a ruse the king and Gawaine devise. Arthur tells his queen he is going hunting, and she makes a rendezvous with Lancelot, who is struggling to escape Camelot yet knows if he looks into Guinevere's eyes, he will be unable to go.

In the shade of a sunlit afternoon, as the end of the old order approaches, the enchanting "white and gold" of Guinevere work their magic upon him. Beset by guilt, Lancelot feels his whole identity challenged.

"Who is this Lancelot that has betrayed
His King, and served him with a cankered honor?
Who is this Lancelot that sees the Light
And waits now in the shadow for the dark?
. . . .
God, what a rain of ashes falls on him
Who sees the new and cannot leave the old!"

Once he and Guinevere have been found out and Lancelot precipitates a civil war by rescuing her from execution, the lovers have time to reflect on the future. It is proposed that she return to Camelot, safe passage guaranteed, as a sort of peace offering, but she rejects this plan. Instead she betakes herself to a

nunnery in Almesbury. She and Lancelot meet there in the powerful concluding section of the poem.

Gone is the resplendent queen, "all white and gold," who had bewitched
Lancelot. Now the golden hair is covered. "The black hood, and the white face
under it, / And the blue frightened eyes, were all he saw." Her wisdom domi-
nates the scene. She asks forgiveness for not letting him go sooner. "God pity
men / When women love too much—and women more." Lancelot offers to
spirit her off to France with him, but she will not accept.

> "There is no place
> For me but where I am; there is no place
> For you save where it is that you are going."

Guinevere will not be alone, she tells Lancelot, for she will keep the memory of
their love. "We have had all there was," and that is enough. They are "going by
two roads to the same end." At last Lancelot sees that he too must choose the
path of renunciation. As he rides off into the night, he asks himself

> "Why should I look for peace
> When I have made the world a ruin of war?"

A Voice within answers that "where the Light falls, death falls." He feels a burden lift as the still face of Guinevere fades "away in a white loneliness." He
reaches as if to touch her, but finds only a black branch of leaves in his hand.
Lancelot's great quest lies ahead, the vision of Guinevere replaced by that of

> Galahad, who had seen and died,
> And was alive, now in a mist of gold.
> He rode on into the dark, under the stars,
> And there were no more faces. There was nothing.
> But always in the darkness he rode on,
> Alone; and in the darkness came the Light.

On an afternoon in the spring of 1926 at the MacDowell Colony, the young
writer Chard Powers Smith discovered Robinson in a state of consternation. He
was carrying a copy of one of the weekly magazines, which he whacked against
his leg. "They call me," he said, spitting out each word, "a dry New England
psychologist! How in God's name do they think I wrote Guinevere?" In his fury,
EAR revealed still more: that Guinevere was a portrait of his "great love."

Significantly, Robinson assigned to Guinevere an unusual characteristic of
Emma Robinson's: that "she used her fingers when talking, and sometimes
paused suddenly and looked at them." In Lancelot, Guinevere does this not
once but twice. The resemblance is more significant, however, in the strength of

character both women showed in setting their lovers free to pursue their call-ing. Not for Robinson a goal so grand as the Light, to be sure, and yet for him the only path—a poet's life—that he was equipped to follow.

A Stay in Brooklyn

As he approached fifty, Robinson's life began to follow a regular course. He was by no means well to do, but could get along on his annual $1,200. He had grown accustomed to a more or less itinerant existence. He wrote steadily dur-ing the summers in New Hampshire, and in the winters he let his reservoir fill as he enjoyed the musical and theatrical inducements of New York. In the territory and time between, there were people to visit. Still, he was often lonely, and never more so than while living alone on West Eighty-third Street in the city.

The Frasers—Jimmy and his sculptor wife Laura Gardin—helped to ward off Robinson's loneliness. James Earle Fraser's career was prospering. In 1913, the same year as his marriage, he submitted the winning design for the buffalo nickel. That coin, together with his "End of the Trail," depicting a disconsolate Indian on horseback, established Fraser as the nation's best-known sculptor. Fraser, like EAR, derived from middle-class roots. He and his wife were both athletic, Laura as an accomplished tennis player and Jimmy as a golfer. The Fra-sers were without pretensions. They went to the symphony and the opera, and they loved to play poker. Childless, they made a home for Laura's mother—and eventually, for Robinson as well. As successful artists, they had no impulse to patronize or lionize him.

FIGURE 21.3 James Earle Fraser working on bust of Teddy Roosevelt at the White House, 1905.

Source: Picture Collection, New York Public Library.

FIGURE 21.4 Laura Gardin Fraser's bust of EAR, 1919.

Source: Colby College Special Colllections.

The Frasers, in short, put Robinson at ease, and he began seeing more of them, both in the city and at their country house near Westport, Connecticut. In the winter of 1919, Laura Gardin sculpted a bust of EAR at her Greenwich Village studio. The bust was dropped on the floor in the course of the work, prompting Robinson to observe that she had "smashed his head to the probable improvement of his appearance." The reassembled plaster bust, it seems, was not converted to bronze, but the Frasers demonstrated their generosity in other ways. For Christmas 1919, they gave Robinson a season ticket to the symphony. "I may get even with my friends in the next world," he said at the time, "though I don't know just how."

Beginning in the winter of 1916, Robinson started disappearing from his New York apartment for the weekends. In his close-mouthed way, he told no one where he was going. Rumors sprang up about clandestine romantic trysts. The truth was less sensational. Robinson was spending the weekends with his old friend from Gardiner, Seth Ellis Pope, who was living and working at the Pratt Institute library in Brooklyn. Like Robinson himself, Pope was a lonely man in need of companionship: his wife Florence had left him. Corpulent, stolid, and ungainly, Pope was hardly prepossessing in appearance or manner, but there was a powerful bond between the two men. Pope regarded Robinson with a worship that traced back beyond the evening meetings of the Quadruped club in Gardiner. Once, in high school, EAR had saved him from a beating by bullies.

In the winter of 1918, Robinson packed his two suitcases, left his room on the Upper West Side, and moved in with Pope at his dingy apartment at 810 Washington Avenue in Brooklyn. This arrangement removed EAR from most of the attractions of Manhattan, but he stayed there until Pope died in the winter of 1922.

Robinson moved to Brooklyn for economic reasons, he told the Perrys. "I found myself living rather beyond my means in Manhattan (all my own fault)," he wrote in January 1918, "and so took advantage of an opportunity to retrench." In his new quarters, EAR taught himself the rudiments of cooking. "No man can boil water, or an egg, or broil a steak or a chop, with more authority and finesse than E. A. R.," he declared. The apartment featured a well-behaved oil-stove for heat, a silent place to work during the day, and—the only mention of Pope—"a laboring friend who comes home at night and doesn't talk too much."

Few of EAR's literary friends ever met Pope. Parker Fillmore did, and found him to be "a most ordinary man," plain, shabbily dressed, and heavy-minded. Robinson made the mistake of asking Fillmore what he thought of Pope.

"He's all right," Fillmore said, "and he's certainly devoted to you."

"You don't sound very enthusiastic about him," Robinson said.

"I don't know that he's anything to be enthusiastic about," Fillmore replied. "He's a friend of your boyhood, and that's that. If you met him now for the first time, I don't believe you and he would strike up a very violent friendship."

At this Robinson flared up in anger. He wouldn't hear anything against Pope. He'd known Pope all his life, and he was a fine man, EAR insisted. Fillmore retreated with apologies. Pope's merits were not a subject for debate.

Malcolm Cowley and S. Foster Damon, two young poets recently graduated from Harvard, made the pilgrimage across the bridge to see Robinson in the spring of 1919. Cowley remembered the visit well. He and Damon stumbled along Washington Avenue, passing rows of identical gray apartment houses. When they found the right building, EAR was waiting for them at the end of a dark hallway. "He was then in his fiftieth year, but looked perhaps thirty-five—a tall, diffident man with the sort of stoop that comes from bending over books." He was struck by Robinson's smile, his high forehead, "his slightly quizzical nose . . . and most of all, his friendly eyes that blinked under thick glasses." They talked, Cowley listening hard to what EAR had to say.

"Poetry is something indefinable, intangible and unmistakable," Robinson said. He compared the process of composition to a miner's search for gold. "We work to find a vein of poetry which may prove to be large or small. It always changes in size as we advance, and sometimes it peters out entirely. Or perhaps, after we've smelted out ore, we find that it isn't gold after all."

Robinson calculated the potential audience for American poetry at a hundred thousand people. He arrived at that estimate, EAR said, on the basis of Gardiner itself. In his home town's population of six thousand people, he found exactly half a dozen who really liked poetry. The ratio was the same as that for confirmed drunkards, he added, but without any crossovers.

What Cowley found most memorable about that visit was Robinson's indifference to his surroundings. Even in his fiftieth year, "the most distinguished

FIGURE 21.5 Malcolm Cowley, man of
letters, in 1934.

Source: Picture Collection, New York Public
Library.

American poet was living in a Brooklyn back-street, in two rooms of an ill
heated, ill lighted railroad apartment, with his books piled in the china closet,
on pine shelves varnished to imitate golden oak." EAR, who did not lack an
aesthetic sense, must have recognized how dismal the place was. It did not
matter. His vocation was large enough to encompass everything in his life. For
Robinson, Cowley believed, "poetry played the part of wife, children, job and
recreation."

Through Pope, Robinson met the slight and impoverished Franklin Schenck,
a painter of landscapes who had studied with the great Thomas Eakins in Philadelphia. Some of his work was quite good, but he knew absolutely nothing about
finding buyers to purchase his canvases. "A mystic, a modern St. Francis," Schenck
lived in a woodland shack near East Northport, Long Island, and eked out a mea-
ger living by raising chickens and vegetables on his "handkerchief of land." He
was sixty when EAR met him in 1919, and he looked even older. But he was a
happy man, deriving pleasure from simple encounters with the natural world.

Schenck got along on three dollars a week, half of which Pope supplied to
him from his own skimpy salary. After Pope died, Robinson took it upon himself to provide Schenck with the minuscule sum required to keep him alive. He
enlisted Lewis Isaacs to help in this endeavor, and the Isaacses subsequently
took an interest in Schenck. On a weekend afternoon, they drove down with the
children to see him on Long Island. Although in poor health, Schenck greeted
his visitors with a radiant smile. The doctors told him he needed iron, so he was
boiling out an old horseshoe in a pot on his one-burner stove. He lacked the
money to buy canvas, so he had painted birds and flowers and running streams
on every window shade in his shack.

FIGURE 21.6 EAR's
painting by Franklin
Schenck, *The Dark
Hills.*

Source: Colby College
Special Collections.

Before his visitors left, Schenck asked the children if they would like to see
the birds come to him when he sang with his guitar. The Iaaacses watched as
he sat under a lilac tree playing and singing an old tune. One by one, the birds
came, some answering his call, some singing with him. It was a scene, Edith
Isaacs said, not to be forgotten.

Robinson kept one painting of Schenck's with him all his days. It depicted a
line of dark hills at evening with a sky of gold and ivory as glowing in color as
in a landscape by Rembrandt or Turner. Precisely when Robinson acquired the
painting is not known, so it is impossible to determine whether the painting
inspired EAR's poem "The Dark Hills," first published in 1920, or the other way
around. The poem, one of Robinson's most lyrical, has been set to music at least
half a dozen times. It runs to only eight lines. The first four lines arrived unbidden, straight from the blue, but it was two years before he could think of the
concluding four. A comparison of two versions of the poem, in published and
manuscript form, demonstrate Robinson in the process of seeking out those
last lines through revision.

Here is "The Dark Hills," in its published version:

Dark hills at evening in the west,
Where sunset hovers like a sound
Of golden horns that sang to rest
Old bones of warriors under ground,
Far now from all the bannered ways
Where flash the legions of the sun,
You fade—as if the last of days
Were fading, and all wars were done.

This is both beautiful and moving. The hills fade away as the light wanes, but the last of days has not yet come and there will be other wars to send other warriors to their rest.

In its first draft, the eight lines of "The Dark Hills" were broken into two quatrains. The first four lines were precisely the same (except for one omitted comma), but they were followed by a different and much less successful conclusion.

> Dark hills at evening in the west
> Where sunset hovers like a sound
> Of golden horns that sang to rest
> Old bones of warriors underground,
>
> No other stillness have I found
> Where Time stays listening as in yours,
> And hears the quivering world go round
> With all its engine-shaken floors.

Leonie Adams and Louise Dauner, in separate essays, discuss the way Robinson improved his poem through revision. The two quatrains of the first draft do not fit together well. At the cost of consistency, the second quatrain shifts its emphasis from the hills themselves to the poet and the abstract Time. The "golden horns" give way to an illogical "stillness," and the remoteness of the buried warriors is lost "in the jangle of a mechanized world." In short, "The Dark Hills" in its manuscript form made little poetic sense. By way of contrast, the eight lines of the poem as revised and published create a single and coherent unit. As Adams observed, "the transformation of mere 'armies' that have come and gone into 'the flashing legions of the sun' was an act of imagination without which the lovely opening lines would have trailed off into flatness."

EAR's tenure in Brooklyn provided another example of keeping companions in discrete compartments—in one pocket the New Yorkers, in a second the Bostonians, loosely aligned with the Gardiner group, including Pope. When Alanson Tucker Schumann died in the spring of 1918, Robinson sent a memorial remembrance to the *Boston Evening Transcript* for publication. In the piece, EAR praised his early mentor's facility and precision as a master of verse forms and included three poems of Schumann's, two sonnets and a ballade, that he thought excellent. With "his highly responsive sense of beauty and his quiet sense of humor," EAR wrote, Dr. Schumann lived "the best part of his life in the land of fancy—a land where he saw much that others might not have seen." The tribute was the least he could do for the man who had taken him, a boy in his teens, into the Gardiner Poetry Society and launched him on his own journey to that same land.

The death of Schumann, together with rooming with Pope in Brooklyn, served to remind Robinson of what he had left behind, and might yet recover, in Gardiner. At Thanksgiving time in 1918, he departed from his usual schedule to make a special trip to Boston. He came to see Emma, and he may well have proposed to her again. In a letter to Betts, he uncovered his yearning for a home and family. "This living outside the hive may look easy from the inside," he said, "but in reality it's a damn poor kind of life."

Robinson and Emma met at Lilla Cabot Perry's studio on Ipswich Street. On that occasion, Emma apparently refused marriage, suggesting instead that Win come to live with her and her daughters at the Shepherd house in Farmingdale. "If I can't have your love," he is supposed to have told her in reply, "I don't want your pity." He took the train back to New York, discouraged. A week later, he wrote Burnham about it. "My last trip to Boston was active but not satisfactory. I don't want another like it, and from present indications I'm not going to have one. Some things die hard, but they die sooner or later." Burnham, more than anyone else among Robinson's friends, knew enough of his emotional life to be able to read between the lines.

To a considerable extent, after 1918 Robinson transferred much of his longing for wife and family from Emma to her three daughters. In his avuncular way, he bestowed his affection on Barbara, the youngest and last to wed; on Marie, who followed her older sister into nursing and eventually married a doctor, and—especially—on the eldest daughter Ruth. "What is all this that I hear in regard to your engagement?" he wrote Ruth in July 1921. "Won't you send me a word about yourself, and let me know, incidentally, whether he is black or white, Jap or German, Yankee or Yahoo?" Yankee was closest. In October 1921, Ruth Robinson gave up her surgical nursing career in Boston to marry William Nivison, master mechanic in the Gardiner paper mill. EAR sent Ruth a note when her son David was born in 1923. "I am glad you have him," he said, "and have no particular advice to offer—except, of course, to drown him if he shows any inclination to write poetry."

Back in the World

In an article for the *North American Review*, Robinson spelled out the wonders of the MacDowell Colony. There he had found

a place in the country, not too far from the civilizing conveniences of life, that would afford comfortable lodging, good food, a large and well-windowed sleeping room with a good bed in it, an easy walk to breakfast at about seven-thirty, a longer walk to a secluded and substantial building in the woods, a large open fireplace and plenty of fuel, a free view from the door of the best kind of New England scenery, a complete assurance of a long day before me without social annoyances or interruptions of any kind, a simple luncheon brought to my door by a punctual but reticent carrier, a good dinner at night with a few congenial people, an evening without enforced solitude or enforced society, and a blessed assurance that no one would ask me to show him or her what I was writing.

As a fixture at the colony, EAR was assigned the Veltin Studio for twenty successive summers, starting in 1915. It made a splendid workplace, as the poet Louise Bogan discovered during her stay there in the summer of 1963. "Built on a slope, of large cobblestones, with a pitched roof inside, and windows high up, *it stayed cool.* Also a view of Monadnock exists, through pine branches—v. Cezanne and Mont-Sainte-Victoire." There Robinson spent his working days. At dusk he walked back to Colony Hall, ubiquitous cane in one hand and lunch basket in the other.

The conditions for creative accomplishment could hardly have been better. Yet they improved with the arrival of Esther Willad Bates, another of Baker's playwriting protégés from Harvard. Bates liked Robinson's poetry, and—amazingly—could decipher his handwriting. For many years, she typed his manuscripts, sometimes receiving no more in return than EAR's gratitude and a dinner and theater engagement in Boston or New York

Bates somehow fought through the poet's formidable inaccessibility. "Mr. Robinson is deaf, shy, and very unapproachable, and he never makes advances conversationally to anyone," Bates wrote her mother upon first encountering him. "Conversations with him are largely questions on my part, pauses on his, and then the briefest possible response. Another question from me, another pause, another telegraphically brief reply, and so on." One morning at breakfast, EAR limbered up enough to ask Bates to pass the butter. "I told him I should tell my grandchildren I had provided the celebrated poet with butter. He said he

FIGURE 21.7 The Veltin Studio at the MacDowell Colony, Robinson's workplace from 1915 to 1934.

Source: Colby College Special Collections.

FIGURE 21.8 Herbert S. Gorman, who reviewed and bonded with Robinson.

Source: Picture Collection, New York Public Library.

had only asked for it, in order that I might." On grounds of such whimsicality, one of Robinson's male-female friendships was forged.

The turnover among colonists also acquainted Robinson with Herbert Gorman, a slender, handsome, and amusing young poet and critic who had written a glowing review of *The Man Against the Sky*. Eventually, Gorman was to publish books about Longfellow and Joyce, but he was only getting established in the literary community when he came to Peterborough in 1918.

Gorman had an Irish charm, a fondness for drink, and a respect for Robinson's work that bordered on reverence. EAR took to him as to no one else at MacDowell. "When Herbert was with him," Parker Fillmore recalled, "or when he spoke of Herbert, he showed a warmth and tenderness that I never knew him to show for any other human being. . . . All E. A.'s reserve, all his inhibitions disappeared and he grew more and more genial, more and more witty. It was as if Herbert were his dear little brother or his son." At the colony, also, Gorman met, fell in love with, and married the flirtatious Jean Wright, a romance encouraged if not quite presided over by Robinson. The couple settled in New York and frequently entertained EAR for dinner.

Gorman's enthusiasm for Robinson may be measured by the five separate pieces about EAR, all laudatory, that he wrote in 1920. In succeeding years, Gorman continued to praise Robinson's books as they appeared, up to and including *Tristram* in 1927. The two men even discussed the possibility that Gorman, instead of the erratic Ranck, might one day write Robinson's biography. Thereafter silence descended.

After Gorman's first marriage broke up, he moved to Paris, remarried, and started a new life. Reluctant to lose the connection, Robinson sent his books to Gorman as they were published, but there was no acknowledgment. It may have been only distance that came between them. Or perhaps Gorman, like many others, thought EAR's production of long, blank-verse poems a mistake. Whatever the reason, to Robinson it seemed like a defection, and he was hurt by it.

When he started writing about King Arthur, Robinson had three separate books in mind—on Merlin, Lancelot and Guinevere, and Tristram and Isolt. But as he neared completion of the draft of *Lancelot* in the summer of 1917, he decided to put off the tale of Tristram for another time. "When [*Lancelot*] is out of the way," he wrote Isaacs, "I intend to get out of Camelot and write another book of shorter poems . . . which will mean going over to my other way of doing things." He felt "on safer ground" that way, inasmuch as it seemed likely that "the shorter things will always have more readers." It would do no harm "to remind a precarious public of my more or less phantom existence."

During the summers of 1918 and 1919, Robinson produced the poetry for *The Three Taverns* (1920): thirty-nine poems of varying lengths, eight sonnets included, along with half a dozen narratives running to nearly ten pages each.

As he grew older, Robinson turned increasingly to literature and history—instead of people on the streets of Tilbury Town or New York City—for his characters. The Bible, still more than Malory or Tennyson, was his greatest source. In his dissertation, "Robinson and the Bible," Nicholas Ayo counted more than 250 biblical allusions in his poetry, as well as seven poems that deal explicitly with biblical subjects. Two of them are in *The Three Taverns*. "Lazarus" concludes the volume, and "The Three Taverns" itself, about the last days of St. Paul, gave EAR the title for his book.

The poem is a dramatic monologue, spoken by Paul to the Christians who come to meet him before he goes, a prisoner, to be judged by Caesar in Rome. Paul knows that he will face a sentence of death. Before his conversion on the road to Damascus, he had "had men slain" himself "for saying Something was beyond the Law, / And in ourselves." Now, with the final judgment impending, he delivers a homily free of bitterness about the power of love:

> I that have done some hating in my time
> See now no time for hate; I that have left,
> Fading behind me like familiar lights
> That are to shine no more for my returning,
> Home, friends, and honors,—I that have lost all else
> For wisdom, and the wealth of it, say now
> To you that out of wisdom has come love,
> That measures and is of itself the measure
> Of works and hope and faith.

In "John Brown," also in *The Three Taverns*, Robinson explores the life and death of another prophet, another man who has sacrificed his life—and the lives of others—for a cause he knows to be right. The poem takes the form of a letter written by Brown to his wife on the eve of his execution. Had he known in the beginning the trouble that lay ahead, Brown admits, he might have wavered. Now he is without fear, though he will be hanged at dawn. His has been a bloody mission.

> If I did ill
> What I did well, let men say I was mad;
> Or let my name forever be a question
> That will not sleep in history.

The poem ends with a powerful valedictory statement from Brown: "I shall have more to say when I am dead."

At fifty, Robinson may have been visited by intimations of his own mortality. The theme of death is pervasive in *The Three Taverns*: the death of prophets and of ordinary folk as well. Two of them take their lives in "The Mill." Esther Bates recalled walking with EAR one summer evening past a deserted settlement at West Peterborough, with its dark, silent mill and velvet-black water. For once, Robinson spoke openly of his hopes for his work. He felt, EAR said, that "he was, perhaps, two hundred years in advance of his time" in his habit of understatement and his absorption in the unconscious and semiconscious feelings and impulses of his characters. He wondered, though, if he wasn't too plain-spoken, if he wasn't overdoing the simple unpoetic phrase. They stood for a long time looking at the water above the dam, and the abandoned mill.

> The miller's wife had waited long,
>   The tea was cold, the fire was dead;
> And there might yet be nothing wrong
>   In how he went and what he said:
> "There are no millers any more,"
>   Was all that she had heard him say
> And he had lingered at the door
>   So long that it seemed yesterday.
>
> Sick with a fear that had no form
>   She knew that she was there at last;
> And in the mill there was a warm
>   And mealy fragrance of the past.
> What else there was would only seem
>   To say again what he had meant;
> And what was hanging from a beam
>   Would not have heeded where she went.
>
> And if she thought it followed her,
>   She may have reasoned in the dark

That one way of the few there were
   Would hide her and would leave no mark:
Black water, smooth above the weir
   Like starry velvet in the night,
Though ruffled once, would soon appear
   The same as ever to the sight.

In what Emery Neff calls "twenty-four perfect lines," "The Mill" portrays the costs in human misery of progress from one era to another. "New arts destroy the old," Ralph Waldo Emerson generalizes the problem in his essay "Circles." "See the investment of capital in aqueducts made useless by hydraulics; fortifications, by gunpowder; roads and canals, by railways; sails, by steam; steam by electricity." Likely with the Emerson passage in mind, Robert Frost describes "The Mill" as "a sinister jest at the expense of all investors of life and capital. The market shifts and leaves them with a car-barn full of dead trolley cars." All this is concentrated in the single spoken phrase of Robinson's poem: "There are no millers any more."

"The Wandering Jew" depicts a man damned for his arrogance to a death-in-life worse than death itself. In twelve eight-line stanzas, Robinson brings his narrator into contact with the title figure, a character drawn not from the Bible but from a medieval legend. According to the legend, the Wandering Jew was a cobbler named Ahaseurus who struck out at Jesus when he paused to rest on his way to Calvary and shouted at him to go faster. "Truly I go away, and that quickly," Jesus replied, "but thou shalt tarry until I come again." The man, in other words, loses the capacity to die and must go on living until the Second Coming.

Robinson took the legend and recast it in a contemporary setting. His narrator encounters the eternally wandering Jew in New York; in his age and loneliness, he resembles an Old Testament figure "who has not been fortunate enough to be gathered to his forefathers." As their eyes meet, the narrator feels a twinge of compassion but fears that to show it might offend the Wanderer. He decides to listen instead, as the old man curses the present world.

Before I pondered long enough
On whence he came and who he was,
I trembled at his ringing wealth
Of manifold anathemas;
I wondered, while he seared the world,
What new defection ailed the race,
And if it mattered how remote
Our fathers were from such a place.

The stanza, as Donald E. Stanford points out in an excellent essay, "presents a vivid picture of spiritual pride in action" and of "the alienated intellectual [who] takes a perverse satisfaction in denouncing the vices" around him. Robinson, as Louis Coxe suggests, must have heard such men—"the doctrinaire, fanatic types that haunt intellectual Bohemia"—holding forth with "vague and bombastic rhetoric." Among them, the most probable model for the Wandering Jew, as for Captain Craig, was Alfred H. Louis.

In 1919, on the streets of New York, Ahasuerus looks back on the past as preferable, although he had once seen nothing good in it, "as he had seen / No good come out of Nazareth." He seems defiant, but the defiance is mingled with a reticence

> That hushed him as if he beheld
> A Presence that would not be gone.

There is nothing left for him but his pride, stiff and intractable through the centuries. He is a man who has willed his blindness. In the final two stanzas, though, the narrator speculates that the Wandering Jew's eyes—eyes that "remembered everything"—may one day betray a terrible self-doubt.

> Whether he still defies or not
> The failure of an angry task
> That relegates him out of time
> To chaos, I can only ask,
> But as I knew him, so he was;
> And somewhere among men to-day
> Those old, unyielding eyes may flash,
> And flinch—and look the other way.

None of Robinson's biographers so much as mention "The Wandering Jew." In early criticism of his work, the poem was generally ignored. Yvor Winters, in 1946, sought to make up for such neglect by calling it "one of the great poems not only of our time but of our language." He singled out the poem because in singularly "plain and generalized diction" it examines the difficult and important subject of a vice "which may occur in any group at a fairly high intellectual and spiritual level." The vice is that of "pride in one's own identity, a pride which will not allow one to accept a greater wisdom from without even when one recognizes that the wisdom is there and is greater than one's own; the result is spiritual sickness." The mythical figure of the Wandering Jew embodies this vice.

Birthday Salute

Two days before "The Wandering Jew" appeared in the *Outlook* for December 24, 1919, Robinson reached his fiftieth birthday. A number of his friends, led by Percy MacKaye, conspired to make it one to remember. The occasion might best be observed, MacKaye decided, by assembling a collection of tributes to Robinson from other leading American poets. He invited seventeen poets to contribute remarks to a joint statement that could be published on or about December 22, 1919.

The list included the most prominent names in the field, together with a few lesser-known figures who were particular friends of EAR: in alphabetical order, Anna Hempstead Branch, Witter Bynner, Arthur Davison Ficke, Robert Frost, Hermann Hagedorn, Louis Ledoux, Vachel Lindsay, Amy Lowell, MacKaye himself, Edwin Markham, Edgar Lee Masters, John G. Neihardt, Josephine Preston Peabody, Corinne Roosevelt Robinson (Teddy's sister), George Sterling, Sara Teasdale, and Ridgely Torrence. In November, MacKaye wrote each of these a letter asking that they send a "a very brief statement" in honor of Robinson to Edward C. Marsh at the Macmillan Company. He then prevailed on Bliss Perry at Harvard to introduce the collection of tributes and on the *New York Times Book Review* to print them in its issue of Sunday, December 21.

Not all of those asked responded with alacrity. Marsh at Macmillan, a bit alarmed, proposed to MacKaye on December 3 that he "send out a hurry call" to a few of the most important poets who had not yet been heard from. He himself would send a note to Amy Lowell, Marsh said, but he wondered if MacKaye might not get two or three others on the telephone and get them to send in their contributions at once. He was "thinking of Frost, Torrence and Markham particularly," Marsh said. The follow-up effort brought in laudatory comments from Torrence, who was between addresses and had missed MacKaye's initial letter, and the elderly Markham, who misunderstood what was expected and wrote several pages that had to be trimmed. Only Robert Frost, of the seventeen invited poets, chose not to participate.

In 1937, Frost provided his account of what happened in a letter to John Holmes. "My being solicited for Robinson some years ago went near to destroying our friendship," Frost wrote. "I got one letter asking me in on a symposium. He knew how much I thought of him. I had put it into a personal letter. I threw the demand (it was from someone named Marsh) into the waste basket. Then I got a second: 'Surely you won't fail to be in on this extraordinarily spontaneous outburst of admiration for E. A. Robinson.' I stayed out and looked ungenerous."

Wilbert Snow, in a 1968 article, recalled asking Frost about the incident. Why hadn't he responded? Snow asked him. "I thought it was an advertising dodge," Frost said. "What of it?" Snow said. "It was advertising a good product." Frost's refusal to answer, as Snow commented, must have "offended Robinson and his admirers." EAR could hardly have been unaware of Frost's absence from the roster of those doing him honor. There is no record, however, that he ever said a word about it to anyone.

The tribute itself led off the book pages of the *Times*. In his introduction, Bliss Perry compared Robinson to Donne, Whitman, and Browning. Amy

Lowell emphasized the duality of vision behind Robinson and his work. "He is a poet for poets, his art becomes only the more interesting the more it is studied," she wrote. "A realist, he is also a foe to materialism; a skeptic, his poems are full of spirituality. . . . Strong, virile, contemptuous of shams, no one has voiced the contradictory elements of the American character better than he."

Edgar Lee Masters, looking backward, celebrated Robinson for his craftsmanship and for fighting through long years of neglect. Nearly half of the poets praised EAR for his insight into the lives of his characters. "A master etcher of human portraits," Josephine Preston Peabody said. "Also a master of music—when he chooses." Several spoke of the humor underlying his portraits.

The surprise had been well kept. Robinson awoke on Sunday, December 21, to find his career celebrated in the *New York Times Book Review*. The next day, his actual birthday, he planned to spend with the Isaacses at their home in Pelham. At the last minute, it was decided to stay in the city. Lewis Isaacs took EAR to see Gilbert and Sullivan's *Mikado* at the Park theater that night, and as if by happenstance a group of his most intimate friends turned up at the same performance. Afterward, there was a supper at the Ledoux's apartment.

"Hagedorn and Ledoux hold you entirely responsible for some recent doings in the *Times*," Robinson wrote MacKaye on Christmas eve, "and if their accusations are correct, you have much to account for." He was glad to know there were "men alive" like MacKaye, EAR said. It was hard to figure out what he had done to deserve such friends. The letter to MacKaye was but the first of a flurry of "thank you" notes Robinson put in the mail. One such communication was posted to Amy Lowell, who replied that she had been delighted to say what she thought of Robinson in the public press. "I suppose that there is no poet in the country more beloved and admired than you are."

FIGURE 21.9 Playwright Percy MacKaye, organizer of EAR's fiftieth-birthday tribute.

Source: Library of Congress.

Periodicals, too, took note of Robinson's fiftieth birthday. MacKaye commented in the *North American Review* that EAR could look back on a quarter century of work as a published poet "and forward—by virtue of that work—to the assured regard of the centuries." Kermit Roosevelt, in an anonymous piece for *Scribner's*, stressed Robinson's universality: he was essentially American and yet like all great poets belonged to every country and age. The tribute was enough to cause a man to take a drink in celebration, even if doing so was against the law.

22

Seasons of Success

A Cause to Fight For

Distrustful of government and most of its practitioners, Robinson customarily stayed on the political sidelines. He did not join groups, resisted signing petitions, and deplored the use of poetry as propaganda. Only once, with the ratification of the Eighteenth Amendment and passage of the Volstead Act in 1919, did he abandon these practices. Prohibition outraged him, and he lashed out against it with uncharacteristic fury.

Robinson's anger derived only in part from his own experience with the bottle. He had been more or less contentedly sober for some time before Congress enacted its legislation forbidding the sale of alcoholic beverages. "I believe now that my demon is dismissed forever," EAR wrote George Burnham in June 1917. He'd never really thought so before, certainly not during his time of compulsive consumption. In a newspaper article, he learned that there were only three gallons of whiskey per capita in the United States. His share "would have lasted about twelve days" when he "was in training," he told Burnham.

Robinson looked back on his drinking days with ambivalence. On the one hand, he felt that when he was down and out liquor had provided him with a necessary if temporary sense of well-being. Talking about Prohibiton with Lewis Isaacs, he flared up when Isaacs suggested that the issue wasn't worth getting excited about. How were young poets supposed to survive the first hard years, if they couldn't make their dreams come true for a few hours at a time? On the other hand, he was aware that drinking crippled his ability to write. One critic described his poetry as the product of "a slow distillation." Well, Robinson responded, for a long time he "was giving so much of [his] attention to other distillations that poetry really didn't have a chance." He scrupulously stayed dry when he was writing at MacDowell, and he was riding the wagon when the Eighteenth Amendment passed.

Then he fell off, deliberately and in protest. "I feel it not only a privilege but a moral duty to take a drink whenever it comes along," he wrote George Sterling in February 1920. When Louis Untermeyer invited him over for dinner, EAR warned him to keep his bottle of Jamaica Rum safely on his side of the table. Since Prohibition, he said, he "was inclined to be rapacious, vindictive and ungovernable in all things alcoholic." In fact, though, he found that he could not drink with the same abandon as in his youth. EAR enjoyed occasional roistering evenings, but he paid for them with hangovers. "The stuff does me no good now unless I take too much, and then it makes me sick all the next day," he lamented.

Like many others, Robinson opposed Prohibition because it didn't—and couldn't—work. Making liquor illegal led to rampant violations of the law. A generation grew up observing the liquor laws flouted with impunity. "New York is full of crime and unrest, all due to prohibition," EAR wrote Ledoux in December 1920. "Nothing looks right, and the world is undoubtedly going to hell—all for the lack of a little knowledge of first principles."

Foremost among those principles, he believed, was that no collective body had the right to invade the personal liberty of the individual. Robinson's social thinking, as Ellsworth Barnard pointed out, stemmed from nineteenth-century liberalism, which regarded government as a necessary evil against whose encroachments men must always be on guard. In EAR's view, Prohibition represented an intolerable encroachment, and heaven only knew what might come next. "They'll have your cigarettes in five years, if you and a few million others . . . are not careful," he wrote Ledoux.

He was so incensed that he broke his own stricture against combining poetry and propaganda to present his convictions in verse, first in "Demos" (1919) and then in two poems of 1925, "Dionysius in Doubt" and "Demos and Dionysius." "Demos" warned of the trouble ahead, if in the name of democracy the majority should continue to exercise its tyranny. The poem, a double sonnet, proposed that "the few shall save / The many, or the many are to fall": an argument, apparently, in favor of oligarchy. In a letter to Jean Gorman of June 1921, Robinson went one step further. He wrote her, smoldering in New York, from his cool studio in New Hampshire. One of the best things for the heat, EAR said, was a "good supply of Budweiser beer in the ice-box, but as you are living in the land of the free, not to mention the home of the brave, you can't have it. Some day we may have a benevolent absolute monarchy, and regain our freedom with a sigh of relief. A king can always be killed, whereas a written constitution can't—or at any rate not so easily."

In a comic piece for the March 1921 *Authors Guild Bulletin*, Robinson's friend and drinking companion Carty Ranck speculated how Prohibition might affect literature in the United States. In other countries, authors might write about wine, women, and song. On native grounds they would have to content themselves with women and song, or possibly women, song, and sarsaparilla. Imagine the prospect, Ranck proposed, of a literary universe drained dry, of Mr. Pickwick's fellow clubmen "enthusiastically quaffing beakers of buttermilk" and

Robin Hood's merry men "boisterously pledging one another in tankards of brown October ginger-ale."

Robinson was too indignant to take the matter lightly. He argued his case in utmost seriousness with Laura Richards in Gardiner, who favored Prohibition. "All human beings who are not made of putty," he asserted, "are going to stimulate themselves in one way or another, and alcohol, in spite of its dangers, is the least harmful." He rejected as "too silly for serious discussion" the proposition that alcohol belonged in the same category as addictive drugs. Besides, everything worth having was dangerous in one way or another, including "poetry and music, not to mention fried onions and cucumbers."

In the summer of 1924, he told Mrs. Richards he had just completed the first draft of a poem about Dionysius which she wouldn't like. "It had to come out," he explained, "for it has been accumulating within me ever since the hypocritical (or worse) action of the so called Supreme Court on the constitutionality of a certain much to be damned amendment." While he was at it, he launched a salvo at the Congress. "One hundred men, who have all they want stowed away in their cellars, could probably put an end to the whole business if they dared to open their mouths except to take a drink." In other correspondence, he inveighed against the "abject timidity of practically every man in public life. They all dose themselves with a nerve-rotting nostrum which they call expediency, and live trembling with a fear of saying or doing something that may not be just what everyone else says and does." Our national bird was "obviously the Ostrich, not the Eagle."

The issues he'd been stewing over since passage of the Eighteenth Amendment found expression in *Dinoysius in Doubt* (1925), a volume framed by two long polemical works. In the opening, title poem, the god Dionysius tells his audience of one that "there are too many sleepers in your land" and that unless they awake, they will find themselves "niched and ticketed and . . . standardized and unexceptional, / To perpetuate complacency and joy / Of uniform size and strength."

> For all I know,
> An ultimate uniformity enthroned
> May trim your vision very well;
> And the poor cringing self, disowned,
> May call it freedom and efficiency.
> Others would somewhat rather call it hell,
> And rather not be quite so free
> To blend themselves with mediocrity.

What had started with an attempt to impose sobriety on the millions might well end, Robinson feared, in universally mandated conformity, with no allowance for individual differences. The point is made forcefully in "Demos and

Dionysius," at the end of *Dionysius in Doubt*. The poem takes the form of a dialogue, in which the false god Demos preaches the doctrine that all should be alike and of a piece:

> Punctual, accurate, tamed and uniform,
> And equal. Then romance and love and art
> And ecstasy will be remembrances
> Of man's young weakness on his way to reason.

What right, Demos asks, has the free individual "to be himself / Since I am here to fix him in his place / And hold him there?" To soothe the few who may rebel against such a regimented existence, Demos plans to distribute a synthetic honey: a procedure eerily predictive of the sedating "soma" in Aldous Huxley's 1932 *Brave New World*. Both writers confronted the same enemy, a Demos or Big Brother who would reduce all his subjects to "amiable automatons."

Robinson's message was clear enough: that democracy, guided by reason and equality, could easily become totalitarianism. He felt he had to say as much, but the poems in which he did so lacked the sharpness required of successful didactic verse. The dice are so heavily loaded against Demos, for instance, that Dionysius need scarcely open his mouth in objection. EAR's poetry only came to life when he looked away from causes to consider the cases of individual human beings.

Drinking figures in one of Robinson's greatest poems, as poignant and moving as anything he wrote. "Mr. Flood's Party" depicts an old man, alone, who pauses to drink on his way to his isolated cabin. The poem is about loneliness, not liquor, but that did not prevent the editors of *Collier's* from turning it down "for alcoholic reasons" in the summer of 1920, a year after prohibition went into effect. EAR put it back in the mail to Carl Van Doren at *The Nation*, who had been asking him for submissions. Van Doren accepted it "with joy," and Mr. Flood "made his disreputable debut" in the November 24, 1920, issue of *The Nation*.

> Old Eben Flood, climbing alone one night
> Over the hill between the town below
> And the forsaken upland hermitage
> That held as much as he should ever know
> On earth again of home, paused warily.
> The road was his with not a native near;
> And Eben, having leisure, said aloud,
> For no man else in Tilbury Town to hear:

"Well, Mr. Flood, we have the harvest moon
Again, and we may not have many more;
The bird is on the wing, the poet says,
And you and I have said it here before.
Drink to the bird." He raised up to the light
The jug that he had gone so far to fill,
And answered huskily: "Well, Mr. Flood,
Since you propose it, I believe I will."

Alone, as if enduring to the end
A valiant armor of scarred hopes outworn,
He stood there in the middle of the road
Like Roland's ghost winding a silent horn.
Below him, in the town among the trees,
Where friends of other days had honored him,
A phantom salutation of the dead
Rang thinly till old Eben's eyes were dim.

Then, as a mother lays her sleeping child
Down tenderly, fearing it may awake,
He set the jug down slowly at his feet
With trembling care, knowing that most things break;
And only when assured that on firm earth
It stood, as the uncertain lives of men
Assuredly did not, he paced away,
And with his hand extended paused again:

"Well, Mr. Flood, we have not met like this
In a long time; and many a change has come
To both of us, I fear, since last it was
We had a drop together. Welcome home!"
Convivially returning with himself,
Again he raised the jug up to the light;
And with an acquiescent quaver said:
"Well, Mr. Flood, if you insist, I might.

"Only a very little, Mr. Flood—
For auld lang syne. No more, sir; that will do."
So, for the time, apparently it did,
And Eben evidently thought so too;
For soon amid the silver loneliness
Of night he lifted up his voice and sang,
Secure, with only two moons listening,
Until the whole harmonious landscape rang—

"For auld lang syne." The weary throat gave out,
The last word wavered, and the song was done.
He raised again the jug regretfully
And shook his head, and was again alone.
There was not much that was ahead of him
And there was nothing in the town below—
Where strangers would have shut the many doors
That many friends had opened long ago.

On an autumn night Eben Flood walks back to his upland hermitage from Tilbury Town, where he has had his jug filled with whiskey. Along the way, he stops to drink with himself and to sing "Auld Lang Syne." That's not much by way of action, yet "it is precisely because Robinson finds such scenes worth recording," as the British critic John Lucas observed, "that he is so invaluable a poet." Robinson "is spokesman for the inarticulate, for those who, whatever the reason, have been forced into incommunicable loneliness."

Robinson accomplishes a great deal at the very beginning. "Old" is the word best linked to Eben Flood, whose very name—*ebb and flood*—invokes the passage of time and tide. A long clause intervenes to establish his situation as a solitary exile before subject is joined with predicate. "Old Eben Flood . . . paused warily." He may well be tired from his climb, but his pause is made "warily" not "wearily." Flood is about to perform a private ritual, and he does not want to be observed.

The second stanza presents the ceremony of Mr. Flood offering himself a drink. The courtliness of the gesture suggests the status he once occupied, and the toast he proposes testifies to his awareness of literature. "The bird on the wing," the first of the poem's three literary allusions, comes from *The Rubaiyat of Omar Khayyam*.

Come, fill the Cup, and in the fire of Spring
Your Winter-garment of Repentance fling:
  The Bird of Time has but a little way
To flutter—and the Bird is on the Wing.

So seize the day, the Persian advises. "Drink to the bird," Mr. Flood heartily agrees, raising his jug to the light as if it were a glass to clink with another's. His alter ego—aware that spring has turned to fall—responds "huskily" that he "believes" he will. The two Mr. Floods are actors.

In the next two stanzas, Robinson uses metaphor to present the old man's plight. First he is compared to the heroic Roland, a captain of Charlemagne's who fought to his death at Roncesvalles, too proud to sound his horn for help until it was too late. There are some superficial similarities linking the situation of old Eben Flood to that of the protagonist of the *Chanson de Roland*. Like the warrior hero, Eben too wears armor, though made "of scarred hopes outworn." But Mr. Flood is no medieval warrior of song and legend. He is a lonely old man suffering the misfortune of having outlived friends and family. But for "Mr. Flood's Party," he would not be remembered at all.

The poet Donald Hall deals brilliantly with the daring comparison in the fourth stanza. Robinson, he writes, "sets us up with a sentimental simile" in these lines:

> Then, as a mother lays her sleeping child
> Down tenderly, fearing it may awake,

"and then swoops the chair from our descendant backsides":

> He set the jug down slowly at his feet
> With trembling care.

"So that, with a gross vaudeville humor, we laugh at the joke—his baby is the jug!—until Robinson takes genius's third step":

> knowing that most things break.

"This lesson Robinson knew from his family and Gardiner, Maine," Hall concludes. And likely, from Emerson's "Compensation" as well, with its observation that "there is a crack in everything that God has made."

In the next two stanzas Mr. Flood again engages in the ritual dialogue—once with others, now with himself—that in happier times preceded taking a drink. Many a change has come to both of them, he fears, since last they had a drop together. He proposes another toast, this time "Welcome home!": which would be too much were it not followed by the humorous "Convivially returning with himself." Again there is the raising of the jug and again the reluctant quavering assent, though on this second occasion he will have only a very little, "for auld lang syne." After making sure again that he is safe from observation, "secure, with only two moons listening," he breaks into Robert Burns's almost unbearably moving song, which appropriately involves two old companions taking "a cup o' kindness" together. "Should auld acquaintance be forgot, / And days of auld lang syne?"

The song continues into the last stanza, when Mr. Flood's weary throat gives out. Lines three and four present a critical problem:

> He raised again the jug regretfully
> And shook his head, and was again alone.

If we conclude from these lines that the jug is empty, we may form a picture of Eben Flood as—the words are those of Cleanth Brooks and Robert Penn Warren—"a drunken derelict, an outcast, a disgrace to the community, a friendless and poverty-bit old nuisance" who once, to be sure, had known better days. Or it may be that Mr. Flood considers taking another drink, and shakes his head against it, even though the jug has temporarily made him feel less alone. The final four lines of the poem make it clear that time, and not any disgraceful behavior, has exiled the old man from Tilbury Town.

> There was not much that was ahead of him,
> And there was nothing in the town below—
> Where strangers would have shut the many doors
> That many friends had opened long ago.

In a manuscript version of "Mr. Flood's Party," apparently a first draft, Robinson presented a concluding stanza entirely different from the one he arrived at for *Avon's Harvest* (1921) and every reprinting since. The original ending followed the clue of the wariness that enables Mr. Flood to speak to himself "for no man else in Tilbury Town to hear" and to find himself "secure" before he bursts into "Auld Lang Syne."

> "For auld lang syne."—The weary throat gave out;
> The last word perished, and the song was done.
> He raised again the jug regretfully,
> And without malice would have ambled on;
> But hearing in the bushes a new sound,
> He smote with new profanity the cause,
> And shook an aged unavailing fist
> At an inhuman barrage of applause.

Issues of technique aside—to make the last line scan we have to emphasize the first syllable of "barrage"—the effect of this ending is to make of Mr. Flood a rather foolish and unsympathetic figure, cursing and shaking an ineffectual fist at those who have concealed themselves to overhear his song.

Robinson did well to change the manuscript ending, even though it may have comported with the behavior of the figure the poem was modeled upon. When the poem appeared in *The Nation*, EAR sent a clipping to Harry Smith. Smith would "detect the direct influence of a story your father told me once in Gardiner," he said. The story was about "old Johnny H ___, who had a habit of returning from town with a little brown jug and, on the way home, conversing with the other half of his split personality."

Robinson's niece Ruth, in annotating his poems, suggested another provenance for the poem. "The incident of Mr. Flood was witnessed by the boys one night on Church Hill," she wrote. "He was old John Esmond who lived out on the Brunswick Road in the cottage now owned by Chas. Skehan." The "boys" presumably meant Robinson and his brothers, or a group of local youths including EAR. And when they observed the old man in conversation with himself (either John Esmond and Johnny H ___ were the same person, or there were two lonely old men in town who chatted with themselves under the influence of liquor) the boys might well have responded with laughter enough to make the poor fellow irate.

In the late 1920s, Robinson said he thought "Mr. Flood's Party" was "the best thing" he'd ever written. He was not always his own soundest critic. This time, though, he may well have been right. Whatever its origins, he fashioned out of this trivial anecdote "one of the most beautifully considerate, tender poems about loneliness ever written."

Robinson has been categorized as a poet obsessed with writing about failures, to which he would answer, weren't the failures *more interesting* than the successes? But he was also masterly in his portraits of people beset by solitude—a group he identified with because he felt himself among their number.

Living mostly within himself, he realized at twenty five that his "one great trouble" would be loneliness. At fifty-five, he reiterated the point in a letter to Arthur Nevin. "We are mostly lonely devils at our age, and the world is full of us. About all we can do is to put on some sort of face and keep our real selves to ourselves, and be glad things are no worse than they are." He was forever reaching out for companionship, yet he felt basically alone, especially at Christmas time. In speaking for Mr. Flood or Aunt Imogen or the poor relation, all of whom "put on some sort of face" to confront the day, he was speaking for himself.

He wrote of these characters with a compassion akin to love, and with extraordinary skill. Robinson deserves some praise for simply noticing them. Yet, as Yvor Winters observed in 1922, "it is not the material that makes a poem great, but the perception and organization of that material. A pigeon's wing may make as great an image as a man's tragedy, and in the poetry of Mr. Wallace Stevens has done so. Mr. Robinson's greatness lies not in the people of whom he has written, but in the perfect balance, the infallible precision, with which he has stated their cases."

Two Books a Year

Robinson's poetic energy reached its peak in his early fifties. Resigned to a life of bachelorhood and no longer troubled by poverty, he produced four books in two years. *The Three Taverns* and *Lancelot* of 1920 were followed by *Avon's Harvest* in the spring of 1921, and by EAR's *Collected Poems* in the fall.

The thirty-page title poem in *Avon's Harvest*, a psychological horror story Robinson referred to as his "metrical dime-novel," depicts a man so consumed by fear that he scares himself to death. It takes the poet some superfluous space to begin "Avon's Harvest," but once underway the tale becomes compelling. As a boy, Avon conceived a hatred for a school companion. This other youth, despicable in his "malignant oily swarthiness," nonetheless succeeds in attaching himself to Avon, a bond that is broken when Avon involuntarily strikes out at him. At that moment, Avon can see vengeance in the eyes of his victim, who utters a terrible warning: "I shall know where you are until you die." Every year thereafter, Avon receives an unsigned card on his birthday repeating that message.

The threat grows more frightening in its annual reiteration, and once, in Rome, Avon and his loathsome tormentor pass each other on the street. Nothing is said, but as Avon recollects,

> "There was the same slow vengeance in his eyes
> When he saw mine, and there was a vicious twist
> On his amphibious face that might have been
> On anything else a smile."

Then Avon reads his antagonist's name among the dead who went down with the Titanic. After that, no more birthday reminders, no vestige of fear.

None, that is, until on an October trip to the Maine woods, alone one frosty night, Avon suffers a paralyzing visitation. He falls into a stupor, unable to move from his bed as the menacing ghost of his enemy "squeezed / His unclean outlines into the dim room," his eyes "aflame as they never had been before." Avon dies there, with the door locked and no sign of visitors. The official verdict is that he died from "a nightmare and an aneurism." The final words come from a doctor who had been Avon's friend.

> "He died, you know, because he had been afraid—
> And he had been afraid for a long time.
> . . . .
>   If I were not a child
> Of science, I should say it was the devil.
> I don't believe it was another woman,
> And surely it was not another man."

There are other ghosts in Robinson's poetry, but "Avon's Harvest" is his only true ghost story. The critics were of two minds about the poem. John Farrar asserted that there was "no more powerful dramatic poem" in all of American literature. Amy Lowell thought it melodramatic and self-indulgent. Carl Van Doren praised it for its style of "steel" and noted that its interest "lies not in the little war between Avon and the spook but in the vaster war within Avon himself." Yvor Winters agreed that "Avon's Harvest" was an exercise in abnormal psychology, but he felt such subject matter was not appropriate for poetry since it "lack[ed] general relevance."

Robinson placed "Mr. Flood's Party" immediately after this title piece in his book and followed it with a dozen sonnets. Some of these deal with love misunderstood. In "Ben Trovato," for instance, a wife makes her sightless, dying husband happy by removing her rings and wearing the furs of his mistress. The neighbors gossip about the apparently chaste Pamela in "The Tree in Pamela's Garden." She should have a cat or a bird to keep her company, they remark,

> And only would have wondered at her smile
> Could they have seen that she had overheard.

Similarly, they express pity for the woman in "Vain Gratuities," who is married to an ugly man. "Let us pray she's a philosopher," they say. Yet after twenty years of marriage, the woman has kept her figure and her happiness and would have laughed at the neighbors' foolishness had *she* overheard.

Another group of sonnets takes up the complications of a life of poetry. "Caput Mortuum" questions whether one's work will survive "in Art's long hazard, where no man may choose / Whether he play to win or toil to lose." Most of those who aspire to emulate Apollo, as "Many are Called" observes, will labor "in ecstasy, in anguish, and in vain." Even Rembrandt, as Robinson depicts him in "Rembrandt to Rembrandt," the long poem that ends the book, is beset by worry about lack of popularity and doubt as to whether his accomplishment really amounts to anything. He must ward off the demon within who reminds him of his

> befrenzied aspiration
> To smear with certain ochres and some oil
> A few more perishable ells of cloth

and listen instead to the wise spirit who advises him to be content with his lot as servant to the muse. He is, after all,

> One of the few that are so fortunate
> As to be told their task and to be given
> A skill to do it with.

Here, surely, Robinson had in mind the long painful years when he toiled in silence. He lived through the dark time and fought off his demon. Like the great Dutch painter, and the others seeking to answer a call from Apollo, he learned that he must go on, never mind the public response. Should an artist let himself sigh for either "distant welcome" or "wayside shouting," he might as well, in the words of Rembrandt's good spirit, "accommodate [his] greatness / To the convenience of an easy ditch."

On an autumn afternoon in 1920, Robinson was walking across the Boston Common with Braithwaite. They had just passed the Park Street church when Braithwaite said, "Don't you think it's time for a collected edition of your poems?" Nonsense, EAR replied. He wasn't done yet, for one thing. Besides, who would want to read or reread all of his work? But the enthusiastic Braithwaite persisted, so that Robinson reluctantly promised to bring up the subject with his publishers.

As it happened, his publishers brought it up first. In mid-November, George Brett at Macmillan wrote him that *The Three Taverns* was going into a second edition and, by the way, if Robinson agreed that a one-volume collected edition of his poetry was a good idea, they'd like to bring it out in the fall of 1921.

The next month, Robinson let Ledoux know about the plan for his collected works, "the paper of which will in all probability be manufactured from the gray fibre of E. A .R.'s unhappy soul." He set about eliminating a number of poems from his first two books and "clearing some of the rubbish" out of *Captain Craig*. By March the editing was over. When he sent off the proofs in April, he could not help feeling that his career might appropriately come to an end with publication of his *Collected Poems*. "It might be rather a neat finish," he observed, "if I were to be struck by lightning this summer in Peterboro."

The collected edition also led him to reflect, as he put it in a midsummer letter to Emma, on what it was "that makes a man turn himself into a book." In his case, he told her, the process had been unavoidable. "I realized long ago that there was only one thing for me to do, and that I should have to do it alone. This is why I have had so little to say, knowing that in my case results would have to say everything." He was in no hurry about future publication, EAR said. " Eight books in one fat volume this fall will serve for the next few years. In fact, they will have to serve (or disappear) for a much longer time."

He did not talk about it publicly, but Robinson came to believe that he was following a path carved out for him by some agency beyond himself. Hagedorn thought that he had "a mystic sense of his calling" and that his poetry stemmed "from subterranean streams deeper than any driven cogitation" of his own. According to Fillmore, EAR felt "appointed by God to be a great poet" and was as confident of his "mission as any prophet of old." His *Collected Poems*, to use the Puritan term, constituted a "justification" of his life.

Whatever their previous attitude toward Robinson, major newspapers and magazines could hardly ignore the substantial accomplishment represented by the 165 titles and 590 pages of his *Collected Poems*. The book was widely reviewed, always with respect and usually with praise. Commentators attempted to sum up the twenty-five years of work encompassed in the volume. What was it about Robinson that made him significantly different from, and superior to, his fellow artists?

In his extensive discussion for the *New York Times Book Review*, Robinson's friend and disciple Herbert Gorman located EAR's distinction in his mastery of the "art of intimation." Robinson, he observed, "possesses the faculty of compelling the reader to build up an untold story." In constructing his Tilbury Town poems, he provided only a "few vivid touches," leaving most of the details to the imagination. "This is one of the secrets of great poetry," Gorman concluded, "to suggest far more than is explicitly stated."

In intimating much that was left unsaid, Robinson ran the risk of being misunderstood. But it was a risk well worth taking, William Rose Benet argued in his essay-review for the *New York Evening Post*. Hailing EAR as "the Merlin of our modern poetry," Benet acknowledged that his poetry was often difficult to interpret because he had a habit of avoiding the obvious. In effect, Robinson paid his readers the compliment of asking them to cooperate in the effort toward understanding. If you managed to reach such an understanding, Benet pointed out, "your delight in your own perspicacity [was] like to make you a Robinsonian forever": a statement that captures much of the poet's lasting appeal.

Yet another distinguishing characteristic of Robinson's poetry was his concentration on character, a point emphasized both by Benet and by Gorman, in a second and more personal review for the *New Republic*. In going over EAR's *Collected Poems*, Gorman said, "the major fact that stands out is that Robinson has almost wholly delivered himself through characterizations. The pageant of figures is enormous, beginning with Luke Havergal and John Evereldown, coming down through even Shakespeare and St. Paul, until an end is reached with Rembrandt." Among them were "the flotsam and jetsam of life, bedraggled figures, characters out-at-elbows . . . 'thwarted clerks and fiddlers,' and majesty hiding a troubled, broken spirit." Robinson made no attempt "to disguise the cruelty of life; he perceives it all but he does not despair." His figures are "the victims of human passions, of delusions. They are all victims, of fear, of envy, of life, of fame, of love."

Unlike the conventional lyric poet, Robinson wrote about these others and not himself, except to the extent that he felt himself involved with mankind, and especially its troubled souls. Robinson's "curiosity about others"—a predilection Thornton Wilder isolated as a basic wellspring of literature—went beyond empathy to love. What EAR was trying to do, Gorman said in conclusion, was "to map the labyrinth of the heart."

Recognition at Last

As Robinson's reputation grew, he began receiving a great deal of attention.. Much of this public acclaim was welcome, for he had labored virtually unnoticed for a long time. Some of it, though, invaded his privacy and challenged his reticence.

Editors and writers who had long ignored Robinson began asking for contributions. Carl Van Doren at *The Nation* wondered if he would review a new book by Thomas Hardy. Robinson wouldn't, for he was busy writing poems and thought it best to stick to his trade and leave the criticism to others. That had been his attitude, Robinson said, for the previous thirty years, and it was one he held to, with only rare exceptions, for the rest of his days. Van Doren also asked Robinson for poems, as did Scofield Thayer at *The Dial* and Ridgely Torrence at the *New Republic*. EAR could be sure of a good audience at the *New Republic*, but with his growing status felt emboldened to complain about the magazine's skimpy fifty-cents-a-line payment rates. "I am getting old and greedy," he wrote Torrence, "and don't like the looks of seven dollars for a sonnet over which I have most likely worked for seven days."

For the princely sum of $100, Robinson agreed to write "a Pilgrim's Chorus" for George Pierce Baker's pageant at Plymouth, Massachusetts, celebrating the tercentenary of the landing on Plymouth Rock on December 21, 1620. The pageant, called "The Pilgrim Spirit," was produced at Plymouth during July and August 1921, with words by Josephine Preston Peabody, Hermann Hagedorn, and Robert Frost, as well as Robinson, and music by various composers Baker had recruited. EAR's contribution was below his usual standard; he disliked doing it and thereafter refrained from writing any poems for special occasions.

He did, however, make a public appearance in connection with another pageant in 1921, this one at Barnard College. Somehow Robinson was persuaded to talk to Barnard students. Before his talk, the poet Leonie Adams escorted Robinson to the opening ceremony of the traditional Greek games at the women's college. For this event, all of the girls donned athletic costumes, some dressed as women, some as men. As they entered the gymnasium in their cross-dressing costumes, with appropriate musical fanfare, EAR "took a deep breath and said, 'Wow.'"

Early in 1922, Mrs. MacDowell made a swing through central Maine on a fundraising trip. In an appearance at the state capitol of Augusta, she extolled the merits of Robinson as a colony regular. "Augusta must be very proud of him," she said, a remark that produced some indignation in Gardiner. It was a queer mistake for Mrs. MacDowell to make, EAR wrote Laura Richards, but he doubted if there were seven people left in Gardiner who remembered him.

Actually, the state of Maine, if not his hometown, was about to launch an investigation into his origins. Henry Dunnack, the state librarian, began accumulating information toward a brief biography. EAR's cousin Clara Palmer alerted him that she was about to be interviewed by a researcher: the sort of news, he said, that made him wish he'd become a housepainter instead of a poet. Any "life" of him would necessarily drag in his early years in Gardiner, as well as his "unfortunate mother and father and even more unfortunate brothers." All of this should be passed over as lightly as possible, he advised Clara. In a separate letter, he reassured his niece Ruth that Clara was under instructions not to rattle the family skeletons. But, he added, it wasn't easy "to stop these things." Someone was "bound to scour the old tombstones."

In the wake of his *Collected Poems*, several books elevated Robinson's reputation precipitously. In *An Introduction to Poetry* (1922), a textbook designed
for college classrooms, Jay B. Hubbell and John O. Beaty acclaimed "The Dark
Hills" as "perfect in conception and phrase" and "Ben Jonson Entertains a Man
from Stratford" as not only one of the best dramatic monologues ever written
but also "the best characterization of Shakespeare . . . in verse." More generally, they described Robinson as "the pioneer of living American poets and the
greatest of them all." Louis Untermeyer, in *American Poetry Since 1900* (1923),
ranked Frost and Robinson as the "twin summits of our poetry—eminences to
which no American poets, since Poe and Whitman, have ever attained."

Also in 1923, Lloyd Morris brought out *The Poetry of Edwin Arlington Robinson: An Essay in Appreciation*, the first book devoted entirely to EAR and his
work. Morris characterized Robinson as a poet "to whom no aspect of human
experience is insignificant, to whom no subject in human life lies outside the
field of art." In his work, Morris wrote, "an intellectual magic" lay beneath "the
immediate emotional effects."

Writing Harry Smith in March 1921, Robinson commented that "after a
rather hard quarter of a century, [his] stock appeared to be picking up a little."
The next royalty statement from Macmillan revealed that sales of his various
books had quadrupled. The *Collected Poems*, emerging in October, sold 5,000
copies in a year, far exceeding the results for any previous book of his. With a
small surplus in the bank, EAR turned to Lewis Isaacs for advice. Isaacs became
Robinson's financial counselor, steering him toward conservative investments
and chiding him for over-generous outlays "to the still down-and-out friends of
his own down-and-out days."

In the early 1920s, collectors began a lively trade in copies of Robinson books,
driving up the prices. In particular demand was Robinson's earliest and rarest,
the blue-backed *Torrent and the Night Before* of which only 312 copies had been
printed. EAR was delighted to learn that "the hunters" were after his first book,
he wrote the bibliophile William Van R. Whitall in November 1920, and he followed the subsequent trade with interest.

Neither Isaacs nor Ledoux owned *The Torrent and the Night Before* when
the book started to appreciate in value, nor did EAR himself. He did what he
could to help them acquire copies. He advised Isaacs to run an advertisement in
the Gardiner newspaper offering to buy a copy of the *Torrent* for $25. A young
man named Carl Marr responded that he would sell the copy that had belonged
to his father, if the Isaacses would assure him it would not be resold for commercial purposes. Edith Isaacs at once agreed, and put a check in the mail, but
it crossed another letter from Marr saying that he'd had second thoughts, and
would send the book directly to Robinson without compensation.

At just this time, in mid-February 1921, another copy came to Robinson
through the good offices of Arthur Spingarn. Spingarn, who was president of
the NAACP, had purchased a collection of odd pamphlets that belonged to the

eminent Algernon Charles Swinburne (1837–1909). Among them was the copy of *The Torrent and the Night Before* that Robinson had inscribed and mailed to the English poet in 1896. Spingarn graciously sent the book to EAR, who was pleased to discover that Swinburne had kept the book and, from the looks of things, apparently spent some time in reading it.

Robinson thus had two copies to dispose of. He gave Swinburne's copy to Isaacs, and the one from Maine went to Ledoux. Meanwhile, the commercial value of the *Torrent* was rapidly escalating. There was a sale for $100 in late January 1921, and in May a copy fetched $250. The following summer in Chicago, a copy sold for $400: more than he would give for it, Robinson commented with a sort of bemused pride. Still, he was at least as interested in *whose* copies came on the market as the prices they sold at. Hardy's didn't turn up, for instance, nor Kipling's.

Grateful though he invariably was when people liked his poetry, Robinson refused to kowtow to his public in search of popularity. He spelled out his position in an October 1920 letter to the young poet Maxwell Bodenheim (1892–1954), who was making a name for himself by way of bohemian excesses in Greenwich Village. "Forget all about 'recognition and reputation' for three or four years and leave those two 'harlots' to do their own running . . . after you," Robinson said, and he went on to excoriate publicity seekers in general. "It appears that nowadays almost anyone who shakes his own tambourine before the populace . . . may acquire a certain amount of recognition etc. and even a few pennies,—but it doesn't amount to anything, and in most cases poisons the performer with the virus of an incurably false standard of poetic value."

Robinson proved his own aversion to even the most respectable form of tambourine shaking when he turned down a request to present the Harvard Phi Beta Kappa poem in the spring of 1922. Although he owed a great deal to the college for his two years there, he believed that any attempt to write such a poem to order would result in disappointment for all concerned. He was inclined to believe that "all Phi Beta Kappa poems [were] bad," and he was constitutionally averse to any public presentation of the self.

He was also a notoriously poor presenter of his own poetry and wise enough to recognize it. Carty Ranck remembered going with Robinson to Sanders theater in Cambridge to hear Alfred Noyes read "The Highwayman" with dramatic force and fervor. He envied Noyes his talent as a performer, Robinson said afterwards; as for himself, he wouldn't read his poems in public for a million dollars. This position he maintained in the face of many requests, even one from his old friend Joseph Ford at Exeter. "I have found it best to decline all invitations to read from my poems or public talks," he told Ford. "I don't enjoy it, and don't do it well; and if such things are not done well, they had far better not be done at all." Mounting a platform would be, for him, "nothing less than a public execution."

Robinson was not a hermit and did not live in a cave, John Farrar pointed out in an appreciative 1923 profile of the poet. But he was, admittedly, notoriously reticent. "He has never seated himself in the middle of the market place and permitted the curious public to stroll about him." He also absented himself from "back slapping dinners," public readings, and the like. As a consequence, John Drinkwater observed, "one of the most distinguished men of his time" managed to hide himself from New York's glare of publicity.

In so doing, Robinson differentiated himself from many modern poets. As Robert Mezey commented, he "belonged to no coterie or movement and had no talent for self-promotion; he had nothing of Pound's gift, or Ginsberg's, for publicity and notoriety—and even if he had known how to operate the levers of advancement, he would have refrained." It went against the down-Maine grain of his personality, and it would have used up time and energy needed for his work. "I don't see how a man can write poetry and do anything else," Robinson told an interviewer.

When the Poetry Society of America was organized in 1910, fifty poets were invited to join as charter members. Robinson was the only one who declined. Writing poems was a solitary occupation. What good would an organization do? Later he relented and joined the Poetry Society, but he rarely attended meetings and steered clear of literary politics.

If it was true, as Robinson remarked, that "all prizes carry sort of a stigma," he was severally stigmatized in the *annus mirabilis* of 1922, in recognition of his *Collected Poems*. The Authors Club, in January, designated EAR's collection as the first winner of an annual award for the most significant book of the year by an American author. In the middle of May, when he was already settled in Peterborough, Robinson got word from the secretary of Columbia University that his book had won the first of his three Pulitzer Prizes for poetry. "The Pulitzer business" was "all very fine," he wrote Fillmore; he wouldn't "even pretend to object" to the thousand dollars that accompanied it.

In June, Robinson surreptitiously stole away from the MacDowell Colony for a long weekend at New Haven, where Yale University gave him a Litt. D. as the nation's foremost poet. "In an age of self-advertising," the citation read, "where many prefer notoriety to obscurity and would rather draw attention by any means than remain unknown, Mr. Robinson has invariably permitted his poems to speak for themselves." As if to illustrate the point, nobody could pry any information from him about the honorary degree when he came back to Peterborough, although the Irish writer Mary Colum detected a new "light in his eyes." In November 1922, the Poetry Society of America chose his *Collected Poems* for its annual award, Robinson's fourth prize of the year.

As he basked in the glow of these awards, steps were being taken to advance Robinson's candidacy for the greatest prize of all. The unlikely promoter of this campaign for the Nobel Prize was Joseph Lewis French, as florid and corpulent and impecunious as ever—and even more mentally unstable. Over the years, French had been abandoned by most of the literary community as a nuisance and a sponge. Robinson and Hagedorn continued to supply him with funds on demand, though, a generosity that French's twisted mind converted into a conspiracy against him.

"I had rather a bad ten minutes with French about two weeks ago," Robinson wrote Hagedorn in December 1919. "He left me, swearing eternal vengeance in some indefinite form or other—and just for what I don't know, unless for giving him money for the past twenty-five years." Still, Robinson counseled Hagedorn to "help the poor devil" whenever he could and ignored the advice of Isaacs and others that he should alert the authorities to French's threats against him. It wasn't as if French "were really responsible" for his actions, he said.

In his demented fashion, French was ready to kill Robinson on some days of the week and eager to secure him the Nobel Prize for Literature on others. Somehow French became acquainted with Otto Dalstrom, a Swedish writer living in New York who was acquainted with members of the Nobel jury. Beginning in 1921, French persuaded Robinson to send Dalstrom copies of his books for forwarding to these jurors. He also attempted to involve Hagedorn in the endeavor, to EAR's embarrassment. "I can imagine your amusement over the whole business—which is surely fantastic enough, though D[alstrom] appears to take it seriously," EAR wrote Hagedorn in November 1921. He couldn't really envision such an award in his future. There were "too many mountains" in the way.

Throughout 1922, Robinson supplied Dalstrom with material to be forwarded overseas, and he even sent him a small sum to defray the mailing expenses. He did not, however, make any attempt to broaden the effort by enlisting literary admirers to send letters. Much as he appreciated Dalstrom's endeavor, Robinson felt it would be "altogether out of order" for him to take any more active part than alerting Dalstrom to an occasional review. He suggested, for example, that the next time Dalstrom was in Brentano's bookstore, he might look at the London *Outlook* for August 26, 1922, which asserted that "Mr. Robinson's poems will be as alive two thousand years hence as they are today."

French's unbalanced mental state remained a central theme in Robinson's letters to Dalstrom. He asked Dalstrom, for instance, to try to convince French that "his fantastic delusions of persecution" had no basis in fact. "The people of whom he suspects the worst enmity are, as is usual in such cases, those who have done their best to help him." Despite repeated insults and ingratitude, EAR would still be glad to help poor French if he could. And if anything should come of "the matter he mentioned to you, and you so kindly considered" (Robinson could not bring himself to commit the words "Nobel Prize" to paper), French would of course "be properly remembered."

He wouldn't have troubled to ask for Dalstrom's intervention, Robinson said, except that the Swede was one of the few people French had spared "in his general condemnation of almost everybody else." Predictably, this did not last. Before long, French unleashed a torrent of abuse on the bewildered Dalstrom, and the Nobel campaign ground to a halt.

Personal Matters

As his career was prospering, Robinson suffered a loss in his personal life. On the morning of Wednesday, March 22, 1922, Craven Langstroth Betts crossed over from Manhattan to visit EAR at the Brooklyn apartment he was sharing with Seth Pope. He found Robinson startled and in distress. Word had just reached him that Pope had dropped dead of a heart attack on the street. Betts took matters in hand, as he so often had done during EAR's earliest years in New York, making arrangements with the undertaker and getting in touch with Pope's relatives in Maine.

The apartment, which had been rented by Pope alone, seemed so gloomy after his death that Robinson had no desire to stay. "Brooklyn with a fellow-lodger" was bad enough; without a companion, it was out of the question. Besides, the landlord was eager to get the place cleaned for a new tenant before the end of the month and allowed Robinson to remain only a few days. Some of Pope's furniture was given away, some left for the landlord to dispose of. The only thing EAR took was the "Century Dictionary of Names," signed as belonging to Pope's former wife Florence.

Lewis Isaacs, who agreed to handle any legal issues concerning the librarian's passing, could not locate Florence Pope for some time. After divorcing Pope, she remarried and moved away, cutting off all ties with her ex-husband. Robinson assured her, when she resurfaced in 1927, that he had never heard Pope say a word against her. In fact, he said, Pope had not once *mentioned* her during the four years he and EAR lived in the same apartment. There followed a sentence that said a great deal about both of these old friends from Maine: "Whatever his feelings may have been, he kept them to himself, and naturally I never tried to draw him out."

With no place to stay, Robinson presented himself at the Frasers' doorstep in Greenwich Village. Would they put him up while he looked for lodgings? They did better than that, installing the poet on the upper floor of their house at 28 W. Eighth Street. The place was conveniently located only a few steps from the Sixth Avenue Elevated Station and only a few minutes from the Christopher Street station on the Seventh Avenue subway line. Robinson moved in with Jimmy and Laura Fraser and Laura's mother, Mrs. James Gardin, late in March 1922, and—in effect—never moved out.

For a number of years, he felt awkward about accepting such generosity. The Frasers could easily have rented the space he occupied to their advantage, he thought, and at times they might occasionally need "his room" for visitors or guests. He did not want to wear out his welcome or become a burden. Time and again he wrote Laura Fraser offering to find a place on his own during his annual five months or so in New York. The answer was always that the Frasers really wanted him around. They proved it in 1925 when they planned their own move to a house at 328 E. Forty-second Street. As part of the remodeling, they prepared a top-floor room for EAR with a view of the East River. "Strange and admirable people!" Robinson exclaimed. He stayed with them the rest of his days.

For some years leading up to 1922, Robinson was doing his best to hold together a marriage as discordant as the Frasers' was harmonious. His friend Carty Ranck had married Reita Lambert, a successful writer of popular fiction for women's magazines, in February 1915. EAR was one of the first to visit the new couple, and he came away moderately impressed. The newlywed Ranck, if "still a little bewildered," was undoubtedly happy as a married man. A cloud hovered on the horizon in the form of "Mrs. R.'s" conviction that her husband's friends were all "terrific highbrows and correspondingly critical." She seemed "a little scared and on trial," but Robinson liked her and thought she would be good for Ranck. For once he was unduly optimistic. The Rancks' marriage went through a series of crises before finally collapsing.

Initially, Robinson was inclined to blame Reita Lambert for much of the problem, despite knowing about Ranck's precarious mental health. But Ranck's behavior became increasingly erratic as time wore on. Unable to achieve success as a playwright, he was convinced that the stars were aligned against him, and not just the stars but a number of people as well. In his frustration, he was liable to strike out physically at these imagined persecutors, seeing "red [where] no such color exists." Finally, in the summer of 1921 he was confined to a sanitarium for treatment of "a nervous breakdown." Robinson wrote him there in September, urging him to remain until he felt "altogether better. . . . I think of you often, as there is no need of my telling you, and hope you won't let your pride get in the way of your recovery by trying to rush things."

Robinson accompanied this advice with the news that Arthur Nevin was teaching and directing the orchestra in Memphis, Tennessee, and the suggestion that Ranck get in touch with him there. Neither as ambitious or musically talented as his older brother Ethelbert, Nevin had established himself as "the most widely liked man" who had ever worked at the MacDowell Colony. He was a particular favorite of Mrs. MacDowell and an amiable drinking companion to both Ranck and Robinson. The three men became the closest of friends. Although Robinson heard the rumors around Peterborough of an affair between Nevin and Ranck's wife, he decided to function as a peacemaker between the two men. "Even a few words would bridge the gap," he told Ranck. And after Ranck was released from the sanitarium—too early, EAR thought—Robinson supplied Nevin with an address and the comment that "a letter from you is always sure to cheer them up."

These attempts at fence mending ended in August 1922 when Reita Lambert and Arthur Nevin bolted for Paris, with her five-year-old daughter in tow. This caused a scandal at the MacDowell Colony, where it was reported that Nevin had "walked off with his best friend's wife." Ranck, naturally furious, wrote Nevin a series of incendiary letters. After a rancorous divorce, Nevin and Lambert married, and in due course, with the encouragement of Robinson, Ranck's anger

FIGURE 22.1 Arthur Nevin, who ran off with . . .

FIGURE 22.2 . . . Reita Lambert, wife of . . .

FIGURE 22.3 Carty Ranck.

Source: Arnold T. Schwab Papers.

subsided. It would be much the best thing for all concerned, EAR told Ranck, to let the past go. He also assured Nevin that his feeling for him had never changed and tried unsuccessfully to persuade him to return to Peterborough.

Parker Fillmore recalled a conversation with Robinson about the Ranck-Nevin fracas. EAR had just come from seeing Ranck, who'd been talking about Reita and Nevin. "Ranck says they're both bad—bad clear through!" Robinson blinked his eyes, smacked his lips, and with a chuckle repeated the verdict: "bad clear through!" Infidelity figured prominently in Robinson's poetry, but it was not, for him, an offense worth breaking a friendship for.

Ranck remained Robinson's devoted admirer throughout this marital difficulty and the series of mental breakdowns that followed. After his divorce, he lived most of the time in a modest Boston hall bedroom close to that of George Burnham, and Robinson saw both of them on his annual swing from New York to Peterborough and back. The likable Nevin, however, drifted away, as did Herbert Gorman, whose own marriage disintegrated in the early 1920s despite EAR's healing efforts.

Fortunately, at just this time of regret for lost companions, another Gardiner native turned up to visit him at the MacDowell Colony. In grade school, Arthur Davis Variell and Win Robinson read their Beadle's Half-Dime Library adventures from behind the covers of their geography texts. They had seen nothing of each other for thirty years until September 1922 when Variell—probably alerted by news of his schoolmate's Pulitzer Prize and honorary degree at Yale—"rolled in on [EAR], driving a giant car and looking generally like a millionaire."

Variell had become first a doctor, next a successful businessman in Waterbury, Connecticut, and finally a practitioner and financial supporter of medical research into leprosy who was knighted and decorated by at least eight countries. In private life, too, Variell was a man of wide accomplishments and interests, in literature and the fine arts as in athletics, in big game hunting as in chess. A man of the world, he fought through EAR's reserve to build a warm comradeship. They saw each other primarily in New York—Robinson apparently never accepted an open invitation to Variell's Waterbury home or to his summer place in Kennebunkport, Maine—and carried on an extensive correspondence until 1929.

When Art Variell came to New York for an evening out with EAR, he brought along a bottle or two of good, illegal liquor and the theater tickets he'd purchased in advance. He sent Robinson cigars and cartons of Sweet Caporal cigarettes, mementoes collected during his travels overseas, and many books. When in February 1923 EAR mentioned "a possible contingency" on the horizon, Variell sent him a generous check. He was in no "immediate need," Robinson responded, but with dental bills accumulating and the cost of a steamship ticket to England in the offing, he hadn't "the moral force to refuse" the money.

Variell, who had literary aspirations himself, wanted to learn whatever Robinson could teach him about a life in poetry. In one of his last letters to Variell,

Robinson discussed the issue at some length. It wasn't fame that the artist paid so much for, EAR wrote, "but the opportunity to do what he wants to do." Money, beyond enough to live on, meant little or nothing. "Some people want money for its own sake, while others, like yourself, want it for what they can get for it. Others—a few others—would rather play the best game of billiards ever played than do anything else." He belonged to the last group, trying to construct poetry as artfully as the billiards player fashioned his perfect game. He'd gone through hard times, it was true. But, he cautioned his old schoolmate, "don't for God's sake be sorry for the price I have paid for whatever I have done. I should have been miserable doing anything else."

In the last weeks of 1922, Robinson served as editorial adviser to Rosalind Richards, the woman he had poured his heart out to twenty-five years before. She had written a novel, and he agreed not only to read and critique it but to do anything he could to advance its chances for acceptance "with the Macmillans." It was not EAR's first venture along these lines on behalf of "R. R." or "the Person," as he referred to Rosalind in his letters to her mother. In 1915, Rosalind sent him the manuscript of *A Northern Countryside*, which was published the following year by Henry Holt, for his comments. The genre—a "nature" book celebrating the seasons in central Maine—was not at all to his liking, but he was able to report that he'd read it "with real pleasure." Robinson liked Rosalind's novel rather less, and he tried to tell her so with more tact than he usually expended when a literary judgment was called for.

Having read only the first eight chapters, Robinson recommended on December 10, 1922, that she cut two of them that seemed "entirely superfluous and beautifully contrived to prohibit the publication of the others." This may have sounded harsh, but it was softened by the observation that he saw "no reason, thus far, why the book should not be accepted."

Five days later, after completing the novel, Robinson changed his mind. In the course of telling her that "as it stands," the novel wouldn't do, he discoursed at length on the benefits of not writing novels. She might be "a much happier and far more valuable Person if [she] were to let others write the novels and pay the almost inevitable payment for discouragement and disillusion. Almost anybody can write a novel, of a sort, and sooner or later get it published. And what of it? Of all novels that are published, ninety-five percent come to nothing; and the other five percent, with woefully few exceptions, don't amount to much."

He'd encountered a long line of disappointed women, Robinson said, who might have been reasonably contented but for their conviction that they must write or die. He felt sure that they would have lived longer and had a much better time, if they hadn't gone so far out of their way to find trouble. "In any event," he concluded, the world was "a different and a better place from [Rosalind's] being in it, "whether or not she wrote novels.

At the same time, Robinson did not quite close the door against R. R.'s manuscript. He proposed certain alterations: excision of "Part First," less detail, less guidebook material (the book was set in Paris, primarily), and he offered to make himself useful should she send him a revised version. But he would not submit the novel to Macmillan "in its present form," for to do so "would practically [kill] its chances with them in the future." Rosalind, apparently, did not revise as suggested; her novel was not published. In signing off on the issue, EAR wished her "every sort of good fortune for the rest of [her] life."

In his role as literary adviser, Robinson involved himself with Rosalind Richards's work-in-progress more closely than with that of anyone else. He obviously wanted to be of service to her and to let her down as gently as he could. In the process, he somehow managed not to damage the relationship between them. She continued to mark up copies of *The Spectator* with articles for him to read, to send him an annual Christmas wreath redolent of the Maine woods—and sometimes, surely, to think back on the summer evening at Camp Cobbossee when he declared his feelings for her.

As an established poet, Robinson was often called upon to advise aspiring writers. Almost always, he proposed, as he had to Rosalind Richards, that they do something else instead. "Generally speaking," he wrote Carl Marr in 1921, "I am slow to recommend any form of literature to any human being strong enough to resist it." In most cases, writing was "a dog's life," and anyone unwilling "to sacrifice everything within reason" for it should find another occupation. If fate decreed that they were to write, they would do so no matter what he said. If they could be sidetracked by his counsel, it served as proof that they were not among the called or chosen or condemned.

Even after they had committed themselves, Robinson invariably counseled young poets to delay publishing their work. Time after time he advised against publishing before thirty (he had been twenty-six when *The Torrent and the Night Before* came out). "You will be glad if you wait until you are thirty," he told Hardwicke Nevin, and the same message went to Maxwell Bodenheim, Lucius Beebe, Malcolm Cowley, and Winfield Townley Scott. When he liked a manuscript, he would still counsel poets to put off publishing for a year or more—advice that infuriated Elinor Wylie, who ignored it to bring out *Black Armour* in 1923, her thirty-eighth year. Where fiction was concerned, Robinson advised still longer delays. "Unless a man is a boiling over genius like Dickens, he is not likely to have a real novel in him before he is forty," he declared.

23

A Sojourn in England

Feeling the pull of his ancestry and of the English literary tradition, Robinson had talked of going to England since he was fresh out of Harvard. But it was not until June 1922 that he began seriously contemplating the possibility of casting loose from his moorings for a journey across the water. Edward Bliss Reed, of the *Yale Review*, was living in Oxford and felt sure EAR would feel at home there. His *Collected Poems* was coming out in an English imprint. He was invited to serve as a delegate to the international PEN banquet in London. A few British writers and editors were urging him to make the trip. And he could through such a journey escape the folly of Prohibition, at least temporarily

By the fall, Robinson's plans for an English sojourn were taking shape. He entered into correspondence with the playwright and poet John Drinkwater, who was to write an introduction to the English edition of his *Collected Poems*, and with J. C. Squire, editor of the *London Mercury*. Drinkwater offered to show him around London, and Squire suggested that he take a room at Garland's hotel in Suffolk Street, a quiet place within a few minutes of Trafalgar Square. "Many people are looking forward to seeing you," Squire assured him.

Robinson sailed April 18, 1923, on the new Cunard boat, the *Tyrrhenia*. "When we are three miles out," he wrote George Burnham before departure, "I shall have [a highball] and think of you." Another farewell letter went to Emma Robinson. Just how long he would stay overseas was still in doubt, he told her. It might be "a year or so." A reporter from the *New York Tribune* stopped by to interview him the day before the boat sailed. Having just come from the dentist, Robinson was tired, still had packing to finish, and was in no mood for an extended discussion of poetry and its practitioners. The best parts of the interview captured the subject's appearance as he rocked back and forth in his chair. "There was static warmth about his dark eyes, and a sensitiveness of the mouth, emphasized by the smoothness of his phrases, which came laconically from the silence [that] had settled over the room."

Louis Ledoux came to see him off on what proved to be a lazy and pleasant crossing. "The people on board haven't bothered me much," he wrote Jean

Ledoux, and in return he had tried not to talk them to death. "That man must be English," he overheard one passenger tell the purser, "he doesn't care a damn about anybody"—which, EAR said, was "entirely untrue."

On arrival Robinson found that Squire had been right. He was warmly welcomed and entertained by the English literary community. Edmund Gosse, to whom he had sent a copy of *The Torrent and the Night Before* in 1896, felt an immediate kinship with Robinson. "We have . . . many sympathies in common, and particularly a tender jealousy for the dignity of Letters," Gosse observed. Robinson went to see Arnold Bennett, who was living in luxury and—EAR decided—letting success dilute the quality of his fiction. At a dinner, he spied May Sinclair across the room. He was hesitant to approach her and renew the acquaintanceship started in New York two decades earlier, but she, nearly as shy as he, sought him out for conversation. She had the brightest eyes he'd ever seen, Robinson thought. During a gathering at John Galsworthy's home, EAR was asked to make a speech. He declined, of course, but agreed to respond to questions and did so with uncommon ease. No speechmaking, no comments at all, were required of him at the PEN International banquet. Robinson was disappointed that so few of the delegates seemed to have heard of him. Still, he was loath to do anything to call attention to himself.

Squire marveled at Robinson's modesty. He'd come to England shortly after publication of his *Collected Poems*, "enjoying the by-ways of London and the beauties of the English spring." Here was an opportunity to familiarize the British public with his name, "had he been addicted to public recitation, lecturing, after-dinner speaking or the furnishing of bright impromptus to interviewers." Yet EAR "did not lecture, he was not interviewed, and when he dined he dined in peace. His arrival was known only to his friends, his departure only by them regretted."

During most of his visit, Robinson was too happily looking about him to indulge in advertisements for himself. Mrs. St. John Irvine drove him about the West End, and through Hyde Park and Kensington Gardens. As they passed the Serpentine, EAR—remembering Harriet Shelley—commented that it looked like a good place to commit suicide. He spent a splendid afternoon with Drinkwater at the Tower of London. Alfred Noyes took him on a tour around the Roman artifacts of St. Albans; he liked Noyes, who impressed him as "a happy man—that is in so far as a poet can be really happy except when he is actually producing poetry." He took a day trip to Cambridge, and returned rhapsodizing about King's College Chapel. "I'm not much in the way of a sight seer," he wrote Isaacs, "but that thing isn't a sight, it's just a miracle."

Literary landmarks interested Robinson more than the usual tourist destinations. As he wrote Drinkwater, "I like to prowl about London and call up the old ghosts which you English are too familiar with to care about." He had no trouble finding guides for these outings. Drinkwater accompanied him on a trip to Rye, where Henry James had lived. The town seemed like one of the "least real" places in the world, EAR wrote Isaacs: he would have gone mad if he had to spend thirty-six hours there. Far more to his liking was an exploration of Shakespeare's London haunts with the expatriate American poet John Gould Fletcher. The most exciting spot in London, for Robinson, was the cemetery at the corner of Wood and Silver Streets, not far from where Shakespeare had lived for some seven years before London's great fire. He tried to capture some of his sense of communion in a poem called "Silver Street."

> Here played the mighty child who for his toy
> Must have the world—king, wizard, sage and clown,
> Queen, fiend and trollop—and with no more renown,
> May be, than friends and envy might annoy.

With an assemblage of literary lights, Robinson made an excursion to Shakespeare's home in Stratford-on-Avon. When the group arrived, they found George Bernard Shaw already ensconced there, acting as self-appointed host in lieu of the bard himself. There was no chance of a talk with Shaw, he told Isaacs. "He took Shakespeare's place and was very busy."

Fletcher was not the only expatriated American Robinson hoped to meet in England. Harold Munro, author, editor, and proprietor of the Poetry Bookshop in Bloomsbury, tried to arrange a meeting for EAR with T. S. Eliot, whose groundbreaking *Waste Land* had been published the previous December. Eliot was living in the country, caring for his ailing wife, and the two poets did not connect. EAR did see Conrad Aiken on at least two occasions, however. Aiken was making a career for himself not only as a poet but as a critic: he had, for example, reviewed both EAR's *Collected Poems* and Eliot's *Waste Land*.

Robinson visited Aiken at his home in Winchelsea, Sussex. Aiken was advised to have Scotch on hand and laid in one bottle, which Robinson finished. Two days later they met in London for "an alcoholiday" that took them to

FIGURE 23.1 Poet Conrad Aiken, EAR's companion on an "alcoholiday."

Source: In House Photo.

Canterbury and back. Robinson drank whisky "as if it were air," Aiken recalled. "We stopped at every pub, from and to Victoria Station, and in Canterbury, going and coming. We missed nothing in Canterbury, except one drink, which he spilled. An enchanting day." Back in London, EAR chose a special lobster restaurant, but first he insisted that they have one final drink. When they did, "two bonny lassies Of The Trade" approached them. One of them kissed Aiken, and said, "Why not take us to dinner?" Amused, Robinson nimbly stepped back. "I fear I'm in the way," he said. Thereupon Aiken dismissed "the nice gal" by explaining that they were poets and poor. Round the corner they went to dinner, where Robinson demonstrated the proper way to eat a lobster. Calling on the skills he had learned growing up in Maine, he performed the operation with the gravity of a Roman rite.

"He knew it all," Aiken recalled. "Ordered 'hen' lobsters, with oil and vinegar. Then proceeded to excavate every mortal morsel—little claws, big claws, tomally, all the meat, even to the flippers, piled it in a luscious pyramid, added a little seasoning, and went to work. It was delicious." Most favorably impressed, Aiken described Robinson as "a charming creature—more of a being than any American litry person I've met."

Unfortunately, Aiken mentioned that memorable day to Lucius Beebe, who altered the facts considerably for a 1930 article for *The Outlook and Independent*. Beebe changed the poets' journey into an overnight train trip from Liverpool to London, and had them consume two bottles of Irish whiskey en route. Then he quoted Robinson as saying that despite the alcohol he felt fine and went to lunch that same day, "but Aiken, pooh, he was no drinker at all. It was a week before he got out of the Charing Cross Turkish Baths."

When Robinson read the piece at the MacDowell Colony, he was rendered "limp and useless" for two days. "Just why," he asked Rollo Walter Brown, "should anybody wish to circulate a yarn like that . . . especially about something that happened seven years ago, and wasn't true in the first place?" His war with prohibition over, he had stopped drinking again in 1926 and did not want his former indulgences paraded in the public press. But most of all, he was appalled by Beebe's account because it made him out to be a braggart at Aiken's expense. In two letters to the much younger Beebe, Robinson speculated that Beebe would probably never have published such a false and sensationalized account had he not spent a year in newspaper work. Beebe might at least have paused "to consider how annoying it must be to a man of sixty when he sees in print things attributed to him [e.g., the wisecrack about the Turkish baths] that he could never possibly have said." Beebe duly apologized, but in back channel communication with Aiken made light of the issue. "Father Robinson has written me in great terror and alarm," he reported. "The anecdote seemed, and still seems, as harmless to me as milk of magnesia."

Robinson liked London and even enjoyed getting lost as he wandered around the city. The place was much as he supposed it would be, he wrote friends after a few weeks. There were a few surprises, though. He was delighted by "the unexpected abundance" of large lobsters. The coffee, on the other hand, was "a pernicious curiosity," and the bread apparently designed as building material. You couldn't buy tobacco, legally, after eight o'clock in the evening. The effects of the Great War persisted "in all sorts of indefinable ways." London was so poor that it couldn't uphold its reputation as a place to get drunk. His own reserve, he found, more than matched the supposed reticence of the English. It seemed to him that they chatted excessively on social occasions, if with rather more wit than he encountered in New York or Boston.

After a month in London, Robinson began to wonder if he would ever work again. Perhaps, he thought, he would be better off in Oxford, and asked Edward Bliss Reed if he could help him locate lodgings for the summer. By the end of May, however, he had given up the idea of going to Oxford, moving instead from Garland's hotel to a room on Hertford Street in Mayfair. It was no more expensive than the hotel "and far more like a place to live in." The chairs seemed more "like things to sit in," though there were no rocking chairs and "the call of the rocker" persisted. Another call beckoned him as well. "I find the call of Peterborough stronger than that of England and Europe together," he wrote Isaacs.

By mid-June Robinson had made up his mind not to extend his vacation much longer. "I could easily stay in England for the rest of my life," he wrote Ledoux. The more he saw of the country, the more he liked it. At the same time, he could foresee that if he stayed, he would never get any work done. He'd talked of a year in England, but the length of time didn't matter. The really important thing was for him to have been in London for a while; he'd needed the change of air. "I have decided to enjoy myself for another month or so," he wrote the Frasers on June 20, "at the end of which time my Puritanical conscience will get the upper hand and send me home." He booked passage on the *President Roosevelt*, sailing July 26, and cabled Mrs. MacDowell to save a place for him when he got back.

Back on home ground, Robinson had nothing bad to say about England. "London makes New York look like Uncle Sam's back yard," he wrote Laura Richards, "and England itself is probably closer to paradise (on the surface) than any other part of this wale." But New England was in his blood and bones, and he was happy to get back to work at Peterborough. EAR felt so closely tied to his origins that he never again ventured far afield. He turned down invitations to Chicago, to Palm Beach, to the University of Michigan. The Grand Canyon was undoubtedly "a grand piece of work," he remarked, but he knew just about how it looked without traveling three thousand miles to see it. During his last dozen years, he sometimes contemplated a repeat journey to England itself, where he'd found everything he dreamed of. Otherwise, he had no interest "in prowling over Europe" or Africa or anywhere else.

Robinson did feel he belonged to a literary tradition that originated on the other side of the Atlantic. Oddly enough, his very devotion to English writers of the past made his poetry less palatable there. He adhered to verse techniques learned from English models, while the public was looking for something like Whitman's "barbaric yawp." As the British writer Theodore Maynard put it, American poets were "usually ignored unless they provide[d] the wildness and wooliness English readers expect." Robinson was acutely aware of the problem. His poetry had a universality of theme and was written in language common to cultivated people on both sides of the ocean. "A careful reader" of Robinson's poems "could hardly tell whether he was English or American," and that would not do, for the English were "inclined to insist that an American must stand on his head to be native and original." So, although several of his books were published in London and praised by Aiken and Fletcher and Drinkwater and Squire, none achieved a wide readership. His work was received much more favorably in France, where critics did not demand flamboyance from American writers.

Restored to his routine at the MacDowell Colony, Robinson wrote a number of sonnets during the late summer of 1923. At least three of them derived in part from his trip to England: "Silver Street," with its emanation of Shakespeare's time in Cheapside, "The Sheaves," one of his loveliest poems, and "New England," one of his most widely misunderstood.

He had to go to England, Robinson said, to see the McCormick "reaper and binder in operation." Hence, "The Sheaves":

> Where long the shadows of the wind had rolled,
> Green wheat was yielding to the change assigned;
> And as by some vast magic undivined
> The world was turning slowly into gold.
> Like nothing that was ever bought or sold
> It waited there, the body and the mind;
> And with a mighty meaning of a kind
> That tells the more the more it is not told.
>
> So in a land where all days are not fair,
> Fair days went on till on another day
> A thousand golden sheaves were lying there,
> Shining and still, but not for long to stay—
> As if a thousand girls with golden hair
> Might rise from where they slept and go away.

In his comments on this sonnet, the poet Henry Taylor emphasizes the artistry of the sestet, particularly the chiasmus in first two lines: "their doubling of *on*, *days*, and *fair*, with *day* (singular) thrown in for good measure." The whole sestet, Taylor observed, read like "a perfect script for a brief moment on film, complete with dissolves that were barely thought of when the poem was written." Taylor also called attention to the ambiguity of lines five through eight:

> Like nothing that was bought or sold
> It waited there, the body and the mind;
> And with a mighty meaning of a kind
> That tells the more the more it is not told.

Here, Taylor felt, Robinson's "mighty meaning" that finds expression by not being expressed ran perilously close to "mere riddling."

While agreeing that the lines quoted above constituted "the heart of the poem," David Nivison has argued persuasively that they may be best interpreted in the context of Indian religious philosophy. That Robinson placed "The Sheaves" immediately before two other sonnets devoted to the topic of human perception with overtly Indian titles, the excellent "Karma" and "Maya," supports this reading, and in this connection it is worth noting that EAR had read and discussed the Bhagavad Gita with George Burnham, a fervent convert to Hinduism.

"The object of attention" in the poem, Nivison pointed out, "is a *field* of growing grain turning to gold, its beauty qualified—no: enhanced—by its impermanence, its constant changing, framed in illusioriness: apparent waves as shadows of wind; fair weather, notoriously changeable; the sheaves transformable by imagination into 'girls with golden hair.'" And in Indian religion, "The Field" is "a standard metaphor . . . for the material world (as a whole or in its stand-in, the human body) as object of enlightened understanding." The cosmic mind-body dualism, a basic concept in Indian thought, may yield such an understanding, albeit not one that can be expressed in words.

Unfortunately, Robinson's "New England," written during the same period, was widely misinterpreted. The poem appeared in the London *Outlook* for November 1, 1923, and was reprinted the following month in two stateside magazines, the *Literary Digest* and the *New Republic*. "To see our own Mr. Robinson in the London *Outlook* on the subject of 'New England' is like reading a challenge," the *Literary Digest* commented. The editors clearly saw the sonnet as an attack on New England, as did many—probably most—readers. "My northern pines are good enough for me," Robinson had announced at the beginning of his career, yet now he was roundly chastised for the supposed crime of disloyalty to his origins.

> Born where the wind is always north-north-east
> And children learn to walk on frozen toes,
> Intolerance tells an envy of all those

Who boil from birth with such a lyric yeast
Of love that you will hear them at a feast
Where demons would appeal for some repose,
Still clamoring where the chalice overflows
And crying wildest who have drunk the least.

Passion is here a soilure of the wits,
It seems, and Love a cross for them to bear;
Joy shivers in the corner where she knits
And Conscience always has the rocking-chair,
Cheerful as when she tortured into fits
The first cat that was ever killed by Care.

This offended David H. Darling, a businessman in Gardiner who wrote a letter to the editor of the *Gardiner Journal* in objection. Robinson's sonnet, he asserted, marked "a phase of New England character familiar enough and much to be deplored." Darling was particularly annoyed because the poem was initially published in England. "The British find rocks to heave at us without our help, and are 'on the target' often enough without our giving them the range." As a corrective, Darling wrote a twelve-line poem of his own for the *Journal*, extolling the virtues of the region. Harry Swanton, a boyhood friend of Win's, followed with another patriotic verse praising New England as a mighty defender of liberty.

Robinson was more or less astounded by the brouhaha in his home town. "I don't see how anything could be plainer than the construction of the octave in the New England sonnet," he wrote Laura Richards, "but somehow I must be in error. 'Intolerance, born where the wind etc., tells an envy of all those (not in New England) who boil, etc.' All which is said sarcastic." On the basis of this communication, Mrs. Richards came to Robinson's defense in the *Gardiner Journal*. The sonnet, she assured the newspaper's readers, "was supposed to be aimed at those who patronize New England." She sent along "The Sheaves," which the *Journal* printed, as an example of the "exquisite beauty and clarity" Robinson was capable of. EAR himself wrote "a few words of explanation" for his home town newspaper. If Mr. Darling would be kind enough to give his "unfortunate sonnet" another reading, Robinson proposed, he might see that the first eight lines constituted "an oblique attack upon all those who are forever throwing dead cats at New England for its alleged emotional and moral frigidity." As for the last six lines, he supposed "that the deliberate insertion of 'It seems' would be enough to indicate the key in which they are written."

Calling attention to one's own irony was "always a little distressing" if in this case "rather necessary," Robinson added. He had manifestly overestimated his audience's capacity to discover irony, even though the poem contained an abundance of clues. The first lines should have aroused immediate suspicion by way of their obvious hyperbole. The wind did not always blow from the same direction, even in New England. Nor was it true that children took their first steps on frozen feet. The passage EAR referred to in his letters to Mrs. Richards and the *Journal* represented a classic example of the Swiftian technique of offering for approval a hideous alternative, inviting envy for a scene of distasteful, noisy, and hypocritical excess.

Further clues were scattered in the sestet. Most notable, as Robinson asserted, was the qualifying "It seems." But he also introduced a cat whose death resulted from a cause contrary to all expectation. Understandably nervous in a room with even one rocking chair, the creature was killed by "Care" instead of the proverbial Curiosity. At the end of his letter to the *Gardiner Journal*, Robinson proposed that if his explanations still left Mr. Darling in doubt, "it may be assumed that I have written an unusually bad sonnet—which is quite possible." Here, though. EAR was being culpably modest. Read with reasonable sensitivity, "New England" belongs among his most entertaining poems. He did make a few alterations before publishing the sonnet in book form, however. "Here" replaced "Born" as the first word, "Intolerance tells" gave way to "Wonder begets" in line three, " boil from birth" was supplanted by "boil elsewhere" in line four, and "It seems" of line ten became the even more obviously qualifying "We're told"—all revisions calculated to make his meaning clearer.

Clippings from the Gardiner newspaper were sent to Robert Frost, then teaching at Amherst. Frost well understood the uses of humor, sarcasm, and irony, as his own poetry demonstrates, and it is unimaginable that he did not detect the irony in "New England." Yet when he discussed the sonnet in class, he chose to present its assertions literally and assured the students that Robinson's letter to the editor was contrived "as an afterthought, for the self-protective purpose of trying to conceal his intent." He forwarded the poem and clippings to Untermeyer with the comment that it was "amusing to see Robinson squirm just like any ordinary person in a tight place trying to keep in with his neighbors."

24

MacDowell's First Citizen

A Place to Belong to

The MacDowell Colony was founded to provide artists with a place to work in peace and in companionship with their peers. Those in residence were supposed to represent an aristocracy of talent—all had a record of accomplishment, or they would not have been admitted—and they were *fellow* aristocrats, bound together by a joint commitment to their work. Yet in this assembly of artistic equals, some were more equal than others.

Dozens of artists came to work for a few weeks, for a month, or for the entire summer at MacDowell. Several of these were in residence for two or three or even more summers. Only Robinson came every year for the whole summer; only he became a permanent summer resident. When the call of the mountains drew him back from England in the summer of 1923, it was his thirteenth summer at the colony, and he had eleven more to go: twenty-four years, every summer at the MacDowell Colony.

From the beginning Mrs. MacDowell intuited Robinson's value as a "stabilizing factor" among his often unstable and unpredictable fellow artists. He set a standard for industry and integrity for others to follow, and as his reputation grew, he served as an advertisement to the outside world. "The MacDowell Colony? Oh, yes. That's where the poet Robinson goes every summer." The colony did wonders for him, and in his quiet way he repaid the debt.

In his memorial reminiscence of Robinson, Parker Fillmore suggests what Robinson's presence meant to his companions. "He was one of us—the man with whom we ate breakfast and dinner, with whom we chatted in the evening, with whom we walked to the Village. His gentle courtesy made him the easiest of comrades and the best man in the world for communal life." He also stood for "decency and order and industry and above all for kindliness."

Some referred Robinson as the King of MacDowell, but he was far too diffident to rule others, or to want to. Hagedorn called him MacDowell's First Citizen, a title earned by seniority as well as distinction, and carrying certain privileges.

FIGURE 24.1 The notch cut in the pines at MacDowell to give EAR a view of Mount Monadnock.

Source: Trinity College Library.

After 1915, Robinson was invariably assigned the Veltin Studio as his place of work. At his request, a notch was cut through the pines to eliminate "thieves of light" and give him a full view of Mount Monadnock from the doorway. In Colony Hall, the white clapboard building, once a cow barn, where all the colonists ate and some slept, he was provided with a room near the end of the hall quiet enough for him to court sleep despite his continual insomnia.

Robinson's special status was most evident, however, in the dining room downstairs. Open seating was the rule at breakfast and dinner. Colonists could sit wherever they found an empty chair. EAR, though, always had the same seat: at a table for six, with the fireplace on his right and his back to the door. No one resented his occupying this particular chair to the exclusion of others. It was an earned entitlement, after all.

At MacDowell, Rollo Brown remembered, Robinson "was not so much a character as a figure. He was something seen on the landscape; he was an integral part of it; he enlivened it; he unwittingly—or at least unintentionally—dominated it." Within the limits of his reserve, EAR tried hard to unbend to newcomers, for he knew that they shared common goals and aspirations. Occasionally the process was speeded up.

Early in July 1924, the young poet Chard Powers Smith arrived at the MacDowell Colony. Still mourning the death of his wife three months before, Smith had been admitted with the sponsorship of Lloyd Morris, whose book on Robinson had recently been published. Morris sent EAR a note about Smith, so that he was more or less on the lookout for the new colonist.

As Smith tells the story, he was still unpacking his bags when the dinner bell clanged, calling him to Colony Hall. By the time he arrived, most of the seats

FIGURE 24.2 Young poet Chard Powers Smith: he usurped EAR's place, once.

Source: Library of Congress.

were taken at the four tables for six in the dining room. But Smith spied an empty place at the table near the fireplace, made an inquiring bow to the others already seated, and sat down. This action produced an audible gasp from the five ladies at the table: two poets, the genteel Virginian Nancy Byrd Turner and the statuesque Leonora Speyer; two dramatists, Elizabeth Marsh who spent much of the year as a librarian at Dartmouth, and Esther Bates, Robinson's faithful amanuensis; and the composer Mabel Daniels.

Smith looked around the room for a glimpse of Robinson without success. Then a door opened beyond the fireplace, and the author of the Pulitzer Prize–winning *Collected Poems* entered. For a moment, he stared at Smith "out of enormous dark eyes, a tall and lean, vertical, moustached, fifty-five-year-old dragonfly. . . . Then he glanced at an empty seat the other side of the room, gave a little jump of decision, and climbed to it with the longest strides of the longest legs I ever saw." A few people looked at Smith and laughed out loud.

Not until dessert did Esther Bates let the newcomer know that he had commandeered Robinson's accustomed place. Upon discovering his faux pas, Smith managed a smile, excused himself, and fled to the safety of his room. The next day, he figured, he could introduce himself to the great man and make amends. But Smith arrived late for breakfast, just in time to watch the disappearing figure of Robinson in his white canvas hat, striding along "down the western road through the meadow towards the pines and distant Monadnock," swinging his cane as he went to decapitate the weeds.

Not until everyone had finished dinner that evening did the two men meet. DuBose and Dorothy Heyward, poet and playwright authors of *Porgy and Bess* and the only married couple in residence, stopped to chat with Robinson before leaving. So did the engaging Thornton Wilder. Essayist and critic Constance Rourke, classically lovely with prematurely white hair, went out with them through the swinging door. The poet Elinor Wylie "sailed magnificently by." On their way out, poet William Rose Benet and artist Grant Reynard exchanged a word with EAR, who nodded in response. Finally, only Robinson and Smith remained in the room, each nibbling second helpings of rice pudding and unwilling to make an overture, the twenty-nine-year-old Smith held back by awe, Robinson, at fifty-four, by shyness.

At last Smith screwed up his courage and started across the dining room to introduce himself. As he did, Robinson rose from his chair and uncoiled his six feet, two inches. Smith advanced, offering his hand for EAR's usual limp handshake. "How do you do, Mr. Robinson. I'm—" he said, but got no further. "I hear you like to play pool," Robinson interrupted, dispensing with any additional formalities. Lloyd Morris had told EAR about Smith and his sorrow over his wife's death. That was enough to include him in Robinson's community of the hurt and broken, the baffled sufferers who made up his inner world of compassion. Besides, Bill Benet and Grant Reynard were waiting to play pool with them.

"I'm really not very good," Smith said as they walked to the pool room.

Robinson half smiled, with what Smith called his rabbit or woodchuck smile. "Fine," he said. "We'll make mincemeat of you."

Robinson introduced him to Benet and Reynard. "This—is—Mister—Smith," he announced, dragging out the sibilants. "He's a—champeen—pool player." So commenced the nightly game of cowboy pool that was part of E.A.'s regular routine at MacDowell.

FIGURE 24.3 William Rose Benet, author and Cowboy Pool competitor.

Source: Picture Collection, New York Public Library.

Robinson was not a gifted player—it was true that he was "born awkward," as he said of himself—but by dint of regular participation had achieved a level of competence. Some of the women came to observe the game, Esther Bates and Mabel Daniels among them. "What everyone liked to watch," Smith wrote, "was his beautiful long left hand on the table, the care with which he placed and shifted it minutely this way and that, aiming. . . . Sometimes he made it, and then he raised his head and walked proudly round for the next shot, glancing at the female gallery. But usually he missed it, and where another man" might have snapped his fingers or cursed or stamped away, EAR made "a single tiny sideways shake of his head," stepped back, and lowered his cue soundlessly. Only to applaud others' shots would he bump the cue vigorously against the floor.

Robinson felt far more at ease around a pool table than a dinner table. Playing with Benet as his partner one evening, EAR was confronted with a particularly difficult shot. "Kiss it in," Benet said. "Kiss it gently. Kiss it as you would your sister." Robinson answered with a quick smile "You never saw me kiss my sister," he said. Then he made the shot, and beamed with delight. He was in his element, relaxed and almost jovial.

The nightly game became part of Robinson's regimen at Peterborough. He played with boyish eagerness to win, then retired to his room to read a detective story and try to get a decent night's sleep. Robinson admired Dickens and Hardy enormously, but as he grew older he preferred tales about Bulldog Drummond and the work of E. Phillips Oppenheim to more serious fiction. His attitude was that he had immersed himself in the best writing of the past and reached a stage where he could justifiably waste time on thrillers as a distraction from the day's creative labors. He told younger writers not to follow his example. "You haven't time for trash now," he said. "Stick to the good things. Read detective stories when you get rickety."

Nothing relaxed Robinson so much as music, in Peterborough as in New York and Boston. Once a week or so, one of the musicians or composers in residence would arrange a performance. EAR would listen, motionless as a statue, lost in reverie. He was "ear-minded" as opposed to "eye-minded," and whereas music could transport him, he had relatively little understanding of visual art. "I simply don't get anything from pictures," he said, "and I can't understand how anyone else does." EAR's tastes in music were far-ranging. He liked almost everything, from opera and symphony to popular songs. He especially delighted in Gilbert and Sullivan. The policeman's chorus in *The Pirates of Penzance*—"tarantara"—struck him as better than "the last act of *Prometheus Unbound*." One winter, he saw *Ruddigore* six times.

Robinson admired the songs of Stephen Foster for their poetry as well as their music, as in the words of "My Old Kentucky Home." "The day goes by like a shadow o'er the heart." "A few more days for to tote the weary load, / No matter 'twill never be light." What could be better than that? Such a happy union

FIGURE 24.4 Esther Bates, faithful amanuensis and friend.

Source: Esther Willard Bates Collection, University of New Mexico Library.

of melody and language occurred only rarely, Robinson thought. At least eight of his poems were set to music by various composers, Aaron Copland among them. Nonetheless, he told Isaacs that "to put most good verse to music was like 'sticking a pin through a butterfly and fastening it down forever.'"

Among Robinson's enthusiasms were old Scottish and English ballads. These reminded him of the happier days of his childhood, the family singing around the piano. "Auld Lang Syne" always tore him "to pieces." One evening at Mac-Dowell, Margaret Widdemer was scheduled to present an assortment of these ballads, only to find her place at the piano preempted by Elinor Wylie, singing a series of childhood airs. The company was generally enchanted, but Wylie's wistfulness and charm bounced off Robinson "as Cleopatra's would have equally." Summoning up his authority as first citizen, Robinson said, "That's enough, Elinor. We came to hear Margaret." And then, so Widdemer recalled, "somehow—I do not know how—she was not there."

Poet and Curmudgeon

Robinson was in most ways an ideal colonist. He didn't make trouble by entering into short-term sexual liaisons. He didn't segregate himself or join exclusive cliques. And, above all, he worked.

From the mid-1920s on, Robinson wrote nearly all of his poetry during his four-month summer terms at MacDowell. New York and Boston wouldn't do: the cities' distractions and interruptions threw his "poetical machine entirely out of gear." With the long poems of his last dozen years, he worked out the sequence of events before arriving at Peterborough, just "as you do the scenario of a play." The actual writing took place in the Veltin Studio, June through September. During that period he drove himself unmercifully, setting a definite time limit for each project "as binding as a contract."

By the end of September, he was exhausted, and he would recover in relative seclusion in Boston. Esther Bates sent him the typescript of the summer's work for revisions there, but he usually did not make revisions until the winter months in New York. Following this schedule, a long Robinson poem begun in June of one year was ready for publication in the spring of the next.

MacDowell became a home for him as well as a workshop, and he arrived every year with a startling cheerfulness and unrestraint. "He was like a boy who had come home from a long visit among distant relatives," fellow colonist Rollo Walter Brown said. Still, when he arrived at Peterborough in late May or early June, it took him a while to get going. As Bates recalled in *Edwin Arlington Robinson and His Manuscripts*, Robinson was usually bright and cheerful the first day. On the second he felt less optimistic. By the third he would mention that he had not gotten under way. On the fourth he was not so sure but that he ought to go back to the city. When on the fifth he said nothing it signaled that all was well. He had started writing his poem.

Situated faithfully at his studio by nine o'clock each morning, he did not usually set pen to paper until eleven or later. During that time he often read from one of the three books that always lay on his work table: the Bible, a collected Shakespeare, and the dictionary. The Bible provided him with much of the material he fashioned into poems. He used *Antony and Cleopatra* to prepare for each day's work on *Tristram*. He actually *read* the dictionary rather than consulting it as a reference tool, and he advised Bates to do the same. Sometimes, when immersed in one of his long blank-verse narratives, he read Milton's blank verse as a model. Occasionally, he used Ibsen's plays as a stimulus.

At one o'clock Robinson ate the light lunch that had been left at his door and drank some strong black tea. Then he walked back to Colony Hall, dropped off his lunch basket, and wandered slowly back to his studio through the hemlock woods. In the late afternoon between four and six, he did some of his best writing. "I have to get things jostled around until the lines begin to come," he said. As he waited for the jostling, he would sit rocking with intense concentration or walk in and out of the studio, letting the slam of the screen door reverberate. Finally, the outer layers of his consciousness peeled away, and he sat down to commit his day's work to paper.

Robinson could become obsessive in his quest for the one perfect word. "For two weeks," he told a young colonist, "I've gone to my studio every morning after breakfast and stayed until after five o'clock. For two weeks I've searched for one word—and I haven't found it yet." According to a story that has become legendary at MacDowell, a brash young newcomer waxed expansive at dinner about the two thousand words he'd written that day. "How about you, Mr. Robinson?" he asked. "Did you have a good day?"

FIGURE 24.5 Robinson on his way back to Colony Hall with walking stick, thermos, and lunch basket.

Source: Colby College Special Collections.

"This morning," EAR dourly replied, "I removed the hyphen from hell-hound. And this afternoon, I put it back."

However haltingly the words came, Robinson's craftsman's conscience and Yankee work ethic drove him to his studio every morning. He took a certain pride in the conviction that writing poetry constituted hard work—the hardest imaginable, he thought. At the same time, though, Robinson knew there was more to it than simply putting in the hours and sweating out elusive diction. During his last decade, he became convinced that when he wrote, he was "only the agent of something-or-other." He disliked the word "inspiration" for its hackneyed connotations. Yet he believed that "the only intelligent way to consider the artist is as an instrument played upon by something he does not understand." Many were called, and somehow, he had been chosen.

In the process of composing a sonnet, it might be that only one line in fourteen came to him "unaccountably, out of the blue ether." He would have to work like a dog to make the other thirteen nonspontaneous lines "sound as though they had come out of the blue ether, too." At least once, an entire poem—and not a short one—arrived unbidden. Robinson was sitting in a theatre when suddenly he saw "Flammonde" and could hear the poem quite clearly. "All the lines were there, and I only had to write them down." On some days, seemingly with the assistance of a higher power, he produced a prodigious volume of poetry. In the late summer of 1926, Robinson set down a hundred and ten lines of *Tristram* in one day. He was good for nothing for the rest of the week.

Everything was not always perfect at MacDowell. Intruders sometimes disturbed the colonists. Robinson was victimized one summer by a singularly noisy and persistent whippoorwill, which called outside his bedroom window much of the night. In an effort to provide Robinson with a decent night's sleep, playwrights Carty Ranck and Fred Ballard went in search of the bird one moonlit night, a rifle in their hands and murder in their hearts. The offending whippoorwill led them a futile chase over hill and dale, and the would-be bird killers wearily returned without accomplishing their mission. Scarcely had they put the rifle away when the whippoorwill resumed singing outside EAR's window.

The next morning, Robinson confessed that during his sleepless night he had started writing a poem to his damnable visitor. He got no further than the first line, which seemed to say all there was to say. The line was: "Unseen, incessant bird of hell."

Summer tourists, having heard about the colony, occasionally snooped around the grounds and peered through studio windows for glimpses of genius at work. EAR was lying down one afternoon when two women appeared outside his window. Pretending to be asleep, he overheard their conversation.

"Isn't it wonderful?" one of them said.

"Yes," the other replied, "but that man's asleep."

"Yes, but isn't it wonderful?"

He did not mind most visitors, taken singly or a few at a time. But he dreaded the larger groups at Mrs. MacDowell's Sunday-evening suppers. "There's nothing in the world I wouldn't do for Mrs. MacDowell," he told Rollo Walter Brown as they observed a series of cars draw up in front of Hillcrest, "and I like the people I see here. But I don't want to see them all at once."

Frances Wright Turner of Ellsworth, Maine, was different from most of the visitors. An ardent admirer of Robinson, she had written two sonnets to him that were printed in Maine newspapers. On an automobile trip, Turner spent an afternoon exploring Peterborough, where she knew her idol did his summer's work. A townsman pointed her in the direction of some of MacDowell's studios, and she followed a footpath that made its way across a field with a brook running alongside. She was resting for a moment, delighting in the brook, when a tall serious-looking man with a book in his hands approached her.

"Is this the way to the MacDowell Colony?" she asked.

Indeed it was, the man answered, and offered to accompany her the rest of the way. Was there someone in particular she was looking for?

"I don't know anyone there," Turner admitted, "but I'd like to see Edwin Arlington Robinson, the poet. Do you know Mr. Robinson?"

Yes, her guide did. In fact, he knew him as well as anyone at the colony. In response to further questions, he said that Robinson was a retiring sort of fellow, that he never said much, that he spent much of the year in Boston and New York, and that he was a bachelor who didn't understand women very well.

Turner objected that in Robinson's poems he seemed to show a very keen understanding of women, citing "Leonora" and "For a Dead Lady" as examples.

"But she was a *dead* lady," the man remarked with a hint of a smile.

That should have given the game away, but her companion changed the subject to tell her about life at the colony: the musical evenings and the lunch baskets left silently, for example. Only some weeks later did Turner discover that she had been in conversation with the poet himself.

Though courtly and genial with the worshipful Turner, Robinson sometimes flared up when he thought too much was expected of him by his fellow colonists. One young woman, recently arrived at the colony, grew restless at the long silences EAR engendered in the evening.

Finally she exclaimed, "I wish somebody would say something."

"Well," Robinson said quietly. "Say something bright yourself."

Robinson adopted a curmudgeonly attitude toward modernity in general and "modern improvements" in particular. "I am pretty well satisfied," he wrote Witter Bynner in 1921, "that free verse, prohibition, and moving pictures are a triumvirate from hell, armed with the devil's instructions to abolish civilization." He would rather see his own poetry go to hell than see it in moving pictures. He realized, though, that most of the people who enjoyed going to the movies "would suffer horribly if compelled to read" his verse.

Robinson took a dim view of the radio and the airplane as well. In a thousand years, perhaps, people wouldn't read at all but instead "listen in" to the radio, fly around the moon, "and chase each other's wives—as they do now." He would have agreed with the novelist Willa Cather, who proclaimed that the "world broke in two in 1922 or thereabouts," separating itself from "yesterday's seven thousand years." Cather, who shared Robinson's passion for music, thought it quite wrong to sit at home in one's work clothes and turn on the radio to hear the Boston symphony. "Something more than passivity should be expected of the recipient of any such bounty as Brahms," she observed.

Airplanes were "all right for some millionaire who needs a surgical operation," but held no appeal for EAR. He further rebelled against meddling with the clock to institute daylight saving time, a practice that led to MacDowell colonists taking their evening meal in a room flooded with sunshine. "I don't like eating in the middle of the afternoon," EAR muttered.

Robinson knew that the world he'd grown up in was extinct and that he was "a misfit" in the new order of things. But he had little tolerance for most of its supposed improvements. He objected strongly to the dehumanizing aspects of standardization and the assembly line and feared the onset of totalitarian governments, both communist and fascist. He thought behaviorism was nonsense. Ernest Hemingway's *Farewell to Arms* (1929), with its sympathetic portrait of love out of wedlock, showed how the times had "changed things at the house of

Scribner," EAR thought, even if the novel was "clever." He considered Gertrude Stein a fraud whose experimental writing did not deserve to be taken seriously.

Despite such reservations, Robinson was impressed by technological improvements that promised to lead to better communication. He was pleased to receive a letter in New York at three p.m. April 1 that had been postmarked in Los Angeles at ten p.m. March 30. Before long, he predicted, we would carry little machines in our pockets that would let us "talk with anybody anywhere on the face of the earth—and some interesting things will be said."

He understood, too, that the role of lamenting the costs of "progress" had been played by many before him. Nearly two thousand years earlier, he noted, Ovid protested that "newfangled ways and inventions . . . were taking all the joy out of life." But people still read Ovid, and that made him think that poetry would "probably last as long as anything that we have with us now." The thought gave him comfort. Even in his grouchiest complaints against the disturbances of modern life, EAR never lost his perspective, or his saving sense of humor.

Humorist at Large

In good part as a consequence of his depictions of the downtrodden and defeated, the humor in Robinson's poetry has been largely overlooked. Yet humor is abundant in his work, ranging from witty wordplay to gentle joshing of his characters. As he insisted early on, his work was liable to "be a waste of time for any reader who has not a fairly well-developed sense of humor."

Robinson liked to exploit the comic effect in complicated meters. In 1918, he sent Lilla Cabot Perry this example of what could be accomplished in alcaics.

> Although his wish was never to baffle us,
> Hamilton Brown was dolichocephalus:
>   His head reached halfway up to heaven;
> Hamilton's hat was a number seven.

That particular frivolity was composed "in the watches of the night," he told her, "with seven thousand katydids doing their best to encourage me."

It was mostly in his characterizations that Robinson's humor came to light. "His regard for the integrity of his characters," Ellsworth Barnard pointed out, "does not permit us to pity or scorn them, but it allows us to laugh at them." As we do, or should, at John Evereldown, "the skirt-crazed old reprobate" EAR immortalized in one of his earliest Tilbury Town poems. This womanizer is given a name with comic overtones: ever he'll down. Moreover, he is presented in a ballad, like the hero of a medieval tale, although there is nothing heroic about John Evereldown's late-night journeys in pursuit of various females.

Evereldown bemoans his fate in drastic misrepresentations of the truth. He would far rather not make his nightly forays, he insists. He only ventures forth because the women were forever calling him. In the last stanza, he makes an appeal for understanding remarkable for its mock solemnity.

> God knows if I pray to be done with it all,
>   But God is no friend to John Evereldown.
> So the clouds may come and the rain may fall,
> The shadows may creep and the dead men crawl,—
> But I follow the women wherever they call.

It is possible to read this poem straightforwardly, without becoming aware of its humorous content. Otherwise intelligent people have done so. Purgatory, Robinson once observed, must be "the place where all one's jokes are taken seriously."

When the subject matter seemed to invite sarcasm, as in several of Robinson's renderings into English of Greek models, he maintained a jocular tone. Here is "A Mighty Runner":

> The day when Charmus ran with five
> In Arcady, as I'm alive,
> He came in seventh.—"Five and one
> Make seven, you say? It can't be done."—
> Well, if you think it needs a note,
> A friend in a fur overcoat
> Ran with him, crying all the while,
> "You'll beat 'em, Charmus, by a mile!"
> And so he came in seventh.
> Therefore, good Zoilus, you see
> The thing is plain as plain can be;
> And with four more for company,
> He would have been eleventh.

In "Old King Cole," Robinson portrayed the plight of a man whose two sons were "The most insufferable pair / Of scamps that ever cheered the devil." People came to see Old King Cole in order to vent their wrath against these youths, and—possibly—to seek recompense, but he refused to lose his equanimity. He merely smoked his pipe and heard them out.

> He beamed as with an inward light
> That had the Lord's assurance in it;
> And once a man was there all night
> Expecting something every minute.

Constance Rourke, in her landmark book *American Humor* (1931), noted Robinson's mastery of an unobtrusive Yankee irony. "A reticent humor runs through much of [his] poetry," she wrote, "so quietly as to pass unnoticed by many readers, yet producing a constant lighting and relief and change, with a balancing of forces against the impending tragedy."

A good deal of evidence attests to Robinson's humorous nature as a person as well as a poet. "Real solid laughter" was almost an impossibility for him, he acknowledged; he did his laughing in his gray matter. He grinned, however, on the slightest provocation, as at the limericks he invented and sent to friends.

> There was a calm man in Sabattis
> Who shot at a skunk through a lattice.
>   The skunk became dead.
>   "I got him," he said.
> "And now let me see where my hat is."

Sabattis, he explained to Daniel Gregory Mason, was a town in Maine. He had never been there, but felt sure it was a calm place.

The play of language figured in much of Robinson's humor. When he was down and out in New York, Robinson told Chard Smith, he used to sit in Battery Park "with the rest of the bums, watching the ships." He saw a sign there in Italian that sounded so beautiful that he thought it must be a quotation from Dante. It read, "Non sputari sui pavimento." Similarly, he was charmed by J. L. Lowes's account of a query supposedly uttered by a small boy in bed, a sentence that supposedly broke all grammatical rules by ending with no fewer than five prepositions: "What did you bring this book that I don't want to be read to out of up for?"

Rather than gamble on gifts they might not want, Robinson often sent small sums of money to his nieces at Christmas. These came with "astringent asides," Richard Cary noted. "Here is a microscopic remembrance for you. You can't buy a motor car with it, but you might be able to get something nourishing for the cat." "Here is another Christmas card with which you may buy rum and jewels."

Robinson was fond of anecdotes that poked fun at his Scottish heritage, "I suppose you heard of the seamen's fund collected on the ocean steamer," he wrote Laura Richards. "'It amounts,' said the purser, 'to the rather unusual sum of fifty seven dollars and three cents. Perhaps there is a Scotchman on board.'" Did Mrs. Richards know "about the Scotchman who spilled a bottle of iodine and then cut his finger"? Was Tom Perry aware of "Dr. McCosh's proof that Shakespeare was at least partly a Scotchman"? "Look at the mon's work," McCosh said.

Robinson had a happy knack for the brief incisive comment. When May Sinclair visited the United States in the 1920s, EAR attended a dinner party in her honor at the home of Lewis and Edith Isaacs. A question then going the rounds was posed for the guests: "If you knew that by pressing a button you could kill a mandarin in China and get twenty thousand dollars and never be found out, what would you do?" The literary folk at table produced a dozen gay answers, Edith Isaacs recalled. When it was EAR's turn, he was busily stirring his after-dinner coffee, and gave his answer without looking up: "I'm on my second mandarin already."

Robinson showed his talent for the perfect putdown in a well-remembered incident at the MacDowell Colony. One evening at twilight, a troubled young poet lay on the grass outside the entrance to Colony Hall, presumably in despair and very much on display. Robinson and the other colonists gazed at the suffering youth for a long time. Finally, EAR spoke. "The ants'll get him," he said.

Frederika Beatty, another young writer at MacDowell, told Robinson one morning that she was sleeping in the room once occupied by a famous and beautiful lyric poet whose wraith had visited her during the night. "How did she manifest her presence?" EAR asked, in all apparent seriousness.

"I felt a chill go through me," Beatty answered.

"No," Robinson said at once, "wrong temperature!"

Another pithy comment came from a taciturn New Englander in a story EAR told Beatty. Robinson was, at the time, drinking more coffee than was good for him, and that reminded him of the Vermont man who drank twenty cups a day. "Oh, my," a summer visitor from the city asked him, "don't you find that it keeps you awake?"

"It helps," said the Vermonter.

Reserved as he usually was, Robinson enjoyed telling stories and was good at it. As a story was swimming into his consciousness, Ranck recalled, "his eyes would twinkle, his moustache would twitch, and out [it] would come." One such story involved a starving young artist who needed a thousand dollars. He went to a wealthy older man who refused him on the grounds that he had no interest in artists or their enterprises. Later, even more desperate, the artist tried again.

"I've got to have the money," he told the older man, "and you've got it to lend. Why not let me have it?"

"I'll tell you what I'll do," the rich man responded. "I have one glass eye, and if you can tell me which one it is, I'll lend you the thousand dollars."

The young artist studied his eyes with great concentration. "Your right eye is the glass eye," he finally said.

"Correct," the older man admitted. "But what made you think so?"

"Well," the artist replied, "I thought your right eye looked just the least bit more sympathetic."

Some of Robinson's stories bordered on the risqué. He told about the unmarried couple who drove out into the country for "a sporting weekend." They stopped at a farmhouse and asked the farmer if he could put them up for the night.

FIGURE 24.6 William Gropper's drawing of Robinson in his ubiquitous rocking chair.

Source: In House Photo.

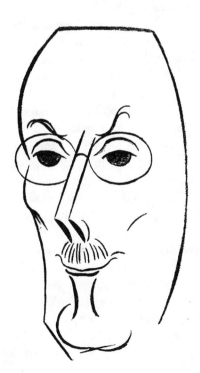

FIGURE 24.7 Eva Herrmann's sketch catches a trace of EAR's humor.

Source: In House Photo.

"You two married?" the farmer wanted to know.

"Of course," said the man.

"Could I see your marriage license?"

"Certainly," the man said, and handed the farmer a dog license.

The couple went upstairs and were unpacking when the farmer knocked at the door loudly. "If you ain't done it," he said through the door, "don't do it. This ain't fer it."

Another favorite Robinson story had to do with the cowboy who ordered a "brushbroom cocktail" at a saloon. The bartender mixed a lethal combination of everything alcoholic he could find, poured out the drink, and stood up a brushbroom beside it. The cowboy tossed down the cocktail, fell writhing on the sawdust floor, got up, brushed himself off, and left.

Women, Especially Sparhawk

A circle of women admirers hovered around Robinson at the Mac-Dowell Colony. "Some of them loved him as if he were a god," Rollo Walter Brown observed. "Some seemed only to be moved by the maternal instinct to make him bodily more comfortable." EAR exhibited a vulnerability surprising in the light of his developing eminence. When she spoke to Robinson the poet, Kathryn White Ryan commented, she felt she was addressing a strong confident person. But to Robinson the man, she spoke her words "carefully as if to a child and with the same search for simplicity, so as to be comprehended and not too easily wound. . . . There was a quality of stunned white helplessness, a doe-like questioning in his big brown eyes, the manner of a child just off the normal that you had to protect."

His female companions at breakfast and dinner were forever on the alert to protect him and to satisfy his needs. As he silently stared around the table, his brow wrinkled in frustration, they were eager to assist. Would he like the bread? The butter? The salt? Their undivided attention? Sometimes, the adoration could embarrass him. A new colonist, female, was sitting at breakfast with Nancy Byrd Turner when Robinson appeared. Turner introduced him, and the newcomer could not contain herself. "Robinson?" she said. "Not E. A. Robinson—not *the* Mr. Robinson?" After a long silence, EAR spoke. "*A* Mr. Robinson," he said.

In *Where the Light Falls*, Chard Powers Smith maintained that the half a dozen or so women devotees of a certain age who shared his table were all in love with Robinson and that individually each of them coveted the slightest signal from him as an indication that he shared her feelings. Smith referred to them as EAR's "harem," a word Esther Bates objected to for its unpleasant connotations.

As best he could manage it, Robinson treated his coterie with chivalry. On a weekend afternoon, he and Nancy Byrd Turner were dragooned into taking an automobile ride. Sitting in the back seat, Turner confessed to feeling chilly. Robinson, all solicitude, saw to it that the windows were closed and proposed that she turn up her collar. Then, Turner recalled, he "made a dive at something on the floor and came up with what he considered a . . . solution of the difficulty, a big, greasy cloth that had done good work, apparently, on the car's innards." "Here, this will do," he said, and cast the filthy cloth around her neck. There was nothing to do but wear it, Turner decided. They continued their drive, EAR "looking fierce" at her side.

Robinson's closest friendships were with men—with Burnham and Betts, Ledoux and Isaacs, Pope and Saben and Ranck. Yet as Ridgely Torrence pointed out in his introduction to EAR's *Selected Letters*, he was "most at his ease in writing to women," particularly older women of accomplishment and stature such as Edith Brower, Lilla Cabot Perry, and Laura Richards. In his correspondence with Mrs. Richards, Torrence commented, Robinson discoursed entertainingly on literature and politics, digging up "old sparking gayeties and slyly contriv[ing] new ones, tossing up the bright fancies before her with the skill of the juggler performing for the madonna."

On the subject of sex, however, he maintained a discreet silence in correspondence as in person. Robinson read Freud, of course, as almost all educated people did in the 1920s, and he read Havelock Ellis as well. But he thought such matters were better read about than talked about.

When Smith brashly suggested to Robinson that an affair might have a therapeutic effect on his well-being and enhance the realism of his verse, Smith "felt the shadow of the guillotine" in the stony silence that followed. Though he was attracted to more than one of the younger female colonists—he stared so at the beautiful sculptress Bashka Paeff when she first crossed the dining room that Arthur Nevin had to kick him under the table—Robinson shied away from physical contact. Jean Gorman, Herbert's flirtatious and attractive wife, was confident that she could break down Robinson's reserve. One evening after dinner, when he was seated in a comfortable chair, she sat down on his knee. He said nothing, neither did he stir. After a time, she peeked around at him. Nothing. At last she slid off his knee and walked away, looking "like a disgruntled cat." Another young woman, who went to see him in his studio, sensed an aura of quietude around him "like a rope of fire."

Nonetheless, almost everyone at the MacDowell Colony thought that the love affairs in Robinson's verse were drawn from his own experience. Rumors circulated as to the identity of the women involved. These annoyed him. "Good Lord," he said to Ranck, "can't they credit poets with imagination enough to visualize the feelings of others without having experienced them ourselves?" One evening, when a woman colonist speculated about the identity of the dark lady in Shakespeare's sonnets, EAR objected that it was not at all necessary that there should have been an actual dark lady. "Anyone can invent a dark lady," he said, and proved it by cranking out a sonnet, "Another Dark Lady," in twenty minutes.

A number of women colonists became emotionally committed to him through the years. Among them was Elizabeth Marsh, playwright and librarian. Marsh was a gentle, charming, and appealingly helpless Southern belle, manifestly wellborn and lovely to look at. On first meeting Robinson, she thought she had never seen a man with so striking a face. EAR liked her and relied on her for a sensitive, intuitive understanding of his poetry in process. Briefly, before the assignment was taken by Esther Bates, Marsh served as typist of his manuscripts. After Robinson's death, she pleaded for possession of the Bible he kept in the Veltin Studio. Ruth Nivison was disposed to let her have it. "From the note she wrote me," she told Lewis Isaacs, "I should say the girl [was] hard hit—though I don't know to what extent the feeling was reciprocated."

By far the closest and longest-standing relationship Robinson forged at Mac-Dowell—one that has been largely ignored—involved him and the talented painter Elizabeth Sparhawk-Jones (1885–1968). Sparhawk-Jones (or Sparhawk, as EAR learned to call her) came to the colony for the first time in the summer of 1922 and immediately and quite openly fell in love with Robinson.

Seeing them together in Colony Hall, a casual observer would have thought them temperamentally unsuited: Robinson withdrawn and silent, Sparhawk-Jones given to lively conversation and bursts of laughter. Yet despite these appearances, as Sparhawk-Jones's biographer Barbara Lehman Smith points out, the painter and the poet were kindred spirits. Sixteen years younger than Robinson, Sparhawk-Jones had suffered through her own extended period of darkness. She sensed the power of his stillness, felt bound to him in a love of the spirit, and was intelligent enough not to demand any overt show of reciprocal feeling from him.

The other women at the colony, even those who had their own affection for Robinson, respected "the simple dignity" of Sparhawk-Jones's devotion and EAR's patent acceptance of its depth and sincerity. In her memoir, Margaret Widdemer presents a persuasive version of the relationship, discreetly omitting Sparhawk-Jones's name. At MacDowell, she wrote, "there was one lady who . . . in a very nice way . . . made a career of being in love with [Robinson]. . . . She was a colonist off and on for years, and everybody liked her; she was cheerful to gaiety, well-bred and friendly, and an excellent raconteuse. She was frank in an understood sort of way to the effect that she loved him, without any expectation of return, for long years." She spoke of her love for him as matter-of-factly as she admitted "her liking for seed-pearl earrings and blueberries."

Robinson understood the situation and welcomed Sparhawk-Jones's company. She left a basket of fruit at his studio, most mornings. He invited her to share lunch once a week, the only person so honored. There was "no question of any scandal." She was a lady and he a gentleman "by old-fashioned standards. 'She didn't hunt him; he didn't flee her. He was aware, courteous, probably a little obliged, and granted her his society exactly as a woman might a man who had loved her without return all his life." He gave her, in other words, "all he *could* give."

Elizabeth Sparhawk-Jones was the daughter of the Reverend John Sparhawk-Jones, pastor of Calvary Presbyterian Church in Philadelphia and a man of considerable eminence. Despite their status as clergyman's children, Elizabeth and her sister Margaret were given free rein. They were not even required to attend Sunday school. Elizabeth showed a remarkable talent for drawing when she was but seven years old, and her mother encouraged her to pursue a career in art.

Elizabeth began her studies at the Pennsylvania Academy of the Fine Arts while still a teenager, under the mentorship of the flamboyant William Merritt Chase. With his handlebar mustache and beard "and palette on his thumb and gold stick, all the paraphernalia," Chase would come down from New York to give weekly criticism to the art students working from life. "He didn't like *anything*," Sparhawk-Jones remembered, but he did like the paintings she was doing of Rittenhouse Square and children and department stores.

She won prizes for her work, and in 1906, at the age of twenty-one, was awarded the academy's coveted traveling scholarship for two years of study in Europe. At this stage, her parents balked. It was one thing to permit Elizabeth to skip Sunday school and attend the Pennsylvania Academy instead of going to college and quite another to let her disappear to Europe for an extended period with no guidance whatever. She turned down the scholarship and stayed at home.

The family fortunes declined as Sparhawk-Jones's father, like Robinson's before him, made a series of bad investments. After he died in 1910, Elizabeth and her mother and sister were compelled to sell their substantial home and relocate to a boarding house. Then, in 1913, the year of the famous Armory Show, her sister Margaret married and moved out. (Margaret's son, Andrew Turnbull, wrote biographies of Thomas Wolfe and F. Scott Fitzgerald.) Left as sole companion to her widowed and increasingly demanding mother, Elizabeth collapsed into severe depression, and for three years she was intermittently hospitalized and entirely unable to paint. When she began to recover in 1916, she immersed herself in art. Painting, she wrote a friend, "is how religion possesses itself in me." She felt called to painting as Robinson was to poetry.

Sparhawk-Jones painted well into her sixties. Her work was acquired by the Metropolitan Museum of Art, the Museum of Modern Art, and the Art Institute of Chicago, among others, and shown in exhibitions at the Whitney Museum, the Brooklyn Museum, and the Corcoran Gallery. She "is first of all an emotional painter," *American Artist* commented in 1944. "Her art is spiritual; her brush answers inner urges, it is a subconscious voice, a yearning voice that strives to translate deep meanings into the language of paint."

This, then, was the woman who chose to worship and adore Robinson. In his way, EAR made occasional gestures of appreciation and understanding in

FIGURE 24.8 The painter Elizabeth
Sparhawk-Jones, who loved Robinson all
her days.

Source: Pennsylvania Academy of the Fine Arts,
Philadelphia. Henry D. Gilpin Fund.

return. One day during their Veltin Studio lunch, he thrilled her by interrupt-
ing a long silence with the remark: "The less I say, the more I feel."

As Sparhawk-Jones saw it, Robinson paid her tribute beyond measure in his
portrayal of Isolt of Brittany in *Tristram*: not Tristram's great love Isolt of Ireland, but "Isolt of the white hands" and grey eyes who was willing to love Tristram without reservation despite knowing that his heart belonged to another.
The poem ends with Isolt searching the horizon for a ship that she knows will
not come. She would have been "the world / And heaven to Tristram," but was
nothing to him.

Devastated by Robinson's death in 1935, Sparhawk-Jones created a suite of
four paintings as an emotional response. The first was called *Mourners* and
the remaining three *A Poet's Burial*, Nos. *1*, *2*, and *3*. These formed the high-
light of her show at the Frank Rehn Gallery in April 1937. The entire series was
"painted with intense feeling," the *New York Times* commented. The fantastic
human drama of *A Poet's Burial, No. 1* unfolded beneath a sky that reminded
the reviewer of El Greco and of the witches in Albert Pinkham Ryder's *Macbeth*.
Fillmore saw the show, and also invoked El Greco in describing Sparhawk-
Jones's memorial paintings. They had "the same rent and tortured skies, painted
in the same brilliant reds and blues, and the figures express[ed] the same single
emotion, [except that] here it is not religious contemplation, but grief so overwhelming that it becomes ecstatic."

Marsden Hartley, like EAR a Maine man and after Robinson's death a frequent
correspondent of Sparhawk-Jones, also attended the exhibition at the Rehn gallery. He emerged with the sense that she was at her best in the representation of
the tragic spirit, where "a peculiar electricity" pervaded the canvas.

In her letters to Hartley, Sparhawk-Jones gave free expression to her passionate feelings for Robinson. In August 1938, she attended a reunion of artists who had worked at MacDowell over the years. Late that night, she wrote Hartley about the powerful sense of loss that overtook her. "I spent a part of the evening in the house in which I lived when I was alive on earth with [Robinson]. I shall never be alive that way again. I met my lost self everywhere tonight, at the doors of that house, in the barn, on the porch, beside the chairs. I think it is because so little was spoken by either of us for fifteen years that the landscape of the spirit is so open for me—not a fence anywhere as if all one had to do was to walk forward and forward."

During Robinson's lifetime, of course, she had been keenly aware of the barriers he erected around himself. As she told Smith, "E. A. locked the door on the inside, threw the key out the window, and thereafter couldn't reach it to let himself out." The protection gave him the space he needed to do his work. If she were actually to meet his ghost, she said, she would apologize to him for having disturbed him with her love.

In another letter to Hartley, Sparhawk-Jones attempted to convey the force of the poet's personality in an extensive passage:

Mr. Robinson could do things with his feelings to people. His coldness was like nothing I have ever met with in a human being. I have faced four people when he passed back of me, and seen the intense effect his anger had on them when it was not directed at them—[n]or did they understand the why, his state of mind. A moment of sympathy with him drew one out of oneself onto the threshold of a mystic union. A dangerous man, because of his charm, a simple man, a very real man never acting parts. A sensitive man who could feel eyes he did not see and cover his eyes from the look. He could punish and then suffer more than he punished—and he was always clearly in the right in the high realm of his personal values. His was no case of a flighty temperament; his nature produced subtle dramas day by day with many who surrounded him. It must sometimes have been tiresome, but he was of a different kind, quite simply that, and those who traveled the road along with him for a time without jealousy know what a man can be—and the mystery of communication he possesses. The ultimate can trace through the air for a minute.

These observations reveal Sparhawk-Jones's abiding spiritual love while uncovering much about Robinson. His "coldness" never met with in anyone else, for instance, and her association of this with his fiercely repressed anger. His "never acting parts" as he never allowed himself to "act out." Her suggestion that everyday life for him was made up of "subtle," unacknowledged dramas with others, most of whom had no idea what was going on. A man of a different kind. Elizabeth Sparhawk-Jones manifestly believed that she shared a communion with this extraordinarily "rare and beautiful person": moments when the ultimate traced through the air.

As Robinson grew older, the prospect of marriage began to seem less unthinkable to him. "Perhaps I ought to get married," he would say. "There comes a time in every man's life when he wants a home to creep into," he wrote Isaacs in a somewhat ambiguous endorsement of matrimony. If his health had not failed, Fillmore believed, Robinson might well have made a convenient match with a cultured and well-do-do woman close to his own age, providing a pleasant companionship for the last years.

Militating against this thought, however, was his conviction that marriage would interfere with his work. "If I had been happily married," he said to Ranck, "I might never have written any poetry at all." In a conversation with Mrs. George Pierce Baker, he insisted that Josephine Preston Peabody should never have married, for her early work was much better than that she produced after marrying Lionel Marks.

"But she wanted to write of life," Christina Baker answered, "and so had to experience love and motherhood."

Robinson shrank back in his chair. "No, no," he exclaimed. "A poet must stand in an alcove and watch life go by."

Visitors: French and Scott

A menacing visitor in the person of Joseph Lewis French invaded the MacDowell Colony on Friday, September 9, 1927.

Through the years Robinson and Hagedorn kept in touch on the subject of French, who was becoming increasingly paranoid with age. "Poor old French rang me up the other day—the first time in nearly two years," EAR reported in December 1925, "informing me to my great surprise that I had instigated two men on The Evening Post (I don't know even one) to have him arrested." French seemed a little worse than ever. Robinson hung up on him.

Eighteen months later, in the middle of August 1927, he received a threatening letter from French. "The poor devil still believes that I have reported him to the police, and apparently his delusions are incurable," Robinson wrote Hagedorn. French said that he was only a few jumps ahead of the law but that he intended to "get" Robinson before he himself was captured. EAR was understandably apprehensive when, three weeks later, the demented French—who was in possession, he made it known, of a revolver—showed up unannounced at MacDowell.

French was directed to EAR's studio by a newcomer to the colony. When Fillmore, who knew about French and his letter, heard this news, he immediately ran to the Veltin Studio, the new colonist at his heels. They found Robinson and French inside, both "standing up and looking rather strained."

Fillmore invented a phone call for Robinson to break up the confrontation. "The fellow said he'd call you at Colony Hall at six o'clock," he told EAR, "and it's ten minutes of six now."

"I'll come along in a few minutes," Robinson said.

"All right," Fillmore replied. "We'll walk slowly and you catch up with us."

Soon enough Robinson caught up with them, his visitor trailing behind.

"That's French, isn't it?" Fillmore asked.

"Yes, but you needn't be concerned. He's not going to do anything." As long as he gave French money, Robinson explained, the "poor fellow" would not shoot him. French was going to come back in the morning for the money, and he promised to leave on the early afternoon train.

All day Saturday, Emil Tonieri, MacDowell's caretaker, hovered in the vicinity of Veltin Studio. French came, collected his money, and went away. But had he really left? After dinner on Saturday evening, Fillmore telephoned the tavern where French was staying and learned that he had not checked out. When he went up to EAR's room with the news, the poet slumped over, and would say nothing for fifteen minutes. Fillmore wanted him to pack up and go to visit the Perrys in Hancock, but Robinson could not be budged. He did agree, however, to stay inside Colony Hall on Sunday, in case French should put in another appearance. At midday the manager of the tavern called to ask if anyone at the colony knew about a man named French, who had absconded without paying his bill.

Upon hearing about the threatening letter and the uninvited visit, Isaacs urged EAR to take action to have French safely put away. Robinson refused. He could not forget that French was a pathological case. "Sooner or later I shall have to have a row with him, I suppose," he wrote Isaacs. "His coming down here was, as you say, about the last straw. I hope to dismiss him peaceably; if not, I may have to ask for assistance." Some time later, he sent Isaacs his "incoherent and irrational and nasty" letters from French for possible use in an emergency.

As Robinson supposed, he was not quit of French. In a letter to the editor of *Commonweal* of February 1932, French fired both barrels in an attack on EAR's poetry. He had written little worth reading since "Captain Craig" thirty years before, French said, and the bulk of his writing consisted of "rather bald prose." This outburst did not prevent French from importuning EAR for money.

As MacDowell's most established literary figure, Robinson was repeatedly asked to read the work of younger writers. He was quick to recognize talent, and to encourage it. Thus he intervened with Mrs. MacDowell to allow young Maxwell Bodenheim to extend his stay at the colony one summer, despite his revulsion toward Bodenheim's rather flashy style of life. In the face of Bodenheim's obvious ability and prodigious energy for work, EAR was willing to set aside a measure of personal dislike.

One night in Colony Hall, Bodenheim criticized Robinson's poetry amid a group of colonists. "Your colors are all grays and blacks," he said.

Robinson's eyes flashed. "Fast colors," he responded, "guaranteed not to fade."

Winfield Townley Scott, who visited EAR at Peterborough on August 22, 1929, combined a precocious gift for poetry with his fervent enthusiasm for Robinson's work. The nineteen-year-old Scott, who went on to achieve an impressive career as poet and essayist, composed "a largely ecstatic essay" about Robinson for an undergraduate magazine at Brown University. He brashly wrote EAR at the MacDowell Colony, offering to call on him and show him the essay. Robinson agreed, and young Scott drove the seventy miles to Peterborough from his summer home in Haverhill, Massachusetts, to see the great man.

Scott was so excited at the prospect of meeting Robinson that he skipped lunch and arrived at the colony hungry. Rollo Walter Brown showed him the way to the Veltin Studio, where Scott gathered up the load of books and manuscripts he had brought along and went inside for the afternoon of his young life. It was a warm day, but the two of them talked on either side of a small fire burning in the fireplace, EAR in his customary rocker. Robinson began to eat his lunch from the picnic basket. "They've sent me more than I can eat," he said, and scraped two pieces of chicken off his sandwich and threw them into the fire. "Burning up food," he said.

Scott had seen pictures of Robinson, but was unprepared for striking features met with in the flesh: the large brown eyes cast downward, preoccupied, and the long, slender, beautiful, masculine hands. Noting the pile of books Scott had brought with him, Robinson agreed to sign them. Some people, he said, his eyes brightening with amusement, had come to him as if "their one desire in life was to have [him] autograph their books. And then . . . they'd sold 'em for two or three dollars more the next week."

After a time, the nineteen-year-old decided to ask what was on his mind. "Have you any particular message for young men who want to be poets?"

FIGURE 24.9 Winfield Townley Scott, a young poet inspired by Robinson.

Source: In House Photo.

"Well, no," Robinson said, chuckling. "If you've got yourself into that trap there's nothing I or anyone else can say to get you out."

"People say a lot of things, among them that poets don't earn money."

"If you keep after it for forty years," EAR said, "you may have about half as much as a good carpenter." He warned against journalism. "It hurts a man's style, every time—even Kipling's." Teaching might be all right, though, with its three months' vacation. "You've got to get money from some other source, whether you steal it or inherit it." Robinson chewed some of his sandwich, grinned, and offered another alternative. "Then there's getting married," he said.

When EAR finished eating and tossing bits of sandwich into the fire, Scott fetched out the essay he'd written about him and read it aloud. A few times, Robinson interrupted with a correction. When Scott referred to an early sonnet as "one of Robinson's few personal utterances," he immediately objected. "Don't go looking for me in my poetry, because you won't find me. . . . Of course, the mood, the thought, but you won't find me."

Afterward, Robinson autographed the books Scott had brought with him, certain that his visitor would not sell them the next week, or any next week. When it was time for Scott to leave, EAR stood outside his car for a moment, then peered in through the window to shake hands. He left Scott with his usual mantra: "Don't publish a book until you're thirty. Thirty's time enough." He'd had a good time talking with him, EAR added. Then, "lunch basket in one hand, trailing his stick with the other, he paused at the [Colony] Hall door, spat, and went slowly in." Scott drove back to Haverhill, starving and inspired.

25

Recognition and Its Consequences

The Triumph of Tristram

In 1925 as in 1922, Robinson enjoyed a springtime of recognition. Word of his second Pulitzer Prize, for *The Man Who Died Twice*, reached him as he was eating breakfast May 2. On the strength of it, he had another cup of coffee. In June he traveled to Maine to accept a Litt. D. from Bowdoin College and to visit friends and family in Gardiner. Bowdoin appealed to him as the college closest to his roots. His brother Dean studied there, and Harry Smith and Seth Pope. Still, he was reluctant to abandon the Veltin Studio for the ceremony. "After this I'll try to stay undoctored," he told Louis Ledoux, and he kept his word. By 1933, EAR wrote Laura Richards, he had "turned down five [honorary degrees], and expect to turn down several more."

Bowdoin saluted Robinson as a "son of Maine, brought up by the shores of the lovely Kennebec; recognized at home and abroad as without a living peer in his own special field of verse." As he sheepishly remarked, "they made quite a fuss over me."

Afterward, he stayed with his niece Ruth in Gardiner. That gave him the opportunity to see Emma, who had returned home to live with Ruth and her family. On Saturday, June 20, they went to Capitol Island, where EAR's grand-nephews, young David and Billy, were staying. Emma made one of her "superior clam chowders," and after supper the two of them walked down to the cottage on the cliff where she and Herman had once become engaged. Later that night, the grownups played poker "for [Uncle Win's] amusement," and a concoction featuring homemade gin was served. EAR partook, copiously. "I didn't expect to be kept up by my family, gambling and drinking," he remarked. Emma was not amused and reminded Win in private how badly his mother would have felt to lose all three of her sons to addiction. Thereafter, Win wrote her, he never took another drink.

On their way back to Gardiner the following day, the group paid a visit to Head Tide. Win looked through the windows—no one was home—and was pleased to find the house where he'd been born still in good condition. Then they paid the visit to EAR's ancient cousins, Clara and Oakes Palmer, that he'd asked Ruth to organize in advance. Cousin Clara, mindful of the Robinson family's history, suggested to Win that he had redeemed its losses by his contribution to poetry. "I don't know if my contribution is as great as Herman's is, in his three daughters," he responded.

The following day, Robinson returned to the MacDowell Colony. The trip to Maine made him feel melancholy. Everything seemed strange and at the same time familiar. He was glad he'd gone and glad to be back in Peterborough, where he belonged. He never saw Gardiner again.

During the mid-1920s Robinson's star was in its ascendancy. Ben Ray Redman, in *Edwin Arlington Robinson* (1926), his contribution to the Modern American Writers series, hailed him as "a biographer of souls . . . bound to humanity by the dual bond of sympathy and humor." Robinson was "less egocentric and less subjective than any other poet of his generation," yet had given his readers "a whole world of his making." Redman concluded by proclaiming him "the greatest poet this country has yet produced."

That was going too far, the *New York Times* commented in its review, but conceded that EAR was nonetheless "the superman among living American poets," superior to Lindsay and Frost and Masters and Pound and Sandburg. Edmund Wilson, in the same year, ranked Robinson with T. S. Eliot as the finest American poets. Robinson had "the authentic lyric gift and the artist's mastery of it," he wrote. He was "the last and, artistically (leaving the happiest flashes of Emerson aside), the most important of the New England poets."

Curiously enough, the most enthusiastic academic advocate of Robinson's poetry emerged at the University of Paris, in the person of Professor Charles Cestre. Cestre came to the United States in the fall of 1925 to deliver a series of six laudatory lectures on Robinson's work at Bryn Mawr. In due course, the lectures were printed in a 1930 book, *An Introduction to Edwin Arlington Robinson*. Written in vague and rather florid prose, the book shows little insight in its interpretations of individual poems. EAR read the galley proofs—the book was brought out by Macmillan in English translation—and asked Cestre to make two "rather important" corrections where the Frenchman totally misunderstood what was going on in *The Man Who Died Twice* (1924) and *Cavender's House* (1929). Robinson could hardly object, however, to Cestre's conclusion that he was no less than "a modern classic." As he wrote Perry, "It is pleasant when a furriner likes one's work and says so."

When Robinson arrived at the Veltin Studio in the summer of 1925, he found Tristram waiting for him "with a club in one hand and . . . a pencil in the other." EAR "succumbed to him," after fighting him off for several years. He got down 550 lines in the week before decamping for Maine and by the end of September had 2,700 lines in first draft. After that, his sole desire was to "get into a hole and hide for a while, and not talk to anybody, and incidentally sleep until noon."

Robinson continued work on *Tristram*, the longest of his poems, throughout the following summer. He found it particularly hard to dispose of Tristram and Isolt in the climactic scenes. "I have already killed them three times," he told Esther Bates, "but they are like cats with nine lives, and I may have to kill them nine times." In September 1926, the poem was finally completed at 4,400 lines, and Robinson was too tired to know if it was any good—or if he could ever write another line of verse, for that matter.

In *Tristram*, Robinson said, he was merely telling a story adapted from an old legend. Unlike *Merlin* and *Lancelot*, the poem had no symbolic significance, no suggestion of worlds collapsing in combat, no metaphysics, no quests for the Grail or the Light. "We have simply two people in love," as Mark Van Doren put it. The "key and color" of the poem differed from anything else Robinson ever wrote. *Tristram* was "all about love," which was what people old and young seemed to want.

He wrote the poem, at least in part, Robinson said, because he was "getting a little tired of hearing about [his] New England reticence." "You know," he said to Esther Bates, "this sort of thing happens every day," and then, to her look of inquiry, added, "I mean, people love the way Tristram and Isolt were supposed to."

For Tristram and Isolt of Ireland, love was all. They discourse on the subject for over four hundred lines, challenging credibility and the reader's attention. "Passion is vaporized into speech," as Ellsworth Barnard put it, "and . . . we begin to question whether a love so much talked about but so rarely evident in real action is as overpowering as it is declared to be." The action of the poem takes place offstage, mostly, for Robinson was primarily interested in the interior lives of his characters. So he "adapted" the legend that had come down from Malory, deleting bloody combat and also, significantly, doing away with the love potion that was supposed to have engendered the disastrous love of Tristram and Isolt. He wanted to tell the story instead "of what might have happened to human beings in those circumstances, without their wits and wiles having been taken away by some impossible and wholly superfluous concoction."

Once again, as in *Lancelot*, EAR took an adulterous love affair as his basic subject matter. Tristram and Isolt fall in love as he performs the mission of delivering her to become the bride of King Mark of Cornwall. When she is married, the lovers' eventual fate is sealed: they must live, and die, of love. No narcotic encouragement is required.

In another departure from previous versions of the medieval romance, Robinson converted Isolt of the White Hands into a significant character. He framed the tempestuous and tragic story of Tristram and Isolt of Ireland (so powerfully evoked in Wagner's *Liebestod*) by the quieter and more persuasive tale of the lesser Isolt and her unrequited love. The other Isolt becomes, at the end, the most persuasive character in the poem. Even King Mark, who had wrongly married Isolt without winning her love, is transformed from the villain of the piece into a bewildered and almost sympathetic figure. These characters are not cardboard figures or automatons, yet the poem as a whole lacks conviction.

In retrospect, it seems incredible that *Tristram*, despite its excessive length and talkiness, should have caught the public fancy and outsold any other book of Robinson's ten times over. Its extraordinary success owed less to artistic merit than to the literary marketplace. The Literary Guild had just been established to send a book each month to its subscribers. Carl Van Doren, who was appointed editor, decided that for its third selection the guild should "surprise the public" and establish its "reputation for taste and courage." He thought *Tristram* would do the job, and associate editors Joseph Wood Krutch and Elinor Wylie agreed. Robinson's Arthurian romance was chosen as the May 1927 selection of the Literary Guild.

On the strength of his two Pulitzers and burgeoning reputation, Robinson was beginning to come into his own as a literary property. And after sticking with Robinson for more than a decade of unrewarding sales, his publishers were reluctant to share the benefits with interlopers. When the Literary Guild took *Tristram*, Macmillan took two actions in retaliation. They courted Robinson by sending him a check for $1,000 in advance of royalties. And they lowered the price of the book to match the guild's discounted price. Inasmuch as the guild depended on discounts earned through buying in bulk to attract members, this action might well have scotched the chances for *Tristram*. The new book club was equal to the challenge. To make purchasing Robinson's poem more appealing, they commissioned the poet Mark Van Doren, Carl's brother, to write—in three weeks!—a monograph about Robinson and his work that would be sent free to subscribers along with *Tristram*.

The guild then put its promotional powers to work. They hired Broadway's Little Theatre for May 8, 1927, the Sunday nearest publication date, with the idea that sections of the poem might be read to an assemblage of Robinson's friends and admirers, as well as influential journalists. To build the house, letters went out to sixty "sponsors" announcing the event. The sponsors were made up of a mixture of those in New York's literary and philanthropic communities. Craven Langstroth Betts, EAR's friend from his bohemian days in New York, was among them, and so was the widow of railroad magnate E. H. Harriman. The Kermit Roosevelts were included, as was Edna St. Vincent Millay.

Each sponsor was asked to suggest still others who should be invited: people "who would naturally be the first to appreciate the poem, and whose appreciation and enthusiasm going with them out of the theatre will be the kind to kindle an interest in the poem in others." Edith Isaacs took on the duties of corresponding with the sponsors and was further instrumental in persuading the well-known actress Eleanor Robson (Mrs. August Belmont) to read from the poem, thereby assuring press attention.

FIGURE 25.1 Writer Carl Van Doren, who orchestrated the Literary Guild *Tristram* campaign.

Source: Picture Collection, New York Public Library.

Robinson would have nothing to do with planning for the event. On the evening itself, he declined a dinner invitation and had to be dragged to the theater where, to his surprise, every seat was filled. Rather than show himself to the audience, EAR stayed in the theater's lounge during Eleanor Robson's reading and words of praise—"the finest Tristram poem in the English language"—from Carl Van Doren. But when it was over, he mingled with the guests at a reception, flushed with pleasure as all of those "distinguished in New York in arts and letters and in social life" congratulated him.

The show went off rather well, EAR wrote Tom Perry in Boston. "There were about 600 people, and they didn't cough." Still, he worried about the "unwholesome amount of publicity" the poem was generating. He felt certain that the guild's "literary lobbyism" would stimulate objections. "You must expect soon to see some brickbats thrown at Tristram, and I only hope they don't knock him down," he wrote Laura Fraser.

Actually, most of the reviews were highly favorable. The *New York Times* ranked Robinson's first among all modern versions of the ancient tale. B. K. Hart in the *Providence Journal* and Herbert Gorman in *The Bookman* went so far as to call *Tristram* the best long poem ever written by an American. More judicious and balanced praise came from Conrad Aiken. On the one hand, Aiken admired Robinson's capacity to make "the thing remarkably his own." His Arthurian characters were "modern and highly self-conscious folk; they move in a world of moral and emotional subtlety which is decidedly more redolent of the age of Proust than of the age of Malory; they take on a psychological reality and intensity which would have astonished, and might have shocked, [such other reinterpreters of the legend as] Tennyson or William Morris." Yet the very introspection of Robinson's heroes prevented them from assuming their roles as men of action. They all resembled "helpless Hamlets." Besides, Aiken thought, *Tristram* was simply too long. The lyricism was often beautiful, the analytic dialogue acute, but there was "a great deal too much of both."

When Carl Van Doren told him that the Literary Guild had purchased 12,000 copies for distribution, Robinson shook his head in sympathy. "I hope you don't have too many left," he said. In fact, the guild's subscribers bought out the entire edition, achieving a success that undoubtedly inspired the rival Book-of-the-Month Club to choose Stephen Vincent Benet's epic Civil War poem, *John Brown's Body*, as one of its 1928 selections.

The sales of *Tristram* in the bookstores surprised Robinson even more. Macmillan disposed of thirteen printings within six months. By July 1928, they sold 57,475 copies of *Tristram*, producing royalties of $12,907.20. "Which isn't so bad for blank verse," EAR dryly noted. And it kept selling, reaching 72,000 copies by the following summer. The poem was so popular that it was presented in dramatic form over NBC radio, accompanied by Wagner's music from *Tristan und Isolde*. "God help us all," Robinson wrote Ledoux, "including Wagner."

All his life Robinson had disparaged people whose primary goal was to amass a private fortune. In his correspondence he declared that he totally lacked the "commercial instinct" and spoke of the "futility of materialism" as a guiding principle. Most of his close friends—the New York social elite aside—were failures in the eyes of the world. Robinson felt comfortable with them, for they shared a similar disenchantment, even resentment, against those who had achieved financial success. Now, suddenly and unexpectedly, such success had sought him out. "The old Bohemian, with indecent speed, became a figure of respectable eminence," as the poet Donald Hall put it.

One of his first thoughts was that considering the popular acclaim he might well have written a bad poem. "Tristram is a 'best seller,'" he remarked, "which may or may not mean that it's no good." Had he worked "for thirty five years for a little noise and smoke"?

Still, Robinson took satisfaction in knowing that the good burghers back in Maine at long last felt compelled to approve of him. One of his Palmer cousins in Whitefield came across his picture in a mail order catalogue (one wonders where this might have happened) and—as Hagedorn put it—"yielded all his doubts."

At the same time, EAR understood that his popular success was sure to arouse the envy of other poets. Hagedorn himself may have been so victimized; his friendship with Robinson cooled in the aftermath *of Tristram*'s triumph. About Frost's jealousy there could be no question. He was infuriated by the orchestrated commercial campaign of the Literary Guild and regarded *Tristram* with a bilious eye. He lashed out at EAR in a letter to Untermeyer of June 6, 1930. "The whole damn thing became disgusting in his romantic mouth. How utterly romantic the enervated old soak is. The way he thinks of poets in the

Browningese of 'Ben Johnson'! The way he thinks of cucolding lovers and cucold husbands in 'Tristram'! . . . I haven't more than half read him since 'The Town Down the River.' I simply couldn't lend a whole ear to all that Arthurian twaddle twiddled over after the Victorians."

At the time he wrote that letter, Frost was anxiously awaiting the reception of his own *Collected Poems*. He need not have worried. The book won the Pulitzer, and the following year Frost was elected to membership in the American Academy of Arts and Letters. Robinson had won similar honors—both the Pulitzer, his third, and election to the American Academy—three years earlier. He was one of the five academy members who nominated Frost for election.

The Late Long Poems

By the late 1920s, Robinson had attained to a position as the preeminent American poet. He had won three Pulitzer prizes in a span of six years, and *Tristram* had become a best-seller. He could easily have slowed down. Instead he did the opposite, producing a remarkable body of poetry in the last decade of his life.

A statistical study dividing EAR's poetry into three chronological periods—his first two decades (1895 to 1914), followed by the ten-year spans from 1915 to 1924 and 1925 to 1934—revealed his enormous productivity during the second half of his career. During his first twenty years, when he was struggling for recognition, he wrote and published an average of but 300 lines a year. In the decade from 1915 to 1924 the average rose to 1,600 lines per year, and between 1925 and 1934 Robinson published at a rate of 2,200 lines a year. Almost all of the increase came in the form of long, blank-verse narrative poems: nine in all beginning with *Roman Bartholow* in 1923 and ending with the posthumously published *King Jasper* in 1935, six appearing in the last seven years of his life.

These long poems are no longer read, and they by no means measure up to the standard he set himself earlier in his career. A poem of any length worth reading demands the full attention of the reader, who must become accustomed to the particular idioms and idiosyncrasies of a distinctive voice and to a mind unlike his own. A long poem asks even more of its audience: an extended period of concentration that few readers are willing—or even able—to expend. This was marginally less true in 1925 than in 2005. There were fewer distractions at the time, fewer entertainments one could lose oneself in without expending any mental energy whatever.

Most of Robinson's friends encouraged him to abandon the long poems and return to shorter ones that were more accessible and more likely to last. He tried his best to do so, but as he approached and passed sixty, the short poems simply stopped coming. Time and again, he announced that as soon as he finished his current long poem, he planned to produce a book made up of shorter ones.

And time and again, he was unable to shake off the demands of the next long poem that urged itself on him "like a big dog, which couldn't be shooed off." It was a frustrating process. If another long poem "shows its head," he declared in 1930, "I'll throw rocks at it." As late as 1934, when he had less than a year to live, he wrote Betts with the forlorn hope that "the Lord, or the Devil" would let him write some short poems when he was through with *King Jasper*.

To stop writing poetry altogether was not an option. Robinson's work ethic would not permit him to contemplate retiring. He felt an inner compulsion to keep writing. It was his calling, and he was bound to pursue it.

Robinson's productivity was motivated as well by a dread of destitution that traced back to his family's financial collapse and his own struggle with poverty. He realized that he was writing too much and publishing too often. "No poet," he said, "can afford to bear a new volume every year. . . . But what could I do? I needed the money." This was not strictly true: after *Tristram*, EAR could have got along on his royalties, and there were people more than willing to help him. Nonetheless, he persuaded himself that poverty lurked around the corner. To stave it off, he seized the opportunities that came his way. In 1928 he was chosen an editor of the new Book League, a short-lived book club formed in the aftermath of the Book-of-the-Month Club and Literary Guild. "I couldn't see my way to turn down a hundred dollars a month," he told Isaacs. He also cooperated with such small publishers as Slide Mountain Press and the Brick Row Book Shop, who brought out expensive limited editions of his work and offered him generous terms for signing copies. And annually he produced another protracted psychological novel in verse that challenged his audience and did his reputation no good. As he said, almost defiantly, "I can turn these things out once a year as long as they want me to."

Several of these long poems depict love gone wrong through the emotional insensitivity of the principal character, a man who has achieved material success. He is married to a woman who cannot love him, knowing that she means no more to him than his other possessions. She has an affair with another man, a friend of the title character, who really loves her. But there is no prospect of divorce or running away together, no possible happiness for the wife trapped in marriage. She can only escape through death. Oddly, the adulterous third figure in the triangle customarily leads the husband toward self-knowledge and a kind of spiritual rebirth. Robinson followed this script, roughly, in five long love poems of his last dozen years, all triangular love stories told from a psychological perspective: *Roman Bartholow* (1923), *Cavender's House* (1929), *The Glory of the Nightingales* (1930), *Matthias at the Door* (1931), and *Talifer* (1933).

Matthias at the Door is typical of these poems in its basic outlines but is more effectively constructed than the others. The brilliantly presented setting, where Matthias's elevated house looks down on treetops enshrouding a "forsaken gorge," gives the work a solid symbolic structure. In the depths of the gorge there is a huge rock with stone pillars on each side, so that it looks like a "dark Egyptian door" to the beyond. This place calls the characters to suicide much as "the western gate" invited Luke Havergal to oblivion in a poem written thirty-five years earlier. Matthias's friend Garth and his wife Natalie take their lives there, and, in retracing their steps, another friend—Timberlake—suffers exposure to the chill and damp that hastens his death.

In *Matthias at the Door*, Robinson shows once again how the attempt to possess other human beings can lead to disaster. The title character—one of Robinson's wealthy capitalists—saves the life of Timberlake by rescuing him from a fire. In gratitude, Timberlake removes himself as a suitor for the hand of Natalie, who marries Matthias instead. But the ceremonial bonds do not obliterate the love between Natalie and Timberlake, which eventually results in an adultery observed by Matthias. Timberlake immediately absents himself as Matthias tries to fight off the demon of jealousy and to reassert his rights of ownership with Natalie.

"My God!" she cries out to him, "what manner of chattel have you made of me?" In a passionate scene, she resists her husband's advances and then, seeking escape from an intolerable situation, leaves a five-word note (*Matthias, I am sorry. Natalie*) and commits suicide.

His religious faith challenged, Matthias struggles on alone, sustained only by a "blindness to his insignificance" that was "like another faith, and would not die." But he is desperately lonely, so that when Timberlake reappears, "wearing clothes almost / As worn-out and wrinkled as his face," Matthias feels "a great wave of joy" and takes him in as a companion. Matthias declares himself done with mysteries and false gods, but Timberlake counsels him to hold fast, for "there's not a man who breathes and believes nothing." But what is Matthias to believe? Natalie comes to him in a dream, first as an angel clinging to him and then as a demon from hell "like a skeleton strangling him." When Timberlake also dies, he feels totally bereft:

A man with nothing left but money and pride,
Neither of which was worth his living for
If there was nothing else.

In his dejection Matthias journeys into the gorge to take his own life, but the ghost of Garth intervenes to stop him. "Not yet, Matthias," he says. "You cannot die, Matthias, till you are born, / You are down here too soon, and must go back." He who has built a tower for himself to live in must return to build another: "a safer one / This time, and one for many to acclaim / And to enjoy." Hence in this poem as in the others, there is a saving grace at the end, when the previously misguided "man of possessions" converts—too late to save those closest to him—from a life of acquisition to one of charity.

The characters in *Matthias at the Door*, particularly Matthias and Timberlake, are successfully realized, and both love and friendship are powerfully conveyed. It is a dark poem that ends in hope of better times to come. Robinson asks whether religious faith can be sustained in a fiercely materialistic society. His answer is a qualified yes.

In two lengthy poems published ten years apart, Robinson set aside romantic triangles to consider the situation of the artist. Both of them—*The Man Who Died Twice* (1924) and *Amaranth* (1934)—rank among the best of his long works.

Fernando Nash, in *The Man Who Died Twice*, is a gifted composer who has let drink and dissipation erode his talent until he is reduced to banging a bass drum with the Salvation Army on New York street corners. Robinson himself liked to listen to such performances. He would stand unobtrusively and look away casually, "as if he had no special reason for being there," while the Salvation Army band played and sang

> Oh, the children of the Lord have a right to shout and sing,
> The way is growing brighter, and our souls are on the wing.

"They sing it with some zip, as if they believed what they said," he told Rollo Walter Brown.

Such a scene opens the poem, from which the narrator flashes back a year earlier to "the ruin of a potential world-shaker," Fernando Nash. Nash descended into the Valley of the Shadow, enslaved to drink, yet still scornful of those who envied him his gift and in his pride repeatedly insisting that he "had it—once."

Nash is observed in his barren room "not much larger than the iron bed" with nothing of music about the place other than a dusty box of orchestrations and a photograph of

> the competent plain face of Bach
> Calm in achievement, looking down on him
> Like an incurious Titan at a worm,
> That once in adolescent insolence
> Would have believed himself another Titan.

The embittered Nash laments the loss of a talent that might have produced great music—"Symphony Number Three. Fernando Nash."—if only he had been patient enough to wait for it to develop into genius. In a long speech, he vituperatively compares himself to a rat trapped in a well, a "less than eminent" dead fish, a greasy burned-out cinder, a phoenix consumed in its own fire, a "fat and unsubstantial" jelly fish, and a "crapulous and overgrown sick lump / Of failure and premeditated ruin."

Beset by the "leprosy of self-contempt," Nash hears "the drums of death" everywhere. He considers suicide but finally achieves an acceptance of his failure, and with it a conviction

That after passion, arrogance and ambition,
Doubt, fear, defeat, sorrow and desperation,
He had wrought out of martyrdom the peace
That passes understanding.

Henceforth he resolves to serve God humbly, playing the drums of life.

In his reborn state, Nash is given a final epiphany. He hears in his mind's ear the great symphony he might have written had he not dissipated his gift away. In a tour de force, Robinson describes the imagined symphony in half a dozen pages of blank verse divided into five distinct movements and a coda.

When Nash dies, the narrator grants him a kind of greatness for his "inviolable distinction" that went up in flames, his communion with older artistic giants, his possession of the "grim nostalgic passion of the great / For glory all but theirs." Robinson suggests here, as in many other places, that success may come from failure. Yet it is difficult, on the basis of the evidence in the poem, to share the narrator's judgment that Nash was a great man.

In tracing the unhappy career of Fernando Nash, Robinson was patently thinking back to his own difficulties in establishing himself as an artist. *The Man Who Died Twice* "would never have been written if I hadn't been through some pretty bad weather and over some rough ground," he told Saben, "but surely Fernando Nash is not E. A. R. or anyone resembling him." Certainly not, but Nash does represent a version of what Robinson might have become had he lacked the staying power to come back to life after his own desolate years in the Valley of the Shadow.

In *Amaranth* (1934) Robinson considered the plight of those misguided souls who waste their lives pursuing an art without the talent to succeed, a far more common problem than that of such a failed genius as Fernando Nash. Amaranth functions in the plot solely as the source of truth. Look into his eyes, and you will discover whether you are among the chosen. In the poem, none of the characters who gaze into Amaranth's eyes—and there are several of them—is so reassured. Genius is rare, and would-be geniuses abound, as EAR had observed both in New York City and at the MacDowell Colony. The issue thus becomes how the aspirants to artistic careers deal with their disappointment.

As Amaranth explains, some of them simply ignore the truth, covering "Their fears and indecisions and misgivings / More resolutely with their vanities." They must then strive and fail and starve. A second group, made up of people strongly committed to their art, come away from the confrontation with Amaranth in despair and choose to kill themselves. The poet Pink, the prolific "Elaine Amelia Watchman, who writes and writes and writes," and the artist Atlas, once a stevedore, all make this choice after discovering the truth from Amaranth. Robinson treats their suicides lightheartedly. Pink accepts his verdict with amusing dispatch. "Excuse me, " he says, "while I go and hang myself." Elaine Amelia Watchman vanishes in a mound of dust. Upon looking into Amaranth's eyes, Atlas shreds his canvases and then himself.

Atlas's death provides an occasion for a third group, those who have resigned themselves to their mediocrity and are content to live "in the wrong world," to deliver memorial speeches at his funeral. These figures include members of various professions. Their very names suggest the lightheartedness of the poem. Among them are lawyer Figg, Doctor Styx, the Reverend Pascal Flax, who no longer preaches but continues to indulge himself in the speechifying that led him to the ministry in the first place. Atlas's passing also gives the engaging Evensong an occasion to compose one of his facile and forgettable musical pieces.

Finally there is Fargo, like Atlas an aspiring painter, and the only character who gives up his misplaced ambition to become useful, as a maker of pumps, "in the right world." As Amaranth observes,

> To a few
> I murmur not in vain: they fly from here
> As you did, and I see no more of them
> Where, far from this miasma of delusion,
> They know the best there is for man to know.

As in other poems, Robinson reiterates how rare it is for any human being to know the truth about him or herself. He suggests, too, how costly it may be to escape from the "insidious region of illusions." For some it may be better to cling to their illusions, for too much knowledge can kill. Living in a "miasma of delusion" has its compensations. As Ipswich, the would-be inventor, tells Fargo,

> I have never
> Invented anything that you have ever heard of,
> But God, the dreams I've had!

Though addressing the deepest of human predicaments in *Amaranth*, Robinson's tone remains cheerful throughout. The presiding voice of the poem is basically comic and celebratory, like that of *Captain Craig* written thirty years earlier.

In 1934 *Amaranth* received scant justice at the hands of reviewers. Only decades later, in the commentary of writer-critics such as Robert Hillyer and Louis Coxe, did *Amaranth* begin to emerge as perhaps—in Hillyer's judgment—EAR's greatest long poem, partly satirical and partly philosophical. Its success, Coxe believed, came in part from its subject matter. Both *Amaranth* and *The Man Who Died Twice*, he pointed out, dealt "with Robinson's central themes: art, failure, self-knowledge." Both of them also came "fairly directly out of the poet's own life and experience."

Coxe also detected a "new terseness and economy of style" in *Amaranth*, evidence that in his last years of exhaustion and illness Robinson was still developing his craft. EAR himself had little doubt about *Amaranth*. "I don't think of anything just like it," he wrote Hagedorn, "and I don't think it is altogether bad."

During the last decade of Robinson's life, he published two books very different from his annual blank verse narratives. In 1928, Macmillan brought out *Sonnets, 1889–1927*, a collection of eighty-nine sonnets that demonstrated the poet's supple mastery. In subject matter, EAR departed from the sonnet's customary concentration on love, instead exploring the lives of other people, or—in the later sonnets—a social, political, or religious issue.

Within the narrow boundaries of the form, he could create an entire drama in miniature. Consider the highly unusual and ironic "Ben Trovato" (1921), for example.

> The deacon thought. "I know them," he began,
> "And they are all you ever heard of them—
> Allurable to no sure theorem,
> The scorn or the humility of man.
> You say, 'Can I believe it?'—and I can;
> And I'm unwilling even to condemn
> The benefaction of a stratagem
> Like hers—and I'm a Presbyterian.
>
> "Though blind, with but a wandering hour to live,
> He felt the other woman in the fur
> That now the wife had on. Could she forgive
> All that? Apparently. Her rings were gone,
> Of course; and when he found that she had none,
> He smiled—as he had never smiled at her."

In the octet, Robinson presents the Calvinist who grants the wife forgiveness. In the sestet, we learn that she has removed her rings and donned the mistress's furs to brighten her husband's dying moments. If the story seems contrived, the title says as much. "Ben Trovato," as EAR pointed out to Untermeyer, was "not a man but a fairly common—I might, say, well-found—Italian phrase." "Well-found" would be, in fact, a literal translation deriving from *bene*, "well," and the past participle of the verb *trovare*, "to find": a tale well-found, well-constructed, well-discovered. An Italian adage gives the expression a looser idiomatic sense. "*Se non è vero, è ben trovato*," or, "If it isn't true, it ought to be." Emma Robinson, in her annotation, suggested a biblical source for the story: "The stratagem—as of Jacob's blessing." In Genesis 27, Jacob seeks the blessing of his father Isaac by pretending, because of the fur on his neck and hands, to be his notoriously hairy brother Esau.

Robinson was to write no more sonnets after his collection appeared in 1928. The last one he produced, "A Christmas Sonnet," was published in December

1927 and sent as a memorial of the season to his friends. EAR used it as the con-cluding sonnet in his book, balanced against "Calvary" (1897) at the beginning. Both poems address the issue of belief. "Calvary" comments bitterly about les-sons unlearned from Christ's sacrifice nineteen hundred years ago, ending, "tell me, O Lord, how long / Are we to keep Christ writhing on the cross!" By way of contrast, "A Christmas Sonnet," subtitled "For One in Doubt," arrives at a hard-won affirmation.

> Though other saviors have in older lore
> A legend, and for older gods have died—
> Though death may wear the crown it always wore,
> And ignorance be still the sword of pride—
> Something is here that was not here before,
> And strangely has not yet been crucified.

The question of religious faith remained on Robinson's mind as he moved into his sixties. In "Nicodemus," the title poem of his 1932 volume, the title character—initially but a lukewarm disciple—presents the case for Jesus' divin-ity to the doubting priest Caiphas, who argues that "this man" whom Nicode-mus worships is either a madman or a charlatan. Nicodemus in reply chastises Caiphas for adopting a "flawed complacency" that amounts to no more than "a fool's armor against revelation." No such conversation takes place in the Bible. Robinson invented it, just as he invented the speech of Saint Paul outside Rome in "The Three Taverns."

In "Sisera," another of the ten medium-length poems that make up the sev-enty pages of *Nicodemus*, Robinson demonstrates how too fervid a belief can lead to inhuman savagery. The Israelite woman Jael brutally drives a nail into the head of the Canaanite Sisera, who comes to her for succor after his defeat in battle. She pretends to be sympathetic, lulling Sisera to sleep before commit-ting her barbarous act. Then she exults that the Lord put her victim to sleep and gave her the strength to destroy him. "Tell Israel to rejoice," she says to Barak, a battle-hardened warrior bewildered by her brutality.

In *Nicodemus*, Robinson was obviously concerned with the end of things. Two poems portray historical figures nearing death. In "Toussaint l'Ouverture," the Haitian independence leader carries on an imaginary conversation in the desolate French prison where Napoleon has confined him. In a vivid dream, Toussaint sees his tormentor Napoleon burning in hell. Soon he himself will die in captivity, to be carried "out of this cold and darkness / To a place where black and white are dark together."

Ponce de Leon, dying in Havana in 1521 at sixty, speaks about his career with the doctor attending him. In his last hours, the Spanish explorer reproves himself for mistreating the natives in the New World. They hailed him as a god, and he revealed himself to be a devil. His doctor, himself an old man who does not have long to live, serves as a confessor to de Leon, who is dying of an arrow wound. Speaking for them both—and for Robinson as well—the doctor offers a few final fatalistic words.

> Our minutes are all arrows. If one strikes,
> There is no balsam for it, and we go;
> And Time has a last arrow for himself.

It was natural for Robinson, his own health declining, to consider such eschatological issues. Impending death is hardly a lightsome subject, and Robinson has usually been regarded as a pessimist. It is important to note, however, that the poems of his last dozen years, whatever their merits, end in hope rather than despair. In each of them, as the critic W. R. Robinson observed, the protagonist passes through spiritual death to rebirth or reawakening. Taken as a group, EAR's late poems relate a story of man moving beyond egotism, vanity, and prideful domination of others "to a higher ground of freedom and peace through self-knowledge and self-realization."

A Reputation for Obscurity

When Robinson was awarded the Gold Medal for Poetry of the National Institute of Arts and Letters in 1929, he welcomed the recognition with characteristic reserve. "At the risk of appearing a little ungracious," he wrote William Lyon Phelps in accepting, "may I ask if anything in the nature of

FIGURE 25.2 Robinson at the peak of success, 1929.

Source: Colby College Special Collections.

a formal presentation may be omitted?" As he grew older, Robinson explained, he felt "less inclined, if possible, to indulge in the luxuries of publicity": a statement, Phelps thought, that had "a humor all its own."

Backward though Robinson may have been, the praise of others still did its damage. In bringing out a new *Collected Poems* in 1929, his publishers introduced the book with embarrassing overstatement. Those who knew his poetry—"its rich intelligence, its deep emotional quality, its magnificent characterizations and philosophical insight"—could not help recognizing Robinson's genius, Macmillan's copywriter asserted. What's more, those readers "entertain small doubt that the future will find Robinson regarded as the greatest poet America has produced."

No doubt there were critics, not to mention other poets, who resented such extravagant puffery, especially as the most perceptive of them noted a definite falling off in quality in Robinson's later poetry. He gave his characters memorable names, Malcolm Cowley observed, but "he sometimes forgot to give them faces." The incessant talk in the long poems sounded "like the conversations of ghosts in unfurnished rooms." Allen Tate, who thought EAR had written "some of the finest lyrics of modern times," found it difficult "to keep the [longer] poems distinct; at a distance they lose outline, blur into one another." The consensus was that EAR wrote too much too long.

Then, too, there remained the problem of obscurity. Some poets believe that poetry has to be difficult to matter. Robinson was not one of them. He did not set out to befuddle his readers. When a bewildered visitor at a MacDowell Sunday tea asked how best to understand his work, he famously recommended that she try reading one word after another. But that procedure did not and does not always work.

For a number of reasons, much of Robinson's poetry is obscure. One such reason, the one with particular application to his late long poems, was that he was forever feinting around the edges, concealing vital information through circumlocution. In this respect, Robinson's late verse strongly resembled Henry James's late prose.

The principal fault shared by Robinson and James, according to the critical commonplace, lay in their common tendency toward hesitancies and elaborations, "weakening modifications, afterthoughts and negations." Their characters talk *around* the subject instead of *about* it. Both writers ordinarily concentrated on the study of a single, rather complicated character whose relations with others are revealed more through thought than through action. In addition to their abnormal sensitivity to psychological undercurrents and reluctance to reach unqualified conclusions, Robinson's verse and James's fiction exhibit several other resemblances that were summed up by the poet-critic Babette Deutsch. "Both rely on a gift for creating atmosphere. Both tend to shove the murders and adulteries offstage, and make the action the subject of endless discussion among the characters. Both are preoccupied with the theme, exemplified in the lives of so many New Englanders and at some period in their own lives, that worldly failure may issue in spiritual triumph."

The essayist Joseph Epstein recalled visiting his local bookstore and observing, on the philosophy table, a book entitled *Clarity Is Not Enough*. "Ah, but it's a start," he thought. Despite Robinson's protestations to the contrary—he said he could not imagine why it was that "for the majority of semi-intelligent readers most of [his] books might as well be written in Sanskrit"—he shied away from too much clarity. Better to confuse his readers than to insult their intelligence or sensitivity. At his worst, he erected "mazes of the incomprehensible." In the late long poems, particularly, it becomes a considerable task to figure out what is going on. Too much has to be surmised that ought to have been made clear.

Yet eschewing the obvious was absolutely essential to those "masterpieces of suggestion," usually in short form, that represent Robinson's best work. In his comments on EAR's obscurity, Louis Coxe proposed a method by which the reader should approach him. If you are not caught up within ten lines, he advised, "forget it and try elsewhere." When Robinson was writing well in his short poems, he "will make us his in the first stanza, often the first line." If, even then, we do not fully understand when we come to the end, it will be because "the poem is, and is about, a mystery, as are most good poems."

In the early 1890s, before Robinson had published anything at all, his friend Harry Smith read a new poem in puzzlement. "Win, what does it mean?" he asked. "That's a hell of a question to ask a poet," Win replied. He was damned if he'd be "his own interpreter." He was trying, after all, to say something that could not be said.

In his great short poems, Robinson practiced an oblique or gnomic style that came down to him from fellow New Englanders Ralph Waldo Emerson and, especially, Emily Dickinson. Tell the truth but tell it slant, she advised. By indirection find direction out. The French writer Jules Bois, a fellow MacDowell colonist, said of Robinson that "he is almost never direct. He suggests, he hints. He is evasive and full of implications, where the ordinary reader comes close to getting lost. But these shadows only give the picture more luster."

The gnomic style mandated a condensation of language so extreme as to make one word do the work of several. "Anything is improved by cutting," Robinson believed, and he fashioned his finest work accordingly. By pursuing such radical economy in his diction, Untermeyer wrote in 1916, EAR "sometimes throws away everything but the meaning—and keeps that to himself."

Robinson read Untermeyer's remarks (in a review of *The Man Against the Sky*) and responded in a private memorandum to Herbert Gorman. "I have been accused in some quarters of not always using a sufficient number of words in my poetry, and I don't deny there is something to be said for this accusation," he began. But, he added, he would rather "run the risk of an occasional obscurity" than tamper with a phrase or a passage he could repeat to himself, months after its composition, "with a certain unmistakable pleasure and without misgivings."

"Ah, what a dusty answer gets the soul / When hot for certainties in this our life!" George Meredith wrote. Those looking for certainties will not find them in Robinson's poetry. He was fascinated by people, and part of the fascination derived from awareness that he could never sound their depths. "A man just called on me who wanted to tell me the whole truth," he told Ridgely Torrence one day. "He ought to be killed!" Oliver Wendell Holmes Jr. had a similar feeling about people who fancied themselves omniscient. "I detest a man who knows that he knows," he said. For seekers like Robinson and Holmes, the truth had value insofar as it remained inaccessible. The only thing we can be sure of is that we can be sure of nothing. This doctrine became for EAR almost an epistemological obsession: one that found expression in his poetry, both early and late.

In "The Tavern" (1897), a passerby imagines he sees the ghost of the murdered Ham Amory as he passes the now-abandoned place: "The Tavern has a story," Robinson comments, "but no man / Can tell us what it is." Nor can anyone divine the fate of the recently deceased "Leffingwell" (1910): "We do not know / How much is ended or how much begun." People conceal themselves, as in the case of "Flammonde" (1916): "How much it was of him we met / We cannot ever know." In "Discovery" (1919), we learn "that earth has not a school where we may go / For wisdom, or for more than we may know." "The best of life . . . is in what we do not know," Saint Paul says in "The Three Taverns" (1919). Laramie Cavender, in *Cavender's House* (1929), wonders at our surpassing ignorance: "Was ever an insect flying between two flowers / Told less than we are told of what we are?" In *Matthias at the Door* (1931), Matthias tells Natalie that

> The trouble with you,
> And me, and a few millions who are like us,
> Is that we live so long to know so little,
> And are not willing then to know ourselves.

Such lack of self-knowledge could be beneficial, even a gift from on high, Robinson came to believe toward the end of his life. "There must be some sort of God, or there wouldn't be so much providential self-esteem to keep most of us from seeing what we are," he wrote Laura Richards in 1931. In *Amaranth* (1934), Robinson illustrated the painful, even deadly consequences of such understanding. "For most, there is more joy, if not more wisdom, / In not seeing too well," the truth-conveying Amaranth tells Pink. And again,

> I should not rush to see myself too well,
> Or to behold myself too finally,
> If I were you.

In "The Whip" (1910), a poem of five quatrains in rhymed trimeter, Robinson combined his notorious obscurity with an acknowledgment of the terrible cost of discovering the truth.

> The doubt you fought so long
> The cynic net you cast,
> The tyranny, the wrong,
> The ruin, they are past;
> And here you are at last,
> Your blood no longer vexed.
> The coffin has you fast,
> The clod will have you next.
>
> But fear you not the clod,
> Nor ever doubt the grave;
> The roses and the sod
> Will not forswear the wave.
> The gift the river gave
> Is now but theirs to cover:
> The mistress and the slave
> Are gone now, and the lover.
>
> You left the two to find
> Their own way to the brink
> Then—shall I call you blind?—
> You chose to plunge and sink.
> God knows the gall we drink
> Is not the mead we cry for,
> Nor was it, I should think—
> For you—a thing to die for.
>
> Could we have done the same
> Had we been in your place?—
> This funeral of your name
> Throws no light on the case.
> Could we have made the chase
> And felt then as you felt?—
> But what's this on your face,
> Blue, curious, like a welt?
>
> There were some ropes of sand
> Recorded long ago,

But none, I understand,
Of water. Is it so?
And she—she struck the blow,
You but a neck behind . . .
You saw the river flow—
Still, shall I call you blind?

"The Whip" has baffled many readers. The words are simple enough, but the meaning escapes a first reading and is liable to remain elusive after rereading. Perhaps, as David Nivison suggests, the puzzlement is but true to life. The speaker of the poem "sees, ponders, begins to grope toward understanding, then leaves us, with a question, to go on ourselves to whatever end we can reach." In this as in other poems, Robinson places us in the difficult position of having to "appraise people and situations."

"In this poem," he admitted in response to a query about "The Whip, " "I may have gone a little too far and given the reader too much to carry. If he refuses to carry it, perhaps I have only myself to blame." But perhaps not, too.

Through the device of the speaker-observer, Robinson invites us to accompany him on a journey toward understanding. The entire poem is written in the form of this speaker's imagined conversation with a recently deceased friend who, in a jealous frenzy, has pursued his wife and her lover, learned the worst, and drowned himself. The speaker (someone very like Robinson himself) is a sensitive person who tries to put himself in the place of the dead man who has suffered through "the tyranny, the wrong, / The ruin." Nonetheless, he is ready to criticize his friend for taking his life. At the midpoint of the poem, he asks "shall I call you blind?" and answers the question in the affirmative. His friend's jealousy must have blinded him. Galling though it certainly was, a wife's unfaithfulness should not have been, for him, "a thing to die for."

This judgment is altered on the basis of the evidence that comes to light at the end of the penultimate quatrain. The speaker, gazing at the dead man in his coffin, suddenly notes the wound, "blue, curious, like a welt" on his face, and begins to reconstruct what must have happened. Frantically chasing the wife and lover on horseback, the husband closed to "but a neck behind" when his wife turned and struck him with her whip. It is apparently this blow, signifying absolute rejection and even hate, that gives him "a thing to die for" and leads him, a slave to love now despairing, to suicide. He has discovered more of the truth than he can stand.

At the end, the speaker repeats the crucial question: "Still, shall I call you blind?" This time, though, it is asked in doubt rather than in judgment. The point of "The Whip," like many Robinson poems, has to do with asking such questions. We cannot really know the answers.

"I like to leave a poem with a fringe around it," EAR said, and his ideal readers admire him for doing so. In his introduction to the *Selected Poems of Edwin Arlington Robinson* (1965), the poet James Dickey speaks of the "artistic virtue, and sometimes a very great one, of arriving at only provisional answers and solutions, of leaving it up to the reader . . . to choose from among them." Unlike the prototypical lyric poet, Robinson was usually an observer looking outward at others, and "he makes of us observers too, outsiders with him." We are in it together, in a happy collaboration of author and reader. In Robinson's universe, and in ours if we share his insights, every human being—even the mundane butcher or banker—is complicated and private enough to resist categorization. Those who pigeonhole other people are worse than foolish. They are the enemy.

Robinson's obscurity arose, then, not from fuzzy thinking or waffling but from conviction. Donald Justice, in an essay called "Benign Obscurity," points out that in "Eros Turannos," "some of the obscurity is expressive of the very understanding the poem is intended to carry." The truth "is held in suspension, unresolved: that itself is the resolution, the final truth." Probably, poets "should know a little more than most of us / Of our obscurities." But Robinson, as Robert Mezey said, does not like to tell us anything he doesn't know for sure, and that includes practically everything.

Any discussion of EAR and obscurity must take into account his temperamental disinclination to reveal himself—or call attention to himself—whether in public or on the page. In his poems, he occasionally offers glimpses of himself in disguise: poignantly in "Aunt Imogen," humorously in "Miniver Cheevy." And in more than a few poems he works variations on the theme of the triangular love relationship in his family. But almost always he remains in the wings. We learn more about him from the sensitivity with which he looked at other people than from any confessional poetry.

Nothing better illustrates Robinson's resistance to self-disclosure than his cryptic and nearly impenetrable handwriting. Interestingly, this difficulty seems to have developed during the time when he was embarking on a life in poetry. His boyhood script is easily readable. After graduating from high school in 1889, for a brief time he studied stenography as a possible avenue toward employment. He even wrote a bad sonnet, marred by blatant alliteration, in praise of Isaac Pitman, the Englishman whose phonological shorthand technique was being taught in the United States. Then, beginning in 1891, he started apologizing to Harry Smith for his "immoral fist."

The single largest barrier to understanding derived from Robinson's exceedingly diminutive hand. He "would give a hundred dollars" (if he had it) to get over his "nasty habit of microscopic handwriting," he wrote Smith in February

1893. Four or five years earlier, he had written legibly enough, but he seemed to be going "steadily down hill in that way (and perhaps in every other)." He acquired a typewriter as a possible remedy but soon abandoned it. He didn't like using the machine for private correspondence, and even less for the composition of poems. By February 1894 he admitted to Smith that he'd given up the struggle. Good penmanship seemed to him nothing more than "a fortunate accident."

Thereafter Robinson adopted a cavalier attitude toward the matter. His handwriting was the way it was, and his correspondents would have to find their own ways of decoding the message. If it was not distinct, at least it was distinctive. A scrap of his script might be "good for two shirts" at a Chinese laundry.

The microscopic nature of the writing was only one of its difficulties. In addition, a number of letters looked more or less exactly alike. "I always make my 'g's' like 'j's," EAR admitted. His capital "I's" were hard to make out because, he said, he didn't believe any man had the "right to make three strokes with his pen every time he refer[red] to himself." He crossed his letter "t's" well to the right of the upright stroke. He warned Esther Bates, who served for twenty years as his faithful copyist, to "look out for my whens and wheres, also for my b's, v's and r's in general. I believe I make them all alike." She discovered, too, that the "c's" looked just like the "e's."

Bates, unfortunately, was not sought out to make accurate transcriptions of Robinson's *Selected Letters* in 1940. An exchange of correspondence between Louis Ledoux and Ruth Nivison suggests how far afield a conscientious but unskilled reader of EAR's handwriting might go. In an early letter to Arthur Gledhill, Robinson referred, so the copyist thought, to "Cousin Sever." Ledoux

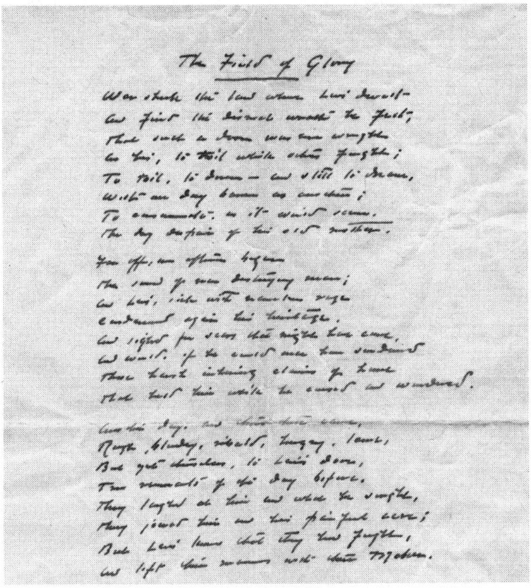

FIGURE 25.3 The first three stanzas of EAR's "Field of Glory" (1913), in his nearly impenetrable handwriting, blown up to improve legibility.

Source: Colby College Special Collections.

wrote Robinson's niece Ruth to ask if there was indeed such a person in the family. There wasn't. On further inspection, "Cousin Sever" turned out to be "common sense." That error was caught before publication. Many others were not. Between page 15 and page 25, *Selected Letters* incorrectly converted "degenerate" into "dogmatic," "world-" into "Thoreau," "congenial" into "English," "becoming" into "burning," "irrepressible" into "impoverished," "I sin against" into "I'm against," "gold mines" into "good news," "indigestion" into "indignation," "carelessness" into "casualness," "undergoing" into "managing," and "grow" into "grand." Substantive mistakes like those warred against the sense of what Robinson meant to say.

A handwriting expert consulted by Robert Gale for his 2006 companion to Robinson examined Robinson's February 11, 1897, letter (and drawing of himself) to Harry Smith, and concluded among other things that the writer "feels apart, alone in the crowd" and suppresses the "physical self." At the very least, the opacity of Robinson's handwriting suggests an unusual degree of repression.

26

Generosities

The money that descended upon him following *Tristram* did not significantly change Robinson or his style of life. "Time may have changed its mind in regard to me, giving me this little illusion of importance as a preparation for oblivion," he wrote John Freeman in August 1927. If he'd achieved such success when he was twenty-five or thirty, "no doubt it would have given me a jingle." Nearing sixty, however, he knew better than to consider himself a great man merely because he was financially self-supporting.

Robinson had learned to get along on so little for so long that the surplus cash didn't much matter. He could have "a lobster or a baked apple" whenever he felt like it, and otherwise satisfy his sweet tooth with Brown Betty at Chard Powers Smith's apartment or chocolate butterscotch from the candy shop on Massachusetts Avenue in Boston. He could afford to buy a new hat, some English neckties and gloves, and even a dinner coat. Otherwise, he did not lavish funds on himself.

Nothing new was added to the spare furnishings of his room with the Frasers. There was a bed, a desk, two rocking chairs (one the Mission rocker the Isaacses gave him) and a table between them. It was a place to sit and think, read and revise. Much as EAR loved music, he didn't add a radio or a phonograph. The very idea of owning a car would have seemed to him "positively sybaritic." Besides, where would he put it?

As before, his entire estate consisted of shelf room and what could be packed into two suitcases and—after his journey to England in 1923—a steamer trunk. He didn't permit books to accumulate. Laura Richards offered to send him a book plate, but—he told her—he had no use for one. It became a spring ritual for him to transfer autographed books that had been sent him to Lewis and Edith Isaacs. "I don't want to own anything that won't go into a suitcase," he said.

Yet in some ways the money did make a significant difference. It meant, for example, that EAR no longer required the annual subsidy provided by Isaacs, Ledoux, and others. He conscientiously paid off outstanding debts, some of them owed for several years. He began to play the stock market a little. "I never knew before how money was made," he wrote Isaacs, who served as financial adviser. "I thought it had something to do with oil, or railroads, or Ford cars, or jazz." Isaacs recommended a conservative investment policy, but Robinson was inclined toward riskier ventures. Why shouldn't he acquire "some calm and well-behaved five per cent stock"? Wasn't it needlessly cautious "to keep so much . . . at two and a half per cent"?

Most importantly, as a consequence of his sudden prosperity Robinson was able to give money to friends and family in need. "Practical people like myself," he wrote Isaacs in June 1931 with tongue in cheek, "are subject to many calls from those whose occupations are less secure and remunerative." Soon there-after he told Isaacs that his "personal expenses" threatened to outrun his bank account. Inasmuch as he rarely spent anything on himself save for doctors' bills and necessities, the Isaacses knew that those "expenses" meant the financial help he was giving others.

Robinson was often of service, too, in ways that had nothing to do with money. In his poetry he was a biographer of souls. In his life he strove to become a succorer of souls. He gave freely of his time and energy and thoughtfulness to those he cared about.

Schenck, the Perrys, Burnham, and Ranck

Social distance lay vast between Franklin Schenck, the impoverished Long Island painter, and Lilla Cabot and her husband, Thomas Sergeant Perry,

FIGURE 26.1 The painter Franklin Schenck on his patch of Long Island land.

Source: Trinity College Library.

the Boston Brahmin painter-poet and gentleman of letters. Robinson did what he could for all three of them.

Following Schenck's death in February 1927, Robinson wrote an appreciation of his life for the local newspaper on Long Island. "Worldly wealth and social conventions meant no more to him than the dirt under his feet, and in truth not half so much," Robinson pointed out. Schenck had no use for money beyond "a few dollars to keep him alive," while the dirt on his patch of land gave him flowers and vegetables and gave his chickens a place to scratch.

Robinson's own mortality may have been on his mind as he said his final words for the saintly Schenck. "All those who really knew the man must have loved him, there was nothing else for them to do. The world is better for his having lived in it—which is perhaps as much as will be said of many of us, and perhaps a little more, when our houses are left empty and our memories are left to flourish or dwindle as they may."

It fell to Robinson to dispose of Schenck's sole legacy—his paintings. They were on exhibition at the Brooklyn Chamber of Commerce at the time of his death, but that institution was not interested in buying them or displaying them permanently. EAR stayed in New York well into April, a month when he was normally in Boston, in an effort to find a place for the paintings. He hated to put them in storage where no one would see them.

Fortunately Nelson White—an old painter friend of Schenck—and his son, also named Nelson, came to the rescue. They took possession of the paintings and arranged an exhibition at the Macbeth Gallery in New York in February 1928, a year after Schenck's death. In a brief piece written for the catalogue, Robinson called attention to the painter's having been a favorite pupil of the great Thomas Eakins. The point was underlined at the exhibition by the display of Eakins's portrait of Schenck, titled *The Bohemian*. A dozen works of Schenck—all landscapes—were also hung, including paintings lent by Isaacs, Fraser, and Mrs. Nelson White. Robinson's gift from Schenck, *The Dark Hills*, stayed on the wall of his room.

In 1923, Robinson wrote some proposed jacket copy for Lilla Cabot Perry's book of poems, *Jar of Dreams*. She was, he said, "a poet who adapts the established forms of verse to the unestablished complexities of human moods and passions." This sort of blurb, unusual for Robinson, was offered in gratitude to Mrs. Perry, who had painted the best portrait of EAR and placed her 30 Ipswich Street studio in Boston at his disposal.

When Tom Perry died in May 1928, the family asked Robinson to edit a collection of his wide-ranging correspondence, with Henry James and William Dean Howells among others. "It is going to be rather a devil of a job," he admitted, "but they want me to do it, and it's no more than right, for many reasons, that I should." Robinson worked on the edition during the winter of 1928–29, and it was published by Macmillan in the fall of 1929. He had no scholarly training to undertake this kind of task, but he did what few scholars

FIGURE 26.2 Thomas Sergeant Perry and EAR outside the Perrys'
Hancock, N.H., home.

Source: Colby College Special Collections.

could have done. In his introduction, he presented a revealing sketch of Perry
himself.

Those who did not know Thomas Sergeant Perry, Robinson began, would
find in his letters a reflection of his powerful personality: "as engaging as it was
unusual, as facetious as it was ferocious, and as amiable as it was annihilating."
Although an aristocrat by birth and instinct, Perry was far more democratic in
his feelings than most of the "professional proletarians" who would have stereotyped him as a plutocrat. And, EAR wrote, "he estimated character and conduct
far beyond accomplishment or glory."

Above all, he depicted Perry as "a man of books." By no means inactive—he
took walks, rode his bicycle, and played tennis—Perry lived for his books with a
passion Robinson conveyed in a memorable metaphor. "Alone in his study, with
a troublesome world forgotten and out of his way, [Perry] made one think sometimes of an experienced and insatiable spider . . . waiting there to suck the living
juice, if he found it, of anything literary that might fall into his clutches." He was
"a great reader, a great friend, and a great gentleman." He might have become a
great writer, too, except that it would have stolen time from his reading.

Robinson's introduction to *Selections from the Letters of Thomas Sergeant
Perry*, written in January 1929, ran to thirteen pages, the longest prose piece
he ever published. A few years later, EAR composed a much briefer and less
impressionistic account of Perry's life (limited to 700 words) for the *Dictionary
of American Biography*. Lilla Perry wanted him to do it, and he would not refuse

her. She herself died at the end of February 1933, almost entirely alone and "angry with Time for taking away her strength, and leaving her in other ways as young as ever." Her daughter Margaret organized an exhibition of her mother's paintings in Boston that fall. Robinson went to see it, and he congratulated Miss Perry for bringing it about. "I like to believe that my friendship meant something to [your parents]," he wrote her, "for you do not have to be told that their friendship meant a great deal to me."

Like the Perrys, George Burnham lived in Boston. Unlike them, he inhabited a single room in a modest house at 257 West Newton Street. More or less always in pain from his wooden legs, Burnham worked as a clerk for the railroad for twenty years. In his devotion to Hinduism, Burnham became something of an ascetic, dressing simply, eating and drinking sparingly, and permitting himself no luxuries. There was "a selfless angelic quality" about him. EAR regarded him as his closest friend, "the man who knows me best, and—so I like to fancy—overlooks the worst of my shortcomings."

In his last decade, Robinson took it upon himself to look after Burnham. Repeatedly, he urged his friend to be more careful about his health and to quit his menial job, which in EAR's eyes amounted to a kind of slavery. He was delighted in the fall of 1928 to learn that Burnham was taking a week off to go to Montreal, where he could escape the confines of his "damned office" and have the few glasses of ale in the evening that Prohibition denied him in the United States. When Burnham was bothered by kidney stones at Christmastime 1930, EAR advised him to take a long rest and to drink a lot of water. Was Burnham getting enough to eat? "If you don't eat, you will die; and we don't want that to happen." To forestall such a fate, he sent a check to finance "some dinners at the Lenox" in Boston. If he used the money for any other purpose, EAR added, Burnham would incur his undying wrath.

There were other checks as well, referred to as "enclosure[s]" or "the enclosed." Fearful of troubling Burnham's pride, EAR assured him that supplying such "slips of paper" didn't "make a damned bit of difference to me . . . except for the satisfaction of knowing" that they couldn't do any harm. Supplying these "small accommodations" was a source of great pleasure to him, EAR said. Burnham was not to trouble himself about them.

Only once did Robinson mention a specific sum in his brief notes to Burnham. In August 1932, he encouraged his friend to delay returning to work as long as possible. If he was running short, EAR could let him "have five hundred, or more, without the smallest inconvenience." There was "absolutely no need" for Burnham to go back to work, Robinson assured him. "The thing that will do you the most good is the privilege of going to bed with no thought of having to get up at any particular time."

Burnham stubbornly stayed on the job. Robinson could no more change his friend's mind about that than he could persuade him to get an overcoat for the Massachusetts winters. He might as well have asked him to don "a pair of riding breeches." Still, he continued to worry that Burnham was too much alone, and in his final years he spent more and more time in Boston so as to be near him.

Robinson did more than care about his friends, and more, even, than give them whatever he could to ease their path. In extreme cases, such as those as George Burnham and Seth Pope, he made himself *responsible* for them, like a parent or a spouse.

Carty Ranck, who headquartered in Boston during much of his career, aligned himself with Burnham as a fellow Robinson enthusiast. In his several reviews of EAR's work, Ranck was so enthusiastic in his praise that Robinson advised him to temper his language. "Please don't mind my asking you to avoid superlatives," he told Ranck, "for they are likely to act in the wrong way." Still, he could not reject so devoted a disciple as Ranck. Although he knew of Ranck's mental instability, Robinson continued to encourage him as an eventual biographer. Ranck was not without talent as a playwright, he believed, and could certainly function as a newspaperman. In the fall of 1930, when EAR was approached about a 2,000-word article on his life and work for the *Boston Herald* and *New York Herald Tribune* magazine sections, he recommended Ranck as the one to write it.

He forwarded "enclosures" to Ranck as he did to Burnham. Ranck paid him back when he could afford to, but Robinson made it clear that this was not necessary. What Ranck needed most of all, he thought, was the tonic of a success on the stage. "It would stiffen him up for the rest of his life," Robinson told Rollo Walter Brown.

In the fall of 1933, it appeared that Ranck's play *The Mountain*, written a decade earlier, might achieve such a success. The Provincetown Players brought it to New York in September. The play had considerable power, EAR felt, and with Ranck he hoped that it might move from its downtown location to Broadway and on to Hollywood. But the reviews were unfavorable, and the production closed. In the aftermath, EAR attempted to brighten Ranck's outlook. Someone important might have seen and liked it during its run, he speculated. The play might yet make it to the "talkies."

That did not come to pass, but the brief flurry of recognition led to a published edition of *The Mountain* in 1934. Robinson wrote a foreword in which he concentrated mostly on the play's subject matter. Zeke Holston, the protagonist, was modeled on Ranck's father. Holston runs afoul of the United States government, in particular its laws against the manufacture and sale of corn liquor. Like other mountain folk, he could not understand "what difference it made to God, who provided so impartially for either product, whether a bushel of corn should be converted ultimately into meal or into whiskey." It was a position EAR shared with Ranck, emphatically. In his own primitive and peculiar way, Robinson wrote, Zeke stood "as upright and as incorruptible as Oliver Cromwell and Abraham Lincoln."

It was unusual for Robinson to give the work of his friends such a sendoff. A few years earlier, he turned down requests from Hermann Hagedorn and

Chard Smith that he write introductions for new volumes of their poetry. It would be awkward for him to provide these, EAR explained, for he had already refused similar proposals from two or three other personal friends. Besides, as he told Smith, "you will be better satisfied in letting your book be entirely yours." He could "see no excuse" for any such introduction "except in a book of poems by a relatively unknown foreign writer, or by a writer who is dead." Neither Smith nor Hagedorn were dead, he was happy to say, nor were they foreign and unknown. In Hagedorn's case, the refusal may have rankled, for it was linked to EAR's resolve to repay him for money lent many years earlier. It must have seemed to Hagedorn that Robinson was breaking off past obligations while not assuming any for the future. The two men drifted apart.

That Robinson would do for Carty Ranck in 1934 what he would not do for Hermann Hagedorn in 1930 and Chard Smith in 1931 was not really surprising. The erratic Ranck, a freelance journalist living from hand to mouth, abandoned by his wife, and subject to mental illness, needed his help. Hagedorn and Smith, both comfortably well off, did not. All three of them, oddly enough, were to vie for the post of Robinson's official biographer.

Saving Mowry Saben

The flamboyant Mowry Saben made no apologies for his excesses in eating, drinking, and sexual adventuring. Saben was widely read in a variety of subjects and entirely persuaded of the value of his own opinions. Robinson often disagreed with Saben, but he respected Saben's breadth of knowledge and his ability to write and talk well about everything under the sun. He supplied Saben with money and encouragement, urged his merits on potential employers, shopped his manuscripts around to publishers, and even intervened with members of Saben's family.

In May 1924 Saben was so strapped for funds that Robinson took it upon himself to write a letter to his more or less estranged brother in an attempt to make things right. In reply, W. M. Saben politely thanked EAR for his interest in his brother but explained that he had never really gotten to know Mowry at all well because of the difference in their ages and professions. "There have been times when he would not write to one for years," he said. The brother, older and living in Arizona, promised to send Mowry some money, though not as much as Robinson had suggested.

The formality and chilliness of the letter came as a disappointment to Robinson, who could hardly imagine Saben's "own people" not making things easier for him. At first, he was inclined to blame Saben for not making the extremity of his situation clear and asking for aid in a diplomatic fashion. Go to see your brother, he urged Saben, who was then living in Montreal. "A few words said the right way" might accomplish "more than reams of distant letters." If he couldn't make such a long trip, Saben should at least "write a good natured letter to [his] brother now and then." It was hard for Robinson to believe that "a small trickle of family oil might not be turned in [Saben's] direction, if encouraged with humor and tact." In the end, though, where the Saben family was concerned, Robinson's efforts to act as a fixer or go-between ended in failure.

Meanwhile, he was sending Saben checks to tide him over—thirty dollars here, fifty dollars there—during a time, the summer of 1924, when he still required outside support to make his own ends meet. He also sent Saben "a perfectly good dark summer suit" he'd fallen heir to. Possibly it had belonged to Seth Pope. It was too large for EAR to wear, and hence better for Saben, who like Pope was overweight.

As a practicing hedonist, Saben regularly abused his health. Robinson commiserated with him about a series of operations in 1925 and trouble with his eyes and ears and "a damned carbuncle" some years later. His own ills, EAR realized, hardly compared with those of Saben and Burnham. "Whenever I am inclined to growl," he wrote the latter, "I think of you and of him, and shut up." He also continued to supply money as needed. "When things are too dark," he assured Saben in March 1926, "you can always count on me for a candle that will burn for at least a short time."

Saben's fortunes improved a few months later, when he secured a job as a researcher and speech writer on Capitol Hill. For the next six years, Saben wrote words on a wide variety of subjects to be spoken by the congressmen and one secretary of the interior who employed him. Like most ghost writers, Saben took a certain sardonic pleasure when the politician in question was praised for language he'd put in his mouth, but these labors did not fully satisfy him. With EAR's approval and support, Saben ambitiously embarked on a series of literary ventures: a book on the Sphinx, a novel, a Dionysian book (unless Saben went "needlessly and wilfully out of [his] way to be raw"), a biography of O. Henry, and a study of the origins of Christianity.

Robinson submitted Saben's book ideas and sometimes his typescripts to Macmillan and Scribner's, the two publishers he had connections with. He had especially high hopes for the O. Henry manuscript, which did not quite make the cut with either firm. He also thought that Saben's autobiography, the one book his friend did not propose writing, might achieve the success he was seeking.

When he left Washington in 1932, Saben tried to start a magazine of his own, where he would have a platform for his ideas. The requisite financing could not be located. As Robinson remarked, most rich men were more inclined to keep a girl than a magazine. Eventually Saben went to the Pacific coast, where, late in 1934, he found a post as editor of a journal of opinion called *The Argonaut* in San Francisco.

Robinson's views diverged markedly from Saben's on the subject of sex. In *The Spirit of Life*, Saben had declared himself an advocate of pleasure for its own sake. He believed in sex, in all its manifestations, as a perfectly natural part of life. Probably bisexual himself, he regarded Robinson as similarly constituted. Why else, he wondered, would EAR have objected so vigorously to Saben's defense of homosexual behavior?

That Robinson did so object emerged in two letters he wrote Saben from MacDowell in August and September 1934. Saben had another book in mind and asked if EAR would permit him to dedicate it to him. He'd be glad to accept the dedication, Robinson replied, if Saben could assure him that no future book of his would "contain any commendation of one particular subject that I particularly don't like." Even to give that "particular subject" a name was taboo. But if he would not write or say the word *homosexuality*, EAR insisted to Saben that he had never let his feelings on the subject interfere with his personal relations. "If I had been born that way, I should be that way myself."

Such a position was enough to persuade Saben that Robinson "had in him a homosexual streak" he was determined to repress. In his memorial for EAR in *The Argonaut*, Saben praised his friend for his total lack of "professional jealousy," for his generosity to fellow creatures in distress, and for his greatness as a poet. But he also thought Robinson a victim of severe repression, a conviction that emerges in the monograph on EAR he wrote during the 1940s.

According to Saben, Robinson's troubles began in Gardiner, Maine, which he described as "a small puritanical community . . . whose more intellectual members believed that virtue is divorced from strong sensations, and that . . . every natural instinct of man is wrong, because at enmity with God." These ideas, not overtly adopted by the poet, nonetheless infiltrated his mind and inhibited his behavior. Instead of rebelling against the restrictions, Robinson let them lead him to a life of sexual abstinence—a renunciation that led to melancholia, Saben contended, summoning Freud's authority to back up his argument.

At no point did Saben submit that Robinson had a homosexual relationship. He did argue, though, that EAR would have been far happier if he had. "I perceive in him," Saben wrote in summary, "one who was bisexually endowed, and at moments dimly conscious of the fact, but who feared the consequences, if the dimly apprehended truth became conscious either to himself or to others." Saben was probably at least partly right about the man he had known for more than forty years. So deep a reserve as EAR's must have had its roots in his subconscious. Yet it should be noted, as a caveat, that in deploring Robinson's repressions, Saben was implicitly defending his own hedonistic style of life.

Family Support

Though Robinson kept physically distant from his home town after 1925, he stayed in touch through correspondence. Only rarely did his correspondence with Laura Richards touch on local matters. EAR's closest connection to Gardiner was maintained with his family: with Emma Robinson, who remained to the end the love of his life, and with her daughter Ruth Nivison. He cared about Emma and her children as he cared about his friends. As he progressed from poor relation to a rather famous Uncle Win, he happily lent them what support he could.

As Richard Cary observes, "for a taciturn, recessive man, Edwin Arlington Robinson had an astounding number" of close friends. He kept them "chambered and isolated" from one another, formed into small circles bound together by various kinds of shared experience and mindset. He placed his New York friends, for instance, in an entirely separate category than his family in Gardiner. Remarkably, Ledoux first discovered the existence of EAR's nieces at his memorial service. Nor was Ledoux acquainted with the unhappy fate of Robinson's brothers. Similarly, Ruth Nivison heard very little about the treasured friends of her uncle's middle and later life in New York. She vaguely understood that they had done much for him, but it was impossible for her to imagine that they could conceivably have known him as well as she did.

A lifelong bachelor, Robinson got along extremely well with his friends' children. The young MacKayes and Ledoux and Isaacses naturally cottoned to him, and he to them. There was something lovable about his unshakable shyness and his willingness to accept children as they were. When she was but a tiny girl, Marion Isaacs opened the door for EAR with words from "John Evereldown." "Come in by the fire, old man, and wait!" she said, a greeting that had him chuckling for days. On another occasion, he watched in quiet terror as young Hermine Isaacs lit every match in his matchbox. "Hermine is teaching me a game," he told Edith Isaacs when she appeared. "She calls it 'house afire.'"

In his contact with children, Robinson managed to put them at ease while maintaining a certain awkward formality. It was an approach he developed back in Maine, when he forged a lasting bond with his nieces. So close was the relationship with Ruth that when she and her husband William Nivison were buying a house in Gardiner in 1930, she consulted her uncle in advance. Would he be interested in coming to live with them? And if so, what kind of house would best suit him? EAR advised her to proceed as if he "were dead or had never been born." He was grateful that she thought of him, he assured Ruth, but his plans for the future were too "vague—or rather non-existent" to be taken into consideration.

EAR took a substantial interest in the Nivison family, including his grand-nephews David and Bill. Both boys showed an interest in music that Robinson supported by paying for music lessons. "Bill may not ever be a Paderewski, but he will always be glad for knowing something of how music is made. David should get all the pleasure out of it that he can." EAR also sent other checks, usually at Christmas time, to pay for the boys' doctor bills. He even offered advice on their diet. The boys should be eating more oatmeal and eggs and fewer sweets in order to lay "a solider foundation for themselves."

A crisis in David Nivison's young life provided a striking example of Robinson's concern. When he was in the second or third grade, the boy—angular and awkward as Win had been growing up—was bullied by his classmates in Gardiner's public schools. His mother looked into the possibility of sending him to private school in Augusta. EAR advised against it. It would be best for David to face down his demons, he felt. Besides, as he wrote Ruth, "a six mile ride back and forth every day would have poisoned my childhood completely." But if it were decided to send David to Augusta and a scholarship could not be arranged, he stood ready to pay the tuition. David stayed in the Gardiner schools and eventually thrived. In later life, he felt a debt of gratitude to his granduncle for discouraging the escape.

Had Robinson come to live under the Nivisons' roof on Dresden Avenue, it would have placed him in the same house with Emma, who had assumed the status of grandmother in residence. Emma was in many ways an ideal grandmother to David and Bill. She was a wonderful cook who made superb doughnuts, letting the boys eat the raw middles. Bill, coming in from school just at doughnut frying time, said, "Oh, Grandma, when I grow up will you marry me?" And then, as an afterthought, "You won't be too old to make doughnuts, will you?" On the other hand, Emma was also used to running her own household and having things her own way. Mother and daughter were often at odds, Ruth feeling that Emma was "appropriating" her children. EAR sensed the trouble brewing—uncannily, Ruth thought—and invited her to come to Boston to talk it out with him.

"I know Emma has a stubborn persistence which can be maddening," Robinson told Ruth, "but it doesn't do you any harm to be patient."

"But it means the childhood of my sons," Ruth objected. "I don't have any children. My mother has two grandsons whom I clothe and feed at her constant disapproval."

"That's the way it has to be," he declared. This response puzzled Ruth at the time. She did not know, then, that her uncle cared so much for her mother that he would invariably side with her in any family dispute.

Ruth was very much her uncle's ally in establishing a memorial to his beloved brother Dean. In the fall of 1930 there was talk in Gardiner of displaying EAR's high school diploma in the school library. It was a little early for that sort of thing, he said, but not too early to pay tribute to Dean, who had drawn "unlucky cards" for the game of living, died while still a young man, and been largely written off in his home town as a drug addict. When Ruth suggested a memorial to Dean, EAR eagerly assented. "It is barely possible," he wrote her with unusual sarcasm, "that there are some who may not quite realize that Dean's unfortunate infirmities had no relation whatever to the fineness of his character. If he hadn't been so fine, he might be alive now and thriving."

Ruth and EAR agreed that a laboratory in the Gardiner hospital, named in Dean's honor, would be an appropriate remembrance. He contributed $1,000 to pay for the laboratory, and relied on Ruth to make the arrangements with the hospital. Laura Richards, hearing of the plan, wrote a memorial piece for the *Kennebec Journal* quoting Win's judgment that Dean "knew more at twenty than I shall ever know."

In another gesture of recognition, Robinson dedicated his 1934 poem *Amaranth* to Dean's memory. Like most of the characters in that poem, Dean Robinson's career had been sacrificed through pursuing the wrong profession. Bending to his father's wishes, Dean had become a physician when, EAR thought, there was "no profession" in the world for which he was less fitted. He might, for example, have become an excellent medical researcher, working in just such a laboratory as the one his brother endowed in his name.

27

Death of a Poet

A Long Animal

As Robinson grew older, he required both a certain degree of social intercourse and "a powerful lot of letting alone." He overflowed with brotherly love, he said, provided there weren't "too many brothers around." As a consequence of this dichotomy, his "chief mission" in life appeared to be that "of a very long animal who barks and snarls when he means to make all sorts of good-natured and affectionate noises." The dilemma worsened with the success of *Tristram* and Robinson's consequent celebrity. A fellow had to build walls around himself, EAR observed, "especially if his name happens to be in the papers now and then."

In his latter years, Robinson cut back on extended visits to the homes of friends. Where he once enjoyed spending two or three weeks with the Ledoux in Cornwall, he could no longer abide the thought of going anywhere for two or three days. An old professor of fine arts at Yale instructed him that visiting was "a very serious matter and requires of us that we shall be at our best, physically and mentally." With these words in mind, EAR visited the Perrys in Hancock and "came back a total wreck after enjoying the hospitality of some of the best friends a man ever had." Hard work may have killed a few people, he told Laura Richards, but visiting had done away with millions.

All he really wanted was a large city with everything available in the way of the arts and about six people in it for him to see from time to time. Whether Boston or New York better met that standard remained in some doubt, although Robinson trended toward longer stays in Boston and shorter ones in New York during his last half dozen years.

When he came to Boston in the spring, the city offered a welcome relief from the busy social life of New York. "I have seen three people here thus far, which isn't bad for two weeks," he declared in April 1928. He felt "rather happy not seeing people and having this place" (Lilla Perry's studio) to himself. In April 1930, he wrote Emma that he had left New York, "which [was] a good thing to do, and getting to be a better thing every year, and [was] once more in hiding" in Boston.

Unlike New York, Boston did not lionize him. He could see his disparate friends and family there—Burnham and Ranck, the Perrys, Marie and Barbara—without having to fend off culturally ambitious hostesses. A few visitors, like the young poet Winfield Townley Scott, were more than welcome. Scott called on Robinson at 30 Ipswich Street in November 1931 and elicited from him a number of unguarded observations about his fellow poets. He spoke of Frost at some length. Frost was "a good fellow," he said. EAR particularly liked "Nothing Gold Can Stay" and preferred Frost's lyrics to his longer poems. "Going back to those 'North of Gloucester' [sic] poems, I find they don't wear so well." What EAR meant was Frost's *North of Boston*, his second book. Gloucester probably came to mind, Scott suggested, in connection with William Vaughn Moody's *Gloucester Moors and Other Poems*. The unconscious association made a certain amount of sense. Where Moody was "the white-headed boy of poetry" during Robinson's early years, Frost was the poet most often cited as his equal or superior in his later years.

There was more than a hint of rivalry in Robinson's final comment about Frost. "I understand they teach Frost and me in the schools now," he said, and then, with a smile, "I don't know which one they teach first." Years later, Frost whacked his thigh in delight when Scott told him about this remark. "*Did* he say that?" Frost asked. "Did he really say that?"

At the end of the evening, EAR complained about New York. It was dirtier and noisier and taller than ever. The city's growth was getting beyond the bounds of material decency, "with fifty and sixty story buildings standing up everywhere" like mushrooms after a warm rain. He wouldn't go there at all, he said, if his friends didn't have the bad taste to live there.

But that was part of the problem, too. With so many friends in New York, Robinson's days were filled with social engagements that taxed his natural reticence, even more so with him permanently on the wagon. He resolved to avoid dinner parties and the like but would break his resolve when, say, the Kermit Roosevelts invited him to a gathering in honor of the English writer G. K. Chesterton. The engaging company, which included Alice Roosevelt Longworth, loosened EAR's tongue. He wrote Lilla Perry afterwards that he had "talked incessantly." He wasn't a hermit at all, he told her. She should have heard him talk.

System Breakdown

All his adult life Robinson was troubled by constipation and insomnia. At Harvard, Mowry Saben prescribed calomel as a remedy for his blockage. That purgative, he maintained, would not only liberate EAR's bowels; it would brighten his entire outlook on life. Calomel did not work for Robinson, and neither did anything else, at least not for long. Robinson tried one corrective after another in search of a panacea, His quest for relief formed a regular theme in his correspondence with Burnham, who was similarly afflicted.

In 1912, Robinson recommended "two tablespoonfuls of castor oil—taken at night on top of an inch or so of lemon-juice and water." In 1919, his doctor told him he needed "a course of sprouts," which he would have known himself if he "hadn't been a natural born idiot." In 1924, he sent Burnham a check to pay for a "pound of agar." In 1928: "Try Sal-Hepatica (any drug store)—one teaspoonful before going to bed and two on getting up. . . . This is really news, and important." In 1930: "If sea-weed is not more than $3.25 a pound you might let them send two pounds." 1931 was a banner year for nostrums: thanking Burnham for the box of meal he'd sent, EAR said he might go back to the seaweed; he reversed directions in favor of the meal, which was "surely unpalatable enough to be beneficial"; then (this to Craven Langstroth Betts) he asked for the correct formula for "the Dr. Mayo powder"; finally, he tried "a new French product called Corein": it cost two dollars a week, but he'd "be glad to pay much more than that for a real thoroughfare." In 1934, he switched to Swiss Kriss, his "elixir of life" for that summer.

Robinson's other "persecuting demon" was his "old enemy Insomnia," linked at Peterborough to an "incongruous companion Early Rising." During his later years, detective stories functioned as a specific against sleeplessness. His only requirement was that these stories make no pretension to literary merit; sometimes he had to read two of them before Morpheus did his work.

EAR's sedentary habits and heavy diet undoubtedly contributed to his digestive and sleeping problems. He loved rich foods, meat and potatoes, and sweets. Alcohol, when he was drinking, was counterproductive to a healthy regimen. Though he *looked* much the same in his fifties as he had in his thirties, he was beginning to realize "that one can't eat and drink everything in sight as he once could." His "internal machinery" could no longer "take care of big dinners."

As for exercise, Robinson walked to get from one place to another, and no further. When Percy MacKaye suffered a fall in 1933, Robinson wondered "why the devil he must climb things." He himself had looked at Mount Monadnock every summer for twenty-three years and "never once disturbed it." Monadnock had been there for a million years or so, and it obviously didn't "care much who does or doesn't climb over it."

During the middle to late 1920s, Robinson's health started deteriorating. In the spring of 1925, for example, he consulted three separate Boston doctors: a dentist, to tinker with his "old soldiers"; an aurist, to relieve the pain in his recurrently troublesome right ear; and "a maker of iron traps," to prop up his ailing feet. These "shoe-traps" were perfect symbols of this life, he told Ranck. He was "not altogether comfortable with them or without them."

Lumbago began to beset him on an annual basis, usually after Robinson left Peterborough in the fall. It was bad enough in November 1926 that EAR had to cancel Thanksgiving with the Perrys. In the fall of 1930, he could barely crawl, his back bent over like Father Time. One specialist wanted to put him in a steel jacket. Robinson resisted that treatment, and in due course he was able to wash his face with both hands "for the first time in two months." He was not uncomfortable, he told Laura Fraser, so long as he didn't "leap and dance too much." Eventually, the orthopedic surgeon Arthur T. Legg, who was to marry his niece Marie, prescribed some spine straightening exercises that seemed to forestall further attacks.

But as one malady disappeared, two or three others came along to take its place. Edith Isaacs, looking back over EAR's letters, decided that he was never really well after 1930. "Either his ear or his back or his foot or his head" was bothering him. He suffered from rheumatism in his left knee, his fingers became arthritic, his jaw hurt, and he had to bathe his eyes with hot water—and avoid fine print—in order to read at all.

Walking in Boston one day in 1931, Robinson was struck in the head and knocked down by a baseball launched his way by boys in a sandlot game. He did not think much of the accident until, two years later, he began to suffer excruciating headaches, "a new woe for me." He had his head x-rayed, but there was no indication that the blow had caused a fracture or infection. The doctors concluded that the headaches were caused by "simply fatigue."

Every fall, Robinson left the MacDowell Colony feeling more and more exhausted. "Probably most of my trouble is due to my being thoroughly used up and tired out—in a way I have never been before," he wrote Lilla Perry in November 1930. "I'm not exactly sick," he told Louis Ledoux in October 1933, "but I'm so thoroughly tired out after another summer at high pressure that I'm not much good." His exhaustion undoubtedly derived, at least in part, from the cancer working its way inside him. It testifies to the strength of Robinson's spirit that he managed to write anything at all after 1930.

Politics and Poetry

After World War I, Robinson took an apocalyptic view of the future. "The whole western world," he wrote Ledoux, "is going to be blown to pieces, asphyxiated, and starved, and then, for a few centuries, we poor artists are going to have a hard time."

Robinson distrusted any political system that threatened to impose conformity. Throughout the 1920s, he regarded communism as the most dangerous of these systems. "The socialistic dark ages" were coming, and he expected the individual to "wither" as a consequence. The only hope was that the Bolsheviks, by doing all things wrong, might be showing their successors how to do them right. At the same time, though, Robinson repeatedly depicted in his long poems the disastrous consequences of unchecked competition in the capitalistic marketplace. Henry Ford and his assembly line came in for particular abuse. "In his way," EAR observed, "[Ford] is greater than Napoleon, and far more terrible." There would be both "a lot of material prosperity and a lot of socialistic and communistic experimenting before Rome falls," he predicted.

The Great Depression only seemed to confirm EAR's foreboding outlook. He made the nation's economic collapse a subject of both comedy and satire in his letter to Laura Richards on Independence Day, 1932. First he told her "the story about the Optimist who said that we shall all be begging in the streets next winter and the Pessimist who asked him from whom we shall beg." Next he repeated Sarah Cleghorn's bitter little poem:

The golf links lie so near the mill
That almost any day
The [work]ing children can look out
And see the men at play.

The hard times naturally affected Robinson's sales. He suffered "a rather bad financial jolt" in 1933: "not a calamitous one, but large enough to make me sit up." Still, he would be all right as long as his "invisible public of hardy perennials who are not afraid of long things in blank verse" did not have to join the bread line.

Back in Maine, the depression struck hard. Robinson's childhood friends Gus and Alice Jordan lost their savings when the bank went under, and, still closer to home, the Nivisons lost their house. EAR made arrangements with Isaacs to raise $3,000 to save the house from foreclosure, and he offered the money to Ruth and Bill Nivison "as a sort of belated wedding present." The Nivisons eventually declined the offer, fearing that even Uncle Win's $3,000 would not enable them to keep the house. They were going through "wicked times," EAR said. He was glad he wasn't beginning at the other end of life, for the future didn't look good.

Robinson's rock-ribbed Republicanism weakened as the crisis wore on. He disliked Woodrow Wilson but could detect little vision in GOP presidents Calvin Coolidge and Herbert Hoover. His inclination was to support Hoover against Franklin Delano Roosevelt in 1932, if only because Hoover had been on the job long enough to learn something. But, he said, he "couldn't get up any steam for either man." Once FDR was in office, EAR granted him his grudging support. He believed in the president's integrity, at least. And even if his policies seemed all wrong as a matter of principle, "in human diseases one poison calls for another, and this may be true of the body economic." But it might also be true that no political remedy short of revolution would work. EAR suspected that "capitalism, with its short-sightedness, [was] hanging itself without knowing it."

The news from overseas was less than reassuring. In some moods, Robinson anticipated a Bolshevik takeover. "All Europe will be Russianized after the next war, and in the meantime we had better learn to eat grass," he wrote Louis Ledoux in October 1933. "Horses and cows think well of it." In others, he foresaw a revolution on the right. "Today I have been thinking of Hitler, and of what one neurotic fanatic may yet do to us and drag us into," he wrote Laura Richards in Feburary 1934. "It's all right to say it can't happen, but unfortunately it can."

Written during the summer of 1934, *King Jasper* represents Robinson's response to the worldwide malaise in general and to socio-economic injustice in particular. He understood that mixing philosophy or economics or sociology with art usually produced an unholy mess. Yet in his last long poem, which was published posthumously, he envisioned nothing less than the incendiary collapse of the capitalist system. The title, *King Jasper*, harked back to the loss of the Robinson family funds, some of them sunk in the Jasper County (Missouri) mines. The poem itself looked ahead to a conflict between communism and capitalism that would end in mutual total destruction.

The depression provided the immediate stimulus for the poem. The idea first occurred to him, Robinson said, as he was walking down Boston's State Street during the bank holiday FDR declared following his inauguration in March 1933. The poem was also influenced by his reading of *The Coming Struggle for Power* (1933) by the English communist John Strachey in the winter of 1934. Robinson came away from that book with a conviction that "something has got to crack before long." *King Jasper*, which Robinson referred to as "my treatise on economics," dramatized the disastrous consequences of that crack-up.

The tycoon Jasper, elevated to the status of royalty by his wealth, achieved his eminence through the same greed and ambition, lust for power, and appropriation of the talent of others that Robinson assigned to the other misguided capitalists of his late poems. Many years earlier, Jasper used the genius of his friend Hebron to advance his own career and then let Hebron waste away and die in poverty. The other characters include Honoria, Jasper's wife; their son, Jasper, who brings home the beautiful and mysterious Zoë, his wife "under the stars" if not legally; and young Hebron, returned to avenge his father by destroying the factory chimneys of Jasper's empire.

Those chimneys come crashing down in the climax of the poem, along with all of the characters but one. Honoria, sensing the impending doom, becomes depressed and kills herself. King Jasper, convalescing from a serious illness when the revolution breaks out, dies of a stroke or heart attack. Young Hebron invades the palace, shoots young Jasper, and attempts to seduce Zoë, who stabs him with a knife. Only Zoë survives.

These are manifestly allegorical figures. King Jasper represents power in a corrupted society of industrial capitalism. Honoria, as her name suggests, stands for traditional values. Young Jasper is the overprivileged and ineffectual liberal who means well, young Hebron the fire-breathing revolutionary who "destroys civilization in avenging the wrong on which it was founded." Zoë, the most complicated character, seems to encompass several qualities at once, but knowledge (or the truth) most of all.

The vagueness of her role may reflect Robinson's own uncertain views about what might emerge after the general conflagration. By leaving its conclusion somewhat hazy, the poem sacrifices its authority as an allegory. Furthermore, by reducing most of its characters to one-dimensional status, *King Jasper* loses the depth of feeling characteristic of Robinson's best work.

Intimations of Mortality

Robinson's attitude toward death remained consistent through the years. When his mother died in 1896, his sense of relief that she had been released from suffering prevented him from grieving in the conventional way. Thirty and forty years later, when tragedy twice struck the Barstow family, he adopted a similarly stoic stance. In August 1926, James and Katherine Barstow's oldest child, Jacqueline, drowned during a vacation at Monhegan Island. Her death would be hard to bear, he wrote Burnham, but his sympathy went to the parents and not the dead child. "I am never sorry for the dead, but I can be damnably sorry for the living."

Release from this "scrappy" existence was not to be lamented, Robinson believed, even if the dead person were a child. And still more so when death claimed an adult like Jacqueline Barstow's uncle Joe, who suffered a disfiguring gunshot wound while rabbit hunting in February 1934. Joe lived only four days after the accident, and EAR wrote Emma that he hoped the doctors had "inadvertently . . . hastened things a little." Nor was death to be regretted for the old. When Robinson's beloved cousin Clara Palmer, who had helped care for him as a child, passed on, he observed that there wasn't much to say. "Poor Clara must have had more than her share of infirmity, and at her age it would not be kindness to wish her more of it."

This sentiment had a precedent in Robinson's ancestry. On the tombstone of his grandfather Edward Robinson, in the cemetery at Alna, Maine, the motto reads:

We would not call thee back
To sorrow, grief and pain,
To tread once more life's weary track,
And sigh with us again.

As his health worsened, Robinson's thoughts turned to his own last days. He dreaded the prospect of a lingering death and thought it might well come to that, for "we are a tough tribe, and pretty hard to kill." Slow dying became almost an obsession with him. In his youth, he worried that he would not live long enough; having passed sixty, he worried that he would live too long. "Apparently, I was born not to be satisfied," he ruefully remarked.

When Hermann Hagedorn joined the Oxford Movement in 1933, Robinson wrote him that it was good to know he had "a light, for without one a fellow is either comfortably blind or wretchedly astray": the message, basically, of his just-completed *Amaranth*. As for himself, Robinson said he had always had a light to keep him going, though at times it was "burning pretty low." His "light" was hardly the same as Lancelot's "Light." He confronted the universe with confidence that he was fulfilling his purpose, with fortitude in the face of its trials, and with hope of a better world to come.

In his letters to Laura Richards as to no one else, Robinson could unselfconsciously discourse on religion. He held no brief for the "theological machinery" of Christianity, he wrote her in February 1933. Had she "heard about the recusant gentleman who said he might believe in the Trinity when he saw one man riding in three carriages"? But religious questions that were no laughing matter increasingly occupied his thoughts. In the spring of 1933, he read John Bunyan's didactic *Pilgrim's Progress* (1678) "with a great deal of satisfaction and admiration, for the first time in half a century." The following year, EAR encountered Geza Roheim's 1934 monograph, "Primitive High Gods," and gleaned from its findings an idea that would have appalled Bunyan. Roheim concluded—as EAR told Mowry Saben—that there was "much to be said for the phallic origin of religion."

When Carty Ranck showed EAR the draft of his 1930 article for the Sunday newspaper magazines, Robinson approved everything except one anecdote. One summer at the MacDowell Colony, Ranck had asked him if he believed in the hereafter. Robinson smiled and cited another writer's response. Asked the same question, O. Henry replied:

I had a little dog
Whose name was Rover,
And when he died,
He died *all over*.

With obvious enjoyment, EAR heavily accented the last two words of the doggerel.

In reporting the incident for his article, Ranck concluded that Robinson was skeptical about a life beyond the grave. That was not at all true, EAR insisted. He'd quoted the Rover lines because they were funny, not because they had "the remotest bearing" on his views of life and death. "I don't believe that this life is all," he wrote Ranck, "and I don't know where anything can be found in my work to indicate any such belief."

This, too, was an issue he explored in his correspondence with Laura Richards. He was inclined to believe in the next world, he wrote her in 1925. "I get no comfort out of turning into grass, and cannot believe that the great What-ever-it-is would have gone to so much trouble as to make you and me (not to mention a few others) for the sake of a little ultimate hay."

Lilla Perry died believing she would meet her friends again, Robinson told Mrs. Richards in March 1933. EAR had his doubts about that. "My notion of immortality . . . doesn't include the memory of this rather trivial—and for most people much worse than that—phase of existence." In a better world to come, he hoped for amnesia about the present one.

When he limped back to Boston from Peterborough in October 1933, Robin-son was ill as he had never been before. Sharp headaches made him miserable. When he tried to read, he felt stabs of pain in his eyes. His ear was worse, his back no better. Fortunately, it was just at this time that he got to know Dr. Mer-rill Moore, a psychiatrist and poet who had settled in Boston after his youth among the Fugitive writers at Vanderbilt. Moore was an amazingly prolific poet who "wrote hundreds of sonnets while waiting at red lights." He also served as "a kind of soul-doctor" for a number of writers. Through conversation if not actual analysis, he was able to make Robinson accept his long-suppressed resentment against a father who paid him little attention. If Moore also man-aged to bring EAR to grips with a mother whose postpartum illness forced her to abandon him as an infant, or with the evident preference both parents bestowed on his brother Herman, there is no record of it.

During the autumn of 1933, Moore hosted a private dinner for Robinson and Frost, another poet he had gone out of his way to befriend. The evening started badly, with Frost berating EAR for having wasted so much of his time retell-ing Arthurian tales. But Robinson gently deflected any hostility by talking of

FIGURE 27.1 Poet and psychiatrist Merrill Moore. EAR opened up to him.

Source: Library of Congress.

Frost poems he admired. It was like a grownup dealing with a child's petulance, Moore thought.

In particular, Robinson told Frost that he thought one quatrain of his was the very best in modern poetry. A friend who knew how much he liked it had given him a woodcut quoting those lines, EAR said, and he'd placed it in a frame to hang on the wall above his bed. Moore corroborated the account; he'd seen the woodcut in Robinson's room. Naturally, Frost wanted to know what the lines were. They came from the end of "Stopping by Woods on a Snowy Evening," and Robinson spoke them for him:

> The woods are lovely, dark and deep,
> But I have promises to keep,
> And miles to go before I sleep,
> And miles to go before I sleep.

After that, good feeling prevailed for the rest of the evening.

Moore's ministrations and a period of extended rest in Boston sent Robinson back to New York in December 1933 feeling somewhat better. He was able to complete revisions on *Amaranth*, participate in social occasions, and put himself out for the benefit of old friends and new. The new one was a young poet named Boris Todrin. Todrin, then a seventeen-year-old high school senior in Brooklyn, sent EAR his first slim book of poems in the fall of 1932. Robinson was enthusiastic enough about them to write Todrin a detailed critique.

On receiving this encouraging letter from Robinson, Todrin immediately came to see him in Boston. Todrin had a favor to ask. He wanted to go to college—Columbia, if possible—but had no money. Could Robinson help? Indeed he could. He wrote Mark Van Doren, then teaching at Columbia, that he suspected Todrin might be a genius and asking if a scholarship might be arranged. After several letters back and forth between EAR and Van Doren, the scholarship came through, and in the fall of 1933 Todrin enrolled at Columbia.

When Robinson got back to New York in December, Todrin visited him several times. In his next book of poems, published in 1936, Todrin suggested something of what Robinson's encouragement had meant to him. The book was titled *The Room by the River* and dedicated to "Edwin Arlington Robinson, The Man in the Room by the River." The room was EAR's at the Frasers on East Forty-second Street, with its view of the East River. The title poem acknowledged the gift that the old poet gave the aspiring one as the two sat in the twin rocking chairs and talked.

> Have you heard of a boy who was dreaming a dream,
> Of the wonderful friend, a father and giver,
> Of quiet and words that he shared like a gleam
> From the quivering hoard in the room by the river?

In the summer of 1934, Robinson wrote Todrin from Peterborough, congratulating him on winning an award that would help defray his college expenses, offering him an additional fifty dollars, and advising him to keep his chin up. Todrin, EAR feared, was subject to the same spells of discouragement he had known in his youth. "You are just at the age when one of your temperament and general make-up is likely to see the dark side of everything. . . . I went through it and know all about it."

Todrin eventually earned both his B.A. and M.A. degrees from Columbia and went on to write six books of poetry and four novels while earning a living as a journalist and advertising man. Before EAR died, he alerted Ridgely Torrence to Todrin's promise, asking that he do what he could to look after him. Torrence helped secure the youth a spot at the MacDowell Colony in the summer of 1937.

Torrence himself was in economic distress in the fall of 1933, having lost his editorial job at the *New Republic*. Upon hearing the news, Robinson wrote Isaacs, asking him to be on the lookout for any openings that might come up. Isaacs heard that Oxford University Press might be expanding its operations, and EAR arranged for George Brett, the head of Macmillan, to write a letter of recommendation about Torrence to Oxford. Robinson then advised Torrence precisely how he should proceed, if he was at all interested. It would be well to apply at once to Oxford. He should endeavor to arrange for an interview by telephone, mentioning Brett's letter. "Mr. B[rett]," he emphasized, "was altogether cordial and pleasant, and glad to be of any possible service to you." As, of course, was Robinson himself.

The summer of 1934 was Robinson's last at MacDowell. He managed to complete the draft of *King Jasper* by fall, despite working shorter hours than in the past. His energy was abating and his body breaking down. One day when he was talking with Esther Bates about *King Jasper*, he seized up, placed his hand on his back, and said, simply, "Pain." Adding to his usual digestive difficulties was an ominous new development. For the first time, he was losing his appetite. Even his favorite foods tasted awful.

Rollo Walter Brown stopped in to see him at the Veltin Studio shortly before Robinson left for Boston in the fall. Finding EAR taking a nap, Brown waited on the porch until he awoke. Then the two men sat together in the September afternoon sun, gazing at Monadnock. "I expect that old mountain will miss me when I stop coming up here," EAR said.

Robinson decided to head back to Colony Hall, and Brown caught a glimpse of the poet as he would always remember him: "a tall man in a dark gray suit and white golf hat swinging along beneath quiet pines over a curving road." EAR held his head high, "as if he were concerned with exceptional possibilities."

In Boston, Robinson placed himself under the nurturing care of Merrill Moore. Dr. Moore supplied him with a useful excuse for avoiding the strain of social life. He was "under doctor's orders," he now could say, "to stay quiet and make as few engagements as possible." He saw Burnham and Ranck, for he felt easy and comfortable with them, and very few others.

It was clear to those who did see him that Robinson did not have long to live. On a bleak day in December, Merrill Moore took him to the Back Bay station to catch the train to New York. Burnham and Ranck were there to see him off. Rollo Brown brought along two young poets who particularly admired EAR, John Holmes and Kenneth Porter, to say their farewells. They were all at the station well in advance of departure time. Brown talked with Burnham, hoping that Porter, sitting next to Robinson, might have a talk with him. It was difficult to say, Porter remarked afterward, which of them struggled harder for words. When the train was ready to leave, the frail poet fussed over his baggage, hoisted himself aboard, and said, "Well, I hope to be up early in the spring."

Robinson interrupted his journey to spend two days in Westport with the Frasers. They played poker, as usual. On the first night, Robinson lost the last hand. On the second night, the same thing happened. This was unusual. Robinson was a good poker player who could read his opponents' holdings while maintaining a calm demeanor himself. It had become a tradition, in games with the Frasers, that he would win the last hand. Not this time: the cards were running against him.

The Last of Days

The auspices were no brighter in New York. The Isaacses were shocked by Robinson's appearance when he arrived but went ahead with plans for the usual dinner-and-theater evening in celebration of EAR's birthday. On December 22, he would be sixty-five. The day before, Robinson telephoned that he did not feel up to the theater: frightening news from a man who enjoyed nothing more than watching a drama unfold on the stage. Lewis Isaacs dined with him instead, and arrangements were made that he should undergo a thorough medical examination.

In advance of Christmas, Robinson phoned Emma not to send her usual gift of apples. He had no taste for apples any more, he said. On Christmas day, which he spent in his room at 328 East Forty-second Street, he sent a note to Betts in California. "This is a Christmas word to let you know that I am here alone with a compound of cold and collywobbles. I hoped to be at Westport with the Frasers, but couldn't quite make it. I'm better than I was, but still 'not so good.'" He remembered, however, to include an "enclosure" as a holiday gift for Betts.

Chard Smith stopped in twice to see Robinson at the Frasers. On the first visit, EAR sat in his rocker, reading and rereading a one-page letter. "I'm afraid Frost is a jealous man," he said, but would say no more. According to Frost, he had written upon hearing of Robinson's illness to express his appreciation of his work. The letter has not come to light.

On Smith's second call, Robinson was not at all himself. He kept getting up and down nervously, moving things around the room. He refused a suggestion that they dine together; he was "off his feed" and wouldn't provide much company. Eventually, he revealed that he was going into the hospital for an examination. "Doesn't amount to a damn," he said, and then, contradicting himself, "there's something wrong."

The purpose of the examination was to discover just what was wrong with EAR and to provide a remedy, if possible. Robinson, thinking of his brother Herman's death, had an abiding fear of spending his last days in the crowded ward of a public hospital. His friends saw to it that it did not happen. Elizabeth Marsh, who had spent many summers with Robinson at the MacDowell Colony, arranged for him to be placed in the care of her cousin, Dr. Eugene DuBois, head of the Department of Medicine at the recently opened New York Hospital on East Sixty-eighth Street. EAR was installed there in a pleasant room early in January 1935.

On January 6, he wrote brief notes to Ruth Nivison and George Burnham from this "new palace on the river." Ruth was not to worry; he was only in the hospital "for a general examination." He thought he had colitis, and possibly ulcers. After the testing was over, in another three or four days, he'd let them know. Meanwhile, he could smoke and read detective stories, so it wasn't so bad. He had a corner room on the seventeenth floor "with the whole town to look at."

FIGURE 27.2 Thin and tired, EAR in his last year.

Source: Colby College Special Collections.

A week later, the tests remained inconclusive. Dr. DuBois—"the big doctor," as EAR called him—could only conclude that Robinson did not have acute colitis and that whatever the trouble was, he didn't think "the ale [had] much to do with it." DuBois took Robinson home with him for a few days. He could see that his patient was weakening and wanted to keep an eye on him. EAR made light of his condition when, back in the hospital, he wrote to Laura Richards apologizing for the break in their correspondence. The letter says much about Robinson's lack of self-pity and concern for others.

New York Hospital
January 20, 1935

Dear Mrs. Richards

Please don't be alarmed, or suspect that I have forgotten you, for I have thought of you as much as I haven't written. I have been rather a sick dog lately and am in this place for inspection and repairs. They expect to have me going again pretty soon, though I shall wobble for a while. The pain has gone from my interior, and the rest will be only a bore.

You must be very careful with your eyes. I doubt if you would care much for Auden or Spender. They are for the youngsters.

Yours as ever
E. A. R.

After more tests and observations, the doctors remained puzzled about the source of Robinson's illness. They were fairly certain that some kind of malignancy was growing inside him but did not know where or what it was. On January 28, Dr. Eugene Poole conducted an exploratory abdominal operation. This revealed the worst: cancer of the pancreas that had metastasized to the lungs and was so far advanced as to be inoperable.

The doctors harbored no hope for his recovery. Robinson, however, was told only that he suffered from an inflammation of the pancreas and that he would be treated for that as soon as the immediate effects of the operation wore off. Whether he believed that diagnosis, and continued to believe it during the ten weeks he stayed in New York Hospital, is not clear. There were good days and bad days, but more of the bad. Food tasted poisonous to him, and he was so tired, most of the time, that he could barely manage to read. Yet throughout he spoke confidently of getting back on his feet and of returning to Boston and Peterborough on his regular spring and summer schedule.

Lewis Isaacs took on the task of seeing Robinson through. He came to the hospital every day, functioned as EAR's advocate with the medical staff, and served as bearer of bad news to Robinson's family and such friends as George Burnham and Merrill Moore in Boston. Isaacs believed that until the very last

EAR did not know he was dying. Edith Isaacs, who saw Robinson nearly as often, felt sure that he did know and that he adopted an optimistic tone in order not to cause discomfort and embarrassment to others.

Ruth Nivison came to New York shortly after the operation with a mission in mind. She knew her uncle was in good hands but wanted to bring him home to Gardiner for his final days. It would be "the perfect place for his convalescence," she told EAR, and she promised to come back and collect him after his incision healed. Robinson seemed pleased about the idea, though he protested that Ruth's husband and sons needed her more than he did.

Robinson's condition deteriorated so badly, though, that a journey to Maine was out of the question. Before the operation, he said he did not dread the surgery so much as the "lying still afterwards." He was right to be concerned about that, for in his bedridden state he developed phlebitis. His legs became badly swollen and gave him considerable pain. During the last few weeks he could not walk at all but occasionally was lifted into a chair. On March 25, he wrote an extraordinary letter to his niece Marie in Boston.

The second paragraph dealt with his illness. Robinson had less than two weeks to live, but he treated his problems as lightheartedly as possible. "I seem to be a fixture in this place, until my rather obstinate phlebitis disappears," EAR wrote. "Perhaps I have never made it quite clear to you that I have been wrestling with a duodenal stasis, an inflamed pancreas, and phlebitis—which should be enough for one visitation." But the real subject of the letter, in its first and third paragraphs, was not his health but Burnham's.

> I have been worrying lately about Mr. Burnham. I am very anxious that you should have a short talk with him, perfectly frank and confidential, giving him to understand that you are an old friend of Dr. Legg's, and that an interview with him could be arranged with no difficulty or expense on his side. I have always suspected something wrong with the legs he is wearing now. . . .
>
> I am sorry to trouble you about Mr. Burnham, but you can easily see how I cannot keep myself from worrying about him. It is desperately important that he should at least have some legs to walk on. If Dr. Legg's bill is not too large, taken along with my present rather exorbitant expenses, I should be glad to pay it and furnish the new pair of legs.

This from a man who would not walk again.

Bedside Visitations

Robinson need not have feared dying alone or neglected. Many friends and admirers came to see him in the hospital. His nurses and doctors felt themselves in the presence of a remarkable human being. "It was a wonderful opportunity," Dr. DuBois said afterwards, "to see so intimately a really great man whose beautiful character was evident in all stages of his illness." Even the hospital interns and resident physicians, hearing of the poet's presence, were eager to stop by his room for, as Edith Isaacs put it, "a few moments of inspiration." EAR received them all with quiet courtesy, doing the utmost within the limits of his flagging strength to put them at ease. Toward the end there were so many who wanted to see him—friends and admirers, as well as members of the medical staff—that Lewis Isaacs and his nurses had to limit the number of callers.

Winfield Townley Scott made his visit a few days after EAR's January 28 operation. Scott found Robinson shockingly changed, "brilliant-eyed, thin, and motionless," his teeth showing "small, yellow, and pitted." His right arm hurt, and he apologized for not being able to shake hands. Scott felt certain he would never see Robinson again. It was hard to think of much to say.

"I mustn't tire you, Mr. Robinson," Scott said after a quarter of an hour.

"It's not so much a matter of your tiring me as it is of my tiring you," EAR replied.

Before Scott left, he stood up and saw the white gulls in the winter sunlight flashing over the East River, "flying and always flying and still flying" like those of the deserted Isolt in *Tristram*. Whether the bedridden Robinson could see the gulls or knew they were there, he could not say.

What Robinson *could* make out, gazing from his high corner room, was the edge of Welfare (now Roosevelt) Island, where the city hospital was located. It spoiled the otherwise splendid view for him. "Think of the old men down there, the suffering, the crowded and dingy quarters, the loneliness," he told Ridgely Torrence. And here he was, on the seventeenth floor of the palatial new hospital, getting every possible attention. It was not in his character not to think of others.

Parker Fillmore, who lived nearby, came to see EAR often after his operation. When he initially proposed frequent visits, Robinson demurred. "You mustn't put yourself out," he told Fillmore. "Just drop in when it happens to be convenient."

"It would be convenient nearly every day," Fillmore replied. He had some arthritis at the base of his spine and was coming to the hospital regularly for treatments.

"Oh, in that case . . . ," EAR said.

Fillmore could barely detect any decline in Robinson's condition from day to day, yet there seemed to be a perceptible change from one week to the next. Midway through EAR's hospitalization, about six weeks before his death, Fillmore fell and broke his right wrist. He was treated in the emergency room of New York Hospital and before going home stopped by, exhausted and shaken, to see Robinson. EAR was at once sympathetic and indignant. It was terrible that Fillmore should have suffered such an accident. Broken wrists might be all right for ordinary people, but not for one of his friends.

The next day, EAR's nurse told Fillmore that the accident may have been hard on him but had done wonders for her patient. "He's been talking of nothing else all morning," she reported. Temporarily at least, Fillmore's broken wrist enabled Robinson to forget his own illness.

In the March *Atlantic Monthly*, Theodore Morrison wrote a favorable review of *Amaranth*, praising Robinson's irony, imagination, and humor. EAR was pleased and excited about the review, which Fillmore brought for him to read. Morrison hadn't much liked his other books of late, nor had most of the other reviewers. "The critics are pretty severe with me nowadays," Robinson said. That shouldn't bother him, Fillmore said. It was simply the price he had to pay for success. Once Robinson became a best-seller, the critics had to jump on him. If he was still struggling for recognition, they'd all be on his side.

At least half believing it, Fillmore also told EAR it was all right to publish a book every year. It didn't matter how much a poet wrote, he said, so long as he put his best into every line. "I don't think you've ever let a careless or slipshod line leave your hands."

Robinson's thin face brightened. "You're right," he said. "I have never scamped my work—never."

The wives of his friends visited Robinson in the hospital, as did his coterie of women artists from the MacDowell Colony. Mrs. MacDowell herself stopped in on her way to a winter in California. Both of them whistling in the dark, they spoke of EAR's return to Peterbrough in a few months. "Yes," he said. "That is home." Elizabeth Marsh was all gaiety. Mabel Daniels tried to make light of his illness. Jean Ledoux chatted about her new hat and her newly bobbed hair, leaving a gardenia on his bedspread.

To them all, Robinson sounded confident about his eventual recovery. He asked Laura Fraser to put his summer suit in mothballs; he'd be wanting to wear it when the weather turned warm. Leonora Speyer, like Edith Isaacs, felt certain that Robinson knew he had little time left. On her last visit, she talked of taking EAR for a drive, now that there was spring in the air. They shook hands, Leonora surprised by the firmness of Robinson's grasp. "I'm coming again, E. A.," she said. "Come soon," he replied.

There were two unwelcome visitors. The bloated Joseph Lewis French, using an assumed name, slipped by the nurses into the poet's bedroom, demanding money. Robinson gave him twenty-five dollars. The parasitical French snatched his prize and scuttled away.

Robinson was also troubled by a more persistent visitor, Edith Isaacs observed. This was a man (nameless in her account) whom Robinson "had known for a long time and whom he had liked and disliked at various times and for good reason." Almost certainly this was Chard Smith, who was making his hospital calls as research toward a poem commemorating Robinson's death. Lewis Isaacs got wind of this when one of EAR's nurses telephoned him that this visitor was causing her patient considerable distress. She herself had asked him not to come again, but he said he had to, and often, because he was writing a poem on the death of a great poet and needed first-hand evidence. His repeated visits troubled EAR, who felt his private world invaded.

Smith did perform the useful service of alerting Carty Ranck (then back in Kentucky) that Robinson was dying. Ranck came at once, and he passed on the dire news to Elizabeth Sparhawk-Jones, who immediately left her home in Westtown, Pennsylvania, to take up the vigil. Burnham also arrived from Boston. The four of them—Burnham, Ranck, Smith, and Sparhawk-Jones—took turns spending the night in the hospital solarium, awaiting the end.

Ranck arrived on Monday, April 1, and saw Robinson the next afternoon. He seemed "quite his old self," Ranck recalled, and EAR dictated a few letters for Ranck to send to others. "Well, Jimmie," said the one to James Barstow, "They've got me on my back at last."

Since coming to the hospital he had been working, as best he could, on *King Jasper*. There was one major change. Robinson decided to call Jasper's wife Honoria instead of Hermione, and he assigned Edith Isaacs to scan the script carefully and change the name all through. With his eyes bothering him, he asked Torrence and Ledoux to read proof for him. On Friday, March 29, Latham brought the page proofs of *King Jasper* for a last read-through. "Come back on Wednesday," Robinson told Latham, "and I'll have everything ready for the printer." Almost at once, EAR found an error: "tailor's hut" for "toiler's hut." Now he'd have to go through the whole poem again, he decided. Isaacs read it to him, marking any passages that seemed doubtful, and EAR laboriously went over them day after day. He was not quite finished when he sank into a coma on Tuesday. The nurse telephoned Latham not to come in the next day; there was no point. But then, miraculously, EAR came out of the coma on Wednesday morning and urgently asked to see Latham. The editor came at once.

As Latham approached the bed, EAR reached feebly for the pile of proofs on the coverlet. "Here it is," he said, placing his last poem in his editor's hands. "I said you were to have it today, and now it is done." Dr. DuBois was astonished that Robinson had broken his coma and recovered his mental comprehension long enough to complete the task. Even when dying, Robinson would not scamp his work.

Robinson's friends came to see him at the end. As he grew more gaunt, it seemed that EAR's great penetrating eyes filled the room. Too tired to talk when Ridgely Torrence arrived, he let his hands talk for him instead, managing a faint smile as he pantomimed buttoning the eleven buttons of the long waistcoats that he and Torrence, both tall and thin men, ordinarily wore. Laura and Jimmy Fraser came and went, sensing that an unspoken goodbye had passed between them. Late on Wednesday afternoon, Ledoux stopped in, and EAR asked for a cigarette.

"Are you allowed to smoke?" Ledoux asked.

"What difference does it make?" Robinson said. "We'll have our cigarettes together."

Elizabeth Sparhawk-Jones, who unabashedly loved EAR, was not allowed to see him. The emotional strain might be too much. She was distressed, but Fillmore assured her—with more tact than honesty—that Robinson did not want to see any of his women friends. Sparhawk-Jones persuaded the nurse to send in a rambler rose to hang at the head of his bed. EAR opened his eyes, looked up, and said "Pretty."

Robinson relapsed into a coma after his exertions on Wednesday. He died at two-thirty in the morning on Saturday, April 6. Burnham and Ranck waited at the hospital through much of the night, hoping that EAR might regain consciousness, and they left an hour before his death. Sparhawk-Jones kept watch until the end. After Robinson was dead, she was permitted to enter his room. She knelt beside his bed and prayed. When she left, she took the rose cutting to be planted at her home. It blossomed wonderfully.

28

Beyond the Sunset

Memorials

Funeral services for Robinson were held at five-thirty P.M., Monday, April 8, at St. George's Protestant Episcopal Church, 207 East Sixteenth Street. About 300 people attended the ceremony. Dr. Karl Railand, rector of the church, read from the epistle of St. Paul to the Romans and from Revelations. The organist played the prelude to Wagner's *Tristan and Isolde*, a group of Bach chorales, the largo from Dvorak's *New World Symphony*, and the Dead March from Handel's *Saul*. "Remember—if the end comes, and if there is any service—to have them play the Dead March in Saul," Laura Richards had cautioned Lewis Isaacs. That music saw Robinson to his rest, as it had his brother Dean.

Everything in the service connected to EAR. Lucius Beebe sent a quantity of red roses to be strewn on the steps leading up to the altar, as in "The Gift of God." Laurel and hemlock from the woods of Peterborough covered his coffin. There was no eulogy—these would come at later observances—and the ceremony lasted but half an hour. Later, Robinson's body was cremated, and the ashes went to Gardiner for burial.

Margaret Perry, who came down from New Hampshire and just missed seeing EAR before his final coma, thought that the services should have been held in a cathedral rather than the small church on Stuyvesant Square. Molly Colum felt strongly that there should have been a national observance. Robinson's poetry "was an expression of the civilization" of the United States, she wrote. "The funeral of this man whose name will be remembered was not as it should have been—something that represented the country." Yet the very simplicity and lack of pretentiousness of the service was much as Robinson would have wished.

Laura Fraser supervised the arrangements for the funeral. A list of twenty-five honorary pallbearers was released to the press: C. C. Auchincloss, James Barstow, William Rose Benet, George Burnham, Dr. Eugene DuBois, Parker Fillmore, Dr. John H. Finley, James Earle Fraser, Robert Frost, Hermann Hagedorn, Lewis M. Isaacs, Harold Latham, Ernest Lawson, Louis V. Ledoux, Daniel Gregory Mason, Percy MacKaye, Edwin Markham, Dr. Eugene Poole, Carty Ranck, Henry H. Richards, Kermit Roosevelt, Ernest Schelling, Chard Powers Smith, Ridgely Torrence, and Thornton Wilder.

A few names were surprising—Auchincloss and Finley, for example, the composer Ernest Schelling, and Frost, a great poet but hardly a friend. Inevitably, a few were omitted who should not have been: EAR's old friend Craven Langstroth Betts and his more recent one Dr. Merrill Moore among them.

Betts was one of but two Robinson friends to whom he bequeathed a fraction of his estate. The estate amounted to about $50,000: "not bad for a poet," as he'd once said. The bulk of the funds went in four equal shares of $11,000 to Emma Robinson and her three daughters. Robinson left $3,000 to Burnham, and $1,000 each to Betts and the MacDowell Colony. In his will, EAR appointed Isaacs and Ledoux as co-executors. In effect, this placed Isaacs in charge of his financial affairs and Ledoux of his literary heritage.

Many metropolitan dailies and magazines noted Robinson's passing with editorials saluting him as the nation's "foremost" or "most illustrious" poet. James Earle Fraser collected two dozen of these commentaries into a booklet called *In Tribute*.

In these retrospective assessments of his career, Robinson was often praised for keeping out of the public limelight and sticking to his art despite long neglect. There was a sense, Malcolm Cowley wrote, in which EAR "was not only the most distinguished but also the only American poet of his generation": the only one who "devoted his whole career to writing verse and refused every opportunity to capitalize [on] his reputation."

The poet Robinson Jeffers, in California, lauded Robinson, for "the dignity with which he wore his fame," for the example of his reticence, and for the single-mindedness with which he pursued his calling. "We are grateful," Jeffers wrote, "that he was not 'a good showman' but gave himself to his work, not his audience, and would have preferred complete failure to any success that had the least taint of charlatanry in it." Dr. DuBois read those remarks in the May 1935 issue of *College Verse* and forwarded them to Ruth Nivison. "Your uncle would have liked that," he said.

Other memorials concentrated on the distinctive qualities of the poetry. Attention was called to EAR's repudiation of the hackneyed, artificial language that dominated American poetry in his youth and to the highly concentrated version of ordinary diction he adopted in its stead. The compression made every word count the more, invited the reader to become an interpreter, and gave the poems much of their power. Some called his poetry prosaic, the *Times* said, and offered in rebuttal the "quiet magic" of the end of "The Sheaves."

A thousand golden sheaves were lying there,
Shining and still, but not for long to stay—

As if a thousand girls with golden hair
Might rise from where they slept and go away.

Radical though Robinson was in his unembarrassed use of commonplace diction, his greatest poems, as the *St. Louis Post-Dispatch* observed, were "almost entirely free of the stylistic devices and the innovations" associated with many poets of the mid-1930s. EAR moved to blank verse but did not take the giant step to free verse or to experimental reinventions of vocabulary and punctuation. "He built upon the shoulders of the classics."

Morton Dauwen Zabel, in an extended evaluation of Robinson's accomplishment for *Poetry*, stressed the "cleansing influence" he exerted on contemporary verse. Through his insistence on "form and toughness of language," EAR "corrected by modest example a slow drift toward slovenly habits and facile impressionism in poetic thought."

The longest and most thoughtful discussion of EAR's achievement, printed as the concluding entry in Fraser's *In Tribute* volume, came from poet and scholar Robert Hillyer in the *Harvard Alumni Bulletin*. Hillyer proposed that Robinson's work fell roughly into three methods. The first produced the series of brief, incisive portraits for which, in part because they are short and easy to anthologize, he is still best remembered: poems like "Richard Cory" and "Luke Havergal." In the second method, midway through his career, Robinson "continued his study of mankind, now reinforced with richer detail and skillfully interpreted by the comments and actions of the characters themselves": "Ben Jonson Entertains a Man from Stratford," for instance. The third method called forth Robinson's "full powers" put to work "on a mistaken errand," resulting in the long verse novels of his last decade. There were "splendid passages" in all of these poems, but they made for dull reading, for EAR analyzed his characters "out of existence." Hillyer, though, detected a welcome rejuvenation of Robinson's powers in the 1934 *Amaranth*, a poem that embodied "the abysmal loneliness of the true artist who, under the impact of successful frauds, questions his own powers."

After summarizing the highs and lows of a career, Hillyer aptly likened Robinson to Thomas Hardy. "Both penetrated, often haltingly, always shyly, the minds of people whom they created . . . and both, Hardy the more pessimistically, Robinson the more hopefully, punctuated their universe with a question mark." In conclusion, he extolled EAR as "a symbol of integrity, of skill, of power." Robinson "was indubitably one of the great poets of the English language."

A few of the memorial pieces drew lines of comparison between Robinson as an artist and as a human being. William Rose Benet hailed him as infinitely kind, "a great man who moved through our hasty and greedy world." Mowry Saben, who had reason to know, commented that "no man ever possessed a more generous nature towards other writers less fortunate than himself. . . . Great as he was as a writer," Saben asserted, "he was even greater as a man." Then, speaking for himself, "one who knew him feels that the poet was the best man he has ever known."

The Harvard and Yale libraries both mounted exhibitions of Robinson's books and manuscripts in the months after his death. In the fall of 1935, Charles Cestre of the Sorbonne returned to the United States to present a series of three lectures at Harvard on the greatest American contemporary poets: two lectures on Robinson and one on Frost and Millay combined. "I hope Mr. Frost and Miss Millay will not feel hurt," Isaacs wrote Laura Richards.

Robinson's home town held two observances in his honor. The first was a memorial gathering on May 12, 1936. The high school auditorium was filled for the ceremony. Governor Louis J. Brann presided, having been introduced by Mayor Edwin P. Ladd. Both men were graduates of Gardiner High School, Ladd in the same 1888 graduating class as Robinson. Bowdoin College president Kenneth O. M. Sills gave an address so lacking in specificity that it might have been made about any poet. Mrs. MacDowell, who was not in attendance, was outraged to learn that Sills had not so much as mentioned the colony.

Henry H. Richards, "Hal" to the family and "Mister Dick" to decades of Groton schoolboys, sought in his remarks to correct the image of EAR as a recluse. To be sure, Robinson was quiet and did not put himself forward, but there was "nothing unapproachable" about him. "I have not known a man who had more friends," Richards said, "or who had a keener sense of humor or a warmer sympathy." The Bowdoin Glee Club sang, twice. Harold T. Pulsifer, president of the Poetry Society of America, read "Richard Cory," "The House on the Hill," "Miniver Cheevy," "Two Gardens in Linndale," and "Credo." At the end came, yet again, the Dead March from *Saul*.

Robinson's ashes were buried the following day in the family plot at Oak Grove Cemetery. The gray stone is not prominent or easy to find. There are seventeen names on it, with EAR's parents on the front and his own among six on the south side.

Before the burial, young Bill Nivison remembers sitting in the music room at home, fascinated by the mechanism that would forever seal the urn containing his granduncle's ashes. Bill and his father were about to close it when Emma brought some dried rose petals to be placed inside. This was done. Then there was a knock on the door—an emissary from the Richardses' Yellow House, with a bunch of forget-me-nots sent by Rosalind and a request that a sprig be put in the urn. This too was done. Two women he loved wanted something of themselves to travel with him.

Eighteen months later, Gardiner installed a permanent memorial to Robinson. Well over eighty, Laura Richards took charge of this endeavor. She and her committee secured the funds—from nearly 400 contributors—and commissioned architect Henry R. Shepley to design a ten-foot granite tablet in Robinson's honor. This was installed on the Gardiner Common, only a few blocks from EAR's boyhood home, and officially unveiled by his two grandnephews as the climax of an impressive ceremony on Sunday, October 18, 1936.

Present governor Louis J. Brann was on the platform again, along with former governor William Tudor Gardiner. Henry Richards, Laura's husband, formally presented the monument to the city on behalf of the many contributors. The seed of Robinson's genius had been sown and germinated before he left Gardiner forty years before, Richards said. Placing it on the common would symbolize his "home-coming" and serve as "an inspiration for future generations." In the principal address, Hermann Hagedorn, his biography underway, spoke eloquently of Robinson as an "anchorite" in the religion of poetry, "outside space and time, conscious of an eternal Eye upon him and upon the work of his hands."

Two short books of reminiscence preceded Hagedorn's 1938 *Edwin Arlington Robinson*. In *E. A. R.* (1936), Laura Richards presented her view of Robinson during his young manhood in Gardiner. In *Next Door to a Poet* (1937), Rollo Walter Brown set down memories of Robinson at the MacDowell Colony.

The colony, Robinson's working home for two dozen years, did not let his passing go unrecognized. "An Hour with E. A. R." was presented at the MacDowell's annual meeting of members in January 1936. Thornton Wilder spoke of what he had learned from Robinson and read from his poems, Mrs. MacDowell revisited Robinson's early years and Kathryn White Ryan his later ones at Peterborough, Lewis Isaacs read some of EAR's letters sent from the colony, and Parker Fillmore in his memorial talk ventured into the personality of the poet.

Fillmore acknowledged in Robinson a reticence about his private life so deep that "intimately as we grew to know him, we never knew about him." But therein lay "a strange contradiction: this man who allowed no one to come very close to himself, of his own volition became very close indeed to us of the Colony—to hundreds of us, men and women alike. We talked to him and he talked to us and the flash of understanding that passed between us . . . was so instant and so complete that we went away happy and satisfied, and always thereafter we knew in our secret hearts that we were friends."

In closing, Fillmore emphasized EAR's modesty. "He was humble about himself as a human being, conscious of his own weaknesses and shortcomings, and even fearful lest unwittingly he offend the least of his associates." Robinson was "never humble in regard to his work," however. "He knew always that a great talent had been entrusted to him and he knew also that he was proving himself a faithful steward."

In September 1938, the MacDowell Colony installed its own memorial to Robinson—a bronze plaque fashioned by Laura Gardin Fraser for permanent installation in the Veltin Studio. Fillmore and Hagedorn spoke, and William Rose Benet read a suite of Robinson poems: "Flammonde," "The Sheaves," "Eros Turannos," "For a Dead Lady," and a section from *Merlin*, concluding with "Mr.

FIGURE 28.1 The Robinson Memorial on the Gardiner Common

Source: Maine Historic Preservation Commission.

Flood's Party." Ruth Nivison drew the cord and the curtain fell away, revealing the bronze plaque. The inscription carried the final words Robinson had given John Brown: "I shall have more to say when I am dead."

Frost and *King Jasper*

Robinson's publishers decided to do something different on behalf of *King Jasper*. To give the book a proper sendoff, they sought out Robert Frost to write an introduction. The book was published in October 1935, to mixed reviews.

Percy Hutchison in the *New York Times Book Review* proclaimed it "both blinding in intensity and fiercely illuminating." John Crowe Ransom in the *Southern Review* found it so "autumn-grey" and vague that only a dedicated Robinsonian could appreciate it. Ransom also commented that Frost's introduction was superior to the poem itself. Frost himself thought it the best prose piece he ever wrote.

The introduction is so well done that some critics have called it "a generous and penetrating tribute" or "a charming, scarcely improvable tribute" to Robinson. Others, however, have labeled it a clever exercise in damning with faint praise. The division of opinion depends on the attitude of the commentators toward Robinson, Frost, and Frost's notorious and often unwarranted jealousy "of just about every poet who had any reputation" at all.

The story of why and how Frost contributed an introduction to *King Jasper* is a long and complicated one. Frost had to be wooed and cajoled into writing it, and persuaded to turn out a second draft after the first one failed to offer much that was specific to or appreciative of Robinson's work. He worked on it over much of the summer of 1935, lamenting to Untermeyer about the expenditure of time involved.

When the American Academy asked Frost, in December, to compose a eulogy for Robinson, he refused to do so. He'd already had his say in the preface to *King Jasper*, he pointed out, and had gone "far far out of [his] way to do honor to Robinson there. What I wrote may not seem enough to his friends, but it was my best and I am sure any attempt on my part to add to it would only take away from it."

Did Frost "do honor" to EAR? In his introduction as revised, he did say a number of laudatory things about Robinson's poetry. "The utmost of ambition is to lodge a few poems where they will be hard to get rid of, to lodge a few irreducible bits where Robinson lodged more than his share." And: "For forty years it was phrase on phrase on phrase with Robinson and every one the closest delineation of something that *is* something. . . . If books of verse were to be indexed by lines first in importance instead of lines first in position, many of Robinson's poems would be represented several times over." And: "Robinson could make lyric talk like drama. He is at his height between quotation marks." And: "Robinson has gone to his place in American literature and left his human place among us vacant. We mourn, but with the qualification that after all, his life was a revel in the felicities of language."

For someone as rivalrous as Frost, statements like those must have come hard, and it *is* a tribute to Robinson that they came at all. What's more, when asked in revision to discuss specific poems, Frost summoned up quotations from no fewer than eight Robinson poems. Presumably he did this from memory and not with a copy of EAR's *Collected Poems* at his elbow, for the punctuation goes askew, and in two of the quotations Frost makes minor changes in the language itself: errors that the editors at Macmillan should have caught and corrected.

On the other hand, it could be argued that Frost's introduction had the effect of stereotyping Robinson as—in Frost's phrase—"the prince of heartachers": a doleful singer, sad and melancholy, plunged into the depths of despair. He repeatedly invoked this image of EAR in the course of commenting on his poetry. From discussing the wit and humor of "Miniver Cheevy," for example, Frost moved to a passage about "a man as sorrowful as Robinson. His death is sad to those who knew him, but nowhere near as sad as the lifetime of poetry to which he attuned our ears." Similarly, he followed his discussion of the cleverness of "Old King Cole" with "his theme was unhappiness itself, but his skill was as happy as it was playful. There is that comforting thought for those who suffered to see him suffer."

In his letter to R. P. T. Coffin in 1938, Frost said that he and Robinson shared many opinions but "parted company over the badness of the world. He was cast in the mold of sadness. I am neither optimist nor pessimist. I never voted either ticket." And in conversation, Frost is said to have criticized EAR for shedding "too many literary tears." Certainly that is the implication one comes away with after reading the introduction to *King Jasper*, with its repeated references to Robinson's grief and sorrow, suffering and sadness.

By and large, the critical consensus has tended to accept Frost's view of the distinction between himself and Robinson. Having been told as much by Frost, Coffin called Frost "a happier poet than Robinson." Floyd Stovall described Robinson's mood as "predominantly sad," Frost's as "predominantly cheerful." Both wrote of ruined cottages and lonely, morbidly obsessed people, Barton St. Armand noted, but "whereas Frost was the poet of survival, Robinson was the poet of defeat."

"Sadness and compassion permeate all of [Robinson's] lines," Henry Steele Commager wrote in *The American Mind* (1950). By focusing on sadness alone, as Frost did in his *King Jasper* piece, one may lose sight of the tremendous compassion that provides another, more accurate way of differentiating Robinson from his fellow poets. Commager's observation does more justice to Robinson and his accomplishment than a pigeonholing phrase like "prince of heart-achers": the title William S. Pritchard borrowed for his assessment of Robinson in his *Lives of the Modern Poets* (1980). To affix that label to EAR and reinforce it with half a dozen repetitions, as Frost did in his introduction to *King Jasper*, effectively diminished the standing of the man then his principal competitor for preeminence among American poets.

The Issue of Reputation

For a decade after his death, little critical material appeared on Robinson. Then, between 1946 to 1954, four full-length studies and forty-six articles on EAR's poetry were published. Far and away the most important of these was Yvor Winters's *Edwin Arlington Robinson* (1946), issued in New Directions' Makers of Modern Literature series. Winters was an influential and extremely controversial critic. His book, as scholar Ronald Moran pointed out, "was instrumental in establishing Robinson as a major American poet." It was not that Winters found no fault in Robinson's works; he found fault in everyone's and in EAR's case mentioned "a certain dryness" and a tendency toward too much "expository statement." But such faults were in his view far outweighed by Robinson's virtues: "the plain style, the rational statement, the psychological insight, the subdued irony, the high seriousness and the stubborn persistence." On balance, Winters adjudged Robinson to be "on certain occasions one of the most remarkable poets in our language."

In 1948, Emery Neff, another well known figure in the academic community, placed Robinson alongside Frost among the greatest American poets in his volume on EAR for the American Men of Letters series. In a lively review of that book, William Carlos Williams brought up a question that has confounded scholars and critics through the years: Where does Robinson belong in American literary history? Should he be considered the last of the nineteenth-century New England poets or rather, as Williams believed him to be, "the great progenitor of the modern in its best sense"? Or, worse yet, allowed to fall between the cracks?

Two full-length studies of the early 1950s—Ellsworth Barnard's critical exploration of the entire Robinson corpus in 1952 and Edwin S. Fussell's examination of the influences that made up "The Literary Background of a Traditional Poet"—contributed to EAR's reputation. There ensued a decade of general silence, broken emphatically by publications leading up to Robinson's centenary in 1969.

Robinson was a famous man when he died in 1935, but thirty years later the fame had shrunk. Trying to ascertain why, the British critic John Lucas asked a class of American undergraduates why Robinson was so little read. "Well," one of them answered, "we know just about where he stands." Where he stood— where he was to be categorized—was, first, as a prince of heartachers, his work permeated with sadness, and second, as a poet who wrote entirely too much and too long. In looking at wonderful poems like "Mr. Flood's Party" and "Isaac and Archibald," Lucas did what he could to dismiss the first half of the stereotype. They communicated "the sadness of incommunicable isolation," to be sure, but escaped desolation through the warmth of affection in the poet's voice and through his fascination with "the mysteriousness of people, no matter how ordinary they may seem." This, Lucas asserted, was what made Robinson "one of the necessary poets."

The charge that Robinson wrote too much and that much of his late work fell below his earlier standard, could hardly be denied. But as the excellent *Selected Poems of Edwin Arlington Robinson* (1965) demonstrated, we would be foolish to abandon many great poems because Robinson did not always write as well as he usually did. Morton Dauwen Zabel, as editor, chose to include not only the usual short anthology pieces for which EAR is still best publicly remembered but also a judicious selection of mid-length poems including "Issac and Archibald" itself, "Ben Jonson Entertains a Man from Stratford," and "Rembrandt to Rembrandt." This book presented readers with the best of Robinson in a paperback one-sixth the length of the 1,500-page *Collected Poems*.

The poet James Dickey, in his introduction to the *Selected Poems*, took issue with the modernists who were inclined, with T. S. Eliot, to repudiate Robinson as "negligible." In Dickey's judgment, "Robinson's considered, unhurried lines, as uncomplicated in syntax as they are difficult in thought," stood as "a constant rebuke to those who conceive[d] of poetry as verbal legerdemain or as the 'superior amusement'" Eliot called it.

Irving Howe also joined the argument on the side of EAR. Those brought up in the modernist tradition of Eliot and Wallace Stevens were liable to regard Robinson as insufficiently dazzling and "merely traditional." But, Howe pointed out, EAR did not set out to bedazzle his readers, and he had in any case made his own significant contribution to the poetic revolution by bringing "commonplace people and commonplace experience into our poetry." As opposed to an experimental poetry determined to surprise, Radcliffe Squires further commented, the "immense surprise" of Robinson's work lay "in its humble poetic fact . . . , the ambition to make the half-known truly known in a way that only the strait geometry of form can make it known."

With the *Selected Poems* available in the bookstore and the college classroom, the stage was set for the burst of critical activity leading up to the Robinson centenary in 1969. Chard Powers Smith's biographical and interpretive *Where the Light Falls* came out in 1965; W. R. Robinson's *Edwin Arlington Robinson: The Poetry of the Act* and Wallace L. Anderson's *Edwin Arlington Robinson: A Critical Introduction* in 1967; Hoyt Franchere's volume on EAR in the Twayne United States Authors series in 1968; and both Louis O. Coxe's *Edwin Arlington Robinson: The Life of Poetry* and *Edwin Arlington Robinson Centenary Essays*, edited by Ellsworth Barnard, in 1969.

In the most penetrating of these books, Coxe celebrated Robinson as a "poet of the middle style" who, "in order to remain faithful to his vision of ordinary men in a recognizably real world, must risk the pedestrian and the banal, just as the poet of originality, in order to fly ever higher, risks the catastrophic fall and disintegration." The times "favored the latter type, obviously" in 1969. Coxe stood with Robinson, however, even if his poetry did not look original enough or difficult enough on the page. In Robinson's best poems, he observed, the poet presented the case for another human being, sometimes with humor, always with pity and terror, and in a voice decidedly his own. "These are the poems . . . readers will go back to for as long as readers read."

Robinson "doesn't write like a demon or a god," James Dickey said in reviewing Coxe's book. "He writes like a man, saying what you and I would say about the people we know, if we knew the way to say it, and if we had the nerve to tell the truth: that is, if we *cared* enough." Manifestly, Robinson does care, and he makes us care too. "The best of his poems are terribly painful, and they are so simply because we believe them; we believe this really happened to someone, and that it happened pretty much as Robinson said it did," Dickey observed, citing "Reuben Bright" for proof.

Attention to Robinson's work sloughed off after the several books of criticism published in the late 1960s, to rise again in the 1990s. This time, the poems themselves and not books about them spurred the renewed interest. Robinson's massive *Collected Poems*, unhandsomely printed in one huge volume, has been out of print for many years, which as Robert Mezey has said constitutes "a national disgrace." Yet when the *Selected Poems* edited by Zabel also went out of print, no fewer than three separate editions appeared to fill the vacuum.

The first of these, *The Essential Robinson* (1994), was edited by the poet Donald Hall. In his foreword, Hall argued that Robinson's reputation had been unjustly sacrificed on the altar of modernism. "We must bring Robinson back," he passionately proclaimed. And again, "We must restore Robinson to the American pantheon." In a concluding paragraph, Hall itemized the qualities that ranked EAR among the best American poets. "Robinson was master of verse and poetry, of metric and diction, of syntax and tone, rhyme and under-standing, ethics, metaphor, and the exposure of greed. The last nouns in this series are not disconnected from the first: Dead metaphors are unethical, and forced rhymes are corrupt. In monkish solitude, with painstaking and moral attention, in long hours of revision, he made great poems."

Robert Faggen, introducing his 1997 *Selected Poems* for Penguin, designated Robinson one of America's greatest poets, who through his mastery of craft and insight into character created a powerful body of poems. This stated the case adequately but without the sense of personal deprivation that motivated both Hall and Mezey, editor of the 1999 Modern Library edition of *The Poetry of E. A. Robinson.*

In his introduction, Mezey harked back to the early 1950s when he and fel-low poet James Wright, both undergraduates at Kenyon, had been captivated by EAR's poetry. By the end of the century, though, Mezey could scarcely remem-ber the last time he'd read "Robinson written of with intelligence and love." What had *happened* to Robinson? "How are we to account for this state of affairs, that one of the greatest poets to have emerged in this country, a poet worthy to be in the company of Emerson, Dickinson, Stevens, and Frost, should be so little read, so little celebrated?"

Attempting to answer the question, Mezey pointed to EAR's adherence to traditional forms of meter and rhyme, to his writing to be understood, and to his conviction that reason as well as imagination had a part to play in poetry, whereas there still existed "among far too many readers, teachers, reviewers, and poets, a stubborn prejudice against metrical verse and against clear rational procedure." The modernist poets who came along only a decade or two later swept Robinson aside for smacking of traditionalism, no matter how revolu-tionary his poems actually were in subject matter and diction.

That very subject matter, Mezey believed, also worked against Robinson's reputation. His concentration on the downcast and defeated, the injured and ignored—"the world that lies just beneath the laugh track"—was hardly "a recipe for popularity."

Then, too, most of us are reluctant to look at others as closely as Robinson did, much less at ourselves. Better to confess such of our sins as may interest and amuse, leaving the darker territory unexamined. Constitutionally averse to unburdening himself on the page, Robinson looked intently around him and put down what he saw, necessarily revealing much about himself—and the rest of us—in the process. Such truth telling can be frightening, even terrifying: we'd rather not know, thank you.

Except sometimes, when we realize that his poems still speak for us. On October 1, 2001, the *New York Times* printed EAR's villanelle "The House on the Hill," as a poem capable of evoking and in some sense exorcising the terrible sense of loss the nation felt in the weeks after the 9/11 attacks. "There is ruin and decay / In the House on the Hill: / They are all gone away, / There is nothing more to say."

A Life in Poetry

We may think of Robinson as a Maine poet, or a New England poet, and that designation makes sense. He was brought up in Gardiner and stayed there until he was almost thirty. Or we may think of him, also with justification, as an urban poet tied, for his last thirty-five years, to New York City. Where he actually *lived* is another matter. In the lifelong dedication to poetry, he was only fully alive when he was writing. Alive in the boyhood room at 67 Lincoln overlooking the road to the cemetery, where he crafted his earliest efforts for the Gardiner Poetry Society. Alive in the sparsely furnished hall bedroom on West Twenty-third Street where he wrote his poems while battling the demons of depression and alcoholism and loneliness. Alive for many summers at a cabin in the New Hampshire woods, doing his work as a professional.

In his correspondence, EAR consistently warned others against the life of a poet. "Whatever [your son] Pierre may or may not do," he wrote Jean Ledoux in September 1929, "you may get down on your knees and be glad that he isn't going to write poetry." He wasn't at all sorry for what he had accomplished as a poet, EAR went on, but he felt mighty sorry "for anyone else who had to do it." He himself *had* to do it because it was his appointed mission. It made for a hard road, for along the way Robinson had to fight "his town, his culture, and his conscience" to suffer "poverty, guilt, neglect, and estrangement," and to write for fifteen years for about fifteen readers. It was as much his ordained journey to make as that of John Bunyan's Christian in *A Pilgrim's Progress*, and against as many obstacles.

People, other artists especially, were in the habit of praising Robinson for all the things he'd renounced to be a poet: home and family, comfort and contentment. That was nonsense, EAR thought. He advised Edith Isaacs, who threatened to write a memoir about him, to make it "clear to those people who say that I gave up great things to write poetry that there was only one thing in all the world I could give up."

"Poetry is not something you do, it is something you are," as Louis Coxe put it. There was a singular appropriateness in EAR's rousing himself from a coma to complete his last task. The deathbed revisions to *King Jasper* prompt a comparison between Robinson and Robert Browning, to whom he was so often inaccurately compared in other terms. Browning, dying in Venice, was brought a copy of *Asolando*, his last book, to hold. He riffled through the pages, said, "I have given my life to that," and tossed it down on the bed. Both men knew, as the inscription on Dr. Johnson's watchcase warned, that "the night is coming when no man can work."

Along with those who congratulated EAR for doing the only thing he could do came a contingent who deplored him for using commitment to his vocation as an excuse to escape the responsibilities of ordinary life. Parker Fillmore defended him against that charge. "I don't think he evaded life," Fillmore said. "E. A. had the conviction that he had a mighty work to do, and I doubt whether it would be fair to call his decision to let nothing stand in the way of that work an evasion of life."

When a teacher of psychology wrote him a fan letter in 1931, EAR replied that he had been called "a psychologist, and a philosopher, and all sorts of names" he didn't deserve. "In truth," he said, "I merely present people as I seem to know them after inventing them." The wonder is how well he knew them, with his powers of insight, and how brilliantly he brought them to life, with his mastery of his craft. Robinson was what Saul Bellow called "a world-class noticer."

Although he would not own up to being a philosopher or a psychologist, Robinson did have something to say about how to confront our troubles. The worst way he spelled out in a fierce condemnation at the end of "Hillcrest" (1916).

> Who sees unchastened here the soul
> Triumphant has no other sight
> Than has a child who sees the whole
> World radiant with his own delight.
>
> Far journeys and hard wandering
> Await him in whose crude surmise
> Peace, like a mask, hides everything
> That is and has been from his eyes;
>
> And all his wisdom is unfound,
> Or like a web that error weaves
> On airy looms that have a sound
> No louder now than falling leaves.

So Robinson inveighed against smug complacency in a world he never stopped regarding as "a hell of a place." Yet at the same time and despite all the darkness, he also expressed in his poetry his conviction that the universe could be "a fine thing" if we only had a light to guide us.

How should we remember Robinson, then? We owe him an immense debt, as the poet Conrad Aiken said, for simply being "the first American thing, the old oak, the first with a classical firmness, that we could, like young mistletoe, live upon." And a substantial debt, as well, for showing poets like James Wright how to make "poems say something humanly important instead of just showing off with language." But not many of us can be poets, and we go to Robinson—those of us who are fortunate enough to have found him—for his powerful and convincing dramatic portraits.

EAR was troubled enough as a human being, heaven knows. He skated on the rim of despair much of his life. But he would not parade his afflictions in the manner of the confessional poets of the late twentieth century. Instead he fixed his gaze on others and, without pretending to know everything about them, worked through their struggles and failures vicariously. As we can too, reading along.

Chard Smith counted 233 "fully drawn characters" in Robinson, more than were created by any other poet in English who did not double as a playwright. But size of population does not compare in importance to the way these characters are presented. The people in Robinson's poems do not resemble mannequins or caricatures or stick figures. They are crafted with a tinge of irony, sometimes, and with highlights of humor, often. They live and breathe and speak like the rest of us. When life treats them harshly, as it usually does, and if we are not terminally afflicted with hardness of heart, we suffer their disappointments and defeats along with them. Reading Robinson is a moving and cathartic experience, constantly reminding us of our involvement with mankind, and of the tears in the things of this world. This is his legacy.

EAR understood from the beginning of his career that recognition would not come quickly and that he might have to wait a hundred years for the judgment of posterity. He accepted the terms as a cost of his calling, confident that in the end "the real poems" would surface and knowing that a dozen titles would be "enough to string wires on" to reach through the centuries. He left more than three times that many "real poems" behind, counting only shorter and mid-length work. A chronologically organized list might include "Luke Havergal," "John Evereldown," "The House on the Hill," "Richard Cory," "Dear Friends," "Aaron Stark," "The Clerks," "Reuben Bright," and "The Tavern"; "Isaac and Archibald," "Aunt Imogen," and "The Growth of 'Lorraine' "; "Calverly's," "Uncle Ananias," "How Annandale Went Out," "Alma Mater," "Miniver Cheevy," "For a Dead Lady," "The White Lights," "The Whip," and "Two Gardens in Linndale"; "Flammonde," "The Gift of God," "Ben Jonson Entertains a Man from Stratford," "Hillcrest," "Old King Cole," "Eros Turannos," "Veteran Sirens," "The Poor Relation," and "The Man Against the Sky"; "The Wandering Jew," "The Mill," "The Dark Hills," "A Song at Shannon's," "John Brown," and "Firelight"; "Mr. Flood's Party," "Ben Trovato," "The Tree in Pamela's Garden,"

"Many Are Called," and "Rembrandt to Rembrandt"; "The Sheaves," "Karma," and "New England."

The list leaves out much, but it may be useful as a guide to aftercomers, now that Robinson has been gone for the better part of a century and his poetry is still in need of the recognition that is its due. That will come when enough of us open his book and—as he recommended—read one word after another.

Acknowledgments

To an unusual extent, this book draws upon the unpublished letters of Edwin Arlington Robinson, as painstakingly and professionally collected, transcribed, and annotated by Wallace L. Anderson. In addition, Robinson's published letters to Harry deForest Smith cast considerable light on his youth and young manhood in Gardiner and at Harvard, while the letters to Edith Brower depict the beginnings of his career as a professional poet.

There are a good many other extremely valuable sources as well that were unavailable to authors of previous biographies. Largely as a consequence, none of these books presents a convincing account of Robinson's life, although each provides interesting information on EAR and his career: Hagedorn on his early days in New York City, for example, and Smith on his life at the MacDowell Colony.

Richard Cary, the eminent Robinson scholar, sought out and presented in print many revelatory documents that would be otherwise extremely difficult to locate in *Early Reception of Edwin Arlington Robinson: The First Twenty Years* (1974) and *Uncollected Poems and Prose of Edwin Arlington Robinson* (1975).

The memoirs by Carty Ranck and Mowry Saben, uncovered in 2003, show EAR as two of his closest friends remember him. Arnold T. Schwab discovered the Ranck memoir, helped lead me to the Saben memoir, and generously shared his detailed fund of information on these and other figures in Robinson's life. Edith Issacs's notes on Robinson's letters to her husband reveal the contrasting figure of a man usually concealed beneath a carapace of reserve yet sometimes bubbling with wry humor. Percy MacKaye's long introduction to William Vaughn Moody's *Letters to Harriet* documents the failed onset on the theatre world that occupied Robinson's energies for nearly a decade.

I discovered to my surprise that much could still be learned from research undertaken by others to assist Hagedorn seventy years ago. Through her extensive interviews with members of her family and others, Rosalind Richards helped to capture the ambience of Gardiner and the position the Robinson family occupied in that community. Parker Fillmore, for his part, sketched perceptive portraits of EAR and his fellow colonists at MacDowell in a series of letters to Hagedorn. Two brief reminiscnces on Robinson at the MacDowell Colony, by Rollo Walter Brown and Esther Willard Bates, also bring him fleetingly to life. Among the several books devoted to Robinson and his poetry, those by Louis O. Coxe and Ellsworth Barnard proved to be the most helpful.

Substantial research for this biography was conducted through libraries with holdings that include letters (or other documents) to or about Robinson, as well as letters from him that have come to light since 1985, and photographs. However briefly, I thank the following people and libraries for their kind cooperation: Wendy Hurlock at the Archives of American Art, Smithsonian Institution; Kathy Kienholz at the American Academy of Arts and Letters; Peter Nelson at the Amherst College Library; Roberta Rosenberg at the Hayden Library, Arizona State University; Carol A. Turley at the University of California, Los Angeles Library; Bernard Crystal and Mary Marshall Clark at the Butler Library, Columbia University; Philip Cronenwett and Sarah Hartwell at the Dartmouth College Library; Alison Dinicola at the Huntington Library; Mary S. Presnell at the Lilly Library, Indiana University; Kathryn Hodson at the University of Iowa Libraries; Alice Birney at the Library of Congress, with gratitude for recommending Carren O. Kasten as a researcher; Benjamin Keating at the Maine State Library; Elizabeth Fairbairn at the Newberry Library; Beth Silbergleit at the Center for Southwest Research, University of New Mexico; Alyssa S. Morein, Loraine Baratti, and Jill Reichenbach at the New-York Historical Society; Rodney Phillips, Mimi Bowling, and Charles J. Liebman at the New York Public Library; Nancy M. Shawcross at the Rare Book and Manuscript Library, University of Pennsylvania; Barbara Katus and Cheryl Leibold at the Pennsylvania Academy of the Fine Arts; AnnaLee Pauls and Margaret Sherry Rich at the Firestone Library, Princeton University; Ken Lavender and Carolyn Davis at the Arents Library, Syracuse University; Jeffrey H. Kaimowitz and Peter J. Knapp at the Watkinson Library, Trinity College; Ann L. S. Southwell at the Alderman Library, University of Virginia; Robert Volz and Wayne G. Hammond at the Chapin Library, Williams College, and Susan Brady and Ruth Carruth at the Beinecke Library, Yale University.

By far my greatest debt as a researcher is owed to Patricia J. Burdick, curator of Special Collections at the Miller Library, Colby College. During three separate trips to Colby's vast holdings of Robinsoniana, she unfailingly did everything possible to expedite my work, arranging for copying equipment, locating hard-to-find materials, and offering professional advice. The Robinson archive could not be in more capable hands.

During the five-year gestation period for this book, I have corresponded with a number of people about it. These include Ellsworth Barnard, Edgar Allen Beem, Patricia J. Burdick, Douglas Van Dyck Brown, Billy Collins, Peter Davison (deceased), Daniel Dyer, Annie Finch, Robert L. Gale, Dana Gioia, Alexander Grinstein, Rachel Hadas, Donald Hall, Burton Hatlen, Nancy Carol

Joyner, Donald Justice (deceased), Robert McDowell, Christopher MacGowan, David Macy, Mark Melnicove, John Merrill, Robert Mezey, Paul Montgomery, David S. Nivison, Robert Pinsky, Josh Porter, Mrs. Eliot T. Putnam (deceased), Robin Rausch, Mark Richardson, Robert J. Scholnick, Arnold T. Schwab, Earle G. Shettleworth Jr., Michael Skupin, Barbara Lehman Smith, Danny D. Smith, Benjamin Sonnenberg, Henry Taylor, Alan Trachtenberg, Thomas J. Travisano, Amanda Vaill, Marjory Whitehurst, and Baron Wormser.

On several sojourns in the state of Maine, I took advantage of Danny D. Smith's ever helpful good nature to investigate Robinson's origins. During the first visit, in 2000, Danny prepared a photographic display of the sites that mattered to the poet during his formative years to guide us as we explored the town of Gardiner from dawn to dark. On subsequent trips he arranged for me to meet Marjory Whitehurst in the Head Tide house where Robinson was born, set up an appointment with Stephen and Sheila Hanley in the home at 67 Lincoln Avenue where he grew up, put me in touch with EAR's grand niece Elizabeth Calloway (who passed away in the spring of 2005) for a fine summer's day at Boothbay Harbor and Capitol Island, and accompanied me on a fall afternoon drive down to Camp Cobbosee, where the twenty-eight-year-old Robinson announced his love for Rosalind Richards. On that same trip to New England, I spent a few profitable hours with Douglas Van Dyck Brown, another acquaintance of Danny's, at Groton school. Brown, a long-time instructor at Groton, supplied an insider's look at the prep school where Kermit Roosevelt encountered EAR's *Children of the Night* and set in motion the extraordinary process by which his father, then president, rescued Robinson from the degradations of poverty.

Smith has been instrumental as well in helping acquire many of the photographs that illustrate and document this biography, through the skill and generosity of his friend Earle G. Shettleworth Jr., the director of the Maine Historic Preservation Commission, the Maine state historian (so designated in 2004), the coauthor, with Smith, of *Gardiner on the Kennebec*, and an expert in all things pictorial. I am also deeply indebted to Gene Nocon at In House Photo in San Diego for his photographic wizardry.

Danny D. Smith functioned as a faithful reader during the nearly two years of actual writing, making constructive suggestions about chapters as they came off the word processor. I relied on my wife, Vivian, to take a first look at everything, however, having learned that she understands better than anyone when my words go awry on the page. Thomas J. Travisano and Steven Gould Axelrod evaluated the beginning sections of the typescript and made gratifying comments about them for the benefit of Columbia University Press. Finally, and far from least, two readers of the work deserve particular mention.

The poet Robert Mezey, who edited the Modern Library's splendid *Poetry of E. A. Robinson* (1999), has been a dedicated supporter of this project from its inception. In the summer of 2005, he read the entire script with the expertise only an accomplished poet and editor can bring to the task, and he produced an extensive critical commentary that has undoubtedly improved the finished book.

Then there is David S. Nivison, EAR's grand nephew, a distinguished scholar of Chinese history and philosophy who has functioned as executor of Robinson's literary estate on behalf of his brother, Admiral William Nivison, Ret., and his cousin, Elizabeth Calloway, for many years. David granted permission to quote from everything Robinson wrote, published or unpublished. This was generosity—and trust—itself, further reinforced by several important documents he let me examine. These included Lawrance Thompson's notes toward a biography of Robinson that was never written, as well as EAR's mother's lengthy and revealing reminiscences, and the letters that his grandfather Herman Robinson wrote to his own beautiful wife, Emma, from an exile unjustly forced upon him.

David Nivison knows his grand uncle's work as well as anyone alive. Anyone interested in the nature of the interplay between Robinson's life and his work, for example, could do no better than to examine Nivison's excellent essay, "Does It Matter How Annandale Went Out?" As the typescript proceeded, he was able to offer insightful and penetrating comments, with close attention to the poems themselves. His reading of "The Sheaves" brilliantly opens up that eloquent and apparently cryptic sonnet.

This biography was written with the assistance of many people. None of them are responsible for its shortcomings. It's my book, after all, my voyage, sink or swim.

Notes

The notes that follow track the text of the book and are keyed to the bibliography that follows.

A number of abbreviations are used.

People

Aiken	Conrad Aiken
WLA	Wallace L. Anderson
Bartlett	Truman H. Bartlett
Bates	Esther Willard Bates
Beebe	Lucius Beebe
Betts	Craven Langstroth Betts
Braithwaite	William Stanley Braithwaite
Brower	Edith Brower
Burnham	George Burnham
Coan	Titus Munson Coan
SD	Scott Donaldson
Fillmore	Parker Fillmore
Ford	Joseph S. Ford
Fraser	James Earle Fraser
French	Joseph Lewis French
Frost	Robert Frost
Gardiner	John Hays Gardiner
Gilder	Richard Watson Gilder
Gledhill	Arthur R. Gledhill
Hagedorn	Hermann Hagedorn
Isaacs	Lewis M. Isaacs
Latham	George W. Latham
Ledoux	Louis V. Ledoux
Lowell	Amy Lowell
Mason	Daniel Gregory Mason
Moody	William Vaughn Moody
Neff	Emery Neff
Nevin	Arthur Nevin

Peabody	Josephine Preston Peabody
L. C. Perry	Lilla Cabot Perry
T. S. Perry	Thomas Sergeant Perry
Ranck	Carty Ranck
EAR	Edwin Arlington Robinson
T. R.	Theodore Roosevelt
Saben	Mowry Saben
Schumann	Alanson Tucker Schumann
C. P. Smith	Chard Powers Smith
Smith	Harry deForest Smith
Sutcliffe	Denham Sutcliffe
Thompson	Lawrance Thompson
Todrin	Boris Todrin
Torrence	Ridgely Torrence
Untermeyer	Louis Untermeyer
Variell	Arthur Davis Variell
Widdemer	Margaret Widdemer

Editions

Essential	*The Essential Robinson*, intro. Donald Hall
Poetry	*The Poetry of E. A. Robinson*, ed. Robert Mezey
Selected	*Edwin Arlington Robinson: Selected Poems*, ed. Robert Faggen
Letters	*Edwin Arlington Robinson's Letters to Edith Brower*
SL	*Selected Letters of Edwin Arlington Robinson*
Stars	*Untriangulated Stars: Letters of Edwin Arlington Robinson to Harry deForest Smith*
Uncollected	*Uncollected Poems and Prose of Edwin Arlington Robinson*, ed. Richard Cary.

Libraries

Colby	Colby College Special Collections
Columbia	Butler Library, Columbia University
Dartmouth	Rauner Special Collections, Dartmouth College Library
Harvard	Houghton Library, Harvard University
Huntington	Huntington Library
Indiana	Lilly Library, Indiana University
LC	Library of Congress
NYPL	New York Public Library
Princeton	Firestone Library, Princeton University
UCLA	Young Research Library, University of California, Los Angeles
UVA	Alderman Library, University of Virginia
Williams	Chapin Library, Williams College
Yale	Beinecke Library, Yale University

Unless otherwise indicated, letters referred to in the notes are to be found in the Wallace L. Anderson Collection at Colby College.

***

Page numbers for individual Robinson poems refer to the 1937 *Collected Poems*.

Introduction

New York Times, 7 April 1935, section 4, p. 8; *Washington Evening Star*, 8 April 1935, p. A10;
Mezey, *Poetry*, pp. xxxv–xlix; Hall, *Essential*, p. 14; *Merwin incident*: e-mail from Paul
Montgomery, 20 August 2003; EAR, "Reuben Bright," p. 92; Scott, *"Dirty Hand,"* p. 66;
MacLeish, "Rereading," 218–19; Redman, *EAR*, p. 95; *"Poetry is a language"*: Cary, *Uncollected*, p. 124; EAR, "Calverly's," p. 330; *"debates . . . battles"*: Wilson, *Shores of Light*, p. 598;
Mason, "Letters," pp. 863–64; Stoppard, quoted in "The Real Outrage," *New York Times
Book Review*, 6 May 2000, p. A16; *"I don't expect"*: Cary, *Early Reception*, opposite frontispiece; *"If you will . . . 2026"*: EAR to Variell, 20 August 1926; *"Byron"*: EAR to Laura E.
Richards, 16 August 1924; *"Wagner"*: EAR to L. C. Perry, 8 March 1931; *"Most great artists"*:
Fillmore to Hagedorn, 15 February 1937, LC.

A Man Almost Without Biography
"Now . . . vouchsafed to anyone": Saben, "EAR," p. 1; *"clam . . . no life to speak of"*: Kaplan, *Philosophy*, p. 16; Cunningham, "EAR," p. 28; *"If I . . . disturb"*: EAR to Brower, 2 April 1897, *Letters*, p. 34; *"E. A. R., born . . . at it"*: EAR to Laura E. Richards, 29 August 1918, *SL*, pp. 110–11;
"How strange it is": Torrence to Laura E. Richards, 4 December 1938, Yellow House Papers,
Gardiner Library Association; *"Some day . . . death"*: Untermeyer, "Unfinished," p. 34.

New Resources
"Sanitized . . . omission": Anderson, "Letters," pp. 52–55; *"lead quiet . . . moments"*: Updike, *On
Literary Biography*, pp. 11–12.

1. A Hell of a Name for a Poet

Anything but Eddie
"Like a tin bathtub . . . for a poet": Cary, *Early Reception*, pp. 14–16; Ranck, memoir, pp. 5–6;
Hall, quoted in Cary, *Early Reception*, p. 35; *"I have . . . pathological"*: EAR to Saben, 26 December 1926; *"You may . . . at all"*: EAR to Brower, 14 April, *Letters*, p. 76; *"my only name"*:
EAR to Variell, 14 August 1922; *"When Laura . . ."*: EAR to Laura E. Richards, 12 April 1931;
"fitted . . . his character": Hall, *Essential*, p. 3.

Edward Arlington Robinson, Pulitzer Prize Winner
EAR to Theodore Roosevelt Jr., 24 July 1930; *"correct error . . . records"*: EAR to "Mr. Ingersoll"
(Authors Club), 3 March 1922; *"high praise"*: Theodore Spencer, review of *Tristram*, by
EAR, Isaacs Collection, NYPL; *"You'd think . . . time"* R. W. Brown, *Next Door*, pp. 77–79;
"something weird . . . Edward": Ranck, memoir, p. 5.

Edward and Mary
Genealogical: Hagedorn, *EAR*, pp. 4–7; Thompson, notes, pp. 2, 10; *"When Ranck . . ."*: Ranck,
memoir, p. 7; *"He was . . . looking at it"*: EAR to Ranck, 14 January 1932; *"Head Tide"*: Bowring, "A Lonely Young Poet"; Mitchell, *Maine Summer*, pp. 174–77; Lord, "Will Head Tide";
Jane, "Journey"; Marjory Whitehurst, interview by SD, 16 August 2000.

Edwin, Drawn from a Hat
Hagedorn, *EAR*, pp. 9–12; Thompson, notes, p. 1: Emma Robinson, comment on Hagedorn's
pp. 9–14; SD, visit to Harpswell Neck, 16 August 2000; Stowe, *The Pearl*, pp. 1–3, 74; Ranck,
memoir, p. 4; Laura E. Richards, *E. A. R.*, pp. 4–5.

EAR as Bestower of Names
EAR, "Two Men," p. 80; *"tilbury"*: Satterfield, "Major Categories," pp. 75–76, Cary, *Early Reception*, pp. 14–15; *"Flammonde"*: Barnard, *Critical Study*, p. 57; *"glove"*: cited in Cary, *Early Reception*, p. 94.

2. A Manor Town in Maine

67 Lincoln and Oaklands
"The original . . . everything": Saben, "EAR," p. 7; *"provincial fastness . . . so acute"*: Gowan, *Puritan*, pp. 22, 27; *description of house*: Thompson, notes, p. 1; Ruth Nivison, memoir, pp. 12–15; Hagedorn, *EAR*, p. 14; Mollman, "Tilbury," pp. 3, 13; *"I know . . . England"*: Lowell, quoted in Gregory and Zaturenska, *A History*, p. 109; *history of Gardiner*: Danny D. Smith, "History"; *City of Gardiner*, p. 91; *"tiny hallmark . . . title"*: Rosalind Richards, notes, interview with Henry Richards.

The Golden Age
Coffin, quoted in Smith and Shettleworth, *Gardiner*, "Introduction," unpaginated; Rosalind Richards, *Northern*, pp. 157–61, 189, 202–03; *ice harvest*: Weightman, pp. 2–10, 20–21, 220–28; Ruth Nivison, memoir, p. 8.

The Duke of Puddledock
Neff, *EAR*, pp. 3–4; *"His whole life . . . man"*: obituary, *Gardiner* (Maine) *Daily Reporter-Journal*, 15 June 1892; *"he and Mr. Swift . . . stock"*: Rosalind Richards, notes, interview Barstow; Hagedorn, *EAR*, pp. 20–21; EAR, *Glory*, pp. 1058–59; *"jolly"*: Rosalind Richards, notes, interviews Laura (Lewis) Macomber and Bertha (Partridge) Allen; *dancer*: Ruth Nivison, memoir, p. 17; *singer*: Thompson, notes, p. 6, and C. P. Smith, p. 72; *"hard-headed"*: EAR to Clara Palmer, 7 March 1922; *drink*: Swanton and Laura E. Richards to Dunnack, 15 November 1935, Maine State Library; *"slight rusticities"*: Rosalind Richards, notes, interview Henry Richards; *"Duke"*: Danny D. Smith, interview by SD, 11 November 2003.

A Pair of Scissors
EAR, *Roman*, p. 735; *mother and son*: Chodorow, *Reproduction*, pp. 59, 71, 76–79; Laura E. Richards, *E. A. R.*, p. 7; *"She had the satiny skin . . ."*: Rosalind Richards, notes, interview Bertha (Partridge) Allen; Betts, p. 5; C. P. Smith, *Light*, pp. 69–70; *"Married people . . . other"*: Hagedorn, *EAR*, pp. 20–23, 85; *"Oedipal"*: Coxe, *EAR* pamphlet, p. 11; [MH: *"the same entity"*: Rosalind Richards, notes,] Saben, "EAR," pp. vii–viii; Martin, *Harvests*, p. 132; Coxe, *Life*, pp. 153–54; Hagedorn, *EAR,*, p. 368.

3. Never So Young Again

First Light
"Tongue": C. P. Smith, *Light*, p. 75; *"I realized . . . Life"*: EAR to Jean Ledoux, 10 December 1915; *"When I . . . born"*: EAR to Lowell, 26 November 1915; Rosalind Richards, notes, interview Laura E. Richards, pp. 3–4; *reading*: Neff, *EAR*, p. 5; Gorman, "Talk,"; Wisehart, " 'By Jove!' "; Brenner, *Modern Poets*, pp. 85–86; *"The proper office"*: Bryant, p. xxiv; *scrapbook poems*: Ranck, memoir, p. 8; *schooldays*: Lord, "Gardiner Childhood" and "Aunt May"; Swanton, "Reminiscences"; Hagedorn, *EAR,*, pp. 25–26; Barstow, *My Tilbury*, p. 10; Emma Robinson to Laura E. Richards, 27 July 1935, Harvard; *Palmers*: Thompson, notes, p. 2; C. P. Smith, *Light*, pp. 77–78; *lure of the sea*: Rosalind Richards, notes, interview Leonard Barnard; *Captain Jordan*: Hagedorn, *EAR*, pp. 14–15, Rosalind Richards, notes; EAR, "Pasa

Thalassa Thalassa," pp. 335–36; *death*: Franchere, *EAR*, p. 15; EAR to Gledhill, 2 April 1895; *ear*: Emma Robinson to Laura E. Richards, 27 July 1935, Harvard; EAR to Gledhill, 28 July 1891, WLA note.

Sibling Connections
EAR to Fred W. Palmer, 5 January 1882, WLA note; Fred W. Palmer, diary, David S. Nivison papers; *Dean*: C. P. Smith, *Light*, p. 74, Hagedorn, *EAR*, pp. 22–23; *"Dean knew more . . .":* Coxe, *Life*, p. 43; *Herman*: Rosalind Richards, notes, interview Bertha (Partridge) Allen; Hagedorn, *EAR*, p, 23; Ruth Nivison, memoir, p. 14, Rosalind Richards, notes, interview Laura (Lewis) Macomber; *accident*: *Gardiner* (Maine) *Daily Reporter-Journal*, undated clipping; *awkwardness*: Rosalind Richards, notes, interview Henry Richards, C. P. Smith, *Light*, p. 79, and Rosalind Richards, notes, interview Herbert Longfellow.

Dickens, Deadwood Dick, and Don Cesar
EAR to Laura E. Richards, 19 June 1929; *dime novels*: Pearson, pp. 45–53, 235–43; EAR to Variell, 7 January 1926; *apple feasts*: Mason, *Music*, p. 88; Olivia H. D. Torrence, "The Poet," pp. 97–99; *Don Cesar*: EAR, *Captain Craig*, p. 133; Rosalind Richards, notes on poems, p. 2; EAR, "Plummer Street," in letter to Moody, 10 May 1900.

The League of Three
"Shin-bones": EAR to Mason, 9 (?) May 1900; *high school*: Hagedorn, *EAR*, pp. 27–30; EAR to Gledhill, 4 January 1891; Neff, *EAR*, p. 8; Hagedorn, *EAR*, pp, 32, 40–43; *"When . . . forgotten"*: EAR to Smith, 15 November 1891, *Stars*, pp. 38–39; *"clandestine symposia"*: EAR to Gledhill, 10 January 1892 and 7 December 1890; Lord, "League of Three"; *"we were all boys"*: EAR, "Romance, II. James Wetherall," *Children*, p. 119; Rosalind Richards, notes, interview with N. C. Barstow; *"cult of friendship"*: Crowder, "Meaning," p. 7; *graduation*: Hagedorn, *EAR*, p. 44; Cary, *Early Reception*, p. 21.

The Gardiner Poetry Society
"Randolph bells": Cary, *Uncollected*, p. xii; EAR to Laura E. Richards, 31 July 1924; *Gardiner Poetry Society*: Dechert, "Study," p. 11–13; Rosalind Richards, notes, interview with Caroline Swan; Smith, quoted in Cary, "'Clam-Digger,'" p. 508; EAR, "Ballade of Broken Flutes," pp. 77–78; Cunningham, quoted in Mezey, *Poetry*, p. xviii; Rosalind Richards, notes, interview with Caroline Swan; *"polish of over-elegance"*: Manheimer, "Speaker's Voice," p. 8; *Schumann*: EAR, "The First Seven Years," Cary, *Uncollected*, pp. 106–7, EAR to Smith, 4 November 1894 and 5 October 1893, *Stars*, pp. 181–82 and p. 111; EAR, "A New England Poet," *Boston Evening Transcript*, 30 March 1918, Section 3, p. 7; Rosalind Richards, notes, interview Bertha (Partridge) Allen; EAR to Peabody, 27 November 1899; Emma Robinson, comment on Hagedorn's p. 33; Rosalind Richards, notes on Kate Vannah and William Henry Thorne; Cary, *Early Reception*, pp. 61–62; Rosalind Richards, notes, interview Miss Milliken, niece of Caroline Swan; *vocation*: EAR, "The First Seven Years," Cary, *Uncollected*, pp. 105–6.

4. Fall of the House of Robinson

Howe, "Tribute," p. 103; Mollman, "Tilbury," pp. 7–8; Waggoner, *American Poetry*, p. 678; EAR to Latham, 15 January 1894; Rosalind Richards, notes, interview Herbert Longfellow, p. 3.

Summer of '88
Father failing: Hagedorn, *EAR*, p. 39; C. P. Smith, *Light*, pp. 100–101; *Emma*: Thompson, notes; C. P. Smith, *Light*, pp. 88–89, 94–95; Emma Robinson and Ruth Nivison, annota-

tions, pp. 7–8; EAR, "The Night Before," *Torrent*, p. 36; EAR to Harry deForest Smith, 27 September 1890, and 10 March 1891, *Stars*, pp. 3, 13–14; *Herman*: Hagedorn, *EAR*, p. 39; C. P. Smith, *Light*, pp. 81–83, Thompson, notes, p. 3; Coxe, *Life*, p. 32; *"capitalist"*: Thompson, notes 1950; C. P. Smith, *Light*, pp. 82–83; *engagement*: Ruth Nivison, memoir, pp. 1–3.

Marking Time

Hagedorn, *EAR*, pp. 45–46; Neff, *EAR*, p. 10; EAR to Gledhill, 21 November 1889 and 3 January 1890; EAR to Smith, 27 September 1890, *Stars*, pp. 3–4; *cat*: Hagedorn, *EAR*, p. 57; EAR to Gledhill, 24 July 1890, and November 1889; *wedding*: *Kennebec* (Maine) *Reporter*, 15 February 1890; Ruth Nivison, memoir, pp. 6–7; Thompson, notes 1950; EAR to Gledhill, 23 February 1894, WLA note; EAR, "Cortege," pp. 221–22; David S Nivison, "Annandale," pp. 181–82; *ventures*: Thompson, notes, p. 4: Ruth Nivison, memoir, pp. 6, 8–10, and C. P. Smith, *Light*, pp. 103–4, 109–10.

Two Invalids

Addiction: Ruth Nivison, memoir, p. 10; Rosalind Richards, notes, interview Laura (Lewis) Macomber; Hagedorn, *EAR*, pp. 38–39, 54–55; EAR, "Charles Carville's Eyes," pp. 87–88; EAR to Gledhill, 24 July 1890; EAR to Gledhill, 4 January 1891, WLA note; EAR to Smith, 25 January 1891, *Stars*, p. 9; *to Harvard*: EAR to Gledhill, 27 September 1890 and 4 January 1891, EAR to Smith, 21 June 1891, *Stars*, p. 21; EAR to Gledhill, 11 March 1891; EAR to Smith, 30 April 1891, *Stars*, p. 18; *ear*: EAR to Gledhill, 28 July 1891; Neff, *EAR*, p. 20; Hagedorn, *EAR*, p. 61.

5. A "Special" at Harvard

College Days

EAR to Smith, 10 March 1891 and 13 September 1891, *Stars*, pp. 14–15, 24–25; Hagedorn, *EAR*, pp. 62–63; EAR to Gledhill, 11 October 1891 and 14 November 1891; Latham, "Robinson," p. 19; Neff, *EAR*, pp. 23–25, 30–31; EAR to Smith, 11 October 1891, 18 October 1891, 25 October 1891, 2 November 1891, and 7 November 1891, *Stars*, pp. 29–37; *Gates*: Tryon, "Harvard Days," pp. 8–10; R. W. Brown, *Harvard Yard*, pp. 13–14, 108–9; Hapgood, quoted in Scholnick, "Children," p. 85; *writing*: Rosalind Richards, notes, interview Herbert Longfellow, p. 4; Santayana, quoted in Scholnick, "Children," p. 7; Ziff, *American 1890s*, p. 308; Coxe, *Life*, p. 35; EAR to Smith, 15 November 1891, *Stars*, p. 40; *Laodicean*: Ziff, *American 1890s*, pp. 310–11; Cowley, quoted in Bak, *Cowley*, p. 52; *Moody*: EAR to Smith, 7 November 1891, *Stars*, p. 37; *Lovett*: EAR to Smith, 8 December 1891, WLA note; Robert Morss Lovett to Emery Neff, 20 May 1947, Columbia; Neff, *EAR*, pp. 26–27; Cary, *Early Reception*, p. 196; EAR, "In Harvard 5," Cary, *Uncollected*, pp. 15–16; C. P. Smith, *Light*, p. 101; Hagedorn, *EAR*, pp. 76–77, 388.

"The Friends of My Life"

Sutcliffe, intro., *Stars*, pp. xix–xx; Coxe, *Life*, p. 35; R. W. Brown, *Harvard Yard*, pp. 14–16; EAR to Smith, 15 November 1891, *Stars*, p. 40; Latham, "Robinson," p. 19; Tryon, "Harvard Days," p. 13; Saben, "EAR," pp. 63–64; Cary, "Mowry Saben," pp. 482–87; *Corn Cob Club*: Hagedorn, *EAR*, pp. 71–73; Tryon, "Harvard Days," p. 15; Saben, "EAR," pp. 8–9; EAR to Smith, 23 May 1892, *Stars*, p. 65; Saben to Burnham, 7 June 1938, Colby; Hagedorn, *EAR*, p. 80; EAR to Saben, 4 April 1896, WLA note; *Burnham*: Hagedorn, *EAR*, pp. 65–66; Neff, *EAR*, p. 29; Saben, "EAR," pp. 81–83.

A Social Education

EAR to Smith, 21 May 1891 and 18 October 1891, *Stars*, pp. 18, 33; Sutcliffe, intro., *Stars*, p. xvii; EAR to Smith, 15 November 1891 and 18 January, 1892, *Stars*. pp. 40 and 49; EAR to Gledhill, 13 February 1892; EAR to Smith, 3 February 1892, *Stars*, p. 52; Beebe, *Aspects*, p. 21; *Sumichrast reception*: Saben to Denham Sutcliffe, 3 June 1947, Colby; Tryon, "Harvard Days," p. 4; EAR to Smith, 29 November 1891 and 18 (?) March 1892, *Stars*, pp. 44, 57–58; EAR to Smith, 21 February 1892 and 1 March 1892, *Stars*, pp. 55–56; EAR to Smith, 13 March 1892, Colby; Cary, "Mowry Saben," p. 487; EAR to Ford, 15 May 1895; *"houses of seclusion"*: EAR to Smith, 7 February 1892, WLA note; EAR to Smith, 6 March 1892 and 13 March 1892, Colby; EAR, "The Growth of 'Lorraine,'" pp. 191–92; Moran, "Firm Address," pp. 48–54; David S. Nivison to SD, 21 May 2005; *theatre*: EAR to Smith, 15 November 1891, *Stars*, p. 40; EAR to Smith, 21 February 1892 and 7 March 1893, *Stars*, pp. 54 and 89; EAR to Ford, 14 May 1894; EAR to Smith, 15 May 1892, Colby; and Laura E. Richards, *E. A. R.*, pp. 36–37; *music*: EAR to Smith, 18 (?) March 1892, *Stars*, p. 59; EAR to Gledhill, 10 December 1892; EAR to Smith, 23 May 1892, *Stars*, p. 66; EAR, "Supremacy," p. 97; Hagedorn, *EAR*, pp. 82–83; EAR to Smith, 23 May 1892, *Stars*, p. 66.

6. Farewell to Carefree Days

Second Time Around
EAR to Smith, 24 April 1892; Ruth Nivison, memoir, p. 10; EAR, "Why He Was There," p. 888; Emma Robinson and Ruth Nivison, annotations, p. 21: *operation*: Hagedorn, *EAR*, p. 69; EAR to Smith, 9 October 1892 and 23 October 1892, *Stars*, pp. 73–74; EAR to Latham, 15 September 1894 and 29 August 1895; EAR to Gledhill, 20 August 1895; EAR to Smith, 1 October 1892 and 21 November 1892, *Stars*, pp. 68–69 and 74–75; EAR to Ford, 14 May 1894; EAR to Gledhill, 13 February 1893; *Norton*: Hagedorn, *EAR*, pp. 78–79; Mason, "Harvard," pp. 63–65; EAR to Smith, 29 November 1892, *Stars*, pp. 76–77; *Royce*: Mason, "Harvard," pp. 68–70; EAR to Smith, 21 February 1893 and 27 February 1893, *Stars*, pp. 87 and 88; Kaplan, *Philosophy*, p. 8.

Willie Butler and Others
Neff, *EAR*, pp. 38–39; *Saben*: EAR to Smith, 5 February 1893 and 7 May 1893, *Stars*, pp. 83–84 and 96; *Latham*: EAR to Smith, 7 May 1893 and 10 June 1894, *Stars*, pp. 95 and 164; EAR to Latham, 5 May 1895; EAR to Latham, 15 January 1894; EAR to Smith, 15 January 1894, Colby; EAR to Latham,10 October 1894,15 September 1894, and 20 December 1893, WLA note; Edel, "Portrait," p. 8; EAR to Smith, 13 May 1894, *Stars*, p. 152; EAR to Ford, 24 January 1894, WLA note; *Butler*: Tryon, "Harvard Days," p. 11; EAR to Smith, 13 January 1893, *Stars*, p. 80; Saben, "EAR," pp. 64–68, 118–20; Saben to Sutcliffe, 5 October 1947, quoted in Cary, "Mowry Saben," pp. 493–94; EAR to Latham,15 January 1894 and 31 March 1894; EAR to Smith, 1 May 1894, *Stars*, p. 147; EAR to Latham, 5 May 1895 and 20 June 1895.

Harvard and Its Effects
EAR to Smith, 19 March 1893, *Stars*, p. 92; EAR to Gledhill, 23 May 1923; EAR to Smith, 4 June 1893, 11 June 1893 and 23 June 1893, *Stars*, pp. 99, 101, and 103; EAR to Latham, 31 March 1894 and 14 December 1895; EAR to Smith, 6 May 1894, *Stars*, p.149; EAR to Gledhill, 8 June 1894; EAR to Smith, 22 April 1894 and 23 May 1896, *Stars*, pp. 144–45 and 248; Coxe, *Life*, p. 35.

7. Shaping a Life

Becoming a Writer
Ruth Nivison, memoir, p. 11; Neff, *EAR*, p. 41–43; Coxe, *Life*, p. 42; EAR to Gledhill, 28 October, 1893, *Selected*, p. 10; EAR to Latham, 20 December 1893; Saben, "EAR," p. 44; EAR

to Gledhill, 23 May 1923; Kaplan, *Philosophy*, p. 5; EAR to Smith, 4 February 1894, *Stars*, p. 126; EAR to Smith, 5 October 1893, *Stars*, p. 111; Barstow, *My Tilbury*, p. 5; *"farming"*: EAR to Ford, 14 May 1894; C. P. Smith, *Light*, pp. 132–33; EAR to Smith, 7 October 1894, *Stars*, p. 169; EAR to Ford, 8 May 1896; EAR to Smith, 22 May 1896, 7 December 1896, and 5 May 1895, *Stars*, pp. 249, 266, and 222; *to be a writer*: EAR to Gledhill, 28 October 1893; C. P. Smith, *Light*, p.132; Neff, p. 44; *sketches*: EAR to Smith, 11 March 1894 and 4 March 1894, *Stars*, pp. 139 and 134–35; WLA, " 'Scattered Lives,' " pp. 498–503; EAR to Latham, 20 December 1893; EAR to Gledhill, 17 December 1893; EAR to Smith, 19 November 1893, *Stars*, pp. 119–20; Neff, p. 51; EAR to Latham, 24 February 1895; *book*: EAR to Smith, 14 April 1895, *Stars*, p. 219; EAR to Ford, 20 October 1894 and 28 January 1895; Hagedorn, *EAR*, p. 102; EAR to Smith, 4 February 1894, *Stars*, pp. 124–25; EAR to Latham, 24 February 1895; EAR, "Aaron Stark," p. 86.

"Dear Friends"

Hanson, quoted in Neff, *EAR*, p. 89; Sutcliffe, "Puritanism," p. 29; Barstow, *My Tilbury*, p. 8; Mollman, "Tilbury," p. 11; Thompson, intro., EAR's *Tilbury Town*, p. xv; EAR to Smith, 1 October 1893 and 5 October 1893, *Stars*, pp. 107 and 110; EAR, "Dear Friends," pp. 83–84; Mollman, "Tilbury," p. 10; Neff, *EAR*, p. 49; EAR to Smith, 6 May 1894, *Stars*, p. 149; EAR to Ford, 5 October 1895, with news clipping, and 12 January 1896; Hagedorn, *EAR*, p.166.

Engagements

Mabel Moore: EAR to Smith, 22 October 1893, 27 January 1894, 1 May 1894, 20 May 1894, and 3 June 1894, *Stars*, pp. 114, 123,148,154, and 159; Thompson, notes, "Mabel Moore"; *Smith*: Rosalind Richards, notes; Hagedorn, *EAR*, pp. 47–48; Sutcliffe, intro., *Stars*, p. x; EAR to Smith, 20 May 1894, *Stars*, pp. 153–57; EAR to Smith, 4 February 1894, *Stars*, p. 125; Weeks, "Antigone," pp. 137–51; EAR to Ford, 14 September 1894; Neff, pp. 54–55; EAR to Smith, 15 June 1895, 26 May 1895, and 9 June 1895, *Stars*, pp. 230–31, 227, and 229–30; *Emma and nieces*: EAR to Smith, 19 November 1894, *Stars*, p. 186; EAR to Ford, 24 January 1894 and 5 October 1895; Ruth Nivison, memoir, pp. 21–22. *"The Night Before"*: Ruth Nivison, annotations 1948, p. 7; C. P. Smith, *Light*, p. 142.

Tilbury Townspeople

EAR to Smith, 14 December 1895, *Stars*, p. 238; Neff, *EAR*, p. 61; Cary, *Early Reception*, pp. 24–25; EAR to Smith, 7 March 1896, *Stars*, p. 243; Scudder, quoted in Cary, *Early Reception*, p. 307; EAR to Ford, 8 May 1896, 27 September 1896 and 14 October 1896; Mezey, *Poetry*, p. 219; EAR to Gledhill, 28 October 1896; *clerks*: EAR, "The Clerks," p. 90; EAR, "The First Seven Years," Cary, *Uncollected*, pp. 107–8; Barnard, *Critical Study*, p. 14; Taylor, "Mission," pp. 10–11; Mezey, *Poetry*, p. 218; Howe, "Tribute," p. 106; Trachtenberg, "Democracy," pp. 17–18; *"Lesson of the Master"*: EAR to Smith, 7 February 1896, *Stars*, p. 239; James, "The Lesson of the Master," *Collected*, pp. 986–87, 1006–8, and Neff, *EAR*, pp. 62–63.

Gardiner in Decline

Thompson, notes, "What Gardiner Has"; *flood*: Laura Richards, quoted in Smith and Shettleworth, *Gardiner*, pp. 82–83; *"picturesque"*: *City of Gardiner*, pp. 3–5, 7, 112; Coffin, *Kennebec*, pp. 188–89; V. W. Brooks, *Indian Summer*, p. 493–94; EAR, "The Dead Village," p. 88; EAR, "The House on the Hill," pp. 81–82; Dechert, "He Shouts"; Cary, *Appreciation*, pp. 341–43; Trachtenberg, "Democracy," pp. 10–11; Howe, "Tribute," p. 105; Coffin, *New Poetry*, p. 37.

The Death of Mary Robinson
Ruth Nivison, memoir, pp. 27, 37; Emma Robinson to Laura E. Richards, 27 July 1935, Harvard; C. P. Smith, *Light*, pp. 150–51; Thompson, notes, p. 3; Ruth Nivison, memoir, p. 28; EAR, "The Book of Annandale," pp. 195–211; Rosalind Richards, notes on "The Book of Annandale"; Rosalind Richards, notes, interview with Laura E. Richards; EAR to Ford, 28 November 1896; EAR to Smith, 15 March 1897, *Stars*, p. 279.

8. Loves Lost

The Torrent Descends
Torrent: EAR to Smith, 7 December 1896, *Stars*, p. 265; Cary, *Early Reception*, pp. 26–27, 44; Hagedorn, *EAR*, p. 108; Cary, *Uncollected*, p. 137; EAR to Smith, 22 December 1896 and 17 January 1897, *Stars*, pp. 268–72; Cary, *Early Reception*, p. 64; Hagedorn, *EAR*, pp. 111–12; EAR to Smith, 3 February 1897, *Stars*, p. 273; EAR to Ford, 28 November 1896; EAR to Chauncey G. Hubbell, 16 December 1896; Neff, *EAR*, p. 82; Cary, *Early Reception*, pp. 66, 28; Bloom, *Ringers*, pp. 305–6; Justice, "Afterword," *Torrent* (1996), unpaginated.

Light Through the Clouds
EAR to Smith, 15 March 1897, *Stars*, pp. 278–79; *Dean*: Ruth Nivison, memoir, p. 24; Weeks, "Antigone," p. 148;. C. P. Smith, *Light*, pp. 153–54, 401; Thompson, notes, p. 8; Rosalind Richards, notes, interview with Laura (Lewis) Macomber; Emma Robinson to Laura E. Richards, 27 July 1935, Harvard; EAR, "The Dark House," p. 43; Ruth Nivison, memoir, p. 7; *Brower*: Brower, "Memories," pp. 204–5; Cary, intro., *Letters*, pp. 1–4; EAR to Brower, 13 (?) January 1897, *Letters*, p. 15; Cary, *Early Reception*, pp. 84–85; EAR to Smith, 17 June 1897, *Stars*, p. 288; Cary, intro., *Letters*, pp. 7–8; EAR to Smith, 4 April 1897 and 17 May 1897, *Stars*, pp. 281 and 286; *Mrs. Richards*: Rosalind Richards, notes, interview with Laura E. Richards, pp. 2–3; Hagedorn, *EAR*, pp. 120–23; Neff, *EAR*, pp. 83–84; Danny D. Smith, "Friendship," p. 1; Faggen, intro., *Selected*, p. xv; EAR to Smith, 24 April 1897 and 17 May 1897, *Stars*, pp. 284 and 286; *Quadruped*: EAR to Smith, 4 May 1897, *Stars*, p. 282; Hagedorn, *EAR*, pp. 92–94; EAR to Brower, 21 April 1897, *Letters*, p. 39; Thompson, notes, p. 4.

Thwarted Love
EAR to Ford, 28 November 1896; George Moore, *Celibates*, pp. 6–7; EAR to Smith, 4 April 1897, *Stars*, pp. 282–83; *Rosalind Richards*: Rosalind Richards to Professor W. A. Jackson, seven-page handwritten letter (15–28 March 1946), Harvard; Rosalind Richards, notes, interview with Laura E. Richards, pp. 4–5; Laura E. Richards, "Recollections," p. 10; H. H. Richards, "Schoolmaster's," pp. 52–53; Hagedorn, *EAR*, p.143; EAR to Rosalind Richards, 22 January 1899. Harvard; EAR to Brower, 15 September 1897 and 29 September 1897, *Letters*, pp. 57–59; Thompson, notes, p. 4; *photo album*: Danny D. Smith papers; *Richard Cory*: EAR, "Richard Cory," p. 82; EAR to Smith, 24 April 1897, *Stars*, p. 285; EAR to Brower, 31 July 1897, *Letters*, p. 54; Winters, "Cool Master," *Robinson*, p. 52; EAR to Robert Haven Schauffler, 4 December 1924, LC; EAR to Hagedorn, 12 April 1928; Hagedorn, *EAR*, pp. 53–54; Condon, "Cory"; Fussell, *EAR*, p. 477; Levenson, "Modernity," pp. 602–3.

A Crisis at Home
Ruth and EAR: Hagedorn, *EAR*, p. 124; Ruth Nivison, memoir, pp. 29–30; Ruth Nivison to Emma Robinson, 8 June 1938, Colby; Hagedorn, *EAR*, pp. 114–15; Laura E. Richards, *E. A. R.*, pp. 42–44, and C. P. Smith, *Light*, p. 149; *tension between brothers*: C. P. Smith, *Light*, pp. 171–72; Ruth Nivison, memoir, pp. 34–35.

9. Breaking Away

The Children of the Night

Idealism: EAR to Smith, 15 March 1897, *Stars*, p. 280; EAR to Latham, 8 February 1897; *Octaves*: EAR to Brower, 7 September 1897, *Letters*, p. 55; Barnard, *Critical Study*, pp. 270–72; EAR, "Octaves," pp. 100–7: especially Octaves 8, 10, 15, and 22; William Henry Thorne review, in Cary, *Early Reception*, pp. 96–99; *Children of the Night*: EAR to Ford, 6 August 1897; Cary, *Early Reception*, pp. 66–67, 176; EAR to Brower, 7 October 1897, *Letters*, pp. 60–61; EAR to Smith, 1 November 1897, *Stars*, p. 289; reviews by Gardiner and Higginson, in Cary, *Early Reception*, pp. 87–90 and 100–101; Laura E. Richards to Thomas Wentworth Higginson, 8 December 1897, Colby; EAR to Coan, 8 June 1898, WLA note; Briggs, quoted in R. W. Brown, *Next Door*, p. 64; Hagedorn, *EAR*, p. 140; Braithwaite, interview, p. 100; Tate and Bogan, in Cary, *Early Reception*, p. 106. *Badger as promoter*; Cary, *Early Reception*, pp. 95–96; Howard G. Schmitt, interview of EAR, 1931, Colby; EAR to Brower, 17 August 1899, *Letters*, pp. 101–2.

Winter in Bohemia

New York: EAR to Smith, 1 November 1897, *Stars*, p. 289; Hagedorn, *EAR*, p. 118; Neff, *EAR*, pp. 87–88; EAR to Brower, 7 October 1897, *Letters*, p. 61; Coxe, *Life*, p. 44; *Coan*: Dekking, "Reminiscences," p. 10; Neff, *EAR*, p. 9; EAR to Brower, 17 December 1897, *Letters*, pp. 65–66; EAR to Smith, 17 December 1897, *Stars*, p. 293; *Betts*: Schwab, "Connection," p. 27; Betts, "Notes," p. 3; *Louis*: EAR to Ranck, 14 January 1932; C. P. Smith, *Light*, pp. 175–76; Hagedorn, *EAR*, pp. 133–36; Neff, *EAR*, p. 92; Betts to Sutcliffe, spring 1939, Colby; Cary, *Uncollected*, pp. 137–38; EAR to Brower, 7 June 1898, WLA note; Alfred H. Louis to EAR, 5 May 1898, Colby; Neff, *EAR*, p. 92; *Stedman*: Scholnick, "Shadowed Years," pp. 510–13; Laura E. Richards to Stedman, 9 January 1898, Colby; EAR to Mary Stuart McKinney, 15 February 1898, WLA note; *Brower visit*: EAR to Ford, 6 August 1897; EAR to Brower, 2 April 1897, 20 November 1897, 29 December 1897, and 6 January 1898, *Letters*, pp. 35, 63, 68–69; Brower, "Memories," pp. 208–9; EAR to Brower, 15 January 1898, *Letters*, p. 70; EAR to Smith, 4 February 1898, *Stars*, pp. 295–96.

Last Days at Home

Return to Gardiner: EAR to Smith, 21 February 1898 and 14 April 1898, *Stars*, pp. 295–96; EAR to Brower, 15 January 1898 and 14 April 1898, *Letters*, pp. 71 and 76; Ruth Nivison, memoir, p. 24; EAR to Coan, 8 June 1898; EAR to Brower, 24 June 1898, *Letters*, p. 79; *Aunt Imogen*: Mason, *Music*, p. 125; Laura E. Richards, *E. A. R.*, p. 59; Cary, *Early Reception*, p. 122; Coxe, *Life*, pp. 72–73; EAR, "Aunt Imogen," pp. 184–89; Weil, " 'Well, She Was a Woman,' " pp. 4–5; Manheimer, "Speaker's Voice," pp. 117–19; Hagedorn, *EAR*, pp. 169–70; *departure*: Neff, *EAR*, p. 96; EAR to Brower, 26 September 1898 and September–October 1898, *Letters*, pp. 83–84; Lord, "Winthrop Once Harbored"; Hagedorn, *EAR*, p. 198; Rosalind Richards, notes, interview with Laura E. Richards, pp. 6–7; Hagedorn, *EAR*, p. 124; EAR to Coan, 1 February 1899; EAR to Gardiner, 2 November 1898, *SL*, pp. 14–15; EAR to Betts, 17 December 1898, Arnold T. Schwab papers.

10. Poetry as a Calling

Six Months in University 5

Harvard and Eliot: EAR to Smith, 12 October 1898 and 5 January 1899, *Stars*, pp. 297–98; EAR to Brower, 29 December 1898, *Letters*, p. 86; R. W. Brown, *Harvard Yard*, pp. 24–27; EAR to Isaacs, 24 August 1930; Betts, "Notes," p. 4; Hagedorn, *EAR*, p. 148; R. W. Brown, *Next Door*, pp. 27–29; EAR to Brower, 20 February 1899, WLA note; EAR to Clara E. Palmer, 3

March 1899; EAR to James S. Barstow, 15 April 1899; EAR to James S. Barstow, 30 August 1899, WLA note; EAR to Brower, 6 June 1899 and 13 June 1899, *Letters*, pp. 94–96; EAR to James S. Barstow, 1 July 1899; Hagedorn, *EAR*, pp. 153–54, EAR to Gardiner, 25 March 1900, *SL*, p. 27; EAR to Mason, 18 April 1900, *SL*, p. 29.

Dan Mason and Josephine Peabody

Mason: Mason, *Music*, pp. 81–83; EAR to Mason, 19 June 1899, WLA note; Neff, *EAR*, pp. 99–100; Hagedorn, *EAR*, p. 149; Betts, "Notes," p. 7; EAR to Mason, 14 July 1899, WLA note; EAR to Mason, 7 September 1899, WLA note; Peabody to Mrs. Edward Mason, 7 September 1899, Harvard; *Peabody*: WLA, "Young Robinson," pp. 71–73; Mason, *Music*, p. 119; Hagedorn, *EAR*, p. 151–52; EAR to Peabody, 25 January 1899, 8 February 1899, and 14 July 1899, WLA notes; EAR to Moody, 27 August 1899; EAR to Peabody, 5 November 1899, WLA note; WLA, "Young Robinson," pp. 76–80; EAR to Peabody, 28 March 1901 and 17 April 1900, WLA note; *French*: Cary, *Early Reception*, pp. 160–61; Hagedorn, *EAR*, pp. 149–51; Neff, *EAR*, pp. 101–2; Winters, *EAR*, p. 7; *Dean's death*: "Sudden Death," *Gardiner* (Maine) *Daily Reporter*, 29 September 1899; Ruth Nivison, memoir, pp. 35, 37; EAR, "How Annandale Went Out," p. 346; David S. Nivison, "Annandale," reprint in Cary, *Appreciation*, pp. 178–90; Ruth Nivison, annotations 1948, p. 15; Edith Isaacs, note on "E. A.'s Humour," NYPL.

New York, New York

Settling in: Hagedorn, *EAR*, pp. 156–57; EAR to Brower, 6 August 1899, *Letters*, p. 99; EAR to Moody, 27 August 1899; Mason, *Music*, pp.86–87; Moody to Mason, 14 November 1900, *Some Letters*, p. 130; EAR to Gardiner, 5 November 1899; Mason, *Music*, p. 88; Olivia H. D. Torrence, "The Poet," p. 98; EAR to Mason, 25 October 1900; Hagedorn, *EAR*, pp. 157–58; Isaacs, "Speaks of Music," p. 501; EAR to Mason, 18 April 1900, *SL*, p. 29; C. P. Smith, *Light*, p. 183; EAR to Ford, 8 November 1899.

New England Ways

New Englander: Bogan, "Tilbury Town," pp. 216–17; Howe, "Tribute," pp. 104–5; EAR to Smith, 11 March 1894, *Stars*, p. 138; *calling*: Gowen, "Puritan," pp. 175–79; C. P. Smith, *Light*, pp. 321–22; Tryon, "Harvard Days," p. 10; EAR to Mason, 19 June 1899; EAR to Smith, 13 May 1896, *Stars*, p. 247; EAR to Ford, 28 November 1896; EAR to Brower, 2 April 1897, *Letters*, p. 36; EAR to Peabody, 14 September 1900; EAR to Betts, March 1905; Hagedorn, *EAR*, p. 286; EAR to Ledoux, 14 December 1920, *SL*, p. 123.

The Climate for Poetry, 1900

Vs. prettiness: Lowell, "Bird's Eye," p. 139; EAR to Latham, 15 September 1894; EAR to Ford, 17 June 1896; Hagedorn, *EAR*, pp. 96–98; EAR, "Sonnet" (Oh for a poet), p. 93; Fussell, *EAR*, p. 44; Ziff, *American 1890s*, pp. 306–7; Cowley, "EAR," p. 269; Cary, *Early Reception*, pp. 3–4; McDowell, "Recovering," p. 62; Mezey, *Poetry*, p. xxiv; Faggen, *Selected*, pp. xx–xxi; *language*: Gorman, "A Talk"; Hagedorn, *EAR*, p. 31; Cary, *Early Reception*, p. 77; Hagedorn, *EAR*, pp. 165–66; Kindilien, *American Poetry*, p. 12; Doyle, "Shorter," reprint in Cary, *Appreciation*, pp. 108–9; Justice, afterword, *Torrent* (1996), unpaginated; Barnard, *Critical Study*, p. 2; Coxe, *Life*, pp. 21–22; Hagedorn, *EAR*, p. 89.

11. City of Artists

Three Benefactors

Betts: EAR to Betts, 17 December 1898, WLA note; EAR to Ranck, 14 January 1932; Betts, *Garland*; Hagedorn, *EAR*, p. 171; EAR to Betts, 15 March 1900; Betts, "Notes," p. 11; EAR

to Betts, 4 April 1901, Arnold T. Schwab papers; EAR to Mason, 25 June 1900 and 7 July
1901; Hagedorn, *EAR*, p. 167; EAR to Brower, 5 April 1900 and 18 October 1900, *Letters*, pp. 124 and 130; EAR to Coan, 23 August 1900; *Stedman and Torrence*: Hagedorn,
EAR, p. 163; EAR to Stedman, 21 December 1899, WLA note; Scholnick, "Shadowed
Years," pp. 520–21; EAR to Peabody, 8 October 1900, WLA note; SD, "Torrence, Frederick Ridgely," *Dictionary of American Biography*, vol. 11, supplement 4, pp. 840–41; Clum,
Torrence, pp. 46–47; Hagedorn, *EAR*, pp. 164–65; EAR to Mason, 27 August 1900; Laura
Richards, quoted in Scholnick, "Shadowed Years," pp. 524; A. M. Williams, "Journalist,"
pp. 715–24; Betts, unnumbered page; EAR to Peabody, 12 April 1901; *Mrs. Richards and
Pope*: Hagedorn, *EAR*, pp. 160–61; Rosalind Richards, notes, interview with Laura E.
Richards, pp. 7–9; Scholnick, "Shadowed Years," p. 518; Rosalind Richards, notes on Seth
Ellis Pope, pp. 1–4; EAR to Mrs. Irving E. Fox, 14 May 1906, WLA note; EAR to Peabody,
12 April 1901, *SL*, p. 41.

The Mason Triangle
EAR to Moody, 27 August 1899; EAR to Mason, 25 June 1900, 8 July 1900, and 24 July 1900;
Mason, *Music*, pp. 89, 125–26; Mason, *Music*, p. 127–29; EAR to Peabody, 17 February 1901;
EAR to Moody, 16 February 1901; EAR to Mason, 26 March 1901; EAR to Peabody, 28
March 1901; EAR to Mason, 30 May 1901 and 7 July 1901; EAR to Peabody, 3 September
1901; EAR, "Partnership," pp. 222–23; EAR to Smith, 22 October 1893, *Stars*, p. 113; EAR to
Mrs. Edward p. Mason, 7 June 1903 and 18 July 1903; EAR to Mrs. Mary L. Mason, 25 April
1904, WLA note; EAR to Mason, 4 October 1904, WLA note.

Circling Moody
Scholnick, "Children," pp. 79, 85; Ziff, *American 1890s*, pp. 319–20; Mason, "Harvard," pp. 48–51; M. F. Brown, "Moody and Robinson," pp. 185–87; Ziff, *American 1890s*, pp. 321–22;
Moody to Mason, 8 May 1898, quoted in M. F. Brown, "Moody and Robinson," p. 185;
EAR to Moody, 27 August 1899, WLA note; EAR to Mason, 7 July 1901; EAR to Mason,
18 April 1900, *SL*, p. 29; EAR to Moody, 3 May 1900, WLA note; EAR to Moody, 10 May
1900; EAR to Mason, 7 May 1900 and 21 September 1900; EAR to Moody, 18 September
1900; EAR to Peabody, 23 October 1900; Betts, "Notes," pp. 9–10; EAR to Betts, 17 December 1898, WLA note; Saben, "EAR," p. 9; EAR to Peabody, 25 November 1900; EAR
to Brower, 10 November 1900 and 16 December 1900, *Letters*, pp. 131 and 134; EAR to
Gardiner, 7 December 1900; Neff, *EAR*, p. 108; EAR to Moody, 4 January 1901, WLA note;
Moody to EAR, 24 January 1901, Colby; Hagedorn, *EAR*, pp. 180–81; EAR to Smith, 29
June 1899, *Stars*, p. 300; EAR to Moody, 16 February 1901; EAR to Brower, 7 January 1901,
Letters, p. 135; EAR to Peabody, 25 December 1900; EAR to Gardiner, 7 January 1901; EAR
to Moody, 22 May 1901; EAR to Mason, 26 September 1901; M. F. Brown, "Moody and
Robinson," pp. 191 and 178; Cary, *Early Reception*, p. 121.

12. The Saga of Captain Craig

The Work in Progress
Cunningham, "EAR," p. 28; EAR to Smith, 17 May 1894, *Stars*, p. 158; EAR to Brower, 8
September 1899, *Letters*, p. 104; Cary, *Early Reception*, p. 111–13; Barnard, *Critical Study*,
pp. 280–81; Coxe, *Life*, pp. 69–70; C. P. Smith, *Light*, p. 177; D. S. Nivison, "Does It Matter?" reprint in Cary, *Appreciation*, p. 186; Barnard, *Critical Study*, pp. 298–99; Hagedorn,
EAR, p. 141; Neff, quoted in Cowley, "Defeat," p. 27; Betts, "Notes," p. 19; Cary, *Early Reception*, p. 107; Scholnick, "Shadowed Years," pp. 526–27; EAR to Brower, 17 September 1900,
Letters, p. 128; EAR to Mason, 6 July 1900; EAR to Moody, 3 May 1900; EAR to Peabody,

2 November 1900; EAR to Smith, 2 June 1900, *Stars*, p. 306; EAR to Mason, 18 April 1900; EAR to Brower, 16 May 1900, *Letters*, p. 114; Cary, *Early Reception*, p. 308.

Captain Craig, Described
EAR, *Captain Craig*, pp. 113–69; Martin, *Harvests*, p. 157; Barnard, *Critical Study*, p. 117.

The Captain's Long Journey
Small Maynard: EAR to Smith, 2 June 1900, *Stars*, p. 306; Neff, *EAR*, p. 104; EAR to Mason, 6 July 1900; Mason, *Music*, p. 126; EAR to T. T. Bouvé, 10 September 1900; EAR to Peabody, 14 September 1900, 29 October 1900, WLA note, and 2 November 1900; Hagedorn, *EAR*, pp. 175–76; EAR to Smith, 22 November 1900, *Stars*, p. 307; EAR to Messrs. Small Maynard & Company, 10 December 1900, WLA note; EAR to Brower, 16 December 1900 and 7 January 1901, *Letters*, pp. 132–35; EAR to Peabody, 1 January 1901, *SL*, p. 36, and 17 February 1901; Hagedorn, *EAR*, pp. 181–82; EAR to Peabody, 1 May 1901, WLA note, 10 May 1901, WLA note, and 13 May 1901, WLA note; EAR to Mason, 30 May 1901; Hagedorn, *EAR*, pp. 182–83; EAR to Peabody, 3 September 1901; EAR to Ford, 26 May 1901; *break with Louis*: EAR to Torrence, 28 September 1901; Blackwood, *Episodes*, pp. 299–310; Sutcliffe, "Original," pp. 424–27; Ranck, memoir, p. 47; Hagedorn, *EAR*, pp. 183–84; EAR to Betts, 21 June 1901; Sutcliffe, "Original," pp. 428–31.

Safe Harbor at Last
Houghton Mifflin: EAR to Ford, 26 May 1901 and 19 August 1901; EAR to Mason, 26 September 1901; EAR to Gardiner, 18 September 1901, 13 October 1901, WLA note, and 25 November 1901, WLA note; Neff, *EAR*, pp. 101–2; Laura E. Richards to Annie Fields, 4 January 1902, Harvard; EAR to Gardiner, 19 February 1902; Bliss Perry to Gardiner, 14 March 1902, Harvard; Hagedorn, *EAR*, pp. 188–89; Neff, *EAR*, pp. 112–13; EAR to Gardiner, 17 March 1902, 25 March 1902, and 22 April 1902; Cary, *Early Reception*, p. 112; Olivia H. D. Torrence, "The Poet," p. 98; EAR to Rosalind Richards, 14 October 1902, Harvard; *reviews*: Cary, *Early Reception*, p. 112; Scollard, in Cary, *Early Reception*, pp. 148–49; Sherman, in Cary, *Early Reception*, p. 131; Carman, in Cary, *Early Reception*, pp. 132–33; Boynton, in Cary, *Early Reception*, p. 152; EAR to Peabody, 1 January 1901, *SL*, pp. 35–37; EAR, "Twilight Song," pp. 223–25; EAR to Nathan Haskell Dole, 21 December 1902, WLA note; Stickney, in Cary, *Early Reception*, pp. 154–56; Ranck, memoir, p. 62; Cowley, "Defeat," p. 27; EAR to Laura E. Richards, 21 November 1922 and 23 October 1934; *Isaac and Archibald*: EAR, "Isaac and Archibald," pp. 169–81; Coxe, *Life*, pp. 70–73; Fussell, *EAR*, p. 141; Hagedorn, *EAR*, p. 168; D. S. Nivison, "Social Criticism?" pp. 1–3; Emma Robinson and Ruth Nivison, annotations, p. 3; Pritchard, *Lives*, p. 95; Lucas, *Moderns*, pp. 41–44; Levenson, "Modernity," p. 610; James, quoted in Cary, *Early Reception*, p. 150; Fussell, *EAR*, p. 79.

13. Down and Out

Descent Into Poverty
EAR to Peabody, 23 October 1900; Mason, *Music*, p. 126; C. P. Smith, *Light*, pp. 400–402; Hagedorn, *EAR*, pp. 184–86; Johnston, "Walk," p. C14; Betts, "Notes," on Burnham; Hagedorn, *EAR*, p. 195; Waldo, "Earlier," p. 534; Betts, "Notes," p. 30; Brower, "Memories," p. 210; EAR to Betts, 19 May 1902; Fillmore to Hagedorn, n.d., on "EAR—Clothes," LC; Barnard, *Critical Study*, p. 296; Hagedorn, *EAR*, p. 347; EAR to Ford, 17 October 1902; Neff, *EAR*, p. 131; Hagedorn, *EAR*, pp. 196, 200; EAR to Peabody, 4 February 1903; EAR to Brower, 13 October 1902, *Letters*, p. 148; Hagedorn, *EAR*, p. 201; Powys, "Big Bed," 2; V. W. Brooks,

Opinions, pp. 25–26, 116–17; Coxe, *Life*, p. 159; EAR to James S. Barstow, 20 October 1902 and 22 January 1903; EAR to Peabody, 23 September 1903 and 27 March 1904.

Herman's Banishment
C. P Smith, *Light*, p. 209; Ruth Nivison, memoir, pp. 45–47; EAR, "Bokardo," pp. 56–59; Mezey, *Poetry*, pp. 230–31; Thompson, notes, p. 10; Ruth Nivison, memoir, pp. 48–50; Emma Robinson to Laura E. Richards, 27 July 1935, Harvard; SD, interview with David S. Nivison, 20 February 2002; Ruth Nivison, memoir, p. 61.

A Hole in the Ground
EAR to Coan, fall 1903; Cary, *Early Reception*, p. 161; Wisehart, "'By Jove!'" pp. 80, 82; Hagedorn, *EAR*, pp. 202–3; Moody, *Letters to Harriet*, p. 172; Ranck, memoir, p. 35; Betts, "Notes," pp. 10–11; Neff, *EAR*, p. 133; Hagedorn, *EAR*, pp. 205–6; French, "Subway," in Cary, *Early Reception*, pp. 157–61; Manheimer, "Speaker's Voice," pp. 45–48; EAR to Mason, 21 April 1902; EAR to Torrence, 15 August 1904; Moody to EAR, 31 March 1905, in Moody, *Letters to Harriet*, pp. 27–28; EAR to Torrence, 15 August 1904; EAR to Gardiner, 15 September 1904; Neff, *EAR*, pp. 134–35; EAR to Torrence, 3 August 1908; Neff, *EAR*, p. 240; Hagedorn, *EAR*, p. 210; EAR to Peabody, 26 January 1905, WLA note; EAR to Betts, 2 May 1905.

Deliverance Through Groton
Views from the Circle, George Biddle, pp. 111–15, and Arnold Whitridge, p. 152; Ashburn, *Fifty*, p. 31; SD, interview with Douglas Van Dyck Brown, 15 April 2003; Douglas Van Dyck Brown to SD, 5 May 2003; H. H. Richards, "Schoolmaster's," pp. 175–76; S. J. Morris, *Edith Kermit Roosevelt*, p. 298; Henry Howe Richards to Laura E. Richards, 5 October 1937, Yellow House papers, Gardiner Library Association; Kermit Roosevelt to Beebe, 4 October 1930, Yale; Ashburn, *Peabody*, p. 175; Ashburn, *Fifty*, pp. 33–34; T. R. to Kermit Roosevelt, *Letters to Kermit*, 3 November 1904, 10 November 1904, and 31 January 1905, pp. 83, 85, and 92; Hagedorn, *Sagamore*, pp. 212–13.

Rough Rider to the Rescue
Sinecure: EAR to Gilder, 30 January 1905, WLA note, and 16 March 1905, WLA note; Hagedorn, *EAR*, pp. 212–14; T. R. to EAR, 27 March 1905, in Weber, "Poet," p. 618; Moody to EAR, 31 March 1905, in Moody, *Letters to Harriet*, pp. 27–28; T. R. to Gilder, 31 March 1905, *Letters of T. R.*, 4:1155; EAR to Peabody, 15 May 1905, WLA note; T. R. to EAR, 1 April 1905 and 3 April 1905, in Weber, "Poet," p. 618; EAR to Betts, 11 April 1905; EAR to Gilder, 11 April 1905; T. R. to Kermit Roosevelt, 7 May 1905, *Letters to Kermit*, p. 99; T. R. to EAR, 12 May 1905, in Weber, "Poet," p. 619; EAR to Peabody, 15 May 1905 (?); EAR to Gardiner, 15 May 1905, WLA note; T. R. to EAR, 23 May 1905, in Weber, "Poet," p. 619; T. R. to Kermit Roosevelt, 1 June 1905, *Letters to Kermit*, p. 103; T. R. to James Hulme Canfield, 16 August 1905, *Letters of T. R.*, 4:1303; Hagedorn, *EAR*, p. 217; *review and backlash*: Hagedorn, "Poetry and Politics" (letter to the editor), p. E9; T. R., review of *Children*, in Cary, *Early Reception*, pp. 170–71; EAR to Mrs. Daniel Gregory Mason, 21 August 1905, WLA note; *Post* review, in Cary, *Early Reception*, pp. 175–76; *Bookman* review, Cary, *Early*, pp. 184–85; *Times* review, Cary, *Early Reception*, pp. 177–78; Cary, *Early Reception*, p. 198; William Loeb Jr. to Scribner's, in Cary, *Early Reception*, p. 168; *Dial* review, in Cary, *Early Reception*, p. 187; *Critic* review, in Cary, *Early Reception*, p. 191; Saben review, in Cary, *Early Reception*, pp. 193–95; T. R. to Lawrence Fraser Abbott, 8 July 1907, *Letters of T. R.*, 5:707; E. Morris, *Theodore Rex*, p. 424; EAR, "Tribute to Theodore Roosevelt," in Cary, *Uncollected*, p. 91; EAR to Kermit Roosevelt, 23 February 1913.

14. Theater Days

Custom House Duty

The job: EAR to Betts, 6 June 1905; Rosenfield, "The Philosopher," p. 33; EAR to Gilder, 30 May 1905; EAR to Peabody, 29 May 1905 (?); EAR to Laura E. Richards [1905, undated], *SL*, p. 62; Hagedorn, *EAR*, pp. 220–22; Betts, "Notes," p. 13; Hagedorn, *EAR*, pp. 234–35; Monteiro, "'The President,'" pp. 512–14; Torrence, quoted in Clum, *Torrence*, p. 92; EAR to Gilder, 30 May 1905, WLA note; Cary, *Early Reception*, p. 209; EAR to Torrence, 11 November 1904; EAR to Betts, 7 October 1904; Torrence to Peabody, April 1905, Princeton; *"bullet hole"*: EAR to Gilder, 15 November 1905; *MacKaye*: EAR to Peabody, 1 December 1905, WLA note; EAR to Jean Ledoux, 23 April 1914; *Sinclair*: EAR to Mrs. Daniel Gregory Mason, 21 August 1905; Moody, *Letters to* Harriet, pp. 245–46; Sinclair, in Cary, *Early Reception*, pp. 201–3; EAR to Josephine Marks, 4 July 1906, WLA note; Lowe, "Some Unpublished Letters," p. 31.

Torrence at the Judson

Neff, *EAR*, pp. 145–46; EAR to Peabody, 28 March 1901; EAR to Torrence, 27 June 1901 and 6 February 1903; Clum, *Torrence*, pp. 92–93; Betts, "Notes," p. 5; New York University handout to students living at the Judson, n.d.; Hagedorn, *EAR*, p. 224–28; Mason, *Music*, pp. 140–44; Ledoux to Rosalind Richards, 14 September 1938, Harvard; Neff, *EAR*, pp. 147–48; EAR to Torrence, January 1922, with Torrence note, Princeton; Clum, *Torrence*, p. 76; EAR to Ledoux, 21 January 1907, WLA note, 19 February 1907, and 26 February 1907, WLA note.

The Siege of Broadway

"Poets' onset": Ziff, *American 1890s*, pp. 322–25; Fryxell, "Dramatist," pp. 7–8; Hagedorn, *EAR*, pp. 239–41; MacKaye, intro. to Moody, *Letters to Harriet*, p. 22; EAR, "White Lights," p. 340; Moody to MacKaye, 15 October 1906, in Moody, *Letters to Harriet*, p. 50; Moody, *Letters to Harriet*, pp. 319–20, 322; *Van Zorn*: EAR to Schumann, 18 October 1907; EAR to MacKaye, 1 May 1907; *Porcupine*: EAR to MacKaye, 20 April 1907 and 23 April 1907; *"seized by the hair"*: EAR to Kermit Roosevelt, 4 April 1907; EAR to Schumann, 24 May 1907, WLA note; EAR to Josephine Marks, 15 July 1907; *Moody and Frohman*: MacKaye, intro. to Moody, *Letters to Harriet*, pp. 28–29; Hagedorn, *EAR*, p. 244; *Herman*: EAR to Herman Robinson, 1907 (?), in Thompson, notes, p. 12; *Mrs. Davidge*: Moody, *Letters*, p. 423; Hagedorn, *EAR*, pp. 233–34; Mason, *Music*, p. 145; *National Institute*: EAR to Robert Underwood Johnson, 9 March 1908; Moody, *Letters to Harriet*, p. 424; *discouragement*: EAR to Josephine Marks, 15 May 1908; EAR to Mason, 22 July 1908; Clum, *Torrence*, p. 92; *fascination with stage*: Hagedorn, *EAR*, p. 239; EAR to Jean Ledoux, 30 August 1915; *one for all*; Moody to EAR, 6 October 1908, NYPL; EAR to Moody, 13 October 1908; Torrence to MacKaye, October 1908, in Moody, *Letters to Harriet*, p. 23; Cary, *Early Reception*, p. 302; Moody, *Letters to Harriet*, p. 417; *Miniver Cheevy*: EAR, "Miniver Cheevy," pp. 347–48; EAR to Harry P. Taber, 27 July 1914; Perrine, "A Reading," p. 70; D. S. Nivison, "Does It Matter?" reprint in Cary, *Appreciation*, p. 180; *Duncan*: MacKaye, intro. Moody, *Letters to Harriet*, pp. 63–64; Kurth, *Isadora*, pp. 236–41; Hagedorn, *EAR*, pp. 230–32; EAR to T. S. Perry, 4 August 1927; W. T. Scott, "To See Robinson," p. 165.

15. The End of Something

Herman in Exile

Herman Robinson, letters to Emma: nineteen letters from the middle of June 1906 to the end of September 1908 tell most of the story. Also see Ruth Nivison, memoir, pp. 62–69.

Herman Robinson to Ruth Robinson, postcard, 11 October 1906, mentioned in Thompson, notes, p. 12; *Emma's promise*: C. P. Smith, *Light*, p. 223; *Herman's death*: Dr. John H. McCollum to Emma Robinson, 4 March 1909; "Death of Herman E. Robinson" and "Funeral of Herman E. Robinson," clippings from *Gardiner* (Maine) *Reporter-Journal*, David S. Nivison papers; Emma Robinson, comment on Hagedorn's p. 248.

Courting Emma

Let go at Customs: EAR to Ledoux, 22 July 1909; EAR to MacKaye, 2 August 1909; *staying with Emma*: Hagedorn, *EAR*, p. 251; Ruth Nivison, memoir, pp. 69–70; EAR to Ledoux, 30 September 1909; *consummation (?)*: C. P. Smith, confidential file, Yale; *"screwdriver"*: Thompson, notes on "Capitol Island: Mrs. Ulmer"; *diverging family views*: C. P. Smith, confidential file, Yale; SD, interview with Barbara Robinson Holt, 16 August 1977; *"My poems will have to tell you"*: Ruth Nivison, annotations 1948, p. 14; EAR, "Late Summer," pp. 525–28, and "The March of the Cameron Men," pp. 1212–28; C. P. Smith, *Light*, pp. 269–76; David S. Nivison, "Social Criticism?" pp. 8–9; *"coil of silk"*: Ruth Nivison, annotations 1948, p. 27; *"dead emotionally"*: Ruth Nivison, annotations 1948, p. 21; *marriage and art*: Neff, *EAR*, pp. 62–63; EAR to Smith, 12 October 1898, *Stars*, p. 298; EAR to Brower, 4 December 1899, *Letters*, p. 107; EAR to Chauncey G. Hubbell, 21 May 1897; EAR, "Exit," pp. 340–41; *nieces*: Holt, reminiscences, pp. 2–3; SD, interview with Elizabeth Calloway, 17 August 2000; Ruth Nivison, memoir, pp. 70, 72, 76–77; EAR to Ruth Robinson, 25 July 1913.

16. Down and Out, Yet Again

Friends in Need

Friendship: Hagedorn, *EAR*, p. 198; EAR, "Fleming Helphenstine," p. 90; "The Corridor," pp. 21–22; "Alma Mater," pp. 346–47, and "A Song at Shannon's," p. 509; EAR to MacKaye, 30 May 1926; Coxe, *Life*, p. 35; *"no man ever lived"*: EAR to Mabel Dodge, n.d. (1915–16?); *"grateful wonder"*: Crowder, "Meaning," p. 7; Halperin, quoted in Hirsch, "'The Man,'" p. 85; *Davidge*: Neff, *EAR*, p. 152; EAR to Betts, 23 October [1909]; EAR to Robert Bridges, 11 March 1910; *Bartlett*: EAR to Betts, 19 July 1910; EAR to Harriet Moody, 29 July 1910; Hagedorn, *EAR*, pp. 256–58; Mason, *Music*, pp. 90–97; EAR to Ledoux, 2 September 1910; EAR to Bartlett, 17 September 1912 and 24 September 1912; *Moody's death*: Mason, *Music*, pp. 146–47; MacKaye to George Pierce Baker, 18 October 1910, Harvard; EAR to MacKaye, 17 October 1910.

The Town Down the River

Reception of book: Cary, *Early Reception*, p. 210; EAR to T. R., 24 October 1910, WLA note; EAR to Smith, 7 October 1894, *Stars*, p. 170; Coxe, *Life*, p. 82; Hagedorn, *EAR*, pp. 259–60; *"brimming river"*: Cary, *Early Reception*, pp. 230–31; Braithwaite review, in Cary, *Early Reception*, pp. 215–19; EAR to Braithwaite, 3 November 1910, WLA note; *For a Dead Lady*: EAR, "For a Dead Lady," p. 355; Hagedorn, *EAR*, p. 238; Coxe, *Life*, pp. 87–91; EAR to Brower, 15 March 1914, *Letters*, p. 155; *"flower withers"*: Super, "For a Dead Lady," item 60; Joyce, *Ulysses*, Modern Library edition, p. 363; Barnard, *Critical Study*, p. 41; *New York poems*: EAR, "Calverly's," pp. 330–31; "Leffingwell," pp. 331–32; "Clavering," pp. 333–34, and "Lingard and the Stars," pp. 334–35; SD, "The Book," pp. 45–49; *MacVeagh essay*: in Cary, *Early Reception*, pp. 281–83.

Borrowings

"Vows of poverty": Cowley, quoted in Mezey, *Poetry*, p. xxxi; Cowley, "Poetry Project," p. 224; Kilmer, *Literature*, pp. 272–73; *loans, Hagedorn*: all indicated by date in the text; *loans, Ledoux*: EAR to Ledoux, 21 January 1907, WLA note; EAR to Ledoux, 2 September 1910;

Braithwaite, interview, p. 101; EAR to Ledoux, 11 June 1912; EAR to Dr. Albert R. Ledoux, 13 December 1912; EAR to Ledoux, 15 May 1913 and 8 June 1913; *novels*: Neff, *EAR*, p. 152; Cary, *Early Reception*, pp. 270–71; EAR to Ledoux, 28 July 1913, WLA note; EAR to Hagedorn, 13 August 1911, WLA note; Martin, "Crisis," pp. 136–37; Moody, *Letters*, p. 431; EAR to Hagedorn, 14 September 1911, 2 August 1912, and 12 January 1914; Vachel Lindsay, quoted in B. Perry, "Poets Celebrate," p. 765; Forster, *Aspects*, pp. 98–99; May Sinclair to EAR, 31 October 1910, Colby; EAR to Hagedorn, 26 August 1912; Martin, "Crisis," p. 137.

17. Life in the Woods, Death in Boston

A Home at the Colony
EAR to Hagedorn, 26 July 1911; EAR to MacKaye, 17 July 1911; *Fillmore*: Hagedorn, *EAR*, p. 268; Fillmore to Hagedorn, 30 August 1937, LC; *conditions*: Ranck, memoir, p. 3; Fillmore to Hagedorn, 10 January 1937, LC; *Sunday teas*: Ranck, memoir, pp. 79–81; Fillmore to Hagedorn, 1 September 1937, LC; *restorative powers*: Fillmore to Hagedorn, 10 January 1937, LC; EAR to Ledoux, 14 August 1911, WLA note; Coxe, *Life*, pp. 94–95; *telegram*: EAR to Coan, 18 August 1911; EAR to Caroline B. Dow, 26 March 1913; EAR to Betts, 19 August 1911; Neff, p. 164; R. W. Brown, *Next Door*, pp. 69–70; *Mrs. MacDowell*: R. W. Brown, "Mrs. MacDowell," pp. 42–43; C. P. Smith, *Light*, p. 384; Gurin, interview, pp. 39–40; *Isaacses*: Hagedorn, *EAR*, p. 269; Fillmore to Hagedorn, 1 September 1937, LC; *Ranck*: Hagedorn, *EAR*, pp. 276–77; C. P. Smith, *Light*, p. 37; Cary, *Early Reception*, p. 251; EAR to Hagedorn, 26 August 1912, WLA note; Ranck, memoir, pp. 3, 145; Fillmore to Hagedorn, 11 December 1936, LC; EAR to Ranck, 3 January 1914; C. P. Smith, *Light*, pp. 37–38; Hagedorn, *EAR*, p. 313; *Perrys*: Harlow, *Perry*, pp. 3–4; EAR to T. S. Perry, 27 August 1913 (?), WLA note; *"best read"*: EAR, *Dictionary of American Biography* entry on Thomas Sergeant Perry, in Cary, *Uncollected*, p. 114; EAR to Smith, 5 February 1893, WLA note; Margaret Perry, reminiscences, p. 1; Harlow, *Perry*, pp. 202–4 and 207; V. W. Brooks, *Autobiography*, p. 497; EAR to L. C. Perry, 11 October 1913, WLA note; EAR to L. C. Perry, 3 May 1914; Harlow, *Perry*, p. 206; EAR to L. C. Perry, 28 December 1915 and 15 January 1916.

Butler and Suicide
Butler: "William E. Butler Suicide," *Boston Evening Transcript*, 2 November 1914, p. 2; "Took His Own Life; W. E. Butler Shoots Himself," *Boston Globe*, 2 November 1912, p. 9; EAR to Braithwaite, 3 November 1910; EAR to Burnham, 7 August 1912; EAR to Mrs. William E. Butler, 19 December 1912 and 23 February 1912, Colby; Edith Isaacs, note to letter of 8 September 1918; *suicide*: Barnard, *Critical Study*, p. 180; Warren, *New England Conscience*, p. 183; EAR to Smith, 15 March 1897, *Stars*, pp. 278–79; EAR to Arthur Davison Ficke, 11 June 1921 and 23 June 1921; EAR to Jean Ledoux, 4 August 1931; *Luke Havergal*: Tate, quoted in Barnard, *Critical Study*, p. 282; EAR, "Luke Havergal," pp. 74–75; T. R., review, in Cary, *Early Reception*, p. 170; EAR to Brower, 21 April 1897, *Letters*, p. 39; Betts, "Notes," pp. 21–22; *"degeneration"*: EAR to Smith, 14 December 1895, *Stars*, p. 238; EAR to Mason, 18 May 1900; EAR to Ford, 9 May 1895, WLA note; EAR, "A Poem for Max Nordau," *Torrent*, p. 33; EAR to Smith, 6 October 1895, p. 233; SD, telephone interview with David S. Nivison, 5 May 2003; EAR, "Credo," *Torrent*, p. 26; Hepburn, in Cary, *Appreciation*, p. 220.

18. Reversal of Fortune

Leaving the Dark House
Going sober: Cary, *Early Reception*, p. 271; Neff, *EAR*, p. 165; Braithwaite, interview, pp. 102–4; EAR to Burnham, 7 August 1912; EAR to Ledoux, 1 October 1912; *"the bottom would drop"*: Hagedorn, *EAR*, pp. 276–79; *La Tourette*: EAR to Jean Ledoux, 27 September 1912; EAR to

Hagedorn, 31 December 1912, WLA note; Hagedorn, *EAR*, pp. 280–83; EAR to Hagedorn, 19 February 1913, WLA note; Luhan, *Movers*, pp. 123–39; EAR to Ledoux, 17 May 1913, 12 June 1913, 26 June 1913, and 22 July 1913.

Turning of the Tide
Hagedorn, *EAR*, p. 283–85; Neff, *EAR*, p. 165; *Kilmer*: Kilmer, "Classic Poet"; Marian Mac-Dowell to Kilmer, 12 September 1912; Fillmore to Kilmer, 17 September 1912, WLA note with EAR to Kilmer, 15 September 1912; Ledoux, "Discussion"; Hagedorn, "EAR"; *Noyes*: F. W. Thompson, "Alfred Noyes"; Ranck, "American Poet"; Braithwaite, "America's Foremost Poet"; *Boston Post*, "Great Among Poets."

A Devil Done Away With
"Devil": EAR to Hagedorn, 10 January 1912; *"real odor"*: EAR to Hagedorn, 2 August 1912; EAR to Hagedorn, 21 July 1912 and 26 July 1912; EAR to Harriet Monroe, 14 January 1913, WLA note; EAR to Hagedorn, 8 September 1912; *Ames*: EAR to Isaacs, 7 March 1913; EAR to Gardiner, 9 March 1913; EAR to Mrs. Percy MacKaye, 5 June 1913 and 10 June 1913; *finances*: C. P. Smith, *Light*, pp. 37–38; *Gardiner bequest*: R. W. Brown, *Next Door*, pp. 66–69; EAR to Dr. Albert R. Ledoux, 24 March 1914 and 26 March 1914; *changing publishers*: EAR to Robert Bridges, 15 May 1914; Robert Bridges to EAR, 18 May 1914, Colby; *Van Zorn and The Porcupine*: EAR to Harriet Moody, 24 September 1914; EAR to Bates, 3 December 1914; Fryxell, "Dramatist," p. 35; EAR to Brower, late 1914, *Letters*, pp. 159–60; EAR, "Broadway," Cary, *Uncollected*, pp. 50–51; *"Defeated Dramatist"*: Bates, *Manuscripts*, p. 9; *"no . . . light and shade"*: Evans, "EAR," p. 677.

19. A Poet Once Again

A New Pattern
Hagedorn, *EAR*, p. 289; Edith Isaacs, note to letter of 28 September 1911; Hagedorn, *EAR*, p. 279; EAR to Hagedorn, 29 December 1913 (?); *Ledoux visits*: Hagedorn, *EAR*, pp. 275–76; EAR to Jean Ledoux, 23 April 1914, 26 June 1915, and 10 August 1914; EAR to Isaacs, 22 October 1919; EAR to Renee Ledoux, 12 June 1918; Ledoux, "Psychologist," p. 1; Ledoux to Gorman, 10 January 1918, UVA; Ledoux, "In Memoriam"; *MacKaye children*: Moody, *Letters to Harriet*, p. 327; EAR to MacKaye, 21 May 1914; MacKaye to EAR, 21 August 1915, Harvard, and EAR to MacKaye, 26 August 1915; *Torrence-Dunbar marriage*: C. P. Smith, pp. 238–40, 404; EAR to the Torrences, 9 February 1914; Torrence to C. P. Smith, 2 April 1946, Yale; Clum, *Torrence*, pp. 100–101, 108; Bates, *Manuscripts*, p. 7.

O Tempora, O Mores
The Spirit of Life: Saben, *Spirit*, on sin, pp. 123, 126; Saben, *Spirit*, on sex, pp. 111, 109, 147, 157, 160–61, 141–42; *"boggy ground"*: EAR to Burnham, 5 December 1914, WLA note; EAR to Saben, 7 July 1924; *issues of the time*: Zabel, "Discipline," p. 222; Nivison, "Social Criticism?" p. 24; EAR to Josephine Marks, 3 February 1914, WLA note; *WWI*: Fillmore to Hagedorn, 30 August 1937; EAR, "Cassandra," pp. 11–12; Fillmore to Hagedorn, 10 January 1937, LC; EAR to Edwin F. Edgett (*Boston Evening Transcript*), 18 December 1914; EAR to Brower, 2 June 1918, *Letters*, p. 172; *Seeger*: EAR to Ledoux, 24 August 1911 and 21 August 1912; EAR to Jean Ledoux, 14 August 1916.

Meeting and Passing
Frost: Frost to Thomas B. Mosher, 17 July 1913, *Selected Letters*, p. 84; Thompson, *Triumph*, p. 43; Braithwaite, *Reader*, pp. 215–16; Thompson to Emery Neff, 3 December 1946, Co-

lumbia; Thompson, *Triumph*, pp. 44–45; Frost to EAR, 13 June 1915, *Selected Letters*, pp. 180–81; EAR to Frost, [1914]; *"two questions"*: Hagedorn, *EAR*, pp. 338–39; Frost to EAR, 15 September 1915, *Selected Letters*, pp. 190–91; Thompson, *Triumph*, pp. 72–74; EAR to Frost, 22 February 1916; Braithwaite, *Reader*, p. 216; EAR to Frost, 2 February 1917; Thompson, *Triumph*, p. 46.

20. A Breakthrough Book

EAR to Ledoux, 23 August 1913; *The Man Against the Sky*, evaluated: Braithwaite, in Cary, *Early Reception*, p. 289–92; *reviews*: quotation from the *New York Times Review of Books*, in Joyner, *Guide*, pp. 9; Lowell, "Robinson's Verse," 96–97, discussed by Neff, *EAR*, pp. 188–89 and Hagedorn, *EAR*, pp. 304–5; *critics "awakened"*: Cary, *Early Reception*, p. 298; Coxe, *Life*, pp. 97–98; *The Gift of God*: EAR, "The Gift of God," pp. 6–8; *The Poor Relation*: EAR, "The Poor Relation," pp. 45–47; Moran, "Firm Address," pp. 134–41; *Eros Turannos*: EAR to Harriet Moody, 18 November 1913, WLA note; Winters, *EAR*, pp. 11, 33; EAR, "Eros Turannos," pp. 32–33; Mezey, *Poetry*, pp. 228–29; Justice, "Obscurity," pp. 73–76; Hall, " 'Long Robinson,' " p. 76; *Ben Jonson*: EAR to Isaacs, 17 December 1912, WLA note; EAR to Ranck, 2 February 1932; EAR to Hagedorn, 17 May 1915; EAR to Jean Ledoux, 30 August 1915; EAR to Arthur Davison Ficke, quoted in Fussell, *EAR*, p. 65; EAR, "Ben Jonson Entertains a Man from Stratford," pp. 20–32; SD, interview with Marjorie Garber, 18 June 2003; Winters, "Cool Master," reprint in Murphy, *A Collection*, p. 12; Hagedorn, *EAR*, p. 295; *Browning*: Cary, *Early Reception*, pp. 5–6; EAR to Smith, 15 April 1894, *Stars*, p. 142; EAR to Peabody, 9 December 1901, *SL*, p. 47; EAR to Brower, 17 August 1899, *Letters*, p. 101; EAR to Helen Grace Adams, 1 January 1930, *SL*, p. 160; Rosenfield, "The Philosopher," p. 34; Winters, *EAR*, pp. 20–21; Cary, *Early Reception*, p. 6; "The Masque of Poets as Seen by William Rose Benet," *Bookman* 45 (July 1917), p. 524; EAR to Lewis N. Chase, 11 January 1917, *SL*, p. 102; EAR to Brower, 9 August 1917, *Letters*, p. 169; Cary, "Soothsayer," p. 240; *The Man Against the Sky*, as poem: EAR, "The Man Against the Sky," pp. 60–69; EAR to Edna Davis Romig, 7 January 1932; Hirsch, " 'The Man,' " pp. 39–40; EAR to Dr. Albert R. Ledoux, 2 March 1916; EAR to Lowell, 18 March 1916; *annual allowance*: Ledoux to MacKaye, 16 August 1916, Harvard; Neff, *EAR*, p. 192; Hagedorn, *EAR*, pp. 315–16; EAR to Isaacs, 14 December 1917; Edith Isaacs, note to letter of 14 December 1917, NYPL; EAR to Isaacs, 25 August 1917.

21. Reaching Fifty

Van Zorn on Stage

EAR to Brower, 17 January 1916, *Letters*, p. 166; Roy Day to MacKaye, 7 June 1935, Harvard; EAR to Brower, 5 February 1917, *Letters*, p. 168; Wright Kramer to MacKaye, 6 June 1935, Harvard; EAR to Kermit Roosevelt, 11 February 1917; Emma Robinson and George Burnham, comment on Hagedorn's p. 321; Fillmore to Hagedorn, 22 July 1938, LC; Skupin, "Robinson's Merlin," pp. 62–63; Hagedorn, *EAR*, p. 321; EAR to Josephine Marks, 31 March 1917; Don Marquis to Wright Kramer, December 1927, with Wright Kramer to MacKaye, 6 June 1935, Harvard; EAR to Scott, 12 August 1932; EAR to Gamaliel Bradford, 3 November 1931; EAR to Ranck, 4 October 1933.

Merlin . . .

EAR to T. S. Perry, 23 March 1916; EAR to Hagedorn, 11 June 1916; *Merlin as character*: Winters, *EAR*, pp. 68–70, cited in Skupin, "Robinson's Merlin," pp. 128–29; Starr, "The Transformation," pp. 116–17; Ruth Nivison, annotations 1948, p. 14; *"two themes"*: EAR, quoted in Gorman, "A Talk;" *King Arthur*: Winters, *EAR*, pp. 73–73; Edward Bliss Reed, review of

Merlin, *Yale Review* 6 (July 1917), pp. 863–64, cited in Skupin, "Robinson's Merlin," pp. 55–56; Aiken, "Three Essays," reprint in Murphy, *A Collection*, pp. 21, 24; Harriet Monroe, "Mr. Robinson in Camelot," *Poetry* 10 (July 1917), pp. 211–13, cited in Skupin, "Robinson's Merlin," pp. 83–84; Lowell, *Tendencies*, quoted in Skupin, "Robinson's Merlin," p. 85; Odell Shepherd, "Versified Henry James," *Dial* 63 (11 October 1917), pp. 339–41, cited in Skupin, "Robinson's Merlin," pp. 53–54; *"butter reviewers"*: Ezra Pound, "Hugh Selwyn Mauberley," in Ellmann, *New Oxford*, pp. 509–10; *Amy Lowell*: EAR to Lowell, 26 November 1915 and 31 October 1916; *"no life to speak of"*: EAR to Lowell, 10 August 1916; Lowell to EAR, 15 June 1917 and 11 October 1917; EAR to Lowell, 22 October 1917; EAR to T. S. Perry, 22 October 1917; *"poisoning people"*: EAR, quoted in Skupin, "Robinson's Merlin," p. 135.

... and Lancelot

EAR to Isaacs, 3 June 1917; EAR to Jean Ledoux, 26 August 1917; EAR to Hagedorn, 3 June 1917; *Roth*: EAR to Isaacs, 4 December 1917 and 12 August 1919, with Edith Isaacs note to letter 12 August 1919, NYPL; EAR to Brower, 17 November 1919, *Letters*, p. 174; *WWI poem*: EAR to Clement Wood, 8 May 1923; EAR to Helen Grace Adams, 1 January 1930, *SL*, p. 102; Starr, "The Transformation," p. 109; EAR to Jean Ledoux, 30 July 1916; EAR to Brower, 24 June 1917, *Letters*, p. 16; EAR to L. C. Perry, 26 November 1918; Celia Morris, "E. A. Robinson," pp. 88–93; *"dry ... psychologist"*: C. P. Smith, *Light*, pp. 56–57; *"used her fingers"*: Skupin, "Robinson's Merlin," p. 39.

A Stay in Brooklyn

Frasers: "Fraser, James Earle," *Current Biography 1951* (New York: H. W. Wilson, 1952), pp. 209–11; *bust*: EAR to Laura Fraser, 4 August 1919 and 6 August 1920; Ledoux to Ruth Nivison, 1 July 1937; EAR to Jean Ledoux, 7 August 1920; EAR to Isaacs, 29 October 1919; *Pope in Brooklyn*: Neff, *EAR*, pp. 192–93; Fillmore to Hagedorn, 10 January 1937; EAR to T. S. Perry, 28 January 1918; Cowley, "The Person," p. 27, and "Edwin Arlington Robinson," p. 269; *Schenck*: Hagedorn, *EAR*, pp. 322–23; Edith Isaacs, note to letter of 17 May 1922, NYPL; EAR, "The Dark Hills," p. 461; Ranck, memoir, p. 96; *revisions*: Dauner, "Two Robinson Revisions," pp. 313–14; Adams, "The Ledoux Collection," p. 13; *Schumann*: EAR, "A New England Poet," in Cary, *Uncollected*, pp. 81–83; *visit to Emma*: Hagedorn, *EAR*, p. 322; EAR to Burnham, 4 December 1918; *nieces*: EAR to Marie Robinson, 3 June 1920; EAR to Ruth Robinson, 3 July 1921; EAR to Ruth Nivison, 20 January 1923.

Back in the World

MacDowell: EAR, "The Peterborough Idea," *North American Review* 204 (September 1916): 448–54, in Cary, *Uncollected*, pp. 71–77; Louise Bogan to Ruth Limmer, 8 September 1963, in *What the Woman*, p. 353; *Bates*: Hagedorn, *EAR*, p. 29; EAR to Bates, 22 November 1930; *"butter"*: Bates, *Manuscripts*, pp. 2–3; *Gorman*: Hagedorn, *EAR*, p. 313; Fillmore to Hagedorn, 10 January 1937, 3 April 1937, and 11 December 1936, LC; *Three Taverns*: EAR to Jean Ledoux, 7 November 1916; EAR to Isaacs, 25 June 1917 and 18 July 1917; Ayo, "Robinson and the Bible," p. 218; Ayo, "Robinson's Use," reprint in Cary, *Appreciation*, pp. 264–65; *The Mill*: EAR, "The Mill," pp. 460–61; Bates, *Manuscripts*, p. 3; Neff, *EAR*, p. 197; Emerson, *Essays*, pp. 403–4; Frost, "Introduction to *King Jasper*," in Mezey, *Poetry*, p. 212; *The Wandering Jew*: EAR, "The Wandering Jew," pp. 456–59; Stanford, "EAR's 'The Wandering Jew,'" p. 100; Coxe, *Life*, pp. 130–32; Winters, *EAR*, pp. 37–42.

Birthday Salute

MacKaye to Bliss Perry, 26 November 1919, NYPL; Edward C. Marsh to MacKaye, 28 November 1919 and 3 December 1919, NYPL; *Frost refusal*: Thompson, *Triumph*, p. 532; *tributes*:

Bliss Perry, "To Edwin Arlington Robinson on His Fiftieth Birthday, Dec. 22, 1919": *New York Times Book Review*, 21 December 1919, p. 765; *surprise party*: Ledoux to MacKaye, 12 December 1919; EAR to MacKaye, 24 December 1919; EAR to Lowell, 24 December 1919; Lowell to EAR, 6 January 1920, Colby; MacKaye, "Milestone," p. 123; [K. Roosevelt], "Appreciation," pp. 763–64.

22. Seasons of Success

A Cause to Fight For

EAR to Burnham, 3 June 1917 and 11 September 1917; Edith Isaacs, note on letter of 28 September 1911, NYPL; Neff, *EAR*, p. 218; *drinking in protest*: EAR to George Sterling, 19 February 1920; EAR to Untermeyer,18 December 1920; *"the stuff does me no good"*: EAR to Laura Fraser, 16 August 1925; *prohibition didn't work*: EAR to Laura Fraser, 6 August 1920; EAR to Ledoux, 14 December 1920 and 4 July 1921; *poetry as propaganda*: Barnard, *Critical Study*, p. 257; EAR, "Demos," pp. 471–72; EAR to Jean Ledoux, 24 June 1921; Ranck, "Prohibition Perils," 54–55; EAR to Laura E. Richards, 31 July 1924 and 20 July 1924; EAR to Saben, 29 February 1928; *"Ostrich"*: EAR to Brower, 24 September 1925, *Letters*, p. 187; EAR, "Dionysius in Doubt," pp. 859–70, and "Demos and Dionysius," pp. 904–18; *Mr. Flood's Party*: C. Van Doren, *Three Worlds*, pp. 160–61; EAR to Ledoux, 14 December 1920; EAR, "Mr. Flood's Party," pp. 573–75; Lucas, *Moderns*, p. 38; Ownbey, "Robinson's 'Mr. Flood's Party,'" item 47; Hall, *Essential*, p. 13; Brooks and Warren, *Understanding*, p. 214; Parish, "The Rehabilitation," pp. 696–97; *revision of last stanza*: Dauner, "Two Revisions," pp. 309–13; Joyner, "Unpublished," pp. 155–57; WLA, "Letters," p. 54; Ruth Nivison, annotations 1948, p. 17; *"the best thing"*: EAR, quoted in Cary, *Uncollected*, p. 162; *loneliness*: Lucas, *Moderns*, p. 36; EAR to Nevin, 20 September 1924; Winters, "Cool Master," reprint in Murphy, *A Collection*, pp. 9–10.

Two Books a Year

EAR, *Avon's Harvest*, pp. 543–73; *comments on*: Boswell, *EAR and the Critics*, pp. 21–25; *as psychologist*: Winters, *EAR*, p. 114; EAR, quoted in Evans, p. 677; *collected edition*: Cary, *Uncollected*, p. ix; George P. Brett (?) to EAR, 12 November 1920; EAR to Ledoux, 14 November 1920; EAR to Brower, 22 January 1921, *Letters*, p. 177; *"struck by lightning"*: EAR to Nevin, 20 April 1921; EAR to Emma Robinson, 2 July 1921; *"mystic sense of his calling"*: Hagedorn, *EAR*, p. 340; Fillmore to Hagedorn, n.d., LC; *"justification"*: Cunningham, "EAR," p. 28; *Collected Poems*, reviewed: Gorman, "Poetry," p. 6; William Rose Benet, "Retrospect," p. 409; Gorman, "EAR," p. 311, 313; Thornton Wilder, quoted by Tappan Wilder, afterword to *The Bridge of San Luis Rey* (1927), reprint, Perennial Classics edition, 1998, p. 114.

Recognition at Last

C. Van Doren, "Post-War," p. 154; EAR to Scofield Thayer, 22 March 1921, Yale; EAR to Torrence, 2 September 1920; *"Pilgrim's Chorus"*: EAR to Jean Ledoux, 2 February 1921; *Barnard*: Alis De Sola, Oral History interview, Columbia; *Maine remembrances*: EAR to Laura E. Richards, 17 January 1922; EAR to Clara Palmer, 17 January 1922; EAR to Ruth Nivison, 12 February 1922; *rise in reputation*: Budd, "EAR Unbends," p. 249; Hubbell, *Who Are*, p. 238; L. Morris, *Poetry of EAR*, p. 78; *money*: EAR to Smith, 29 March 1921; EAR to Brower, 23 August 1921, *Letters*, p. 178; EAR to Isaacs, 8 December 1921, with note by Edith Issacs, NYPL; *collectors*: EAR to William Van R. Whitall, 28 November 1920; EAR to Isaacs, 28 February 1921, with note by Edith Isaacs, NYPL; *price of Torrent*: EAR to Dr. Albert R. Ledoux, 26 January 1921, 20 April 1921, and 17 June 1922; EAR to William Van R. Whitall, 16 September 1921; *publicity*: EAR to Maxwell Bodenheim, 25 October

1920; EAR to Mr. Palmer (Phi Beta Kappa), 7 November 1921; Lord, "Friendly Contacts"; EAR to Ford, 5 September 1927; Farrar, "The Literary Spotlight," p. 565; Drinkwater, *Muse*, p. 251; EAR, in Mezey, *Poetry*, p, xxxix; Stark, in Cary, *Uncollected*, p.133; *Poetry Society*: Grebanier, foreword, p. 9; *annus mirabilis*: EAR to Authors Club, 30 January 1922; *Pulitzer*: EAR to Untermeyer, 20 May 1922; EAR to Fillmore, 25 May 1922; *Yale*: "in an age of self-advertising": Neff, *EAR*, p. 207; Fraser, *In Tribute*, p. 59; Mary M. Colum, quoted in Bates, *Manuscripts*, p. 11; EAR to John Erskine, 6 November 1922; *French and the Nobel*: EAR to Hagedorn, 17 December 1919; Braithwaite, *Reader*, pp. 217–18; French to William Rose Benet, 12 February 1922; EAR to Otto Dalstrom, 11 April 1921; EAR to Hagedorn, 27 November 1921 and 7 December 1921; EAR to Otto Dalstrom, 18 May 1922, 3 June 1922, 14 July 1922, 17 July 1922, 14 August 1922, 6 September 1922, and 5 April 1923.

Personal Matters
Pope's death: Betts, "Some Notes," unpaginated; EAR to Nevin, 21 March 1922; EAR to Florence Leonard, 4 August 1927; *moving in with Frasers*: Neff, *EAR*, p. 209; EAR to Hagedorn, 26 April 1922; EAR to Ledoux, 21 September 1924; EAR to Laura Fraser, 31 July 1922; EAR to Jean Ledoux, 16 April 1925; EAR to Ledoux, 20 April 1925; *Rancks' marriage*: EAR to Hagedorn, 16 November 1919; EAR to Isaacs, 27 July 1921 and 6 August 1921, with note by Edith Isaacs, NYPL; *Nevin*: EAR to Nevin, 29 August 1924; EAR to Ranck, 6 September 1921; EAR to Nevin, 28 October 1921, 31 December 1921, 14 July 1925, and 13 May 1927; *"bad clear through"*: Fillmore to Hagedorn, n.d.; *Variell*: Cary, "Robinson's Friend," pp. 372–85; EAR to Variell, 14 August 1922; *"driving a giant car"*: EAR to Smith, 1 September 1922; EAR to Variell, 15 February 1923 and 30 June 1929; *R. R.'s novel*: EAR to Rosalind Richards, 16 June 1915 and 28 June 1915, Harvard; EAR to Rosalind Richards, 28 November 1922, 10 December 1922, 15 December 1922, 20 December 1922, 25 December 1922, and 10 January 1923, Harvard; *advice to young writers*: EAR to Carl Marr, 25 March 1921; *"not until thirty"*: Harry Salpeter, "E. A. Robinson, Poet," *New York World*, 15 May 1927, p. 8M, in Cary, *Uncollected*, p. 135; EAR to Hardwicke Nevin, 12 May 1922, Williams; EAR to Maxwell Bodenheim, 25 October 1920; EAR to Beebe, 18 November 1924; EAR to Cowley and EAR to Scott, in Cary, *Early Reception*, p. 57; C. P. Smith, *Light*, p. 20; EAR to W. H. Gerry, 9 April 1934, *SL*, p.177.

23. A Sojourn in England

Making the trip: EAR to Ledoux, 25 June 1922; EAR to John Drinkwater, 30 December 1922 and 1 March 1923; J. C. Squire to EAR, 4 December 1922, 11 January 1923, and 13 March 1923, UCLA; EAR to J. C. Squire, 1 March 1923; EAR to Burnham, 5 April 1923; EAR to Emma Robinson, 8 April 1923 and 22 April 1923; [Stark], "Young Boswell," p. 13; EAR to Jean Ledoux, 26 April 1923; *welcome*: Hagedorn, *EAR*, pp. 334–36; Neff, *EAR*, pp. 215–16; Squire, "Contemporary," p. 401; EAR to Isaacs, 9 August 1923; *literary sightseeing*: Rye: EAR to John Drinkwater, 2 July 1923, and EAR to Isaacs, 28 May 1923; Silver Street and Stratford: Fussell, *EAR*, pp. 66–67; EAR to Isaacs, 9 August 1923; EAR, "Silver Street," p. 873; Ranck, memoir, p. 130; EAR to Isaacs, 8 September 1923; *Eliot*: EAR to Harold Munro, 29 May 1923; Ackroyd, *T. S. E.*, p. 134; *Aiken*: Aiken, "Three Meetings," p. 346; Aiken to Robert N. Linscott, 20 June 1923, *Selected Letters*, pp. 77–78; Beebe, "Faun," p. 649; R. W. Brown, *Next Door*, pp. 21–22; EAR to Beebe, 30 August 1930 and 5 September 1930; Beebe to Aiken, 1 September 1930, Huntington; *impressions*: EAR to Gorman, 9 May 1923; *coffee and bread*: Hagedorn, *EAR*, p. 335; EAR to Saben, 21 June 1923; EAR to Isaacs, 16 May 1923; Tittle, p. 191; *Oxford*: EAR to L. C. Perry, 18 May 1923; EAR to Edward Bliss Reed, 23 May 1923 and 1 June 1923; EAR to Isaacs, 28 May 1923; EAR to Ledoux, 11 June 1923; *called home*: EAR to Isaacs, 9 July 1923; Hagedorn, *EAR*, p. 336; EAR to the Frasers, 20 June 1923; EAR to Ledoux, 11 July 1923; *retrospective reflections*: EAR to Laura E. Richards, 10 August 1923; *Grand Canyon*: EAR, quoted in Barnard, *Study*, p. 269; EAR to Variell, 28 March 1926; *English reputation*: Neff, *EAR*, p. 216; Maynard, "EAR," p. 267; EAR to John Freeman, 23 September 1924, Williams; *The Sheaves*: EAR to Ranck, 2 February 1932; EAR, "The Sheaves," pp. 870–71; Taylor, "The Mission," pp. 20–21; David S. Nivison to SD, 21 May 2005; *New England*: EAR, "New England," pp. 900–901; Satterfield, "Major Categories," p. 28–34; *northern pines*: EAR, "Boston," p. 83; EAR to Laura E. Richards, 2 February 1924; *Frost's reaction*: Thompson, *Triumph*, pp. 254–56.

24. MacDowell's First Citizen

A Place to Belong To
Status: R. W. Brown, *Next Door*, p. 89; Hagedorn, *EAR*, pp. 348–350; Fillmore, "In Memoriam," Annual Meeting of the Allied Members of the MacDowell Colony, 5 January 1936; *privileges*: R. W. Brown, *Next Door*, pp. 2, 9; Daniels, "EAR," p. 6; *Chard Smith*: C. P. Smith, *Light*, pp. 3–16; *cowboy pool*: Farrar, "The Literary Spotlight," pp. 567–68; Ranck, memoir, pp. 143–44; R. W. Brown, *Next Door*, p. 10; *light reading*: Neff, *EAR*, p. 238; Fillmore to Hagedorn, n.d., LC; Scott, "To See Robinson," reprint in *Exiles*, p. 168; *music*: Hagedorn, *EAR*, p. 300, 370–71; EAR to Mason, 18 April 1900, *SL*, p. 29; EAR to Jean Ledoux, 26 June 1915, *SL*, p. 86; Ranck, memoir, pp. 85, 88; Isaacs, "Speaks of Music," p. 503; SD, "Robinson and Music," p. 65.

Poet and Curmudgeon
Work schedule: EAR to Saben, 27 August 1932; *"scenario"*: Bates, *Manuscripts*, p. 24; *"contract"*: Beatty, "EAR," p. 379; *getting started*: Lord, "Friendly Contacts"; Bates, *Manuscripts*, pp. 25, 29–30; Grebanier, foreword, p. 10; Beatty, "EAR," p. 379; *"hell-hound"*: EAR, quoted in Cary, *Uncollected*, p. x; *inspiration*: Cary, *Uncollected*, p. xi; Beebe, "Faun," p. 649; *"out of the blue ether"*: EAR, *CLQ* 8 (June 1969), p. 308; *"Suddenly I saw Flammonde"*: Cary, *Uncollected*, p. 149; R. W. Brown, *Next Door*, p. 74; *intruders*: EAR to Isaacs, 29 May 1920; Ranck, memoir, pp. 100, 148; R. W. Brown, *Next Door*, pp. 16–17; *incognito*: Frances Wright Turner to Henry E. Dunnack, 29 April 1935, Maine State Library; *vs. modernity*: Rosenfield, "The Philosopher," p. 32; EAR to Witter Bynner, 14 October 1921; EAR to Braithwaite, 13 October 1920; EAR to Betts, 5 May 1925; EAR to Brower, 9 September 1924, *Letters*, pp. 184–85; *Cather*: Hilgart, "Death Comes," pp. 378–79; Daniels, "EAR," p. 7: EAR to Saben, 17 February 1929; *"misfit"*: EAR to Saben, 15 April 1928; *Hemingway and Stein*: EAR to Variell, 6 August 1929; EAR to Laura E. Richards, 2 December 1934; *technological wonders*: EAR to Laura E. Richards, 3 April 1932; EAR to Gorman, 16 June 1929; *Ovid*: EAR to Theodore Roosevelt Jr., 30 November 1930.

Humorist at Large
"Waste of time": EAR, quoted in Pritchard, *Lives*, p. 96; EAR to L. C. Perry, 11 October 1918; Barnard, *Study*, p. 182; EAR, "John Evereldown," pp. 73–74; *"purgatory"*: EAR, quoted in Kaplan, *Philosophy*, p. 19; EAR, "A Mighty Runner," p. 226; EAR, "Old King Cole," p. 19; Rourke, *American Humor*, pp. 271–72; *"real solid laughter"*: EAR to Smith, 4 March 1894, *Stars*, p. 135; *limerick*: EAR to Mason, 27 May 1900; C. P. Smith, *Light*, p. 43; *"five prepositions"*: EAR to Laura E. Richards, 18 May 1929; Cary, "Nieces," p. 199; *Scottish*: EAR to Laura E. Richards, 4 August 1929 and 8 July 1929; EAR to T. S. Perry, 25 July 1926; *"mandarin"*: Edith Isaacs, note on "E. A.'s Humour," NYPL; *"ants"*: Hagedorn, *EAR*, pp. 314–15; Beatty, "EAR," p. 381; Ranck, memoir, p. 59; *"glass eye"*: R. W. Brown, *Next Door*, pp. 42–43; *"sporting weekend"* and *"brushbroom cocktail"*: C. P. Smith, *Light*, pp. 44–45.

Women, Especially Sparhawk

R. W. Brown, *Next Door*, p. 58; Hagedorn, *EAR*, p. 352; C. P. Smith, *Light*, pp. 18, 46, 50; *"sparkling gayeties"*: Torrence, intro. to EAR, *SL*, p. ix; *Jean Gorman*: C. P. Smith, *Light*, pp. 48–49; *"rope of fire"*: R. W. Brown, "A Letter," p. 14; *rumors*: Ranck, memoir, p. 151; *"dark lady"*: Hagedorn, *EAR*, p. 296; *Marsh*: Fillmore to Hagedorn, 1 September 1937, LC; Hagedorn, *EAR*, pp. 298–99; Ruth Nivison to Isaacs, 11 April 1935, NYPL; *Sparhawk-Jones*: B. L. Smith, "Talented," pp. 20–27; Esther Willard Bates to C. P. Smith, n.d., Yale; Widdemer, *Golden*, pp.78–79; Gurin, interview with Sparhawk-Jones: on family, pp. 26, 33; on Chase: pp. 25, 7–8; note on *American Artist* (September 1944) article, Barbara Lehman Smith papers; *"the less I say"*: C. P. Smith, *Light*, p. 180; EAR, *Tristram*, pp. 728–29; *"Poet's Burial"*: "New Gallery Openings," *New York Times*, 11 April 1937, Fillmore to Hagedorn, 13 April 1937, LC; Marsden Hartley, quoted in B. L. Smith, "Talented," p. 25; Elizabeth Sparhawk-Jones to Marsden Hartley, 6 August 1938 and 22 December 1938, Yale; *"locked the door"*: C. P. Smith, *Light*, p. 48; *marriage*: Hagedorn, *EAR*, pp. 310–11; Fillmore to Hagedorn, 15 February 1937, LC; Maynard, *World*, p. 236; Ranck, memoir, p. 154; Mrs. George Pierce Baker to Emery Neff, 22 December 1948, Columbia.

Visitors: French and Scott

French again: EAR to Hagedorn, 27 December 1925 and 14 August 1927; Fillmore to Isaacs, 16 September 1927, NYPL; EAR to Isaacs, 29 September 1927, 14 March 1929, and 24 March 1929: French, "An Interregnum"; EAR to French, 27 September 1933 and 16 October 1933; *Bodenheim*: EAR to Ledoux, 5 August 1921; Ranck, memoir, p. 99; Fillmore to Hagedorn, 11 December 1936, LC; *Scott*: Scott, "To See Robinson," reprint in *Exiles*, pp. 154–61.

25. Success and Its Consequences

The Triumph of Tristram

Pulitzer: EAR to Isaacs, 27 April 1925 and 2 May 1925; *Bowdoin*: EAR to Ledoux, 14 June 1925; EAR to Laura E. Richards, 11 June 1933; Neff, *EAR*, p. 222; *"quite a fuss"*: Daniels, "EAR," p. 6; *Gardiner*: Ruth Nivison, memoir, pp. 104–5; EAR to Isaacs, 26 June 1925; Ruth Nivison, annotations 1948, p. 26; Thompson, notes, p. 13; *"ghosts"*: EAR to Ledoux, 19 June 1925; *star in ascendancy*: Redman, *EAR*, p. 95; "Poetry, Particularly Mr. Robinson's," *New York Times Book Review*, 28 November 1926; Wilson, quoted in Hubbell, *Who Are*, p. 216; *Cestre*: EAR to Ledoux, 16 October 1925; EAR to Charles Cestre, 20 March 1930; EAR to Laura E. Richards, 27 August 1930; EAR to T. S. Perry, 23 January 1928; *writing Tristram*: EAR to Laura Fraser, 10 June 1925; Hagedorn, *EAR*, pp. 340–43; EAR to Ledoux, 20 September 1925; EAR to Bates, 3 August 1926; EAR to Saben, 19 August 1926; *love as theme*: Carpenter, "Transcendent," reprint in Cary, *Appreciation*, p. 77; EAR to Emma Robinson, 18 May 1927; *"New England reticence"*: EAR to Jean Ledoux, 3 August 1925; *"every day"*: EAR, quoted in Bates, *Manuscripts*, p. 19; Barnard, *Study*, pp. 151–53; *potion*: EAR to Laura E. Richards, 26 July 1925; *promoting the book*: C. Van Doren, *Three Worlds*, pp. 202–5; *Little Theatre reading*: Edith Isaacs (for the committee) to MacKaye, 22 April 1927; invitation with list of sponsors, Colby; Hagedorn, p. 344; EAR to T. S. Perry, 11 May 1927; *reviews*: *"brickbats"*: EAR to Laura Fraser, 11 May 1927; Hutchison, "American Poetry," p. 27; Hart and Gorman, in Boswell, *EAR and the Critics*, p. 49; Aiken, "Three Essays," reprint in Murphy, *A Collection*, pp. 26–28; *sales*: C. Van Doren, *Three Worlds*, pp. 205–6; EAR to John Freeman, 1 November 1927; EAR to Isaacs, 27 June 1928; EAR to Ledoux, 28 September 1928; *E. A.'s reaction*: Crowder, "'Here Are the Men,'" reprint in Cary, *Appreciation*, p. 159; Hall, *Essential*, p. 8; *"best seller"*: EAR to Ford, 12 June 1927; *"noise and smoke"*: EAR to Saben, 13 June 1927; *rural cousin*: Hagedorn, *EAR*, p. 345; *envy*: C. Van Doren, *Three*

Worlds, pp. 206–7; *"Hagedorn . . . cooled"*: Margaret Perry, reminiscences; *"enervated old soak"*: Frost, quoted in Thompson, *Triumph*, pp. 380–81, 389.

The Late Long Poems

Productivity: Stovall, "EAR in Perspective," pp. 250–51; Coxe, *Life*, p. 145; *"big dog"*: EAR, quoted in Ranck, "Edwin Arlington Robinson" (1930); *"throw rocks"*: EAR to Ledoux, 30 October 1930; Warren, *New England Conscience*, pp. 191–82; EAR, *Matthias at the Door*, pp. 1077–155; EAR to Ranck, 8 October 1933; Winters, *EAR*, p. 132; Blackmur, " 'Verse,' " p. 224; EAR, *The Man Who Died Twice*, pp. 921–57; *Salvation Army band*: R. W. Brown, *Next Door*, pp. 41–42; EAR to Saben, 21 December 1926; EAR, *Amaranth*, pp. 1311–93; Robert Hillyer, *In Pursuit of Poetry* (New York: McGraw-Hill, 1960), pp. 82–97, quoted in Boswell, *EAR and the Critics*, p. 127–28; Coxe, *Life*, p. 146, 151; EAR, *Sonnets, 1889–1927*; Barnard, *Study*, p. 65; EAR, "Ben Trovato," pp. 575–76; EAR to Untermeyer, in Cary, *Uncollected*, p. 163; Mezey, *Poetry*, p. 236; EAR, "Calvary," p. 83, and "A Christmas Sonnet," p. 903; EAR, "Nicodemus," pp. 1159–69; EAR, "Sisera," pp. 1169–79; EAR, "Toussaint l'Ouverture," pp. 1179–87; EAR, "Ponce de Leon," pp. 1187–99; *message*: Stovall, *American Idealism*, p.175; W. R. Robinson, *EAR*, pp. 102–4.

A Reputation for Obscurity

"Luxuries of publicity": EAR to William Lyon Phelps, 18 November 1929; Phelps, "EAR," pp. 325–26; *"falling off in quality"*: Barnard, *Study*, pp. 82–83; Cowley, quoted in Untermeyer, *Makers*, p. 103, and in Franchere, *EAR*, p. 73; Tate, quoted in Grebanier, foreword, p. 24; Murphy, *A Collection*, p. 5; *"one word after another"*: R. W. Brown, *Next Door*, p. 19; *like late James*: Bogan, "Tilbury Town," p. 220; Winters, *EAR*, pp. 119–20; Deutsch, *Poetry*, p. 56; Epstein, *The Middle*, p. 138; *"Sanskrit"*: EAR, quoted in Barnard, *Study*, pp. 25–26; *"mazes"*: Millett, *Contemporary*, p. 131; *"eschewing the obvious"*: W. R. Robinson, *EAR*, p. 62; Lascelles Abercrombie, quoted in Boswell, *EAR and the Critics*, p. 25; Coxe, *Life*, p. 119; *"What does it mean?"*: C. P. Smith, *Light*, p. 342; Barnard, *Study*, p. 28; *oblique style*: Jules Bois, quoted in Skupin, "Robinson's Merlin," p. 89; *"improved by cutting"*: EAR, quoted in C. P. Smith, *Light*, p. 338; *"throws away everything"*: Untermeyer, review of *The Man Against the Sky*, in Boswell, *EAR and the Critics*, p. 12; EAR, penciled statement on draft of "The Unforgiven," UVA; *"dusty answer"*: quoted in Sonnenberg, *Lost Property*, p. 100; *"the whole truth"*: Martin, "Crisis," p. 144; *"a man that knows that he knows"*: Holmes, quoted in Menand, *Metaphysical*, p. 62; EAR, quotations from poems, "The Tavern" through *Amaranth*; EAR to Laura E. Richards, 1 October 1931; *The Whip*: EAR, "The Whip," pp. 338–39; L. Thompson, intro. to *Tilbury Town*, p. xii; D. S. Nivison, "Does It Matter?" reprint in Cary, *Appreciation*, p. 184; *"a little too far"*: EAR to Carl J. Weber, 28 January 1923; McDowell, "Recovering," p. 66; *"a fringe around it"*: Cary, *Uncollected*, p. 132; Justice, "Obscurity," pp. 75–76; *handwriting*: Ranck, memoir, p. 8; EAR, "Isaac Pitman," in Hogan, "Phonic," pp. 359–60; EAR to Smith, 8 February 1891, *Stars*, p. 12; EAR to Smith, 21 February 1893 and 11 February 1894, *Stars*, pp. 86–87 and 126; EAR to Jean Gorman, 7 November 1926; *"good for two shirts"*: EAR to Ford, 21 December 1895; *peculiarities*: EAR to Latham, 22 September 1895; EAR to Stedman, 10 September 1900; EAR to Bates, 14 September 1917; Lord, "Friendly Contacts;" *"Cousin Sever"*: Ledoux to Ruth Nivison, 14 August 1939 and 17 August 1939, Colby; corrections to *SL* made by Wallace L. Anderson in transcribing originals, Colby.

26. Generosities

"A jingle": EAR to John Freeman, 19 August 1927, Williams; C. P. Smith, *Light*, p. 354; EAR to Burnham, 3 January 1933; *"positively sybaritic"*: Maynard, "EAR," p. 272; Edith Isaacs,

note to letter of 10 June 1930, NYPL; *"oil . . . or jazz"*: EAR to Isaacs, 1 June 1930 and 10 April 1932,

Schenck, the Perrys, Burnham, and Ranck

Schenck: EAR, "A Tribute to Franklin L. Schenck," *Northport* (N.Y.) *Observer*, 18 February 1927, in Cary, *Uncollected*, pp. 92–83; *"sole legacy"*: EAR to Saben, 8 April 1927; EAR to Nelson C. White, 2 April 1928; *exhibition*: EAR to Isaacs, 24 October 1927; "Paintings by Franklin L. Schenck, 1856–1927" (New York: Macbeth Gallery, 1928); *The Perrys*: EAR, dust jacket copy for Lilla Cabot Perry, *The Jar of Dreams* (Boston: Houghton Mifflin, 1923); EAR to Laura E. Richards, 30 September 1924; *editing letters*: EAR to Mrs. John E. Gardin, 16 November 1928; EAR, intro. *The Letters of Thomas Sergeant Perry* (New York: Macmillan, 1929), pp. 1–14, in Cary, *Uncollected*, pp. 94–102; EAR, "Perry, Thomas Sergeant," *Dictionary of American Biography*, vol. 14 (New York: Scribner's, 1934), pp. 493–94, in Cary, *Uncollected*, pp. 113–15; EAR to Laura E. Richards, 3 March 1933; EAR to Margaret Perry, 29 October 1933 and 23 December 1933; *Burnham*: *"selfless angelic"*: Rosalind Richards, notes on Pope, p. 4; *menial job*: EAR to Saben, 13 June 1927 and 28 February 1928; *kidney stones*: EAR to Burnham, 25 December 1930 and 15 January 1931; EAR to Burnham, 23 September 1931 and 14 June 1933; *"slips of paper"*: EAR to Burnham, 31 July 1931, 25 September 1933, and 26 December 1933; *"five hundred"*: EAR to Burnham, 7 August 1932, 22 September 1932, and 3 January 1934; *"riding breeches"*: EAR to Burnham, 15 February 1931; EAR to Laura E. Richards, 3 April 1932; Coxe, *Life*, p. 154; *Ranck*: Joyner, *Guide*, p. 212, lists fourteen reviews and articles by Ranck about EAR between 1913 and 1935; *"superlatives"*: EAR to Ranck, 6 October 1926; EAR to Mrs. William Brown Meloney (*Boston Herald*), 5 September 1930 and 17 December 1930; *"enclosures"*: EAR to Ranck, 11 September 1929; R. W. Brown, *Next Door*, p. 50; *The Mountain*: EAR to Burnham, 6 August 1933 and 19 September 1933; EAR to Saben, 16 September 1933; EAR, foreword to Carty Ranck, *The Mountain* (Rock Island, Ill.: Frederick B. Ingram, 1934), in Cary, *Uncollected*, pp. 115–17; Hagedorn to EAR, 17 January 1930; EAR to Hagedorn, 23 January 1930 and 25 December 1930; EAR to C. P. Smith, 10 October 1931.

Saving Mowry Saben

Family appeals: EAR to Saben, 21 May 1924; W. M. Saben to EAR, 1 June 1924; EAR to Saben, 15 June 1924, 18 July 1924, 3 March 1926, and 28 August 1930; *"summer suit"*: EAR to Saben, 7 July 1924; *health*: EAR to Saben, 20 April 1925, 21 April 1925, 20 May 1925, 3 February 1933, 25 June 1933, and 29 August 1933; *"count on me for a candle"*: EAR to Saben, 18 March 1926; *book proposals*: EAR to Saben, 12 July 1927, 23 July 1927, and 22 February 1934; EAR to Burnham, 3 January 1934; *"one particular subject"*: EAR to Saben, 21 August 1934 and 4 September 1934; Saben, "EAR," pp. 22, 112.

Family Support

Rosalind Richards, notes, interview Herbert Longfellow, p. 2; Edith Isaacs, note to letter of 9 August 1915, NYPL; *Marion and Hermine Isaacs*: Edith Isaacs, note to letter of 22 October 1919, NYPL; *relationship with Ruth Nivison*: EAR to Ruth Nivison, 1 January 1930 and 8 February 1930; *David and Bill*: EAR to Ruth Nivison, n.d. (December 1931 or January 1932); EAR to Emma Robinson, 1 January 1933; EAR to Ruth Nivison, 4 September 1930; *grandmother tension*: Ruth Nivison, memoir, pp. 113, 107; *memorial for Dean*: EAR to Ruth Nivison, 4 September 1930; Laura E. Richards, "Horace Dean Robinson," *Kennebec* (Maine) *Journal*, 15 November 1930, *SL*, pp. 190–91; EAR to Laura E. Richards, 7 December 1930; Ruth Nivison, annotations 1948, p. 29; *"no profession"*: Ranck, memoir, p. 49.

27. Death of a Poet

A Long Animal

"Letting alone": EAR to Mrs. John E. Gardin, 11 April 1928; EAR to Bates, 21 May 1924; *"barks and snarls"*: EAR, quoted in Boswell, *EAR and the Critics*, p. 99; EAR to Saben, 13 December 1927; *visiting*: EAR to Laura Fraser, 30 July 1931; EAR to Laura E. Richards, 22 December 1924; *Boston vs. New York*: EAR to Jean Ledoux, 2 September 1926; R. W. Brown, *Next Door*, pp. 86–89; EAR to Mrs. John E. Gardin, 11 April 1928; EAR to Isaacs, 7 May 1928; EAR to Emma Robinson, 3 April 1930; Scott, "To See Robinson," reprint in *Exiles*, pp. 166–68; EAR to Jean Ledoux, 17 February 1929; EAR to Brower, 5 February 1928, *Letters*, p. 193; EAR to L.C. Perry, 8 January 1931.

System Breakdown

Constipation: EAR to Burnham, 27 August 1912, 2 January 1919, 29 May 1924, 21 January 1928, 26 June 1930, 12 July 1931, 16 August 1931; EAR to Betts, 30 (?) November 1931; EAR to Burnham, 8 July 1931, 15 July 1934, and 1 August 1934; *insomnia*: EAR to Isaacs, 22 July 1918; Ryan, p. 33; *digestion*: EAR to Frederic H. Nash, 1925; EAR to Emma Robinson, 23 October 1931; *exercise*: EAR to Mrs. Percy MacKaye, 12 November 1933; EAR to Betts, 13 July 1934; *various maladies*: EAR to Gorman, 20 April 1925; EAR to Saben, 20 May 1925; EAR to Nevin, 14 July 1925; EAR to Ranck, 30 May 1926 and 16 November 1926; EAR to L. C. Perry, 20 November 1926; EAR to Laura Fraser, 3 December 1930; EAR to Ruth Nivison, 8 May 1934; Edith Isaacs, note to letter of 16 December 1930, NYPL; EAR to Gamaliel Bradford, 3 November 1931; EAR to Saben, 29 August 1933; EAR to Ruth Nivison, 2 September 1933; EAR to Ranck, 24 June 1934; EAR to Laura E. Richards, 29 July 1934; *baseball*: Hagedorn, *EAR*, p. 367; EAR to Isaacs, 5 November 1933; EAR to Ledoux, 10 November 1933; *exhaustion*: EAR to L. C. Perry, 9 November 1930; EAR to Ledoux, 18 October 1933.

Politics and Poetry

Apocalyptic views: EAR to Ledoux, 2 February 1921; Cary, "Soothsayer," reprint in Cary, *Appreciation*, p. 207; EAR to MacKaye, 18 February 1921; *Henry Ford*: EAR to Laura E. Richards, 30 May 1926; *Great Depression*: EAR to Laura E. Richards, 4 July 1932; EAR to Ruth Nivison, 20 August 1933; EAR to Laura E. Richards, June 1932; EAR to Ledoux, 10 November 1933; EAR to Ruth Nivison, 2 September 1933 and 6 September 1933; EAR to Isaacs, 2 September 1933 and 11 September 1933; *Hoover-F.D.R.*: EAR to L. C. Perry, 22 October 1932; EAR to Laura E. Richards, 29 March 1934; *"Russianized"*: EAR to Ledoux, 18 October 1933; *"Hitler"*: EAR to Laura E. Richards, 12 February 1934; *King Jasper*: EAR to Saben, 5 May 1928; *Strachey*: Cary, "Mowry Saben," p. 489; EAR to Saben, 5 February 1934; Winters, *EAR*, pp. 139–42.

Intimations of Mortality

Confronting death: EAR to Burnham, 13 August 1926; EAR to Emma Robinson, 25 February 1934; EAR to Belle Palmer, 14 June 1930; EAR to Saben, 13 December 1927; C. P. Smith, *Light*, p. 360; EAR to Mrs. John E. Gardin, 21 June 1928, *SL*, p. 155; *religious views*: EAR to Hagedorn, 17 September 1933, *SL*, p. 172; EAR to Laura E. Richards, 13 February 1933 and 16 April 1933; *Roheim*: Ledoux to Ruth Nivison, 2 July 1935; Roheim, "Primitive," pp. 3–7; EAR to Saben, 11 June 1934; *afterlife*: Ranck, memoir, p. 50; EAR to Laura E. Richards, 19 January 1925 and 3 March 1923; *Moore and Frost*: Coxe, *Life*, p. 153; C. P. Smith, *Light*, p. 360; Thompson, *Triumph*, pp. 418–19, 666–67; *Boris Todrin*: EAR to Todrin, 11 October 1932, 13 October 1932, and 21 October 1932; EAR to Mark Van Doren, 23 October 1932 and 29 October 1932; EAR to Todrin, 16 August 1933 and 22 October 1933; Todrin, *Room*, p. 78;

Wally Schoop, "Remembering Boris Todrin," *Columbia College Today* (November 1999), p. 4; EAR to Todrin, 2 July 1934; Ledoux to Ruth Nivison, 1 July 1937; *Torrence*: EAR to Isaacs, 10 September 1933; EAR to Torrence, 20 January 1934; *farewells*: C. P. Smith, *Light*, p. 360; R. W. Brown, *Next Door*, pp. 94–95, 98; *"doctor's orders"*: Peltier, "EAR," p. 14; R. W. Brown, "A Letter," p. 24; *poker*: Hagedorn, *EAR*, p. 372.

The Last of Days

Edith Isaacs, note to letter of 8 December 1934, NYPL; Olivia H. D. Torrence, "The Poet," p. 96; EAR to Betts, 25 December 1934; C. P. Smith, *Light*, pp. 361–63; Frost, quoted in Thompson, *Triumph*, pp. 666–67; Edith Isaacs, note to letter of 8 December 1921, NYPL; *New York Hospital*: EAR to Burnham, 6 January 1935 and 10 January 1935; EAR to Ruth Nivison, 6 January 1935 and 14 January 1935; EAR to Ranck, 9 January 1935; EAR to Laura E. Richards, 20 January 1935; *terminal diagnosis*: Isaacs to Merrill Moore, 3 February 1935, LC; Ruth Nivison, memoir, pp. 113–14; Ruth Nivison to Isaacs, 15 February 1935, NYPL; EAR to Marie Robinson, 25 March 1935.

Bedside Visitations

"Inspiration": Edith Isaacs, note to letter of 8 December 1934, NYPL; Scott, "To See Robinson," reprint in *Exiles*, p. 169; *Welfare Island*: Hagedorn, *EAR*, pp. 374–75; Fillmore to Hagedorn, "Those Last Weeks," n.d., pp. 2–3, LC; Fillmore to Hagedorn, 10 January 1937, pp. 9–10, LC; *women*: Hagedorn, *EAR*, pp. 377–79; *unwelcome callers*: Hagedorn, *EAR*, p. 379; Neff, *EAR*, p. 248; Edith Isaacs, note to letter of 8 December 1934, NYPL; Ranck to Bates, 13 April 1935, UVA; Barstow, p. 11; *last visitors*: Edith Isaacs, note to letter of 8 December 1934, NYPL; H. S. Latham, *My Life*, pp. 46–47; C. P. Smith, *Light*, p. 366; Hagedorn, *EAR*, pp. 380–81.

28. Beyond the Sunset

Memorials

Laura E. Richards to Isaacs, 13 February 1935, NYPL; *"roses"*: David S. Nivison to SD, 21 May 2005; Margaret Perry, reminiscences, p. 2; Colum, "Poets," pp. 343–44; *will and estate*: Lewis M. Isaacs collection and Macmillan Co. records, NYPL; *tributes*: Cowley, "Defeat," p. 268; Jeffers, quoted in Eugene DuBois to Ruth Nivison, 1 May 1935, Colby; *diction*: Fraser, *In Tribute*, p. 6; Berryman, "Note"; *form*: Fraser, *In Tribute*, p. 63; Zabel, "Robinson in America," p. 162; Hillyer, in Fraser, *In Tribute*, pp. 87–90; *poet and person*: Benet, in Fraser, *In Tribute*, p. 9; Saben, "EAR," p. 5; *exhibitions*: Ledoux to Ruth Nivison, 26 April 1935; *Gardiner memorial (12 May 1935)*: "Robinson's Literary Eminence Secure," *Daily Kennebec* (Maine) *Journal*, 13 May 1935; Margaret Perry to Ruth Nivison, 23 May 1935, Colby; Rosalind Richards, "E. A. R. Memorial Meeting," Richards Home Log, 15 May 1935, Yellow House papers, Gardiner Library Association; *closing the urn*: David S. Nivison to Danny D. Smith, c.c. SD, 19 February 2003; *Gardiner memorial (18 October 1936)*: Henry Richards remarks, Richards Home Log, Yellow House papers, Gardiner Library Association; program, "Unveiling of the Memorial Tablet," with speech by Hagedorn, Gardiner Library Association; *MacDowell memorial (5 January 1936)*: Fillmore, "In Memoriam," Minutes of the Annual Meeting of the Allied Members of the MacDowell Colony, 5 January 1936, Colby; Fillmore to Ruth Nivison, 13 January 1936; *MacDowell memorial (17 September 1938)*: Lord, 24 September 1938.

Frost and *King Jasper*

Hutchison, "Robinson's Satire," p. 5; Ransom, "Autumn," pp. 612–14; Auslander, "Posthumous Poem," pp. 375–76; Berthoff, "The 'New' Poetry," reprint in Murphy, *A Collection*, p. 122;

"faint praise": Coxe, *Life*, p. 155; C. P. Smith, *Light*, p. 221; R. McDowell, "Recovering," pp. 63–64; Mezey to SD, 8 July 2005; Frost, "Introduction to King Jasper," in Mezey, *Poetry*, pp. 205–13; *"far far out of my way"*: Frost to Grace D. Vanamee, 21 January 1936, *Selected Letters*, p. 425; Frost to Untermeyer, 21 September 1935, *Letters to Untermeyer*, p. 265; *quotations*: Taylor, "The Mission," p. 25; *stereotyping*: *"too many tears"*: St. Armand, p. 564; Frost to Robert P. Tristram Coffin, 24 February 1938, *Selected Letters*, pp. 461–62; Coffin, *New Poetry*, p. 25; Stovall, *American Idealism*, p. 179; Commager, *American Mind*, p. 158.

The Issue of Reputation

Moran, "Firm Address," p. 7; Winters, *EAR*, pp. 161–65; Neff, *EAR*, p. xvii; W. C. Williams, "'Eat Rocks,'" pp. 498–99; Wilson, *Shores of Light*, p. 37; Lucas, *Moderns*, pp. 37, 44; Dickey, "Many Truths," reprint in Murphy, *A Collection*, p. 90; Howe, "Tribute," p. 106; Squires, "Tilbury Town Today," in Barnard, *Centenary Essays*, p. 178; Coxe, *Life*, pp. 162–63, 24–25; Dickey, "Secret Lives," p. 1; *"honesty"*: Winters, quoted by R. McDowell, "Recovering," p. 64; *1990s editions*: Hall, *Essential*, p. 14; Faggen, *Selected*, p. xi; Mezey, *Poetry*, pp. xxxv–xxxvii, xlii–xliii; Justice to SD, 30 January 2000.

A Life in Poetry

EAR to Jean Ledoux, 298 September 1929; W. R. Robinson, *EAR*, p. 27; *"fifteen readers"*: Hubbell, *Who Are*, p. 318; *"night is coming"*: Coxe, *Life*, p. 96; *Browning*: Scott, "In Palazzo Rezzonico," in *New and Selected*, p. 117; Dr. Johnson, quoted in Dowie, *James Salter*, p. 1; *life and love*: Fillmore to Hagedorn, 15 February 1937, LC; *"psychologist"*: EAR to Sarah Payne, 27 December 1931; EAR, "Hillcrest," p. 17; Aiken, "Three Meetings," p. 345; James Wright, quoted in Breslin, *Modern to Contemporary*, pp. 185–86; *population*: C. P. Smith, *Light*, p. xiv; EAR to Mason, 22 July 1908.

Bibliography

Works by E. A. Robinson

Poems and Plays

The Torrent and the Night Before. Cambridge, Mass.: Privately printed, 1896. Reprint, Gardiner, Maine: Tilbury House, 1996.

The Children of the Night. Boston: Badger, 1897.

Captain Craig. Boston: Houghton Mifflin, 1902.

The Town Down the River. New York: Scribner's, 1910.

Van Zorn. New York: Macmillan, 1914.

The Porcupine. New York: Macmillan, 1915.

The Man Against the Sky. New York: Macmillan, 1916.

Merlin. New York: Macmillan, 1917.

Lancelot. New York: Seltzer, 1920.

The Three Taverns. New York: Macmillan, 1920.

Avon's Harvest. New York: Macmillan, 1921.

Collected Poems. New York: Macmillan, 1921.

Roman Bartholow. New York: Macmillan, 1923.

The Man Who Died Twice. New York: Macmillan, 1924.

Dionysius in Doubt. New York: Macmillan, 1925.

Tristram. New York: Macmillan, 1927.

Sonnets, 1889–1927 New York: Macmillan, 1928.

Cavender's House. New York: Macmillan, 1929.

Collected Poems. New York: Macmillan, 1929.

The Glory of the Nightingales. New York: Macmillan, 1930.

Matthias at the Door. New York: Macmillan, 1931.

Nicodemus. New York: Macmillan, 1932.

Talifer. New York: Macmillan, 1933.

Amaranth. New York: Macmillan, 1934.

King Jasper. New York: Macmillan, 1935.

Collected Poems. New York: Macmillan, 1937.

Letters

Selected Letters of Edwin Arlington Robinson. Intro. Ridgely Torrence. New York: Macmilllan, 1940.

Letters of Edwin Arlington Robinson to Howard George Schmitt. Ed. Carl J. Weber. Waterville, Maine: Colby College Library, 1943.

Untriangulated Stars: Letters of Edwin Arlington Robinson to Harry deForest Smith, 1890–1905. Ed. Denham Sutcliffe. Cambridge, Mass.: Harvard University Press, 1947.

Edwin Arlington Robinson's Letters to Edith Brower. Ed. Richard Cary. Cambridge, Mass.: Harvard University Press, 1968.

Selected Editions

Tilbury Town: Selected Poems of Edwin Arlington Robinson. Intro. Lawrance Thompson. New York: Macmillan, 1953.

Edwin Arlington Robinson: Selected Early Poems and Letters. Ed. Charles T. Davis. New York: Holt Rinehart and Winston, 1960.

Selected Poems of Edwin Arlington Robinson. Ed. Morton Dauwen Zabel. New York: Macmillan, 1965.

Uncollected Poems and Prose of Edwin Arlington Robinson. Ed. Richard Cary. Waterville, Maine: Colby College Press, 1975.

The Essential Robinson. Intro. Donald Hall. Hopewell, N.J.: Ecco, 1994.

Edwin Arlington Robinson: Selected Poems. Ed. Robert Faggen. New York: Penguin, 1997.

The Poetry of E. A. Robinson. Ed. Robert Mezey. New York: Modern Library, 1999.

Bibliographies

Boswell, Jeanetta. *Edwin Arlington Robinson and the Critics: A Bibliography of Secondary Sources with Selective Annotations.* Metuchen, N.J.: Scarecrow, 1988.

Hogan, Charles Beecher. *A Bibliography of Edwin Arlington Robinson.* New Haven, Conn.: Yale University Press, 1936.

Humphrey, James, III. *The Library of Edwin Arlington Robinson.* Waterville, Maine: Colby College Press, 1950.

Joyner, Nancy Carol. *Edwin Arlington Robinson: A Reference Guide.* Boston: G. K. Hall, 1978.

Lippincott, Lillian. *A Bibliography of the Writings and Criticism of Edwin Arlington Robinson.* Boston: F. W. Faxon, 1937.

White, William. *Edwin Arlington Robinson: A Supplementary Bibliography.* Kent, Ohio: Kent State University Press, 1971.

General Bibliography

Ackroyd, Peter. *T. S. Eliot.* London: Hamish Hamilton, 1984.

Adams, Leonie. "The Ledoux Collection of Edwin Arlington Robinson Manuscripts." *Library of Congress Quarterly Journal of Current Acquisitions* 7 (November 1949): 9–13.

Aiken, Conrad. "Three Essays on Robinson." In *A Reviewer's ABC*, 333–46. New York: Meridian, 1958. Reprint, in *Edwin Arlington Robinson: A Collection Of Critical Essays*, ed. Francis Murphy, 15–28. Englewood Cliffs, N.J.: Prentice-Hall, 1970.

——. "Three Meetings with Robinson." *Colby Library Quarterly* 8 (September 1969): 345–46.

——. *Selected Letters of Conrad Aiken.* Ed. Joseph Killorin. New Haven, Conn.: Yale University Press, 1978.

Allen, James L., Jr. "Symbol and Theme in 'Mr. Flood's Party.'" *Mississippi Quarterly* 15 (Fall 1962): 139–43.

Anderson, Wallace L. *Edwin Arlington Robinson: A Critical Introduction.* Boston: Houghton Mifflin, 1967.

——. "E. A. Robinson's 'Scattered Lives.'" *American Literature* 38 (January 1967): 498–507.

——. "The Young Robinson as Critic and Self-Critic." In *Edwin Arlington Robinson: Centenary Essays*, ed. Ellsworth Barnard, 68–87. Athens: University of Georgia Press, 1969.

——. "The Letters of E. A. Robinson: A Sampler." *Colby Library Quarterly* 16 (March 1980): 51–62.

Andrews, Wayne, ed. *Concise Dictionary of American History*. New York: Scribner's, 1962.

Ashburn, Frank D. *Fifty Years On: Groton School, 1884–1934*. New York: Privately printed, 1934.

——. *Peabody of Groton: A Portrait*. New York: Coward McCann, 1944.

Auslander, Joseph. "A Posthumous Poem: Review of *King Jasper*." *North American Review* 241 (June 1936): 375–76.

Axelrod, Steven Gould, Camille Roman, and Thomas Travisano, eds. *The New Anthology of American Poetry*. Vol. 1. New Brunswick, N.J.: Rutgers University Press, 2003.

Ayo, Nicholas. "Robinson and the Bible." Ph. D. diss., Duke University, 1965.

——. "Robinson's Use of the Bible." *Colby Library Quarterly* 8 (March 1969): 250–65. Reprint, in *Appreciation of Edwin Arlington Robinson: Twenty-eight Interpretive Essays*, ed. Richard Cary, 263–75. Waterville, Maine: Colby College Press, 1969.

Bak, Hans. *Malcolm Cowley: The Formative Years*. Athens: University of Georgia Press, 1993.

Baker, Carlos. "'The Jug Makes the Paradise': New Light on Eben Flood." *Colby Library Quarterly* 10 (June 1974): 327–35.

Ballou, Ellen B. *The Building of the House: Houghton Mifflin's Formative Years*. Boston: Houghton Mifflin, 1970.

Barnard, Ellsworth. *Edwin Arlington Robinson: A Critical Study*. New York: Macmillan, 1952.

——, ed. *Edwin Arlington Robinson: Centenary Essays*. Athens: University of Georgia Press, 1969.

——. "'Of This or That Estate': Robinson's Literary Reputation." In *Edwin Arlington Robinson: Centenary Essays*, ed. Ellsworth Barnard, 1–14. Athens: University of Georgia Press, 1969.

Barstow, James S. *My Tilbury Town*. New York: Privately printed, 1939.

Bates, Esther Willard. *Edwin Arlington Robinson and His Manuscripts*. Waterville, Maine: Colby College Library, 1944.

Beatty, Frederika. "Edwin Arlington Robinson as I Knew Him." *South Atlantic Quarterly* 43 (October 1944): 375–81.

Becker, Ernest. *The Denial of Death*. New York: Free Press, 1975.

Beebe, Lucius. *Aspects of the Poetry of Edwin Arlington Robinson*. Cambridge, Mass.: Privately printed, 1928.

——. "Dignified Faun: A Portrait of E. A. R." *Outlook and Independent* 155 (27 August 1930): 647–49, 677.

Beem, Edgar Allen. "The Mayor of Tilbury Town," *Down East* 49 (October 2002): 66–69.

Benet, William Rose. "Robinson in Retrospect." *New York Evening Post Literary Review* (11 February 1922): 409–10.

——. "The Phoenix Nest." *Saturday Review of Literature* 11 (13 April 1935): 628.

——. "E. A." *Forum and Century* 93 (June 1935): 381.

——. "The Phoenix Nest." *Saturday Review of Literature*, 20 February 1943, 18–19.

Berryman, John. "Note on E. A. Robinson" (poem). *Nation*, 10 July 1935, 38.

Berthoff, Warner. "The 'New' Poetry: Robinson and Frost." In *The Ferment of Realism*, 263–77. New York: Free Press, 1965. Reprint, in *Edwin Arlington Robinson: A Collection Of Critical Essays*, ed. Francis Murphy, 117–27. Englewood Cliffs, N.J.: Prentice-Hall, 1970.

Betts, Craven Langstroth. *A Garland of Sonnets*. New York: Mansfield and Wessels, 1899.

——. "Some Notes on Edwin Arlington Robinson." Manuscript, c. 1930. Chapin Library, Williams College.

Blackmur, R. P. "'Verse that is to Easie.'" *Poetry* 43 (January 1934): 221–25.

Blackwood, Algernon. *Episodes Before Thirty*. New York: E. P. Dutton, 1924.

Bloom, Harold. *The Ringers in the Tower: Studies in Romantic Tradition*. Chicago: University of Chicago Press, 1971.

——, ed. *Edwin Arlington Robinson*. Modern Critical Views. New York: Chelsea House, 1988.

Blumenthal, Anna Sabol. "The New England Oblique Style: The Poetry of Ralph Waldo Emerson, Emily Dickinson, and Edwin Arlington Robinson." Ph D. diss., Washington University of Saint Louis, 1986.

Bogan, Louise. "Tilbury Town and Beyond." *Poetry* 37 (January 1931): 216–21.

——. *What the Woman Lived: Selected Letters of Louise Bogan, 1920–1970*. Ed. Ruth Limmer. New York: Harcourt Brace Jovanovich, 1973.

Boston Herald. "Surgeon's Wife Blast Victim" (Marie Robinson Legg). 10 May 1938.

Boston Post. "Great Among Poets Hides in Modesty." 30 May 1913. Colby College Special Collections. Reprint, in *Early Reception of Edwin Arlington Robinson: The First Twenty Years*, ed. Richard Cary, 256–59. Waterville, Maine: Colby College Press, 1974.

Bowring, Dick. "A Lonely Young Poet." *Daily Kennebec* (Maine) *Journal*, 11 July 1964, 28.

Braithwaite, William Stanley. "America's Foremost Poet." *Boston Evening Transcript*, 8 May 1913, 21. Reprint, in *Early Reception of Edwin Arlington Robinson: The First Twenty Years*, ed. Richard Cary, 251–55. Waterville, Maine: Colby College Press, 1974.

——. Interview. 10 May 1956. Oral History Archives, Columbia University.

——. *The William Stanley Braithwaite Reader*. Ed. Philip Butcher. Ann Arbor: University of Michigan Press, 1972.

Brenner, Rica. *The Modern Poets*. New York: Harcourt Brace, 1930.

Breslin, James E. B. *From Modern to Contemporary: American Poetry, 1945–1965*. Chicago: University of Chicago Press, 1984.

Brookhouse, Christopher. "Imagery and Theme in *Lancelot*." In *Edwin Arlington Robinson: Centenary Essays*, ed. Ellsworth Barnard, 120–29. Athens: University of Georgia Press, 1969.

Brooks, Cleanth. "Edwin Arlington Robinson." 1951 Library of Congress lecture. Beinecke Library, Yale University.

Brooks, Cleanth, R. W. B. Lewis, and Robert Penn Warren, eds. *American Literature: The Makers and the Making*. Vol. 2. New York: St. Martin's, 1973.

Brooks, Cleanth, and Robert Penn Warren. *Understanding Poetry*. 3rd ed. New York: Holt Rinehart and Winston, 1966.

Brooks, Van Wyck. *An Autobiography*. New York: E. P. Dutton, 1965.

——. *New England: Indian Summer, 1865–1915*. New York: E. P. Dutton, 1940.

——. *Opinions of Oliver Allston*. New York: E. P. Dutton, 1941.

Brower, Edith. "Memories of E. A. R., 1920." Fifty-two-page manuscript. Miller Library, Colby College.

——. Appendix 1 of *Edwin Arlington Robinson's Letters to Edith Brower*, ed. Richard Cary, 203–15. Cambridge, Mass.: Harvard University Press, 1968.

Brown, David. "Some Rejected Poems of Edwin Arlington Robinson." *American Literature* 7 (January 1936): 395–414.

——. "E. A. Robinson's Later Poems." *New England Quarterly* 10 (September 1937): 487–502.

Brown, Maurice F. "Moody and Robinson." *Colby Library Quarterly* 5 (December 1960): 185–94.

Brown, Rollo Walter. *Next Door to a Poet*. New York: D. Appleton, 1937.

——. "A Letter." *Mark Twain Quarterly* 2 (Spring 1938): 14, 24.

——. *Harvard Yard in the Golden Age*. New York: Current Books, 1948.

——. "Mrs. MacDowell and Her Colony." *Atlantic Monthly* 184, July 1949, 42–46.

Bryant, William Cullen, ed. *A Library of Poetry and Song*. New York: J. S. Ford, 1873.

Bryer, Jackson R., ed. *Fifteen Modern American Authors*. Durham, N.C.: Duke University Press, 1969.

——. *Sixteen Modern American Authors*. Vol. 2. Durham, N.C.: Duke University Press, 1990.

Budd, Louis J. "E. A. Robinson Unbends for Academe." *Colby Library Quarterly* 16 (December 1980): 248–51.

Burlingame, Roger. *Of Making Many Books*. New York: Scribner's, 1946.

Burnshaw, Stanley. *Robert Frost Himself*. New York: George Braziller, 1988.

Burton, David H. *Edwin Arlington Robinson: Stages in a New England Poet's Search*. Studies in New England Thought and Literature. Lewiston, N.Y.: Edwin Mellen, 1987.

Butscher, Edward. *Conrad Aiken: Poet of White Horse Vale*. Athens: University of Georgia Press, 1988.

Carlson, C. Lennart. "Robinsoniana." *Colby Mercury* 6 (December 1939): 281–84.

Carpenter, Frederic Ives. "Tristram the Transcendent." *New England Quarterly* 11 (September 1938): 501–23. Reprint, in *Appreciation of Edwin Arlington Robinson: Twenty-eight Interpretive Essays*, ed. Richard Cary, 75–90. Waterville, Maine: Colby College Press, 1969.

Cary, Richard. "Robinson's Notes to His Nieces." *Colby Library Quarterly* 5 (December 1960): 195–202.

——. "Robinson on Moody." *Colby Library Quarterly* 6 (December 1962): 176–83.

——. "E. A. Robinson as Soothsayer." *Colby Library Quarterly* 6 (June 1963): 233–45.

——, ed. *Appreciation of Edwin Arlington Robinson: Twenty-eight Interpretive Essays*. Waterville, Maine: Colby College Press, 1969.

——. "Mowry Saben About Edwin Arlington Robinson." *Colby Library Quarterly* 9 (March 1972): 482–97.

——. *Early Reception of Edwin Arlington Robinson: The First Twenty Years*. Waterville, Maine: Colby College Press, 1974.

——. "Robinson's Friend Arthur Davis Variell." *Colby Library Quarterly* 10 (June 1974): 372–85.

——. " 'The Clam-Digger: Capitol Island': A Robinson Sonnet Recovered." *Colby Library Quarterly* 10 (December 1974): 505–11.

Cestre, Charles. *An Introduction to Edwin Arlington Robinson*. New York: Macmillan, 1930.

Childers, William C. "Edwin Arlington Robinson's Proper Names." *Names* 3 (December 1955): 223–29.

Chodorow, Nancy. *The Reproduction of Mothering: Psychoanalysis and the Sociology of Gender*. 2nd ed. Berkeley: University of California Press, 1999.

The City of Gardiner, Maine, U.S.A.: Its Water Power, Industries, Water Front, Picturesque Avenues, Attractions and Surroundings. Gardiner, Maine: Board of Trade, 1896.

Clum, John M. *Ridgely Torrence*. New York: Twayne, 1972.

Coffin, Robert P. Tristram. *Kennebec: Cradle of Americans*. New York: Rinehart, 1937.

——. *New Poetry of New England: Frost and Robinson*. Baltimore, Md.: Johns Hopkins University Press, 1938.

Collamore, H. B. "Robinson and the War." *Colby Library Quarterly* 1 (March 1943): 30–31.

Coleridge, Samuel Taylor, *Selected Letters*. Ed. H. J. Jackson. Oxford: Clarendon Press, 1987.

Colum, Mary. "Poets and Their Problems." *Forum and Century* 93 (June 1935): 343–44.

Commager, Henry Steele. *The American Mind*. New Haven, Conn.: Yale University Press, 1950.

Condon, Mark. "Richard Cory: Solution to a Literary Mystery." *Maine Sunday Telegram*, 17 February 1980.

Cowley, Malcolm. "Edwin Arlington Robinson: The Person and the Poet." *Brentano's Book Chat* 6 (March–April 1927): 24–28.

——. "Edwin Arlington Robinson." *New Republic*, 17 April 1935, 268–69.

——. "Poetry Project." *Poetry* 52 (July 1938): 224–27.

——. "Edwin Arlington Robinson: Defeat and Triumph." *New Republic*, 6 December 1948, 26–30.

——. *The Flower and the Leaf.* New York: Viking, 1985.

Coxe, Louis. "E. A. Robinson: The Lost Tradition." *Sewanee Review* 62 (Spring 1954): 247–66.

——. *Edwin Arlington Robinson.* Pamphlets on American Writers. Minneapolis: University of Minnesota Press, 1962.

——. *Edwin Arlington Robinson: The Life of Poetry.* New York: Pegasus, 1969.

Crowder, Richard. "'Here Are the Men . . .': E. A. Robinson's Male Character Types." *New England Quarterly* 18 (September 1945): 346–67. Reprint, in *Appreciation of Edwin Arlington Robinson: Twenty-eight Interpretive Essays*, ed. Richard Cary, 147–63. Waterville, Maine: Colby College Press, 1969.

——. "E. A. Robinson's Craftsmanship: Opinions of Contemporary Poets." *Modern Language Notes* 61 (January 1946): 1–14.

——. "'Man Against the Sky.'" *College English* 14 (February 1953): 269–76.

——. "E. A. Robinson and the Meaning of Life." *Chicago Review* 15 (Summer 1961): 5–17.

——. "Robinson's Reputation: Six Observations." *Colby Library Quarterly* 8 (March 1969): 220–38.

Crowley, John W. "E. A. Robinson and Henry Cabot Lodge." *New England Quarterly* 43 (March 1970): 115–24.

Cunningham, J. V. "Edwin Arlington Robinson: A Brief Biography." *Denver Quarterly* 3 (Spring 1968): 28–31.

Daniels, Mabel. "Edwin Arlington Robinson—a Musical Memoir." *Radcliffe Quarterly* 46 (November 1962): 5–11.

Dauner, Louise. "The Pernicious Rib: E. A. Robinson's Concept of Feminine Character." *American Literature* 15 (May 1943): 139–58.

——. "Two Robinson Revisions: 'Mr. Flood's Party' and 'The Dark Hills.'" *Colby Library Quarterly* 8 (June 1969): 309–16.

Dechert, Peter. "Edwin Arlington Robinson and Alanson Tucker Schumann: A Study in Influence." Ph.D. diss., University of Pennsylvania, 1955.

——. "He Shouts to See Them Scamper So: E. A. Robinson and the French Forms." *Colby Library Quarterly* 8 (September 1969): 386–98. Reprint, in *Appreciation of Edwin Arlington Robinson: Twenty-eight Interpretive Essays*, ed. Richard Cary, 335–45. Waterville, Maine: Colby College Press, 1969.

Dekking, Mary. "Reminiscences." 13-page typescript. Interview, 11 October 1979. Arnold T. Schwab papers.

Derrick, Peter. *Tunneling to the Future.* New York: New York University Press, 2001.

Deutsch, Babette. *Poetry in Our Time.* New York: Henry Holt, 1952.

Dickey, James. "Edwin Arlington Robinson: The Many Truths." Intro. to *Selected Poems of Edwin Arlington Robinson*, ed. Morton Dauwen Zabel, xi–xxviii. New York: Macmillan, 1965. Reprint, in *Edwin Arlington Robinson: A Collection Of Critical Essays*, ed. Francis Murphy, 77–94. Englewood Cliffs, N.J.: Prentice-Hall, 1970.

——. "The Poet of Secret Lives and Misspent Opportunities." *New York Times Book Review*, 18 May 1969, 1, 10.

Donaldson, Scott. "The Alien Pity: A Study of Character in E. A. Robinson's Poetry." *American Literature* 38 (May 1966): 219–29.

——. "The Book of Scattered Lives." In *Edwin Arlington Robinson: Centenary Essays*, ed. Ellsworth Barnard, 42–53. Athens: University of Georgia Press, 1969.

——. *Poet in America: Winfield Townley Scott.* Austin: University of Texas Press, 1972.

——. "Robinson and Music." *Colby Library Quarterly* 16 (March 1980): 63–72.

——. "Edwin Arlington Robinson." In *Oxford Encyclopedia of American Literature*, ed. Jay Parini, 3:471–76. New York: Oxford University Press, 2003.

Donoghue, Denis, "Frost: the Icon and the Man." *New York Review of Books*, 21 October 1999, 17–18, 20–21.

Dowie, William. *James Salter*. New York: Twayne, 1998.

Doyle, John R. "The Shorter Poems of E. A. Robinson." *Bulletin of the Citadel* 6 (1942): 3–18. Reprint, in *Appreciation of Edwin Arlington Robinson: Twenty-eight Interpretive Essays*, ed. Richard Cary, 107–16. Waterville, Maine: Colby College Press, 1969.

Drinkwater, John. *The Muse in Council*. Boston: Houghton Mifflin, 1925.

Dunbar, Olivia Howard. *A House in Chicago*. Chicago: University of Chicago Press, 1947.

Dunn, Stephen. "Mr. Flood's Party." In *Touchstones*, ed. Robert Pack and Jay Parini, 52–56. Hanover, N.H.: University Press of New England, 1996.

Edel, Leon. "Portrait of a Professor: G. W. Latham (1871–1947)." *McGill News* (Summer 1947): 8–10.

Elliott, Emory, et al., eds. *Columbia Literary History of the United States*. New York: Columbia University Press, 1988.

Ellmann, Richard, ed. *The New Oxford Book of American Verse*. New York: Oxford University Press, 1976.

Emerson, Ralph Waldo. *Essays and Lectures*. Ed. Joel Porte. New York: Library of America, 1983.

Epstein, Joseph. *The Middle of My Tether*. New York: Norton, 1983.

Evans, Nancy. "Edwin Arlington Robinson." *Bookman* 75 (November 1932): 675–81.

Faggen, Robert, ed. *The Cambridge Companion to Robert Frost*. New York: Cambridge University Press, 2001.

Farrar, John. "The Literary Spotlight." *Bookman* 56 (January 1923): 565–69. Reprint, in *The Literary Spotlight*, 116–24. New York: Doran, 1924.

Fillmore, Parker. Notes. Sent to Hagedorn, 1936–37. Library of Congress.

Finch, Annie. "Robinson's Mysteries: Houses, Nature, Women." Talk at 1997 E. A. Robinson festival. Gardiner, Maine.

Fletcher, John Gould. "Portrait of Edwin Arlington Robinson" (poem). *North American Review* 244 (August 1937): 24–26.

——. *Selected Essays of John Gould Fletcher*. Fayetteville: University of Arkansas Press, 1989.

Forster, E. M. *Aspects of the Novel*. New York: Harcourt Brace, 1927.

Foy, J. Vail. "Robinson's Impulse for Narrative." *Colby Library Quarterly* 8 (March 1969): 238–49.

Franchere, Hoyt. *Edwin Arlington Robinson*. New York: Twayne, 1968.

Fraser, James Earle, ed. *In Tribute: Edwin Arlington Robinson, 1869–1935*. New York: Privately printed, 1935.

——. "A Dakota Boyhood." *American Heritage* 20 (December 1968): 81–88.

Free, William J. "The Strategy of 'Flammonde.'" In *Edwin Arlington Robinson: Centenary Essays*, ed. Ellsworth Barnard, 15–30. Athens: University of Georgia Press, 1969.

French, Joseph Lewis. "A Poet in the Subway," *New York World Magazine*, 15 May 1904, 10. Reprint, in *Early Reception of Edwin Arlington Robinson: The First Twenty Years*, ed. Richard Cary, 157–63. Waterville, Maine: Colby College Press, 1974.

——. "The Younger Poets of New England." *New England Magazine* 33 (December 1905): 425–26.

——. "An Interregnum of Genius." *Commonweal* 15 (10 February 1932): 412.

Frost, Robert. *The Letters of Robert Frost to Louis Untermeyer*. New York: Holt Rinehart and Winston, 1963.

——. *Selected Letters of Robert Frost*. Ed. Lawrance Thompson. New York: Holt Rinehart and Winston, 1964.

——. *Collected Poems, Prose, and Plays.* Ed. Richard Poirier and Mark Richardson. New York: Library of America, 1995.

——. "Introduction to *King Jasper.*" Appendix to *The Poetry of E. A. Robinson*, ed. Robert Mezey, 205–13. New York: Modern Library, 1999.

Fryxell, Lucy Dickinson. "Edwin Arlington Robinson as Dramatist and Dramatic Poet." Ph.D. diss., University of Kentucky, 1955.

Fussell, Edwin S. *Edwin Arlington Robinson: The Literary Background of a Traditional Poet.* Berkeley: University of California Press, 1954.

Fust, John. "Fust of the Hutch." *Old York* (Maine) *Transcript*, 12 April 1935.

Gass, William. "The Test of Time." In *The Best American Essays 1998*, ed. Cynthia Ozick, 125–45. Boston: Houghton Mifflin, 1998.

Gorman, Herbert S. "Edwin Arlington Robinson, and a Talk with Him." *New York Sun*, Books and the Book World, 4 January 1920, 7.

——. "Edwin Arlington Robinson's Poetry." *New York Times Book Review*, 30 October 1921, 6.

——. "Edwin Arlington Robinson." *New Republic*, 8 February 1922, 311–13.

——. *The Procession of Masks.* Boston: B. J. Brimmer, 1923.

Gorman, Jean Wright, and Herbert S. Gorman, eds. *The Peterborough Anthology.* New York: Theatre Arts, 1923.

Gowen, James A. "Some Puritan Characteristics of the Poetry of Edwin Arlington Robinson." Ph.D. diss., Stanford University, 1968.

Graff, Gerald E. "Statement and Poetry." *Southern Review* n.s. 2 (Summer 1960): 499–515.

Graham, Peter. "'How Annandale Went Out'—a Doctor's Decision." In *The Culture of Biomedicine*, ed. D. Heyward Brock, pp. 158–64. Studies in Science and Culture, vol. 1. Newark: University of Delaware Press, 1984.

Grebanier, Bernard. Foreword to *Edwin Arlington Robinson: A Centenary Memoir-Anthology*, 9–25. South Brunswick, N.J.: A. S. Barnes for Poetry Society of America, 1971.

Gregory, Horace, and Marya Zaturenska. *A History of American Poetry, 1900–1940.* New York: Harcourt Brace, 1946.

Grimm, Clyde L. "Robinson's 'For a Dead Lady': An Exercise in Evaluation." *Colby Library Quarterly* 7 (December 1967): 535–47.

Grover, Edwin Osgood, ed. *Annals of an Era: Percy MacKaye and the MacKaye Family, 1826–1932.* Washington, D.C.: Pioneer Press, 1932.

Guerin, Philip J., Jr., ed. *Family Therapy: Theory and Practice.* New York: Gardner Press, 1976.

Gurin, Ruth. Interview with Elizabeth Sparhawk-Jones. 26 April 1964. Archives of American Art.

Gurney, A. R. *Richard Cory.* In *Collected Plays, 1974–1983.* 2:51–95. Lyme, N.H.: Smith and Kraus, 1997.

Hagedorn, Hermann. "Edwin Arlington Robinson." Letter to the editor, *New York Times Review of Books*, 1 December 1912. Reprint, in *Early Reception of Edwin Arlington Robinson: The First Twenty Years*, ed. Richard Cary, 246–47. Waterville, Maine: Colby College Press, 1974.

——. *Edwin Arlington Robinson: A Biography.* New York: Macmillan, 1938.

——. "Poetry and Politics." Letter to the editor, *New York Times*, 13 June 1943.

——. *The Roosevelt Family of Sagamore Hill.* New York: Macmillan, 1954.

Hall, Donald. "'Long Robinson.'" In *Breakfast Served Any Time All Day*, 70–80. Ann Arbor: University of Michigan Press, 2003.

Hamilton, Ian, ed. *The Oxford Companion to Twentieth-Century Poetry in English.* New York: Oxford University Press, 1994.

Hanson, J. W. *History of Gardiner, Pittston, and West Gardiner*. Gardiner, Maine: William Palmer, 1852.

Hardy, Thomas. *Life's Little Ironies*. New York: Harper & Brothers, 1894.

Harlow, Virginia. *Thomas Sergeant Perry: A Biography*. Durham, N.C.: Duke University Press, 1950.

Harraden, Beatrice. *Ships That Pass in the Night*. New York: G. P. Putnam's Sons, 1894.

Hazzard, Shirley. *Greene on Capri*. New York: Farrar Straus Giroux, 2000.

Henderson, L. J. "Edwin Arlington Robinson (1869–1935)." *Proceedings of the American Academy of Arts and Sciences* 70 (1936): 569–72.

Hepburn, James G. "E. A. Robinson's System of Opposites." *PMLA* 80 (June 1965): 266–74.

Herrmann, Eva. *On Parade: Caricatures*. Ed. Erich Posselt. New York: Coward-McCann, 1929.

Hilgart, John. "Death Comes for the Aesthete: Commodity Culture and the Artifact in Cather's *The Professor's House*." *Studies in the Novel* 30 (Fall 1998): 377–404.

Hillyer, Robert. "Edwin Arlington Robinson." *Harvard Alumni Bulletin* (24 May 1935): 992–94.

Hirsch, David H. "'The Man Against the Sky' and the Problem of Faith." In *Edwin Arlington Robinson: Centenary Essays*, ed. Ellsworth Barnard, 31–42. Athens: University of Georgia Press, 1969.

Hirsch, Edward. *How to Read a Poem*. San Diego: Harcourt, 1999.

Hoffenstein, Samuel. *Poems in Praise of Practically Nothing*. New York: Boni & Liveright, 1928.

Hogan, Charles Beecher. "A Poet at the Phonic Shrine." *Colophon* n.s. 3 (Summer 1938): 359–63.

Holt, Barbara Robinson. Reminiscences. Three-page typescript. Gardiner Library Association.

Hopper, V. Foster. "Robinson and Frost." Letter to the editor, *Saturday Review of Literature*, 2 November 1935, 9.

Howe, Irving. "Tribute to an American Poet." *Harper's* 240 (June 1970): 103–8.

Hubbell, Jay B. *Who Are the Major American Writers?* Durham, N.C.: Duke University Press, 1972.

Hutchison, Percy. "American Poetry at Its Best." Review of *Tristram*, by Edawin Arlington Robinson. *New York Times*, 8 May 1927.

——. "Robinson's Satire and Symbolism." Review of *King Jasper*. *New York Times Book Review*, 10 November 1935, 5.

——. "A Revealing Biography of E. A. Robinson." Review of Hagedorn's biography. *New York Times Book Review*, 16 October 1938, 5.

Isaacs, Edith. Notes on Robinson's correspondence with Lewis M. Isaacs. New York Public Library.

Isaacs, Lewis M. "E. A. Robinson Speaks of Music." *New England Quarterly* 22 (December 1949): 499–510.

James, Henry. *Collected Stories*. Vol. 1. New York: Everyman's Library, 1999.

Jane, Mary C. "Journey to Head Tide." *Christian Science Monitor*, 25 February 1950, 10.

Johannsen, Albert. *The House of Beadle and Adams and Its Dime and Nickel Novels*. Vol. 2. Norman: University of Oklahoma Press, 1950.

Johnston, Laurie. "A Walk Through Chelsea's Literary Past." *New York Times*, 25 May 1979.

Jonson, Ben. *The Complete Poems*. Ed. George Parfitt. New Haven, Conn.: Yale University Press, 1975.

Joyner, Nancy Carol. "Edwin Arlington Robinson's View of Poetry: A Study of His Theory and His Technique in the Late Narratives." Ph.D. diss., University of North Carolina, 1966.

——. "An Unpublished Version of 'Mr. Flood's Party.'" *English Language Notes* 7 (September 1969): 55–57.

——. "Robinson's Poets." *Colby Library Quarterly* 9 (March 1972): 48–53.

Justice, Donald. *Oblivion: On Writers and Writing*. Ashland, Ore.: Story Line Press, 1998.

——. "Benign Obscurity." *New Criterion* 15 (February 1997): 70–76.

Kaplan, Estelle. *Philosophy in the Poetry of Edwin Arlington Robinson*. New York: Columbia University Press, 1940.

Kenin, Richard, and Justin Wintle, eds. *The Dictionary of Biographical Quotation of British and American Subjects*. New York: Knopf, 1978.

Kennebec (Maine) *Journal*. "Memorial for Poet Robinson Draws Distinguished Company." 13 May 1935. Colby College Special Collections.

Kennedy, X. J. *An Introduction to Poetry*. Boston: Little Brown, 1966.

Kilmer, Joyce. "A Classic Poet." *New York Times Review of Books*, 8 September 1912. Reprint, in *Early Reception of Edwin Arlington Robinson: The First Twenty Years*, ed. Richard Cary, 236–39. Waterville, Maine: Colby College Press, 1974.

——. *Literature in the Making by Some of Its Makers*. 1917. Reprint, Port Washington, N.Y.: Kennikat Press, 1968.

Kindilien, Carlin T. *American Poetry in the Eighteen Nineties*. Providence, R.I.: Brown University Press, 1956.

Kunitz, Stanley [Dilly Tante], ed. *Living Authors: A Book of Biographies*. New York: H. W. Wilson, 1931.

Kuntz, Joseph M., and Nancy C. Martinez. *Poetry Explication: A Checklist of Interpretation Since 1925*. Boston: G. K. Hall, 1980.

Kurth, Peter. *Isadora: A Sensational Life*. Boston: Little Brown, 2001.

Latham, George W. "Robinson at Harvard." *Mark Twain Quarterly* 2 (Spring 1938): 19–20.

Latham, Harold S. *My Life in Publishing*. New York: E. P. Dutton, 1965.

Ledoux, Louis V. "A Discussion of the Exact Value of Robinson's Poetry." Letter to the editor, *New York Times Review of Books*, 29 September 1912. Reprint, in *Early Reception of Edwin Arlington Robinson: The First Twenty Years*, ed. Richard Cary, 240–42. Waterville, Maine: Colby College Press, 1974.

——. "Psychologist of New England." *Saturday Review of Literature*, 19 October 1935, 3–4, 16, 18.

——. "In Memoriam: Written in 1935." *Mark Twain Quarterly* 2 (Spring 1938): 10.

——. "Robinson, Edwin Arlington." In *Dictionary of American Biography*. Vol. 11, supplement 1, 632–34. New York: Scribner's, 1944.

Levenson, J. C. "Robinson's Modernity." *Virginia Quarterly Review* 44 (Autumn 1968): 590–610.

Library of America. *American Poetry: The Twentieth Century*. Vol. 1. New York: Library of America, 2000.

Lord, Alice Frost. "Will Head Tide Become Literary Shrine?" *Lewiston* (Maine) *Journal*, 28 October 1933, magazine section, 1, 4.

——"Gardiner Poet Was Friend of Edwin Arlington Robinson." *Lewiston* (Maine) *Journal*, 27 January 1934, magazine section, 9.

——. "Gardiner's One-Time 'League of Three' Dates Back to E. A. Robinson's Youth." *Lewiston* (Maine) *Journal*, 3 March 1934, magazine section, 2.

——. "Laura E. Richards Recalled Edwin Arlington Robinson." *Lewiston* (Maine) *Journal*, 17 March 1934, magazine section, 9.

——. "Gardiner Neighbors Knew Robinson as Infant." *Lewiston* (Maine) *Journal*, October [?] 1934.

——. "H. Dean Robinson." *Lewiston* (Maine) *Journal*, 27 October 1934, magazine section, 9.

——. "Gardiner School Authorities Sponsor Memorial to Poet Robinson." *Lewiston* (Maine) *Journal*, 11 May 1935, magazine section, 9.

——. "Sunlit Trails." *Lewiston* (Maine) *Journal*, 12 February 1938.

——. Account of MacDowell Memorial to Robinson. *Lewiston* (Maine) *Journal*, 24 September 1938.

——. "Hagedorn's Biography of Poet Robinson is Ready." *Lewiston* (Maine) *Journal*, 8 October 1938, magazine section.

——. "Barstow House in Gardiner Was Frequented by Robinson." *Lewiston* (Maine) *Journal*, 16 March 1940, magazine section, A8.

——. "Gardiner Associations of Poet Recalled." *Lewiston* (Maine) *Journal*, 30 March 1940, magazine section, A8.

——. "Gardiner Library Treasures Unique Robinson Collection." *Lewiston* (Maine) *Journal*, 6 April 1940, magazine section, A8.

——. "Gardiner Woman Cherishes Letters from Poet Robinson." *Lewiston* (Maine) *Journal*, 13 April 1940, magazine section, A8.

——. "Glimpse of Robinson House Interior at Gardiner." *Lewiston* (Maine) *Journal*, 20 April 1940, Magazine Section, A8.

——. "Colby College Acquires New Literary Distinction Through H. Bacon Collamore's Gift of Robinsoniana." *Lewiston* (Maine) *Journal*, 16 November 1940, magazine section, A8.

——. "Winthrop Once Harbored Gardiner's Poet, Robinson." *Lewiston* (Maine) *Journal*, 4 January 1941, magazine section, A8.

——. "Gardiner Childhood of Auburn Banker Goes Back to Robinson." *Lewiston* (Maine) *Journal*, 1 February 1941, magazine section, A8.

——. "This is 'Aunt May' Who Taught Gardiner Poet." *Lewiston* (Maine) *Journal*, 1 March 1941, magazine section, A8.

——. "The Journal Wayfarer." *Lewiston* (Maine) *Journal*, 16 May 1942.

——. "Friendly Contacts with Maine Poet Reveal Personality." *Lewiston* (Maine) *Journal*, 23 October 1943, magazine section, A8.

Lowe, Robert Liddell. "Edwin Arlington Robinson to Harriet Monroe: Some Unpublished Letters." *Modern Philology* 60 (August 1962): 31–40.

Lowell, Amy. "E. A. Robinson's Verse." *New Republic*, 27 May 1916, 96–97.

——. *Tendencies in Modern American Poetry*. Boston: Houghton Mifflin, 1917.

——. "A Bird's-Eye View of E. A. Robinson." *Dial* 72 (February 1922): 130–42.

——. *A Critical Fable*. Boston: Houghton Mifflin, 1922.

Lucas, John. *Moderns and Contemporaries: Novelists, Poets, Critics*. Totowa, N.J.: Barnes & Noble, 1985.

Luhan, Mabel Dodge. *Movers and Shakers*. Vol. 3 of *Intimate Memories*. New York: Harcourt Brace, 1936.

MacDowell, Mrs. Edward. "Robinson at the MacDowell Colony." *Mark Twain Quarterly* 2 (Summer 1938): 16.

MacGowan, Christopher. *Twentieth-Century American Poetry*. Blackwell Guides to Literature. Malden, Mass.: Blackwell, 2004.

MacGregor, Tiree. "The Principle of Plainness: A Study of English and American Poetry, 1798–1935." Ph.D. diss., University of Alberta, 1993.

MacKaye, Percy. *Poems and Plays*. Vol. 1, *Poems*. New York: Macmillan, 1916.

——. " 'E. A.'—a Milestone for America." *North American Review* 211 (January 1920): 121–27.

MacLeish, Archibald. "On Rereading Robinson." *Colby Library Quarterly* 8 (March 1969): 217–19.

Mallon, Thomas. "On Not Being a Poet." *American Scholar* 69 (Spring 2000): 5–11.

Manheimer, Joan. "A Study of the Speaker's Voice in the Poetry of Edwin Arlington Robinson." Ph.D. diss., Brandeis University, 1974.

——. "Edwin Arlington Robinson's 'Eros Turannos': Narrative Reconsidered." *Literary Review* 20 (Spring 1977): 253–69.

Mark Twain Quarterly 2 (Spring 1938). Special issue on Robinson.

Martin, Jay. *Harvests of Change: American Literature, 1865–1914.* Englewood Cliffs, N.J.: Prentice-Hall, 1967.

——. "A Crisis of Achievement: Robinson's Late Narratives." In *Edwin Arlington Robinson: Centenary Essays,* ed. Ellsworth Barnard, 130–55. Athens: University of Georgia Press, 1969.

Martindale, Meredith. *Lilla Cabot Perry: An American Impressionist.* Washington, D.C.: National Museum of Women in the Arts, 1990.

Mason, Daniel Gregory. "At Harvard in the Nineties." *New England Quarterly* 9 (March 1936): 43–71.

——. "Edwin Arlington Robinson: A Group of Letters." *Yale Review* 25 (June 1936): 860–64.

——. *Music in My Time and Other Reminiscences.* 1938. Reprint, Westport, Conn.: Greenwood Press, 1970.

Maynard, Theodore. "Edwin Arlington Robinson." *Catholic World* 141 (June 1935): 266–75.

——. *The World I Saw.* Milwaukee, Wis.: Bruce Publishing, 1938.

Mazzaro, Jerome, ed. *Modern American Poetry: Essays in Criticism.* New York: David McKay, 1970.

McClatchy, J. D. "Feeding on Havoc: The Poetics of Edna St. Vincent Millay." *American Scholar* 72 (Spring 2003): 45–52.

McDowell, Robert. "Recovering E. A. R. and the Narrative of Talk." *New England Review and Bread Loaf Quarterly* 8 (Autumn 1985): 62–69.

McNair, Wesley. "Places in the Dark." *Sewanee Review* 109 (Winter 2001): 102–7.

Melnicove, Mark. "A Peck of Poets." *Down East* (June 2004): 35–36, 38.

Menand, Louis. *The Metaphysical Club.* New York: Farrar Straus Giroux, 2001.

Merwin, W. S. *The Drunk in the Furnace.* New York: Macmillan, 1960..

Millett, Fred B. *Contemporary American Authors.* New York: Harcourt Brace, 1940.

——. *Reading Poetry.* New York: Harper & Row, 1950.

Mitchell, Edwin Valentine. *Maine Summer.* New York: Coward-McCann, 1939.

Mollman, Jane. "Tilbury Town." 14-page typescript. October 1976, Gardiner Library Association.

Monroe, Anne Shannon. *The World I Saw.* Garden City, N.Y.: Doubleday Doran, 1928.

Monroe, Harriet. "Robinson as Man and Poet." *Poetry* 46 (June 1935): 150–57.

Monteiro, George. " 'The President and the Poet': Robinson, Roosevelt, and *The Touchstone.*" *Colby Library Quarterly* 10 (December 1974): 512–14.

Moody, William Vaughn. *Some Letters of William Vaughn Moody.* Ed. Daniel Gregory Mason. Boston: Houghton Mifflin, 1913.

——. *Letters to Harriet.* Ed. Percy MacKaye. Boston: Houghton Mifflin, 1935.

Moore, George. *Celibates.* London: Walter Scott, 1895.

Moore, Marianne. "The Man Who Died Twice" (review). *Dial* 77 (August 1924): 168–70.

Moran, Ronald. "With Firm Address: A Critical Study of Twenty-six Shorter Poems of E. A. Robinson." Ph.D. diss., Louisiana State University, 1966.

——. "The Octaves of E. A. Robinson." *Colby Library Quarterly* 8 (September 1969): 363–70.

——. "Lorraine and the Sirens: Courtesans in Two Poems by E. A. Robinson." In *Essays in Honor of Esmond Linworth Marilla,* ed. Thomas Austin Kirby and William John Olive, 312–19. Baton Rouge: Louisiana State University Press, 1970.

Morrill, Paul H. "Psychological Aspects of the Poetry of Edwin Arlington Robinson." Ph.D. diss., Northwestern University, 1956.

——. " 'The World is . . . a Kind of Spiritual Kindergarten.' " *Colby Library Quarterly* 8 (December 1969): 435–38.

Morris, Celia. "E. A. Robinson and 'The Golden Horoscope of Imperfection.'" *Colby Library Quarterly* 11 (June 1975): 88–97.

Morris, Edmund. *Theodore Rex*. New York: Random House, 2001.

Morris, Lloyd. *The Poetry of Edwin Arlington Robinson: An Essay in Appreciation*. New York: George H. Doran, 1923.

Morris, Sylvia Jukes. *Edith Kermit Roosevelt*. New York: Coward McCann & Geoghegan, 1980.

Mott, Sara L. "The Happy Ending as a Controlling Comic Element in the Poetic Philosophy of Edwin Arlington Robinson." Ph.D. diss., University of South Carolina, 1965.

Munson, Gorham. *Destinations: A Canvass of American Literature Since 1900*. 1928. Reprint, New York: AMS Press, 1970.

Murphy, Cullen. "Setting the Bar." *Atlantic Monthly* (December 2003): 135–36.

Murphy, Francis, ed. *Edwin Arlington Robinson: A Collection of Critical Essays*. Englewood Cliffs, N.J.: Prentice-Hall, 1970.

——. Introduction to *Edwin Arlington Robinson: A Collection Of Critical Essays*, ed. Francis Murphy, 1–7. Englewood Cliffs, N.J.: Prentice-Hall, 1970.

Neff, Emery. *Edwin Arlington Robinson*. American Men of Letters Series. New York: William Sloane, 1948.

Nelson, Cary, ed. *Oxford Anthology of Modern American Poetry*. New York: Oxford University Press, 2000.

——. "Modern American Poetry." Online Journal and Multimedia Companion to the *Oxford Anthology of Modern American Poetry*, 2000.

Newcomb, John Timberman. *Would Poetry Disappear? American Verse and the Crisis of Modernity*. Columbus: Ohio State University Press, 2004.

"New Gallery Openings" (Elizabeth Sparhawk-Jones). *New York Times*, 11 April 1937, section 9.

New York Times. "Edwin A. Robinson, Poet, Is Dead at 66." 7 April 1938.

Nivison, David S. "Does It Matter How Annandale Went Out?" *Colby Library Quarterly* 5 (December 1960): 170–85. Reprint, in *Appreciation of Edwin Arlington Robinson: Twenty-eight Interpretive Essays*, ed. Richard Cary, 178–90. Waterville, Maine: Colby College Press, 1969.

——. "Robinson's Poetry as Social Criticism?" Talk at 1997 E. A. Robinson festival, Gardiner, Maine.

Nivison, Ruth. Notes on Hagedorn's biography. 20-page typescript with comments by George Burnham. July 1939. Colby College Special Collections.

——. Memoir. 116-page typescript with annotations by David S. Nivison. 1956–57. Gardiner Library Association,

Notopoulos, James A. "Mike the Teacher." *Amherst Graduates' Quarterly* 29 (November 1939): 1–7.

Oaklander, Christine I. "Clara Davidge's Madison Art Gallery: Sowing the Seed for the Armory Show." *Archives of American Art Journal* 36 (1987): 20–37.

Ownbey, E. Sydnor. "Robinson's 'Mr. Flood's Party.'" *Explicator* 8 (April 1950), item 47.

Palmer, Carl F. "Their Names Were Palmer Too." Family history. 1947–48. David S. Nivison papers.

Papero, Daniel V. *Bowen Family Systems Theory*. Boston: Allyn and Bacon, 1990.

Parini, Jay. *Robert Frost: A Life*. New York: Henry Holt, 1999.

Parish, John E. "The Rehabilitation of Eben Flood." *English Journal* 55 (September 1966): 696–99.

Parisi, Joseph, and Stephen Young, eds. *Dear Editor: A History of "Poetry" In Letters, the First Fifty Years, 1912–1962*. New York: Norton, 2002.

Pearce, Roy Harvey. *The Continuity of American Poetry*. Princeton, N.J.: Princeton University Press, 1961.

Pearson, Edmund. *Dime Novels*. 1929. Reprint, Port Washington, N.Y.: Kennikat Press, 1968.

Peltier, Florence. "Edwin Arlington Robinson, Himself." *Mark Twain Quarterly* 1 (Summer 1937): 14.

Perrine, Lawrence. "A Reading of 'Miniver Cheevy.'" *Colby Library Quarterly* 6 (June 1962): 65–74.

Perry, Bliss. "Poets Celebrate E. A. Robinson's Birthday." *New York Times Book Review*, 21 December 1919, 765–66.

Perry, Margaret. Reminiscences of Edwin Arlington Robinson. 21 May 1938. Three-page typescript recorded by Carl J. Weber. Colby College Special Collections.

Perry, Thomas Sergeant. *Selections from the Letters of Thomas Sergeant Perry*. Ed. Edwin Arlington Robinson. New York: Macmillan, 1929.

Peschel, Bill. "Robinson, Edwin Arlington (22 Dec. 1869–6 Apr. 1935)." *American National Biography*, ed. John A. Garraty and Mark C. Carnes, 18:652–54. New York: Oxford University Press, 1999.

Phelps, William Lyon. "Edwin Arlington Robinson." *Commemorative Tributes of the American Academy of Arts and Letters, 1905–1941*, 323–28. New York: American Academy, 1942.

Pinsky, Robert. *Poetry and the World*. New York: Ecco Press, 1988.

Pipkin, E. Edith. "The Arthur of Edwin Arlington Robinson." *English Journal* 19 (March 1930): 183–95.

Powell, Dawn. *Selected Letters of Dawn Powell, 1913–1965*. Ed. Tim Page. New York: Henry Holt, 1999.

Powys, John Cowper. "The Big Bed." *Mark Twain Quarterly* 2 (Summer 1938): 2.

Pritchard, William H. *Lives of the Modern Poets*. New York: Oxford University Press, 1980.

Quiller-Couch, Sir Arthur, ed. *The Oxford Book of English Verse, 1250–1918*. New York: Oxford University Press, 1955.

Raleigh, Walter Alexander. *On Writing and Writers*. London: Edward Arnold, 1926.

Ranck, Carty. "An American Poet with a Message." *Boston Evening Transcript*, 12 May 1913. Reprint, in *Early Reception of Edwin Arlington Robinson: The First Twenty Years*, ed. Richard Cary, 248–51. Waterville, Maine: Colby College Press, 1974.

——. "Prohibition Perils in Fiction." *Authors League Bulletin* (March 1921). Reprint, in *Authors Guild Bulletin* (Fall 1999): 54–55.

——. "Edwin Arlington Robinson" (poem). In *The Peterborough Anthology*, ed. Jean Wright Gorman and Herbert S. Gorman, 135. New York: Theatre Arts, 1923.

——. "Edwin Arlington Robinson." *New York Herald Tribune Magazine*, 14 December 1930, 8–9, 24.

——. "Last Work, and a Great One, from 'E. A.'" *Boston Evening Transcript*, 27 November 1935, section 3, p. 2.

——. "My Friend Robinson." 162-page typescript memoir, c. 1950. Arnold T. Schwab papers.

Randall, David A. *Dukedom Large Enough*. New York: Random House, 1969.

Ransom, John Crowe. "Autumn of Poetry." *Southern Review* 1 (Winter 1936): 612–14.

——. *Selected Essays of John Crowe Ransom*. Ed. Thomas Daniel Young and John Hindle. Baton Rouge: Louisiana State University Press, 1984.

Razak, Ajmal M. "The Concept of Mystery in Edwin Arlington Robinson's Murder Mystery Poems: Between Knowing and Not Knowing." Ph.D. diss., Ball State University, 1993.

Redman, Ben Ray. *Edwin Arlington Robinson*. Modern American Writers. New York: McBride, 1926.

Reynolds, Michael. *Hemingway: The Paris Years*. Oxford: Basil Blackwell, 1989.

Richards, Henry Howe. "Schoolmaster's Scrapbook." Manuscript. 1958. Groton School.

Richards, Laura E. *Stepping Westward*. New York: D. Appleton, 1931.

——. "Recollections of 'E. A.' as a Boy in Gardiner." *New York Herald Tribune Books*, 12 May 1935, 10, 17.

——. *E. A. R.* Cambridge, Mass.: Harvard University Press, 1936.

Richards, Rosalind. *A Northern Countryside*. New York: Henry Holt, 1916.

——. Notes and interviews on EAR. 1937–38. Houghton Library, Harvard University.

Richardson, Mark. "Collected Prose of Robert Frost: A New Critical Edition, Together with 'The Ordeal of Robert Frost: A Study of Biography and Style in His Poetics.'" Ph.D. diss., Rutgers University, 1993.

——. "Editing Robert Frost." *Robert Frost Review* (Fall 2000): 84–123.

Ridge, Lola. "To E. A. R." (poem). In *Sun-Up and Other Poems*, 73. New York: B. W. Heubsch, 1920.

Riis, Jacob A. *How the Other Half Lives*. 1890. Reprint, New York: Hill and Wang, 1957.

Rittenhouse, Jessie B. *My House of Life: An Autobiography*. Boston: Houghton Mifflin, 1934.

Robbins, J. Albert, ed. *American Literary Manuscripts*. 2nd edition. Athens: University of Georgia Press, 1977.

Robinson, Emma, and George Burnham. Handwritten comments on Hagedorn, *EAR*, keyed to page numbers. 1939–1940. Colby College Special Collections.

Robinson, Emma, and Ruth Nivison. Annotations of Robinson's *Collected Poems*. 1940, 1948. Colby College Special Collections.

Robinson, Herman. Letters to his wife, Emma, 15 June 1906–30 September 1908. Transcribed by David S. Nivison, 1996. Thirty-six-page typescript. David S. Nivison papers.

Robinson, W. R. *Edwin Arlington Robinson: A Poetry of the Act*. Cleveland, Ohio: Western Reserve University Press, 1967.

Roheim, Geza. "Primitive High Gods." *Psychoanalytic Quarterly* 3 (1934): 1–133.

[Roosevelt, Kermit]. "An Appreciation of the Poetry of Edwin Arlington Robinson." *Scribner's* 66 (December 1919): 763–64.

Roosevelt, Theodore. Review of *The Children of the Night*, by EAR. *Outlook* 80 (12 August 1905): 913–14.

——. *Letters to Kermit from Theodore Roosevelt, 1902–1908*. Ed. Will Irwin. New York: Scribner's, 1946.

——. *The Letters of Theodore Roosevelt*. Vols. 4–5. Cambridge, Mass.: Harvard University Press, 1951.

Rosenfield, Leonora Cohen. "The Philosopher and the Poet." *Palinurus* 1 (April 1959): 24–40.

Rosenthal, M. L. *The Modern Poets: A Critical Introduction*. New York: Oxford University Press, 1960.

Rourke, Constance. *American Humor: A Study of the National Character*. New York: Harcourt Brace, 1931.

Ryan, Kathryn White. "Tristram." *Voices* 83 (Autumn 1935): 32–36.

Saben, Mowry. *The Spirit of Life: A Book of Essays*. New York: Mitchell Kennerley, 1914.

[——]. "Edwin Arlington Robinson." *Argonaut* 113 (12 April 1935): 4–5.

——. "Memories of Edwin Arlington Robinson." *Colby Mercury* 7 (January 1941): 13–14.

——. "Edwin Arlington Robinson: An Essay." Typescript memoir, 145 pages, 1949. Colby College Special Collections.

St. Armand, Barton L. "The Power of Sympathy in the Poetry of Robinson and Frost: The 'Inside' vs. the 'Outside' Narrative." *American Literature* 19 (Fall 1967): 564–74.

Satterfield, Leon J. "Major Categories of Irony in the Poetry of Edwin Arlington Robinson." Ph.D. diss., University of Nebraska, 1969.

—— "Bubble-Work in Gardiner, Maine: The Poetry War of 1924." *New England Quarterly* 57 (March 1984): 25–43.

Scholnick, Robert J. "The Children of the Night: The Situation for Poetry in the American 1890s." Ph.D. diss., Brandeis University, 1969.

——. "The Shadowed Years: Mrs. Richards, Mr. Stedman, and Robinson." *Colby Library Quarterly* 9 (June 1972): 510–31.

Schriftgiesser Karl. "An American Poet Speaks His Mind." *Boston Evening Transcript*, 4 November 1933, book section, 1–2.

——. "Robinson the Poet." *Washington Post*, 14 April 1935, 8.

Schwab, Arnold T. "The Robinson Connection: New Jeffers Letters." *Robinson Jeffers Newsletter* 57 (November 1980): 26–35.

Scott, Winfield Townley. *Elegy for Robinson*. New York: Privately printed, 1936.

——. "Robinson to Robinson." Review of Hagedorn, *EAR. Poetry* 54 (May 1939): 92–100.

——. "To See Robinson." *New Mexico Quarterly* 26 (Summer 1956): 161–78.

——. *Exiles and Fabrications*. Garden City, N.Y.: Doubleday, 1961.

——. *New and Selected Poems*. Ed. George P. Elliott. Garden City, N.Y.: Doubleday, 1967.

——. *"A Dirty Hand": The Literary Notebooks of Winfield Townley Scott*. Austin: University of Texas Press, 1969.

Shand-Tucci, Douglas. *The Crimson Letter: Harvard, Homosexuality, and the Shaping of American Culture*. New York: St. Martin's, 2003.

Shinn, Thelma J. "The Art of a Verse Novelist: Approaching Robinson's Late Narratives Through James's *The Art of the Novel." Colby Library Quarterly* 12 (September 1976): 91–100.

Sills, Kenneth C. M. Address at Memorial Meeting in Honor of Edwin Arlington Robinson. 12 May 1935. Gardiner Library Association.

Sinclair, May. "Three American Poets of Today." *Atlantic Monthly* 98 (September 1906): 429–34.

Skupin, Michael. "Robinson's Merlin and Its Context." Available at www.skupinbooks.com, pp. 24–154.

Smith, Barbara Lehman. "Talented Tragic and Triumphant: The Life and Career of Elizabeth Sparhawk-Jones." *Pennsylvania Heritage* (Spring 1995): 20–27.

Smith, Chard Powers. *Annals of the Poets*. New York: Scribner's, 1935.

——. "Final and Inclusive." Letter to the editor, *Saturday Review of Literature*, 20 April 1935, 632.

——. *Prelude to Man*. Mount Vernon, N.Y.: Peter Pauper Press, 1936.

——. *Where the Light Falls: A Portrait of Edwin Arlington Robinson*. New York: Macmillan, 1965.

Smith, Danny D. *Gardiner's Yellow House*. Gardiner, Maine: Privately printed, 1988.

——. "E. A. R. and L. E. R.: The Robinson-Richards Friendship." Lecture, 30 April 1996. Gardiner Library Association.

——. "The Literary Relationship Between John Hays Gardiner and Edwin Arlington Robinson." Lecture, 16 May 1997. Gardiner Library Association.

——. "History of Gardiner, Maine." Leaflet, Gardiner Sesquicentennial. 1999. Gardiner Library Association.

Smith, Danny D., and Earle G. Shettleworth Jr. *Gardiner on the Kennebec*. Dover, N.H.: Arcadia Publishing, 1996.

Smith, Henry Nash. "Emerson's Problem of Vocation." In *Emerson: A Collection of Critical Essays*, ed. Milton R. Konvitz and Stephen E. Whicher, 60–71. Englewood Cliffs, N.J.: Prentice-Hall, 1962.

Sonnenberg, Ben. *Lost Property*. Washington, D.C.: Counterpoint, 1999.

——. "The Modernist from Maine." *New York Times Book Review*, 18 July 1999, 31.

Spencer, Elizabeth. *Landscapes of the Heart: A Memoir*. New York: Random House, 1998.

Squire, J. C. "Contemporary American Authors: IV: Edwin Arlington Robinson." *London Mercury* 13 (February 1926): 401–13.

Squires, Radcliffe. "Tilbury Town Today." In *Edwin Arlington Robinson: Centenary Essays*, ed. Ellsworth Barnard, 175–83. Athens: University of Georgia Press, 1969.

Stageberg, Norman C., and Wallace L. Anderson. *Poetry as Experience*. New York: American Book Company, 1952.

Stanford, Donald E. "Edwin Arlington Robinson's 'The Wandering Jew.'" *Tulane Studies in English* 23 (1978): 95–108.

[Stark, Harold]. "Young Boswell Interviews E. A. Robinson." *New York Tribune*, 18 April 1923, 13.

Starr, Nathan Comfort. "The Transformation of Merlin." In *Edwin Arlington Robinson: Centenary Essays*, ed. Ellsworth Barnard, 106–19. Athens: University of Georgia Press, 1969.

Stevick, Robert D. "Formulation of E. A. Robinson's Principles of Poetry." *Colby Library Quarterly* 8 (June 1969): 295–308.

——. "The Metrical Style of E. A. Robinson," In *Edwin Arlington Robinson: Centenary Essays*, ed. Ellsworth Barnard, 54–67. Athens: University of Georgia Press, 1969.

Stovall, Floyd. "The Optimism Behind Robinson's Tragedies." *American Literature* 10 (March 1938): 1–23.

——. *American Idealism*. Norman: University of Oklahoma Press, 1943.

——. "Edwin Arlington Robinson in Perspective." In *Essays on American Literature in Honor of Jay B. Hubbell*, ed. Clarence Gohdes, 241–58. Durham, N.C.: Duke University Press, 1967.

Stowe, Harriet Beecher. *The Pearl of Orr's Island*. 1862. Reprint, Boston: Houghton Mifflin, 1896.

Sullivan, Winifred H. "'The Double-Edged Irony of E. A. Robinson's 'Miniver Cheevy.'" *Colby Library Quarterly* 22 (September 1986): 185–91.

Super, R. H. "For a Dead Lady." *Explicator* 3 (June 1945), item 60.

Suss, Irving D. "The Plays of Edwin Arlington Robinson." *Colby Library Quarterly* 8 (September 1969): 347–63.

Sutcliffe, Denham. "Edwin Arlington Robinson: A Product of Seventeenth-Century Puritanism." (Bates College) *Garnet* (May 1935): 29–32.

——. "The Original of Robinson's Captain Craig." *New England Quarterly* 16 (September 1943): 407–31.

Swanton, Harry. "Reminiscences of the Early Years of Edwin Arlington Robinson." Seven-page typescript. 1935. Maine State Library.

Tate, Allen. *Essays of Four Decades*. Chicago: Swallow Press, 1968.

Taylor, Henry. "In the Mode of Robinson and Frost." In *The Pure Clear Word: Essays on the Poetry of James Wright*, ed. Dave Smith, 49–64. Urbana: University of Illinois Press, 1982.

——. "The Mission of His Bondage: Robinson's Sonnets." Talk at 1997 E. A. Robinson Festival. Gardiner, Maine.

Thompson, Fred W. "Alfred Noyes Sees American Poets Leading World Movement." *Boston Sunday Post*, 2 March 1913. Reprint, in *Early Reception of Edwin Arlington Robinson: The First Twenty Years*, ed. Richard Cary, 247–48. Waterville, Maine: Colby College Press, 1974.

Thompson, Lawrance. Notes toward a biography of E. A. Robinson. 1939–1950. David S. Nivison papers.

——. *Robert Frost: The Early Years, 1874–1915*. New York: Holt Rinehart and Winston, 1966.

——. *Robert Frost: The Years of Triumph, 1915–1938*. New York: Holt Rinehart and Winston, 1970.

Thompson, Lawrance, and R. H. Winnick. *Robert Frost: The Later Years, 1938–1963*. New York: Holt Rinehart and Winston, 1976.

Tittle, Walter. "Glimpses of Interesting Americans." *Century* 110 (June 1925): 189–92.

Todrin, Boris. "Edwin Arlington Robinson." *Book Collector's Journal* 1 (July 1936): 1, 4.

——. *The Room by the River*. Chicago: Black Cat Press, 1936.

Torrence, Olivia H. D. "The Poet at the Dinner Table." *Colophon* n.s. 3 (Winter 1938): 93–99.

Trachtenberg, Alan. "Democracy and the Poet: Walt Whitman and E. A. Robinson." Talk at 1997 E. A. Robinson festival. Gardiner, Maine.

Tryon, James L. "Harvard Days with Edwin Arlington Robinson." Sixteen-page pamphlet. Talk to Colby Chapter, Phi Beta Kappa. 16 April 1940. Colby College Special Collections.

Untermeyer, Jean Starr. "Edwin Arlington Robinson." Twenty-page typescript memoir with handwritten addenda. Undated. Poetry/Rare Books, State University of New York at Buffalo.

Untermeyer, Louis. "Unfinished Portrait." Review of *Edwin Arlington Robinson: A Biography*, by Hermann Hagedorn. *Saturday Review of Literature*, 15 October 1938, 34.

——. *From Another World: The Autobiography of Louis Untermeyer*. New York: Harcourt Brace, 1939.

——. *Makers of the Modern World*. New York: Simon and Schuster, 1955.

——. "Edwin Arlington Robinson: A Reappraisal." Robinson Exhibit. Washington, D.C.: Library of Congress, 1963.

Updike, John. *On Literary Biography*. Columbia: University of South Carolina Press, 1999.

Van Doren, Carl. "Post-War: The Literary Twenties." *Harper's* 173 (July 1936): 148–56.

——. *Three Worlds*. New York: Harper and Brothers, 1936.

Van Doren, Carl, and Mark Van Doren. *American and British Literature Since 1890*. New York: Century, 1925.

Van Doren, Mark. *Edwin Arlington Robinson*. New York: Literary Guild, 1927.

——. "The Last Look" (poem). *Mark Twain Quarterly* 2 (Summer 1938): 21.

——. "Great Books of the Twentieth Century in Literature: Lyric Poetry." In *The Great Ideas Today*, 285–91. Chicago: Encyclopedia Britannica, 1969.

Views from the Circle: Seventy-five Years of Groton School. Groton, Mass.: The Trustees of Groton School, 1960.

Vincent, Sybil Korff. "Flat Breasted Miracles: Realistic Treatment of the Woman's Problem in the Poetry of Edwin Arlington Robinson." *Markham Review* 6 (Fall 1976): 14–15.

Wagenknecht, Edward. *The Seven Worlds of Theodore Roosevelt*. New York: Longmans Green, 1958.

Waggoner, Hyatt. *American Poetry from the Puritans to the Present*. Boston: Houghton Mifflin, 1968.

Waldo, Fullerton. "The Earlier E. A. R.: Some Memories of a Poet in the Making." *Outlook*, 30 November 1921, 531–32, 534.

Warren, Austin. *The New England Conscience*. Ann Arbor: University of Michigan Press, 1966.

Weber, Carl J. "The Cottage Lights of Wessex." *Colby Mercury* (February 1936): 64–67.

——. "Poet and President." *New England Quarterly* 16 (December 1943): 615–26.

Weeks, Lewis E., Jr. "E. A. Robinson's Poetics." *Twentieth-Century Literature* 11 (October 1965): 131–45.

——. "Edwin Arlington Robinson's *Antigone*." *Colby Library Quarterly* 20 (September 1984): 137–51.

Weightman, Gavin. *The Frozen-Water Trade*. New York: Hyperion, 2003.

Weil, Eric A. " 'Well, She Was a Woman': Female Characters in the Poetry of Edwin Arlington Robinson." Ph.D. diss., University of North Carolina at Greensboro,1993.

Wheelock, John Hall. "A Friend of Young Poets." *Mark Twain Quarterly* 2 (Summer 1938): 20.

——. Interview. Oral History Archives, Columbia University.

Whipple, T. K. *Spokesmen*. Berkeley: University of California Press, 1963.

Widdemer, Margaret. *Golden Friends I Had*. Garden City, N.Y.: Doubleday, 1964.

Williams, Alice Meacham. "Edwin Arlington Robinson, Journalist." *New England Quarterly* 15 (December 1942): 715–24.

Williams, Stanley. "Edwin Arlington Robinson." In *Literary History of the United States*, ed. Robert E. Spiller et al., 1157–70. New York: Macmillan, 1948.

Williams, William Carlos. " 'Eat Rocks.' " Review of Neff, *EAR*. *Nation*, 30 October 1948, 498–99.

Wilson, Edmund. *The Shores of Light: A Literary Chronicle of the Twenties and Thirties*. New York: Farrar Straus and Young, 1952.

Winters, Yvor. "A Cool Master." Review of *Collected Poems*, by EAR. *Poetry* 19 (February 1922): 277–88. Reprint, in *Edwin Arlington Robinson: A Collection Of Critical Essays*, ed. Francis Murphy, 8–14. Englewood Cliffs, N.J.: Prentice-Hall, 1970.

——. *Edwin Arlington Robinson*. New York: New Directions, 1947.

Wisehart, M. K. " 'By Jove!' said Roosevelt, 'It Reads like the Real Thing!' " *American Magazine* 105 (April 1928): 34, 76, 78, 80, 82, 84.

Wolf, H. R. "E. A. Robinson and the Integration of Self." In *Modern American Poetry: Essays in Criticism*, ed. Jerome Mazzaro, 40–59. New York: David McKay, 1970.

Wood, Frederick S. *Roosevelt as We Knew Him*. Philadelphia: John C. Winston, 1927.

Wormser, Baron, and David Cappella. *A Surge of Language: Teaching Poetry Day by Day*. Portsmouth, N.H.: Heinemann, 2004.

Ziff, Larzer. *The American 1890s*. New York: Viking, 1966.

Zabel, Morton Dauwen. "Robinson in America." *Poetry* 46 (June 1935): 157–62.

——. "Robinson: The Ironic Discipline." *Nation* 145 (28 August 1937): 222–23.

Zietlow, Paul. "The Meaning of Tilbury Town: Robinson as a Regional Poet." *New England Quarterly* 40 (June 1967): 188–211.

Zinsser, William. *Writing About Your Life*. New York: Marlowe and Company, 2004.

Index

Page locators in italics refer to figures